AF790597

RETENTION OF TITLE IN SECURED TRANSACTIONS LAW FROM A CREDITOR'S PERSPECTIVE

Retention of Title in Secured Transactions Law from a Creditor's Perspective

A comparative analysis of selected (non-)functional approaches

Inge Van de Plas

INTERSENTIA

Cambridge – Antwerp – Chicago

Intersentia Ltd
8 Wellington Mews | Wellington Street
Cambridge | CB1 1HW | United Kingdom
Tel.: +44 1223 736 170
Email: mail@intersentia.co.uk
www.intersentia.com | www.intersentia.co.uk

Distribution for the UK and the rest of the world (incl. Eastern Europe):
NBN International
1 Deltic Avenue, Rooksley
Milton Keynes MK13 8LD
United Kingdom
Tel.: +44 1752 202 301 | Fax: +44 1752 202 331
Email: orders@nbninternational.com

Distribution for Europe:
Lefebvre Sarrut Belgium NV
Hoogstraat 139/6
1000 Brussels
Belgium
Tel.: 0800 39 067 | Fax: 0800 39 068
Email: contact@larcier-intersentia.com

Distribution for the USA and Canada:
Independent Publishers Group
Order Department
814 North Franklin Street
Chicago, IL60610
USA
Tel.: +1 800 888 4741 (toll free) | Fax: +1312 337 5985
Email: orders@ipgbook.com

Retention of Title in Secured Transactions Law from a Creditor's Perspective.
A comparative analysis of selected (non-)functional approaches
© Inge Van de Plas 2023

The author has asserted the right under the Copyright, Designs and Patents Act 1988, to be identified as authors of this work.

No part of this book may be reproduced, stored in a retrieval system, or transmitted, in any form, or by any means, without prior written permission from Intersentia, or as expressly permitted by law or under the terms agreed with the appropriate reprographic rights organisation. Enquiries concerning reproduction which may not be covered by the above should be addressed to Intersentia at the address above.

Cover design by Danny Juchtmans / www.dsigngraphics.be

ISBN 978-1-83970-370-6
D/2023/7849/62

British Library Cataloguing in Publication Data. A catalogue record for this book is available from the British Library.

FOREWORD

Mastery is a function of time and intense focus applied to a particular field of knowledge (R. Greene)

In the past few years, Inge Van de Plas dedicated herself entirely to the analysis of the functional approach and its application to retention of title. This research was inspired and fostered by the scholarly insights gained in her master's and LLM studies.

The love for (the modernisation of) secured transactions law sparked in 2013 while preparing her master thesis as a student researcher at the University of Antwerp. Mid 2014 Inge left to pursue an LLM degree at the University of Toronto. In her LLM thesis she analysed and compared the Belgian Securities Rights Acts with secured transaction laws in New Zealand and Australia against the backdrop of the UNCITRAL Legislative Guide and Model Law. During these initial research activities, Inge developed a profound passion for 'the functional approach' as a tool to modernize secured transaction law. In simple terms the functional approach is aimed at creating equivalent legal outcomes for functionally similar mechanisms. This may sound obvious, but the practical implementation of such functional approach faces many challenges in legal systems around the globe.

Fast forward to September 2016 when Inge began her doctoral studies at her *alma mater* focussing her attention on unravelling and comparing retention of title mechanisms from a functional approach perspective. From day one Inge demonstrated a discipline to continually clarify and deepen her personal understanding and vision. Her research visit at the New York University Law School – Law Library and her research stay at the Max Planck Institute for Comparative and International Private Law in Hamburg are examples of Inge's hunger to grasp all the details of her research. Six exciting years later, on 23 September 2022, Inge defended with brio her PhD dissertation. With natural ease and confidence Inge captivated both the members of the jury and the audience explaining the relevance of the functional approach for retention of title devices.

The findings of Inge's years-long research are compiled and clearly explained in this book. The text offers a comprehensive and logically structured analysis, divided into three core sections, each dealing with one specific perspective. The book delivers on its intention to present a well-balanced report integrating descriptive, comparative, explanatory and evaluative components.

Introductory part 1 provides an explanation of the research topic and the methodology. This prologue sets the scene to make the abstract and technical research topic (more) accessible to the reader.

The second part of the book examines divergent approaches to the regulation of retention of title through a functional comparative law analysis. The detailed studies of the selected jurisdictions (United States and Germany) and international instruments (UNCITRAL legislative guide and model law on secured transactions and Book IX of the Draft Common Frame of Reference) offer the reader new insights on both the functional approach with and without recharacterization and the non-functional approach to retention of title.

Part 3 of the book presents an in-depth investigation of retention of title in Belgium from a functional approach perspective. The descriptive core is enriched with helpful comparative insights drawn from part 2 and concluded with recommendations concerning the direction the Belgian legislator could take with regards to the regulation of retention of title.

The concluding part 4 consolidates and merges the findings stemming from part 2 and 3. In this concluding part the reader is given a systematic answer to the research questions. Various possibilities to (not) integrate retention of title are discussed, pointing out the (dis)advantages of the different solutions and outlining what should happen if the (Belgian) legislator were to make one choice or the other. The author formulates clear recommendations, but pays equal attention to alternative solutions and the specific context in which the solutions should be used

This book is original in the sense that the author not only pays attention to the mechanism of retention of title itself, but also to the consequences for the creditors in the various scenarios. When weighing the different solutions, it is not only important to examine how the framework can be more coherent as such, but also what the impact of a certain adaptation is on the parties directly involved, in this case the creditors.

Readers will undoubtedly appreciate the book's accessible style: the text is concise and well written. Each chapter or part of the book closes with a practical overview, in which the author critically summarises the findings and lessons learned. In the same vein the diagrams and tables included throughout the book and especially in part 4 are very helpful to understand the different applications of the functional approach in respect of retention of title.

The book is relevant to both a national and international audience. From a national perspective, the research is filling a gap by clarifying how the functional approach in Belgium should be understood in relation to retention of title and illustrates where the obstacles lie. This analysis is particularly valuable because it indicates how retention of title can be fitted into secured transactions law in a (more) coherent manner. The findings provide the legislator with clear guidance when preparing Book 9 Security Interests in the new Civil Code.

Furthermore, the book offers a fascinating case study for international policy makers. The Belgian retention of title regulations and practice provide a nice illustration of how the functional approach was applied in a (minimal) way in a national secured transactions framework. The thorough analysis of this Belgian case, which identifies a number of clear inconsistencies, can give law reform institutions and other national legislators more insight into the way in which the functional approach is given shape and what the pitfalls are in this concrete case. The lessons learned from the Belgian case might be helpful for other initiatives to implement the functional approach in other secured transactions law regimes.

Finally, I would like to congratulate and extend my heartfelt thanks to Inge. It was a delight to work with her during the past years and I cherish our time together. Her enthusiasm and curiosity, her cheerfulness and genuine interest, marked every step of our journey. I am proud of her achievements and look forward to the meaningful ideas and projects that she will bring into the future world.

Antwerpen, 28 april 2023
Prof. dr. Melissa Vanmeenen, Universiteit Antwerpen

ACKNOWLEDGEMENTS

My defense marks the end of a long journey. It was a journey I did not go on alone and I could not have brought it to this conclusion without the help of many people. First I would like to thank the University of Antwerp and specifically the faculty of law for giving me the opportunity and very pleasant working environment to work on my PhD. I would like to especially thank Inge Jongbloet and Ulrike Loos from the support staff who were instrumental in organizing the "International seminar on law reform in secured transactions and insolvency proceedings" and making it the beautiful event that it is. Next I would like to thank my doctoral jury. Some of you have been part of this project since the first day, others have joined mid-trip, but each of you has given much of his/her valuable time, effort and insights into making my research the best it can be.

A special word of thanks is reserved for my doctoral advisor, professor Vanmeenen. Our working relationship started when I became her aspiring doctoral assistant in the last year of my masters of law. After a few years in which I went to explore different cities and countries, I had the very good fortune of typing in "jobs for master of law" in Google right at the moment that the University of Antwerp had extended the application deadline for the position of PhD student under professor Vanmeenen. This very lucky confluence of events brought me back to work with professor Vanmeenen, who from the start was a mentor, a critical but very fair judge of my work, a confidant, a one-woman motivational team and a very good city-trip companion. I could not have wished for a better advisor and I count my lucky stars that Google and the VDAB jobsite brought me back to work for her.

A PhD is often described as a solitary and even lonely experience, but thanks to many co-workers at the faculty it never felt that way for me. You were there for lunches, wine tastings or long chats around the coffee machine or printer where we could vent and commiserate about everything under the sun. I would like to give a special thanks to Aïda, Sarah, Leontien, Charlotte, Tine, Inès and Mathieu for making the office such a fun and easy going place.

I would not have been able to arrive at my destination without some very special people that have always been there. First I would like to thank my friends for providing much needed moments of relaxation and fun to take my mind of looming deadlines, reframing of research questions and other PhD stuff.

Next a big thanks to my family for always being supportive of my endeavors, be it moving to Canada or the US and then suddenly coming back to start a 6 year PhD program. I felt your unconditional support all the way through this program and I cannot thank you enough. Finally a very special word of thanks to my two most cherished travel companions. Edward, you have been with me on this trip from the very moment that I found the job application, the one weekend in which I wrote my research proposal and everything that came after. You were without a doubt the best person to have with me on this ride. Not only because you are a PhD yourself and therefore knew with half a word what I meant and could relate to my experience, but more importantly because you are my favorite person in the world and every problem becomes easy or manageable after I have talked to you about it. I already loved you before I started this project, but when you without hesitation said that I should take this job at the University of Antwerp, which meant me moving back to Belgium, it really hit home how much you trusted me and our relationship. Finally, Freya, you made your appearance towards the tail end of the trip and you were the best hard deadline a PhD could wish for. As your presence became more and more evident you provided the perfect incentive and motivation I needed to land this plane.

To my family, I can never thank you enough.

CONTENTS

PART 1
GENERAL INTRODUCTION

1. *Overview* – This part sets the scene for this dissertation. First, I set out the starting point for my research, the research problems, objectives and questions (ch. 1). This is followed by the methodology (ch. 2) and a brief explanation concerning the use of terminology (ch. 3).

CHAPTER 1

STARTING POINT, RESEARCH PROBLEMS, OBJECTIVES AND QUESTIONS

SECTION 1 – STARTING POINT: INTEGRATION OF RETENTION OF TITLE IN THE BELGIAN SECURITY RIGHTS ACT (2013)[1]

2. *The integration of retention of title and the functional approach* – In 2013 the Security Rights Act (hereafter also, SRA) was introduced in Belgium. A significant change following the Security Rights Act was the explicit inclusion of retention of title[2] in the category of security rights in movable goods. This inclusion, in part, was based on the functional approach which aims at creating equivalent legal outcomes for functionally equivalent secured transactions in movable goods despite their potential conceptual differences.[3] Following this approach, the previous amalgam of security rights in movable goods, such as the pledge in movable goods in the former Civil Code[4], the pledge in movable goods in the former Commercial Code[5], the pledge in business assets[6] and the

1 Wet van 11 juli 2013 tot wijziging van het Burgerlijk Wetboek wat de zakelijke zekerheden op roerende goederen betreft en tot opheffing van diverse bepalingen ter zake, *Belgian State Gazette* 2 August 2013, 48463. This law was implemented as a separate chapter in the Civil Code. When I refer to the Security Rights Act (SRA) in this dissertation, I refer to the provisions of this Act as they can be found in Chapter XVII of the Civil Code. There are a few provisions that can only be found in the actual law that amends the Civil Code concerning *in rem* security rights in movables and abrogation of various dispositions. When referring to these provisions I will refer to the wet van 11 juli 2013 tot wijziging van het Burgerlijk Wetboek wat de zakelijke zekerheden op roerende goederen betreft en tot opheffing van diverse bepalingen ter zake, *Belgian State Gazette* 2 August 2013, 48463.

2 Retention of title in the broadest sense is a security mechanism in which the creditor retains title to a movable good delivered to the debtor to guarantee the credit that enabled the debtor to acquire the encumbered good.

3 Explanatory memorandum for the law to amend the Civil Code concerning *in rem* security rights in movables and abrogation of various dispositions, *Parl. St.* Kamer 2012–13, no. 2463/001, 10 (hereafter, explanatory memorandum Security Rights Act, no. 2463/001).

4 Art. 2071 - 2084 CC.

5 Art. 1–11 Pledge in the Commercial Code.

6 Business asset Pledge Act 1919.

warrant or warehouse receipt[7], is replaced by one form of pledge (*pand/gage*) in movable goods[8] that can be possessory[9] and non-possessory.[10] Likewise, the functional approach is applied to transfer of title (*fiduciaire eigendomsoverdracht tot zekerheid/cession fiduciaire à tire de sûreté*) by limiting transfer of title in its effect to a pledge.[11]

As mentioned, the functional approach is also applied to integrate retention of title (*eigendomsvoorbehoud/réserve de propriété*) in the Security Rights Act. Interestingly, for retention of title the functional approach is mainly used to explicitly include retention of title in the category of full-fledged security rights in movable goods[12], together with the pledge[13] and the right of retention of possession (*retentierecht/droit de rétention*).[14] The explicit classification of retention of title as a security right implies that retention of title is now subjected to the same principles that govern security rights in movable goods, such as the specificity principle, the prohibition against unjust enrichment of the security right holder and the first in time rule to settle priority conflicts among different security rights.[15] Additionally, following the functional approach the legislator decided to expand some of the provisions concerning the non-possessory pledge to retention of title.[16] The expanded provisions concern the extension of retention of title into proceeds[17], altered goods[18] and mixed goods[19] and the transfer of retention of title in the event the guaranteed debt is transferred.[20] Notably, the Security Rights Act does not recharacterize retention of title or limits retention of title in its effect to another security right in movable goods. Schematically, the Security Rights Act can be visualized as follows:

7 Wet 18 november 1862 houdende invoering van het warrantstelsel, *Belgian State Gazette* 20 November 1862, 5.305 (hereafterWarehouse Receipt Act 1862).

8 Chapter 1 SRA.

9 Art. 39 SRA.

10 Art. 15 SRA.

11 Art. 62 SRA.

12 Explanatory memorandum Security Rights Act, no. 2463/001, 18.

13 Chapter 1 SRA.

14 Chapter 3 SRA.

15 E. DIRIX and R. DE CORTE, 'Zekerheidsrechten' in *Beginselen van Belgisch privaatrecht*, (5th edn., Mechelen: Wolters Kluwer, 2006), 3–4.

16 Art. 70 SRA; Explanatory memorandum Security Rights Act, no. 2463/001, 30–31.

17 Art. 9 SRA.

18 Art. 18 SRA.

19 Art. 20 SRA.

20 Art. 23, par. 1 SRA.

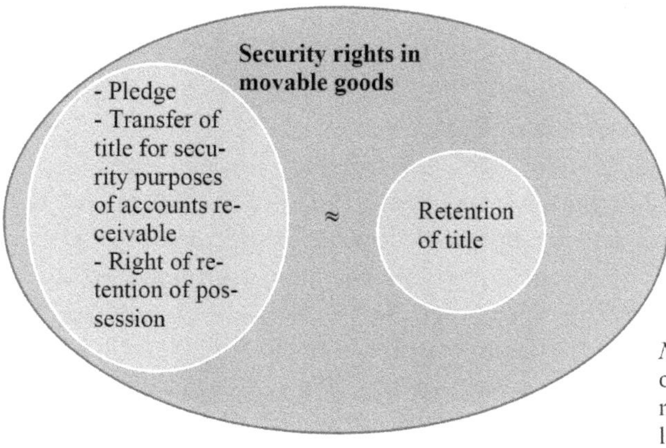

Not included in the SRA: other security rights in movable goods e.g. legislative liens in movable goods, security rights in financial collateral

3. *International trend to create consolidated security right frameworks for all secured transactions in movable goods that perform the same function* – The functional approach in the context of security rights in movable goods was originally found in the United States with the introduction of Article 9 of the Uniform Commercial Code (UCC). Article 9 UCC contains one set of rules for all interests in personal property or fixtures which secure payment or performance of an obligation.[21] This approach was transplanted to some other jurisdictions, such as the majority of the Canadian territories[22], New Zealand[23] and Australia[24], and in most international instruments concerning secured transactions in movable goods.[25]

---

21 §9–109 (a) Uniform Commercial Code (UCC) (2010). The Uniform Commercial Codes were an initiative of the National Conference of Commissioners on Uniform State Laws, who were later joined by the which was later joined by the renowned American Law Institute. See, P. WINSHIP, 'An historical overview of UCC Article 9' in L. GULLIFER and O. AKSELI (eds.), *Secured transactions law reform: principles, policies and practice*, (Oxford: Hart Publisher, 2016), (21) 24.

22 Art. 2 Personal Property Security Act, RSO 1990, Cp. 10 (Ontario, Canada); Art. 3 (1) Personal Property Security Act, SS 1993, c P-6.2 (Saskatchewan, Canada); Art. 2 Personal Property Security Act, RSBC 1996, Cp. 359 (British Columbia, Canada); Art. 2 Personal Property Security Act, RSY 2002, C.169 (Yukon, Canada); Art. 2 Personal Property Security Act, SNWT (Nu) 1994, c 8 (Northwestern Territories and Nunavut, Canada); Art. 3 (1) Personal Property Security Act, RSA 2000, P-7 (Alberta, Canada); Art. 3 (1) Personal Property Security Act, CCSM 1993, c. P35 (Manitoba, Canada); Art. 4 (1) Personal Property Security Act, SNL 1998, C. P-7.1 (St. John's, Newfoundland and Labrador, Canada); Art. 3 (1) Personal Property Security Act, SNB 1993, C. P-7.1 (New Brunswick, Canada); Art. 4 (1) Personal Property Security Act, SNS 1995–96, C.13 (Nova Scotia, Canada); Art. 3 (1) Personal Property Security Act, RSPEI 1988, c P-3.1 (Prince Edward Island, Canada).

23 Art. 26 (1) Personal Property Securities Act (1999), New Zealand.

24 Sec. 6 Personal Property Security Act 2009, Australia (Cth).

25 Legislative guide on secured transactions, United nations commission on international trade law, (New York, 2010), 62–63 (UNCITRAL Guide); art. 1 (1) of the model law on secured

SECTION 2 – RESEARCH PROBLEMS

4. *Different approaches to treatment of retention of title in secured transactions law* – The pursuit of equivalent legal outcomes for retention of title and functionally equivalent security rights in tangible, movable goods (i.e. the functional approach) has gained in popularity.[26] However, the concept of the functional approach and its operation in view of retention of title is not generally defined. With regards to its operation, we see that some jurisdictions and international instruments, like the United States[27], Canadian territories[28], New Zealand[29], Australia[30] and the unitary approach of the UNCITRAL legislative guide on secured transactions (hereafter, the UNCITRAL Guide) and UNCITRAL model law on secured transactions (hereafter, UNCITRAL Model Law)[31] apply, what will be referred to as a *functional approach with recharacterization.* In these jurisdictions and international instruments, a choice is made to recharacterize retention of title to a purchase money security interest (PMSI)[32], an acquisition

transactions, United nations commission on international trade law, (New York, 2016) (UNCITRAL Model Law); art. 1.1 of the Model Law on Secured Transactions, European Bank for Reconstruction and Development, 2010 (EBRD Model Law); art. 1 of the Model Inter-American Law on Secured Transactions, Organization of American States, 2002 (OAS Model Law); IX.-1:101 Draft Common Frame of Reference, Study Group and Acquis Group, (Munich: 2008) (DCFR).

26 R. CUMING, 'The internationalization of secured financing law: the spreading influence of the concepts of UCC, Article 9 and its progeny' in R. CRANSTON (ed.), *Making commercial law: essays in honour of Roy Goode*, (499) 502–508.

27 §1–201 (b) (35) UCC (2001) *juncto* §9–109 (a) UCC (2010).

28 Art. 1 (1) Personal Property Security Act, RSO 1990, Cp. 10 (Ontario, Canada); Art. 1 (qq) Personal Property Security Act, SS 1993, c P-6.2 (Saskatchewan, Canada); Art. 2 Personal Property Security Act, RSBC 1996, Cp. 359 (British Columbia, Canada); Art. 1 (1) Personal Property Security Act, RSY 2002, C.169 (Yukon, Canada); Art. 1.1 Personal Property Security Act, SNWT (Nu) 1994, c 8 (Northwestern Territories and Nunavut, Canada); Art. 1 (1), (tt) Personal Property Security Act, RSA 2000, P-7 (Alberta, Canada); Art. 1 (1) Personal Property Security Act, CCSM 1993, c. P35 (Manitoba, Canada); Art. 2 (1), (pp) Personal Property Security Act, SNL 1998, C. P-7.1 (St. John's, Newfoundland and Labrador, Canada); Art. 1 (1) Personal Property Security Act, SNB 1993, C. P-7.1 (New Brunswick, Canada); Art. 2 (1), (ar) Personal Property Security Act, SNS 1995–96, C.13 (Nova Scotia, Canada); Art. 1 (1), (rr) Personal Property Security Act, RSPEI 1988, c P-3.1 (Prince Edward Island, Canada).

29 Art. 17 Personal Property Securities Act (1999), New Zealand.

30 Sec. 12 Personal Property Security Act 2009, Australia (Cth).

31 UNCITRAL Guide, 57–58; Art. 2 (b) UNCITRAL Model Law.

32 §9–103 UCC; Art. 1 (1) Personal Property Security Act, RSO 1990, Cp. 10 (Ontario, Canada); Art. 2 (1), (jj) Personal Property Security Act, SS 1993, c P-6.2 (Saskatchewan, Canada); Art. 1 (1) Personal Property Security Act, RSBC 1996, Cp. 359 (British Columbia, Canada); Art. 1 (1) Personal Property Security Act, RSY 2002, C.169 (Yukon, Canada); Art. 1.1 Personal Property Security Act, SNWT (Nu) 1994, c 8 (Northwest Territories and Nunavut, Canada); Art. 1 (1), (ll) Personal Property Security Act, RSA 2000, P-7 (Alberta, Canada); Art. 1 (1) Personal Property Security Act, CCSM 1993, c. P35 (Manitoba, Canada); Art. 2 (1), (hh) Personal Property Security Act, SNL 1998, C. P-7.1 (St. John's, Newfoundland and Labrador, Canada); Art. 1 (1) Personal Property Security Act, SNB 1993, C. P-7.1 (New Brunswick, Canada); Art. 2 (1), (ai) Personal Property Security Act, SNS 1995–96, C.13 (Nova Scotia, Canada);

security right[33] or an acquisition security interest.[34] A different approach is found in the non-unitary approach of the UNCITRAL Guide[35] and Book IX of the Draft Common Frame of Reference (hereafter, DCFR).[36] Here the term retention of title is maintained in a larger security right framework, but with the explicit intention to create equivalent legal outcomes for retention of title and functionally equivalent secured transactions. This will also be referred to as the *functional approach without recharacterization.* More specifically, in the UNCITRAL Guide and the DCFR the drafters state that the legal outcomes for retention of title should be equated to the outcomes for acquisition security rights.[37] This variety in functional approaches complicates the understanding of the functional approach as a concept and its application to retention of title.

5. *Other approaches to the treatment of retention of title in secured transactions law* – The integration of retention of title in consolidated security right frameworks via the functional approach has not been universally adopted. This is especially the case in European jurisdictions, where the functional approach for security rights in movable goods in general and for retention of title in particular has not been very popular.[38] For example, Germany[39] and the Netherlands[40] do not pursue the functional approach for retention of title. These jurisdictions do not formally pursue the creation of functionally equivalent legal outcomes for retention of title and functionally similar security mechanisms.

6. *Uncertainty concerning the application of the functional approach* – First, the variety in approaches to retention of title in movable goods causes uncertainty as to how retention of title is and should be treated in the Belgian law. More specifically, the application of a functional approach to retention of title in the Security Rights Act creates uncertainty. As mentioned, the functional approach is aimed at creating equivalent legal outcomes for functionally similar mechanisms.[41] However, this objective can be achieved in various ways (e.g. with or without recharacterization). Furthermore, the assessment of what

---

Art. 1 (1), (ii) Personal Property Security Act, RSPEI 1988, c P-3.1 (Prince Edward Island, Canada); Art. 16 Personal Property Securities Act (1999), New Zealand; Sec. 14 Personal Property Security Act 2009, Australia (Cth).

33 Recommendation 9 (a) UNCITRAL Guide; art. 2 (b) UNCITRAL Model Law.

34 Art. 3, IX OAS Model Law.

35 UNCITRAL Guide, 58 and 63 (hereafter,).

36 IX.-1:103 DCFR.

37 Recommendation 9, (b), (ii) UNCITRAL Guide; comments to art. IX.- 1:104 DCFR, p. 4458.

38 E. M. KIENINGER, 'Evaluation: a common? Convergences, subsisting differences and possible ways for harmonisation' in E.-M. KIENINGER (ed.), *Security rights in movable property in European private law*, (Cambridge: Cambridge University Press, 2004), (647) 648–649.

39 §449 Bürgerliches Gesetzbuch (BGB).

40 Art. 3:93 Nederlands Burgerlijk Wetboek (NBW).

41 Explanatory memorandum Security Rights Act, no. 2463/001, 10.

exactly constitutes functionally equivalent security mechanisms is not entirely clear. The continuation of the term retention of title in the Security Rights Act indicates that the Belgian legislator has opted for the application of the functional approach without recharacterization. However, the Belgian legislator does not further specify their application of the functional approach and the pursuit of this objective remains obscure with regards to retention of title. Is this objective achieved by placing retention of title in the category of security rights in movable goods, together with the pledge and the right of retention of possession or does this require additional steps in which outcomes between specific security rights are equated via legislative changes? In case of the latter, with which other security right is and should retention of title be equated in order to achieve functional equivalence and does the Belgian legislator pursue these steps? Furthermore, given the non-functional approaches to regulate retention of title in Germany and the Netherlands, should Belgium even pursue functional equivalence for retention of title and functionally similar security rights in movable goods?

Second, the potential consequences of the functional approach for retention of title creditors in Belgium are uncertain. Are the rights of retention of title creditors changed in order to create equivalent legal outcomes with functionally similar security mechanisms? If the rights of retention of title creditors are altered, does this change the protection that retention of title creditors now enjoy both prior to and during corporate bankruptcy proceedings? Given that the Security Rights Act is aimed at increasing access to credit[42], it is important that retention of title creditors are confident in their rights in order for them to grant credit with retention of title as security. If uncertainty concerning the meaning and application of the functional approach casts doubts on the rights of retention of title creditors, this should be addressed.

Third, the Security Rights Act aims to create a more predictable, coherent and clear secured transactions law.[43] Given that the functional approach is one of the underlying principles of the Security Rights Act, this raises the question whether and to what extent the functional approach as applied to retention of title contributes to these goals. For example, does it simplify the interpretation and classification of retention of title? Does it create a system that brings together the different security rights in movable goods in a cohesive and logical way? Does it make the rights of retention of title creditors (more) predictable both prior to and during corporate bankruptcy proceedings?

---

[42] Explanatory memorandum Security Rights Act, no. 2463/001, 9–10.

[43] Explanatory memorandum Security Rights Act, no. 2463/001, 9–10.

SECTION 3 – RESEARCH OBJECTIVES AND QUESTIONS

7. *Research objectives* – Following these research problems concerning the treatment of retention of title in secured transactions law in general and in the Belgian Security Rights Act in particular, I formulated these research objectives:

1) Clarify the selected functional approaches to retention of title;
2) Compare the selected functional and non-functional approaches to retention of title and more specifically the rights of retention of title creditors within and across the selected jurisdictions and international instruments;
3) Evaluate the Belgian functional approach and legislation on retention of title and, if applicable, suggest recommendations to improve the Belgian legislation.

8. *Research questions* – The three research objectives of this dissertation give rise to one overarching research question:

What is the meaning and role of the (Belgian) functional approach with regards to retention of title and what is its impact on retention of title creditors?

This question breaks down in three sub-questions:

1) What were the leading examples for the Belgian legislator with respect to the functional approach, how is the functional approach applied to retention of title in these frameworks and what is the impact for retention of title creditors?

To better understand the functional approach in the Belgian Security Rights Act, this question examines the functional approaches that served as inspiration for the Belgian Security Rights Act (i.e. Article 9 UCC, the UNICTRAL Guide and Model Law and the DCFR). The focus is on the specific functional approach these jurisdiction and instruments have developed and how they apply to retention of title and retention of title creditors. The assessment of impact focuses on whether the application of the functional approach has affected the rights of retention of title creditors after retention of title has been recharacterized to functionally similar security rights in movable goods or their legal outcomes have been equated with those of functionally similar security rights. This question is addressed in Part 2, chapter 1 of this dissertation in which the different selected functional approaches are analyzed.

2) How is the functional approach applied to retention of title, and more specifically retention of title creditors, in the Security Rights Act and how does this compare to retention of title in the other selected jurisdictions and international instruments?

Once the different functional approaches and their application to retention of title are better understood, the application of the functional approach to retention of title in the Security Rights Act is examined and its potential impact on retention of title creditors assessed in part 3 of this dissertation. When looking at the potential impact of the functional approach, the focus is on whether retention of title creditors lose any of their rights or protections following their integration in the Security Rights Act. Furthermore, retention of title in the Security Rights Act is compared to retention of title or its functional equivalent in the other selected jurisdictions and international instruments: PMSI in Article 9 UCC (part 2, ch. 1, section 1), acquisition security rights, retention of title and finance leasing in the UNICTRAL Guide and Model Law (part 2, ch. 1, section 2), retention of ownership devices in the DCFR (part 2, ch. 1, section 3) and retention of title in Germany (part 2, ch. 2).

3) What can we learn from the analysis and the comparison of the different approaches to retention of title in the selected jurisdictions and frameworks and how can the Belgian legislation with regards to retention of title be improved upon?

The analysis of the application of the functional approach to retention of title in the Belgian Security Rights Act allows for the identification of the success, but also potential problem areas concerning the Belgian functional approach to retention of title and to make recommendations for improvements. These recommendations are formulated in part 3, ch. 3 of this dissertation. For these recommendations, I turn on the one hand to the different functional approaches in the United States, the UNCITRAL Guide and Model Law and DCFR, and on the other hand to the alternative approach followed in Germany. More specifically, should Belgium follow through on its choice to pursue a functional approach, as in Article 9 UCC, the UNCITRAL Guide and Model Law and DCFR, or should Belgium revert back to a non-functional approach, such as in Germany? These recommendations can be useful in the development of the new Book 9 of the Belgian Civil Code concerning security rights in movable goods. Rather than the legislator just copying the current Security Rights Act to the new Civil Code, the reform can be used as momentum to either improve the application of the functional approach or to re-evaluate the use of the functional approach as method to integrate retention of title in secured transactions law.

CHAPTER 2
METHODOLOGY

9. *Overview* – In order to achieve these research objectives appropriate research subjects were selected and a suitable methodology was developed. The justification for the different research subjects and the different phases of the selected methodology are described in further detail below.

SECTION 1 – SELECTION OF RESEARCH SUBJECTS

1. COUNTRY AND INTERNATIONAL INSTRUMENT SELECTION

10. *Country selection based on inspiration for the functional approach in the Security Rights Act* – The first objective of this research is to clarify the functional approach and its application to retention of title in Belgium. Consequently, Belgium and more specifically retention of title in the Security Rights Act is selected as a research subject. Additionally, the explanatory memorandum to the Security Rights Act explicitly mentions Article 9 UCC of the United States, the UNCITRAL Guide and the DCFR as sources of inspiration for the functional approach in the Belgian Security Rights Act.[44] Therefore, this jurisdiction and these international instruments are well suited to provide more insight into the functional approach as it is developed in the Security Rights Act, but also offer new insights into different approaches to the functional approach, their application to retention of title and how these are adopted in jurisdictions and translated to international instruments.

11. *Country selection based on contrast* – The functional approach in Belgium is contrasted with a jurisdiction that takes a different approach to retention of title: Germany. As mentioned, Germany has steered away from applying the functional approach to retention of title and maintained retention of title as a mechanism entirely separate from security rights in movable goods. Moreover, in Germany there is a greater recognition of title-based security mechanisms which includes not only retention of title, but also transfer of title

[44] Explanatory memorandum Security Rights Act, no. 2463/001, 15–16.

mechanisms.[45] Consequently, Germany offers an entirely different approach to the regulation of retention of title, and title-based security by extension, which makes for an interesting contrast with Belgium in particular and the functional security rights frameworks in general. More specifically, the comparison between retention of title in Belgium and Germany provides insight into what a different approach to retention of title may look like and whether this approach can be an alternative for the current approach in the Security Rights Act.

2. TYPE OF GOOD ENCUMBERED WITH RETENTION OF TITLE

12. *Choice for retention of title in movable, tangible goods* – Title can be retained to a myriad of goods: tangible, intangible, movable and immovable goods. Nevertheless, a choice was made to focus the dissertation on retention of title in tangible and movable goods.

First, the focus on retention of title in tangible and not intangible goods stems from the fact that traditionally title is retained to tangible goods. Theoretically title can be retained to intangible goods, such as accounts receivable and shares, but this is less common and much more complex. Consequently, if the research would include retention of title in intangible goods, the analysis would likely get bogged down in the complexities of retention of title in intangible goods. This would distract from the research objective: the analysis of the different regulatory approaches to retention of title.

Furthermore, the choice to exclude retention of title in immovable goods stems from the scope of the legal frameworks in the selected jurisdictions. In Article 9 UCC[46], the Security Rights Act[47], retention of title in the *Bundesgezetsbuch*[48] (hereafter, BGB), the UNCITRAL Guide and Model Law[49] and DCFR[50] the scope of retention of title is explicitly limited to movable goods only. Consequently, this dissertation only examines retention of title with regards to movable goods.

45 W. WIEGAND, '§929–931' in W. WIEGAND (ed.), *J. Von Staudingers Kommentar zum Bürgerlichen Gesetzbuch mit Einführungsgesetz und Nebengesetzen*, vol. 3, (Berlin: Sellier, 2017), par. 1 *et seq.*

46 §9–109 UCC (2010).

47 Art. 69 SRA.

48 §449 BGB.

49 UNCITRAL Guide, 32; art. 1 UNCITRAL Model Law.

50 Art. IX. – 1:101 DCFR.

SECTION 2 – FUNCTIONAL COMPARATIVE RESEARCH

13. *Tertium comparationis* – To achieve the set research objectives, a functional comparative research methodology is applied. The *tertium comparationis*[51] is the treatment of retention of title and its functional equivalents (i.e. PMSI, acquisition security rights, retention of ownership devices, *Eigentumsvorbehalt*) in the secured transactions and corporate bankruptcy laws of the selected jurisdictions and international instruments. The functional comparative methodology compares how different jurisdictions and international instruments tackle similar problems differently, but with functionally similar results.[52] In this dissertation, the common problem that is solved via different means is the treatment of retention of title from a secured transactions and corporate bankruptcy law perspective: the functional approach with or without recharacterization or the non-functional approach.

14. *Internal and external comparison*[53] – The internal comparison looks at how the functional approach is applied to retention of title within the selected jurisdictions and whether this approach has resulted in any changes to the rights of retention of title creditors. On an external level, the functional approach towards retention of title in the Belgian Security Rights Act is compared with (1) the functional approach with recharacterization in Article 9 UCC and the UNCITRAL unitary approach, (2) the functional approach without recharacterization of the UNCITRAL non-unitary approach and DCFR and (3) the non-functional approach in Germany. The comparison of the treatment and regulation of retention of title across jurisdictions and international instruments with and without the functional approach allows for a better understanding of the different (functional) approaches to retention of title and allows for an evaluation of the role and meaning of the functional approach as a method to integrate retention of title in the Belgian Security Rights Act.

The functional comparative research is divided in: (1.) a descriptive component, (2.) a comparative component and (3.) an explanatory and evaluative component.[54]

---

51 The *tertium comparationis* is the point of comparison among all the selected jurisdictions and international instruments (L. KESTEMONT, *Handbook on legal methodology*, (Antwerp: Intersentia, 2018), 38–39).

52 K. ZWEIGERT and H. KÖTZ, *Introduction to comparative law*, (Oxford: Clarendon Press, 1998), 34 *et seq.*; L. KESTEMONT, *Handbook on legal methodology*, (Antwerp: Intersentia, 2018), 44.

53 L. KESTEMONT, *Handbook on legal methodology*, (Antwerp: Intersentia, 2018), 12–13.

54 L. KESTEMONT, *Handbook on legal methodology*, (Antwerp: Intersentia, 2018), 48–54.

1. DESCRIPTIVE COMPONENT

15. *Description with the aim to clarify the functional approach and compare different treatments of retention of title* – The first research objective sets out to clarify the functional approach and its application to retention of title. To achieve this objective, I start this dissertation with a descriptive analysis of the application of the functional approach to retention of title in the jurisdiction and international instruments that served as inspiration for the Security Rights Act (i.e. Article 9 UCC of the United States, the UNCITRAL Guide and Model Law and the DCFR). The analysis is conducted from a creditor perspective and allows for an assessment of whether and to what extent the functional approach results in equivalent legal outcomes for retention of title and functionally similar mechanisms.

This is followed by a descriptive analysis of retention of title in Germany. In this section, the focus is on the treatment of retention of title and the rights of retention of title creditors in a jurisdiction that does not apply the functional approach and maintains a strict distinction between the different forms of secured transactions.[55] This analysis is used to present an alternative option, besides the functional approach, to treat and regulate retention of title.

Finally, the treatment and approach taken towards retention of title in the Belgian Security Rights Act is also described. Here, the focus is on the attempt the Belgian legislator made to apply the functional approach to retention of title in the Security Rights Act. More specifically, the examination looks at the mechanisms with which retention of title is functionally equated, the extent to which the Belgian legislator creates equivalent legal outcomes for retention of title and functionally similar mechanisms and whether this is in line with the application of the functional approach in the other selected jurisdictions.

16. *Source material* – The descriptive examinations are based on primary sources, such as statutes and case law and secondary sources, such as legal doctrine and explanatory memoranda. These sources are analyzed by making use of a variety of interpretation techniques[56], such as a systemic interpretation[57], legal-historic interpretation, teleological interpretation and interpretation based on jurisprudence, doctrine and non-binding legal sources (i.e. non-binding international instruments).

---

55 See *supra* no. 5.

56 L. KESTEMONT, *Handbook on legal methodology*, (Antwerp: Intersentia, 2018), 21–31.

57 Legal provisions concerning retention of title are interpreted as part of a larger legal act or code and a larger legal system. See specifically on systematic interpretation, L. KESTEMONT, *Handbook on legal methodology*, (Antwerp: Intersentia, 2018), 24–26.

2. COMPARATIVE COMPONENT

17. *Internal and external comparisons* – The functional comparison takes place in two phases: (1) comparison of retention of title before and after the application of the functional approach in the selected jurisdictions and international instruments that apply the functional approach and (2) comparison of retention of title in the Security Rights Act with retention of title or its functional equivalent in the selected jurisdictions and international instruments (i.e. Article 9 UCC of the United States, the UNCITRAL Guide and Model Law, the DCFR and the BGB in Germany).

The first comparison is aimed at gaining more insight in the application of the functional approach, whether this leads to changes to retention of title and the rights of retention of title creditors and an evaluation of the application of the functional approach in Article 9 UCC and the Security Rights Act. The second comparison enables the determination of similarities and differences between retention of title in jurisdictions and international instruments that have taken different approaches to the treatment of retention of title.

3. EXPLANATORY AND EVALUATIVE COMPONENT

18. *Clarification of the functional approach and comparison of retention within the selected jurisdictions and international instrument with functional approach* – The internal analysis of retention of title in the selected jurisdiction and international instruments with different functional approaches allows for a clarification of the operation of the different functional approaches. Furthermore, it enables an evaluation of whether and to what extent the functional approach in the selected jurisdictions and international instruments with functional approach creates equivalent legal outcomes for retention of title and functionally similar security mechanisms.

The internal, functional comparison of retention of title prior to and after the application of the functional approach makes an evaluation of what the potential consequences are of this approach for the rights of retention of title creditors possible. Finally, the comparison of retention of title before and after the application of the functional approach in Belgium allows for an evaluation of whether and to what extent the functional approach as applied to retention of title has helped in the creation of a more coherent, clear and predictable security rights framework as set out in the objectives of the explanatory memorandum.[58]

19. *Threefold evaluation following the external comparison of retention of title* – First, the comparison of the different functional approaches for retention of

[58] Explanatory memorandum Security Rights Act, no. 2463/001, 9.

title enables an evaluation of the different functional approaches and whether there is a need for different functional approaches to retention of title. Second, from a Belgian perspective, the external, functional comparison of retention of title in the Security Rights Act with retention of title and finance leases under the non-unitary approach in the UNCITRAL Guide and retention of ownership in the DCFR allows me to evaluate the application of the functional approach without recharacterization in the Security Rights Act. Third, the external, functional comparison of retention of title makes it possible to evaluate the alternative approaches to retention of title, such as the functional approach with recharacterization to a PMSI or acquisition security right (i.e. Article 9 UCC and the UNCITRAL unitary approach) or the non-functional approach (i.e. Germany) and to formulate recommendations on the direction of the Security Rights Act.

CHAPTER 3

USE OF TERMINOLOGY FOR THE PURPOSE OF THIS BOOK

20. *Retention of title and security rights as catch-all terms throughout this dissertation* – Throughout this dissertation the term retention of title is used to refer to the different retention of title mechanisms in the selected jurisdictions and international instruments: conditional sale, finance leasing, retention of ownership devices, *Eigentumsvorbehalt* and *eigendomsvoorbehoud*. Similarly, the term security right is used as an overarching term to refer to all types of security interest (Article 9 UCC), security right (UNCITRAL Guide and Model and Book IX DCFR) and *zakelijke zekerheden in roerende goederen/sûretés réelles mobilières* (Belgian Security Rights Act).

However, in the event a situation or rule is specific to a certain retention of title mechanism or security right in a particular jurisdiction or international instrument, its specific term is used to indicate this difference.

PART 2

DIFFERENT APPROACHES TO THE REGULATION OF RETENTION OF TITLE

21. *Introduction* – In this part, I examine two divergent approaches to the regulation of retention of title: (1) the functional approach with and without recharacterization and (2) the non-functional approach to retention of title.

CHAPTER 1
THE MANY FACES OF THE FUNCTIONAL APPROACH

22. *Overview* – In this chapter I discuss the main sources of inspiration of the functional approach in the Security Rights Act: Article 9 of the Uniform Commercial Code (UCC) (section 1) and the selected international instruments (section 2). For each jurisdiction and international instrument, I set out how the functional approach was developed, applied to retention of title and potentially affected the rights of retention of title creditors.

SECTION 1 – ARTICLE 9 UCC: FROM CONDITIONAL SALE TO PMSI

23. *Historical setting of the analysis of Article 9 UCC* – The background and development towards the functional approach as applied to retention of title in Article 9 UCC is detailed in this chapter. I start with a brief introduction to the treatment of retention of title prior to Article 9 UCC via an assessment of case law and doctrine starting around the 1800s (1.). This is followed by a brief discussion of the introduction of the functional approach in Article 9 UCC (2.). Finally, I discuss how the functional approach is specifically applied to retention of title and the consequences of the functional approach for retention of title creditors (3.) and its potential impact on retention of title during corporate bankruptcy proceedings (4.). For this section, the focus is on the latest version of Article 9 UCC (2010). However, earlier versions and changes to Article 9 UCC are discussed when relevant.

1. RETENTION OF TITLE PRE-ARTICLE 9 UCC: CONDITIONAL SALE AND LEASING

24. *Introduction of the terms conditional sale and leasing* – Pre-Article 9 UCC retention of title clauses could be found in either a conditional sale or a lease agreement. Evidently, conditional sales are a type of sale and are agreed upon between a seller and a buyer.[59] In a conditional sale the goods are intended to become the buyer's property once the final payment to the seller is made.[60] Conversely, a lease is traditionally a transaction in which the lessee leases or rents a movable good from the lessor and pays regular installments for the use of the good.[61] At the end of the lease agreement, the leased goods are expected to return to the lessor.

25. *Conflicting views on the acceptance of conditional sales* – Initially there was some division as to whether conditional sales were valid and could be enforced against the buyer and third parties. The majority of courts[62] and

59 G. GILMORE and A. AXELROD, 'Chattel security: I', (1947–48) 57 Yale L. J., (517) 542. As of 1918 defined in art. 1.1 of the Uniform Conditional Sales Act.

60 J. WILFORD, E. DAVISSON and N. CHARLES, *Lease as a financing and selling device*, (An Arbor: School of Business and Administration, 1951), 27.

61 W. C. DALZELL, 'Lease-contracts as a means of conveying title to chattels', (1921) 1 Ore. L. Rev., (9) 13; J. WILFORD, E. DAVISSON and N. CHARLES, *Lease as a financing and selling device*, (An Arbor: School of Business and Administration, 1951), 25.

62 Supreme Judicial Court of Massachusetts, 1 May 1808, Hussey v. Thornton, 4 Mass., (405) 407; Supreme Judicial Court of Massachusetts 1 November 1830, Reed v. Upton, 10 Pick, (522) 536; Court of Appeals of Law and Equity of South Carolina 1 May 1830, Reeves v. Harris, 1 Bail., (563) 564; Supreme Court of Errors and Appeals of Tennessee 1 March 1835, Bradshaw v. Thomas, 15 Tenn., (497) 499; Supreme Court of Vermont 1 January 1836, Bigelow v. Huntley, 8 Vt., (151) 154–155; Court of Errors of South Carolina 1 May 1839, Bennett v. Sims, Rice, (421) 423; Supreme Court of Errors of Connecticut 1 June 1843, Forbes v. Marsh, 15 Conn., (384) 392; Supreme Judicial Court of Massachusetts 1 October 1849, Heath v. Randall, 58 Mass., (195) 196; Supreme Court of Vermont 1 January 1850, Buckmaster v. Smith, 22 Vt., (203) 204; Supreme Judicial Court of Massachusetts 1 October 1855, Sargent v. Metcalf, 5 Gray, (306) 308; Court of Appeals of Kentucky 1 July 1855, Patton v. McCane, 15 B. Mon., (555) 558; Supreme Judicial Court of Massachusetts 1 October 1856, Blancherd v. Child, 7 Gray, (155) 157; Court of Appeals of New York 1 June 1857, Herring v. Hoppock, 15 N.Y., (409) 413; Supreme Court of New York 13 October 1857, Fleeman v. McKean, 25 Barb., (474) 480; Supreme Court of Missouri 1 March 1858, Dannefelser v. Weigel, 27 Mo., (45) 47; Supreme Court of Tennessee 1 September 1859, Price v. Jones, 3 Head, (84) 86; Supreme Court of Iowa 14 April 1859, Bailey v. Harris, 8 Iowa, (331) 331; Court of Appeals of New York 1 January 1869, Ballard v. Burgett, 1 Hand, (314) 315–316; Supreme Court of Indiana 12 June 1860, Shireman v. Jackson, 14 Ind., (459) 460; Circuit Court Connecticut 20 September 1870, Bauendahl v. Horr, 7 Blatchf. 548, 2 F. Cas., (1040) 1041; Supreme Court of California 1 April 1871, Kohler v. Hayes, 41 Cal., (455) 457–458; Supreme Court of Ohio 1 December 1872, Sage v. Sleutz, 23 Ohio St., (1) 4; Supreme Court of Ohio 1 December 1872, Sage v. Sleutz, 23 Ohio St., (1) 8–9; Supreme Court of Arkansas, 1 November 1875, Carroll v. Wiggins, 30 Ark., (402) 477 and the case law there cited; Supreme Judicial Court of Massachusetts 23 March 1875, Currier v. Knapp, 117 Mass., (324) 325–326; Supreme Court of Indiana 1 May 1875, Lester v. East, 49 Ind., (588) 592; Supreme Court of Ohio 1 December 1876, Sanders v. Keber, 28 Ohio St., (630) 636–637; Circuit Court District of Missouri 1 November 1877, Rogers' Locomotive Works v. Lewis, 4 Dill. 158, 20 F. Cas., (1134) 1135; District Court District of California 5 March 1878, Truman v. Hardin, 5 Sawy. 115, 24 F. Cas., (249) 250–251; Supreme Court of the United States 1 October 1878, Fosdick v. Schall, 99 U.S., (235) 247; Supreme Court of the United States 1 October 1878, Fosdick v. Schall, 99 U.S., (235) 247; Supreme Court of Missouri 1 October 1879, Wangler v. Franklin, 70 Mo., (659) 660; Supreme Court of North Carolina 1 January 1879, Clayton v. Hester, 80 N.C., (275) 278; Supreme Court of Ohio 1 January 1884, Call v. Seymour, 40 Ohio St., (670) 673; Supreme Court of the Territory of Montana 31 January 1885, Heinbockel v. Zugbaum, 5 Mont. 344, (897) 900; Supreme Court of Missouri 1 October 1885, Coover v. Johnson, 86 Mo., (533) 537; Supreme Court of Georgia 20 October 1885, Bowen v. Frick, 75 Ga., (786) 788; Supreme Court of Arkansas, 16 October

doctrine[63] had a positive view on the validity and third-party effectiveness of conditional sales. In states that recognized conditional sales it was described as follows:

> *Where the buyer is by the contract bound to do anything as a condition, either precedent or concurrent, on which the passing of the property depends, the property will not pass until the condition be fulfilled, even though the goods may have been actually delivered into the possession of the buyer.*[64]

However, in some states, such as Illinois, conditional sales were considered fraudulent and were recharacterized as chattel mortgages[65], which required the fulfillment of certain formalities to be effective.[66] This minority opinion

---

1886, McIntosh v. Hill, 1. S. W., (680) 681; St. Louis Court of Appeals, Missouri 23 February 1886, Defiance Mach. Works v. Trisler, 21 Mo. App., (69) 71; Supreme Court of Pennsylvania 1 January 1909, Powell v. Clawson, 38 Pa. Super, (245) 250.

63 A. B. PEARSON and H. F. BOYD, *Benjamin's treatise on the law of sale of personal property*, (Boston: Charles Edson & Co. Publishers, 1888), 477; C. R. MILLER, *A treatise on the law of conditional sales of personal property*, (Cincinnati: R. Clarke, 1888), 60; A. H. FENN, 'Conditional sales', (1890) 24 Am. L. Rev., (64) 65; F. B. HARING, *The law of conditional sales*, (New York: The Ronald Press, 1907), 11.

64 A. B. PEARSON and H. F. BOYD, *Benjamin's treatise on the law of sale of personal property*, (Boston: Charles Edson & Co. Publishers, 1888), 474. See also, Carroll v. Wiggins, 30 Ark., (402) 404; Supreme Judicial Court of Massachusetts, 1 May 1808, Hussey v. Thornton, 4 Mass., (405) 407; Supreme Court of California, 1 July 1879, Hegler v. Eddy, 53 Cal., (597) 598; Supreme Court of Indiana 31 May 1859, Thomas v. Winters, 12 Ind., (322) 323–324; Supreme Court of Indiana 1 May 1861, Plummer v. Shirley, 16 Ind., (380) 382; Supreme Court of Indiana 1 November 1867, Dunbar v. Rawles, 28 Ind., (225) 231–232; Supreme Court of Iowa 14 June 1876, Moseley v. Shattuck, 43 Iowa, (540) 543; Supreme Court of Indiana 1 November 1876, Bradshaw v. Warner, 54 Ind., (58) 60; Supreme Court of California 1 October 1877, Cardinell v. Bennett, 52 Cal., (476) 477; Supreme Court of Georgia 1 January 1877, Flanders & Huguenin v. Maynard, 58 Ga., (56) 57; Supreme Court of Indiana 1 November 1877, Hodson v. Warner, 60 Ind. (214) 215; Supreme Court of Georgia 1 January 1877, Jowers v. Blandy, 58 Ga., (379) 383; Supreme Court of Indiana 1 November 1878, Domestic Sewing Mach. Co. v. Arthurhultz, 63 Ind., (322) 325–326; Supreme Judicial Court of Massachusetts 1 September 1854, Henry Coggill & another v. Hartford and New Haven Railroad Company, 3 Gray, (545) 546–547; Supreme Court of New York 3 September 1855, Brewster v. Baker, 20 Barb., (364) 369; Supreme Court of Indiana 15 December 1858, King v. Wilkins, 11 Ind., (347) 349; Supreme Court of Missouri 1 March 1858, Dannefelser v. Weigel, 27 Mo., (45) 47; Supreme Court of Michigan July 7 1871, Preston v. Whitney, 23 Mich., (260) 267; Supreme Court of Missouri 1 February 1873, Ridgeway v. Kennedy, 52 Mo., (24) 25; Supreme Judicial Court of Massachusetts 1 January 1874, Burnham C. Benner & another v. Asaheld D. Puffer & another, 114 Mass., (376) 378; Superior Court of Judicature of New Hampshire 11 August 1876, King v. Bates, 57 N. H., (446) 450; Supreme Judicial Court of Massachusetts 1 January 1879, Drury v. Hervey, 126 Mass., (519) 519; Supreme Judicial Court of Massachusetts 1 October 1824, Barrett v. Pitchard, 2 Pick., (512) 547;.

65 Chattel mortgage is a secured transaction in which the title to a good is transferred to a mortgagee as security for the payment of a debt or for the performance of an obligation (A. B. GRIFFIN and A. F. CURTIS, *The law of chattel mortgages and conditional sales under the Uniform Conditional Sales Act, adapted to New York State*, (4 edn., Albany: Bender, 1925), 2; J. SCHOULER, *Treatise on the law of personal property*, (Albany: M. Bender & Co., 1918), 621–622).

66 Supreme Court of Illinois 1 January 1859, Brundage v. Camp, 21 Ill., (330) 335–336; Supreme Court of Illinois 1 April 1865, McCormick v. Hadden, 37 Ill., (370) 372; Supreme Court of Illinois 1 January 1868, Murch v. Wright, 46 Ill., (487) 488–489; Supreme Court of Illinois

concerning the effectiveness of retention of title in conditional sale agreements was due to the influence of English bankruptcy law. One of the English bankruptcy provisions set out that any goods in the bankrupt's possession, of which he is the reputed or presumed owner, will be to the benefit of the bankrupt's creditors and not the creditor with the retained title.[67] The effect of this provision was compounded by the fact that English case law already had a negative view towards non-possessory secured transactions.[68] It had been standing case law since the *Twyne* case that any transfer of possession of a movable good without publicity is fraudulent.[69] This reasoning was then applied in American cases, although no such bankruptcy provision or case law existed in the United States.[70] To end this debate, the United States Supreme Court intervened and confirmed in 1886 that there was no legal foundation for this interpretation and it was accepted that a sale and delivery of a movable good under the condition to retain title with the vendor until payment of the purchase price was a valid and enforceable sale agreement in which title remained with the vendor.[71]

States not only varied in the recognition, but also in the regulation of conditional sale agreements. The disparity was most pronounced in the context of third-party effectiveness. For example, Alabama, Arkansas, Arizona, Colorado, Connecticut, Florida, Georgia, Iowa, Kansas, Maine, Massachusetts, Minnesota, Missouri, Montana, Nebraska, New Hampshire, New Jersey, New York, North Carolina, North Dakota, Ohio, Oklahoma, South Dakota, Texas, Vermont, Virginia, Washington, West Virginia, Wisconsin and Wyoming enacted a registration requirement for conditional sales agreements to be effective against third parties.[72] However, lease agreements were often exempt from the filing requirement all together.[73] This disparate regulation

1 September 1871, Michigan Cent. R. Co. v. Phillips, 60 Ill., (190) 195; Supreme Court of Illinois 1 January 1878, Lucas v. Campbell, 88 Ill., (447) 449–450; Supreme Court of Illinois 1 September 1878, Van Duzor v. Allen, 90 Ill., (499) 502.

67 S. 10 & 11, 21 Jac. 1, c. 19 (1623).

68 Court of King's Bench 29 January 1808, Horn v. Baker, 9 East, (215) 237–238; Court of Common Pleas 23 November 1809, Holroyd v. Gwynne, 2 Taunton, (176) 180.

69 Court of the King's Bench 1 January 1601, Twyne's case, 76 E.R., (809) 814. See also, D. G. BAIRD and T. H. JACKSON, 'Possession and ownership: an examination of the scope of article 9', (1983) 35 Stan. L. Rev., (175) 180 *et seq.*

70 X., *Principles of the law of conditional sales and chattel mortgages: a monograph*, (St. Paul: West Publishing, 1899), 3.

71 Supreme Court of the United States 8 November 1886, Harkness v. Russel, 118 U.S., (663) 670 and 682.

72 W. W. MORILL, *Conditional sales and bailments with forms*, (Albany: Mathew Bender, 1901), 4 *et seq.*

73 Court of Appeals of Kentucky 19 November 1877, Greer v. Church, 13 Bush, (430) 434; Supreme Court of New York 6 February 1888, Marvin Safe Co. v. Emanuel, 21 Abb. N. Cas., (181) 192; Supreme Judicial Court of Maine 1 September 1898, Campbell v. Atherton, 92 Me. 66, 42 A., (323) 233; Supreme Court of Rhode Island 31 December 1881, Carpenter v. Scott, 13 R. I., (477) 479; Supreme Court of Vermont 1 January 1882, Whitcomb v. Woodworth, 54 Vt., (544) 547; Supreme Judicial Court of Maine 22 March 1887, Gorham v. Holden, 79 Me. 317,

of conditional sales and lease agreements led to an undesirable situation in which the treatment of retention of title could vary from state to state, thereby complicating interstate trade.[74]

26. *Retention of title in lease agreements* – On the surface, one would distinguish leasing from conditional sale agreements, since the leased goods are supposed to return to the lessor at the end of the lease agreement. However, courts were quick to realize that there are many instances where lease agreements show great similarities with conditional sales. For example, when title passes automatically when the last rent installment is paid[75], when the rent installments make up the full value of the leased good[76], or when the intentions of the parties[77] or all the conditions, clauses and covenants that make up the agreement indicate that a transaction is a conditional sale instead of lease agreement.[78] In these instances, courts intervened and recharacterized the lease agreement as a conditional sale in which title was only retained to secure the outstanding credit.[79] The reasoning behind this recharacterization

9 A., (894) 894; Supreme Court of California 23 March 1900, Lundy Furniture Co. v. White, 128 Cal., (170) 171; Supreme Court of South Dakota 6 July 1905, Pringle v. Canfield, 19 S. D. 506, 104 N. W., (223) 223; Supreme Court of Pennsylvania 14 May 1906, Kelly Springfield Road Roller Co. v. Spyker, 215 Pa., (332) 333. See also, R. J. LONG, 'Conditional sale' in D. S. GARLAND and L. P. MCGEHEE (eds.), *The American and English encyclopaedia of law*, vol. 6, (New York: Edward Thompson Co., 1898), 447.

74 G. G. BOGERT, 'Proposed uniform conditional sales act', (1917) 3 Cornell L. Rev., (1) 1–2.

75 Supreme Court of New Hampshire 16 March 1888, Gerrish v. Clark, 64 N. H. 492, 13 A., (870) 870; District Court of Pennsylvania 8 July 1907, In re Morris, 16 Pa. D. 875, 156 F., (597) 600.

76 Supreme Court of Rhode Island 31 December 1881, Carpenter v. Scott, 13 R. I., (477) 479; Supreme Court of Vermont 1 January 1882, Whitcomb v. Woodworth, 54 Vt., (544) 547; Supreme Judicial Court of Maine 22 March 1887, Gorham v. Holden, 79 Me. 317, 9 A., (894) 894; Supreme Court of California 23 March 1900, Lundy Furniture Co. v. White, 128 Cal., (170) 171; Supreme Court of South Dakota 6 July 1905, Pringle v. Canfield, 19 S. D. 506, 104 N. W., (223) 223; Supreme Court of Pennsylvania 14 May 1906, Kelly Springfield Road Roller Co. v. Spyker, 215 Pa., (332) 333.

77 Supreme Court of Illinois 1 January 1878, Lucas v. Campbell, 88 Ill., (447) 449; Supreme Court of Georgia 28 July 1890, Hays v. Jordan, 85 Ga. 741, 11 S. E., (833) 835; Supreme Court of California 23 March 1900, Lundy Furniture Co. v. White, 128 Cal., (170) 171; Supreme Judicial Court of Massachusetts 3 January 1902, Smith v. Aldrich, 180 Mass., (367) 368; Superior Court of Delaware 10 December 1906, Staunton v. Smith, 6 Penne. 193, 65 A., (593) 594–595.

78 Supreme Court of South Dakota 6 July 1905, Pringle v. Canfield, 19 S. D. 506, 104 N. W., (223) 223; Supreme Court of Colorado 6 July 1908, Coors v. Reagan, 44 Colo., (126) 130.

79 Court of Appeals of Kentucky 19 November 1877, Greer v. Church, 13 Bush, (430) 434; Supreme Court of New York 6 February 1888, Marvin Safe Co. v. Emanuel, 21 Abb. N. Cas., (181) 192; Supreme Judicial Court of Maine 1 September 1898, Campbell v. Atherton, 92 Me. 66, 42 A., (323) 233; Supreme Court of Rhode Island 31 December 1881, Carpenter v. Scott, 13 R. I., (477) 479; Supreme Court of Vermont 1 January 1882, Whitcomb v. Woodworth, 54 Vt., (544) 547; Supreme Judicial Court of Maine 22 March 1887, Gorham v. Holden, 79 Me. 317, 9 A., (894) 894; Supreme Court of California 23 March 1900, Lundy Furniture Co. v. White, 128 Cal., (170) 171; Supreme Court of South Dakota 6 July 1905, Pringle v. Canfield, 19 S. D. 506, 104 N. W., (223) 223; Supreme Court of Pennsylvania 14 May 1906, Kelly Springfield

was that conditional sales, unlike true lease agreements[80], were often subjected to additional requirements, such as a filing requirement.[81] Consequently, parties could not be allowed to circumvent the rules concerning conditional sales by simply casting their agreement under a different name.

27. *Introduction of the Uniform Conditional Sales Act* – The amalgam of conditional sale regulations and the lack of regulation for leasing led the Uniform Law Commission to take the initiative in 1918 to draft the Uniform Conditional Sales Act (hereafter also, UCSA). The fundamental aspects of the UCSA were:

> *"(1) That the reservation of title by the seller shall be void as to innocent purchasers or attaching creditors unless the contract is recorded; (2) That the seller shall not by stipulations as to forfeiture, and by seizure of the chattel and attempted termination of the contract secure for himself anything in excess of the satisfaction of his claim for the purchase price but shall account to the buyer for any sur- plus; and (3) that risk of loss shall be on the buyer."*[82]

Furthermore, given this trend to recharacterize certain lease agreements as conditional sales in case law, the drafters of the UCSA explicitly included leasing in the scope of the UCSA:

> *(2) any bailment or leasing of goods where payments are made over time that are equivalent to the value of the goods and for which it is agreed that the bailee or lessee is bound to become or has the option to become the owner of the goods when he complies with the conditions of the contract."*[83]

It was reasoned that in each of these transactions the intention of the seller, lessor or bailor was to only retain title while the credit was still outstanding and to transfer title the movable good to the lessee at the end of the transaction. Consequently, the drafters decided that such lease agreements and bailments should be governed by the same rules as conditional sales. Otherwise, the classification of the agreement as a lease or bailment could be used to evade the rules of the UCSA and would result in different treatment and formalities for functionally similar contracts.[84] The fact that ownership did not always

---

Road Roller Co. v. Spyker, 215 Pa., (332) 333. See also, R. J. LONG, 'Conditional sale' in D. S. GARLAND and L. P. MCGEHEE (eds.), *The American and English encyclopaedia of law*, vol. 6, (New York: Edward Thompson Co., 1898), 447.

80 X, 'Acquisition of industrial and commercial equipment through leasing arrangements', (1957) 66 Yale L. J., (751) 764 and 770.

81 See *supra* no. 25.

82 W. G. HALE, 'The Uniform Conditional Sales Act', (1922–1923) 2 Or. L. Rev., (1) 2.

83 §1 (1) and (2) UCSA.

84 G. G. BOGERT, 'Proposed uniform conditional sales act', (1917) 3 Cornell L. Rev., (1) 3–4; H. NOYES GREENE, 'Uniform Conditional Sales Act and commentary' in H. NOYES GREEN (ed.), *Uniform laws, annotated*, vol. 2, (Northport: Edward Thompson Co., 1922), 3.

automatically pass at the end of a lease agreement or bailment, as it did in a conditional sale, was considered of small importance, since the drafters assumed that the lessee nearly always wanted to obtain ownership of the movable good once he had paid the value of the good.[85] With this legislative move certain lease agreements were explicitly recharacterized to conditional sales under the UCSA and subjected to its rules and requirements.

2. ARTICLE 9 UCC AND THE FUNCTIONAL APPROACH

28. *Overview* – In this section, a brief introduction is given to the Uniform Commercial Code and Article 9's place in it (2.1.). Furthermore, the introduction of the functional approach and its main tenets are also discussed (2.2.).

2.1. Article 9 of the Uniform Commercial Code

29. *Introduction* – The functional approach in the United States was introduced in Article 9 UCC. Article 9 is part of the larger Uniform Commercial Code series which were developed in the 1940's and promulgated in the 1950's. The Uniform Commercial Code generally and Article 9 UCC specifically are briefly introduced here.

2.1.1. The Uniform Commercial Code

30. *Incentive to introduce the Uniform Commercial Code (UCC)* – Before the UCC, commercial law in the United States was a combination of trade practices, common law and a sprinkling of Uniform Acts.[86] Despite their name, the Uniform Acts were not uniformly adopted[87] and the interaction between the different Uniform Acts did not always lead to desirable results.[88] Therefore, the suggestion was made to draft a new code that would encompass the various Uniform Acts and commercial transactions in general.[89]

---

85 H. NOYES GREENE, 'Uniform Conditional Sales Act and commentary' in H. NOYES GREEN (ed.), *Uniform laws, annotated*, vol. 2, (Northport: Edward Thompson Co., 1922), 3.

86 The Uniform Negotiable Instruments Law (1896), the Uniform Sales Act (1906), the Uniform Warehouse Receipt Act (1906), the Uniform Bills of Lading Act (1909), the Uniform Stock Transfer Act (1909), the Uniform Conditional Sales Act (1918), the Uniform Trust Receipts Act (1933), the Uniform Conditional Sales Act (1918) and the Uniform Negotiable Instruments Act (1896). See also, W. A. SCHNADER, 'A short history of the preparation and enactment of the Uniform Commercial Code' (1967) 22 U. Miami L. Rev. (1) 2.

87 K. N. LLEWELLYN, 'Why we need the Uniform Commercial Code', (1957) 10 U. Fla. L. Rev. (367) 370–372; W. A. SCHNADER, 'A short history of the preparation and enactment of the Uniform Commercial Code', (1967) 22 U. Miami L. Rev., (1) 2.

88 W. A. SCHNADER, 'A short history of the preparation and enactment of the Uniform Commercial Code', (1967) 22 U. Miami L. Rev., (1) 2.

89 K. N. LLEWELLYN, 'Why we need the Uniform Commercial Code', (1957) 10 U. Fla. L. Rev. (367) 372; W. L. BEERS, 'The new commercial code', (1947) 2 Bus. Law (14) 14–15.

31. *Timeline of the introduction of the Uniform Commercial Code* – The idea to create a Uniform Commercial Code was formulated in 1940 under the auspices of the National Conference of Commissioners on Uniform State Laws, which was later joined by the renowned American Law Institute.[90] Professor LLEWELLYN of Columbia Law School was appointed chief reporter on the Uniform Commercial Code.[91] He created sub-committees which were each responsible for a specific commercial transaction or section of the Code. The actual drafting of the Code commenced in 1945[92] and the first draft of the entire UCC was presented to the public in 1949. However, the first version of the UCC caused considerable commotion and was the topic of much debate.[93] As a result, the 1949 draft was heavily revised and re-evaluated in order to find a compromise between the views of the drafters and the views of different interest groups.[94] Therefore, the process to get the drafts past the Conference of Commissioners on Uniform State Laws and the American Law Institute took much longer than anticipated.[95] Finally, the UCC was promulgated in 1952 and consisted of 10 sections or articles.[96] This version of the UCC was immediately amended in 1953 following some further concerns by various interest groups.[97] In 1953 Pennsylvania was the first American state to put the enactment of the UCC to a vote and the UCC became effective in Pennsylvania on July 1st, 1954.

Since then both the number of member states in which the UCC is enacted, as well as the number of articles of the UCC have increased. First, after the enactment of the UCC in Pennsylvania in 1954 more and more States have enacted the UCC, reaching all fifty States in 1990 with the partial enactment of

---

90 Before the UCC the American Law Institute's most famous achievement were the Restatements of Law. The Restatement of Laws are an authoritative source of secondary legal materials in which the American Law Institute has written rules based on the accumulated case law on this issue, see P. WINSHIP, 'An historical overview of UCC article 9' in L. GULLIFER and O. AKSELI (eds.), *Secured transactions law reform: principles, policies and practice*, (Oxford: Hart Publisher, 2016), (21) 25.

91 W. A. SCHNADER, 'A short history of the preparation and enactment of the Uniform Commercial Code', (1967) 22 U. Miami L. Rev., (1) 4; P. WINSHIP, 'An historical overview of UCC article 9' in L. GULLIFER and O. AKSELI (eds.), *Secured transactions law reform: principles, policies and practice*, (Oxford: Hart Publisher, 2016), (21) 25.

92 P. WINSHIP, 'An historical overview of UCC article 9' in L. GULLIFER and O. AKSELI (eds.), *Secured transactions law reform: principles, policies and practice*, (Oxford: Hart Publisher, 2016), (21) 25.

93 A. R. KAMP, 'Uptown act: a history of the Uniform Commercial Code: 1940–49', (1997–98) 51 S. M. U. L. Rev. (275) 336 *et seq.*

94 Due to the strong reactions to the first public draft of the UCC, the 1949 version of the UCC is very different from the UCC that was finally offered for approval and promulgated amongst the different states. See, A. R. KAMP, 'Downtown code: a history of the Uniform Commercial Code 1949–1954', (2001) 49 Buffalo L. Rev. (359) 392.

95 W. A. SCHNADER, 'A short history of the preparation and enactment of the Uniform Commercial Code', (1967) 22 U. Miami L. Rev., (1) 5.

96 F. K. BEUTEL, 'The proposed Uniform Commercial Code as a problem in codification', (1951) 16 Law & Contemp. Probs. (141) 158–159.

97 W. A. SCHNADER, 'A short history of the preparation and enactment of the Uniform Commercial Code', (1967) 22 U. Miami L. Rev., (1) 7.

the UCC in Louisiana.[98] Second, new articles have been added to the UCC such as Article 2A on true leases and Article 4A on the transfers of funds, bringing the total now to 13 articles.

2.1.2. Article 9 UCC

32. *Innovating secured transactions law in Article 9 UCC* – The innovative nature of Article 9 UCC is mostly due to the fact that unlike other Articles of the UCC, the drafters did not merely restructure and redraft the problem areas of the existing common law and Uniform Acts. In Article 9 UCC, the drafters took the array of secured transactions in movable goods that existed across the United States prior to the UCC and created an entirely new and unified secured transactions law.[99]

33. *Panoply of secured transactions in movable goods pre-Article 9 UCC* – Prior to Article 9 UCC there was a multitude of secured transactions in movable goods in different laws and codes. LLEWELLYN listed the following pre-article 9 UCC secured transactions in movable goods:

> *"The chattel mortgage, the conditional sale, the pledge of documents of title with its now rather well developed "field warehouse" variant; there is the trust receipt; there are the two rather different types of assignment of contract rights: that of accounts receivable in bloc and that of a single executory production contract; there is the bailment variation of the sale on installments, familiar especially in railroad equipment financing as "the Pennsylvania plan"; there is the true factor's (i.e., selling agent's) possessory lien, and the banker-"factor's" statutory lien on the New York model. There is the introduction of banker's responsibility for the price of goods by way of the letter of credit, there is the device of suretyship or guaranty, there is the discount of customers' acceptances or consumers' notes."*[100]

The reason for the many secured transactions in movable goods was that originally the common law in most of the United States required the secured creditor to be in possession of the encumbered good.[101] Non-possessory

---

98 Louisiana has only accepted Article 1, 3, 4, 4A, 5, 7, 8 and 9.

99 J. J. WHITE and others, *Principles of secured transactions*, (St. Paul: West Academic Publishing, 2018), 2; G. GILMORE, 'The secured transactions article of the Commercial Code', (1951) 16 Law & Contemp. Probs., (27) 34; J. F. IRETON, 'Proposed commercial code: a new deal in chattel security', (1949) 43 Ill. L. Rev. (794) 796.

100 K. N. LLEWELLYN, 'Problems of codifying security law', (1948) 13 Law & Contemp. Probs. (687) 687. See also P. F. COOGAN, 'The lazy lawyer's guide to secured transactions under the Code' (1961–62) 60 Mich. L. Rev. (685) 704; H. KRIPKE, 'The modernization of commercial security under the Uniform Commercial Code' (1951) 16 Law & Contemp. Probs. (183) 183; J. BROOK, Secured transactions, (New York City: Aspen Publishers, 2011), 4 (hereafter, BROOK, Secured transactions).

101 R. A. HAKES, *The ABC's of the UCC: Article 9 secured transactions*, (3 edn., Chicago: American Bar Association, 2013), 3.

secured transactions in movable goods were generally considered as fraudulent conveyances and could be voided by the trustee in bankruptcy.[102] Consequently, only the possessory pledge originally existed. Nevertheless, many other types of secured transactions in movable goods were soon developed to circumvent this limitation to possessory secured transactions.[103] There were numerous problems with this uncoordinated development of new secured transactions mechanisms. First, the sheer amount of secured transactions made the field a very difficult legal domain to navigate. Second, the type of law in which these secured transactions were regulated would vary from state to state. Some states would rely on common law, others on specific laws or Uniform Acts.[104] Finally, the formalities for the different secured transactions and the rights for the holders of the different secured transactions could vary significantly from state to state making everything increasingly confusing and inefficient.[105]

Given the complex and uncoordinated nature of secured transactions in movable goods prior to the UCC, the head drafters for Article 9 UCC, GILMORE and DUNHAM, set out to simplify and streamline the field of secured transactions law.[106]

34. *Ongoing amendments made to Article 9 UCC* – Since its original enactment, Article 9 UCC has undergone several amendments in 1972, 1999, 2000, 2001 and 2010.[107] The analysis in this dissertation mainly works with the most recent version of Article 9 UCC (2010). However, when significant changes have been made to Article 9 UCC that had an impact on the application of the functional approach or the integration of retention of title, these will be mentioned.

---

102 The most notable example of the problems associated with non-possessory secured transactions was the case *Benedict v. Ratner* in which Justice Brandeis decided that the assignment of accounts receivables constituted a fraudulent conveyance under New York law and was therefore voidable by the trustee in bankruptcy (Supreme Court of the United States 25 May 1925, Benedict v. Ratner, 268 U. S., (353) 361).

103 R. A. HAKES, *The ABC's of the UCC: Article 9 secured transactions*, (3 edn., Chicago: American Bar Association, 2013), 3; G. GILMORE, A. AXELROD, 'Chattel security: I', (1947–48) 57 Yale L. J., (517) 522; G. GILMORE, 'Security law, formalism and Article 9', (1968) 47 Neb. L. Rev., (659) 660; J. J. WHITE, R. S. SUMMERS and R. A. HILMAN, *Uniform Commercial Code*, vol. 4, (6th edn., Eagan: Thomson Reuters, 2015), 3.

104 P. WINSHIP, 'An historical overview of UCC article 9' in L. GULLIFER and O. AKSELI (eds.), *Secured transactions law reform: principles, policies and practice*, (Oxford: Hart Publisher, 2016), (21) 22. See for examples, the Uniform Trust Receipt Act or the Uniform Conditional Sale Act.

105 J. J. WHITE and others, *Principles of secured transactions*, (St. Paul: West Academic Publishing, 2018), 2; R. A. HAKES, *The ABC's of the UCC: Article 9 secured transactions*, (3 edn., Chicago: American Bar Association, 2013), 3.

106 G. GILMORE, 'Security law, formalism and Article 9', (1968) 47 Neb. L. Rev., (659) 668;

107 Uniform Law Commission, online: https://my.uniformlaws.org/acts/ucc (date: January 9th, 2022).

2.2. *The functional approach in Article 9 UCC: substance over form*

35. *Introduction of the functional approach in Article 9 UCC* – Interestingly, the functional approach was initially considered as something to be avoided in the context of Article 9 UCC. At first the drafters had divided Article 9 UCC in different security interests that each guaranteed a specific type of financing, such as agricultural financing, consumer good financing and equipment financing.[108] In that sense the functional approach referred to the different functions the security rights performed and the different rules that were developed for each security interest. However, after further critical analysis of this approach DUNHAM found that there were many similarities between the rules for the different security interests. This prompted him to suggest to recharacterize all the different secured transactions in movable goods as security interests in a movable good belonging to the debtor and governing them by one set of rules.[109] This unitary approach to secured transactions[110] is realized by the substance over form principle: if the transaction in substance secures credit by vesting a proprietary interest in a movable good, it is considered a security interest and governed by the rules of Article 9 UCC.[111] Consequently, Article 9 UCC is a prime example of *the functional approach with recharacterization*. The substance over form principle is made explicit in §9–109(a)(1) UCC on the scope of article 9 UCC[112]:

---

108 P. WINSHIP, 'An historical overview of UCC article 9' in L. GULLIFER and O. AKSELI (eds.), *Secured transactions law reform: principles, policies and practice*, (Oxford: Hart Publisher, 2016), (21) 27;

109 G. GILMORE, 'The secured transactions article of the Commercial Code', (1951) 16 Law & Contemp. Probs., (27) 33–34; S. MENTSCHIKOFF, 'Reflections of a drafter', (1982) 43 Ohio St. L. Rev., (537) 542;

110 R. CUMING, The internationalization of secured financing law: the spreading influence of the concepts of UCC, Article 9 and its progeny' in R. CRANSTON (ed.), *Making commercial law: essays in honour of Roy Goode*, (499) 504 *et seq*; W. H. LAWRENCE, W. H. HENNING and R. W. FREYERMUTH, *Understanding secured transactions*, (2 edn., New York City: Matthew Bender, 1999), 9.

111 W. H. LAWRENCE, W. H. HENNING and R. W. FREYERMUTH, *Understanding secured transactions*, (2 edn., New York City: Matthew Bender, 1999), 9; J. J. WHITE, R. S. SUMMERS and R. A. HILMAN, *Uniform Commercial Code*, vol. 4, (6th edn., Eagan: Thomson Reuters, 2015), 13; B. CLARK, *The law of secured transactions under the Uniform Commercial Code*, vol. 1, (loosel., 3 edn., New York City: LexisNexis, 2014), 1–29; J. J. WHITE and others, *Principles of secured transactions*, (St. Paul: West Academic Publishing, 2018), 8.

112 This is a departure from other common law jurisdictions, such as the United Kingdom, where substance over form in the domain of secured transactions is still a judicial construct thereby also resulting in different interpretations by different courts. For a more detailed overview of substance over form in the common law of the United Kingdom, see P. M. SPINK and C. A. ONG, 'Substance versus form: Anglo-Australian perspectives on title financing transactions', (2004) 63 Cambridge L. J., 199.

Except as otherwise provided in subsections (c) and (d), this article applies to:
(1) *a transaction, regardless of its form, that creates a security interest in personal property or fixtures by contract;* (emphasis added)

Surprisingly, the transition to this all-encompassing security interest that covers all conceivable secured transactions in movable goods was not strongly debated at the time. It seemed that both scholars and practitioners were tired of the existing myriad of secured transactions in movable goods and welcomed an overarching regime that brought all secured transactions in movable goods under one roof.[113] The substance over form principle has two main components: the irrelevance of the name that is given to a secured transaction (2.2.1.) and the irrelevance of which party holds title to the encumbered good (2.2.2.).

2.2.1. Irrelevance of name

36. *Broad definition security interests* – Evidently, the substance over form principle aims to create a regime in which the substance or function of the transaction is more important than the name or form given to the transaction. Consequently, the drafters developed a very broad definition of security interest that represents the core function of a secured transaction and thereby encompasses all secured transactions that perform this function despite their name[114]:

> *'Security interest' means an interest in personal property or fixtures which secures payment or performance of an obligation.*

Following this definition, any transaction that meets this description is considered a security interest and governed by the rules of Article 9 UCC. As a result, parties can still use the old terminology for secured transactions that existed prior to the Code, such as conditional sale or chattel mortgage, without it affecting their treatment as security interest in Article 9 UCC[115]

37. *Explicit inclusion of certain transactions* – Furthermore, certain specific transactions are named in the definition to leave no mistake that they fall under the definition of security interest:

> *"Security interest" includes any interest of a consignor and a buyer of accounts, chattel paper, a payment intangible, or a promissory note in a transaction that is subject to Article 9.*

---

113 G. GILMORE, *Security interests in personal property*, vol. 1, (Boston: Little Brown and Co., 1965), 298–299.

114 §1-201 (b) (35) UCC (2001).

115 W. H. LAWRENCE, W. H. HENNING and R. W. FREYERMUTH, *Understanding secured transactions*, (2 edn., New York City: Matthew Bender, 1999), 9.

A consignment is a transaction in which the owner of movable goods puts goods in the possession of a consignee and allows the consignee to sell the consigned goods to third parties. On the surface consignments are not secured transactions, since they do not secure an outstanding obligation and the consignee can simply return the consigned goods to the consignor if they are not sold.[116] However, consignments can have security-like features, such as an obligation for the consignee to pay for the consigned goods when they are not sold to third parties.[117] In that case, the consignment is viewed as a construction in which the consignor delivered the goods on credit to the consignee and maintained an interest in the goods to secure his payment.[118] Furthermore, consignment agreements carry the risk of misleading third parties due to the indicia of ownership they bestow on the consignee.[119] Given the security-like features and the lack of publicity of consignments, all consignments[120] are characterized as security interests and explicitly subjected to the same notification requirements as other security interests.[121] A similar approach was taken towards the sale of certain intangible goods, such as accounts, chattel paper or promissory notes. For these transactions, there was also debate on whether they were an outright sale or a financing technique.[122] Consequently, there was debate on which rules needed to be followed concerning the creation and third-party effectiveness of the sale of such goods. Bringing these transactions explicitly within the scope of Article 9 UCC avoids any debate on which rules need to be followed.[123]

38. *Explicit exclusions from Article 9 UCC* – Given the broad definition of security interests, certain specific transactions are explicitly excluded from the definition of security interest to avoid their automatic inclusion in the

---

116 X., 'Comments', (1936) 36 Col. L. Rev., (1362) 1362.

117 Circuit Court of Appeals, Ninth Circuit 1 June 1936, Kemp-Booth Co. v. Calvin, 84 F. 2d, (377) 381; X., 'Comments', (1936) 36 Col. L. Rev., (1362) 1363 W. D. HAWKLAND, 'Consignment selling under the Uniform Commercial Code', (1962) 67 Com. L. J., (146) 146; G. GILMORE, *Security interests in personal property*, vol. 1, (Boston: Little Brown and Co., 1965), 338;

118 R. F. MAGILL, 'Legal advantages and disadvantages of the various methods of selling goods on credit', (1923) 8 Cornell L. Q., (210) 211; J. J. WHITE and others, *Principles of secured transactions*, (St. Paul: West Academic Publishing, 2018), 25.

119 D. HAWKLAND, 'Consignment selling under the Uniform Commercial Code', (1962) 67 Com. L. J., (146) 146; W. H. LAWRENCE, W. H. HENNING and R. W. FREYERMUTH, *Understanding secured transactions*, (2 edn., New York City: Matthew Bender, 1999), 16; B. CLARK, *The law of secured transactions under the Uniform Commercial Code*, vol. 1, (3 edn., New York City: LexisNexis, 2015), 115.

120 §1-201(35) UCC (2001) *juncto* §9-109(a)(4) UCC (2010).

121 B. CLARK, *The law of secured transactions under the Uniform Commercial Code*, vol. 1, (3 edn., New York City: LexisNexis, 2015), 115.

122 H. J. BAILEY and R. B. HAGEDORN, *Secured transactions in a nutshell*, (4 edn., St. Paul: West Group, 2000), 17–18.

123 R. A. HAKES, *The ABC's of the UCC: Article 9 secured transactions*, (3 edn., Chicago: American Bar Association, 2013), 14.

definition.[124] This is for example the case with the purchase of goods on identification:

> *"Security interest" does not include the special property interest of a buyer of goods on identification of those goods to a contract for sale under Section 2-401, but a buyer may also acquire a "security interest" by complying with Article 9.*

The default rule in Article 2 UCC is that title to the sold goods does not pass unless the sold goods have been identified and the seller has physically delivered the goods to the buyer.[125] If the sold goods are identified prior to the delivery of the goods to the buyer, then the buyer obtains a special interest in the sold goods which protects him against other creditors of the seller and good faith purchasers.[126] Given the broad definition of security interest, the buyer's special interest upon identification of the sold goods could be considered a security interest. The seller has an obligation to deliver the identified goods to the buyer and the performance is guaranteed by a proprietary interest in the sold goods. Following this reasoning, the buyer would be under an obligation to follow the requirements of Article 9 UCC in order to obtain a fully effective security interest against third parties. An explicit reason for the exclusion of such sale agreements from the definition of security interest is lacking in the official commentary to Article 1 and 9 UCC, but presumably the requirements of Article 9 UCC are considered too burdensome for such buyers. Consequently, they are excluded from the scope of security interests to avoid automatic inclusion. Nevertheless, these buyers are given the option to comply with Article 9 UCC and thereby obtain a security interest.

Likewise, the seller or lessor's right of retention of possession in a sale or true lease agreement is not considered a security interest. However, the seller or lessor is also allowed to comply with Article 9 UCC and thereby obtain a security interest. The specific division between security interests and true leases is discussed in more detail below.[127]

> *Except as otherwise provided in Section 2-505, the right of a seller or lessor of goods under Article 2 or 2A to retain or acquire possession of the goods is not a "security interest", but a seller or lessor may also acquire a "security interest" by complying with Article 9.*

---

124 M. BRIDGE, 'The scope and limits of security interests', (2008) 5 ECFR, (180) 214.

125 §2-401 (1)-(2) UCC (2002). See also, H. D. GABRIEL, *The ABC's of the UCC - Article 2 sales*, (3 edn., Chicago: American Bar Association, 2013), 113-114; G. GILMORE, *Security interests in personal property*, vol. 1, (Boston: Little Brown and Co., 1965), 340-341.

126 Commentary to §2-401 UCC (2002).

127 See *infra* no. 50 *et seq.*

39. *Explicit inclusion of retention of title within the scope of Article 9 UCC* – Finally, the security interest definition explicitly mentions retention or reservation of title:

> *The retention or reservation of title by a seller of goods notwithstanding shipment or delivery to the buyer under Section 2-401 is limited in effect to a reservation of a "security interest." Whether a transaction in the form of a lease creates a "security interest" is determined pursuant to Section 1-203.*

As with consignments and the transfer of accounts receivable or chattel paper, the drafters wanted to make abundantly clear that agreements in which the seller reserves or retains title to the sold good until the purchase price is paid, are nothing more than the reservation of a security interest. As with consignments, the characterization of retention of title as a security interest is to address potential ostensible ownership issues that can arise when sale agreements with retention of title fall outside of Article 9 UCC and would not require any notification requirements towards third parties.[128] Furthermore, conditional sales perform a very similar function as other secured transactions: retaining a proprietary interest in a movable good to secure the performance of an obligation. Therefore, it makes sense in the spirit of the unitary approach towards secured transactions that conditional sales are governed by the same rules as other secured transactions.[129] The recharacterization of certain lease agreements as security interests is discussed below.[130]

40. *Summary concerning the different categories of security interests in Article 9 UCC* – The drafters of the UCC did not aim to abolish all existing secured transactions, nor force parties to adopt an entire new language or terminology in the drafting of their security agreements.[131] On the contrary, the drafters merely set out to define security interest as widely as possible in order to include all the existing secured transactions and bring them within the Article 9 UCC framework, regardless of the name and form the parties have given to the transaction in the agreement. Article 9 UCC only makes use of the new term, security interest, but its application does not oppose the use of old terminology

---

128 H. D. GABRIEL, *The ABC's of the UCC – Article 2 sales*, (3 edn., Chicago: American Bar Association, 2013), 114; B. CLARK, *The law of secured transactions under the Uniform Commercial Code*, vol. 1, (3 edn., New York City: LexisNexis, 2015), 123.

129 J. J. WHITE and others, *Principles of secured transactions*, (St. Paul: West Academic Publishing, 2018), 2-3.

130 In the original version of the UCC, the definition of security interest included the guidelines concerning the distinction between security interests and true leases (§1-201 (37) UCC (1952)). In 1987, these rules were moved to their own provision in §1-203 UCC. See, E. E. HUDDLESON, 'Old wine in new bottles: UCC articles 2A – leases', (1987-88) 39 Ala. L. Rev., (615) 617.

131 G. GILMORE, *Security interests in personal property*, vol. 2, (Boston: Little Brown and Co., 1965), 297-298.

in the security agreement itself. Furthermore, the drafters went out of their way to explicitly list certain transactions, among which conditional sales with retention of title, to ensure that they would be characterized and treated as security interests despite the name the parties gave to the transaction.

2.2.2. Irrelevance of title

41. *Holding title to an encumbered good loses its significance in Article 9 UCC* – The second important component of the substance over form principle is the irrelevance of title. The drafters explicate in Article 9 UCC that "*the provisions of this article with regard to rights and obligations apply whether title to collateral is in the secured party or the debtor.*"[132] In other words, a transaction is considered in substance a security interest, regardless of whether the secured party or creditor retained title to the encumbered good or the debtor transferred title to the creditor to guarantee an outstanding obligation.[133]

This move away from a title-based application of the law was inspired by the changes made in Article 2 UCC concerning sales. It had been established in the context of sale agreements that reliance on the concept of title to determine the rights and duties of parties often resulted in more confusion and debate, since the concept of title and where it resided, was very elusive. Consequently, the outcomes in similar cases often varied among states and jurisdictions.[134] It was therefore thought more practical to move away from the concept of title and towards a more explicit division of rights and duties among parties regardless of title.[135]

In the domain of secured transactions there were similar issues concerning the use of title to secure credit. Pre-UCC creditors often used their retained or obtained title to the encumbered good to maintain a stronger position as opposed to other creditors. For example, title in the hands of the creditor allowed the creditor to repossess the encumbered goods immediately upon default by the retention of title debtor instead of following more arduous enforcement proceedings that applied to non-title based secured transactions.[136] Following the choice away from title in Article 2 UCC it made sense to limit the effect of a conditional sale to that of a security interest in Article 9 UCC, since

---

132 §9-202 UCC (2010).

133 Commentary to §9-202 UCC (2010).

134 R. F. MAGILL, 'Legal advantages and disadvantages of the various methods of selling goods on credit', (1923) 8 Cornell L. Q., (210) 215; E. R. LATTY, 'Sales and title and the proposed code', (1951) 16 Law & Contemp. Probs. (3) 10; H. L. HALL, 'Article 2 – from status to contract', (1952) Wis. L. Rev., (209) 217 *et seq.*

135 G. M. TRAVALIO, R. J. NORDSTROM and A. L. CLOVIS, *Nordstrom on sales and leases of goods*, (2nd edn., New York: Aspen law and business, 2000), 667–669.

136 J. WILFORD, E. DAVISSON and N. CHARLES, *Lease as a financing and selling device*, (An Arbor: School of Business and Administration, 1951), 27; H. J. BAILEY and R. B. HAGEDORN, *Secured transactions in a nutshell*, (4 edn., St. Paul: West Group, 2000), 54–55.

maintaining a title-based conditional sale agreement would run counter to this new approach in Article 2 UCC. As a result, a conditional sale results in no more than a security interest and the conditional seller has to fulfill the necessary requirements for a valid and effective security interest to enjoy the protection of a secured creditor. Moreover, the recharacterization of the conditional sale to a security interest also means that the retention of title debtor is considered the owner of the encumbered good and the secured creditor only holds a proprietary security interest in the encumbered good.[137] There are some exceptions to the broad scope of application of Article 9 UCC. For example, if a conditional sale does not include delivery of the good to the buyer, the seller does not have to comply with the formalities or requirements of Article 9 UCC. In that case, the transaction falls within the scope of Article 2 UCC and the provisions concerning sales apply.[138]

42. *Summary* – In Article 9 UCC the functional approach takes the form of substance over form by focusing on the essence of secured transactions: the security of credit by obtaining or retaining a proprietary interest in a movable good. Furthermore, the drafters then pushed the functional approach further by recharacterizing each secured transaction in movable goods that meets the definition of security interest in a security interest in a movable good and subject it to one set of rules. This recharacterization happens regardless of the name the parties have given to the agreement or the rights the creditor claims to have obtained or retained to the encumbered good.

3. APPLICATION OF THE FUNCTIONAL APPROACH TO RETENTION OF TITLE

43. *Introduction to the functional approach as applied to retention of title in Article 9 UCC* – On the one hand, the application of the functional approach to retention or reservation of title in conditional sales or leases seems fairly straight forward: a retention or reservation of title is limited in its effect to a security interest.[139] Consequently, retention of title is treated as all other security interests and governed by the rules applicable to security interests. On the other hand, how conditional sales are limited in their effect to security interests is not further explained. The phrase "limited in their effect" suggests that the protection of a security interest is weaker than that of a conditional sale with retention of title and that conditional sellers see their protection diminished

137 R. CUMING, The internationalization of secured financing law: the spreading influence of the concepts of UCC, Article 9 and its progeny' in R. CRANSTON (ed.), *Making commercial law: essays in honour of Roy Goode*, (499) 523.

138 §9-110 UCC (2010) (originally §9-113 UCC (1952)).

139 §1-201(b)(35) UCC (2001).

due to the application of the functional approach. Furthermore, most retention of title agreements fall into the sub-category of purchase money security interests (PMSIs), which are security interests that specifically guarantee credit that enabled the debtor to acquire a new movable good and are in some cases governed by specific rules. This means that retention of title agreements are not in all respects treated as general security interests. The application and potential impact of the functional approach on these two levels is set out in the following sections.

3.1. Scope

44. *Schematic overview of the scope of Article 9 UCC* – The first question that comes up with regards to the application of the functional approach to retention of title is how broad the new categories of security interests are.

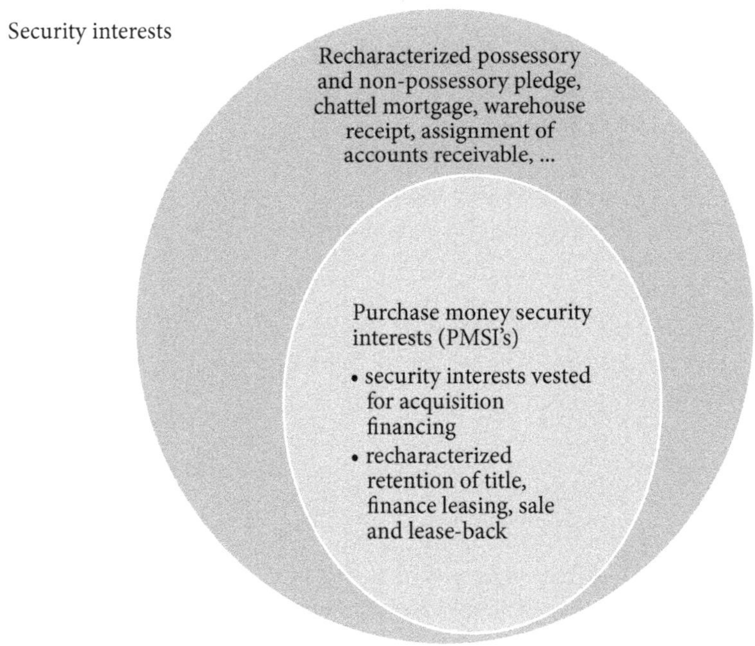

3.1.1. Security interests

45. *Main category of security interests in movable goods* – In Article 9 UCC, the application of the functional approach to retention of title happens in two phases. On a general level retention of title is recharacterized to a general security interest, since it secures credit via a proprietary interest in a movable good. Consequently, a reservation or retention of title is limited in its effect to a security interest.[140] A security interest is defined in Article 1 UCC as:

> *'Security interest' means an interest in personal property or fixtures which secures payment or performance of an obligation.*
>
> *"Security interest" includes any interest of a consignor and a buyer of accounts, chattel paper, a payment intangible, or a promissory note in a transaction that is subject to Article 9.*
>
> *"Security interest" does not include the special property interest of a buyer of goods on identification of those goods to a contract for sale under Section 2-401, but a buyer may also acquire a "security interest" by complying with Article 9.*
>
> *Except as otherwise provided in Section 2-505, the right of a seller or lessor of goods under Article 2 or 2A to retain or acquire possession of the goods is not a "security interest", but a seller or lessor may also acquire a "security interest" by complying with Article 9.*
>
> *The retention or reservation of title by a seller of goods notwithstanding shipment or delivery to the buyer under Section 2-401 is limited in effect to a reservation of a "security interest." Whether a transaction in the form of a lease creates a "security interest" is determined pursuant to Section 1-203.*[141]

The drafters made a choice to recharacterize all secured transactions in movable goods to security interests, which the secured creditor retains in the encumbered, movable good, regardless of the fact that the agreement between the parties claims that the secured creditor retains title. In that sense, the recharacterization of retention of title to a security interest can be seen as a diminishing in protection for former retention of title creditors. However, the extent to which the recharacterization of retention of title to a security interest results in actual loss of rights is assessed in the section concerning the rights of PMSI creditors.

3.1.2. PMSIs

46. *The general definition of PMSI* – Within the broad category of security interests, the drafters identify a sub-category of purchase money security interests (PMSIs) that secure not just credit, but credit that enables the debtor to acquire a new good (i.e. acquisition credit).[142] Specific for PMSIs is (1) that

---

140 §1-201(b)(35) UCC (2001).

141 §1-201(b)(35) UCC (2001).

142 §9-103 UCC (2010). See also, W. E. HOGAN, 'Financing the acquisition of new goods under the Uniform Commercial Code', (1962) 3 B. C. Indus. & Com. L. Rev., (115) 117; G.

they guarantee credit that enables the debtor to acquire new goods and (2) that the claim is guaranteed by vesting the security interest in the newly acquired good.[143]

Transactions are also recharacterized to PMSIs following the substance over form principle: when a transaction meets the definition of a PMSI, it is considered as such and governed by its specific rules. The name the parties may give to this agreement plays no part in the charachterization.[144] Consequently, a conditional sale, in which the seller has sold a good on credit and reserved title in the sold good, is limited in its effect to a security interest and additionally falls in the PMSI sub-category.[145] However, the definition of PMSI also applies to other security interests and therefore the term PMSI encompasses different security interests that secure acquisition credit.

47. *Terminology* – In the next sections, I outline which transactions are included in the definition of PMSI in Article 9 UCC. Moving forward, whenever the rules apply to all security interests, including PMSIs, the dissertation uses the term security interest. Only when the rules are specific to PMSIs, is the term PMSIs specifically used.

A. Purchase money obligation

48. *Relevant terminology concerning PMSIs* – Like security interests, PMSIs are broadly defined in order to encompass all transactions in which acquisition credit is secured. Following the definition in Article 9 UCC, PMSIs are security interests that secure purchase money obligations by vesting a security interest in purchase money collateral.[146] Purchase money collateral are goods that secure purchase money obligations[147] and purchase money obligations in turn are obligations incurred as all or part of the price of the encumbered good or for value given to enable the debtor to acquire rights in or the use of the encumbered good.[148] In other words, PMSIs secure credit, that enables a debtor to acquire the encumbered good, by vesting a security interest in the acquired good.

GILMORE, *Security interests in personal property*, vol. 1, (Boston: Little Brown and Co., 1965), 780; K. MEYER, 'A primer on purchase money security interests under revised Article 9 of the Uniform Commercial Code', (2001–02) 50 U. Kan. L. Rev., (143) 152; J. J. WHITE and others, *Principles of secured transactions*, (St. Paul: West Academic Publishing, 2018), 177–178.

143 §9–103 UCC (2010). See also, A. M. CHRISTENFELD and A. KOPEC, ‹Purchase money security interests›, (2009) 41 Uniform Com. Code L. J., (291) 292.

144 J. J. WHITE and others, *Principles of secured transactions*, (St. Paul: West Academic Publishing, 2018), 64.

145 W. H. LAWRENCE, W. H. HENNING and R. W. FREYERMUTH, *Understanding secured transactions*, (2 edn., New York City: Matthew Bender, 1999), 46.

146 §9–103 UCC (2010).

147 §9–103(a)(1) UCC (2010).

148 §9–103(a)(2) UCC (2010).

49. *Scope of PMSIs* – Evidently, conditional sales are PMSIs in Article 9 UCC. In a conditional sale, the seller sells a movable good on credit to the debtor and retains title to the sold good to secure payment of the outstanding purchase price. The sold good is the purchase money collateral which secures the debtor's payment obligation to the seller (i.e. the purchase money obligation). To what extent this recharacterization affects the rights of former conditional sellers is discussed in the following sections.

An interesting feature of Article 9 UCC is that the term PMSI also encompasses transactions in which a financer provides credit specifically for the acquisition of a movable good and secures this credit by vesting a security interest in the acquired good.[149] Prior to Article 9 UCC, the only codified secured transaction that catered specifically to acquisition financing was the conditional sale. Theoretically, acquisition financiers could not make use of the conditional sale, since they were not sellers who could retain title until the purchase price was paid. Therefore, acquisition financiers had to rely on the existing non-possessory secured transactions, such as the warehouse receipt, trust receipt or chattel mortgage, which were available for all lenders.[150] Practically, however, acquisition financiers could place themselves in the same position as a conditional seller by obtaining a good via an absolute bill of sale from the debtor and selling it back to the debtor upon condition of payment of the purchase price.[151] Unfortunately, these constructions were often recharacterized by the courts as masked chattel mortgages and would be considered ineffective due to lack of registration.[152] This changed in 1952 with the introduction of the PMSI in Article 9 UCC, which not only covers conditional sales, but all secured transactions that secure purchase money obligations and thus can be extended to credit outside of a sale context.[153] However, for these transactions it is important that the financer makes sure that the debtor actually uses the credit for the acquisition of new goods and that he can prove this.[154] Unlike with the conditional sale, which automatically secures a purchase money obligation, one cannot simply assume that the provided credit secures the acquisition of a new good. As a solution the acquisition financier can transfer the money directly to the manufacturer or retailer of the good and thus

149 G. GILMORE, *Security interests in personal property*, vol. 1, (Boston: Little Brown and Co., 1965), 781; W. H. LAWRENCE, W. H. HENNING and R. W. FREYERMUTH, *Understanding secured transactions*, (2 edn., New York City: Matthew Bender, 1999), 45; P. WANGERIN, 'Floating liens, proceeds, and PMSIs: perfection and priority in three closely connected cases', (2017) 47 UCC L. J., (287) 315.

150 G. GILMORE and A. AXELROD, 'Chattel security: I', (1947–48) 57 Yale L. J., (517) 538.

151 G. GILMORE and A. AXELROD, 'Chattel security: I', (1947–48) 57 Yale L. J., (517) 542.

152 Circuit Court of Appeal, Second Circuit, 7 January 1929, In re James, 30 F.2d., (555) 557; Circuit Court of Appeals, Fourth Circuit, 16 January 1929, In re Sachs, 30 F.2d, (510) 512.

153 M. BRIDGE, 'The scope and limits of security interests', (2008) 5 ECFR, (180) 197.

154 Court of Appeals of Tennessee 4 February 1992, Mays v. Brighton Bank, 18 UCC Rep. Serv. 2d. 621, 18 UCC Rep. Serv. 2d., (621) 629. See also, J. J. WHITE and others, *Principles of secured transactions*, (St. Paul: West Academic Publishing, 2018), 65.

guarantee that his credit can be traced to the acquired good.[155] In that case, a security interest vested to guarantee acquisition credit is considered a PMSI and is also treated as a PMSI.

B. Leasing: security or true lease?

50. *Emergence of the leasing debate in Article 9 UCC* – Once the drafters decided to opt for a substance over form approach in Article 9 UCC, the debate concerning the distinction between lease agreements and secured transactions was bound to come up again. A security interest is broadly defined as any interest vested to secure the performance of an obligation.[156] Given the similarities between some lease agreements and conditional sales and the automatic recharacterization of conditional sales as security interests, the recharacterization of some lease agreements as a security interest and PMSI was a logical consequence. The distinction is not without importance, since a lease for security purposes has to fulfill the requirements for third-party effectiveness for security interests, whereas the true lease does not.[157] However, in practice, many lessors have started to always register their lease agreement, regardless of its characterization, in order to avoid discussions about its third-party effectiveness later.[158]

51. *Explicit inclusion of leasing for security purposes within the scope of Article 9 UCC* – The drafters decided to address this discussion head on by immediately including lease agreements into the definition of security interest in the first version of Article 1 UCC.[159] However, unlike conditional sales, the drafters did not have the intention to simply characterize all lease agreements as security interests and bring them within the scope of Article 9 UCC. Instead, they aimed to draft a provision that would distinguish the nuanced difference between a lease for security purposes and a true lease in which the lessee simply rents a movable good for a set amount of time and has a clear intention of returning the leased good to the lessor. This provision set out that the determination of

---

155 G. GILMORE, *Security interests in personal property*, vol. 1, (Boston: Little Brown and Co., 1965), 782; W. H. LAWRENCE, W. H. HENNING and R. W. FREYERMUTH, *Understanding secured transactions*, (2 edn., New York City: Matthew Bender, 1999), 47; K. MEYER, 'A primer on purchase money security interests under revised Article 9 of the Uniform Commercial Code', (2001–02) 50 U. Kan. L. Rev., (143) 153.

156 §1-201(37) UCC (2010).

157 United States District Court, N.D. Georgia, 29 October 1965, In re Transcontinental Industries, Inc., 3 UCC Rep. Serv., (235) 244; R. L. HILLER, 'Security Aspects of Chattel Leases in Bankruptcy', (1965–66) 34 Fordham L. Rev., (439) 440.

158 D. G. BAIRD and T. H. JACKSON, 'Possession and ownership: an examination of the scope of article 9', (1983) 35 Stan. L. Rev., (175) 187.

159 §1-201(37), par. 2 UCC (1952).

whether a lease was intended as a security interest depended on the facts of the case. However, the Code continues that

> (a) *the inclusion of an option to purchase does not of itself make the lease one intended for security, and*
> (b) *an agreement that upon compliance with the terms of the lease the lessee shall become or has the option to become the owner of the property for no additional consideration or for a nominal consideration does make the lease one intended for security.*[160]

Beyond that the Code did not give any specific factors that were critical for the determination of either a security interest or a true lease.[161] GILMORE, one of the drafters of Article 9 UCC, merely pointed out that the word "*intention*" in this provision should not be viewed as the subjective intention of the parties.[162] However, how the intentions of the parties should be interpreted is not further explained.[163] Relying on the intentions of the parties in this context seems illogical, since parties may have clear intentions to circumvent specific regulations and to classify a transaction as a true lease for tax or other purposes.[164] It seems counterintuitive then that their intentions should be taken into account.[165] PEDEN argued that an objective test should determine whether a transaction had the intention of being a security interest.[166] Examples of such objective factors were: length of the lease in relation to the economic life of the collateral, relation of the rental price to the market value rental price, the acquisition of the leased good by the lessor specifically for the lessee or the intention of the lessee to permanently attach the leased good to his premises.[167]

---

160 §1-201 (37), par. 2 *in fine* UCC (1952).

161 P. F. COOGAN, 'Leases of equipment and some other unconventional security devices: an analysis of UCC section 1-201(37) and Article 9', (1973) Duke L. J., (909) 918; J. D. AYER, 'On the vacuity of the sale/lease distinction', (1983) 68 Iowa L. Rev. (667) 669.

162 G. GILMORE, *Security interests in personal property*, vol. 1, (Boston: Little Brown and Co., 1965), 338;

163 S. L. SHAPIRO, 'The ABC's of leasing', (1972) U. Ill. L. F., (433) 440-441; C. COOPER, 'Identifying a personal property lease under the UCC', (1988-89) 49 Ohio St. L. J., (195) 200;

164 J. WILFORD, E. DAVISSON and N. CHARLES, *Lease as a financing and selling device*, (An Arbor: School of Business and Administration, 1951), 27-28; X., 'Acquisition of industrial and commercial equipment through leasing arrangements', (1957) 66 Yale L. J., (751) 753; P. F. COOGAN, 'Leasing and the Uniform Commercial Code' in B. E. FRITCH and A. F. REISMAN (eds.), *Equipment leasing - leveraged leasing*, (2 edn., New York City: Practicing Law Institute, 1980), 692.

165 W. R. REISS, 'Security aspects of equipment leasing', (1962) U. Ill. L. F., (77) 81; P. F. COOGAN, 'Leases of equipment and some other unconventional security devices: an analysis of UCC section 1-201(37) and Article 9', (1973) Duke L. J., (909) 916.

166 J. R. PEDEN, 'The treatment of equipment leases as security agreements under the Uniform Commercial Code', (1971) 13 Wm. & Mary L. Rev., (110) 137;

167 J. R. PEDEN, 'The treatment of equipment leases as security agreements under the Uniform Commercial Code', (1971) 13 Wm. & Mary L. Rev., (110) 137.

The two additional indicators concerning security leasing were anything but clear. The first guideline stated that the mere presence of a purchase option for the lessee did not automatically ("*of itself*") result in a characterization as a security interest. It was not the presence of the purchase option, but the amount of the purchase option in relation to the market value of the leased good that determined the nature of the transaction.[168] Consequently, transactions without a purchase option were more likely to be true leases, but this was not always the case.[169] The second guideline stated that a transaction in which the lessee could become owner at the end of the lease agreement without having to make any payments or by paying only a minimal amount would make the lease one intended for security. However, how these guidelines had to be further interpreted, was again not further indicated.[170] Consequently, courts were left to their own devices to assess whether the purchase price at the end of the agreement or lack of purchase price could be considered nominal or minimal. This again led to different views in case law and doctrine concerning the relevant factors in the distinction between lease agreements for security purposes and true leases.[171] Interestingly, this lack of guidance made courts return to pre-Code case law and the UCSA to further fine-tune these principles.[172] Specifically, courts got bogged down in making an economic analysis of the market value of the leased good, the relation of the market value to the rental payments over time and the potential optional purchase price at the end of the lease agreement.[173] Furthermore, financiers would pick up on certain approaches courts would take

168 C. COOPER, 'Identifying a personal property lease under the UCC', (1988–89) 49 Ohio St. L. J., (195) 222.

169 G. GILMORE, *Security interests in personal property*, vol. 1, (Boston: Little Brown and Co., 1965), 338–339.

170 P. F. COOGAN, 'Leasing and the Uniform Commercial Code' in B. E. FRITCH and A. F. REISMAN (eds.), *Equipment leasing - leveraged leasing*, (2 edn., New York City: Practicing Law Institute, 1980), 685;

171 United States District Court of California 19 October 1967, In re Pomona Valley Inn, 4 UCC Rep. Serv., (893) 893–894; United States District Court of Wisconsin 18 December 1969, In re Lakeshore Transit-Kenosha, Inc., 7 UCC Rep. Serv., (607) 609–611; United States District Court of New York 17 May 1971, In re Brothers Coach Corp., 9 UCC Rep. Serv., (502) 504–505; W. D. HAWKLAND, 'The impact of the Uniform Commercial Code on equipment leasing', (1972) U. Ill. L. F., (446) 468; J. H. STROH, 'Peripheral security interests - the expanded net of Article 9', (1967) 22 U. Miami L. Rev., (67) 74; P. F. COOGAN, 'Leasing and the Uniform Commercial Code' in B. E. FRITCH and A. F. REISMAN (eds.), *Equipment leasing - leveraged leasing*, (2 edn., New York City: Practicing Law Institute, 1980), 696.

172 P. F. COOGAN, 'Leasing and the Uniform Commercial Code' in B. E. FRITCH and A. F. REISMAN (eds.), *Equipment leasing - leveraged leasing*, (2 edn., New York City: Practicing Law Institute, 1980), 720 *et seq.*

173 Court of Appeals Maryland 7 June 1963, United Rental Equipment Co. v. Potts & Callahan Contracting Co., 231 Md., (552) 558; United States District Court S.D. New York 6 May 1963, In re Herold Radio & Electronics Corp.,, 218 F.Supp., (284) 285; United States District Court W.D. Pennsylvania 9 December 1964, In re Wheatland Elec. Products Co., 237 F.Supp., (820) 821–822. See also, J. S. BROWN, 'Notes - Leases: Security Interests: Uniform Commercial Code', (1963–64) 49 Cornell L. Q., (672) 675; H. M. WELSH, 'Judicial interpretations of the filing requirements under Article 9 of the Code', (1970) 37 Tenn. L. Rev., (273) 282 *et seq.*; C.

and would tailor their transactions to avoid a characterization they considered unfavorable.[174] Consequently, courts were constantly trying to catch up with new developments.[175]

52. *Amendments concerning leasing in Article 9 UCC* – It was not until 1987 that the Uniform Law Commission decided to amend the provision concerning leasing in the UCC.[176] This amendment was partly a reaction to the difficulties parties and courts were having with the interpretation of §1–201 (37) UCC and partly a reaction to the introduction of Article 2A in the Uniform Commercial Code.[177] Following this amendment, the guidelines for distinguishing leasing from security interests became:

> *Whether a transaction creates a lease or security interest is determined by the facts of each case; however, a transaction creates a security interest if the consideration the lessee is to pay the lessor for the right to possession and use of the goods is an obligation for the term of the lease not subject to termination by the lessee, and*
>
> *(a) the original term of the lease is equal to or greater than the remaining economic life of the goods,*
> *(b) the lessee is bound to renew the lease for the remaining economic life of the goods or is bound to become the owner of the goods,*
> *(c) the lessee has an option to renew the lease for the remaining economic life of the goods for no additional consideration or nominal additional consideration upon compliance with the lease agreement, or*
> *(d) the lessee has an option to become the owner of the goods for no additional consideration or nominal additional consideration upon compliance with the lease agreement.*

What is immediately noticeable, is that the amended version of §1–201(37) UCC gives more guidelines on how to determine when a transaction should be considered a security interest and not a true lease. First, the drafters did away with the intent portion of the provision. As had been pointed out before, the intention of the parties was probably not a good place to start the assessment of the true nature of an agreement.[178] Second, the drafters made it clear that an

---

COOPER, 'Identifying a personal property lease under the UCC', (1988–89) 49 Ohio St. L. J., (195) 224.

174 J. H. STROH, 'Peripheral security interests – the expanded net of Article 9', (1967) 22 U. Miami L. Rev., (67) 80.

175 R. L. HILLER, 'Security Aspects of Chattel Leases in Bankruptcy', (1965–66) 34 Fordham L. Rev., (439) 442.

176 E. E. HUDDLESON, 'Old wine in new bottles: UCC articles 2A – leases', (1987–88) 39 Ala. L. Rev., (615) 625.

177 Uniform Law Commission, online: https://www.uniformlaws.org/acts/ucc; E. E. HUDDLESON, 'Old wine in new bottles: UCC articles 2A – leases', (1987–88) 39 Ala. L. Rev., (615) 617–618.

178 See *supra* no. 46.

obvious indication for a security interest is when the lessee cannot terminate the lease agreement[179] combined with one of the four abovementioned elements. The emphasis in these guidelines is placed on the economic positions of the parties.[180] The overarching theme of the four additional elements that signify a security interest instead of a true lease is that the lessee makes use of the leased good for the duration of its economic life and/or is bound to become owner of the leased good without or for only a nominal consideration. In other words, a transaction would be likely classified as a security interest when the lessor has no reasonable expectation of meaningful residual value in the goods left.[181] To aid courts in the interpretation of these guidelines, the drafters provided interpretations of "*nominal consideration*"[182], "*reasonably predictable*"[183] and "*remaining economic life of the goods*"[184] and "*present value.*"[185]

53. *Further indicators for the distinction between true and security leasing* – Additionally, the UCC identified some elements that do not automatically create a security interest:

> *A transaction does not create a security interest merely because it provides that*
>
> *(a) the present value of the consideration the lessee is obligated to pay the lessor for the right to possession and use of the goods is substantially equal to or is greater than the fair market value of the goods at the time the lease is entered into,*
> *(b) the lessee assumes risk of loss of the goods, or agrees to pay taxes, insurance, filing, recording, or registration fees, or service or maintenance costs with respect to the goods,*
> *(c) the lessee has an option to renew the lease or to become the owner of the goods,*
> *(d) the lessee has an option to renew the lease for a fixed rent that is equal to or greater than the reasonably predictable fair market rent for the use of the goods for the term of the renewal at the time the option is to be performed, or*
> *(e) the lessee has an option to become the owner of the goods for a fixed price that is equal to or greater than the reasonably predictable fair market value of the goods at the time the option is to be performed.*

179 §1-201 (37), 2nd par. UCC (1987).

180 C. COOPER, 'Identifying a personal property lease under the UCC', (1988–89) 49 Ohio St. L. J., (195) 202; Official comments to amendment of §1-201 (37) UCC.

181 United States Court of Appeals, Third Circuit 14 November 2003, In re Pillowtex, Inc., 349 F.3d, (711) 720; C. W. Jr. MOONEY, 'The mystery and myth of ostensible ownership and article 9 filing: a critique of proposals to extend filing requirements to leases', (1987–1988) 39 Ala. L. Rev., (683) 692; W. H. LAWRENCE, W. H. HENNING and R. W. FREYERMUTH, *Understanding secured transactions*, (2 edn., New York City: Matthew Bender, 1999), 14; P. W. SCHROTH, 'Financial leasing of equipment in the law of the United States', (2010) 16 Unif. L. Rev., (437) 448; J. J. WHITE, R. S. SUMMERS, and R. A. HILMAN, *Uniform Commercial Code*, vol. 4, (6th edn., Eagan: Thomson Reuters, 2015), 27.

182 §1-201 (37) (x) UCC (1987).

183 §1-201 (37) (y) UCC (1987).

184 §1-201 (37) (y) UCC (1987).

185 §1-201 (37) (z) UCC (1987).

With this the drafters wanted to make it clear that the specific economics and the facts of each transaction play an important role in the determination of the true nature of a transaction.[186] In other words, the mere presence of one of these elements is not sufficient to recharacterize a transaction as a security interest. For example, a transaction with a fixed price option at the end of the transaction does not automatically mean the transaction is a security interest.[187] Only when the purchase price is nominal, will the transaction shift from a lease agreement to a security interest.[188] This was already the case in the original guidelines concerning the distinction between true leases and security interests[189] and was made more explicit and detailed in the amended version. Furthermore, the drafters also made it more explicit that specific indicators of ownership in the hands of the lessee, such as the assumption of risk or paying for insurance or taxes, is not enough to recharacterize the lease as a security interest.[190] This again aligns with the Code's approach that does not attach much weight anymore to the concept of title to allocate certain rights and duties and the classification of transactions.[191]

Despite the additional guidelines, there are still issues with the distinction between true leases and security interests. First, some authors are of the opinion that more regulation would only lead to more confusion and unnecessary complicate the differentiation between security interests and true leases.[192] Second, parties could still come up with a myriad of different transactions that are not explicitly classified as either a security interest or a true lease.[193] A response to this is that it was never the intention of the drafters to list all the provisions or situations that could give rise to a security interest over a true lease. Such a list would be impossible to make, since it would simply give parties examples of which transactions to avoid when trying to escape the application of Article 9 UCC. Instead, the drafters only attempted to cast the guidelines for the distinction between a security interest and true leases in more economic terms, thereby moving courts to assess the true nature of these transactions from this angle.[194] The ongoing debates concerning true leases and security interests has

---

186 Official comment to §1-201 (37), 3rd par. UCC. See also, W. H. LAWRENCE, W. H. HENNING and R. W. FREYERMUTH, *Understanding secured transactions*, (2 edn., New York City: Matthew Bender, 1999), 13.

187 §1-201 (37), 3rd par., (e) UCC (1987).

188 Official comment to §1-201 (37), 3rd par. UCC. See also, C. COOPER, 'Identifying a personal property lease under the UCC', (1988-89) 49 Ohio St. L. J., (195) 238.

189 §1-201 (37) UCC (1952).

190 C. COOPER, 'Identifying a personal property lease under the UCC', (1988-89) 49 Ohio St. L. J., (195) 238.

191 See *supra* no. 41.

192 J. D. AYER, 'Further thoughts on lease and sale', (1983) Ariz. St. L. J., (341) 354.

193 C. COOPER, 'Identifying a personal property lease under the UCC', (1988-89) 49 Ohio St. L. J., (195) 244 *et seq.*

194 C. COOPER, 'Identifying a personal property lease under the UCC', (1988-89) 49 Ohio St. L. J., (195) 247.

prompted some scholars to argue that the distinction between true leases and security interests should be abandoned altogether and that true leases should be outright included in the scope of Article 9 UCC. Alternatively, they suggest that true leases should be distinguished on more concrete grounds, such as the consumer status of the lessor or the value of the leased good.[195]

54. *Conclusion concerning the inclusion of leasing for security purposes within the scope of Article 9 UCC* – The fact that the provision concerning the distinction between security interests and true leasing have not been amended after 1987 and is still the same in the current version of Article 9 UCC[196] should not be interpreted to mean that the provision has worked perfectly and all discussions concerning the true nature of lease transactions have been resolved. It only suggests that as of yet the drafters have not found a better way to further regulate the distinction between security interests and true leases. Consequently, even under the current versions of the UCC there is still not a clear-cut rule on when a lease agreement should be considered a true lease or a security interest.[197] Nevertheless, the more nuanced steps the drafters of the UCC have developed in this field have to be commended. When transactions are being recharacterized following their functional similarities with security interests, the debate concerning the distinction between true leases and leases for security purposes will inevitably come up. At minimum the provisions provide a preliminary answer to the problem of distinguishing between true leases and leases for security purposes.

3.2. *Creating effective PMSIs*

55. *Overview* – Because conditional sales are PMSIs and a type of security interests under Article 9 UCC, they are created and made effective against third parties following the general rules for security interests. However, since PMSIs are also a sub-category of security interests, there are some specific rules concerning third-party effectiveness that only apply to PMSIs. In the following sections, the creation and third-party effectiveness of PMSIs is discussed in more detail and the extent to which the functional approach to creating and vesting security interests affected the creation and third-party effectiveness of conditional sellers.

---

195 D. G. BAIRD and T. H. JACKSON, 'Possession and ownership: an examination of the scope of article 9', (1983) 35 Stan. L. Rev., (175) 201.

196 §1-201 (37) UCC (1987) was later divided over §1-201(b)(35) UCC (2001) and §1-203 UCC (2001). However, the wording of the provision was not changed.

197 J. J. WHITE, R. S. SUMMERS, and R. A. HILMAN, *Uniform Commercial Code*, vol. 4, (6th edn., Eagan: Thomson Reuters, 2015), 22 *et seq*; M. BRIDGE, 'The scope and limits of security interests', (2008) 5 ECFR, (180) 206.

3.2.1. Creating a PMSI between parties

56. *Requirements for the creation of a security interest between parties* – Originally, the creation of a security interest (also known as attachment)[198] required that the secured creditor gave value to the debtor and the debtor had rights in the encumbered good.[199] Following later amendments, these requirements are still in place, but are now accompanied by more specific requirements concerning the security agreement[200]:

1) value has been given;
2) the debtor has rights in the collateral or the power to transfer rights in the collateral to a secured party; and
3) one of the following conditions is met:
  (A) the debtor has authenticated a security agreement that provides a description of the collateral and, if the security interest covers timber to be cut, a description of the land concerned;
  (B) the collateral is not a certificated security and is in the possession of the secured party under Section 9-313 pursuant to the debtor's security agreement;
  (C) the collateral is a certificated security in registered form and the security certificate has been delivered to the secured party under Section 8-301 pursuant to the debtor's security agreement; or
  (D) the collateral is deposit accounts, electronic chattel paper, investment property, letter-of-credit rights, or electronic documents, and the secured party has control under Section 7-106, 9-104, 9-105, 9-106, or 9-107 pursuant to the debtor's security agreement.[201, 202]

In most conditional sale or lease agreements with retention of title the abovementioned elements are present and the conditional sale or lease agreement fulfills the requirements for creating a security interest. The only potentially problematic part from the perspective of a retention of title creditor is that the debtor must have rights in the encumbered good or collateral or the power to transfer rights in the collateral to a secured party in order for the security interest to be created. This provision does not require that the debtor must have title to or ownership of the encumbered good to grant a security interest.[203] Any rights beyond the physical possession of movable goods, such as the power to transfer

198 J. J. WHITE and others, *Principles of secured transactions*, (St. Paul: West Academic Publishing, 2018), 48.
199 §9-204 (1) UCC (1952).
200 §9-203 (a) UCC (2010).
201 §9-203 (b) UCC (2010).
202 §9-203 (c) – (i) UCC (2010) gives further exceptions to this rule.
203 W. E. HOGAN, 'Financing the acquisition of new goods under the Uniform Commercial Code', (1962) 3 B. C. Indus. & Com. L. Rev., (115)

rights in the collateral or the right of enjoyment of the collateral, are sufficient.[204] For example, a joint owner of a good can grant a security interest in his share of the good or a lessee can grant a security interest in his right of enjoyment and use of the leased good.[205] However, the security interest only attaches to the rights the debtor has in the collateral[206] and mere physical possession of the good does not suffice for attachment.[207] In the context of a conditional sale with retention of title or security lease this requirement does raise an interesting question. If the seller has retained title to the collateral, how can the debtor have sufficient rights in the collateral for a security interest to attach? For the answer to this question, we have to return to the definition of security interest in Article 1 UCC.[208] Here it was made clear that a retention or reservation of title by a seller is limited in its effect to a security interest. Moreover, a retention of title is recharacterized as a security interest.[209] Following this definition, in a conditional sale the reserved or retained title to the encumbered good actually passes to the debtor and the debtor grants a PMSI to the seller in the newly acquired good.[210] In other words, the debtor becomes the owner of the encumbered good and the secured creditor only retains a PMSI.[211] Consequently, the debtor has sufficient rights in the newly acquired good to grant other security interests in the good to other

204 Superior Court of Connecticut 24 July 1964, Cain v. Country Club Delicatessen of Saybrook Inc., 25 Conn. Supp., (327) 333; United States Court of Appeals, Tenth Circuit 14 April 1983, Kinetics Technology Intern. Corp. v. Fourth Nat. Bank of Tulsa, 705 F.2d, (396) 399. See also, R. A. HAKES, *The ABC's of the UCC: Article 9 secured transactions*, (3 edn., Chicago: American Bar Association, 2013), 26; T. M. ANDERSON, M. B. CULHANDE and C. L. WILSON, 'Attachment and perfection of security interests under revised Article 9: a nuts and bolts primer', (2001) 9 Am. Bankr. L. Rev., (179) 186.

205 B. CLARK, *The law of secured transactions under the Uniform Commercial Code*, vol. 1, (3 edn., New York City: LexisNexis, 2015), 2–89; J. J. WHITE and others, *Principles of secured transactions*, (St. Paul: West Academic Publishing, 2018), 59.

206 R. A. HAKES, *The ABC's of the UCC: Article 9 secured transactions*, (3 edn., Chicago: American Bar Association, 2013), 27; B. CLARK, *The law of secured transactions under the Uniform Commercial Code*, vol. 1, (3 edn., New York City: LexisNexis, 2015), 2–90.

207 W. H. LAWRENCE, W. H. HENNING and R. W. FREYERMUTH, *Understanding secured transactions*, (2 edn., New York City: Matthew Bender, 1999), 91.

208 §1–201 (b) (35) UCC (2010). See also, *supra* no. 36.

209 United States Court of Appeals 15 March 1988, Crocker Nat. Bank v. Ideco Div. of Dresser Industries Inc., 839 F. 2d, (1104) 1106.

210 B. CLARK, *The law of secured transactions under the Uniform Commercial Code*, vol. 1, (3 edn., New York City: LexisNexis, 2015), 2–89. See also, Supreme Court of Oregon 30 December 1966, Evans Products Co. v. Jorgensen, 245 Or., (362) 366; Court of Appeals of Ohio, Eight District 26 June 1969, Sussen Rubber Co. v. Hertz, 19 Ohio App. 2d, (1) 6; Supreme Court of Oklahoma 15 March 1977, Morton Booth Co. v. Tiara Furniture Inc., 564 P.2d, (210) 212; Supreme Court of Minnesota 11 February 1972, James Talcott Inc. v. Franklin Nat. Bank of Minneapolis, 292 Minn., (277) 285.

211 R. CUMING, The internationalization of secured financing law: the spreading influence of the concepts of UCC, Article 9 and its progeny' in R. CRANSTON (ed.), *Making commercial law: essays in honour of Roy Goode*, (499) 523.

secured creditors.[212] Furthermore, the PMSI creditor has to make sure to comply with the requirements of Article 9 UCC to make his PMSI effective against third parties or he risks losing his priority as opposed to potential conflicting secured creditors.[213]

57. *Authenticated security agreement* – Besides the substantive requirements for the creation of a security interest, the security interest has to be formalized via an authenticated security agreement[214], possession of the encumbered good in the hands of the creditor, delivery of a security certificate or control of the encumbered good by the creditor.[215] For the purposes of this research, I focus on the authenticated security agreement. In a conditional sale agreement, it is unlikely that the creditor remains in possession of the encumbered good. The other two requirements are more applicable to financial collateral, such as shares and bank accounts. These types of goods fall outside the scope of this research.

The requirements for the security agreement are relatively flexible. For example, the agreement does not have to be named security agreement to be considered as such.[216] The essential elements of the security agreement are: the debtor's intention to transfer an interest in personal property as security to a creditor, description of the collateral and a signature of the security agreement.[217] A minority of courts and scholars are more formalistic and of the opinion that a security agreement must be a specific document and must also include explicit granting language.[218] Conversely, a majority of courts and scholars are of the opinion that a security agreement can be cobbled together from different documents, if the essential elements of a security agreement can be found in those documents.[219] For example, a security agreement has been found by reading together a promissory note and a financing

212 United States Court of Appeals, Fifth Cicruit 17 February 1976, Matter of Samuals & Co., 526 F.2d, (1238) 1246; Court of Appeals Arizona 8 July 1980, Amfac. Mortgage Corp. v. Arizona Mall of Tempe Inc., 127 Ariz., (70) 74.

213 See *infra* 3.2.2. Perfection and 3.3.3. super-priority.

214 Security agreement is an agreement that creates or provides for a security interest (§9–102 (a) (74) UCC (2010)).

215 §9–203 (a) (3) UCC (2010).

216 J. J. WHITE and others, *Principles of secured transactions*, (St. Paul: West Academic Publishing, 2018), 51.

217 B. CLARK, *The law of secured transactions under the Uniform Commercial Code*, vol. 1, (3 edn., New York City: LexisNexis, 2015), 21–22.

218 United states Circuit Court of Appeals, 8th circuit 7 February 1973, Shelton v. Erwin, 11 UCC Rep. Serv., (1239) 1240; United States Court of Appeals, Tenth Circuit 26 June 1975, Transport Equipment Co. v. Guaranty State Bank, 518 F.2d, (377) 380. See also, J. J. WHITE and others, *Principles of secured transactions*, (St. Paul: West Academic Publishing, 2018), 51.

219 Court of Appeals First Circuit 17 October 1973, In re numeric corp., 485 F. 2d, (1328) 1331–1332; H. J. BAILEY and R. B. HAGEDORN, *Secured transactions in a nutshell*, (4 edn., St. Paul: West Group, 2000), 82; J. J. WHITE and others, *Principles of secured transactions*, (St. Paul: West Academic Publishing, 2018), 52–53.

statement.[220] If the necessary elements can be found in different documents, a security agreement can be discerned. Following this opinion, a sale or lease agreement, that explicitly retains title to the sold goods in the hands of the seller until payment of the purchase price, generally contains the essential elements of a security agreement and is considered as a security agreement even though it does not contain explicit language concerning the granting of a security interest.[221] As a result, the recharacterization of a conditional sale to a security interest following the application of the functional approach and the creation of uniform rules with respect to the creation of security interests did not change much for former retention of title creditors in the drafting of their conditional sale agreements.

3.2.2. Third-party effectiveness (perfection) of PMSIs

58. *Overview of general notification requirements for third-party effectiveness of security interests* – Similar to the rules concerning creation, Article 9 UCC has a general set of rules for the third-party effectiveness of security interests or perfection.[222] The different methods of perfection are: filing a financing statement[223], possession of the encumbered good[224], control over the encumbered good[225] and in some cases automatic perfection at the moment of creation of the security interest.[226] For non-possessory security interest, such as conditional sales and lease agreements, the most relevant method of perfection is filing a financing statement in the security interest registry.[227] Prior to Article 9 UCC there was already a trend to subject conditional sales to filing requirements.[228] The reasoning went that third parties should be put on notice of the encumbrance the retention of title creditor placed on the debtor's estate

---

220 United States Court of Appeals, Third Circuit 8 February 1980, Matter of Bollinger Corp., 614 F.2d, (924) 927; United States Bankruptcy Court, W.D. Texas, Austin Division 4 November 1988, In re Maddox, 92 B.R., (707) 710 *et seq.*; United States Bankruptcy Court, D. Connecticut 21 August 1995, In re S.O.M.B., Inc., 1995 WL, (542512); United States Bankruptcy Court, N.D. West Virginia 28 June 2006, In re Weir-Penn, Inc., 344 B.R., (791) 794.

221 J. J. WHITE and others, *Principles of secured transactions*, (St. Paul: West Academic Publishing, 2018), 51.

222 J. J. WHITE and others, *Principles of secured transactions*, (St. Paul: West Academic Publishing, 2018), 60.

223 §9-310 UCC (2010).

224 §9-313 UCC (2010).

225 §9-312(b)(3) UCC (2010).

226 §9-309 UCC (2010).

227 §9-302 (1) UCC (1952); §9-310 (a) UCC (2010); D. G. BAIRD and T. H. JACKSON, ‹Possession and ownership: an examination of the scope of article 9', (1983) 35 Stan. L. Rev., (175) 183; W. H. LAWRENCE, W. H. HENNING and R. W. FREYERMUTH, *Understanding secured transactions*, (2 edn., New York City: Matthew Bender, 1999), 122; J. J. WHITE and others, *Principles of secured transactions*, (St. Paul: West Academic Publishing, 2018), 60.

228 *Supra* no. 25.

and to avoid ostensible ownership problems.[229] However, what sets the filing system of Article 9 UCC apart, is that now the filing system applies to all security interests, including PMSIs. Before different filing systems existed for conditional sales, chattel mortgages and trust receipts, resulting in a very complicated and cumbersome system.[230] The uniform filing system of Article 9 UCC made an end to the disparity in registration requirements and systems.[231] Furthermore, the introduction of Article 9 UCC at state level made it possible to encourage state filing instead of local filing.[232] Initially, the drafters still left it up to the states to decide whether they would introduce centralized state filing or would maintain local filing. However, in 1999 with the wider acceptance of electronic filing, revised Article 9 UCC only recommended state filing.[233] In summary, in many states the implementation of a uniform filing requirement for all security interests, such as conditional sales, did not come as a surprise and was even welcomed because it streamlined and simplified existing systems. Ideally, the filing system would be expanded to the national level, creating one system in which all interested parties can verify the encumbrance of their debtor's estate instead of having a system state by state. However, that would require a uniform regulation of secured transactions on a federal level. At the moment there does not seem to be much appetite for such an approach.

59. *Exceptions to notifications requirements for PMSIs* – Article 9 UCC allows some security interests to be perfected automatically, among which PMSIs in consumer goods.[234] The underlying reasoning for automatic perfection for PMSIs in consumer goods is that consumer transactions on credit are so common that subjecting them to filing requirements would overburden the filing system.[235] Furthermore, consumer goods are often low in value and depreciate quickly. Therefore, it is usually not worth it for the other creditors to verify whether they can obtain a security interest in a consumer good.[236] Finally, the automatic third-party effectiveness of PMSIs in consumer goods

---

229 G. GILMORE, *Security interests in personal property*, vol. 1, (Boston: Little Brown and Co., 1965), 438 *et seq.*

230 G. GILMORE, *Security interests in personal property*, vol. 1, (Boston: Little Brown and Co., 1965), 463.

231 G. GILMORE, *Security interests in personal property*, vol. 1, (Boston: Little Brown and Co., 1965), 462–463.

232 Local filing usually took place at the local court house at the municipal or county level instead of the state level. See also, J. J. WHITE and others, *Principles of secured transactions*, (St. Paul: West Academic Publishing, 2018), 88.

233 J. J. WHITE and others, *Principles of secured transactions*, (St. Paul: West Academic Publishing, 2018), 88–89.

234 §9–302 (1) (d) UCC (1952); R§9–309 (1) UCC.

235 W. H. LAWRENCE, W. H. HENNING and R. W. FREYERMUTH, *Understanding secured transactions*, (2 edn., New York City: Matthew Bender, 1999), 205.

236 D. G. BAIRD and T. H. JACKSON, 'Possession and ownership: an examination of the scope of article 9', (1983) 35 Stan. L. Rev., (175) 192; J. J. WHITE and others, *Principles of secured transactions*, (St. Paul: West Academic Publishing, 2018), 64.

has been long established so creditors are sufficiently on guard when a debtor wants to loan against consumer goods, despite the lack of filing.[237] There is one exception to the automatic perfection for PMSIs in consumer goods: a PMSI in consumer goods that is attached to immovable property. In that case, the PMSI holder always has to file a financing statement to maintain his protection and priority against creditors with an interest in the immovable good.[238] The PMSI creditor's right to trace his PMSI into fixtures is discussed in more detail in the following section.[239]

60. *Delineation of consumer goods* – Evidently, to be eligible for automatic perfection the security interest must be vested in consumer goods and must guarantee a purchase money obligation. Consumer goods are defined in the UCC as *"goods that are used or bought for use primarily for personal, family, or household purposes."*[240] Understandably, there can be debate about the consumer nature of goods. An example of this is when goods are purchased for both private and professional use, such as when a doctor buys a car for both personal and private use.[241]

61. *Conclusion* – The application of the functional approach to retention of title has not resulted in an increase of requirements to achieve third-party effectiveness. Prior to and under the UCSA many states already implemented a registration requirement for conditional sales and lease agreements. Consequently, the uniform perfection rules for all security rights in movable goods, with an emphasis on the filing of a financing statement, was not a big change for former retention of title creditors. Furthermore, the exception to the perfection rules for PMSIs in consumer goods shows that a functional approach does not necessarily has to lead to identical rules for all security interests. A policy choice to exempt PMSIs in consumer goods from perfection requirements is possible. Moreover, the underlying principle of the functional approach to value substance over form ensures that these separate rules apply to all security interests that are substantively the same and for which the same policy logically should apply. This distinguishes this exemption or separate rule for the third-party effectiveness for PMSIs in in consumer goods from previous exemptions

---

237 J. J. WHITE and others, *Principles of secured transactions*, (St. Paul: West Academic Publishing, 2018), 64;

238 §9-302 (d) *juncto* §9-313 UCC (1952); §9-309 (1) *juncto* R§9-334 UCC (2010); R. A. HAKES, *The ABC's of the UCC: Article 9 secured transactions*, (3 edn., Chicago: American Bar Association, 2013), 53; W. H. LAWRENCE, W. H. HENNING and R. W. FREYERMUTH, *Understanding secured transactions*, (2 edn., New York City: Matthew Bender, 1999), 206.

239 See *infra* no. 73.

240 §9-102(a)(23) UCC (2010).

241 J. J. WHITE and others, *Principles of secured transactions*, (St. Paul: West Academic Publishing, 2018), 68.

for conditional sales or lease agreements, which were only based on the name of the transaction and not the function they performed.

3.3. *Rights of PMSI creditors*

62. *Overview* – In the next section I discuss the rights that PMSI creditors have and whether these rights differ from the rights retention of title creditors had prior to the enactment of Article 9 UCC. The rights are divided in the PMSI creditor's right to dispose (3.3.1.), right to trace (3.3.2.), super-priority (3.3.3.) and enforcement (3.3.4.).

3.3.1. Right to dispose of the encumbered good

63. *Right to dispose prior to Article 9 UCC* – The explicit retention of title in a conditional sale or lease agreement raised the question whether the retention of title creditor retained sufficient title to the encumbered good to dispose of the encumbered good a second time. The answer to this question was twofold. If the retention of title creditor was of the opinion that payment of the purchase price by the debtor was uncertain, the creditor was allowed to resell the encumbered good.[242] Furthermore, when the debtor did not fulfill his obligations, the retention of title creditors could give good title to a new debtor without having to retake possession from the first debtor.[243]

When the conditional buyer was not in default, the seller was not allowed to dispose a second time of the sold good despite the title he retained to the good. The reasoning for this limitation on the seller's right to dispose of the title a second time when the debtor was not in default stemmed from general contract law principles. When the seller sold the good to the buyer under condition of payment of the purchase price, he took upon himself the obligation to deliver the good to the buyer and transfer title when the purchase price was paid. This obligation to transfer ownership after completion of the condition meant that the seller could not in good faith dispose of the good a second time to a new buyer when the original buyer was not in default. This would go against the conditional seller's standing obligation with the original buyer and could result in damages for the buyer.[244] If the seller did dispose of the good a second time,

---

242 ***Conditional sale***: Supreme Court of Ohio 1 January 1884, Call v. Seymour, 40 Ohio St., (670) 673–674. ***Leasing***: L. D. ADKINS and T. B. BARDOS, 'The leasing transaction', (1962) U. Ill. L. F., (16) 30.

243 Supreme Judicial Court of Massachusetts 1 September 1866, Hubbard v. Bliss, 12 Allen, (590) 591; R. S. WHITE, 'Right, duties and remedies of the parties to a sale of personal property which is to be delivered and paid for in instalments', (1897) 7 Yale L. J., (117) 131.

244 M. POTHIER, *A treatise on the law of obligations, or contracts*, vol. 1, (Philadelphia: Robert H. Small, 1839), 64–65; L. VOLD, 'Dividend Property Interests in Conditional Sales', (1929–30) 78 Univ. Penn. L. Rev., (713) 722.

despite his earlier conditional sale, and the new buyer came to revendicate the collateral, the original buyer could rely on his possession of the good to ward of the revindication by the new buyer. In the event that a good was conveyed twice, the buyer in possession was given preference.[245] However, the conditional buyer would not be able to invoke his right of retention of possession to protect against a second sale of the encumbered good, if the conditional buyer was in default. In that case the retention of title creditor was allowed to transfer the retained title. This would entitle the third party to the outstanding purchase price and continue the retention of title in hands of the new third-party transferee.

With regard to true lease agreements, the lessor could dispose of the leased good to a third party and the lease agreement would remain attached to the re-disposed good. This was for example the case when the leased goods were themselves encumbered with a chattel mortgage. If the lessor would default, then the secured creditor with a chattel mortgage could foreclose on the leased goods, acquire the lessor's interests in the leased goods and become entitled to the lease payments.[246] If a foreclosure did not terminate the lessee's obligation, then a disposition of the leased good to a new owner would also not. In other words, the third party would become the new lessor and the leased good would be returned to him at the end of the lease agreement. In the event that the lease was a masked conditional sale, then the same contract law principles would apply and the lessor was not allowed to dispose a second time of the leased good in contradiction with the standing obligation between the lessor and the lessee.

64. *Right to dispose post-Article 9 UCC* – Following the introduction of Article 9 UCC all conditional sales and lease agreements for security purposes are limited in their effect to security interests. As previously mentioned this means that now title is presumed to have transferred to the debtor and the PMSI creditor has retained a PMSI in the movable good. Given this recharacterization of all secured transactions for acquisition financing to a PMSI, there is no longer any debate whether the PMSI creditor could potentially dispose of the encumbered good a second time. At any rate, this new approach under Article 9 UCC does not significantly change the conditional seller's or lessor's right to dispose, since they were already limited in their right to dispose of the good after the conditional sale or lease.

---

245 T. PARSONS, *Law of contracts*, (Boston: Little Brown, 1864), 529; Supreme Judicial Court of Massachusetts 1 March 1815, Lamb v. Durant, 12 Mass., (54) 57; Supreme Judicial Court of Massachusetts 1 March 1821, Lanfear v. Sumner, 17 Mass., (110) 113; Supreme Court of Vermont 1 January 1826, Fletcher v. Howard, 1826 WL 1235, 2 Aik., (115) 116.

246 X., 'Acquisition of industrial and commercial equipment through leasing arrangements', (1957) 66 Yale L. J., (751) 764.

3.3.2. Tracing

65. *Introduction to general tracing rules and principles* – Tracing refers to the secured creditor's right to follow the encumbered good after it has been altered, such as processing, mixing, incorporation or a transfer in the hands of third-party transferee. Notable for Article 9 UCC is that the drafters opted to make the rules concerning tracing explicit and uniform for all security interests and no longer dependent on the application of property law principles. Pre-UCC the retention of title creditor's retained title to the encumbered good gave him an advantage in conflicts with other creditors or third parties concerning altered goods. The irrelevance of title and the creation of one set of rules concerning tracing in Article 9 UCC raises the question whether the retention of title creditor comes out less protected under Article 9 UCC.

A. Tracing into the hands of a third-party transferee

66. *Pre-Article 9 UCC* – The retention of title creditor mainly relied on his retained title to retain an effective claim against third parties in the event the encumbered goods were transferred. For example, after an unauthorized transfer the conditional seller was allowed to trace the goods in the hands of a third-party transferee, regardless of third party's good or bad faith, and to revendicate the good if it could still be identified.[247] This was based on two roman law maxims: *nemo dat quod non habet* and *caveat emptor.* The first principle, *nemo dat quod non habet*, states that the retention of title debtor cannot give what he does not have to a third-party transferee.[248] For example, if the first buyer bought under conditional sale, he did not obtain title. Consequently, the buyer without title did not have the proper authority or power to dispose of the good to a third party.[249]

---

247 Circuit Court District of Massachusetts 1 October 1823, Thompson v. Perkins, 23 F. Cas., (1066) 1067; Supreme Judicial Court of Massachusetts 1 March 1824, Denston v. Perkins, 19 Mass., (86) 93; Supreme Judicial Court of Massachusetts 1 January 1837, Merril v. Bank of Norfolk, 19 Pick, (32) 34; Supreme Court of Errors of Connecticut 1 May 1881, Lewis v. McCabe, 49 Conn., (141) 155.

248 Court of Appeals of New York 1 January 1869, Ballard v. Burgett, 1 Hand, (314) 315–316 and 321.

249 The right to dispose is generally reserved for the owner of the good. If the buyer did not obtain title or ownership, he normally does not have the authority or power to dispose of the good. See, O. BUMP, Fraudulent conveyances – a treatise upon conveyances made by debtors to defraud creditors, (2 edn., New York: Bakes, Voorhis & Co. Publishers, 1876), 62; J. DUKIMINIER, J. E. KRIER, G. S. ALEXANDER, M. H. SCHILL and L. J. STRAHILEVITZ, *Property*, (New York: Wolters Kluwer, 2018), 205; R. A. EPSTEIN, 'Property and necessity', (1990) 2 Harv. L. J. & Pub. Pol'y. (2) 3; MERRILL and SMITH, *Property- principles and policy*, 16; C. A. ARNOLD, 'The reconstitution of property: property as a web of interests', (2002) 26 Harv. Envtl. L. Rev. (281) 285; A. MOSSOFF, 'What is property? Putting the pieces back together' (2003) 45 Ar. L. Rev. (371) 376. See also specifically with regards to the rights vendors in conditional sales, R. S. WHITE, 'Right, duties and remedies of the parties to a sale of personal property which is to be delivered and paid for in instalments', (1897)

Furthermore, the third-party purchaser could not stand in any better situation than his seller with respect to the personal property.[250] Since the seller did not have title to the good, the third-party purchaser did not obtain title and thus could not invoke title against the original seller.[251] The second principle, *caveat emptor*, meant that the third-party purchaser had a responsibility to investigate the possible encumbrances on the sold good.[252] The fact that the retention of title debtor was in possession of the good did not protect the good faith purchaser, whose right always yielded to the actual title in the good and would have to suffer the loss of the good.[253] According to this maxim, the responsibility and risk fell to the third-party transferee to determine in whom title to the sold good was vested. Furthermore, the amount of due diligence the third-party purchaser exerted in this investigation for the actual title to the good, did not protect him if it turned out that his seller did not have the proper title or authority to sell the good. In other words, third-party purchasers suffered the consequences of any mistakes they made in their investigations.[254]

As mentioned above, in certain states the right to trace into the hands of a third-party transferee could be made dependent on additional requirements, such as registration of the conditional sale.[255] In the UCSA this requirement was generalized and a conditional seller could only trace the encumbered good in the hands of a third-party transferee when the conditional sale had been properly registered.[256] Furthermore, the conditional seller could not enforce his retained title against a third-party transferee, when the buyer was implicitly or expressly given the authority to resell the goods prior to the fulfillment of the condition

---

7 Yale L. J., (117) 131; Supreme Court of Florida 22 June 1886, Campbell Printing Press & Co. v. Walker, 22 Fla., (412) 422; Supreme Judicial Court of Massachusetts 1 September 1854, Henry Coggill & another v. Hartford and New Haven Railroad Company, 3 Gray, (545) 549; Supreme Judicial Court of Massachusetts 1 March 1857, Daniel Deshon v. Edward B. Bigelow & others, 8 Gray, (159) 160; Supreme Judicial Court of Massachusetts 1 October 1824, Barrett v. Pitchard, 2 Pick., (512) 548; Supreme Judicial Court of Massachusetts 1 November 1830, Reed v. Upton, 10 Pick, (522) 536.

250 Supreme Court of California 1 October 1868, Putnam v. Lamphier, 35 Cal., (151) 158; Supreme Court of Indiana 1 November 1876, Bradshaw v. Warner, 54 Ind., (58) 61.

251 Supreme Court of Indiana 12 June 1860, Shireman v. Jackson, 14 Ind., (459) 460.

252 Supreme Court of Georgia 1 June 1857, Goodwin v. May, 23 Ga., (205) 210; Supreme Judicial Court of Massachusetts 1 October 1864, Gilmore v. Newton, 9 Allen, (171) 172; Court of Appeals of New York 1 June 1868, Spraight v. Hawley, 12 Tiffany, (441) 445; Supreme Court of Oregon 2 January 1888, Velzian v. Lewis, 15 Oreg., (539) 541–542; Supreme Court of North Carolina 1 January 1879, Clayton v. Hester, 80 N.C., (275) 279.

253 Supreme Court of Indiana 1 November 1867, Dunbar v. Rawles, 28 Ind., (225) 229; Supreme Court of Arkansas, 16 October 1886, McIntosh v. Hill, 1. S. W., (680) 681; Supreme Court of Mississipi, Ketchum v. Brennan, 1 October 1876, 53 Miss., (596) 608; Circuit Court, E. D. Arkansas, 1 January 1880, Blackwell v. Walker, 5 F., (419) 422.

254 Supreme Court of Tennessee 1 September 1859, Price v. Jones, 3 Head, (84) 86; Supreme Court of Oregon 2 January 1888, Velzian v. Lewis, 15 Oreg., (539) 541–542. See also, N. NEWMARK, 'Conversion by purchase', (1881) 15 Am. L. Rev. (363) 364.

255 See *supra* no. 25.

256 §5 USCA.

and the goods were suited to resale.[257] This provision aligned with case law in which it was viewed inconsistent to retain title in the hands of the seller until performance of a preceding condition, while also authorizing the conditional buyer, implicitly or explicitly, to resell the conditionally sold goods.[258] This rule applied, regardless of the registration of the conditional sale agreement.[259] The reasoning went that third-party transferees could not be expected to check the records each time they made a purchase of retail goods to verify whether their buyer had sufficient title to sell the goods.[260] However, according to the UCSA this rule did not apply to mortgagees, pledgees and creditors. They were not considered to operate in the normal course of business and could be expected to investigate the records whether the good their debtor was offering as collateral actually belonged to him.[261] However, case law did not unify after the promulgation of the UCSA.[262] Some courts agreed that a conditional sale combined with the authority for resale for the conditional buyer, ostensibly clothed the conditional buyer with the indicia of ownership and ownership should therefore be considered as absolutely transferred to the conditional buyer, who can then do with the good as he pleases.[263] Conversely, other courts held that only good faith transferees could obtain the encumbered good without the condition precedent attached, whereas an executing creditor of a conditional

257 §9 UCSA. See also, L. VOLD, 'Dividend Property Interests in Conditional Sales', (1929–30) 78 Univ. Penn. L. Rev., (713) 733.

258 Supreme Court of New York 3 April 1860, Ludden v. Hazen, 31 Barb., (650) 652; Supreme Court of Indiana 5 January 1887, Winchester Wagon Works Co. v. Carman, 109 Ind. 31, 9 N.E., (707) 709–710; Supreme Court of Mississippi 24 February 1896, Columbus Buggy Co. v. Turley, 73 Miss. 529, 19 So., (232) 233; Supreme Court of Tennessee 2 February 1907, Star Clothing Mfg. v. Nordeman, 10 Cates 384, 100 S.W., (93) 94–95; Supreme Court of Georgia 12 May 1909, Clarke Bros. v. McNatt, 132 Ga. 610, 64 S.E., (795) 799; Supreme Court of Alabama 15 November 1910, Bass v. International Harvester Co. of America, 169 Ala., (154) 159; Superior Court of Delaware 24 October 1911, Flint Wagon Works v. Maloney, 3 Boyce 137, 81 A., (502) 503; Supreme Court of Idaho 12 November 1913, Trousdale v. Winona Wagon Co., 25 Idaho, 130, 137 P., (372) 374; Supreme Court of Wisconsin 13 January 1914, Oconto Land Co. v. Wallschlaeger, 155 Wis. 418, 144 N.W., (979) 981–982.

259 P. CAVENDER, 'Notes and comments', (1930) 5 Wash. L. Rev., (65) 69.

260 Supreme Court of Washington 28 Augustus 1922, Gramm-Bernstein Motor Truck Co. v. Todd, 121 Wash., (145) 148. *Contra*: Court of Appeals Maryland 1 February 1924, Finance & Guaranty Co. v. Defiance Motor Truck Co., 145 Md. 94, 125 A., (585) 588; P. CAVENDER, 'Notes and comments', (1930) 5 Wash. L. Rev., (65) 70.

261 H. NOYES GREENE, 'Uniform Conditional Sales Act and commentary' in H. NOYES GREEN (ed.), *Uniform laws, annotated*, vol. 2, (Northport: Edward Thompson Co., 1922), 16.

262 P. CAVENDER, 'Notes and comments', (1930) 5 Wash. L. Rev., (65) 71.

263 Supreme Court of New York 3 April 1860, Ludden v. Hazen, 31 Barb., (650) 653; District Court of New York 20 June 1901, In re Howland, 109 F., (869) 871; Circuit Court of Appeals 22 April 1902, In re Garcewich, 115 F., (87) 89; District Court New York 14 December 1909, In re Penny & Anderson, 176 F., (141) 144; Circuit Court of Appeals 16 June 1908, Coweta Fertilizer Co. v. Brown, 163 F., (162) 166–167.

buyer merely succeeded in the rights of the conditional buyer in the encumbered goods and was thus bound by the condition.[264]

67. *Tracing into the hands of a third-party transferee in Article 9 UCC* – Despite the fact that the retention of title creditor no longer has title in the encumbered good, a security interest, including the PMSI, follows in the hands of a third-party transferee after a sale, exchange or disposition of the encumbered good.[265] This rule also applies when the encumbered good is sold as part of an enforcement proceeding.[266] Furthermore, the security right holder may enforce his security interest in both the transferred collateral or the proceeds.[267] Of course, the secured creditor's enforcement is limited by the size of his claim. Moreover, the secured creditor is not allowed to enforce both the proceeds and the collateral beyond what he is owed.[268]

However, there are exceptions to this rule. First, the third-party transferee obtains the good free from the security interest when the secured creditor gave permission for the transfer of the collateral.[269] This makes sense. If the secured creditor has given permission to dispose of the encumbered goods, then it would be contradictory for him to also want to maintain a claim in the sold good after transfer. The authorization for the right to dispose can be explicit or implied.[270] Second, the third-party transferee also obtains the good free from the security interest, if the transferee acquired in good faith. A third party is considered to act in good faith even if the security interest is perfected and the third-party transferee knows of its existence.[271] The idea is that a free flow of goods means that good faith purchasers can buy goods from sellers in the ordinary course of business free of a security interest and without having to check the registry.[272] Additionally, the fact that buyers in the ordinary course of business do not have to check the registry before acquiring the good, aligns with the underlying goal of registration to inform other creditors and not to protect the secured creditor

264 Supreme Court of the United States 24 May 1909, Bryant v. Swofford Bros. Dry Goods Co., 214 U.S., (279) 285–292; Superior Court of Delaware 24 October 1911, Flint Wagon Works v. Maloney, 3 Boyce 137, 81 A., (502) 506–507.

265 §9-315 (a) (1) UCC (2010). See also, J. J. WHITE and others, *Principles of secured transactions*, (St. Paul: West Academic Publishing, 2018), 204.

266 §9-317 (a) (2) UCC (2010).

267 W. H. LAWRENCE, W. H. HENNING and R. W. FREYERMUTH, *Understanding secured transactions*, (2 edn., New York City: Matthew Bender, 1999), 301.

268 W. H. LAWRENCE, W. H. HENNING and R. W. FREYERMUTH, *Understanding secured transactions*, (2 edn., New York City: Matthew Bender, 1999), 301, fn. 9.

269 §9-315 (a) (1) UCC (2010). See also, P. WANGERIN, 'Floating liens, proceeds, and PMSIs: perfection and priority in three closely connected cases', (2017) 47 UCC L. J., (287) 322.

270 W. H. LAWRENCE, W. H. HENNING and R. W. FREYERMUTH, *Understanding secured transactions*, (2 edn., New York City: Matthew Bender, 1999), 302.

271 §9-320 (a) UCC (2010).

272 W. H. LAWRENCE, W. H. HENNING and R. W. FREYERMUTH, *Understanding secured transactions*, (2 edn., New York City: Matthew Bender, 1999), 309.

against third-party transfers. Nevertheless, this provision offers a significant protection for third-party transferees and limits the usefulness of registration in this context. To offer some counter-balance, the buyers in the ordinary course of business only enjoy the assumption of good faith and thus the exemption of checking the registry when: the goods are sold to a (1) good faith purchaser, who (2) buys goods in the ordinary course of business, (3) does not buy in bulk, and (4) does not buy farm products, (5) from a seller who ordinarily deals in such goods (6) in which the competing PMSI was vested by the good faith buyer's seller.[273] Understandably, there have been debates about some of the requirements of this rule. For example, when a sale takes place outside the seller's usual business. This was the case for a car rental agency that also occasionally sold cars. The New York State Supreme Court decided that the sale of these cars by the rental company were incidental and should not be considered as the rental agency's ordinary business. Therefore, the purchaser could not be considered to act in good faith.[274]

Another point of contention is the contradiction that seems to exist between the definition of good faith buyer in Article 1 UCC and the protection given to good faith buyers in Article 9 UCC. The definition in Article 1 UCC states that a person buys goods in good faith when he does not have knowledge that the sale violates the rights of another person in the goods.[275] In turn, Article 9 UCC sets out that the good faith buyer takes free of a security interest, including PMSIs, even if the security interest is perfected and the buyer knows of its existence.[276] At first glance, these provisions seem to contradict one another and more importantly, the definition in Article 1 UCC indicates that the buyer cannot buy in good faith once he has knowledge of the perfected security interest. However, the definition in Article 1 UCC actually states that the buyer cannot buy in good faith if he knows that the sale of the encumbered good will violate the conditions of the security agreement. For example, when the security agreement prohibits the debtor from selling the good and the buyer knows of this prohibition, then the buyer cannot buy in good faith. However, this is different from the buyer knowing that there is a perfected security interest and still buying it as is set out in Article 9 UCC. The third-party transferee's knowledge of the perfected security interest does not prevent the buyer from purchasing the good in good faith, since this does not necessarily violate another person's right. Security agreements often implicitly or explicitly allow the debtor to dispose of the

---

273 §1–201 (b) (9) *juncto* §9–320 (a) UCC (2010). See also, W. H. LAWRENCE, W. H. HENNING and R. W. FREYERMUTH, *Understanding secured transactions*, (2 edn., New York City: Matthew Bender, 1999), 309.

274 New York Supreme Court 6 July 1970, Hempstead Bank v. Andy's Car Rental System, 35 A.D. 2d., (35) 39.

275 §1–201 (b) (9) UCC (2001).

276 §9–320 (a) UCC (2010).

collateral so the knowledge of the perfected security interest, nor its sale prevents the good faith purchaser's protection.[277]

B. Tracing into proceeds

68. *Pre-Article 9 UCC* – The case law varied with regards to the extension of the retention of title creditor's right in the proceeds of the encumbered collateral. On the one hand, the idea of tracing the retention of title creditor's right in the proceeds of the conditionally sold good was foreign to commercial law before the introduction of the UCC.[278] Disposing of the encumbered sold good was generally at the transferee's risk who was likely to obtain the good with the retention of title creditor's claim still attached.[279] Given the retention of title creditor's right to follow the good in the hands of the third-party transferee, there was no immediate need to introduce a right to trace into the proceeds. On the other hand, some courts allowed tracing into proceeds, but only when the parties explicitly agreed to extend the retention of title creditor's right in the proceeds and the proceeds could still be identified.[280] For example, if the payment was made in promissory notes, then the proceeds could still be identified in the hands of the transferee and traced. If the encumbered goods were sold for cash, then the retention of title creditor's claim was lost due to the specificity principle. Cash money cannot be earmarked and was therefore not sufficiently specific to maintain the conditional seller's claim.[281] Tracing into proceeds was not addressed in the UCSA, so the case law remained applicable after its promulgation and enactment.

69. *Tracing into proceeds in Article 9 UCC* – With the introduction of a general non-possessory security interest in Article 9 UCC, the need for explicit rules concerning tracing of the security interest into proceeds of the encumbered good became more important. In Article 9 UCC the issue of tracing security interests into proceeds is addressed explicitly. Any security interest extends into the proceeds of the encumbered goods, if the financing statement covers

277 J. J. WHITE and others, *Principles of secured transactions*, (St. Paul: West Academic Publishing, 2018), 206–207.

278 Supreme Court of Arkansas 2 November 1889, Deadman v. Earle, 52 Ark. 164, 12 S. W., (330) 330–331; Supreme Court of Arkansas 6 December 1890, Nattin v. Riley, 54 Ark. 30, 14 S. W., (1100) 1100; J. J. WHITE and others, *Principles of secured transactions*, (St. Paul: West Academic Publishing, 2018), 128.

279 See *supra* no. 63.

280 Supreme Court of Vermont 1 February 1846, Paris v. Vail, 18 Vt., (277) 283; Supreme Court of Vermont 1 August 1875, Kelsey v. Kendall, 48 Vt., (24) 26; Supreme Court of North Carolina 5 May 1890, Perry v. Young, 105 N. C. 463, 11 S. E., (511) 512; R. J. LONG, 'Conditional sale' in D. S. GARLAND and L. P. MCGEHEE (eds.), *The American and English encyclopaedia of law*, vol. 6, (New York: Edward Thompson Co., 1898), 485;

281 Court of Common Pleas 10 February 1742, Scott v. Surman, 125 E.R., (1235) 1237.

"all of the debtor's assets". In that scenario, the security interest in the proceeds is automatically perfected[282] and the secured creditor can avoid any headache concerning the continued perfection of his security interest into the proceeds of the originally encumbered good.[283] However, with regards to PMSIs, the PMSI creditor's super-priority still depends on whether the proceeds stemming from the original goods were directly financed with credit from the PMSI creditor[284] and the PMSI creditor has correctly fulfilled the additional perfection requirements for super-priority.[285] In other words, the extension of the PMSI creditor's collateral to all the debtor's assets to ensure continued perfection in the original good's proceeds does not mean that the PMSI creditor is given super-priority status in the proceeds. It is merely a method to ensure continued perfection after resale of the originally encumbered goods.

In many cases, a PMSI is vested in the context of conditional sale or lease agreement. In these situations, it is unlikely that the PMSI creditor explicitly extends his security to all of the debtor's assets. Nevertheless, even if the secured creditor did not opt for a broad description of collateral, Article 9 UCC includes provisions that regulate the extension of the security interest into identifiable proceeds of the original collateral.[286] The extension of security interests into proceeds was made explicit in the 1972 version of Article 9 UCC and applies even when parties have not explicitly mentioned the extension of their security interest to proceeds.[287] For the first 20 days the extended security interest into proceeds is automatically perfected in all proceeds.[288] After 20 days, the temporary automatic perfection in proceeds, in most cases, changes into permanent automatic perfection if one of the following conditions is met. In the first scenario, the temporary perfection of a security interest into proceeds automatically transfers to permanent perfection, if the financing statement for the security interest in the proceeds is filed at the same office as the one where the financing statement for the security interest in the originally encumbered good was filed and the proceeds were not acquired with cash proceeds.[289] The idea with regards to the office of registration is that the financing statement concerning the original collateral should give third parties sufficient warning

---

282 G. R. WARNER, 'The anti-bankruptcy act: revised Article 9 and bankruptcy', (2001) 9 Am. Bankr. L. Rev., (3) 59.

283 G. R. WARNER, 'The anti-bankruptcy act: revised Article 9 and bankruptcy', (2001) 9 Am. Bankr. L. Rev., (3) 59 *et seq.*

284 See *supra* no. 49.

285 See *infra* no. 78.

286 §9-315(a)(2) UCC (2010). See also, R. A. HAKES, *The ABC's of the UCC: Article 9 secured transactions*, (3 edn., Chicago: American Bar Association, 2013), 32; C. J. CHERNUCHIN, 'Security interests in proceeds of collateral', (2012) 1 Bus. L. Today, (1) 1.

287 J. J. WHITE and others, *Principles of secured transactions*, (St. Paul: West Academic Publishing, 2018), 124.

288 §9-315(d) UCC (2010).

289 §9-315(d)(1) UCC (2010).

that the proceeds in the original good are likely covered by the security interest in the original good. For example, if a security interest is in inventory and the debtor's business consists of reselling inventory, then a third party checking the registry can be expected to deduce that the originally encumbered good will be sold and that the security interest will extend to the proceeds. As a result, the filing of another financing statement concerning the proceeds in the same office is considered unnecessary.[290] The other condition for automatic perfection in this scenario is that the proceeds cannot be purchased with cash proceeds.[291] This condition tackles the situation of second-generation proceeds.[292] Let's take the previous example and presume that the debtor uses the proceeds of the inventory to buy a new good that is not inventory. In this scenario, it is very difficult for a potential creditor to deduce whether the good acquired with the cash proceeds is also covered by the security interest in the original collateral. It would ask too much from third parties to consider all assets of the debtor as potential proceeds of the original collateral and would likely deter them from granting credit. Therefore, the condition was added that the automatic extension of the security into proceeds only applies when the proceeds were not acquired with cash proceeds. In other words, this condition aims to strike a balance between the extension of the security interest into proceeds and the extent to which a third party should be able to ascertain which assets or proceeds thereof are potentially encumbered with a security interest.

Furthermore, the perfection into proceeds continues automatically when the proceeds are identifiable cash proceeds.[293] An important exception to this rule is that accounts receivable are not considered cash proceeds. Consequently, in such proceeds the temporary perfection does not automatically transfer to permanent perfection.[294] In that case the secured creditor has to make sure that he has made separate arrangements for the perfection of his security interest into the accounts receivable.[295] Only when none of these rules regarding the automatic transfer from temporary to permanent perfection apply, does the secured creditor have to separately perfect the security interest into proceeds before the 21st day.[296]

70. *The concept of proceeds* – The term proceeds itself did and to some extent still results in some case law. Originally, the definition of proceeds put a lot of emphasis on proceeds being the result of an exchange, sale or other disposition

290 P. WANGERIN, 'Floating liens, proceeds, and PMSIs: perfection and priority in three closely connected cases', (2017) 47 UCC L. J., (287) 309.
291 §9-315(d)(1)(C) UCC (2010).
292 P. WANGERIN, 'Floating liens, proceeds, and PMSIs: perfection and priority in three closely connected cases', (2017) 47 UCC L. J., (287) 310.
293 §9-315(d)(2) UCC (2010).
294 P. WANGERIN, 'Floating liens, proceeds, and PMSIs: perfection and priority in three closely connected cases', (2017) 47 UCC L. J., (287) 307-308.
295 §9-315(d) UCC (2010).
296 §9-315(d)(1) UCC (2010).

of the underlying collateral.[297] This led some courts to apply a "(permanent) passage-of-title approach" that denies proceeds status, unless the debtor parts with the title to the original collateral.[298] This approach overlooks the fact that an asset can generate proceeds in a myriad of ways that does not necessarily involve the transfer of title. For example, this approach would not consider insurance payments or lease payments for an encumbered good as proceeds.[299] In the revised definition, proceeds outside of a transfer of rights context are included, such as lease payments and insurance payments.[300] This broader version of proceeds makes clear that proceeds should not be interpreted in a formalistic manner (i.e. based on a transfer of title), but in a functional manner that focuses on whether some event has consumed the economic value or the productive capacity of the collateral.[301]

Furthermore, proceeds can be all sort of goods: cash, cheques, promissory notes or other tangible goods.[302] The only thing that matters for the secured party to enforce his right is that the proceeds are identifiable. Basically, the identifiable nature means that outsiders have to be able to discern that the new goods are proceeds from the originally encumbered goods. In the event of a sale of goods for cash this will be evident, but when encumbered goods are directly exchanged for new goods, these new goods will theoretically fit the description of proceeds but will be harder to identify and could lose their determination.[303] The problem of identifying the proceeds in the debtor's estate mainly rises when the proceeds take the form of cash. In that case, the proceeds are likely to get mixed with the debtor's other money or in his bank account. To counter this courts have allowed secured parties to trace their cash proceeds via equitable rules, such as the lowest intermediate balance rule.[304] This rule has now been explicitly acknowledged in Article 9 UCC.[305] This rule presumes that a debtor first uses his own money and that the proceeds of the secured party are the last amount to

297 §9-306 (1) UCC (2010).

298 W. H. LAWRENCE, W. H. HENNING and R. W. FREYERMUTH, *Understanding secured transactions*, (2 edn., New York City: Matthew Bender, 1999), 97.

299 R. W. FREYERMUTH, 'Rethinking proceeds: the history of misrepresentation and revision of UCC section 9-306', (1994-95) 69 Tul. L. Rev., (645) 660; J. J. WHITE and others, *Principles of secured transactions*, (St. Paul: West Academic Publishing, 2018), 125.

300 R§9-102 (a) (64) UCC (2010). See also, P. WANGERIN, 'Floating liens, proceeds, and PMSIs: perfection and priority in three closely connected cases', (2017) 47 UCC L. J., (287) 301-302.

301 R. W. FREYERMUTH, 'Rethinking proceeds: the history of misrepresentation and revision of UCC section 9-306', (1994-95) 69 Tul. L. Rev., (645) 655.

302 W. H. LAWRENCE, W. H. HENNING and R. W. FREYERMUTH, *Understanding secured transactions*, (2 edn., New York City: Matthew Bender, 1999), 96.

303 P. WANGERIN, 'Floating liens, proceeds, and PMSIs: perfection and priority in three closely connected cases', (2017) 47 UCC L. J., (287) 305.

304 United States District Court Missouri 12 March 1973, Universal C. I. T. Credit Corp v. Farmers Bank of Portageville, 358 F. Supp., (317) 325-327.

305 §9-315(b)(2) UCC (2010). See also, R. A. HAKES, *The ABC's of the UCC: Article 9 secured transactions*, (3 edn., Chicago: American Bar Association, 2013), 33;

be removed from an account.[306] For example, 1000 euro proceeds are deposited in an account that already contains 1000 euro from the debtor. Then the debtor takes out 1500 euro and later deposits another 1000 euro. During this period, the lowest intermediate balance in the account was 500 euro. Consequently, the secured creditors claim will be limited to 500 euro.[307]

c. Tracing into accessions or mixed goods

71. *Pre- Article 9 UCC* – When dealing with non-possessory secured transactions in movable goods there is always a risk that the encumbered goods become attached to or mixed with another movable good. Pre-Article 9 UCC the accession or mixing of the encumbered good with another movable good likely spelled the end of the retention of title creditor's claim to the good.[308] This risk for the retention of title creditor stemmed from the principle: *accessorium sequitur principale*. Following this maxim the owner of the principal good would automatically extend his claim to the accessory good that had been added.[309] Consequently, the retention of title creditor could only maintain his retained title, if his good was considered the principal good after the manufacturing process.[310] This raised the question whether this principle would still apply once the retention of title creditor became the holder of a PMSI.

Interestingly, the retention of title creditor was less at risk following the mixing of the encumbered good with other movable goods. If the encumbered good became part of a mixed mass of goods, then the retention of title creditor was entitled to a part of the mass in proportion to his original collateral.[311] In this scenario the retention of title creditor did not lose his claim to the mixed goods due to the specificity principle. The fact that he no longer could identify which goods specifically had been his did not matter. He was still entitled to a portion of the entire mass in which the original goods had been mixed.

72. *Tracing into accessions and mixed goods in Article 9 UCC* – Article 9 UCC considers a good an accession when it has been affixed to another movable

306 R. A. HAKES, *The ABC's of the UCC: Article 9 secured transactions*, (3 edn., Chicago: American Bar Association, 2013), 33.

307 United States District Court Missouri 12 March 1973, Universal C. I. T. Credit Corp v. Farmers Bank of Portageville, 358 F. Supp., (317) 326.

308 F. B. HARING, *The law of conditional sales*, (New York: The Ronald Press, 1907), 11.

309 Supreme Judicial Court of Maine 1 Janaury 1851, Pulcifer v. Page, 32 Me., (404) 405; J. KENT, *Commentaries on American Law* (4 edn., New York: E. B. Clayton, 1840), 360; G. GILMORE, *Security interests in personal property*, vol. 1, (Boston: Little Brown and Co., 1965) 837.

310 G. GILMORE, *Security interests in personal property*, vol. 1, (Boston: Little Brown and Co., 1965), 837.

311 G. GILMORE, *Security interests in personal property*, vol. 1, (Boston: Little Brown and Co., 1965), 841.

good in such a manner that the identity of the original good is not lost.[312] An accession is different from a processed good, since an accession can still be identified from the good to which it is attached. Conversely, a processed good refers to a good in which another good has been integrated so completely that it can no longer be identified.[313] Notably, a good does not lose its status as an accession due to the cost or difficulty of removing the accession from the other goods or because the accession has become an integral part of the other goods.[314] Since Article 9 UCC, there is no denying that a security interest continues in the affixed good that has become an accession. However, in the pre-revised version of Article 9 UCC the extension of the security interest in the accession was only allowed, if the security interest was created and made effective against third parties (i.e. attached) before the encumbered good was attached to the other movable good.[315] Conversely, security interests that attached after the good became attached to the other movable good would be invalid and could not be enforced.[316] This distinction was addressed in the revised version of Article 9 UCC. Now a security interest always continues in the affixed good.[317] However, its priority as opposed to the (secured) creditor, who has an interest in the good to which the encumbered good was affixed, is determined by the general priority rules of Article 9 UCC.[318]

The problem concerning mixed goods was addressed in the revised version of Article 9 UCC. Now the provision concerning mixed goods only deals with situations in which the separate goods are no longer identifiable.[319] The secured creditor of an unidentifiable mixed good continues to have a security interest in the entire mass or new product in proportion to the value of his original encumbered good, if the security interest or PMSI was perfected before the goods were mixed or processed.[320] Notably, the rules concerning mixed or processed goods no longer regulated the situation where the encumbered goods are still identifiable after they have been processed or mixed. In that case the encumbered goods are not in fact mixed, nor processed, but have merely turned into accessions. Therefore, if the encumbered goods remain identifiable after they have been processed or mixed, then the secured creditor can rely on the

312 §9-102(a)(1) UCC (2010).

313 W. H. LAWRENCE, W. H. HENNING and R. W. FREYERMUTH, *Understanding secured transactions*, (2 edn., New York City: Matthew Bender, 1999), 363.

314 J. J. WHITE and others, *Principles of secured transactions*, (St. Paul: West Academic Publishing, 2018), 199;

315 §9-314 (2) UCC. See also, W. H. LAWRENCE, W. H. HENNING and R. W. FREYERMUTH, *Understanding secured transactions*, (2 edn., New York City: Matthew Bender, 1999), 365.

316 §9-314(3) UCC (2010).

317 §9-335(a) UCC (2010).

318 §9-335(c) UCC (2010). See also, J. J. WHITE and others, *Principles of secured transactions*, (St. Paul: West Academic Publishing, 2018), 199.

319 §9-336(c) UCC (2010).

320 J. J. WHITE and others, *Principles of secured transactions*, (St. Paul: West Academic Publishing, 2018), 200.

rules concerning accession or choose to apply the rules applicable to mixed or processed goods even though the encumbered good is an accession.[321]

D. Tracing into fixtures

73. *Impact of incorporation pre-Article 9 UCC* – Finally, the retention of title creditor's claim to the encumbered good was threatened by the attachment to or incorporation of the encumbered good in an immovable good. The general rule to determine whether movable goods had become part of the immovable good and would transfer as part of the immovable good depended on whether the incorporated movable goods were permanent in nature and essential for the purpose of the immovable good. This assessment did not take into account the fact that the movable goods could be severed from the immovable good without physical or lasting injury to either.[322] If the attached goods were permanent in nature and essential to the purpose of the immovable good, then the movable goods became permanently affixed to the immovable good and could no longer be individualized, nor revendicated by the retention of title creditor. However, if it could be shown that the owner of the movable good agreed with the owner of the immovable good that the goods would remain movable property, then this agreement would be sustained and the movable good would not transfer to a third party in the event the immovable good was transferred.[323] In other words, a clear intention between the parties concerning the incorporated nature of the encumbered good could protect the conditional seller's retained title in an incorporated good.[324]

In the UCSA, the drafters made a choice to hinge the continuation of the retention of title on whether or not the encumbered sold good could be severed from the immovable good without damage to the immovable good.[325] In other words, if the movable good could be removed from the immovable good without damage, title to the incorporated good would remain in the hands of the retention of title creditor. The concept of damage or injury to the immovable good was left open in the USCA and led to different interpretations. In Pennsylvania and New Jersey, for example, courts interpreted this as economic injury to the real estate referring to the potential damage the removal could have on the economic integrity of the real estate. In other UCSA states, the concept

321 W. H. LAWRENCE, W. H. HENNING and R. W. FREYERMUTH, *Understanding secured transactions*, (2 edn., New York City: Matthew Bender, 1999), 367.

322 Supreme Court of Appeals of Virginia 18 September 1875, Green v. Phillips, 26 Gratt., (752) 759; Supreme Court of Appeals of Virginia 12 February 1880, Shelton v. Ficklin, 32 Gratt., (727) 735; Supreme Court of California 1 May 1881, Fratt v. Whittier, 8 P.C.L.J. 149, 58 Cal., (126) 131.

323 Supreme Court of Vermont 1 March 1845, Cross v. Marston, 17 Vt., (533) 541; Supreme Court of New York 6 June 1853, Godard v. Gould & Strong, 14 Barb., (662) 666.

324 X., 'Conditional sales' 9 Pac. Coast L. J., (545) 564.

325 §7, sec. 1 UCSA.

of damage or injury to the immovable good was interpreted to mean physical and irreparable damage to the immovable good. In other words, removal that had resulted in the structural destruction of the immovable good.[326] The different interpretations of damage or injury to the immovable good led to new differentiations between different UCSA states. Nevertheless, there was at least a general assumption that title to incorporated goods could be maintained and was not immediately lost.

Furthermore, the drafters also made clear rules regarding tracing the encumbered good after it had been incorporated in an immovable good which was in turn sold to a third party. Following the UCSA, the retention of title would be void against purchasers of the immovable good in which the encumbered good was incorporated, unless the conditional sale contract or a copy thereof was filed together with a statement signed by the seller in which he described the immovable good and the goods that were affixed to it.[327] If the conditional sale contract and the statement were filed and the good could be severed without damage, then the retention of title creditor was allowed to trace his reserved title in the incorporated good in the hands of a third-party transferee.[328] This provision moved away from the case law that existed at that time in the United States which held that a retention of title creditor could not enforce his reserved title in an incorporated good against a third-party purchaser of the immovable good.[329]

74. *Fixtures in Article 9 UCC?* – In Article 9 UCC, security interests continue into fixtures (i.e. movable goods that have become attached to immovable goods).[330] The only problem is that the concept of fixture is not explicitly defined in the UCC. The definition of fixture in Article 9 UCC merely refers to goods that have become so related to a particular real property that an interest in them arises under real property law.[331] States are in charge of setting out real property

---

326 G. GILMORE, *Security interests in personal property*, vol. 1, (Boston: Little Brown and Co., 1965), 804.

327 §7, sec. 2 UCSA.

328 H. NOYES GREENE, 'Uniform Conditional Sales Act and commentary' in H. NOYES GREEN (ed.), *Uniform laws, annotated*, vol. 2, (Northport: Edward Thompson Co., 1922), 12–13.

329 Supreme Court of Vermont 1 Feburary 1870, Davenport v. John G. Shants & Co., 43 Vt., (546) 552; Supreme Court of Kansas 7 March 1885, Rowand v. Anderson, 33 Kan. 264, 6 P., (255) 258–259; Supreme Court of Michigan 23 June 1887, Jenks v. Colwell, 66 Mich., (420) 428; Supreme Court of New Hampshire 1 December 1888, Tibbets v. Horne, 65 N.H. 242, 23 A., (145) 146; Supreme Court of Tennessee 11 February 1905, Union Bank Trust Co. v. Fred w. Wolf Co., 114 Tenn. 255, 86 S.W., (310) 312; Supreme Court of Oregon 28 June 1910, Washburn v. Inter-Mountain Mining Co., 56 Or., (578) 584; Supreme Court of Georgia 28 October 1911, J. S. Schofield's Sons Co. v. Woodward, 137 Ga. 65, 72 S. E., (509) 509; Supreme Court of Iowa 13 December 1913, Allis-Chambers Co. v. Atlantic, 164 Ia. 8, 144 N. W., (346) 349.

330 §9–334 (a) UCC (2010).

331 §9–201(a)(41) UCC (2010).

law. Consequently, state real estate law determines when a good is considered a fixture.[332] Generally, a good is considered a fixture when it is so attached to the immovable good that a buyer of the land would believe that the fixture would transfer with the immovable good.[333] Furthermore, a movable good can only be a fixture when the movable good is still identifiable and has not fully merged with the immovable good to which it has been attached.[334] Courts generally take following factors into account when determining if a movable good has become a fixture or not: the intention of the annexor, the degree of physical attachment to the immovable good and the degree to which the movable good adapted to the characteristics of the immovable good.[335] Once it has been determined that the encumbered good has become a fixture, the next question is whether this means that the good has thereby become an immovable good or falls into a separate category (i.e. fixtures) that is part movable and part immovable good. The drafters of Article 9 UCC presumed that a fixture was a mixed good with both movable and immovable characteristics.[336] However, in the early days of Article 9 UCC certain states did not always see it this way and still worked with only two categories: movable and immovable goods.[337] Consequently, in these states a fixture meant a good that had become part of an immovable good and was thus excluded from the scope of Article 9 UCC. This interpretation went against the policy of Article 9 UCC that security interests continue to exist in fixtures. Furthermore, this interpretation was detrimental to the uniform approach to fixtures across states that the UCC envisioned. In Article 9 UCC, the

332 P. F. COOGAN, 'Security interests in fixtures under the Uniform Commercial Code', (1962) 75 Harv. L. Rev., (1319) 1347; J. J. WHITE and others, *Principles of secured transactions*, (St. Paul: West Academic Publishing, 2018), 188.

333 P. F. COOGAN, 'Security interests in fixtures under the Uniform Commercial Code', (1962) 75 Harv. L. Rev., (1319) 1344; H. KRIPKE, 'Fixtures under the Uniform Commercial Code', (1964) 64 Colum. L. Rev., (44) 44; W. H. LAWRENCE, W. H. HENNING and R. W. FREYERMUTH, *Understanding secured transactions*, (2 edn., New York City: Matthew Bender, 1999), 350; J. J. WHITE and others, *Principles of secured transactions*, (St. Paul: West Academic Publishing, 2018), 187.

334 H. KRIPKE, 'Fixtures under the Uniform Commercial Code', (1964) 64 Colum. L. Rev., (44) 49; P. F. COOGAN, 'Security interests in fixtures under the Uniform Commercial Code', (1962) 75 Harv. L. Rev., (1319) 1345; J. J. WHITE and others, *Principles of secured transactions*, (St. Paul: West Academic Publishing, 2018), 186.

335 Supreme Court of Ohio 1 January 1853, Teaff v. Hewitt, 1 Ohio St., (511) 530; Supreme Court of Missouri 18 December 1975, Sears, Roebuck & Co. v. Seven Palms Motor Inn, 530 S. W. 2d., (695) 696; United States Bankruptcy Court 23 March 1994, In re Hot Shots Burgers & Fries Inc., 169 B. R., (920) 924–925; W. H. LAWRENCE, W. H. HENNING and R. W. FREYERMUTH, *Understanding secured transactions*, (2 edn., New York City: Matthew Bender, 1999), 350.

336 P. F. COOGAN, 'Security interests in fixtures under the Uniform Commercial Code', (1962) 75 Harv. L. Rev., (1319) 1344.

337 Massachusetts was one of the states that considered a fixture as a non-removable part of the immovable good (Supreme Judicial Court of Massachusetts 7 March 1922, Ferdinand v. Earle, 241 Mass., (92) 94).

idea of fixture as a separate category besides pure movable and pure immovable goods is more accepted.[338]

Nevertheless, the dividing line between a movable good, an immovable good and a fixture has not been made more explicit in Article 9 UCC. Consequently, states still have to rely on their own case law to determine when a good will be a fixture. The only good Article 9 UCC has explicitly excluded from the fixture's category are ordinary building materials incorporated into an improvement on land. The reasoning went that it would be too damaging to the immovable good to remove them. Furthermore, most state laws consider such materials as immovable goods, once they have been incorporated under their state real estate law.[339] This led some authors to argue that the dividing line between a fixture and an immovable good was whether or not the movable good had been incorporated into the immovable good.[340] However, a definition based on whether or not the movable good had been incorporated or not would merely shift the debate to what would be considered incorporation. As a result, there is still no definition of a fixture.

75. *Specific requirements for tracing into fixtures* – The determination of whether a good has become a fixture is important, because specific filing requirements have to be followed for the security interest to continue in the fixture and to remain effective against all competing claims in the fixture.[341] The secured creditor with a security interest in a fixture will likely come into conflict with creditors or third parties who have or are going to obtain an interest in the immovable good to which the fixture has been attached. To maintain an effective security interest against these creditors or purchasers, the secured creditor has to make a fixture filing in the office where a record of the mortgage in the real property would be filed.[342] The idea is that creditors or purchasers of the immovable good, who obtain an interest after the fixture has been attached, should have an opportunity to find out about the prior interest in the fixture since they are likely to encumber or buy the immovable good under the impression that the fixture is included in their collateral.[343] However, in the event the encumbered good is not considered a fixture, the secured creditor's claim can come into conflict with other secured creditors or lien creditors, who have an overlapping claim in the same movable goods. To protect against

338 §9-102(41) UCC (2010).
339 §9-334 (a) UCC (2010).
340 P. F. COOGAN, 'Security interests in fixtures under the Uniform Commercial Code', (1962) 75 Harv. L. Rev., (1319) 1348.
341 §9-501 (a) (1) (B) UCC (2010).
342 §9-501 (a) (1) UCC (2010).
343 W. H. LAWRENCE, W. H. HENNING and R. W. FREYERMUTH, *Understanding secured transactions*, (2 edn., New York City: Matthew Bender, 1999), 352; J. J. WHITE and others, *Principles of secured transactions*, (St. Paul: West Academic Publishing, 2018), 188.

these creditors the secured creditor should also file a financing statement in the regular security interest registry.[344] Given the difficulty of determining whether a good becomes a fixture or not under the applicable real estate law, the recommendation is that secured creditors should always make both a fixture filing and security interest filing to make sure that they their security interest remains effective against all types of conflicting claims.[345]

76. *Conclusion* – Security interests continue in fixtures, but fixtures are not further defined in Article 9 UCC, nor uniformly interpreted in the various states. As a result, secured creditors cannot be sure when their encumbered good will be considered a fixture and whether additional measures need to be taken to obtain protection against creditors or purchasers with a conflicting claim in the immovable good. Therefore, secured creditors are advised to take all possible steps to obtain effectiveness in order to guarantee that their security interest is maintained in the event of attachment to an immovable good.

E. Conclusions on tracing for PMSI creditors

77. *Summary on impact of recharacterization on tracing* – The default rule in Article 9 UCC is that security interests, including PMSIs, continue in the altered goods, barring certain requirements that need to be fulfilled in some situations, such as the extra filing requirement to trace into fixtures. In other words, the functional approach with recharacterization of retention of title in conditional sales and lease agreements to PMSIs has not altered, nor limited their protection in the altered, encumbered goods. If anything, the rules in Article 9 UCC concerning tracing for security interests, including PMSIs, allow more extensive tracing than was the case for retention of title prior to Article 9 UCC. This leads to the conclusion that the recharacterization of retention of title to a PMSI does not automatically mean a reduction in protection.

3.3.3. Super-priority

78. *Introduction of super-priority* – An innovative feature of Article 9 UCC was the introduction of super-priority status for PMSIs. Super-priority means that a PMSI creditor always surpasses a conflicting creditor, even if he has a more senior claim to the encumbered good.[346] In the following section, I discuss the

344 J. J. WHITE and others, *Principles of secured transactions*, (St. Paul: West Academic Publishing, 2018), 188.

345 J. J. WHITE and others, *Principles of secured transactions*, (St. Paul: West Academic Publishing, 2018), 188.

346 J. J. WHITE and others, *Principles of secured transactions*, (St. Paul: West Academic Publishing, 2018), 177.

PMSI creditor's super-priority status in the originally encumbered good (a.) and in the encumbered good after alterations (b.).

A. In the originally encumbered good

79. *Recharacterization and conflicts with competing creditors* – The limitation in effect of a retention of title to a security interest means that the retention of title creditor no longer holds title to the encumbered good, but only has a security interest.[347] Consequently, the PMSI creditor no longer automatically holds the strongest proprietary claim to the encumbered good which would give him the upper hand in potential conflicts with other creditors.[348]

80. *The first in time principle and its limitations* – The general approach for resolving conflicts between security interests in Article 9 UCC is the first in time rule: the first secured creditor to perfect his security interest has priority.[349] The application of the first in time rule to retention of title creditors would mean a decrease in the protection of retention of title creditors. The retention of title creditor could come after other security interests that were vested at an earlier time and apply to after-acquired property of the debtor. For example, the debtor obtains a line of credit and grants a security interest in all his current and after-acquired inventory, which is correctly perfected. If later the same debtor purchases new inventory under retention of title, the new inventory is automatically encumbered with the previously vested security interest which would outrank the PMSI based on the first in time rule.

The drafters of Article 9 UCC argued that the application of the first in time rule to all security interests would lead to unsatisfactory outcomes. First, the first in time rule can create a monopoly in the hands of the first creditor. Often a debtor has a continuing line of credit with a financer. This creditor usually has a first ranking security interest in the debtor's present and after-acquired property. Consequently, when the debtor wants to acquire new goods on credit, the seller or manufacturer of the goods is not inclined to grant credit in return for a security interest in the new goods, since he will always be outranked by the financer with a first ranking security interest in the current and after-acquired goods. This situation would drive the debtor back into the hands of the first financer, thereby giving him a monopoly on the credit extended to the debtor.[350]

---

347 See *supra* no. 39.

348 G. GILMORE, 'The purchase money priority', (1963) 57 Harv. L. Rev., (1333) 1337; P. WANGERIN, 'Floating liens, proceeds, and PMSIs: perfection and priority in three closely connected cases', (2017) 47 UCC L. J., (287) 319 *et seq.*

349 W. H. LAWRENCE, W. H. HENNING and R. W. FREYERMUTH, *Understanding secured transactions*, (2 edn., New York City: Matthew Bender, 1999), 272.

350 P. WANGERIN, 'Floating liens, proceeds, and PMSIs: perfection and priority in three closely connected cases', (2017) 47 UCC L. J., (287) 290.

Second, the credit provided by the PMSI creditor makes the acquisition of the goods possible and contributes to the debtor's estate. Therefore, it would be unjust to subordinate the PMSI creditor to the first-ranked secured creditor, who did not rely on these goods when vesting their security interests and did not directly make their acquisition possible.[351] In other words, the first in time priority rule can create a windfall for the first-ranked creditor at the acquisition-financer's expense.

81. *Introduction of super-priority* – Super-priority means that the holder of a super-prioritized security interest can jump to the head of the line even though his security interest was created and perfected later in time. Notably, the super-priority for retention of title creditors and other acquisition financiers is based on a policy choice to favor acquisition financing over other forms of financing. The super-priority status does not stem from retaining title to the encumbered good. The advantage of basing super-priority on policy over title is that it gives retention of title creditors a similar protection as retaining title when they come into conflict with third parties, but without the need to actually retain title.[352] As a result, other PMSI creditors that do not hold title, such as acquisition-credit financiers, can also enjoy super-priority status based on the type of credit they secure instead of the proprietary interest they hold in the encumbered good. In other words, super-priority ensures a functionally equivalent outcome for all security interests that secure acquisition credit.[353] This was lacking prior to Article 9 UCC, where acquisition financiers had to take additional steps, such as substituting themselves in the shoes of the supplier or manufacturer, to obtain the same strong protection as conditional seller or lessors with retention of title.

82. *Specific requirements for super-priority* – The protection of super-priority does not always come automatically. For some goods super-priority requires the completion of additional formalities.[354] For super-priority in inventory three conditions have to be met: (1) the PMSI is perfected at the time the debtor takes physical possession of the inventory[355] and (2) the PMSI creditor notifies in writing the holder of conflicting security interests in the same collateral if the competing secured creditor has filed a financing statement covering the same types of inventory (i) before the date of the filing made by the PMSI creditor, or (ii) before the beginning of the 21 day period where the PMSI is temporarily

---

351 W. H. LAWRENCE, W. H. HENNING and R. W. FREYERMUTH, *Understanding secured transactions*, (2 edn., New York City: Matthew Bender, 1999), 287.

352 M. BRIDGE, 'The scope and limits of security interests', (2008) 5 ECFR, (180) 192.

353 M. BRIDGE, 'The scope and limits of security interests', (2008) 5 ECFR, (180) 197.

354 W. H. LAWRENCE, W. H. HENNING and R. W. FREYERMUTH, *Understanding secured transactions*, (2 edn., New York City: Matthew Bender, 1999), 288.

355 G. GILMORE, *Security interests in personal property*, vol. 1, (Boston: Little Brown and Co., 1965), 788; W. H. LAWRENCE, W. H. HENNING and R. W. FREYERMUTH, *Understanding secured transactions*, (2 edn., New York City: Matthew Bender, 1999), 291.

perfected without filing or possession. Finally, (3) the notification states that the PMSI creditors has or expects to acquire a PMSI in inventory of the debtor, describing such inventory by item or type.[356] The notification will be valid for 5 years following the notification.[357] Consequently, the notification provides protection not only for this transaction, but for all subsequent transactions concerning inventory in the next five years.[358] The notification of creditors with a potentially conflicting security interest in the inventory stems from the idea that revolving credit is often secured by present and after-acquired inventory. However, this could lead the inventory financer to grant additional finances based on inventory that is actually covered by a PMSI. To prevent this, the financer with a conflicting claim in the inventory has to be notified of the PMSI in the newly acquired inventory.[359]

The rules are slightly different for super-priority in goods other than inventory. For these goods, in most cases equipment, a PMSI takes priority over all conflicting security interests in the same collateral, if the PMSI is perfected at the moment the debtor receives possession[360] or 20 days thereafter.[361] Furthermore, the PMSI creditor not only takes priority over more senior security interests that already attached before the PMSI attached, but also takes priority over the rights of a buyer, lessee or lien creditor which arise between the time the PMSI attaches and the time of filing.[362] The 20 days grace period for PMSIs stems from the fact that in these transactions it is often more difficult to file in advance and ensure your perfection and priority status. Therefore, PMSI creditors are given a grace period to perfect their PMSI, to ensure that the PMSI creditor does not have to delay the delivery of the encumbered good to the debtor because they want to make sure that their PMSI is perfected[363] However, the grace period can also be seen as a way to keep the potential super-priority status of PMSIs in check. In Article 9 UCC, PMSIs are given super-priority, thereby making it irrelevant when they are perfected as long as they are perfected prior to the enforcement of another creditor or bankruptcy proceedings. This would also mean that a PMSI creditor could perfect at any time and surpass any older and more senior security interest in the same good. Due to the 20 days grace

---

356 §9–324 (b) UCC (2010).

357 §9–324 (b) (3) UCC (2010).

358 G. GILMORE, *Security interests in personal property*, vol. 1, (Boston: Little Brown and Co., 1965), 789.

359 W. H. LAWRENCE, W. H. HENNING and R. W. FREYERMUTH, *Understanding secured transactions*, (2 edn., New York City: Matthew Bender, 1999), 293; J. J. WHITE and others, *Principles of secured transactions*, (St. Paul: West Academic Publishing, 2018), 183.

360 §9–312(4) UCC (2010).

361 §9–312(4) UCC (2010)

362 §9–317(e) UCC (2010).

363 G. GILMORE, *Security interests in personal property*, vol. 1, (Boston: Little Brown and Co., 1965), 498; W. H. LAWRENCE, W. H. HENNING and R. W. FREYERMUTH, *Understanding secured transactions*, (2 edn., New York City: Matthew Bender, 1999), 288–289.

period, PMSI creditors are obligated to perfect their PMSI at least 20 days after delivering the good and thus put third parties and other creditors on notice of the potential super-priority of their claim. Notably, for these goods the PMSI creditor does not have to send an additional notification to the secured creditors with a conflicting claim in the encumbered goods. The idea is that for these goods it is less likely that they will already be encumbered with more senior claims or that the distribution of additional credit by a more senior creditor depends on the acquisition of that good in the debtor's estate.[364]

Lastly, there are exceptions to the rule that super-priority requires the fulfilment of additional formalities. For example, the automatic perfection of PMSIs in consumer goods[365] means that PMSI creditors with a PMSI in consumer goods do not have to fulfill additional formalities.[366]

83. *Competing PMSIs* – The fact that the term PMSI encompasses all acquisition financiers meant that the drafters had to provide a solution for the situation in which two PMSI creditors had competing conflicts in the same collateral. Prior to Article 9 UCC, there was no concept of super-priority that could be granted to different secured creditors. Only the retention of title creditor had a stronger position than other secured creditors due to his title, but his retained title also meant to no one else could come into conflict with him.[367] Now under Article 9 UCC, different acquisition-credit financiers can theoretically obtain super-priority status. For example, it is possible that a debtor gets part of his credit for the acquired good from a financer and part from the manufacturer or supplier, who sells the good on credit. In such a conflict, the drafters decided to favor the PMSI creditor who sells the good on credit over the PMSI creditor who provides the acquisition financing.[368] This solution is based on the approach for real property mortgages. The idea is that the vendor will not let go of the good on credit, unless he is assured that he has the highest ranking claim to the sold good.[369] When the acquisition of a good is financed by two acquisition financers and both have taken a PMSI in the acquired good, priority will be determined by the first to file rule.[370]

84. *PMSIs securing mixed obligations* – Finally, the drafters had to decide whether the PMSI super-priority status still applies if the PMSI guaranteed more

---

364 J. J. WHITE and others, *Principles of secured transactions*, (St. Paul: West Academic Publishing, 2018), 183.

365 See *supra* no. 59 *et seq*.

366 P. WANGERIN, 'Floating liens, proceeds, and PMSIs: perfection and priority in three closely connected cases', (2017) 47 UCC L. J., (287) 320.

367 See *supra* no. 78.

368 §9-324(g)(1) UCC (2010).

369 Official commentary to §9-324 UCC.

370 §9-324(g)(2) UCC (2010). See also, official comments to §9-324 UCC.

than the acquisition financing. Some courts transformed a PMSI to a regular security interest, when the acquired good no longer purely guaranteed a purchase money obligation.[371] Other courts rejected the transformation rule and allowed creditors to retain their PMSI status, if the PMSI creditor can prove the extent to which the outstanding loan balance at any given time retains its purchase money security character.[372] This approach allows for a dual status where an obligation can be guaranteed by partly a PMSI and partly a security interest. This approach is more explicitly embraced in the revised version of Article 9 UCC where the possible dual status of a security interest is explicitly confirmed.[373]

B. IN ALTERED COLLATERAL

85. *Introduction* – Given the power the debtor has over the encumbered goods; the next question is whether the PMSI creditor can maintain his super-priority in altered collateral. In this section, I discuss whether the secured creditor maintains super-priority in proceeds (i), accessions (ii), mixed goods (iii) and fixtures (iv).

i. Super-priority in proceeds

86. *First attempts at super-priority and proceeds* – In the initial version of Article 9 UCC there was no explicit solution for a conflict between a PMSI in inventory that was turned into proceeds and another security interest in all the debtor's accounts receivable.[374] Article 9 UCC only stated that the PMSI creditor jumped over a more senior secured creditor with a regular security interest in the same collateral.[375] Since proceeds could not be considered as "same collateral", the PMSI creditor would not have super-priority over conflicting claims in the proceeds.[376]

This situation was amended in 1972 when the super-priority for PMSIs was explicitly extended to proceeds of the original collateral.[377] This extension has

371 United States Court of Appeals 10 February 1975, In re Manuel, 507 F.2d, (990) 993–994; United States Court of Appeals 21 May 1985, Southtrust Bank of Alabama v. Borg-Warner Acceptance Corp., 40 UCC Rep. Serv., (1601) 1605; W. H. LAWRENCE, W. H. HENNING and R. W. FREYERMUTH, *Understanding secured transactions*, (2 edn., New York City: Matthew Bender, 1999), 47; J. J. WHITE and others, *Principles of secured transactions*, (St. Paul: West Academic Publishing, 2018), 68.

372 W. H. LAWRENCE, W. H. HENNING and R. W. FREYERMUTH, *Understanding secured transactions*, (2 edn., New York City: Matthew Bender, 1999), 47; J. J. WHITE and others, *Principles of secured transactions*, (St. Paul: West Academic Publishing, 2018), 65 *et seq*.

373 §9–103(f) UCC (2010).

374 G. GILMORE, *Security interests in personal property*, vol. 1, (Boston: Little Brown and Co., 1965), 792.

375 §9–312 UCC (1952).

376 G. GILMORE, *Security interests in personal property*, vol. 1, (Boston: Little Brown and Co., 1965), 792–793;

377 §9–312 (4) UCC (1972).

been maintained in the revised versions of Article 9 UCC.[378] Notably, the PMSI creditor can still lose his super-priority, if the proceeds can no longer be traced or identified due to the mixing of the proceeds with other similar goods, such as losing the identification of cash proceeds after they have been deposited in a bank account, despite the application of principles, such as the lowest intermediate balance rule.[379]

87. *Types of proceeds* – Furthermore, the PMSI's super-priority does not extend to all types of proceeds. With regards to inventory, the super-priority is limited to identifiable cash proceeds.[380] Cash proceeds are money, checks, deposit accounts and the like.[381] If the proceeds take the form of non-cash proceeds, such as accounts receivable or promissory notes, then the super-priority does not automatically extend.[382] This limitation to cash proceeds was made explicit in the revision of Article 9 UCC.[383] The limitation of super-priority of PMSIs in inventory to cash proceeds is a significant limitation on the protection of PMSI creditors. The reasoning for this is a balancing act between the interests of PMSI creditors and account financiers. Financing based on security interests in accounts receivable is a serious market. Therefore, the subordination of security interests in accounts receivable to secured creditors with a potential PMSI in proceeds would discourage too many financiers from providing credit. Consequently, to strike a balance between PMSI creditors on the one hand and account financiers on the other the decision was made to only grant PMSI creditors super priority in cash proceeds and not further.[384] Furthermore, the assumption is that the debtor will use the incoming funds to pay the PMSI creditor and thus that the PMSI creditor benefits from the generation of accounts receivable without the need for having a super-priority PMSI in these goods.[385] Finally, the PMSI creditor must keep in mind that prior to Article 9 UCC the extension of super-priority into proceeds was not guaranteed and thus that any

378 §9-324 (a) UCC (2010). See also, P. WANGERIN, 'Floating liens, proceeds, and PMSIs: perfection and priority in three closely connected cases', (2017) 47 UCC L. J., (287) 326; J. J. WHITE and others, *Principles of secured transactions*, (St. Paul: West Academic Publishing, 2018), 182.

379 J. J. WHITE and others, *Principles of secured transactions*, (St. Paul: West Academic Publishing, 2018), 184.

380 §9-312 (3) UCC (1972).

381 §9-102 (9) UCC (2010).

382 United States Court of Appeal 31 October 1989, MBank Alamo Nat. Ass'n v. Raytheon Co., 10 UCC Rep. Serv. 2d., (35) 39–40; W. H. LAWRENCE, W. H. HENNING and R. W. FREYERMUTH, *Understanding secured transactions*, (2 edn., New York City: Matthew Bender, 1999), 297.

383 §9-324(b) and (c) UCC (2010).

384 W. H. LAWRENCE, W. H. HENNING and R. W. FREYERMUTH, *Understanding secured transactions*, (2 edn., New York City: Matthew Bender, 1999), 298; J. J. WHITE and others, *Principles of secured transactions*, (St. Paul: West Academic Publishing, 2018), 184.

385 W. H. LAWRENCE, W. H. HENNING and R. W. FREYERMUTH, *Understanding secured transactions*, (2 edn., New York City: Matthew Bender, 1999), 298.

protection offered under Article 9 UCC is superior to the grey area concerning proceeds under common law.[386]

ii. Super-priority in accessions

88. *Definition* – An accession is the attachment of a movable good to another movable good, such as attaching or installing a motor in a car.[387] In this scenario, the conflict will likely be between a secured creditor with a PMSI in the affixed good and a third party with a claim to the whole good[388]

89. *Super-priority and accessions throughout the different versions of Article 9 UCC* – Prior to the revision of Article 9 UCC, the determination of priority hinged on whether the PMSI was created (i.e. attached) before or after the encumbered good was affixed to the other movable good. Once the movable good was affixed to another movable good, an unattached security interest in the affixed good was not valid against a third party with an interest in the whole good. However, if a PMSI attached to the movable good before the encumbered good was affixed to the movable good, then the PMSI creditor took priority over creditors or third parties with an interest in the whole good.[389]

After the revision of Article 9 UCC, conflicts between secured creditors with an interest in the whole and PMSI creditors with a PMSI in the affixed good are governed by the general priority rules of Article 9 UCC.[390] In most cases, priority is determined by the rules of PMSI super-priority, since the person with a claim on the accession will typically be a PMSI seller or a lender who financed the acquisition of the accession.[391] Therefore, a PMSI in the accession takes super-priority over pre-existing security interests, if the PMSI creditor fulfilled the specific requirements for super-priority. If the PMSI creditor did not fulfill the specific requirements for super-priority, then the more senior security interest in the whole good takes priority due to the first in time rule. Finally, if the PMSI creditor perfected his PMSI in the attached movable good in a timely manner and the whole good is then sold, the PMSI creditor will have priority over the

386 See *supra* no. 24 *et seq.*

387 W. H. LAWRENCE, W. H. HENNING and R. W. FREYERMUTH, *Understanding secured transactions*, (2 edn., New York City: Matthew Bender, 1999), 364.

388 W. H. LAWRENCE, W. H. HENNING and R. W. FREYERMUTH, *Understanding secured transactions*, (2 edn., New York City: Matthew Bender, 1999), 364.

389 §9-334 UCC (2010); W. H. LAWRENCE, W. H. HENNING and R. W. FREYERMUTH, *Understanding secured transactions*, (2 edn., New York City: Matthew Bender, 1999), 365.

390 §9-335(c) UCC (2010); W. H. LAWRENCE, W. H. HENNING and R. W. FREYERMUTH, *Understanding secured transactions*, (2 edn., New York City: Matthew Bender, 1999), 365.

391 J. J. WHITE and others, *Principles of secured transactions*, (St. Paul: West Academic Publishing, 2018), 199;

purchaser for the attached good, unless the purchaser bought the whole good including the accession in good faith.[392]

iii. Super-priority in mixed goods

90. *Super-priority and different claimants to mixed goods* – As previously mentioned, Article 9 UCC allows for PMSIs and regular security interests to extend into mixed goods.[393] Consequently, rules had to be developed for the priority of multiple claims in the mixed goods. First, if the encumbered good is only mixed with goods belonging to the debtor, then the PMSI attaches to the mass of mixed goods and the PMSI creditor is allowed to revendicate the equivalent of originally encumbered goods.[394]

Second, Article 9 UCC provides rules for when multiple secured creditors have claims to the mixed goods. Initially, creditors had a right to the new good in proportion to the costs made by the various parties.[395] Basing the ratio on the costs for the various parties made the calculation of the ratio unnecessarily difficult, since the cost seemed to be based not only on the pure cost of the goods but also on the labor and additional investment the debtor put into the collateral.[396] This meant that a rather complicated fact-based analysis had to be made to determine each of the secured creditors' claims.

Since the revision of Article 9 UCC, conflicting security interests in mixed or processed goods are entitled to a proportion based on the value of the collateral at the time of it becoming co-mingled or processed goods.[397]

Example

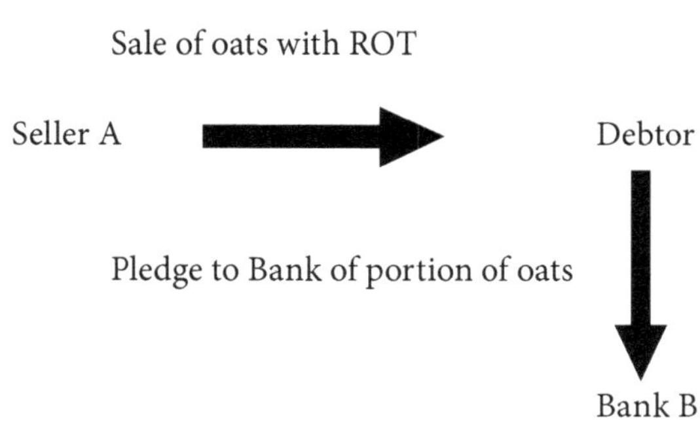

[392] W. H. LAWRENCE, W. H. HENNING and R. W. FREYERMUTH, *Understanding secured transactions*, (2 edn., New York City: Matthew Bender, 1999), 366.

[393] See *supra* no. 71 *et seq.*

[394] §9-336 (b) UCC (2010).

[395] §9-315 (2) UCC (1972).

[396] G. GILMORE, *Security interests in personal property*, vol. 1, (Boston: Little Brown and Co., 1965), 852–853.

[397] §9-336(f)(2) UCC (2010); W. H. LAWRENCE, W. H. HENNING and R. W. FREYERMUTH, *Understanding secured transactions*, (2 edn., New York City: Matthew Bender, 1999), 368.

In this scenario, seller A has a perfected PMSI in 800 000 euro worth of mixed oats and bank B had a perfected security interest in 400 000 euro of mixed oats. If the debtor default, then Seller A is entitled to a share twice as large as bank B's share. This outcome is regardless of the claim they have on the debtor or the costs made or the order in which they perfected their security interest.[398]

iv. Super-priority in fixtures

91. *Priority and fixtures pre-Article 9 UCC* – For the super-priority in fixtures, the drafters built on the rule for conditional sales in fixtures.[399] In the UCSA the defining characteristic was whether the good could be severed completely or in part from the immovable good without material injury to the immovable good. If it could be severed without material injury, then the conditional sale in that good could continue. If it could not be severed without material injury, then the conditional sale in the affixed good could no longer be enforced.

92. *Super-priority and fixtures in Article 9 UCC* – In the first versions of Article 9 UCC, a PMSI that had been correctly perfected (i.e. via a fixture filing)[400] before the encumbered good was affixed to the immovable good, took priority over all earlier claims in the immovable good.[401] The reasoning went that the creditors with an earlier claim in the immovable good provided their credit without counting on the later affixed good and thus did not lose out by being subordinated by the PMSI creditor.[402] However, if the PMSI in the movable good was created after the encumbered good had been affixed to an immovable good, then the PMSI creditor would not be able to rely on his super-priority but the first to file rule would apply.[403] The reasoning went that in that scenario other creditors or third parties with an interest in the immovable good could be mistaken by the incorporation of the movable good and thus the effectiveness of the PMSI would depend on the correct perfection of the PMSI in the registries for security interests and mortgages.[404]

In the revised version of Article 9 UCC the super-priority of security interests over senior interests in the immovable good were limited to PMSIs. PMSIs still

---

398 J. J. WHITE and others, *Principles of secured transactions*, (St. Paul: West Academic Publishing, 2018), 201;

399 §7 UCSA. See *supra* no. 24 *et seq.* H. KRIPKE, 'Fixtures under the Uniform Commercial Code', (1964) 64 Colum. L. Rev., (44) 46; G. GILMORE, *Security interests in personal property*, vol. 1, (Boston: Little Brown and Co., 1965)801–802.

400 See *supra* no. 75.

401 §9–313 UCC (1952).

402 H. KRIPKE, 'Fixtures under the Uniform Commercial Code', (1964) 64 Colum. L. Rev., (44) 50.

403 §9–334(e)(1) UCC (2010).

404 H. KRIPKE, 'Fixtures under the Uniform Commercial Code', (1964) 64 Colum. L. Rev., (44) 50; W. H. LAWRENCE, W. H. HENNING and R. W. FREYERMUTH, *Understanding secured transactions*, (2 edn., New York City: Matthew Bender, 1999), 354.

have priority over existing interests in the immovable good, if (1) the security interest is a PMSI, (2) the PMSI is created before the good becomes a fixture and (3) the PMSI is perfected by a fixture filing before the goods become fixtures or within 20 days thereafter.[405] The super-priority over the older interest in the immovable good is based on the same reasoning that gives super-priority to PMSIs over senior interests in the same movable good.[406] Once the movable good is affixed to the immovable good, the PMSI creditor will only take priority over security and other interests that come into existence after the PMSI was created and only if the PMSI has been properly perfected.[407]

3.3.4. Enforcement

93. *Article 9 UCC's uniform approach to enforcement* – In Article 9 UCC a whole chapter is dedicated to the rights and limitations of secured creditors when enforcing their security interest.[408] A first innovation of Article 9 UCC is that the enforcement for all security interests is governed by the same set of rules. Prior to Article 9 UCC, secured creditors had to look at the specific legislation and case law that governed their specific secured transaction.[409] This inefficient approach has been addressed in a uniform approach for the enforcement of all security interests, including PMSIs.

94. *Debtor's default and its possible remedies* – Logically, the enforcement of security interests starts with the debtor's default. This was already the case prior to Article 9 UCC and is explicitly maintained in Article 9 UCC.[410] Default is not defined in Article 9 UCC, but must be determined in the security agreement and following general contract law principles.[411] In most cases, default is the debtor's failure to pay the secured creditor when his claim is due.[412]

---

405 §9-335(d) UCC (2010).

406 J. J. WHITE and others, *Principles of secured transactions*, (St. Paul: West Academic Publishing, 2018), 190.

407 §9-334(e) UCC (2010).

408 Part 5 of Article 9 UCC (1952); Part 6 of revised Article 9 UCC.

409 G. GILMORE, *Security interests in personal property*, vol. 2, (Boston: Little Brown and Co., 1965), 1184–1189.

410 §9-501 UCC (1952); G. GILMORE, *Security interests in personal property*, vol. 2, (Boston: Little Brown and Co., 1965), 1190.

411 J. S. BROWN, 'Notes – Leases: Security Interests: Uniform Commercial Code', (1963–64) 49 Cornell L. Q., (672) 678; L. LAKIN and H. J. BERGER, 'The secured party: enforcement of his security interest under Article 9 after the debtor's default', (1970) 8 Am. Bus. Law. J., (1) 2; W. H. LAWRENCE, W. H. HENNING and R. W. FREYERMUTH, *Understanding secured transactions*, (2 edn., New York City: Matthew Bender, 1999), 437; J. J. WHITE and others, *Principles of secured transactions*, (St. Paul: West Academic Publishing, 2018), 232.

412 United States Court of Appeals, Eleventh Circuit 6 August 1996, Cofield v. Randolph County Com'n, 90 F.3d, (468) 471; Court of Appeals of Tennessee 10 April 1996, Nationsbank v. Clegg, 29 UCC Rep.Serv.2d, (1366) 1366.

Once the debtor has defaulted, the secured creditor has access to several remedies.[413] In Article 9 UCC the debtor can cumulate the different remedies. The secured creditor can sue *in personam* for the outstanding claim or can pursue *in rem* actions based on his security interest.[414] The revised version of Article 9 UCC even explicates that the different actions can be pursued cumulatively and simultaneously.[415] This was a big departure from the common law approach where retention of title creditors had to choose between either suing for the outstanding debt[416] or revendicate the encumbered good.[417] Pre-Article 9 UCC, the reasoning went that the revindication of the conditionally sold good rescinded the contract between the conditional seller and the conditional buyer, thereby removing any basis for suing for the outstanding claim. Conversely, if the conditional seller opted to sue for the outstanding claim, then the sale was considered absolute. This meant that the title to the encumbered good was considered absolutely transferred to the buyer and removed the seller's possibility to reclaim the sold good.[418] This changed in the UCSA, in which the drafters clarified that an action for the payment of single installment did not rule out a later action of the seller for the recovery of the good.[419] Moreover, the commentary to the UCSA explicated that an action for deficiency did not mean that the buyer should be considered the owner of the conditionally sold good and excluded the seller from retaking the good as the owner.[420] Only when the conditional seller commenced an action for the entire outstanding purchase price, could he be prevented from retaking the goods at a later time.[421] Under Article 9 UCC multiple remedies can be pursued to achieve payment of the outstanding claim. Furthermore, in the UCC holding title to a

---

413 §9-601(c) UCC (2010). See also, J. J. WHITE and others, *Principles of secured transactions*, (St. Paul: West Academic Publishing, 2018), 240–241.

414 §9-601 UCC (2010).

415 §9-601(c) UCC (2010).

416 G. GILMORE, *Security interests in personal property*, vol. 2, (Boston: Little Brown and Co., 1965), 1202 *et seq.*

417 Supreme Court of Arkansas 15 January 1887, McRae v. Merrifield, 48 Ark. 160, 2 S. W., (780) 782; Supreme Judicial Court of Massachusetts 19 June 1883, Bailey v. Hervey, 135 Mass., (172) 174; Supreme Court of California, 1 July 1879, Hegler v. Eddy, 53 Cal., (597) 598; Supreme Court of California 1 July 1880, March v. McKoy, 56 Cal., (85) 88; County Court of Rockland County 1 August 1897, Iserman v. Conklin, 21 Misc., (194) 195; C. R. MILLER, *A treatise on the law of conditional sales of personal property*, (Cincinnati: R. Clarke, 1888), 63; A. H. FENN, 'Conditional sales', (1890) 24 Am. L. Rev., (64) 73; A. B. PEARSON and H. F. BOYD, *Benjamin's treatise on the law of sale of personal property*, (Boston: Charles Edson & Co. Publishers, 1888), 479; X., 'Conditional sales' 9 Pac. Coast L. J., (545) 545.

418 Supreme Court of Washington 22 July 1913, Stewart & Holmes Drug Co. v. Ross, 74 Wash., (401) 405; Supreme Court of Minnesota 1 May 1914, A. F. Chase & Co. v. Kelly, 125 Minn., (317) 319.

419 §24 UCSA.

420 §24, *in fine* UCSA.

421 H. NOYES GREENE, 'Uniform Conditional Sales Act and commentary' in H. NOYES GREEN (ed.), *Uniform laws, annotated*, vol. 2, (Northport: Edward Thompson Co., 1922), 37.

good is no longer relevant, so the transfer of title to the debtor is not a relevant factor in the enforcement proceeding of the secured creditor.

95. *Repossession of the encumbered good* – The first step in the enforcement process is the repossession of the collateral.[422] Taking possession does not mean that the good itself will be used as payment for the outstanding claim. The repossession of the encumbered good is merely the first step in the enforcement process, unless the good is already in the secured creditor's possession.[423] The secured creditor has the right to take possession of the good without having to go through the courts.[424] However, as was already the case under common law[425] and under the UCSA[426], the secured creditor cannot breach the peace when repossessing the encumbered collateral.[427] Article 9 UCC does not define breach of the peace, so the common law principles apply.[428] Any excessive force, violent or not, is considered a breach of peace and thus an unlawful repossession.[429] In the event the encumbered good is very large or imbedded and repossession would be very difficult or costly, the secured creditor may also make the encumbered good unusable to protect his security interest.[430] However, the secured creditor must be commercially reasonable in his efforts to maintain his security interest and thus cannot make the encumbered good unusable to such an extent that the good loses commercial value.[431] In the case that the secured creditor cannot pursue his self-help repossession of the encumbered good and he will have to rely on the judicial process.[432]

---

422 §9–609(a) UCC (2010).

423 G. GILMORE, *Security interests in personal property*, vol. 2, (Boston: Little Brown and Co., 1965), 1214; L. LAKIN and H. J. BERGER, 'The secured party: enforcement of his security interest under Article 9 after the debtor's default', (1970) 8 Am. Bus. Law. J., (1) 4.

424 §9–609(b)(2) UCC (2010).

425 Supreme Judicial Court of Massachusetts 1 September 1831, Sampson v. Henry, 11 Pick, (379) 394; Supreme Judicial Court of Massachusetts 1 March 1860, McNeal v. Emerson, 15 Gray, (384) 385.

426 §16 UCSA.

427 §9–609(b)(2) UCC (2010).

428 L. LAKIN and H. J. BERGER, 'The secured party: enforcement of his security interest under Article 9 after the debtor's default', (1970) 8 Am. Bus. Law. J., (1) 4; J. R. PEDEN, 'The treatment of equipment leases as security agreements under the Uniform Commercial Code', (1971) 13 Wm. & Mary L. Rev., (110) 129; W. H. LAWRENCE, W. H. HENNING and R. W. FREYERMUTH, *Understanding secured transactions*, (2 edn., New York City: Matthew Bender, 1999), 450; J. J. WHITE and others, *Principles of secured transactions*, (St. Paul: West Academic Publishing, 2018), 245.

429 W. H. LAWRENCE, W. H. HENNING and R. W. FREYERMUTH, *Understanding secured transactions*, (2 edn., New York City: Matthew Bender, 1999), 451.

430 §9–609 (a) (2) UCC (2010).

431 See comment to R§9–609 UCC.

432 W. H. LAWRENCE, W. H. HENNING and R. W. FREYERMUTH, *Understanding secured transactions*, (2 edn., New York City: Matthew Bender, 1999), 455.

Furthermore, the secured party does not have to give notice of his intention to repossess the encumbered good.[433] Under the UCSA the conditional seller could only revendicate without notification, if he gave the debtor time to use his right of redemption[434] while the good was already repossessed by the conditional seller. If the conditional seller wanted to repossess without having to provide time in which the debtor could use his right of redemption, he had to notify the debtor of his intention to repossess. It seems that the drafters of Article 9 UCC realized that the advantage of not having to provide time in which the debtor could retake the goods from the secured creditor via his right of redemption did not outweigh the disadvantage of having to first notify your debtor of your intention to revendicate.[435] Therefore, in Article 9 UCC the secured creditor can always repossess without notification, without it having any effect on the debtor's right of redemption.[436] Nevertheless, the debtor has a right of redemption which allows him to recover the encumbered good in return for payment of the outstanding claim and costs.[437] As mentioned, the period during which the debtor can invoke his right of redemption does not hinge on whether or not the secured creditor notified the debtor.

96. *Different methods to realize the encumbered good* – Once the PMSI creditor is in possession of the encumbered good, the default enforcement rule is that he disposes of the good in a public or private sale[438] for either cash or on credit.[439] Article 9 UCC does not provide a timeline in which the encumbered good has to be sold.[440] The idea behind the flexible rules concerning foreclosure in Article 9 UCC is to generate the highest price possible.[441] The drafters had noticed that in previous laws, such as the UCSA, the guidelines for foreclosure were too strict and led to lower proceeds. For example, if the conditional buyer had already paid 50% of the purchase price or more, the seller was obligated to resale the good via a public sale and return the surplus to the buyer.[442] However, public sales generally do not raise a lot of money. Furthermore, potential buyers had

---

433 G. GILMORE, *Security interests in personal property*, vol. 2, (Boston: Little Brown and Co., 1965), 1213;

434 The right of redemption is a grace period during which he could pay of the outstanding claim and halt the enforcement proceedings (§17 UCSA).

435 G. GILMORE, *Security interests in personal property*, vol. 2, (Boston: Little Brown and Co., 1965), 1213–1214.

436 §9–609(a) UCC (2010).

437 §9–623(b) UCC (2010).

438 §9–610 UCC (2010).

439 W. H. LAWRENCE, W. H. HENNING and R. W. FREYERMUTH, *Understanding secured transactions*, (2 edn., New York City: Matthew Bender, 1999), 456.

440 W. H. LAWRENCE, W. H. HENNING and R. W. FREYERMUTH, *Understanding secured transactions*, (2 edn., New York City: Matthew Bender, 1999), 458–460.

441 J. J. WHITE and others, *Principles of secured transactions*, (St. Paul: West Academic Publishing, 2018), 238–239.

442 §19 UCSA.

to be able to pay the price in cash immediately, thereby further decreasing the potential group of buyers.[443] These rules were made more flexible under Article 9 UCC. Nevertheless, during the enforcement the secured creditor is obligated to dispose of the collateral in a commercially reasonable manner.[444] The concept of commercially reasonable is not defined in Article 9 UCC. The drafters only describe certain situations in which it is presumed that the sale takes place in a commercially reasonable manner.[445] Furthermore, the enforcing creditor has to give the debtor and other secured creditors proper notice of his intention to sell the encumbered good.[446] The only exception to this notification requirement is when the encumbered goods are perishable and the foreclosure proceedings have to happen quickly to avoid the goods losing their value.[447] Finally, like under the UCSA[448], the enforcing creditor cannot simply assign the proceeds of the foreclosure sale as he sees fit. Article 9 UCC provides a specific order in which the proceeds of the foreclosure sale have to be distributed.[449] If the sale resulted in any surplus, then the surplus has to be returned to the debtor.[450]

A second option in the event of default is that the secured creditor accepts the good itself as payment.[451] The acceptance of the good as payment for the outstanding claim and additional costs is also a remnant of the common law and the UCSA.[452] Prior to the UCSA and Article 9 UCC it was common for the retention of title creditor to revendicate the encumbered collateral based on his retained title.[453] In Article 9 UCC, this option to foreclose on the encumbered good is expanded so that all secured creditors can accept the repossessed good as payment when the debtor is not a consumer or when the debtor-consumer has paid off less than 60% of his debt.[454] Once the debtor has paid off more than 60% of the outstanding debt, then the assumption is that the secured creditor will enrich himself by accepting the good as payment.[455] If the secured creditor can accept the encumbered good as payment for his outstanding claim, he still has to notify the debtor and all other secured creditors with a filed financing

443 W. H. LAWRENCE, W. H. HENNING and R. W. FREYERMUTH, *Understanding secured transactions*, (2 edn., New York City: Matthew Bender, 1999), 456.
444 §9-610(b) UCC (2010).
445 §9-627(b) UCC (2010).
446 §9-611 UCC (2010).
447 §9-611(d) UCC (2010).
448 §21 UCSA.
449 §9-615(a)(1) UCC (2010).
450 §9-615(d) UCC (2010).
451 §9-620(a)-(d) UCC (2010).
452 J. J. WHITE and others, *Principles of secured transactions*, (St. Paul: West Academic Publishing, 2018), 248.
453 See *supra* no. 70.
454 §9-620(e)-(f) UCC (2010).
455 G. GILMORE, *Security interests in personal property*, vol. 2, (Boston: Little Brown and Co., 1965), 1222; W. H. LAWRENCE, W. H. HENNING and R. W. FREYERMUTH, *Understanding secured transactions*, (2 edn., New York City: Matthew Bender, 1999), 487.

statement. If either the debtor or any of the other secured creditors object to the acceptance of the good as payment, then the secured creditor has to dispose of the encumbered good instead.[456] Notably, the lack of notification to the other secured creditors does not invalidate the acceptance of the encumbered good as payment. However, the unnotified secured creditor can sue the enforcing secured creditor for any damages that the lack of notification may have caused.[457]

In revised Article 9 UCC, the formalities for accepting the good as payment are further specified. In the revised version, the debtor has to give his consent to the acceptance of the good as payment.[458] The debtor's consent can be tacit when the encumbered good is taken in satisfaction of the full debt, but has to be explicit when the acceptance is only a partial satisfaction of the debt.[459] The reason behind the explicit consent for the acceptance of the encumbered good in partial satisfaction is to avoid that the secured creditor will enrich himself. For example, the secured creditor who is owed 10.000 euro could accept the encumbered good with a value of 10.000 euro as payment for 1.000 euro of the outstanding claim and then sue the debtor for the remaining 9.000 euro. To make the debtor aware of such potential schemes, the debtor has to very explicitly agree before a partial satisfaction can take place. In the event of an acceptance of the good in full satisfaction of the good, the chance is much smaller that the encumbered good will be worth more than what is owed to the secured creditor. Consequently, the secured creditor still has to send the proposal for accepting the good in satisfaction of the entire claim to the debtor, but if the debtor does not object against this proposal in 20 days, then the secured creditor can proceed.[460] In any case, the debtor has the authority to object to the acceptance of the encumbered good in satisfaction of the claim and will likely do so when there is a chance that the encumbered good is worth more than the outstanding claim. In other words, the secured creditor cannot unilaterally impose this method of enforcement. Furthermore, revised Article 9 UCC provides extra guidelines for the notification to the other secured parties.[461] The more detailed rules concerning notification are aimed at clarifying the notification formalities and thereby further increasing the awareness and vigilance from the debtor and the other secured creditors to make sure that the appropriating creditor does not obtain a windfall. The fact that the acceptance of the encumbered good in satisfaction of the outstanding debt can only happen with the (explicit or tacit)

---

456 §9-620(a)-(d) UCC (2010). See also, W. H. LAWRENCE, W. H. HENNING and R. W. FREYERMUTH, *Understanding secured transactions*, (2 edn., New York City: Matthew Bender, 1999), 486.

457 Comment to §9-620 UCC (2010).

458 §9-620(a)(1) and (c) UCC (2010).

459 §9-620 (c) UCC (2010).

460 J. J. WHITE and others, *Principles of secured transactions*, (St. Paul: West Academic Publishing, 2018), 251.

461 §9-620(d) UCC (2010).

consent of the debtor explains why there are no specific rules concerning surplus value. If the debtor or other creditors were of the opinion that the good is worth more than the outstanding claim of the appropriating creditor, they would never agree to the acceptance of the encumbered good in satisfaction of the outstanding claim. The consent operates as a failsafe against unjust enrichment. Moreover, if the debtor and the other secured creditors do not object in timely manner against the appropriation, then each interested party is still given standing in court to object against such an acceptance of payment on the basis of fraud and will be allowed to protest against this acceptance of payment.[462]

4. PMSIS DURING CORPORATE BANKRUPTCY PROCEEDINGS

97. *Introduction PMSIs in bankruptcy* – Once the debtor's situation really deteriorates, bankruptcy proceedings are generally just around the corner. In this dissertation, the scope is limited to corporate bankruptcy proceedings in which the debtor is a corporation and not a consumer.

The initiation of bankruptcy proceedings raises the question to what extent the PMSI creditor are protected during these collective insolvency proceedings and whether this protection is different from the protection the retention of title creditor enjoyed prior to their recharacterization in Article 9 UCC. Furthermore, bankruptcy law has undergone several changes as well. After the promulgation of Article 9 UCC, federal bankruptcy law changed from the 1938 version of the Bankruptcy Act[463] to Title 11 of the United States Code (hereafter, Bankruptcy Code).[464] Moreover, prior to Article 9 UCC federal bankruptcy law already underwent several changes that impacted the treatment of retention of title creditors during bankruptcy. To provide sufficient background on the different versions of bankruptcy law with which retention of title creditors comes into contact, I will first give a brief overview of the evolution of corporate bankruptcy proceedings in the United States (3.4.1.), followed by the protection of the PMSI creditor in the event of the debtor's bankruptcy (3.4.2.) and the PMSI creditor's bankruptcy (3.4.2.).

---

462 G. GILMORE, *Security interests in personal property*, vol. 2, (Boston: Little Brown and Co., 1965), 1224–1225.

463 An act to amend an Act entitled "An Act to establish a uniform system of bankruptcy throughout the United States", approved July 1, 1898, and Acts amendatory thereof and supplementary thereto; and to repeal section 76 thereof and all Acts and parts of Acts inconsistent therewith, (1938) 52 Stat., 840.

464 An act of 6 November 1978 to establish a uniform law on the subject of bankruptcies, 92 Stat. 2549 (hereafter, Title 11 U.S.C.).

4.1. *Brief overview of the US corporate bankruptcy proceedings*

98. *American bankruptcy law throughout the years* – Prior to formal bankruptcy proceedings, most states relied on state regulated assignment laws.[465] These were very limited in scope and did not have extra-territorial effect.[466] Furthermore, the rules regarding distribution and priority varied from state to state, thereby differentiating between creditors based on the state in which they pursued the payment of their claim. The limited application and different approaches of state bankruptcy or assignment laws paved the way for the introduction of uniform federal laws concerning bankruptcy.[467]

Corporate bankruptcy in the United States initially focused on liquidation proceedings in which the debtor was divested of all or parts of his assets and the proceeds of these assets were distributed among the bankrupt's creditors.[468] Later Bankruptcy Acts included some provisions concerning reorganization[469], but the chapter 7 liquidation and 11 reorganization proceedings that we know today were only introduced in 1978 with the introduction of title 11 in the U.S Code.[470] The first federal bankruptcy act was enacted on April 4th, 1800.[471] This act was mainly a consolidation of English statutes.[472] It was only applicable to traders[473] and only allowed for involuntary bankruptcy proceedings (i.e. proceedings initiated by creditors).[474] The reasoning was that voluntary bankruptcy would make it too easy for the debtor to file for bankruptcy, be discharged of his debts and then leave the creditor empty handed. Under this Act the debtor could only obtain a discharge when 2/3rd of the creditors voted in favor of discharging the debtor. The bankruptcy act of 1800 was repealed in 1803.[475]

---

465 W. E. BULLOCK, 'Assignments for the benefit of creditors' in D. S. GARLAND DS and L. P. MCGEHEE (eds.), *The American and English encyclopaedia of law*, vol. 3, (2 edn., Northport: Edward Thompson 1897), 5 *et seq*.

466 W. D. COLES, 'Bankruptcy legislation in the United States' (St Louis Law Society, 1898), 6.

467 W. D. COLES, 'Bankruptcy legislation in the United States' (St Louis Law Society, 1898), 6 *et seq*.

468 W. D. COLES, 'Bankruptcy legislation in the United States' (St Louis Law Society, 1898), 4.

469 An act of 25 June 1910 to amend an act entitled an act to establish a uniform system of bankruptcy throughout the United States," approved July-first, eighteen hundred and ninety-eight, as amended by an act approved February fifth, nineteen hundred and three, and as further amended by an act approved June fifteenth, nineteen hundred and six, (1910) 36 Stat., 838.

470 An act of 6 November 1978 to establish a uniform law on the subject of bankruptcies, 92 Stat. 2549.

471 An act of 4 April 1800 to establish a uniform system of bankruptcy throughout the United States, 2 Stat. 19.

472 W. D. COLES, 'Bankruptcy legislation in the United States' (St. Louis Law Society, 1898), 7.

473 Sec. 1 of an act of 4 April 1800 to establish a uniform system of bankruptcy throughout the United States, 2 Stat. 19.

474 Sec. 2 of an act of 4 April 1800 to establish a uniform system of bankruptcy throughout the United States, 2 Stat. 19.

475 An act of 19 December 1803 to repeal an act intitled "An act to establish an uniform system of bankruptcy throughout the United States" 2 Stat. 248.

The next federal bankruptcy act came about in 1841.[476] This act introduced for the first time the concept of voluntary bankruptcies.[477] The act also allowed for a discharge of the debtor[478], unless it could be proven that the debtor was guilty of fraud or willful concealment of property, had preferred one of his creditors contrary to the provisions of this act or willfully omitted or refused to comply with the orders and directions of the bankruptcy court.[479] The act enabled many debtors to be discharged of their debts.[480] Following this increase in discharges, creditors lobbied for the repeal of the act which took place only thirteen months after the bankruptcy act had been implemented.[481]

The next bankruptcy act was enacted in 1867.[482] This law attempted a more equal treatment of debtors and creditors. Debtors were eager to regain access to a discharge of their debts following the civil war and were willing to make concessions to creditors to make this possible.[483] This more balanced approach took the form of more easily refusing the debtor's discharge. As in previous bankruptcy acts the debtor was divested from all or parts of his assets and an assignee was charged with the sale and distribution of the proceeds. Furthermore, the debtor could only file for a discharge six months after the opening of the bankruptcy proceedings and his discharge could be refused, if the debtor was found guilty of any of the fraudulent acts listed in the bankruptcy law.[484] This act contained a more detailed and extensive list of the different acts for which the debtor could be refused a discharge than was the case in the 1841 bankruptcy act. Moreover, a debtor, who enjoyed a discharge and became a voluntary bankrupt again, would only be discharged if his estate was able to fulfill 70% of the creditors' claims on the estate. As a result, debtors had access to a discharge, but measures were put in place to protect a creditor against debtors who committed acts that hindered the fair distribution of the bankruptcy estate or attempted to repeatedly use the bankruptcy regime to discharge themselves of debts. Unfortunately, the tenure of this act was also short lived and the 1867 Bankruptcy Act was repealed in 1878.[485]

476 An act of 19 August 1841 to establish a uniform system of bankruptcy throughout the United States, 5 Stat. 440.

477 Sec. 1 of an act of 19 August 1841 to establish a uniform system of bankruptcy throughout the United States, 5 Stat. 440.

478 Sec. 4 of an act of 19 August 1841 to establish a uniform system of bankruptcy throughout the United States, 5 Stat. 440.

479 Sec. 4, par. 2 of an act of 19 August 1841 to establish a uniform system of bankruptcy throughout the United States, 5 Stat. 440.

480 W. D. COLES, 'Bankruptcy legislation in the United States' (St. Louis Law Society, 1898), 9.

481 An Act of 3 March 1843 to repeal the bankrupt act, 5 Stat. 614.

482 An act of 2 March 1867 to establish a uniform system of bankruptcy throughout the United States, 14 Stat. 517.

483 W. D. COLES, 'Bankruptcy legislation in the United States' (St Louis Law Society, 1898), 9–10.

484 Sec. 29 of an act of 2 March 1867 to establish a uniform system of bankruptcy throughout the United States, 14 Stat. 517; W. D. COLES, 'Bankruptcy legislation in the United States' (St. Louis Law Society, 1898), 11.

485 An act of 7 June 1878 to repeal the bankrupt law, 20 Stat. 99.

99. *The federal bankruptcy law of 1898*[486] – On the one hand, this law implemented a uniform bankruptcy procedure in which the debtor would be divested of all or parts of his property and the appointed trustee in bankruptcy distributed the proceeds among the creditors.[487] Furthermore, it provided clear rules on the avoidance of preferences to certain creditors or third parties in the lead-up towards a bankruptcy proceeding.[488] On the other hand, as with its predecessors, this bankruptcy act also gave rise to debate on whether debtors should be allowed to voluntarily file for bankruptcy and obtain a discharge for their outstanding debts.[489] Especially the limited number of grounds on which a discharge could be refused[490] and the fact that the act could be so interpreted to allow a discharge for corporations was cause for concern for creditors. The latter issue stemmed from section 14 of the act that stated that any person who had been adjudged a bankrupt could file an application for a discharge. According to section 1, (19) the term person would include corporations. Based on these provisions it would be possible to argue that corporations were also entitled to a discharge even though it was the more common approach to limit the fresh-start principle to natural persons.[491] Nevertheless, the concerns regarding the bankrupt's discharge did not outweigh the benefits for having a uniform bankruptcy regime that applied to all states.[492] The overall benefits of a more balanced uniform bankruptcy regime explains why the act remained in effect until 1978, until it was superseded by title 11 of the U.S. Code. However, the act was amended a few times. Once in 1910[493], thereby indirectly affecting the protection of conditional seller's during corporate bankruptcy proceedings, and a second time in 1938.[494]

---

486 An act of 1 July 1898 to establish a uniform system of bankruptcy throughout the United States, 30 Stat., 544. See also, C. WILDE, 'The Chandler Act', (1938) 14 Ind. L. J., (93) 93; B. A. BLUM, *Bankruptcy and debtor/creditor*, (New York: Aspen publisher, 2006), 91.

487 Sec. 39 of an act of 1 July 1898 to establish a uniform system of bankruptcy throughout the United States, 30 Stat. 544.

488 Sec. 65, e of an act of 1 July 1898 to establish a uniform system of bankruptcy throughout the United States, 30 Stat. 544; A. B. THOMPSON, 'The bankruptcy act in operation', (1900) 6 W. Res. L. J., (157) 159.

489 A. B. THOMPSON, 'The bankruptcy act in operation', (1900) 6 W. Res. L. J., (157) 158.

490 Sec. 14, b of an act of 1 July 1898 to establish a uniform system of bankruptcy throughout the United States, 30 Stat. 544.

491 A. B. THOMPSON, 'The bankruptcy act in operation', (1900) 6 W. Res. L. J., (157)

492 H. C. BLACK, 'Corporations under the bankruptcy act of 1898', (1898) 8 Yale L J. (105) 117–118.

493 To amend an act entitled An act to establish a uniform system of bankruptcy throughout the United States," approved July-first, eighteen hundred and ninety-eight, as amended by an act approved February fifth, nineteen hundred and three, and as further amended by an act approved June fifteenth, nineteen hundred and six, (1910) 36 Stat., 838.

494 An act to amend an Act entitled "An Act to establish a uniform system of bankruptcy throughout the United States", approved July 1, 1898, and Acts amendatory thereof and supplementary thereto; and to repeal section 76 thereof and all Acts and parts of Acts inconsistent therewith, (1938) 52 Stat., 840.

4.2. *Corporate bankruptcy of the PMSI debtor*

100. *Treatment of PMSI creditors during corporate bankruptcy* – A big aspect of any bankruptcy procedure is the delineation of the bankruptcy estate. For the trustee in bankruptcy, it will be essential to include as many goods as possible in the estate to increase the potential distributions for the creditors. For secured creditors, it will be paramount to have their encumbered goods excluded from the bankruptcy estate so that they can simply carry on unaffected by the bankruptcy proceedings. Based on this reasoning, transactions with retention of title offered seemingly the perfect protection for secured creditors. The retained title ensured that the good would not be considered as part of the debtor's estate and thus that the retention of title creditor's claim would remain unaffected by corporate bankruptcy proceedings. This creditor friendly approach was exemplified in section 70 of the 1898 Bankruptcy Act. Following this provision, the trustee in bankruptcy would be vested with the title of the bankrupt from the moment of his appointment.[495] The trustee in bankruptcy thus became the retention of title debtor in relation to the retention of title creditor. Consequently, bankruptcy courts and the United States Supreme Court were of the opinion that the trustee in bankruptcy would not have a better title to the sold good than the bankrupt.[496] The fact that the retention of title debtor defaulted on the purchase price and did not yet obtain title, meant that the trustee in bankruptcy also did not acquire title to the good. Therefore, the retention of title creditor was unaffected by the bankruptcy proceedings and could simply recover the sold goods.

101. *Interaction UCSA and corporate bankruptcy* – At first, the enactment of the UCSA did not change the treatment of the retention of title creditor during corporate bankruptcy. Corporate bankruptcy was still regulated by the 1898 Bankruptcy Act in which the retention of title creditor was considered the owner of the encumbered good and thus the encumbered good fell outside of the

---

495 Sec. 70 of an act of 1 July 1898 to establish a uniform system of bankruptcy throughout the United States, 30 Stat. (544) 565.

496 Supreme Court of the United States 1 October 1877, Yeatman v. New Orleans Sav. Inst., 95 U.S., (764) 766; Supreme Court of the United States 1 October 1879, Stewart v. Platt, 101 U.S., (731) 738–739; Supreme Judicial Court of Maine 29 May 1880, Rogers v. Whitehouse, 71 Me., (222) 226; Supreme Court of the United States 16 May 1904, Hewit v. Berlin Mach. Works, 194 U.S., (296) 302–303; Circuit Court District of Louisiana 1 April 1872, Goddard v. Weaver, 1 Woods 257, 10 F. Cas., (513) 514; Supreme Court of the United States 1 December 1871, Gibson v. Warden, 81 U.S., (244) 248; Supreme Court of Illinois 1 December 1848, Strong v. Clawson, 5 Gilman, (346) 349; Supreme Court of Illinois 1 December 1843, Talcott v. Dudley, 5 Ill., (427) 435; Circuit Court District of Maine 1 October 1843, Mitchell v. Winslow, 2 Story 630, 17 F. Cass., (527) 530; Circuit Court District of Massachusetts 1 October 1843, Winsor v. McLellan, 2 Story 492, 30, F. Cas., (323) 324; Circuit Court District of Massachusetts 1 May 1842, Ex Parte Newhall, 2 Story 360, 18 F. Cass., (74) 75. See also, M. ISAAC, 'Conditional sale contracts in bankruptcy proceedings', (1902) 10 Am Law. (535) 535.

bankruptcy estate.[497] The retention of title creditor under the UCSA was even protected in the event the conditional sale was not registered and registration was required for third-party effectiveness. The trustee could not be considered a third party, because the trustee in bankruptcy was considered to step into the shoes of the bankrupt retention of title debtor.[498] Consequently, the lack of registration did not harm the retention of title creditor in the event of the debtor's bankruptcy, since the conditional sale was still effective between the parties (i.e. the trustee in bankruptcy who took the place of the conditional buyer).

However, in 1910 the position of the trustee in bankruptcy changed due to an amendment to the Bankruptcy Act of 1898. With this amendment, the trustee in bankruptcy was to be considered vested with all the rights, remedies and powers of a creditor holding a lien by legal or equitable proceedings.[499] Following this change the trustee in bankruptcy no longer just stepped into the shoes of the bankrupt retention of title debtor, but became vested with the rights and remedies of a creditor or third party.[500] Moreover, this change implied that the lack of registration of the conditional sale under the UCSA could affect the effectiveness and enforcement of the conditional sale, since the trustee in bankruptcy could be considered a third party or creditor against whom an unregistered conditional sale was not effective.[501] This change to the trustee's position was maintained after the 1938 amendment to the bankruptcy act.[502] This amendment was a significant departure from the previous understanding in

---

497 L. VOLD, 'Dividend Property Interests in Conditional Sales', (1929–30) 78 Univ. Penn. L. Rev., (713) 729

498 Sec. 70 of an act of 1 July 1898 to establish a uniform system of bankruptcy throughout the United States, 30 Stat., (544) 565.

499 Sec. 8 of an act to amend an act entitled an act to establish a uniform system of bankruptcy throughout the United States," approved July-first, eighteen hundred and ninety-eight, as amended by an act approved February fifth, nineteen hundred and three, and as further amended by an act approved June fifteenth, nineteen hundred and six, (1910) 36 Stat., (838) 840. See also, H. S. WILCOX, 'The new amendments to the national Bankruptcy Act', (1910) 9 Okla. L. J. (85) 87. In the 1938 amendment of the Bankruptcy Act the trustee remains vested "*with all the rights, remedies, and powers of a creditor then holding a lien*" but this provision is moved from section 47 to section 68 (An act to amend an Act entitled "An Act to establish a uniform system of bankruptcy throughout the United States", approved July 1, 1898, and Acts amendatory thereof and supplementary thereto; and to repeal section 76 thereof and all Acts and parts of Acts inconsistent therewith, (1938) 52 Stat., (840) 878).

500 Circuit Court of Appeals 30 June 1913, Gage Lumber Co. v. McEldowney, 207 F., (255) 262.

501 W. T. PLUMB, 'The new Uniform Conditional Sales Law', (1922) 27 Com. L. League Bull., (571) 571; R. F. MAGILL, 'Legal advantages and disadvantages of the various methods of selling goods on credit', (1923) 8 Cornell L. Q., (210) 220–221. See for New York: Supreme Court Appelate Division of New York 10 May 1933, General Motors Acceptance Corp. v. Raz Delivery, 238 A.D., (277) 279.

502 Sec. 70 of an act to amend an Act entitled "An Act to establish a uniform system of bankruptcy throughout the United States", approved July 1, 1898, and Acts amendatory thereof and supplementary thereto; and to repeal section 76 thereof and all Acts and parts of Acts inconsistent therewith, (1938) 52 Stat., 840. See also, W. CHANDLER, 'The revised Bankruptcy Act of 1938', (1938) 24 A. B. A. J., 880; C. WILDE, 'The Chandler Act', (1938) 14 Ind. L. J., (93) 135.

which the trustee in bankruptcy was seen merely as an extension of the bankrupt retention of title debtor against whom a conditional sale could nearly always be enforced. As a result, it became even more important for the retention of title creditor to correctly register his conditional sale agreement in order to avoid losing his enforcement options during corporate bankruptcy proceedings.[503] However, if the conditional sale was correctly vested and made effective against third parties, then the goods were considered to fall outside of the bankruptcy estate and the retention of title creditor could still proceed as if the bankruptcy proceedings were not taking place.[504]

102. *Article 9 UCC and corporate bankruptcy proceedings* – With the introduction of Article 9 UCC, the conditional sale became limited in its effect to the reservation of a security interest.[505] As a result, the retention of title creditor or now PMSI creditor could no longer claim that title resided with him and that the encumbered good fell outside of the bankruptcy estate.[506] In the 1938 version of the Bankruptcy Act, this meant that the PMSI creditor had to be considered a secured creditor and the encumbered good part of the bankruptcy estate. Nevertheless, correctly vested and perfected security interests in personal property were not disturbed and were upheld during corporate bankruptcy proceedings.[507] Whether a security interest was correctly vested and perfected was determined by state law, in this context the state enactments of Article 9 UCC.[508] However, the trustee in bankruptcy was given the power to void security interests in goods in the bankruptcy estate when the security interest was considered an improper preference for the secured creditor.[509] Furthermore, the trustee in bankruptcy was vested with all the rights, remedies and powers of a judgment lien creditor which gave the trustee in bankruptcy priority over all unperfected security interests.[510]

During the bankruptcy procedure, the enforcement of the goods in the bankruptcy estate fell under the jurisdiction of the bankruptcy court.[511] All individual claims by creditors against the bankrupt's estate were stayed for the duration of the bankruptcy procedure.[512] However, the bankruptcy court

---

503 G. GLENN, 'The conditional sale at common law and as a statutory security', (1938–39) 25 Va. L. Rev., (559) 585.

504 Circuit court of appeals (federal) 29 July 1935, In re Lake's Laundry, 59 F. 2d, (326) 328.

505 §1-201(b)(35) UCC (2001).

506 See *supra* no. 101.

507 G. GILMORE, *Security interests in personal property*, vol. 2, (Boston: Little Brown and Co., 1965), 1284.

508 G. GILMORE, *Security interests in personal property*, vol. 2, (Boston: Little Brown and Co., 1965), 1284.

509 Sec. 60 of the Bankruptcy Act (1938). See also, G. GILMORE, *Security interests in personal property*, vol. 2, (Boston: Little Brown and Co., 1965), 1285.

510 Sec. 70 Bankruptcy Act (1938).

511 Sec. 2 (7) Bankruptcy Act (1938).

512 Sec. 11 Bankruptcy Act (1938).

could decide to abandon certain assets or to permit enforcement outside the bankruptcy procedure by either the secured creditor or another court.[513] Either way, under the bankruptcy act the PMSI creditor was at the mercy of the bankruptcy court with regards to the enforcement of the encumbered good.

103. *Title 11 of the U.S. Code: a quick introduction* – In 1978, Title 11 of the United States Code was enacted which regulates corporate bankruptcy. This part of the U.S. Code is itself divided into different chapters. The first chapters (1, 3 and 5) consist of general provisions concerning case administration, creditors, the debtor and the estate. The following chapters each regulate a specific type of bankruptcy proceeding, such as liquidation (ch. 7), adjustment of debts of a municipality (ch. 9), reorganization (ch. 11), adjustment of debts of a family farmer or fishermen (ch. 12) and adjustment of debts of individual with a regular income (ch. 13). In this dissertation, the scope of the research is limited to the liquidation proceedings in chapter 7.

104. *Treatment of PMSIs in the Bankruptcy Code 1978* – In the Bankruptcy Code of 1978, a correctly vested and perfected security interest is upheld and left undisturbed during corporate bankruptcy proceedings.[514] Furthermore, just as in the bankruptcy act of 1938, the PMSI creditor is stayed in his enforcement for the duration of the bankruptcy procedure.[515] However, the PMSI creditor can obtain relief from the automatic stay when the debtor offers inadequate protection to the encumbered good.[516] During the bankruptcy proceedings, the encumbered good often remains in the debtor's possession and the secured creditor cannot enforce upon the encumbered collateral. If the secured creditor can show that the continued stay of the encumbered good in the hands of the debtor will result in the depreciation of the encumbered collateral, the secured creditor is granted a relief of the automatic stay.[517] Once the stay is lifted for these assets, the secured creditor can simply commence or continue his enforcement under Article 9 UCC.

The secured creditor can also obtain relief from the automatic stay, if the debtor does not have equity in the encumbered good and the good is not necessary for an effective organization[518] The debtor does not have equity in the encumbered good, when the sum of all encumbrances on that good exceed

---

513 District Court, S.D. New York 24 March 1931, In re Schulte-United, 50 F.2d, (243) 244; J. HANNA, 'The secured creditor in bankruptcy', (1960) 14 Rutgers L. Rev., (471) 477.

514 J. HANNA, 'The secured creditor in Bankruptcy', (1960) 14 Rutgers L. Rev., (471) 477; W. H. LAWRENCE, W. H. HENNING and R. W. FREYERMUTH, *Understanding secured transactions*, (2 edn., New York City: Matthew Bender, 1999), 375.

515 §362 Title 11 U.S.C.

516 §362, (d) (1) Title 11 U. S. C.

517 W. H. LAWRENCE, W. H. HENNING and R. W. FREYERMUTH, *Understanding secured transactions*, (2 edn., New York City: Matthew Bender, 1999), 380.

518 §362 (d) (2) Title 11 U.S.C.

the value of the good.[519] This analysis requires an assessment of the value of the encumbered good for which there are no specific guidelines in the Bankruptcy Code.[520] The Supreme Court intervened in 1997 by stating that the value of the encumbered good should be determined via the replacement value. This is the value that represents the price a willing buyer in the debtor's trade, business or situation would pay to obtain similar property from a willing seller.[521] However, the Supreme Court then confused the point again by stating in a footnote that whether the replacement value is the equivalent of the wholesale value, the retail value or another value depends on the type of property and the type of debtor.[522] The second requirement in order for the secured creditor to obtain a relief of stay is to show that the good is not necessary for a successful reorganization.[523] This requirement can be considered automatically fulfilled in a chapter 7 liquidation proceeding, since the goal of chapter 7 is liquidation and not reorganization. Consequently, in chapter 7 proceedings the secured creditor only has to show that due to the PMSIs, security interests and other liens covering the good, the debtor does not have sufficient equity in the good to warrant a stay of enforcement.[524]

Requesting relief from the automatic stay is also important in the event the encumbered good is abandoned by the trustee in bankruptcy.[525] The Bankruptcy Code allows the trustee in bankruptcy to abandon goods when they are so encumbered with security interests or other encumbrances that they are valueless to the bankruptcy estate. In such a scenario, all proceeds of the sale will go to the secured creditors and it will only cost the bankruptcy estate money to hold on to this good.[526] However, the abandonment of the encumbered good does not mean that the good automatically falls in the secured creditor's hands. Only when the debtor has no interest or any equity in the good, can the good be released to the secured creditor.[527] If the debtor still has an interest or any equity in the encumbered good, then the abandoned good will be turned over to the debtor. In that case, the secured creditor has to ask for relief of stay against the debtor to enforce his security interest in the encumbered good.[528]

---

519 United States Bankruptcy Court Appelate Panel 8 August 1994, In re Sun Valley Newspapers Inc., 171 B. R., (71) 75;United States Bankruptcy Court Tennessee Western District 18 September 1997, In re Hurst, 212 B. R., (890) 892.

520 W. H. LAWRENCE, W. H. HENNING and R. W. FREYERMUTH, *Understanding secured transactions*, (2 edn., New York City: Matthew Bender, 1999), 385;

521 Supreme Court of the United States 16 June 1997, Associates Commercial Corp. v. Rash, 117 S.Ct., (1879) 1885–1886.

522 Supreme Court of the United States 16 June 1997 Associates Commercial Corp. v. Rash, 520 U.S., (953) 1886, fn. 6.

523 §524 (c) Title 11 U.S.C.; J. J. WHITE and G. E. J. BRUNSTADT, *Secured transactions teaching materials*, (4 edn, St. Paul: West Publishing, 2013), 151.

524 W. H. LAWRENCE, W. H. HENNING and R. W. FREYERMUTH, *Understanding secured transactions*, (2 edn., New York City: Matthew Bender, 1999), 387, fn. 97.

525 §554 Title 11 U.S.C.

526 B. A. BLUM, *Bankruptcy and debtor/creditor*, (New York: Aspen publisher, 2006), 287.

527 B. A. BLUM, *Bankruptcy and debtor/creditor*, (New York: Aspen publisher, 2006), 243.

528 B. A. BLUM, *Bankruptcy and debtor/creditor*, (New York: Aspen publisher, 2006), 288.

105. *Treatment of leasing during corporate bankruptcy* – Finally, like in the UCC, the distinction between true leases and security interests is relevant in the Bankruptcy Code. If a transaction is classified as a true lease and not a security interest, then the true lease is considered an executory contract that continues after the bankruptcy petition has been filed. A true lease is not affected by the automatic stay. Moreover, the trustee in bankruptcy has to decide whether to assume the lease and honor its ongoing obligations or reject the lease and return the leased good to the lessor.[529] Furthermore, a true lease does not need to be perfected via the filing of a financing statement.[530] Consequently, the trustee in bankruptcy cannot look to the perfection rules to potentially declare a true lease void and thus ignore its operation during bankruptcy.[531] These specific rules for true leases indicate that true leases are less impacted by bankruptcy proceedings and that, when impacted, the treatment of true leases during bankruptcy is more beneficial. Therefore, debates concerning the true nature of transactions as either a security interest or true lease are likely to continue during corporate bankruptcy proceedings.

4.3. Corporate bankruptcy of the PMSI creditor

106. *The impact of the PMSI creditor's bankruptcy prior to and after Article 9 UCC* – One of the big advantages of retention of title in a conditional sale or lease agreement was the fact that the retained title kept the encumbered good out of the bankruptcy estate.[532] However, the flip side of this advantage was that the encumbered good could get caught up in the retention of title creditor's bankruptcy due to the retention of title creditor's retained title.

Prior to Article 9 UCC, it was understood that retention of title implied that the encumbered goods fell in the retention of title creditor's estate and could be sold and distributed among his creditors in the event of a corporate bankruptcy proceeding. However, this interpretation was more difficult to apply in the event the buyer was making regular payments for the conditionally sold good and he had been gradually appropriating the good.[533] As a result, the retention of title debtor who made regular payments would not necessarily be negatively

529 §365 (a) Title 11 U.S.C.

530 See *supra* no. 26.

531 J. J. WHITE and G. E. J. BRUNSTADT, *Secured transactions teaching materials*, (4 edn., St. Paul: West Publishing, 2013), 215.

532 See *supra* no. 100.

533 ***United Kingdom***: Court of King's Bench 26 June 1822, Woods v. Russell, 106 E. R., (1436) 1438–1439; Court of Queen's Bench 12 January 1856, Wood v. Bell, 119 E.R., (669) 678. ***United States***: Supreme Judicial Court of Massachusetts 1 March 1828, Glover v. Austin, 23 Mass., (209) 220; Supreme Court of California 12 June 1902, Yukon River Steamboat Co. v. Gratto, 136 Cal., (538) 542 (the buyer had made progress payments but payment of the full purchase price was considered a condition precedent for title to transfer); Court of Errors and Appeals of Delaware 1 June 1858, Hall v. Green, 6 Del., (546) 554–555.

affected by the retention of title creditor's bankruptcy, but would be awarded the goods on the basis of an equitable lien the buyer acquired on the good through his payments.[534] This lien was respected in the retention of title creditor's bankruptcy and ensured that the retention of title debtor could continue his payments of the conditionally sold good and gradually acquire title.

Under the UCSA, the retention of title creditor was still considered the owner of the encumbered good and the good part of the bankruptcy estate. However, following the UCSA the retention of title debtor had the right to retain possession of the conditionally sold good as long as he was not in default.[535] Consequently, in the event the trustee in bankruptcy attempted to reclaim the conditionally sold good, the retention of title debtor could invoke his right to ward of recovery by the trustee. This protection explicated the protections established in case law for retention of title debtors based on the rights they built up via their pre-payments.[536]

107. *Effect of the PMSI creditor's bankruptcy on PMSIs under Article 9 UCC* – The risk of the encumbered goods getting caught up in the retention of title creditor's bankruptcy proceedings went away with the introduction of Article 9 UCC. In Article 9 UCC, the PMSI creditor is no longer considered to have title to the encumbered good but a PMSI. This also means that the encumbered good is not considered part of the PMSI creditor's estate in event the PMSI creditor goes bankrupt. In other words, the bankruptcy of the PMSI creditor does not impact the PMSI in the encumbered good, nor the rights of the PMSI debtor.

5. CONCLUSIONS

108. *Irrelevance of title* – A first conclusion, is that the drafters of Article 9 UCC made a clear choice to move away from the use of title in the domain of secured transactions in movable goods. Consequently, the drafters abandon title-based mechanisms, such as condition sales, leases and transfers of title for security purposes, in favor of security interests in which the debtor is the owner of the encumbered good and the secured creditor acquires a limited proprietary interest in the movable good.

109. *Creating functionally equivalent outcomes for functionally similar mechanisms via recharacterization* – A cornerstone of Article 9 UCC is the recharacterization of all secured transactions in movable goods that

534 X., 'The effect of prepayment upon the buyer's right to the goods', (1937) 37 Colum. L. Rev., (630) 643; Supreme Court of the United States 5 April 1909, Hurley v. Atchison, 213 U.S., (126) 134; Circuit Court of Appeals 24 July 1915, Sieg v. Greene, 225 F., (955) 959–960.

535 §2 UCSA.

536 See *supra* no. 63.

create interests in personal property or fixtures which secures payment or performance of an obligation to security interests.[537] For retention of title the recharacterization takes place on two levels. On a first level, conditional sales and lease agreements for security purposes are recharacterized to general security interests. Consequently, former conditional sellers and lessors are governed by a uniform set of rules that regulate the creation, third-party effectiveness, tracing and enforcement of all security interests in movable goods. Furthermore, on a second level, Article 9 UCC also creates equivalent legal outcomes for all security interests that guarantee acquisition credit, by recharacterizing these transactions to PMSIs, a sub-category of security interests, and subjecting them to specific uniform rules. Following this approach, retention of title mechanisms, such as conditional sales and lease agreements, are recharacterized to the sub-category of PMSIs that guarantee acquisition credit. Moreover, PMSIs are defined so broadly that this category not only covers former retention of title in conditional sale and lease agreements, but also other credit agreements in which financing is provided for the acquisition of the encumbered good. This subdivision based on function also allows for the assignment of specific rules to PMSI', such as the assignment of super-priority which applies to PMSIs that fulfill the necessary requirements[538], and also certain exceptions to the registration requirement.[539] As a result, Article 9 UCC succeeds in creating equivalent legal outcomes for mechanisms that perform similar functions on both a general and specific level.

110. *The impact of the functional approach with recharacterization on the rights of retention of title creditors* – The recharacterization from a retention of title to a security interest in general and a PMSI in particular did not significantly affect the requirements for the creation or third-party effectiveness of former retention of title mechanisms, nor the rights of former retention of title creditors. For example, the implementation of notification requirements for all security interests, including PMSIs, is not that big of a change for former retention of title creditors, since the UCSA already imposed a general registration requirement for conditional sales.[540] Similarly, with regards to priority and enforcement the comparison of the rights of retention of title creditors and PMSI holders shows that PMSI holders still enjoy super-priority, albeit after the fulfillment of certain formalities[541], and that the enforcement proceedings for PMSI holders are not that more stringent than the pre-Article 9 UCC enforcement rules for retention of title creditors.[542] The only area where the recharacterization of retention of title to PMSIs had somewhat of an impact is in the context of

[537] §1-201(b)(35) UCC (2001).
[538] See *supra* no. 82.
[539] See *supra* no. 59.
[540] See *supra* no. 25.
[541] See *supra* no. 82.
[542] See *supra* no. 93 *et seq.*

corporate bankruptcy. In a conditional sale, the seller retained full title and the conditionally sold good fell outside of the bankruptcy estate. Evidently, with the recharacterization of a retention of title to a PMSI, the encumbered good becomes part of the debtor's estate. Consequently, the encumbered good is part of the bankruptcy estate and the PMSI creditor is stayed in his enforcement. However, correctly vested PMSIs are protected during corporate bankruptcy proceedings, so the PMSI creditor is likely to receive some proceeds when the encumbered good is liquidated. Furthermore, the PMSI creditor can request a relief of stay or the trustee in bankruptcy can abandon the encumbered good, thereby giving power back to the PMSI creditor to continue his enforcement. Therefore, the loss of the title protection, nor the recharacterization to a PMSI is detrimental to PMSI creditor's protection, since his secured status remains protected during bankruptcy proceedings and the PMSI creditor can request for relief from the stay of proceedings if necessary.[543]

The minimal effect of the recharacterization from retention of title to PMSI on the rights of retention of title creditors leads to the conclusion that conditional sales and leases for security purposes were already operating more as secured transactions with a limited proprietary interest in the movable good instead of title. This explains why the drafters felt comfortable reharacterizing conditional sales and leases for security purposes to PMSIs and why the implementation of this new regime went smoothly and did not encounter much resistance.

SECTION 2 – INTERNATIONAL INSTRUMENTS: UNCITRAL AND DCFR

111. *Overview* – In this chapter the background and development of the specific functional approaches to retention of title in each of the international instruments is discussed. The focus is on the specific recommendations for retention of title, as well as the policies underlying the choices made in these instruments.

1. UNCITRAL LEGISLATIVE GUIDE AND MODEL LAW ON SECURED TRANSACTIONS

1.1. Background and purpose

112. *Historical background* – The first steps towards the UNCITRAL Legislative Guide on Secured Transactions (hereafter, the UNCITRAL Guide)[544]

543 See *supra* no. 104 *et seq.*

544 United Nations Commission on International Trade Law (UNCITRAL), *UNCITRAL Legislative guide on secured transactions*, (New York City: United Nations, 2010).

were taken in 1977. At that time the UNCITRAL sent out professor DROBNIG to examine the possibilities of creating a harmonized set of rules for security rights in movable goods.[545] Unfortunately, the outcome of that study was that although harmonization could potentially be very positive for the global economic system, secured transactions law was too interwoven with the culture and traditions of states to allow for the distillation of a common denominator.[546]

The UNCITRAL launched another attempt in 2002 when a specific Working Group was founded to investigate the possibility of a legislative guide concerning secured transactions.[547] This time the UNCITRAL was more successful and the UNCITRAL Guide was adopted by consensus in 2007.[548]

113. *Reasoning behind the introduction of a legislative Guide* – The choice by the Working Group for a legislative guide was deliberate. The reasoning went that a legislative guide would be preferable over a convention or model law, since it would be difficult to come up with a one-size-fits-all model with regards to secured transactions.[549] Consequently, states can theoretically choose which recommendations they implement from the UNCITRAL Guide.[550] Furthermore, within the different aspects of secured transactions, the UNCITRAL Guide gives a lot of options for states to choose from. However, given that the framework recommended in the UNCITRAL Guide is a tightly interwoven system it is not so easy to lift out certain components of the UNCITRAL Guide and still maintain a coherent and logical framework.[551]

---

545 U. DROBNIG, 'Report of the Secretary-General: study on security interests (A/CN.9/131)', (1977) 8 UNCITRAL Yearbook, 171.

546 U. DROBNIG, 'Report of the Secretary-General: study on security interests (A/CN.9/131)', (1977) 8 UNCITRAL Yearbook, 171; S. BAZINAS, 'The work of UNCITRAL on security interest: an overview', (2010) 15 Unif. L. Rev., (315) 316; J.-H. ROVER, 'The EBRD's Model Law on Secured Transactions and its implications for an UNCITRAL Model Law on Secured Transactions', (2010) 15 Unif. L. Rev., (479) 480. See also, G. G. CASTELLANO, 'Reforming non-possessory secured transactions law: a new strategy?', (2015) 78 MLR, (611) 632.

547 Official Records of the General Assembly, Fifty-seventh Session, Supplement No. 17 (A/57/17), 32. See also, S. BAZINAS, 'The work of UNCITRAL on security interest: an overview', (2010) 15 Unif. L. Rev., (315) 317.

548 S. BAZINAS, 'The work of UNCITRAL on security interest: an overview', (2010) 15 Unif. L. Rev., (315) 318.

549 S. BAZINAS, 'The utility and efficacy of the UNCITRAL legislative guide on secured transactions' in O. AKSELI (ed.), *Availibility of credit in a time of crisis*, (Cambridge: Cambridge University Press, 2013), (133) 135; S. MITSDÖRFFER, *Sicherungsrechte an Schutzrechten – Ein Vergleich zwischen dem deutschen Recht and dem UNCITRAL Legislative Guide on Secured Transactions*, (Karlsruhe: Mohr Siebeck, 2013), 8.

550 S. BAZINAS, 'The utility and efficacy of the UNCITRAL legislative guide on secured transactions' in O. AKSELI (ed.), *Availibility of credit in a time of crisis*, (Cambridge: Cambridge University Press, 2013), (133) 137.

551 H. BEALE, 'The UNCITRAL Legislative Guide on Secured Transactions as a model for law reform: some conclusions' in O. AKSELI (ed.), *Availibility of credit and secured transactions in a time of crisis*, (Cambridge: Cambridge University Press, 2013), (275) 278.

114. *Objectives and policies of the Guide and Model Law* – The UNCITRAL Guide very explicit states the objectives and the policies it wants to achieve via its recommendations. On its most basic level, the UNCITRAL Guide aims to help states with the adoption of a modern secured transactions law to facilitate the access to and distribution of credit.[552] More specifically, its objectives are: (1) to promote low-cost credit by enhancing the availability of secured credit; (2) to allow debtors to use the full value inherent in their assets to support credit; (3) to enable parties to obtain security rights in a simple and efficient manner; (4) to provide for equal treatment of diverse sources of credit and of diverse forms of secured transaction; (5) to validate non-possessory security rights in all types of assets; (6) to enhance certainty and transparency by providing for registration of a notice (hereafter also, financing statement) in a general security rights registry; (7) to establish clear and predictable priority rules; (8) to facilitate efficient enforcement of secured creditors' rights; (9) to allow parties maximum flexibility to negotiate the terms of their security agreement, (10) to balance the interests of persons affected by a secured transaction and; (11) to harmonize secured transactions laws, including conflict-of-laws rules.[553]

Additionally, to help states correctly interpret and implement the recommendations from the UNCITRAL Guide, the drafters also provided the policies they are pursuing with these recommendations. Consequently, this can help steer legislators in the right direction when adapting these recommendations to their own framework.[554] The policies are: (1) comprehensiveness in scope; (2) functional approach; (3) allowing security rights in future assets and proceeds; (4) clear rules on effectiveness between parties and towards third parties; (5) creation of a security rights registry; (6) allowing multiple security rights in the same collateral; (7) priority rights and; (8) effective enforcement rights.[555]

115. *Introduction of the UNCITRAL Model Law on Secured Transactions* – After the adoption of the UNCITRAL Guide in 2007, the idea was thrown around to continue the work of the Security Interest Working Group at UNCITRAL and create a Model Law on Secured Transactions (hereafter, the UNCITRAL Model Law). Initially, the idea was not met with a lot of enthusiasm. Among the counterarguments was the idea that the drafting of a model law would reopen some of the debates that took place during the drafting of the UNCITRAL Guide and would potentially lead to divergences between the UNCITRAL Guide

---

552 UNCITRAL Guide, 1; J. D. DUNN, 'UNCITRAL Adopts Legislative Guide on Secured Transactions', (2008) 2 Insolv. & Restruct. Int'l., (40) 40; J. KLEIN, 'UNCITRAL Legislative Guide on Secured Transactions: an introduction and overview', (2009) Am. Bankr. Inst. L. J., (28) 28.

553 UNCITRAL Guide, recommendation 1, 30.

554 UNCITRAL Guide, 22.

555 UNCITRAL Guide, 23–26.

and the UNCITRAL Model Law. Furthermore, critics were not convinced that a model law would add a lot of value and would just mean more costs for the UNCITRAL. Especially, since there were already a lot of model laws concerning secured transactions crowding the field, such as the EBRD Model Law on secured transactions or the OAS Model Law.[556] Finally, there was significant skepticism that a one-size-fits-all model law could be developed in the field of secured transactions.[557]

Nevertheless, in 2016 the UNCITRAL Model Law on Secured Transactions was adopted by the UNCITRAL (hereafter, the UNCITRAL Model Law).[558] The arguments in favor of the development of the UNCITRAL Model Law were that it would offer a less complex and shorter document that legislators could use to develop their modern secured transactions regime.[559] With regards to the existence of other model laws, the drafters were of the opinion that a model law with a global appeal developed by an international organization did not yet exist and could add value.[560] Finally, the UNCITRAL Model Law should not be viewed as a one-size-fits-all approach, since it still leaves a lot of alternatives to its users and does not try to shoehorn the rules of the UNCITRAL Model Law in existing frameworks.

As expected, the UNCITRAL Model Law is very similar to the UNCITRAL Guide. However, the UNCITRAL Model Law is much shorter, broader in scope and includes less exceptions.[561] This is to make it easier for states to potentially adopt the regime recommended by the UNCITRAL. In the following sections, both the UNCITRAL Guide and UNCITRAL Model Law are discussed and their differences, when present, are highlighted.

116. *American influence in the development of the UNCITRAL Guide and Model Law* – There is one topic that frequently recurs when discussing the UNCITRAL

556 N. COHEN, 'Should UNCITRAL prepare a model law on secured transactions', (2010) 15 Unif. L. Rev., (325) 327; R. MACDONDALD, 'A model law on secured transactions. A representation of structure? An object of idealized imitation? A type, template or design?', (2010) 15 Unif. L. Rev., (419) 421.

557 N. COHEN, 'Should UNCITRAL prepare a model law on secured transactions', (2010) 15 Unif. L. Rev., (325) 327; R. MACDONDALD, 'A model law on secured transactions. A representation of structure? An object of idealized imitation? A type, template or design?', (2010) 15 Unif. L. Rev., (419) 421.

558 S. BAZINAS, 'The UNCITRAL legislative guide on secured transactions and draft UNCITRAL model law on secured transactions compared' in L. GULLIFER and O. AKSELI (eds.), *Secured transactions law reform*, (Oxford: Hart Publishing, 2016), (481) 481.

559 S. BAZINAS, 'The UNCITRAL legislative guide on secured transactions and draft UNCITRAL model law on secured transactions compared' in L. GULLIFER and O. AKSELI (eds.), *Secured transactions law reform*, (Oxford: Hart Publishing, 2016), (481) 482.

560 J.-H. ROVER, 'The EBRD's Model Law on Secured Transactions and its implications for an UNCITRAL Model Law on Secured Transactions', (2010) 15 Unif. L. Rev., (479) 504.

561 S. BAZINAS, 'The UNCITRAL legislative guide on secured transactions and draft UNCITRAL model law on secured transactions compared' in L. GULLIFER and O. AKSELI (eds.), *Secured transactions law reform*, (Oxford: Hart Publishing, 2016), (481) 482.

Guide and the UNCITRAL Model Law: its perceived similarity with Article 9 UCC of the United States.[562] As we will see in more detail later, the UNCITRAL Guide and UNCITRAL Model Law introduce a functional approach in which all secured transactions in movable goods that perform the same function (i.e. guaranteeing credit by obtaining or retaining a proprietary interest in a movable good) are governed by one set of rules or at least different sets of rules that result in equivalent legal outcomes.[563] Undeniably, this approach is very similar to the approach in Article 9 UCC.[564] For some authors, this similarity to Article 9 UCC is perceived as a significant problem in the promulgation and potential adoption of the UNCITRAL Guide and UNCITRAL Model Law.[565] More specifically, there is a worry that the UNCITRAL Guide and UNCITRAL Model Law are in fact neo-liberal instruments that will rewrite secured transactions law on a global level on the basis of an American playbook.[566] The drafters of the UNCITRAL counter the perceived influence of the United States by stating that the UNCITRAL Guide and UNCITRAL Model Law are not an international convention and do not have the power, nor intention to rewrite secured transactions law on such a scale.[567] Additionally, the drafters refer to the other sources were they got their inspiration for the development of the UNCITRAL Guide and UNCITRAL Model Law (i.e. the PPSA's of the Canadian territories, Australia, New Zealand, etc.).[568] Unfortunately, it does not help their case that these regimes themselves are heavily based on Article 9 UCC.

Evidently, the idea that one jurisdiction steered the development of two instruments that are supposed to be a global framework for secured transactions does not look good. However, the problem of similarity between Article 9 UCC on the one hand and the UNCITRAL Guide and UNCITRAL Model Law on the other hand seems to be blown out of proportion. The Working Group was always clear that it wanted to modernize what they deem outdated legal frameworks for secured transactions.[569] Given the inefficiencies it saw in many unreformed

562 S. BAZINAS, 'The utility and efficacy of the UNCITRAL legislative guide on secured transactions' in O. AKSELI (ed.), *Availibility of credit in a time of crisis*, (Cambridge: Cambridge University Press, 2013), (133) 172–173.

563 See *infra* no. 117.

564 See *supra* no. 35.

565 G. MCCORMACK, 'American private law writ large? The UNCITRAL secured transactions guide', (2011) 60 Int'l. & Comp. L. Q., (597) 598 and 602.

566 S. BAZINAS, 'The utility and efficacy of the UNCITRAL legislative guide on secured transactions' in O. AKSELI (ed.), *Availibility of credit in a time of crisis*, (Cambridge: Cambridge University Press, 2013), (133) 172–173.

567 S. BAZINAS, 'The utility and efficacy of the UNCITRAL legislative guide on secured transactions' in O. AKSELI (ed.), *Availibility of credit in a time of crisis*, (Cambridge: Cambridge University Press, 2013), (133) 173.

568 S. BAZINAS, 'The utility and efficacy of the UNCITRAL legislative guide on secured transactions' in O. AKSELI (ed.), *Availability of credit in a time of crisis*, (Cambridge: Cambridge University Press, 2013), (133) 175.

569 Working Group VI (Security Interests), Draft legislative guide on secured transactions – background remarks, UNCITRAL, (New York, 2007), 1 *et seq.*

jurisdictions, such as panoply of possessory and non-possessory security rights, lack of registration system and outdated enforcement methods, I can understand the drafters went to look for inspirations in jurisdictions where they have gone in an entirely different direction, such as Article 9 UCC and the PPSA's from Canada, Australia and New Zealand. The inspiration upon these regimes was not part of a nefarious imperialistic plot to secretly indoctrinate all jurisdictions into the Article 9 UCC framework, but was simply pragmatic since these systems offer a new and, according to the drafters, a more modern and efficient approach to secured transactions. Certain rules and policies from the UNCITRAL Guide and UNCITRAL Model law should not be rejected out of hand because they can be found in Article 9 UCC. Likewise, policies and rules should not simply be accepted because they can also be found in Article 9 UCC.[570] Furthermore, the goal of the UNCITRAL drafters was not to create a neutral amalgam or common denominator of all existing secured transactions regimes in the world without preference for any particular approach or even regime. The drafters developed what they consider a more efficient and modern way to regulate secured transactions.[571] Evidently, authors and states have the prerogative to disagree with this assessment, but the choice to take inspiration in some regards from Article 9 UCC does not automatically undermine the value or usefulness of the UNCITRAL Guide or UNCITRAL Model Law.

1.2. Functional approach in the UNCITRAL Guide and Model Law

117. *The functional approach as policy choice* – As mentioned, the UNCITRAL Guide and UNCITRAL Model Law adopt a functional approach for their secured transactions regime.[572] The choice for the functional approach is even listed as one of the main policies upon which the UNCITRAL Guide is based:

> *Many States have secured transactions regimes that permit grantors (especially companies) to offer security to creditors based upon all (or substantially all) of their assets. Nonetheless, in many of these States different legislative regimes govern different types of assets. Moreover, in many of these States different legislative regimes govern different types of transactions, such as pledges, mortgages, fiduciary transfers and*

570 H. BEALE, 'The UNCITRAL Legislative Guide on Secured Transactions as a model for law reform: some conclusions' in O. AKSELI (ed.), *Availibility of credit and secured transactions in a time of crisis*, (Cambridge: Cambridge University Press, 2013), (275) 280.

571 O. AKSELI, *International secured transactions law – Facilitation of credit and international conventions and instruments*, (London: Routledge, 2001), 16.

572 S. BAZINAS, 'Key objectives and fundamental principles of the UNCITRAL legislative guide on secured transactions', (2008) 2 Insolvency & Restructuring Int'l., (42) 42; S. BAZINAS, 'Acquisition financing under the UNCITRAL legislative guide on secured transactions', (2011) 16 Unif. L. Rev., (483) 484; G. CASTELLANO and A. TOSATO, 'Personal property security law: international ambitions and local realities' in L. GHIA (ed.), *International business law*, (Wolters Kluwer, 2019), (283) 302.

> *hypothecs. Finally, in many States, the rights of sellers are treated differently from the rights of other providers of credit and are often not considered to be security rights at all. In contrast to this diversity, the Guide adopts what might be characterized as an integrated and functional approach. It takes the position that, to the maximum extent possible, all transactions that create a right in any type of asset meant to secure the performance of an obligation (that is, to fulfil security functions) should be considered to be secured transactions and regulated by the same rules or, at least, by the same principles.*[573] (emphasis added)

The idea for this approach stems from the observation that many non-possessory security rights, possessory security rights, transfer of title and retention of title mechanisms are based on identical guiding principles that aim at achieving the same economic outcomes and the same economic function of securing repayment of an obligation.[574] For most secured transactions in movable goods, the adoption of the functional and integrated approach in the UNCITRAL Guide will not only imply a unification of rules and requirements across formerly different secured transactions in movable goods, such as pledge and floating charges, but also the recharacterization of these categories of secured transactions to the general category of security right.

The functional approach in the UNCITRAL Guide and UNCITRAL Model Law is very similar to the substance over form approach in Article 9 UCC. Nevertheless, the drafters clarify that the choice for the functional and integrated approach is not due to a certain preference for one or another legal system. It is mainly introduced to address the fragmentation of security mechanisms that in fact perform the same function.[575] According to the drafters of the UNCITRAL Guide there is no viable alternative to the functional approach as a way of addressing the gaps and inconsistencies of legal systems that do not have a comprehensive and rational code on secured transactions in movable goods.[576]

118. *Advantages and disadvantages to the adoption of the functional approach* – According to the UNCITRAL Guide, there are several advantages to adopting the functional approach. First, all statutes and provisions concerning non-possessory security rights can be merged in one text together with the possessory security rights.[577] This reasoning is based on the fact that in many,

---

573 UNCITRAL Guide, 23.

574 UNCITRAL Guide, 56 and 320.

575 S. BAZINAS, 'The utility and efficacy of the UNCITRAL legislative guide on secured transactions' in O. AKSELI (ed.), *Availibility of credit in a time of crisis*, (Cambridge: Cambridge University Press, 2013), (133) 141; S. MITSDÖRFFER, *Sicherungsrechte an Schutzrechten – Ein Vergleich zwischen dem deutschen Recht and dem UNCITRAL Legislative Guide on Secured Transactions*, (Karlsruhe: Mohr Siebeck, 2013), 13.

576 S. BAZINAS, 'The utility and efficacy of the UNCITRAL legislative guide on secured transactions' in O. AKSELI (ed.), *Availibility of credit in a time of crisis*, (Cambridge: Cambridge University Press, 2013), (133) 174.

577 UNCITRAL Guide, 56.

especially civil law, jurisdictions various forms of non-possessory secured transactions in movable goods have come into existence, often to avoid the more stringent rules concerning the possessory pledge.[578] By adopting a functional and integrated approach the rules governing these different transactions can be unified in one text that includes rules for both possessory and non-possessory security rights. Second, the provisions concerning possessory security rights can be modernized.[579] However, the UNCITRAL Guide does not further explain what it means by modernizing. Does this mean that possessory security rights should be abandoned or that possessory security rights should remain possible but with more modern features, such as extra-judicial enforcement? It is hard to imagine a modern form of a possessory security right, since it is inherently an old-fashioned form of securing credit. Third, security mechanisms based on title (transfer and retention of title mechanisms) can be integrated in a way that gives the creditor sufficient protection while providing the debtor with sufficient rights in the encumbered good to make use of it. Fourth, contractual security mechanisms (such as leasing, sale and resale, sale and lease-back) can be included without creating confusion on their priority in conflict with other creditors. Fifth, the approach increases competition by placing sellers, lessors and lenders on a level playing field. Finally, the functional and integrated approach simplifies cross-border transactions, since a comprehensive security right has a better chance of being recognized.[580] This last argument is interesting, since the drafters of the DCFR explicitly choose not to recharacterize retention of title devices to acquisition security rights to avoid that this new type of security right would not be recognized in cross-border transactions.[581]

There are also disadvantages associated with the introduction of the integrated and functional approach, especially the recharacterization aspect. First, the functional approach combined with recharacterization of secured transactions will likely require training programs and re-education for practitioners. Second, the adoption of the functional approach in many jurisdictions will mean an adjustment to a fundamental and logical underpinning of many secured transactions regimes: the *numerus clausus*. Most jurisdictions have a limited set of security rights that can only be vested in certain goods and for certain obligations. Conversely, the functional approach adheres to a general principle that favors the distribution of secured credit and thus not limits itself to certain transactions with a certain name, certain assets or certain obligations. Finally, the functional approach is best introduced in a

---

578 E. M. KIENINGER, 'Introduction: security rights in movable property within the common market and the approach of the study' in E.-M. KIENINGER (ed.), *Security rights in movable property in European private law*, (Cambridge: Cambridge University Press, 2004), (1) 10.

579 UNCITRAL Guide, 56.

580 UNCITRAL Guide, 56.

581 See *infra* no. 160.

single piece of legislation. However, for many states this will include significant changes to their existing civil and commercial codes.[582]

Notwithstanding the disadvantages, the UNCITRAL Guide recommends the adoption of a comprehensive, functional and integrated approach to secured transactions.[583] This means that states should enact frameworks that achieve functionally equivalent outcomes for functionally equivalent mechanisms.[584] Or in other words that to the maximum extent possible, all transactions that create a right in a movable good meant to secure the performance of an obligation should be considered as a secured transaction and regulated by the same rules[585], regardless of the form of the transaction or the used terminology.[586]

119. *Introduction of the unitary and non-unitary approach* – However, to address some of the criticisms concerning the functional and integrated approach the drafters developed two methods of achieving a functional and integrated framework: the unitary and the non-unitary approach.[587] Basically, under the unitary approach, all secured transactions in movable goods that perform the same function are recharacterized to either security rights or acquisition security rights, depending on the type of financing they guarantee[588] (i.e. *functional approach with recharacterization*).[589] Under the non-unitary approach, the drafters allow that title-based secured transactions, more specifically retention of title and finance leasing, that guarantee acquisition financing maintain their original names and remain governed by their own rules. However, the rules governing retention of title and finance leasing would still have to be amended to make sure that equivalent legal outcomes are achieved between acquisition security, retention of title and finance leasing[590] (i.e. *functional approach without recharacterization*).[591] How these different approaches are specifically applied to

---

582 UNCITRAL Guide, 57.

583 UNCITRAL Guide, recommendation 8.

584 UNCITRAL Guide, 336.

585 S. BAZINAS, 'Key objectives and fundamental principles of the UNCITRAL legislative guide on secured transactions', (2008) 2 Insolvency & Restructuring Int'l., (42) 45; S. BAZINAS, 'Acquisition financing under the UNCITRAL legislative guide on secured transactions', (2011) 16 Unif. L. Rev., (483) 485.

586 J. KLEIN, 'UNCITRAL Legislative Guide on Secured Transactions: an introduction and overview', (2009) Am. Bankr. Inst. L. J., (28) 30; S. BAZINAS, 'The work of UNCITRAL on security interest: an overview', (2010) 15 Unif. L. Rev., (315) 319; O. AKSELI, *International secured transactions law – Facilitation of credit and international conventions and instruments*, (London: Routledge, 2001), 88; S. BAZINAS, 'The utility and efficacy of the UNCITRAL legislative guide on secured transactions' in O. AKSELI (ed.), *Availibility of credit in a time of crisis*, (Cambridge: Cambridge University Press, 2013), (133) 139–140.

587 UNCITRAL Guide, 58.

588 See *supra* no. 3.

589 See *supra* no. 123.

590 UNCITRAL Guide, 58. See also, O. AKSELI, *International secured transactions law – Facilitation of credit and international conventions and instruments*, (London: Routledge, 2001), 243.

591 See *supra* no. 4.

retention of title and finance leasing is discussed in the section concerning the scope of the UNCITRAL Guide and the UNCITRAL Model Law.

1.3. Application of the functional approach to retention of title and finance leasing

120. *Overview* – In the following section, I discuss how the two functional approaches (i.e. the unitary and non-unitary approach) are applied to retention of title in sale and finance lease agreements. More specifically, these sections focus on the scope of the UNCITRAL Guide and UNCITRAL Model Law (1.3.1.), the creation and third-party effectiveness of retention of title (1.3.2.) and the rights of retention of title creditors (1.3.3.).

1.3.1. Scope

121. *Advantages of broad scope for security rights* – The UNCITRAL Guide works under the assumption that the broader the scope of the secured transactions regime, the more efficient and effective it will be.[592] The regime should govern a broad range of transactions that serve a security function, including those that are not named as security rights but serve the same purpose.[593] Examples are: transfers of title in tangible assets and receivables for security purposes, retention of title and finance leasing.[594]

122. *Impact of unitary and non-unitary approach on scope of (acquisition) security rights* – A big difference between the two approaches in the UNCITRAL Guide is that under the unitary approach, all secured transactions that perform the same function are recharacterized to a security right and potentially an acquisition security right if they guarantee acquisition financing. Consequently, all these transactions fall within the scope of security rights and acquisition security rights. However, under the non-unitary approach certain title-based secured transactions that guarantee acquisition financing, such as retention of title and finance leasing, are not recharacterized. Nevertheless, under the non-unitary approach these transactions still fall within the scope of the UNCITRAL Guide. In this scenario, these transactions are not recharacterized but the rules governing these transactions are amended where necessary to guarantee that equivalent legal outcomes with acquisition security rights are achieved.

---

592 UNCITRAL Guide, 32.

593 UNCITRAL Guide, 34 and recommendation 2, (d).

594 UNCITRAL Guide, 35.

A. UNITARY APPROACH

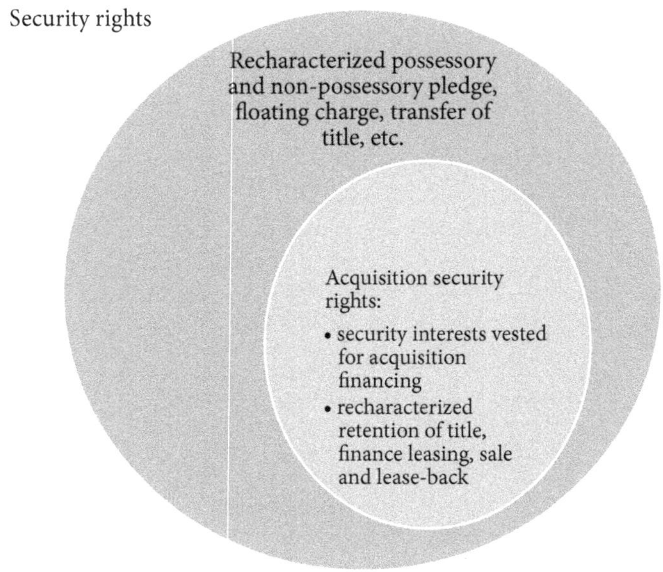

123. *Definitions of (acquisition) security rights under the unitary approach* – In the unitary approach, all types of secured transactions in movable goods are abolished and subsumed into a single, uniform notion of security right. According to the UNCITRAL Guide and Model Law a security right is:

> *A property right in a movable asset that is created by an agreement to secure payment or other performance of an obligation, regardless of whether the parties have denominated it as a security right, and regardless of the type of asset, the status of the grantor or secured creditor, or the nature of the secured obligation.*[595]

Within the category of security rights there is a sub-category of acquisition security rights. According to the definition in the UNCITRAL Guide and Model Law, an acquisition security right is:

> *A security right in a tangible asset (other than a negotiable instrument or negotiable document) that secures the obligation to pay any unpaid portion of the purchase price*

[595] UNCITRAL Guide, 13; art. 2, (kk) UNCITRAL Model Law. In the UNCITRAL Guide, the drafters make adjustments to the definition for the application of either the unitary or non-unitary approach: *In the context of the unitary approach to acquisition financing, the term includes both acquisition security rights and non-acquisition security rights. In the context of the non-unitary approach to acquisition financing, it does not include a retention-of-title or financial lease right. Although an outright transfer of a receivable does not secure payment or other performance of an obligation, for convenience of reference the term also includes the right of the assignee in an outright transfer of a receivable. The term does not include a personal right against a guarantor or other person liable for the payment of the secured obligation.*

of the asset or an obligation incurred or credit otherwise provided to enable the grantor to acquire the asset.[596]

Under the unitary approach, the category of acquisition security rights also includes recharacterized retention of title clauses in sale agreements and finance leases for security purposes.[597] The key features of acquisition security rights are: (a) the credit is used for the specific purpose of enabling the buyer or lessee to acquire a tangible asset; (b) the rights being claimed or retained relate directly to the asset being acquired; and (c) the rights being claimed arise by virtue of an agreement[598]

124. *Specific impact of the unitary approach on title-based mechanisms* – An important consequence of the unitary approach is that the debtor is considered the owner of the encumbered goods even though the goods were acquired via what would be considered a retention of title transaction under the pre-unitary approach, such as a sale with retention of title or a finance lease.[599] Following this consequence, states have to decide whether the debtor will be considered the owner of the encumbered good in all legal domains (such as tax law) or only in the context of secured transactions law.[600]

B. Non-unitary approach

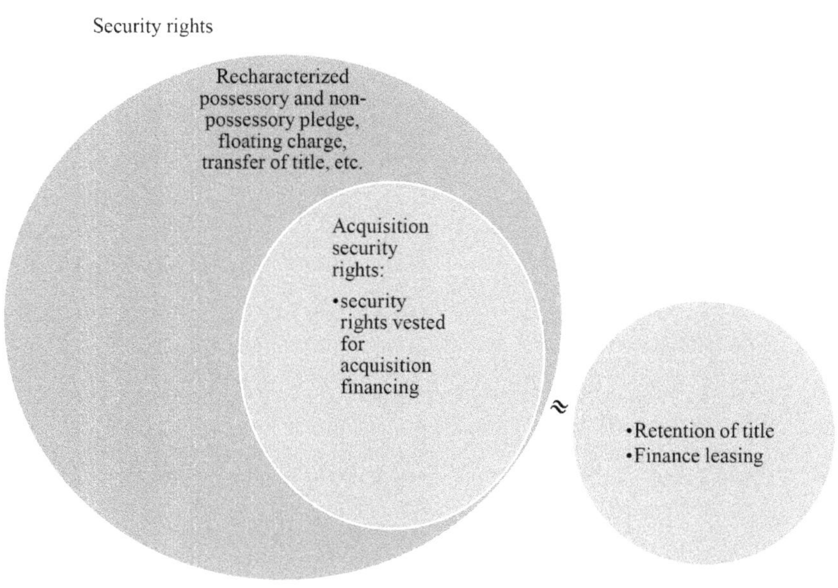

596 UNCITRAL Guide, 6 and 320; art. 2, (b) UNCITRAL Model Law.
597 UNCITRAL Guide, 58.
598 UNCITRAL Guide, 58, 320 and recommendation 9, (b).
599 UNCITRAL Guide, 337.
600 UNCITRAL Guide, 337.

125. *The non-unitary approach* – Only in the UNCITRAL Guide and only for secured transactions that guarantee acquisition financing[601], the drafters offer an alternative method to achieve functional equivalence between functionally similar secured transactions: the UNCITRAL non-unitary approach.[602] Basically, under this approach title-based secured transactions that guarantee acquisition financing, such as retention of title[603] in sale agreements and finance leases[604], are maintained and are not recharacterized as a security right.[605] However, to ensure that functional equivalence results in equivalent legal outcomes, the rules governing retention of title and finance leasing are adjusted, where necessary, to have the same legal outcomes as the rules governing acquisition security rights.[606] The hope is that this approach makes states more receptive to the idea of a consolidated framework for all secured transactions in movable goods, including those based on title.[607]

126. *Two approaches to adoption of the non-unitary approach* – The non-unitary approach can be achieved in two ways: (1) the rights of retention of title creditors can be modeled after the rights of acquisition security holders or (2) the rights of acquisition security right holders can be modeled after the rights of retention of title creditors and financial lessors.[608] The UNCITRAL Guide prefers the system where the rights of retention of title creditors and financial lessors are modeled after those of acquisition security right holders.[609] This approach is preferred for various reasons. First, it would be hard to treat lenders

---

601 Acquisition financing refers to credit in the form of an unpaid portion of the purchase price or credit otherwise provided to enable the grantor to acquire a good (UNCITRAL Guide, 6).

602 UNCITRAL Guide, 58.

603 *A seller's right in a tangible asset (other than a negotiable instrument or a negotiable document) pursuant to an arrangement with the buyer by which ownership of the asset is not transferred (or is not transferred irrevocably) from the seller to the buyer until the unpaid portion of the purchase price is paid* (UNCITRAL Guide, 12).

604 *A lessor's right in a tangible asset (other than a negotiable instrument or negotiable document) that is the object of a lease agreement under which, at the end of the lease:*
(a) The lessee automatically becomes the owner of the asset that is the object of the lease;
(b) The lessee may acquire ownership of the asset by paying no more than a nominal price; or
(c) The asset has no more than a nominal residual value.
The term includes a hire-purchase agreement, even if not nominally referred to as a lease, provided that it meets the requirements of subparagraph (a), (b) or (c) (UNCITRAL Guide, 9).

605 O. AKSELI, *International secured transactions law – Facilitation of credit and international conventions and instruments*, (London: Routledge, 2001), 236.

606 S. BAZINAS, 'Acquisition financing under the UNCITRAL legislative guide on secured transactions', (2011) 16 Unif. L. Rev., (483) 486 – 487; G. MCCORMACK, 'American private law writ large? The UNCITRAL secured transactions guide', (2011) 60 Int'l. & Comp. L. Q., (597) 618.

607 O. AKSELI, *International secured transactions law – Facilitation of credit and international conventions and instruments*, (London: Routledge, 2001), 17.

608 UNCITRAL Guide, 338.

609 UNCITRAL Guide, 338.

like owners and to adjust the rules concerning these transactions accordingly. Second, these lenders would never be able to achieve the full status of absolute owner, since their enforcement rights would have to be adjusted to account for certain rights of third parties that have obtained rights in the encumbered good. Third, it is considered too complicated to design a set of rules that would distinguish between the ordinary secured lenders, who would only have a proprietary interest in the encumbered good, and acquisition secured lenders, who under the second approach would have to be viewed as owners. Finally, it would benefit the overall coherence of the secured transactions regime when retention of title and finance leases are modeled after security rights, since they make up the bulk of the secured transactions.[610]

The arguments that (1) it would be difficult to treat acquisition security right holders as owners, (2) acquisition security right holders could never obtain the same protection as absolute owners of a good and (3) that the distinction between ordinary security rights and acquisition security rights would be hard to make are not that convincing. First, it would arguably be as difficult to treat an acquisition security right as a form of ownership as it would be to treat retention of title creditors and lessors as merely secured lenders. Both approaches require a thorough analysis of the applicable rules and their legal outcomes to then make adjustments that would put both mechanisms on a level playing field. Moreover, one can even argue that it might be easier to convince creditors weary of this new system that they will be upgraded to "owner" than to convince retention of title creditors and financial lessors that they will be "downgraded" to secured lender. In the same vein, the argument that it would be impossible to protect acquisition security right holders as owners as opposed to third parties seems an exaggeration. In the end, the protection of creditor-owners is determined by the legislator and if the legislator chooses to expand this to acquisition security rights based on their functional similarity, I see no reason why this cannot be done. Whether this will fit with jurisdictions' legal tradition, culture or history is a different matter. However, this is a matter that each jurisdiction would have to decide for themselves, but should not be immediately ruled out by the UNCITRAL Guide. Of course, a lot of the perceived difficulty has to do with how much retention of title creditors and financial lessors are still treated as owners. In jurisdictions were the position of retention of title creditor or lessor is still associated with the protection of an absolute owner, the transition to a secured acquisition lender can be perceived as a downgrade or the transition to a creditor-owner can be perceived as an upgrade. However, in jurisdictions where the protection of retention of title creditors and lessors has already been somewhat equated with those of secured lenders, the transition in either direction will likely not have a significant impact. The third argument concerning the problems discerning between normal secured lenders and

610 UNCITRAL Guide, 338.

acquisition secured lenders is less convincing, because this problem is not resolved by treating retention of title and finance leasing as acquisition security rights. In that scenario, a distinction will still have to be made between ordinary security rights and acquisition security rights, since, as we will see hereafter, acquisition security rights have some special features, such as super-priority and specific rules concerning third-party effectiveness.[611] Consequently, there will always be some rules specific for acquisition security rights and thus a need for characteristics or criteria that allow to distinguish between the two.

I do agree with the argument that the adjustment of retention of title and finance leasing to acquisition security rights fits better with the overall coherence of the recommended legal framework in the UNCITRAL Guide. The drafters made a clear choice for a security right-based approach in the UNCITRAL Guide, and even more so in the UNCITRAL Model Law. It would then be strange to within that system have security rights that are actually more akin to ownership. The coherence argument is sufficient to favor the model based on acquisition security rights over the model based on retention of title and leasing. In the end, the drafters aim to create a more efficient secured transactions regime and presumably the more coherent the regime is, the more efficient it can be implemented and operate.

1.3.2. Creation and third-party effectiveness

127. *Overview* – In this section, I set out the rules for (a) the creation and (b) third-party effectiveness of security rights in the UNCITRAL Guide and UNCITRAL Model Law and the extent to which these rules extend to retention of title mechanisms and finance leases.

A. Creation

128. *Separating creation from third-party effectiveness* – The UNCITRAL Guide and UNCITRAL Model Law make a clear distinction between the creation of a security right and its third-party effectiveness.[612] The reasoning goes that by separating these two actions, the creation of a security right can be kept as simple as possible. Generally, when the creation and third-party effectiveness happen simultaneously, additional formalities are added in order to guarantee that third parties are made aware of the security right and are protected.[613] This would go against the UNCITRAL Guide's and UNCITRAL Model Law's policy

[611] See *infra* no. 131 *et seq.* and 143 *et seq.*

[612] UNCITRAL Guide, 65; S. BAZINAS, 'Acquisition financing under the UNCITRAL legislative guide on secured transactions', (2011) 16 Unif. L. Rev., (483) 488.

[613] UNCITRAL Guide, 66.

to make the creation of security rights as uncomplicated as possible.[614] Therefore, the creation of the security right only creates effects between the parties to the security agreement.

129. *Requirements for creation of security rights* – With regards to the rules for the creation of security rights, a distinction has to be made between the unitary and non-unitary approach. Under the unitary approach, a retention of title transaction and finance lease are recharacterized as acquisition security rights. Furthermore, acquisition security rights are created in the same way as security rights.[615] Consequently, the rules concerning the creation of security rights apply to acquisition security rights and thus to former retention of title agreements and finance leases.[616]

According to the UNCITRAL Guide, a security agreement must meet the following requirements:

(a) reflect the intent of the parties to create a security right;
(b) identify the secured creditor and the grantor;
(c) describe the secured obligation;
(d) describe the encumbered assets in a manner that reasonably allows their identification; and
(e) indicate the maximum monetary amount for which the security right may be enforced, if the State determines that such an indication would be helpful to facilitate subordinate lending.[617]

In the UNCITRAL Model Law similar requirements are imposed[618], except that the UNCITRAL Model Law does not mention the intention of the parties as a specific requirement for the creation of the security right in the security agreement. Furthermore, in both the UNCITRAL Guide and UNCITRAL Model Law, the creation of an acquisition security right does not require parties to mention that they are creating a specific acquisition security right. In other words, the intention to create an acquisition security right can only be deduced from the fact that the security right guarantees acquisition financing. With regards to the formalities, the security agreement does not have to be in writing, unless the debtor remains in or obtains possession of the encumbered

614 S. BAZINAS, 'Acquisition financing under the UNCITRAL legislative guide on secured transactions', (2011) 16 Unif. L. Rev., (483) 488; A. M. GARRO, 'The creation of a security right and its extension to acquisition financing devices', (2010) 15 Unif. L. Rev., (375) 380.
615 S. BAZINAS, 'Acquisition financing under the UNCITRAL legislative guide on secured transactions', (2011) 16 Unif. L. Rev., (483) 489.
616 UNCITRAL Guide, recommendation 189; S. BAZINAS, 'Acquisition financing under the UNCITRAL legislative guide on secured transactions', (2011) 16 Unif. L. Rev., (483) 489.
617 UNCITRAL Guide, recommendation 14.
618 Art. 6 UNCITRAL Model Law.

good.[619] Moreover, both the UNCITRAL Guide and UNCITRAL Model Law seem to adopt a relatively flexible interpretation of what they consider a written agreement for the creation of a security right, such as electronic communications or general terms and conditions.[620]

Fortunately for retention of title creditors and financial lessors, the requirements for the creation of a security right and the formalities for the security agreement can generally be found in a sale with retention of title or financial lease agreement. Consequently, retention of title creditors and financial lessors would not have to significantly adjust the way in which they draft their agreements in order to conform with these requirements.

130. *Non-unitary requirements for creation of an acquisition security right* – Under the non-unitary approach, the UNCITRAL Guide recommends that states develop a regime for the creation of acquisition security rights that permits the acquisition security right creditor to achieve the same status as a retention of title creditor or financial lessor.[621] This phrasing is somewhat strange, since earlier in the UNCITRAL Guide it is recommended that retention of title and finance leasing should be modeled after acquisition security rights and not the other way around. This means that the requirements for creating a retention of title or finance lease would have to be mirrored after the requirements for the creation of an acquisition security right. In practice this should not be so difficult since many of the requirements for the creation of an acquisition security right, such as the intention of the parties, the identification of the encumbered good and secured obligation, are present in most sale agreements with retention of title and finance leases. Consequently, the rules concerning the creation of retention of title and finance leasing will likely not have to be adjusted significantly. What can be a significant adjustment for retention of title and finance leasing is that now the creation of the retention of title and finance lease only has effect between the parties, but is not yet effective against third parties. In many jurisdictions, the simple act of creating a retention of title or finance lease also makes it effective against third parties.[622] The separation of the creation of retention of title and finance leases from its third-party effectiveness can be an impactful change in many jurisdictions.

The UNCITRAL Guide continues that to achieve equivalent legal outcomes for acquisition security rights, retention of title and finance leasing, states would have to ensure that the rules governing creation as between the parties would

619 UNCITRAL Guide, recommendation 15, art. 6, 4 Model Law.

620 UNCITRAL Guide, 72; J. KLEIN, 'UNCITRAL Legislative Guide on Secured Transactions: an introduction and overview', (2009) Am. Bankr. Inst. L. J., (28) 29.

621 UNCITRAL Guide, 342; G. CASTELLANO and A. TOSATO, 'Personal property security law: international ambitions and local realities' in L. GHIA (ed.), *International business law*, (Wolters Kluwer, 2019), (283) 303.

622 UNCITRAL Guide, 54.

be equivalent, regardless of the form of the acquisition financing transaction. In particular, the rules governing: (a) the capacity of parties to the contract; (b) the specific character and modalities of the obligation secured; (c) the assets in which the acquisition financing right might be taken; (d) evidentiary obligations such as a writing and signature; and (e) the time of effectiveness of the agreement between the parties would have to be closely coordinated so as not to favor one type of acquisition financing transaction over another.[623] For example, states using the non-unitary approach would have to decide what will be considered a newly acquired good in which the secured creditor can vest an acquisition security right and whether the position of acquisition security right holder can be extended beyond the immediate acquisition financing. Generally, in states adhering to the non-unitary approach, these limitations will be set in the retention of title or lease agreement itself. For example, a typical sale with retention of title automatically limits the protection of the retained title to the outstanding purchase price and potentially some associated costs. However, in the case of an acquisition security right it would have to be clearly stipulated in the security agreement which debt is secured with which newly acquired good. Conversely, the creation of retention of title and finance lease agreement may have to be become somewhat more formalistic in order to be functionally equivalent with the creation of acquisition security rights. As the UNCITRAL Guide points out, in many states that seem prone to adopt the non-unitary approach, retention of title can be vested very informally as part of a sale agreement with minimum information requirement or sometimes even orally.[624] Were such states to adopt the non-unitary approach, they would have to extend the formalities for the creation of acquisition security rights to retention of title and leasing to ensure a level playing field.

B. Third-party effectiveness

131. *Methods of achieving third-party effectiveness* – As mentioned, the UNCITRAL Guide and UNCITRAL Model Law require a second step to make a security right effective against third parties.[625] Consequently, until a security right is made effective the secured creditor can only enforce his security right against the debtor.[626] There are several arguments in favor of the implementation of a notification requirement for security rights: (1) it provides third parties with objective evidence that a good is already encumbered, (2) there is no need for

623 UNCITRAL Guide, 342; G. CASTELLANO and A. TOSATO, 'Personal property security law: international ambitions and local realities' in L. GHIA (ed.), *International business law*, (Wolters Kluwer, 2019), (283) 303.

624 UNCITRAL Guide, 340.

625 UNCITRAL Guide, 103; J. KLEIN, 'UNCITRAL Legislative Guide on Secured Transactions: an introduction and overview', (2009) Am. Bankr. Inst. L. J., (28) 29.

626 UNCITRAL Guide, 104.

special rules protecting third parties against the risk posed by secret security rights in the debtor's assets and (3) the notification requirement generally establishes a defined temporal event that can easily be used to determine the order of priority between a secured creditor and a competing claimant.[627]

The UNCITRAL Guide recommends that security rights are made effective against third parties via either possession[628], control[629] or registration.[630] The general method of obtaining third-party effectiveness is registration of a security right notice in a general security right registry.[631] The notice is a document with minimal information[632] in which the grantor of the security right and the secured creditor[633], the encumbered assets[634], the duration of the registration[635] and, if the adopting state so chooses, the maximum monetary amount for which the security right may be enforced, are identified. Furthermore, states can decide to let the parties to the security, retention of title or finance lease agreement to indicate in the notice that they are vesting an acquisition security right, retention of title or lease.[636] This will then signal to third parties checking the registry that they are dealing with a secured transaction that guarantees acquisition financing and may be entitled to specific protections, such as super-priority.[637] Since this notice is a separate document from the security agreement, it can be filed prior to the actual closing of the security agreement.[638]

For the two other methods of third-party effectiveness the formalities are less stringent. For third-party effectiveness via possession, the debtor simply has to transfer physical possession of the encumbered good to the secured creditor[639] or a third party.[640] Constructive or symbolic possession of the encumbered good in the hands of the secured creditor is not accepted.[641] The third-party effectiveness via control is a specific method that applies to security rights in intangible assets, such as the right to payment of funds credited to a bank account.[642] Since the

---

627 UNCITRAL Guide, 103.

628 UNCITRAL Guide, recommendation 34 (a) (i).

629 UNCITRAL Guide, recommendation 34 (a) (v).

630 UNCITRAL Guide, recommendation 32.

631 UNCITRAL Guide, 108 and recommendation 32; art. 18 UNCITRAL Model Law; G. CASTELLANO and A. TOSATO, 'Personal property security law: international ambitions and local realities' in L. GHIA (ed.), *International business law*, (Wolters Kluwer, 2019), (283) 303.

632 UNCITRAL Guide, recommendation 57; art. 8 UNCITRAL Model Law.

633 UNCITRAL Guide, recommendation 58–60; art. 9–10 UNCITRAL Model Law.

634 UNCITRAL Guide, recommendation 63 *juncto* recommendation 14; art. 11 UNCITRAL Model Law.

635 UNCITRAL Guide, recommendation 69.

636 UNCITRAL Guide, 345.

637 See *infra* no. 143 *et seq.*

638 UNCITRAL Guide, 111 and 344; art. 18 UNCITRAL Model Law.

639 UNCITRAL Guide, recommendation 37.

640 UNCITRAL Guide, recommendation 15 and 32; art. 18, par. 2 UNCITRAL Model Law.

641 UNCITRAL Guide, 116.

642 UNCITRAL Guide, recommendation 49; art. 25 UNCITRAL Model Law.

scope of this research is limited to tangible, movable goods, the method of achieving third-party effectiveness via control is not further discussed.

132. *Distinction in requirements under the unitary and non-unitary approach* – Under the unitary approach, the rules concerning third-party effectiveness uniformly applies to all security rights, including acquisition security rights, which include recharacterized retention of title and financial lease devices.[643]

Under the non-unitary approach, the UNCITRAL Guide recommends that retention of title agreements and finance leases are subjected to similar requirements for third-party effectiveness.[644] More specifically, retention of title and finance leases also need to be made effective against third parties via either registration of the retention of title or financial lease agreement, or any of the alternative forms of third-party effectiveness that are made available in the UNCITRAL Guide, such as possession or registration in a specialized registry.[645] For many states this will be a significant adjustment, since in many, especially civil law, jurisdictions, retention of title and financial lease agreements are exempt from any third-party effectiveness requirements.[646]

133. *Exceptions to requirements for third-party effectiveness* – The UNCITRAL Guide and UNCITRAL Model Law provide in exceptions for the requirements for third-party effectiveness of acquisition security rights and functionally equivalent mechanisms. For example, acquisition security rights, usually in equipment, can be given a grace period for their third-party effectiveness without it affecting their effectiveness or priority as opposed to competing third parties.[647] In other words, if the secured creditor registers the acquisition security right, retention of title or finance lease within the grace period, then he will still be given super-priority status.[648] Second, the UNCITRAL Guide and UNCITRAL Model Law also provide in an exception for acquisition security rights in consumer goods.[649] Under the non-unitary approach, these exceptions are extended to retention of title and finance lease agreements.[650]

---

643 S. BAZINAS, 'Acquisition financing under the UNCITRAL legislative guide on secured transactions', (2011) 16 Unif. L. Rev., (483) 490.

644 UNCITRAL Guide, 344; G. MCCORMACK, 'American private law writ large? The UNCITRAL secured transactions guide', (2011) 60 Int'l. & Comp. L. Q., (597) 617.

645 UNCITRAL Guide, 344.

646 UNCITRAL Guide, 342; E.-M. KIENINGER, 'Evaluation: a common? Convergences, subsisting differences and possible ways for harmonisation' in E.-M. KIENINGER (ed.), *Security rights in movable property in European private law*, (Cambridge: Cambridge University Press, 2004), (647) 658.

647 UNCITRAL Guide, 346 and recommendation 192.

648 UNCITRAL Guide, 346; art. 38 UNCITRAL Model Law.

649 UNCITRAL Guide, 347 and recommendation 179; S. BAZINAS, 'Acquisition financing under the UNCITRAL legislative guide on secured transactions', (2011) 16 Unif. L. Rev., (483) 488 and 491.

650 UNCITRAL Guide, 346.

1.3.3. Rights of retention of title creditors and financial lessors under the Guide

134. *Overview* – In this section, I set out the rights of retention of title creditors and financial lessors under both approaches in the UNCITRAL Guide and UNCITRAL Model Law. More specifically, I discuss (a) the right to dispose, (b) the right to (super-)priority and (c) the right to enforcement.

A. Right to dispose of the encumbered good

135. *Conflicting views on the right to dispose* – On the one hand, the retention of title in a sale or finance lease agreement implies that the retention of title creditor or lessor is still in a position to dispose of the encumbered good a second time. On the other hand, the recharacterization of retention of title and finance leasing under the unitary approach and the functional equivalence with acquisition security rights under the non-unitary approach raise the question whether this remains the case in the UNCITRAL Guide and UNCITRAL Model Law.

136. *The right to dispose under the unitary and non-unitary approach* – Under the unitary approach, the retention of title and finance leases are recharacterized to acquisition security rights. Following this recharacterization, title to the encumbered good is assumed to have transferred to the debtor and no longer resides with the retention of title creditor or financial lessor.[651] Consequently, the retention of title creditor and financial lessor do not have title to the encumbered good to potentially dispose of the good a second time.

Under the non-unitary approach, retention of title and finance leases are not recharacterized, maintaining the possibility that retention of title creditors and financial lessors can dispose of the encumbered good while it is encumbered with a retention of title or finance lease. However, the UNCITRAL Guide addresses this issue head on and recommends that the default rules concerning ownership, which is presumed to reside with the retention of title creditor or lessor, are reversed. Consequently, the retention of title creditor or lessor no longer has the right to the fruits of the encumbered good or the right to further encumber or dispose of the encumbered good.[652] This reversal makes sense, since otherwise acquisition security rights, retention of title and finance leasing would not result in equivalent legal outcomes. An acquisition security right holder only holds a security right in the encumbered good and this proprietary interest does not include the right to dispose of the collateral. Therefore, if retention of title creditors and financial lessors would have the right to dispose of the encumbered

[651] UNCITRAL Guide, 337 and 365.
[652] UNCITRAL Guide, 366–367.

good, this would undermine the goal of equivalent legal outcomes among the different types of acquisition financing.[653]

137. *The debtor's right to dispose?* – Logically, if the right to dispose no longer resides with the (former) retention of title creditor or financial lessor, it can be found in the hands of the debtor. However, the debtor cannot do as he pleases with the encumbered good. According to the UNCITRAL Guide and UNCITRAL Model Law, every (acquisition) security right comes with a right to trace the encumbered good into the hands of the third-party transferee[654], unless the encumbered good is sold within the ordinary course of business[655] or with the authorization of the creditor.[656] Under the non-unitary approach it is recommended that the rules concerning retention of title and finance leasing are adjusted to make sales of the encumbered good in the ordinary course of business possible. This adjustment of rights between the retention of title creditor/lessor and debtor falls under the general reversal of the default presumptions concerning the prerogatives of ownership, such as the right to dispose and the right to trace the encumbered good.[657] Consequently, under both approaches, the debtor has the right to dispose of the encumbered good but whether he can do it free of the attached encumbrance depends on the situation.

Fortunately for secured creditors, the UNCITRAL Guide recommends that acquisition security right holders can always trace their claim in the proceeds of the originally encumbered good[658] and that the rules for retention of title and finance leases should be similarly adapted.[659] This way, retention of title creditors, financial lessors and acquisition security right holders still have some collateral upon which they can enforce their claim in the event the encumbered good is sold in the ordinary course of business and the secured creditor cannot trace the encumbered good. However, in that case secured creditors have to make sure that the proceeds of the originally encumbered good can be identified.[660]

---

653 A. M. GARRO, 'The creation of a security right and its extension to acquisition financing devices', (2010) 15 Unif. L. Rev., (375) 386.

654 UNCITRAL Guide, 200; art. 34, 1 Model Law; S. BAZINAS, 'Acquisition financing under the UNCITRAL legislative guide on secured transactions', (2011) 16 Unif. L. Rev., (483) 492. See also *infra* no. 139.

655 In order for the third-party transferee to obtain the good free of the encumbrance: (1) the seller must be in the ordinary business of selling these goods and (2) the buyer must not have any knowledge that the sale violates the rights of a secured creditor (UNCITRAL Guide, 202; UNCITRAL Guide, 202; art. 34, 4–5 UNCITRAL Model Law).

656 UNCITRAL Guide, Art. 34, 2–3 Model Law.

657 UNCITRAL Guide, 366.

658 UNCITRAL Guide, 86 and recommendation 19; art 19 UNCITRAL Model Law; A. M. GARRO, 'The creation of a security right and its extension to acquisition financing devices', (2010) 15 Unif. L. Rev., (375) 382. See also *infra* no. 140

659 UNCITRAL Guide, 359 and recommendation 197.

660 A. M. GARRO, 'The creation of a security right and its extension to acquisition financing devices', (2010) 15 Unif. L. Rev., (375) 382.

For example, in the event the proceeds take the form of money the UNCITRAL Guide recommends that the money proceeds can still be identified in the mixed account as long as the amount of value of the mixed money is more than the amount of the proceeds themselves.[661]

B. Right to trace

138. *Overview* – The UNCITRAL Guide and Model Law provide unified rules concerning the tracing of retention of title or acquisition security rights in the encumbered good after it has undergone alterations. In the following sections, I look at tracing into the hands of the third-party transferee (i.), tracing into proceeds (ii.) and tracing into attachments and comingled goods (iii.).

i. *Tracing into the hands of a third-party transferee*

139. *General rules concerning tracing into the hands of a third-party transferee* – Under the UNCITRAL Guide and Model Law the secured creditor has the right to follow the encumbered asset into the hands of a third-party transferee when the security right was correctly made effective against third parties.[662] However, the UNCITRAL Guide and Model Law also provide exceptions to the right to follow when the encumbered good was sold in the ordinary course of business or with the permission of the secured creditor.[663]

Under both the unitary and non-unitary approach, retention of title and finance leases enjoy the same protection against third-party transferees. Under the unitary approach, the protection stems from the fact that effective acquisition security rights have the same effect as opposed to third parties as general security rights. Consequently, acquisition security rights also follow the encumbered good in the hands of the third-party transferee, unless the transfer falls under one of the abovementioned exceptions.[664] Under the non-unitary approach, the rules concerning retention of title and finance leasing are so adjusted that they achieve third-party effectiveness in the same manner as acquisition security rights and thereby are also effective against third-party transferees.[665]

ii. *Tracing into proceeds*

140. *General rules concerning tracing into proceeds* – Under the UNCITRAL Guide and Model Law, the goods encumbered with an acquisition security

661 UNCITRAL Guide, 88 and recommendation 20; art. 10 UNCITRAL Model Law. See also, A. M. GARRO, 'The creation of a security right and its extension to acquisition financing devices', (2010) 15 Unif. L. Rev., (375) 383.

662 UNCITRAL Guide, 107 and recommendation 31; art. 34 UNCITRAL Model Law.

663 UNCITRAL Guide, 107 and recommendation 80–81; art. 34, sec. 2–5 UNCITRAL Model Law.

664 UNCITRAL Guide, 344 and recommendations 178 and 188; art. 18 UNCITRAL Model Law.

665 UNCITRAL Guide, 345 and recommendations 191 *et seq.*

right or retention of title can be disposed of.[666] Fortunately for the security right holder, a security right automatically continues into the proceeds.[667] Furthermore, the UNCITRAL Guide and Model Law both have a broad definition of proceeds:

> *whatever is received in respect of encumbered assets, including what is received as a result of sale or other disposition or collection, lease or license of an encumbered asset, proceeds of proceeds, natural and civil fruits or revenues, dividends, distributions, insurance proceeds and claims arising from defects in, damage to or loss of an encumbered asset.*[668]

The drafters of the UNCITRAL Guide and Model Law are of the opinion that it is the usual expectation of the parties that their secured transaction extends to the proceeds of the originally encumbered good.[669] Consequently, no additional steps are necessary to create a security right that extends into the proceeds.[670] However, with regards to third-party effectiveness, the security right only automatically extends to proceeds when the proceeds take the form of money, receivables, negotiable instruments and rights to payment of funds credited to a bank account.[671] For other types of proceeds the secured creditor is given a short amount of time to make his security interest effective against third parties.[672] The reasoning goes that otherwise secured creditors could describe the encumbered assets so broadly that it would be very difficult for third parties to take notice of the debtor's encumbered collateral. For example, a security right vested in all the debtor's present and future field equipment could potentially extend to a tractor traded for a milking machine. It would be very difficult for third parties to discern based on the description in the registry that this milking machine was also part of the secured creditor's collateral. Consequently, the UNCITRAL Guide and Model Law recommend that an additional step is taken towards third-party effectiveness. A counterargument to this approach is that the description of the originally encumbered goods is usually broad enough to also cover the milking machine and that a third party can deduce from that description that the milking machine is covered by a security right, regardless of whether it is a form of proceeds or not.

---

666 See *supra* no. 136.

667 UNCITRAL Guide 124 and recommendation 19; art. 10 UNCITRAL Model Law. See also, A. M. GARRO, 'The creation of a security right and its extension to acquisition financing devices', (2010) 15 Unif. L. Rev., (375) 382.

668 UNCITRAL Guide,12; art. 2, (bb) Model Law.

669 UNCITRAL Guide, 86.

670 UNCITRAL Guide, recommendation 19 and 39.

671 UNCITRAL Guide, recommendation 39; art. 19, sec. 1 UNCITRAL Model Law.

672 UNCITRAL Guide, 127 and recommendation 40; art. 19, sec. 2 UNCITRAL Model Law.

141. *Distinction between unitary and non-unitary approach* – With regards to the extension to proceeds for acquisition security rights and proceeds, the same reasoning applies as before. Under the unitary approach, the extension of security rights automatically applies to acquisition security rights and under the non-unitary approach the rules concerning retention of title and leasing are adjusted to allow for the extension of retention of title and finance leasing to proceeds.[673] However, in the latter case, the retention of title creditor or financial lessor is not holding title to the proceeds, but a security right.[674] The priority of these creditors in proceeds is discussed in more detail in the section on super-priority.[675]

iii. *Tracing into attachments and comingled goods*

142. *General rules concerning attachments and comingled goods* – The UNCITRAL Guide and Model Law provide that security rights continue after they have been comingled with or attached to other movable or immovable goods.[676] There is one specific rule with regards to the extension of security rights into attachments to immovable goods. In this scenario, the secured creditor also has to register his security right in the registry for secured transactions in immovable property, in most cases the mortgage registry. This to make sure that the secured creditor with a mortgage in the immovable good to which the encumbered movable good is attached, can take notice of the security right.[677] This approach is extended to acquisition security rights under the unitary approach and to retention of title and finance leasing under the non-unitary approach. In other words, acquisition security rights, retention of title and finance leases continue in the comingled mass or the movable or immovable good to which the encumbered good is attached.[678]

c. Super-priority

143. *First in time, first in right* – The basic principle of priority in the UNCITRAL Guide and UNCITRAL Model Law is first in time, first in right: the first security right to be effective against third parties is given priority.[679] More specifically, the moment in time upon which priority is based, is in most cases the moment at which the security right notice is registered, even if this moment

673 UNCITRAL Guide, 359.
674 UNCITRAL Guide, 359 and recommendation 197.
675 See *infra* no. 143.
676 UNCITRAL Guide, 88–91; art. 11 UNCITRAL Model Law.
677 UNCITRAL Guide, 214 and recommendation 184.
678 UNCITRAL Guide, 356 *et seq*; art. 42 UNCITRAL Model Law.
679 UNCITRAL Guide, 195; art. 29 UNCITRAL Model Law; G. CASTELLANO and A. TOSATO, 'Personal property security law: international ambitions and local realities' in L. GHIA (ed.), *International business law*, (Wolters Kluwer, 2019), (283) 304.

takes place before the security right is agreed upon and created between the parties.[680] With this approach, the UNCITRAL Guide and UNCITRAL Model Law want to distinguish themselves from other regimes in which priority is regulated via a variety of rules for specific situations and secured transactions.[681]

144. *Introduction of super-priority* – Nevertheless, the UNCITRAL Guide and UNCITRAL Model Law assign super-priority for retention of title, finance leasing and acquisition security rights.[682] Super-priority means the right to overtake conflicting creditors even if their right was made effective against third parties at an earlier point in time. In the UNCITRAL Guide and UNCITRAL Model Law the reasons for granting super-priority vary depending on the type of secured transaction. For acquisition security rights super-priority is based on economic policy. For example, without the acquisition financing the debtor would not have acquired the asset and any other secured creditor would not have rights in this asset. Consequently, it would be unfair if other secured creditors would have priority over the acquisition creditor based on his first in time third-party effectiveness, when he has not contributed to the acquisition of this asset.[683] For retention of title-creditors and financial lessors there is actually no need to explicitly assign super-priority.[684] Due to their retained title, no other security rights can be vested in the encumbered good and the retention of title creditor and financial lessor cannot come into conflict with other creditors.[685] As a result, retention of title creditors and financial lessors always have the highest ranking claim to the encumbered good.

Despite these reasons, not everyone agrees with bestowing super-priority status upon acquisition financiers. Specifically, MCCORMACK argues that non-acquisition financing also serves a valuable purpose, such as paying wages and other general investments and that acquisition financing should not automatically be placed upon a pedestal.[686] This is true, however, by granting super-priority status to acquisition financing, the UNCITRAL Guide and UNCITRAL Model Law do not remove all priority from non-acquisition financing. Non-acquisition financiers still enjoy priority over non-secured creditors and more

680 UNCITRAL Guide, 196.

681 UNCITRAL Guide, 191; S. BAZINAS, 'The utility and efficacy of the UNCITRAL legislative guide on secured transactions' in O. AKSELI (ed.), *Availibility of credit in a time of crisis*, (Cambridge: Cambridge University Press, 2013), (133) 151.

682 UNCITRAL Guide, recommendation 180 and 192; art. 38 UNCITRAL Model Law.

683 S. BAZINAS, 'Acquisition financing under the UNCITRAL legislative guide on secured transactions', (2011) 16 Unif. L. Rev., (483) 494.

684 UNCITRAL Guide, 348. See also, O. AKSELI, *International secured transactions law – Facilitation of credit and international conventions and instruments*, (London: Routledge, 2001), 234.

685 S. BAZINAS, 'Acquisition financing under the UNCITRAL legislative guide on secured transactions', (2011) 16 Unif. L. Rev., (483) 493.

686 G. MCCORMACK, 'American private law writ large? The UNCITRAL secured transactions guide', (2011) 60 Int'l. & Comp. L. Q., (597) 620–621.

junior secured creditors. Only when it comes to newly acquired goods for which specific acquisition financing was used, do the drafters of the UNCITRAL Guide and UNCITRAL Model Law find that acquisition financiers should be given preference in the newly acquired goods over more senior general creditors. A second argument against the assignment of super-priority status for acquisition financing in the UNCITRAL Guide and UNCITRAL Model Law is that not all international instruments automatically assign super-priority to acquisition financing. For example, in the EBRD Model Law creditors are free to arrange the order of priorities among themselves. If super-priority is really beneficial for acquisition lenders, then one could argue that they would come to this arrangement via their own negotiations.[687] This argument is not entirely correct. It is true that the EBRD Model Law allows secured creditors to further negotiate the order of priorities concerning a certain encumbered good.[688] However, this option also exists in the UNCITRAL Guide and UNCITRAL Model Law.[689] In the UNCITRAL instruments this is known as a subordination agreement. Furthermore, the EBRD Model Law also gives super-priority to the vendor's charge (the EBRD's term for retention of title in sale agreements).[690] Consequently, the system in the UNCITRAL Guide and UNCITRAL Model Law and EBRD Model Law are very similar. Each of these instruments give super-priority to acquisition financing, but leave room for the parties to negotiate a different order in priority. In other words, the drafters of the EBRD Model Law also believe that, as a default, super-priority should be given to acquisition financing, but that secured creditors can potentially change their ranking via negotiations. Whether this actually happens in practice is a different matter, but it is hard to imagine why an acquisition creditor would trade his super-priority status for the general first in time priority of a general lender.

145. *Requirements for obtaining super-priority* – Despite the difference in reasons for granting super-priority to retention of title, financial leasing and acquisition security rights, the requirements for obtaining super-priority are the same under both the unitary and non-unitary approach. Under the unitary approach, all acquisition financiers are subject to the same regime and governed by one set of rules.[691] Consequently, recharacterized retention of title and finance leases are subject to the priority regime, but also granted super-priority if they follow the necessary requirements. The requirements for super-priority depend on whether the regime makes a distinction between acquisition security rights in inventory and equipment. In the case that the regime does not make

---

687 G. MCCORMACK, 'American private law writ large? The UNCITRAL secured transactions guide', (2011) 60 Int'l. & Comp. L. Q., (597) 620–621.

688 Art. 17.8 EBRD Model Law.

689 UNCITRAL Guide, 219 and recommendation 94; art. 43 UNCITRAL Model Law.

690 Art. 17.3 EBRD Model Law.

691 UNCITRAL Guide, 349 and recommendation 178.

the distinction, the acquisition security right will simply obtain super-priority by registering the notice of the acquisition security right in the security right registry within a grace period.[692] If the regime does make the distinction between inventory and equipment, then the acquisition financier only obtains super-priority in the inventory after filing a notice in the security registry in a timely manner and notifying potential competing claimants in the inventory.[693] The reasoning goes that often revolving credit is provided to debtors for which the debtor's inventory operates as the collateral. To avoid that the secured creditor grants new credit on the debtor's inventory without knowing that the new goods were provided by and secured for an acquisition creditor, the acquisition creditor has to notify creditors with a competing and more senior claim in the inventory before he can rely on his super-priority status.[694] Given that the UNCITRAL Guide and the UNCITRAL Model Law do not recommend one alternative over another and the approach in which the requirements for super-priority in equipment and inventory are the same is much easier, one can presume that states will be inclined to choose the alternative in which no distinction is made between inventory and equipment.

Under the non-unitary approach, super-priority of retention of title and finance leasing is theoretically still based on their retained title. Consequently, once the retention of title of financial lease is effective against third parties, the secured creditor cannot come into conflict with other secured creditors in the same good and will thus have super-priority over these creditors. However, to achieve equivalent legal outcomes between retention of title, finance leasing and acquisition security rights, the UNCITRAL Guide recommends that the requirements for obtaining third-party effectiveness for retention of title and finance leasing are made the same as the requirements for obtaining super-priority for acquisition security rights.[695] For example, under the non-unitary approach, the retention of title-creditor also has to take possession of the encumbered good or register a security notice within 20 or 30 days after the encumbered good is delivered to the debtor to obtain third-party effectiveness and thus super-priority.[696] If a distinction is made between retention of title or finance leases in inventory and equipment, then the third-party effectiveness requires either possession of the encumbered good or the registration of a security notice combined with a notification of secured creditors with an

692 UNCITRAL Guide, 353 and recommendations 180 and 190, alternative B; art. 38, option B UNCITRAL Model Law; G. MCCORMACK, 'American private law writ large? The UNCITRAL secured transactions guide', (2011) 60 Int'l. & Comp. L. Q., (597) 622.

693 UNCITRAL Guide, 353 and recommendation 180, alternative A; art. 38, option A UNCITRAL Model Law. See also, S. BAZINAS, 'Acquisition financing under the UNCITRAL legislative guide on secured transactions', (2011) 16 Unif. L. Rev., (483) 494.

694 UNCITRAL Guide, 353.

695 UNCITRAL Guide, 350.

696 UNCITRAL Guide, recommendation 192.

earlier security right in the encumbered good.[697] Consequently, retention of title, finance leasing and acquisition security rights have to fulfill the same requirements to avoid conflict with more senior secured creditors with potentially competing claims in the acquired goods.

Furthermore, acquisition security rights, retention of title and finance leasing are given the same exemptions to these requirements in both the unitary and non-unitary approach. Under both systems, acquisition security rights, retention of title and finance leasing in consumer goods are effective against third parties and take priority over pre-existing security rights in the same good from the moment the acquisition security right is created.[698] In many jurisdictions, this will not require an adjustment of the rules but simply a continuation of the lack of third-party effectiveness requirements for retention of title and finance leasing.

146. *Super-priority in altered goods* – Additionally, the UNCITRAL Guide and UNCITRAL Model Law recommend that acquisition security rights, retention of title and financial leases maintain their super-priority status in attachments, co-mingled masses and proceeds.[699] However, for acquisition security rights, retention of title and finance leases in attachments to immovable goods the secured creditor has to remember to register his acquisition security right, retention of title or finance lease in the registry for secured transactions in immovable goods. Otherwise, the creditor with a secured claim in the immovable good will take priority over the acquisition security right holder, retention of title creditor or financial lessor.[700]

With regards to proceeds, a distinction can again be made between proceeds of inventory and proceeds of goods other than inventory. If a distinction is made, the acquisition security right does not extend to receivables and other payment rights that stem from the sale of the inventory.[701] This exception is mainly provided to allow creditors to take security in the debtor's receivables without fearing that they might be overtaken by acquisition security rights. When the distinction between proceeds of inventory and equipment is not made, the acquisition security right again simply extends to all proceeds.[702] However, in that case the acquisition security right holder's priority will become time-based priority in the proceeds and not a super-priority.[703] This again to allow

---

697 UNCITRAL Guide, recommendation 192, alternative A.

698 UNCITRAL Guide, 351 and 355; art. 24 UNCITRAL Model Law.

699 UNCITRAL Guide, 357–359; art. 42 Model Law.

700 UNCITRAL Guide, 358.

701 UNCITRAL Guide, recommendation 185, alternative A and recommendation 199, alternative A; art. 41, option A Model Law.

702 UNCITRAL Guide, recommendation 185, alternative B and recommendation 199, alternative B; art. 41, option B Model Law.

703 S. BAZINAS, 'Acquisition financing under the UNCITRAL legislative guide on secured transactions', (2011) 16 Unif. L. Rev., (483) 496.

creditors to obtain a competitive security right in the debtor's receivables. With regards to the extension of retention of title and finance leases into proceeds, the UNCITRAL Guide recommends that here the extension is limited to a security right and not ownership.[704] Therefore, even under the non-unitary approach some recharacterization finds its way into the regime in an attempt to create a level playing field between the different secured creditors.

Finally, when two acquisition security rights come into conflict with each other, the conflict will generally be resolved by determining who fulfilled the third-party effectiveness requirements first.[705] This situation can happen when a debtor borrows part of the acquisition price from a lender, such as a bank, and receives part of the credit of the acquisition price from the supplier or seller of the acquired good. When one of the competing acquisition security rights is vested by a supplier, the supplier is given priority over the acquisition lender.[706] This rule mainly comes into play, if the encumbered good has decreased in value while in possession of the debtor. In an ideal situation, the encumbered good maintains its original value and in the event of default the value of the good will cover perfectly the debts owed to both acquisition financiers. However, if the good has diminished in value, then the proceeds of the good following execution no longer covers both claims and there will be a need for a priority rule among the acquisition financiers to determine who gets paid first.

147. *Loss of super-priority* – The fact that super-priority in most cases now hinges on the fulfillment of requirements for third-party effectiveness also means that failure to fulfill these requirements results in a loss of super-priority. Consequently, if an acquisition security right holder fails to register in a timely manner, the security right remains effective between the parties but cannot be enforced against competing third parties. However, if the secured creditor takes the necessary steps to achieve third-party effectiveness even after the expiry of the grace period, the acquisition security right holder is treated as an ordinary, non-acquisition secured creditor.[707]

The situation is slightly different when a retention of title creditor or a financial lessor fails to make its rights effective against third parties in a timely manner. In these cases, the seller or lessor loses the benefit of its ownership as opposed to third parties and the creditor becomes the holder of an unperfected security right.[708] Without the fulfilment of the third-party effectiveness requirement, title to the asset being sold or leased is transferred to the buyer

704 UNCITRAL Guide, 359, 361.
705 UNCITRAL Guide, 364 and recommendation 182; art. 39, 1 UNCITRAL Model Law.
706 UNCITRAL Guide, 350 and recommendation 182; art. 39, 2 UNCITRAL Model Law.
707 UNCITRAL Guide, 365–366.
708 O. AKSELI, *International secured transactions law – Facilitation of credit and international conventions and instruments*, (London: Routledge, 2001), 236.

or lessee.[709] The loss of rights is a severe consequence to attach to the failure to take the steps necessary to achieve third-party effectiveness in a timely manner. Therefore, the UNCITRAL Guide mitigates these consequences by converting the right of the seller or lessor that does not become effective against third parties within the grace period into an ordinary security right and subjecting it to the general priority rules applicable to security rights.[710] Additionally, this approach also furthers the equivalent legal outcomes between retention of title creditors, financial lessors and acquisition security right holders.[711]

D. Enforcement

148. *Enforcement under the unitary approach* – Finally, the UNCITRAL Guide and UNCITRAL Model Law provide rules for secured creditors to enforce their security right in the event the debtor defaults. Under the unitary approach, retention of title and finance leases have become acquisition security rights and thus their enforcement follows the recommendations concerning the enforcement of security rights. In other words, the assumption is that the secured creditor is enforcing upon a good that is owned by the debtor and in which the secured creditor has vested a security right. Not a good to which the secured creditor has retained title.[712]

Specific to the enforcement of security rights in the UNCITRAL Guide and UNCITRAL Model Law, is that the creditor is offered self-help and extra-judicial tools to realize their security right.[713] For example, the secured creditor can enforce his security right without going to court. However, the secured creditor has to notify the debtor of the impending action.[714] Furthermore, the secured creditor has an automatic right to obtain possession of the encumbered good when the debtor is in default.[715] However, the manner in which the secured creditor takes possession is regulated.[716] More precisely, the debtor has to consent to the dispossession in the security agreement, the secured creditor has notified the debtor, and the debtor does not object at the time of the possession being sought.[717] Once the encumbered good is in the secured creditor's possession, the

709 S. BAZINAS, 'Acquisition financing under the UNCITRAL legislative guide on secured transactions', (2011) 16 Unif. L. Rev., (483) 492.

710 UNCITRAL Guide, 366.

711 UNCITRAL Guide, 366.

712 S. BAZINAS, 'Acquisition financing under the UNCITRAL legislative guide on secured transactions', (2011) 16 Unif. L. Rev., (483) 497.

713 G. CASTELLANO and A. TOSATO, 'Personal property security law: international ambitions and local realities' in L. GHIA (ed.), *International business law*, (Wolters Kluwer, 2019), (283) 305.

714 UNCITRAL Guide, 288 and recommendation 147; art 73 UNCITRAL Model Law.

715 UNCITRAL Guide, 286 and recommendation 146.

716 UNCITRAL Guide, 292.

717 UNCITRAL Guide, 292 and recommendation 147; art. 74 Model Law; S. BAZINAS, 'The utility and efficacy of the UNCITRAL legislative guide on secured transactions' in O. AKSELI

secured creditor can choose between sale of the encumbered asset or acquisition of the encumbered asset in satisfaction of the outstanding debt. For the sale of the encumbered goods, the secured creditor can do this outside of the court but the secured creditor has to notify the interested parties.[718] If the encumbered good is sold and the proceeds distributed, the secured creditor has to follow a ranking in the distribution of the proceeds. For example, any remaining surplus value will go to the debtor.[719] Alternatively, the secured creditor and debtor can also agree that the encumbered good is taken in full or partial satisfaction of the outstanding debt.[720] In that case, the secured creditor has to send out a notification in which he indicates the assets that will be acquired, the amount owed and the amount of this obligation that will be satisfied.[721]

149. *Enforcement under the non-unitary approach* – Unsurprisingly, under the non-unitary approach the UNCITRAL Guide recommends that the enforcement of retention of title and finance leases follows the method that is equivalent to the enforcement of the functionally equivalent acquisition security rights.[722] There is a presumption that the achievement of equivalent legal outcomes in this domain requires significant adjustments to the rules concerning enforcement of retention of title and finance leasing. Given their retained ownership, these secured creditors often have a very strong position in the event of the debtor's default.[723] For example, in many jurisdictions a retention of title creditor or financial lessor can terminate the agreement upon the debtor's default and can demand the return of the assets.[724]

Consequently, to achieve equivalent legal outcomes considerable adjustments may have to be made. For example, the debtor, and any secured creditor with a right in the buyer's or lessee's expectancy right, could be given the right to compel the retention of title creditor or lessor to sell the encumbered good, rather than letting them assert ownership to regain possession of and ultimately to retain or dispose of the encumbered good.[725] Another possible adjustment is that the retention of title creditor and lessors would have to return any surplus value to the debtor or competing creditors, rather than keeping the surplus value following their revindication of the encumbered good as owner.[726]

(ed.), *Availibility of credit in a time of crisis*, (Cambridge: Cambridge University Press, 2013), (133) 155.

718 UNCITRAL Guide, 293 and recommendation 150–151; art. 78 UNCITRAL Model Law.

719 UNCITRAL Guide, 294 and recommendation 152; art. 79 UNCITRAL Model Law.

720 UNCITRAL Guide, 297 and recommendation 156 and 159; art. 80 UNCITRAL Model Law.

721 UNCITRAL Guide, 297 and recommendation 157; art. 80 UNCITRAL Model Law.

722 UNCITRAL Guide, 369.

723 S. BAZINAS, 'Acquisition financing under the UNCITRAL legislative guide on secured transactions', (2011) 16 Unif. L. Rev., (483) 498.

724 UNCITRAL Guide, 368.

725 UNCITRAL Guide, 369; S. BAZINAS, 'Acquisition financing under the UNCITRAL legislative guide on secured transactions', (2011) 16 Unif. L. Rev., (483) 499.

726 UNCITRAL Guide, 369.

Notably, the UNCITRAL Guide allows exceptions to the adjustments for retention of title and finance leasing to the extent that these exceptions are necessary to preserve the coherence of the regime applicable to sale and lease.[727] However, this exception seems to leave room for states to avoid adjusting their enforcement proceedings for retention of title and finance leasing in accordance with the rules of enforcement of acquisition security rights by simply stating that this would threaten the coherence of the regime for sales and leasing. Furthermore, this recommendation seems rather self-evident. Evidently, states should not adjust the rules concerning the enforcement of retention of title and leasing in an incoherent way. Therefore, I am not convinced that the recommendation adds very much except providing states with a justification for not adjusting the enforcement proceedings of retention of title and leasing to acquisition financing. What's more, this recommendation is not made in other areas of secured transactions law, such as creation, third-party effectiveness or priority, so it seems strange that it is explicitly mentioned here. A better recommendation would be to state that the coherence of the legal regime should be paramount when making adjustments in general and not only with regards to the enforcement of retention of title and finance leasing. This way the UNCITRAL Guide would still emphasize the importance of coherence, but without offering states the opportunity to avoid making adjustments in service of functional equivalence.

1.4. Conclusion

150. *Functional equivalence between retention of title and acquisition security rights* – The UNCITRAL Guide and UNCITRAL Model Law are clear that under both the unitary and non-unitary approach, retention of title and finance leasing, whether they are recharacterized or not, have to have the same legal outcomes as acquisition security rights. This can either be directly achieved by recharacterizing retention of title and finance leasing to acquisition security rights and subjecting them to a uniform set of rules for all acquisition security rights. Conversely, the UNCITRAL Guide offers an alternative approach where the original terms of retention of title and finance leasing are maintained, but their rules are adjusted to such an extent that they still achieve the same legal outcomes as acquisition security rights. The UNCITRAL Guide is clear that under this approach, achieving functionally equivalent legal outcomes between the different forms of acquisition financing is paramount. How difficult the application of the non-unitary approach will be, depends on how similar retention of title, finance leasing and acquisition security rights are already

[727] UNCITRAL Guide, recommendation 200, (b); S. BAZINAS, 'The utility and efficacy of the UNCITRAL legislative guide on secured transactions' in O. AKSELI (ed.), *Availibility of credit in a time of crisis*, (Cambridge: Cambridge University Press, 2013), (133) 159.

treated in the states contemplating adoption. In any case, simply adding acquisition security right to the menu of secured transactions in movable goods alongside retention of title and finance leasing will likely not be enough. Adopting states will have to go through their rules concerning retention of title and leasing and their legal outcomes to determine whether these are equivalent to those for acquisition security rights and, if not, how they can be made to be so. In any event, regardless of the adopted approach, the legal outcomes for retention of title and finance leasing in the UNCITRAL Guide and UNCITRAL Model Law will become equivalent to the legal outcomes of acquisition security rights.

151. *Added value of the UNCITRAL non-unitary approach* – The fact that under both approaches, retention of title and finance leasing are recharacterized or legally amended to have the same legal outcomes as acquisition security rights raises the question whether it is necessary to offer states the option between these two approaches. On the one hand, the non-unitary approach can be seen as a good way to ease states into the idea of acquisition security rights and bringing retention of title and finance leasing gently into the fold of secured transactions law. On the other hand, the drafters themselves seem less convinced of the actual usefulness and practicality of the non-unitary approach. In chapter IX on acquisition financing, the UNCITRAL Guide ends the section concerning the application of the non-unitary approach to the enforcement of retention of title and finance leasing by stating that under the non-unitary approach functionally equivalent legal outcomes can be achieved by making sufficient adjustments to the current enforcement proceedings for retention of title and leasing. However, in the same paragraph, the UNCITRAL Guide points out that it may preferable for states to simply adopt the unitary approach to avoid the many adjustments that might be necessary to achieve functionally equivalent legal outcomes.[728] I wonder if this sentiment cannot be extended to the application of the non-unitary approach in all aspects of the UNCITRAL Guide. Theoretically, states can maintain their original concepts of acquisition financing in the forms of retention of title and leasing, but they will have to make sufficient adjustments to the rules governing these mechanisms in order for them to have the same legal outcomes as acquisition security rights. In other words, the rules of retention of title and financial leasing become the legal equivalent of acquisition security rights, except in name. Furthermore, these adjustments not only have to happen in a way that preserves the coherence and logic of the sale and leasing system, but also have to take into account the potential domino effect these adjustments can have in other fields of law. It stands to reason that this will not be an easy exercise for legislators and is prone to lead to mistakes, inconsistencies and incoherence. The difficulty of the application of the non-unitary approach is somewhat ironic given that it is introduced as the approach that should convince

[728] UNCITRAL Guide, 370.

reluctant states to adopt the vision of the UNCITRAL Guide and UNCITRAL Model Law. Given this state of affairs, I conclude that the non-unitary approach in the UNCITRAL does not offer sufficient advantages to make up for its many complexities. Therefore, I applaud the choice the drafters made in the UNCITRAL Model Law to simply prescribe the unitary approach and I would argue that if the UNCITRAL Guide were up for revision, the possibility for the non-unitary approach were to be removed.

2. DRAFT COMMON FRAME OF REFERENCE

152. *Overview* – In this part, a second international instrument that applies the functional approach without recharacterization is examined. More specifically, some background is given to the DCFR (2.1.), the introduction of the functional approach (2.2.) and the application of the functional approach to retention of ownership devices (2.3.).

2.1. Background and aspirations

153. *Drafters of the DCFR* – The Draft Common Frame of Reference (DCFR) was part of the European Commission's Action Plan to create a more coherent European contract law.[729] The DCFR was developed by two main groups[730]: the Study Group on a European Civil Code (create rules on private law issues that had not yet been affected by European law)[731] and the European Research Group on the existing EC Private Law or Acquis Group (restating the European *acquis communautaire*).[732] Furthermore, the DCFR took a lot of inspiration from the Principles of European Contract Law (PECL) prepared by the Lando

729 European Commission, Communication from the Commission to the European Parliament and the Council – a more coherent European Contract Law – An action plan (2003), COM (2003) final, OJ C-63, 11–12.

730 H. EIDENMULLER, F. FAUST, H. C. GRIGOLEIT, N. JANSEN, G. WAGNER, R. ZIMMERMANN, 'The common frame of reference for European private law -- policy choices and codification problems', (2008) 28 Oxford J. L. Studies, (659) 665; W. ERNST, 'Der 'Common Frame of Reference' aus juristischer Sicht', (2008) 208 AcP, (249) 252; S. WHITTAKER, The 'Draft Common Frame of Reference' – An assessment, (United Kingdom: Ministry of Justice, 2008), 3 and 31.

731 M. W. HESSELINK, 'The Common Frame of Reference as a source of European private law', (2009) 83 Tul. L. Rev., (919) 951.

732 This group set out to develop certain common principles based on the existing European law (H. EIDENMULLER, F. FAUST, H. C. GRIGOLEIT, N. JANSEN, G. WAGNER, R. ZIMMERMANN, 'The common frame of reference for European private law -- policy choices and codification problems', (2008) 28 Oxford J. L.Studies, (659) 667); M. W. HESSELINK, 'The Common Frame of Reference as a source of European private law', (2009) 83 Tul. L. Rev., (919) 951.

Commission.[733] Given the name of the groups involved in the development of the DCFR, there was a lot of suspicion that the European Commission had the intention to create a European Civil Code.[734] The possible creation of a European Civil Code was a very sensitive issue.[735] The European Commission and the drafters of the DCFR did not want to step on the toes of larger European member states by suggesting that they wanted to replace for example the French Code Civil or take over the English common law (when the U.K. was still part of the EU).[736] Consequently, the drafters went out of their way to remove this impression[737] by stating explicitly in the introduction that the DCFR is mainly an academic endeavor.[738]

154. *Different objectives for the DCFR* – First, the DCFR could be a model for a political Common Frame of Reference (CFR).[739] According to the European Commission, the CFR would be a politically supported document that contains fundamental principles, definitions and model rules.[740] Such an optional

---

733 The Lando Commission developed the Principles of European Contract Law in 2000. See O. LANDO and H. BEALE, *Principles of European Contract Law, Parts I and II* (The Hague: Kluwer, 2000); O. LANDO and H. BEALE, *Principles of European Contract Law, Part III*, (The Hague: Kluwer, 2000.

734 H. EIDENMULLER, F. FAUST, H. C. GRIGOLEIT, N. JANSEN, G. WAGNER, R. ZIMMERMANN, 'The common frame of reference for European private law -- policy choices and codification problems', (2008) 28 Oxford J. L. Studies, (659) 668 *et seq.*

735 H. BEALE, 'The European Commission's Common Frame of Reference project: a progress report', (2006) 2 ECLR, (303) 304; C. VON BAR, 'Coverage and structure of the academic common frame of reference', (2007) 3 ERCL, (350) 353.

736 M. W. HESSLINK, 'The politics of a European civil code', (2004) 10 ELJ, (675) 689; G. MCORMACK, 'The CFR and credit securities – a suitable case for treatment?' in A. VAQUER (ed.), *European private law beyond the Common Frame of Reference*, (Groningen: Europa Law Publishing, 2008), (99) 99.

737 H. BEALE, 'The future of the Common Frame of Reference', (2007) 3 ERCL, (257) 259; H. BEALE, 'The nature and purposes of the Common Frame of Reference', (2008) 14 Juridica International, (10) 11; S. WHITTAKER, The 'Draft Common Frame of Reference' – An assessment, (United Kingdom: Ministry of Justice, 2008), 34.

738 Study Group on a European Civil Code and Research Group on EC Private Law (Acquis Group), *Principles, definitions and model rules of European private law – Draft common frame of reference (DCFR)*, (Munich: Sellier European Law Publishers, 2009), 7; J. M. SMITS, 'The Draft Common Frame of Reference for a European private law: fit for purpose?', (2008) 15 Maastricht J. Eur. & Comp. L., (145) 146.

739 Study Group on a European Civil Code and Research Group on EC Private Law (Acquis Group), *Principles, definitions and model rules of European private law – Draft common frame of reference (DCFR)*, (Munich: Sellier European Law Publishers, 2009), 8; H. EIDENMULLER, F. FAUST, H. C. GRIGOLEIT, N. JANSEN, G. WAGNER, R. ZIMMERMANN, 'The common frame of reference for European private law – policy choices and codification problems', (2008) 28 Oxford J. L. Studies, (659) 669.

740 Study Group on a European Civil Code and Research Group on EC Private Law (Acquis Group), *Principles, definitions and model rules of European private law – Draft common frame of reference (DCFR)*, (Munich: Sellier European Law Publishers, 2009), 30–31; H. BEALE, 'The future of the Common Frame of Reference', (2007) 3 ERCL, (257) 257; M. KUNEVA, 'Introduction', (2007) 3 ERCL, (239) 239; O. LANDO, 'The structure and the legal values of the Common Frame of Reference (CFR)', (2007) 3 ECLR, (245) 246.

instrument could have taken the form of a interinstitutional document that would set a standard for the further development of European law in the domain of contract law.[741] However, the European Commission reiterates that the CFR would only be a legislative guide or toolbox and would not take on the form of a European Civil Code.[742] As a toolbox, the CFR could still perform a myriad of roles. The CFR toolbox can, for example, help with interpretation problems that face both national courts and judges at the European Court of Justice.[743] However, there is a risk that the open-ended nature of the CFR can lead to different interpretations from national judges with no clear guidance on the "right" interpretation.[744] Alternatively, the CFR toolbox can help with the creation of European and national law that adheres to the common principles distilled in the DCFR.[745]

Second, the DCFR has a purpose and function separate from its potential political recognition in a CFR. The DCFR is an academic text that contains an enormous amount of information on European private law and its comparison. Therefore, it enlarges the awareness of private law in Europe and the similarities that already exist in private law across the different European member states.[746] In other words, the DCFR does not need to be politically acknowledged for it to serve as a source of information for further legal research and education (this research being a case in point). In the same vein, the DCFR, regardless

741 H. COLLINS, 'Review – Principles, Definitions and Model Rules of European Private Law: Draft Common Frame of Reference (DCFR)', (2008) 71 Mod. L. Rev., (840) 844.

742 Study Group on a European Civil Code and Research Group on EC Private Law (Acquis Group), *Principles, definitions and model rules of European private law – Draft common frame of reference (DCFR)*, (Munich: Sellier European Law Publishers, 2009), 31; S. VAN ERP, *European and National Property Law: Osmosis or Growing Antagonism?*, (Leuven: European Law Publishing, 2007), 10; J. M. SMITS, 'The Draft Common Frame of Reference: how to improve it?' in H. W. MICKLITZ and F. CAFAGGI (eds.), *European private law after the common frame of reference*, (Cheltenham: Elgar, 2010), (90) 91; R. SEFTON-GREEN, 'The DCFR: a technical or political toolbox?' in A. SOMMA (ed.), *The politics of the Draft Common Frame of Reference*, vol. 16, (Alphen on the Rhine: Kluwer Law International, 2009), (39) 40.

743 S. WHITTAKER, The 'Draft Common Frame of Reference' – An assessment, (United Kingdom: Ministry of Justice, 2008), 40 and 92; R. SEFTON-GREEN, 'The DCFR: a technical or political toolbox?' in A. SOMMA (ed.), *The politics of the Draft Common Frame of Reference*, vol. 16, (Alphen on the Rhine: Kluwer Law International, 2009), (39) 48; M. HAENTJENS, 'DCFR en goederenrecht in de praktijk over zekerheid en rafelranden', (2011) NTBR, (54) 55.

744 R. SEFTON-GREEN, 'The DCFR: a technical or political toolbox?' in A. SOMMA (ed.), *The politics of the Draft Common Frame of Reference*, vol. 16, (Alphen on the Rhine: Kluwer Law International, 2009), (39) 48.

745 R. SEFTON-GREEN, 'The DCFR: a technical or political toolbox?' in A. SOMMA (ed.), *The politics of the Draft Common Frame of Reference*, vol. 16, (Alphen on the Rhine: Kluwer Law International, 2009), (39) 48; M. W. HESSELINK, 'The Common Frame of Reference as a source of European private law', (2009) 83 Tul. L. Rev., (919) 921.

746 Study Group on a European Civil Code and Research Group on EC Private Law (Acquis Group), *Principles, definitions and model rules of European private law – Draft common frame of reference (DCFR)*, (Munich: Sellier European Law Publishers, 2009), 8–9.

of its political recognition, can serve as an important source of inspiration for lawmakers and courts both inside and outside of the European Union.[747]

Following the publication of the DCFR in 2008 there has not been much political development concerning the DCFR. Given the sensitive nature of the further political development of the DCFR, especially its perceived intention to create a European Civil Code, the European Commission opted to mainly pursue the inspirational purpose of the DCFR and abandon its further political evolution. As a result, the DCFR does not have any direct impact on national legal systems or even the European legal system. However, as predicted, the DCFR does have a significant inspirational value. An example being the Belgian Security Rights Act, which explicitly refers to the DCFR as a source of inspiration.[748]

155. *Outline of the DCFR* – Notwithstanding the drafters' intention to steer clear of a European Civil Code, the DCFR is presented not as a list of principles, guidelines or recommendations but as a set of rules that make the DCFR look very much like a Civil Code.[749] The DCFR starts with general provisions (Book I) and is then followed by different Books that cover the relevant aspects of contract law, such as what are the relevant contracts and juridical acts in the DCFR (Book II), the obligations and corresponding rights of contract parties (Book III), specific contracts (Book IV), intervention in other's affairs (Book V), non-contractual liability (Book VI), unjustified enrichment (Book VII), acquisition and loss of ownership of goods (Book VIII), proprietary security interests in movable goods (Book IX) and trusts (Book X). In this dissertation the focus is on Book IX DCFR.

156. *The introduction and outline of book IX* – Book IX concerning security interests was a later addition to the DCFR.[750] Initially, the drafters focused on the common frame for European contract law. Property law was considered too closely intertwined with the legal frameworks and national culture of the

747 Study Group on a European Civil Code and Research Group on EC Private Law (Acquis Group), *Principles, definitions and model rules of European private law – Draft common frame of reference (DCFR)*, (Munich: Sellier European Law Publishers, 2009), 8; G. MCORMACK, 'The CFR and credit securities – a suitable case for treatment?' in A. VAQUER (ed.), *European private law beyond the Common Frame of Reference*, (Groningen: Europa Law Publishing, 2008), (99) 102; J. M. SMITS, 'The Draft Common Frame of Reference: how to improve it?' in H. W. MICKLITZ and F. CAFAGGI (eds.), *European private law after the common frame of reference*, (Cheltenham: Elgar, 2010), (90) 94.

748 Explanatory memorandum Security Rights Act, no. 2463/001, 12; W. FABER, 'Proprietary security rights in movables – European developments', (2014) 22 Juridica Int'l., (27) 29.

749 S. WHITTAKER, The 'Draft Common Frame of Reference' – An assessment, (United Kingdom: Ministry of Justice, 2008), 49.

750 Study Group on a European Civil Code and Research Group on EC Private Law (Acquis Group), *Principles, definitions and model rules of European private law – Draft common frame of reference (DCFR)*, (Munich: Sellier European Law Publishers, 2009), 6.

European member states to allow for generalizations and the determination of a common denominator.[751] For example, some jurisdictions have a *numerus clausus* for *in rem* rights[752] or specific rules on the transfer of ownership.[753] It would be near impossible to come up with a European approach that would accommodate each member state's approach to property issues and the drafters were initially unsure to make a choice for a "best solution" or the creation of an entirely new approach.[754] However, it was quickly discovered that a comprehensive framework on contract law would inevitably collide with property law and that a logical framework would have to incorporate the interactions between contract and property law.[755] Consequently, the drafters embraced the idea of drafting a common frame of reference for more proprietary aspects of private law and selecting one approach over another. As a result, the later version of the DCFR included three additional books in which the drafters selected an approach towards transfer and acquisition of ownership rights[756], created a new and more modern system of security interests in movable goods[757] and set out a common frame of reference for trusts.[758]

Book IX follows the life of a security interest: creation, third-party effectiveness, priority, relation between secured creditor and debtor, termination of the proprietary interest in the movable good and its enforcement.[759] As mentioned, for this Book the drafters went further than describing the *status quo* in security rights in movable goods in Europe, but actually developed a system that incorporates modern developments in security rights in movable goods.[760] Among these modern developments are: a generalization of non-possessory

---

751 E. CASHIN RITAINE, 'Common Frame of Reference and property law: a general introduction' in S. VAN ERP, A. SALOMONS and B. AKKERMANS (eds.), *The future of European property law*, (Munich: Sellier European Law, 2012), (1) 6.

752 E. CASHIN RITAINE, 'Common Frame of Reference and property law: a general introduction' in S. VAN ERP, A. SALOMONS and B. AKKERMANS (eds.), *The future of European property law*, (Munich: Sellier European Law, 2012), (1) 15.

753 A. STADLER, 'Die Vorschläge des Gemeinsamen Referensrahmens für ein europäisches Sachenrecht - Grundprinzipien und Eigentumserwerb', (2010) 8 JZ, (380) 380–381.

754 G. MCORMACK, 'The CFR and credit securities – a suitable case for treatment?' in A. VAQUER (ed.), *European private law beyond the Common Frame of Reference*, (Groningen: Europa Law Publishing, 2008), (99) 104; E. CASHIN RITAINE, 'Common Frame of Reference and property law: a general introduction' in S. VAN ERP, A. SALOMONS and B. AKKERMANS (eds.), *The future of European property law*, (Munich: Sellier European Law, 2012), (1) 16.

755 E. CASHIN RITAINE, 'Common Frame of Reference and property law: a general introduction' in S. VAN ERP, A. SALOMONS and B. AKKERMANS (eds.), *The future of European property law*, (Munich: Sellier European Law, 2012), (1) 5–6.

756 Book VIII DCFR.

757 Book IX DCFR.

758 Book X DCFR.

759 A. J. VAN DER WEIDE, '(On)zekerheden in het DCFR. Boek IX Proprietary security in movable assets', (2011) NTBR, (53) 54.

760 U. DROBNIG and O. BÖGER, *Proprietary security in movable assets (PEL Prop. Sec.)*, vol. 6, (Principles on European Law, Munich: Sellier Publishers, 2015), 211; A. J. VAN DER WEIDE,

security rights in movable goods[761] including proprietary rights in intangible goods[762], publicity of non-possessory security rights via registration[763] and the adoption of the functional approach.[764]

2.2. Functional approach in the DCFR

157. *Introduction of the functional approach* – In the pursuit of a more modern approach to security rights, the drafters decided to adopt a unitary and functional approach[765] in the vein of the UNCITRAL Legislative Guide.[766] Notably, the drafters avoid listing Article 9 UCC as a direct influence in the creation of the DCFR. Listing Article 9 UCC as a source of inspiration would likely have attracted criticism of undue influence of the American system in Europe. Moreover, DROBNIG and BÖGER even state that a wholesale adoption of the American system would not be compatible with the European legal tradition and would thus be impossible.[767] Nevertheless, the similarities between Book IX and Article 9 UCC are a clear indication of Article 9's influence. Furthermore, many of the instruments from which the drafters did draw inspiration, such as the UNCITRAL Legislative Guide, are themselves in large parts based on Article 9 UCC. Therefore, Article 9 UCC still finds its way into the DCFR via these sources.

158. *The broad definition of security rights in the DCFR* – The unitary and functional approach aims to bring different secured transactions that perform the same function in one category.[768] The seeds for such a functional approach could already be found in the European directive on financial collateral

---

'(On)zekerheden in het DCFR. Boek IX Proprietary security in movable assets', (2011) NTBR, (53) 53.

761 Art. IX.-2:103 DCFR.

762 Art. IX.-1:201 (6) DCFR.

763 Art. IX.-3:102 (2) (a) DCFR.

764 Art. IX.-1:101 DCFR.

765 E. M. KIENINGER, 'The scope and limits of security interests: commentary', (2008) 5 ECFR, (215) 216; U. DROBNIG and O. BÖGER, *Proprietary security in movable assets (PEL Prop. Sec.)*, vol. 6, (Principles on European Law, Munich: Sellier Publishers, 2015), 212; M. HAENTJENS, 'DCFR en goederenrecht in de praktijk over zekerheid en rafelranden', (2011) NTBR, (54) 56; A. VENEZIANO, 'The DCFR Book on Secured Transactions: some policy choices made by the Working Group' in S. VAN ERP, A. SALOMONS and B. AKKERMANS (eds.), *The future of European property law*, (Munich: Sellier European Law, 2012), (123) 128.

766 U. DROBNIG and O. BÖGER, *Proprietary security in movable assets (PEL Prop. Sec.)*, vol. 6, (Principles on European Law, Munich: Sellier Publishers, 2015), 210–211.

767 U. DROBNIG and O. BÖGER, *Proprietary security in movable assets (PEL Prop. Sec.)*, vol. 6, (Principles on European Law, Munich: Sellier Publishers, 2015), 211.

768 H. BEALE, 'Secured transactions', (2008) 14 Juridica International, (96) 100; E. M. KIENINGER, 'The scope and limits of security interests: commentary', (2008) 5 ECFR, (215) 216; U. DROBNIG, 'Choosing the right approach for European law making: commentary', (2008) 5 ECFR, (102) 103.

arrangements[769], which treats security rights in financial collateral similarly as transfers of title to financial collateral for security purposes.[770] Following this unitary and functional approach, Book IX adopted a broad definition of security rights in movable goods that includes not only traditional security rights in movable goods, such as the pledge and non-possessory security rights, but also their functional equivalents, such as transfer of ownerships for security purposes.[771]

159. *Separate rules for retention of ownership devices* – The DCFR maintains an important distinction between security rights and retention of ownership devices[772] (i.e. *functional approach without recharacterization*).[773] Retention of ownership devices are not considered as security rights in movable goods and are, in the domain of creation[774], priority[775] and enforcement[776], governed by their own rules.[777] However, the phrasing of the provision concerning the applicable rules leaves much to be desired.

> (1) *Retention of ownership devices are subject to the following rules on security rights, unless specifically provided otherwise:*
> (a) *IX.–2:104 (Specific issues of transferability, existence and specification) paragraphs (2) to (4);*
> (b) *Chapter 2, Sections 3 and 4;*
> (c) *Chapters 3 to 6; and*
> (d) *Chapter 7, Section 1.*[778]

---

769 Directive 2002/47/EC of the European Parliament and of the Council of 6 June 2002 on financial collateral arrangements, 168 *Pb. L.*, 43 (hereafter, Financial Collateral Directive).

770 H. BEALE, 'Secured transactions', (2008) 14 Juridica International, (96) 97; B. AKKERMANS, 'The European Union development of European property law' in C. GODT (ed.), *Hanse Law School in Perspective – Legal Teaching and Cross Border Research after Lisbon*, (The Hague: Kluwer, 2011), 5.

771 Art. IX.-1:101 DCFR. See also, W. FABER, 'Proprietary security rights in movables – European developments', (2014) 22 Juridica Int'l., (27) 29.

772 W. FABER, 'Proprietary security rights in movables – European developments', (2014) 22 Juridica Int'l., (27) 30.

773 See *supra* no. 4.

774 Art. IX. – 2:201 DCFR.

775 Art. IX. – 4:102 (1) DCFR.

776 Art. IX. – 7:301 *et seq.* DCFR.

777 Art. IX. – 1:104 DCFR; Study Group on a European Civil Code and Research Group on EC Private Law (Acquis Group), *Principles, definitions and model rules of European private law – Draft common frame of reference (DCFR)*, (Munich: Sellier European Law Publishers, 2009), 5401; U. DROBNIG and O. BÖGER, *Proprietary security in movable assets (PEL Prop. Sec.)*, vol. 6, (Principles on European Law, Munich: Sellier Publishers, 2015), 213; A. VENEZIANO, 'Security rights in movables in the DCFR: general presentation' in V. SAGAERT, M. E. STORME and E. TERRYN (eds.), *The Draft Common Frame of Reference: national and comparative perspectives*, (Antwerp: Intersentia, 2012), (305) 310; A. VENEZIANO, 'The DCFR Book on Secured Transactions: some policy choices made by the Working Group' in S. VAN ERP, A. SALOMONS and B. AKKERMANS (eds.), *The future of European property law*, (Munich: Sellier European Law, 2012), (123) 133.

778 Art. IX.-1:104 (1) DCFR.

On the basis of this provision, retention of ownership devices are subjected only to the rules listed in this paragraph. However, when you then read the commentary to this provision you find that the drafters say that

> *In the Sections and Chapters mentioned in paragraph (1), those rules that deviate from the corresponding rules for security rights, are set out explicitly. Retention of ownership devices are subject to the rules on security rights, unless otherwise provided.*[779]

This is a very different statement than the provision itself and even in direct contradiction. Either retention of ownership devices are only governed by the provisions concerning security rights listed in the provision or the list makes up the provisions where the rules for retention of ownership devices deviate from these for security rights. For the answer to this contradiction, one has to look in the commentary of yet another provision, article IX. – 2:101 DCFR. Here we find that the creation of retention of ownership devices is dealt with in its own rules in section 2 of chapter 2 on the creation and coverage of security rights and retention of ownership devices. The commentary continues that only provision IX. – 2:104 DCFR is partially applicable to retention of ownership devices.[780] Since this provision is also listed in paragraph one of the provision concerning the applicable rules for retention of ownership devices, the conclusion must be that the provisions applicable to both retention of ownership devices and security rights are limited to the provisions listed in this paragraph instead of being all provisions concerning security rights unless specifically provided otherwise.

160. *Reasons for separate treatment of retention of ownership devices* – The selective differentiation in the rules for security rights and retention of ownership devices was seen as a compromise between the full recharacterization method of Article 9 UCC[781] and the UNCITRAL unitary approach[782] on the one hand and the complete exclusion of retention of ownership devices from the domain of proprietary interests in movable goods for security purposes on the other hand.[783]

The reasons for the separate treatment of retention of ownership devices in the DCFR vary from rule to rule. With regards to the different rules for creation

779 Study Group on a European Civil Code and Research Group on EC Private Law (Acquis Group), *Principles, definitions and model rules of European private law – Draft common frame of reference (DCFR)*, (Munich: Sellier European Law Publishers, 2009), 5401.

780 Study Group on a European Civil Code and Research Group on EC Private Law (Acquis Group), *Principles, definitions and model rules of European private law – Draft common frame of reference (DCFR)*, (Munich: Sellier European Law Publishers, 2009), 5401.

781 See *supra* no. 35 *et seq.*

782 See *supra* no. 123 *et seq.*

783 A. VENEZIANO, 'A secured transactions' regime for Europe: treatment of acquisition finance devices and creditor's enforcement rights', (2008) 14 Juridica International. (89) 90.

of retention of ownership devices the reasoning is rather formal. The retention of ownership creditor has to retain ownership instead of retaining or granting a limited proprietary interest in the encumbered good. Consequently, the creation of a retention of ownership device has to be regulated in a separate set of rules.[784] Alternatively, the reason for the special priority rules for retention of ownership devices (i.e. super-priority) is economic. According to the DCFR, retention of ownership devices are mainly used by suppliers or manufacturers, who provide their wares on credit and thereby finance the acquisition of new goods for the retention of ownership debtor. However, without super-priority protection, retention of ownership creditors may be less willing to provide credit for the new acquisition of goods. The reasoning goes that often banks or other financiers have an all-encompassing, non-possessory security right in the debtor's present and future goods.[785] Consequently, under a first-in-time priority system, the newly acquired goods will likely fall under the bank's or financier's all-encompassing security right and make the retention of ownership creditor a second-ranking creditor in the goods he helped the debtor acquire. This would likely discourage retention of ownership creditors from providing acquisition credit. Therefore, the DCFR decided to provide the retention of ownership creditor with super-priority to give some other creditors the chance to obtain a first-ranking security position and to make sure that retention of ownership creditors are rewarded for the contribution they made to the debtor's pool of assets.[786] The drafters did realize that other creditors can provide a similar type of credit without selling or supplying goods on credit and retaining title, but by providing specific financing that enables the debtor to acquire a new movable good. In the spirit of a functional and unitary approach, these security rights are considered of the same economic importance and placed in the overarching category of acquisition finance devices[787], which are also entitled to super-priority.[788]

Finally, the different treatment of retention of ownership devices in the context of enforcement, is due to the fact that the secured creditor holds title to the encumbered good and an owner can generally count on a stronger

784 Study Group on a European Civil Code and Research Group on EC Private Law (Acquis Group), *Principles, definitions and model rules of European private law – Draft common frame of reference (DCFR)*, (Munich: Sellier European Law Publishers, 2009), 5448.

785 Study Group on a European Civil Code and Research Group on EC Private Law (Acquis Group), *Principles, definitions and model rules of European private law – Draft common frame of reference (DCFR)*, (Munich: Sellier European Law Publishers, 2009), 5554.

786 Study Group on a European Civil Code and Research Group on EC Private Law (Acquis Group), *Principles, definitions and model rules of European private law – Draft common frame of reference (DCFR)*, (Munich: Sellier European Law Publishers, 2009), 5555.

787 Art. IX.-1:201 (3) DCFR.

788 Art. IX.-4:102 (1) DCFR; Study Group on a European Civil Code and Research Group on EC Private Law (Acquis Group), *Principles, definitions and model rules of European private law – Draft common frame of reference (DCFR)*, (Munich: Sellier European Law Publishers, 2009), 5555; U. DROBNIG and O. BÖGER, *Proprietary security in movable assets (PEL Prop. Sec.)*, vol. 6, (Principles on European Law, Munich: Sellier Publishers, 2015), 4459.

protection.[789] The creditor's retained title means that the creditor simply has to regain possession of the encumbered good and terminate the underlying contract in which ownership was retained. Interestingly, this increased protection during enforcement proceedings is not offered to a creditor to whom ownership is transferred with the intention of guaranteeing a debt even though these creditors also technically hold title to the encumbered good and could count on the same protection.[790] Nevertheless, such creditor-owners are placed in the category of security rights and are considered as holders of a limited proprietary right in the encumbered good and not title.[791]

161. *Conclusion on the different treatment for retention of ownership devices* – In summary, the drafters did not have one specific reason for maintaining some separate rules for retention of ownership devices. Sometimes the different rule stems from the specific economic function retention of ownership devices perform, while at other times the different approach stems from the fact that retention of ownership creditors retain ownership to the encumbered good and not a limited proprietary interest. This bifurcated approach to the regulation of retention of ownership devices explains why the functional approach is not fully pursued. The recognition of the specific economic function of retention of ownership devices allows for a similar treatment with other functionally equivalent acquisition finance devices. However, the continued recognition of the ownership in hands of the retention of ownership creditor means that retention of ownership devices cannot be fully treated as other security rights even though they perform the same function.

2.3. *Application of the functional approach to retention of ownership devices*

162. *Overview* – In the next sections I set out how the functional approach of the DCFR is applied to retention of ownership devices and the potential consequences of the functional approach for retention of ownership devices. More specifically, I focus on the scope of the secured transactions in the DCFR (2.3.1.), the creation and third-party effectiveness of retention of ownership devices (2.3.2.) and the rights of retention of ownership creditors (2.3.3.).

---

789 Study Group on a European Civil Code and Research Group on EC Private Law (Acquis Group), *Principles, definitions and model rules of European private law – Draft common frame of reference (DCFR)*, (Munich: Sellier European Law Publishers, 2009), 5401; A. VENEZIANO, 'A secured transactions' regime for Europe: treatment of acquisition finance devices and creditor's enforcement rights', (2008) 14 Juridica International, (89) 90.

790 U. DROBNIG and O. BÖGER, *Proprietary security in movable assets (PEL Prop. Sec.)*, vol. 6, (Principles on European Law, Munich: Sellier Publishers, 2015), 212.

791 Art. IX.1:102 (3) DCFR; Study Group on a European Civil Code and Research Group on EC Private Law (Acquis Group), *Principles, definitions and model rules of European private law – Draft common frame of reference (DCFR)*, (Munich: Sellier European Law Publishers, 2009), 5392.

2.3.1. Scope

163. *Main categories of secured transactions* – Evidently, the functional approach has an effect on the scope of the DCFR. Classifying transactions on the basis of their function over their name results in broader categories and some recharacterization. Book IX DCFR contains two categories: (a) security rights and (b) acquisition financing devices. However, within the category of acquisition finance devices there is a carve-out for retention of ownership devices which goes against the otherwise functional approach in the DCFR. Visually, the different categories of proprietary interests in movable goods in the DCFR look as follows.

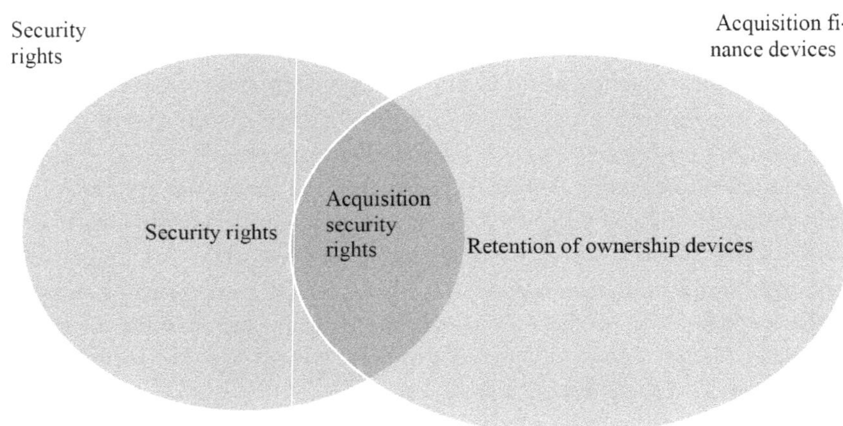

A. Security rights

164. *Definition of security rights* – In the DCFR security rights in movable goods are given a broad definition that encompasses:

> *any limited proprietary right in the asset which entitles the secured creditor to preferential satisfaction of the secured right from the encumbered asset.*
>
> *The term security right includes:*
>
> *(a) limited proprietary rights of a type which is generally recognised as designed to serve as proprietary security, especially the pledge;*
>
> *(b) limited proprietary rights, however named, that are based upon a contract for proprietary security and that are either intended by the parties to entitle the secured creditor to preferential satisfaction of the secured right from the encumbered asset or have this effect under the contract; and*

(c) *other rights which are regarded as security rights under the rules of this Book, such as the right referred to in IX. – 2:114 (Right of retention of possession) and the rights covered by paragraph (3)*[792]

This definition focuses on the function of a proprietary security right and generalizes the function that the variety of different secured transactions perform in most member states. Furthermore, the drafters explicate that the right of retention of possession will be considered a security right[793] and that the transfer of ownership of a movable asset with the intention or the effect of securing the satisfaction of an outstanding debt can create only a security right in the asset for the transferee.[794] As mentioned, this approach is based on the Financial Collateral Arrangements Directive, which also classifies transfers of ownership for security purposes as a type of secured transaction.[795] With regards to transfers of ownership for security purposes, the drafters further list that this includes a security transfer of ownership of corporeal assets, a security assignment, a sale and lease-back and a sale and resale.[796] In other words, the fact that the credit is guaranteed by means of transferring ownership from the debtor to the creditor does not exclude it from the category of security rights.

165. *Components of a security right* – The main elements of a security interest are its limited proprietary nature and the entitlement to preferential satisfaction from the enforcement of the encumbered asset.[797] The first element indicates that a security right in the DCFR is merely an encumbrance on the movable good, as opposed to the full ownership in a movable good. Book IX takes the position that the security right debtor is the owner of the encumbered good, even in cases where the security right debtor has supposedly transferred ownership of the encumbered good to the security right holder to secure an outstanding

---

792 Art. IX.-1:102 (1) DCFR.

793 Art. IX.-1:102 (2) (c) DCFR.

794 Art. IX.-1:102 (3) DCFR. See also, A. VENEZIANO, 'Security rights in movables in the DCFR: general presentation' in V. SAGAERT, M. E. STORME and E. TERRYN (eds.), *The Draft Common Frame of Reference: national and comparative perspectives*, (Antwerp: Intersentia, 2012), (305) 307.

795 Art. 2 Financial Collateral Directive. See also, A. VENEZIANO, 'Security rights in movables in the DCFR: general presentation' in V. SAGAERT, M. E. STORME and E. TERRYN (eds.), *The Draft Common Frame of Reference: national and comparative perspectives*, (Antwerp: Intersentia, 2012), (305) 307; H. BEALE, 'Secured transactions', (2008) 14 Juridica International, (96) 97; B. AKKERMANS, 'The European Union Development of European property law' in C. GODT (ed.), *Hanse Law School in Perspective – Legal Teaching and Cross Border Research after Lisbon*, (The Hague: Kluwer, 2011), 5.

796 Art. IX.-1:102 (4) DCFR.

797 Study Group on a European Civil Code and Research Group on EC Private Law (Acquis Group), *Principles, definitions and model rules of European private law – Draft common frame of reference (DCFR)*, (Munich: Sellier European Law Publishers, 2009), 5392.

debt.[798] The second element is the preferential treatment the security right holder enjoys when he comes into conflict with competing creditors. From a practical standpoint the preferential treatment of security rights is the most important aspect of security rights.[799]

To further guide the use of this broad definition of security rights, two additional criteria were formulated to determine whether a transaction is a security right: (1) the intentions of the parties or (2) the effect the transaction has.[800] The DCFR also employs a type of substance over form approach which looks at the actual effect of a transaction to determine its classification and not necessarily the name the parties have given to it.[801] The criterion of the intention of the parties on the one hand and the real-life effect of transactions on the other hand seem at first glance contradictory. Often, parties have the intention to avoid secured transactions law, especially if secured transactions law requires additional formalities, such as registration or limitations on enforcement. Consequently, the parties' intention would be a bad indicator for the classification of their transaction as a security right. However, in the context of the DCFR, the intention of the parties to the security agreement has to be understood as their intention to create a security right in a movable good, even though this specific transaction or this specific type of collateral has thus far not been explicitly classified as a security right.[802]

These criteria are also used to bring transfer of ownership devices within the scope of security rights. When parties have the intention or the transaction has the effect of securing a debt by transferring ownership to a movable good to a secured creditor, then the transaction is a security right.[803] The drafters continue with a list of transactions that are considered a transfer of ownership with the intention or effect of creating a security right.[804] However, this wording does suggest that such a transaction can be considered outside of the scope of security

---

798 Study Group on a European Civil Code and Research Group on EC Private Law (Acquis Group), *Principles, definitions and model rules of European private law – Draft common frame of reference (DCFR)*, (Munich: Sellier European Law Publishers, 2009), 5392.

799 Study Group on a European Civil Code and Research Group on EC Private Law (Acquis Group), *Principles, definitions and model rules of European private law – Draft common frame of reference (DCFR)*, (Munich: Sellier European Law Publishers, 2009), 5392.

800 Study Group on a European Civil Code and Research Group on EC Private Law (Acquis Group), *Principles, definitions and model rules of European private law – Draft common frame of reference (DCFR)*, (Munich: Sellier European Law Publishers, 2009), 5393.

801 Study Group on a European Civil Code and Research Group on EC Private Law (Acquis Group), *Principles, definitions and model rules of European private law – Draft common frame of reference (DCFR)*, (Munich: Sellier European Law Publishers, 2009), 5393.

802 Study Group on a European Civil Code and Research Group on EC Private Law (Acquis Group), *Principles, definitions and model rules of European private law – Draft common frame of reference (DCFR)*, (Munich: Sellier European Law Publishers, 2009), 5394.

803 Study Group on a European Civil Code and Research Group on EC Private Law (Acquis Group), *Principles, definitions and model rules of European private law – Draft common frame of reference (DCFR)*, (Munich: Sellier European Law Publishers, 2009), 5394.

804 Art. IX.-1:102 (4) DCFR.

rights when the parties do not have the intention of creating a security right or this transaction does not create that effect.[805] Consequently, the list in the last paragraph does not add very much except that it alerts creditors and debtors that such transactions could be considered a security right if they were created with that intention or have that effect. In other words, the list should not be read as an automatic inclusion of these transactions in the scope of Book IX DCFR.

B. Acquisition finance devices

166. *Scope of acquisition finance devices* – The second main category of proprietary interests in movable goods in the DCFR are the acquisition finance devices. The idea is that proprietary interests that secure acquisition financing deserve specific protection, regardless of whether the proprietary interests came about via retaining ownership or vesting a security right in a movable good to guarantee the acquisition price.[806] Following the functional equivalence between these mechanisms, the drafters decided that they should be governed by the same specific rules.[807] Interestingly enough, acquisition financing devices are not given their own provision, like security rights[808] or retention of ownership devices.[809] They are simply listed and defined among other relevant terms for Book IX DCFR even though this term makes up the second main category of proprietary interests in Book IX.[810] Consequently, the current order in Book IX of the DCFR could give the wrong impression that there are just security rights and retention of ownership devices, whereas acquisition finance devices make up a significant group of secured transactions in the DCFR. Following the definition of acquisition finance devices, the category of acquisition finance devices is made up of: (i) specific security rights for acquisition financing (hereafter, acquisition security rights) and (ii) retention of ownership devices.

i. Acquisition security rights

167. *Absence of definition for acquisition security rights* – According to the DCFR, the category of acquisition finance devices consists of retention of ownership devices and security rights which:

---

805 Study Group on a European Civil Code and Research Group on EC Private Law (Acquis Group), *Principles, definitions and model rules of European private law – Draft common frame of reference (DCFR)*, (Munich: Sellier European Law Publishers, 2009), 5394–5395.

806 A. VENEZIANO, 'The DCFR Book on Secured Transactions: some policy choices made by the Working Group' in S. VAN ERP, A. SALOMONS and B. AKKERMANS (eds.), *The future of European property law*, (Munich: Sellier European Law, 2012), (123) 134.

807 Study Group on a European Civil Code and Research Group on EC Private Law (Acquis Group), *Principles, definitions and model rules of European private law – Draft common frame of reference (DCFR)*, (Munich: Sellier European Law Publishers, 2009), 5404.

808 Art. IX-1:102 DCFR.

809 Art. IX.-1:103 DCFR.

810 Art. IX.-1:201 (3) DCFR.

- *secure the right of the seller to payment of the purchase price for the encumbered asset under a contract of sale*[811];
- *secure the right of a lender of repayment of a loan granted to the buyer for payment of the purchase price for the encumbered asset*[812];

For simplicity, I have recharacterized the second group of acquisition finance devices as acquisition security rights. As the name suggests, acquisition security rights are like the other security rights in the DCFR and grant the acquisition security right holder a limited proprietary interest in the encumbered asset. For the most part, acquisition security rights are governed by the same rules as normal security rights. However, due to the fact that acquisition security rights guarantee acquisition financing and are acquisition financing devices, they are subjected to some specific rules. For example, acquisition security rights are also given super-priority status[813] and, with regards to third-party effectiveness, acquisition security rights have a grace period of 35 days during which they can register their acquisition security right without loss of their super-priority status.[814]

The drafters make it very clear that acquisition security rights perform the same function as retention of ownership devices and should therefore be given the same treatment in the DCFR.[815] The inspiration for the introduction of a special security right for acquisition financiers can also be found in Sweden[816], Article 9 UCC and its many spin-offs in Canada, Australia and New Zealand.[817] However, the DCFR does not specify that acquisition security rights have to be created or are registered in a specific way that would signal the acquisition security right status to other creditors. Furthermore, the drafters do not give further guidance on how creditors can make sure that their credit is truly given for the acquisition of a new movable good and thus their security right will be classified as an acquisition financing device. This is especially relevant for financiers, who provide credit for the acquisition of a new good and want to enjoy the advantage of having an acquisition security right in the newly acquired good. Given that the introduction of an acquisition security right was inspired

811 Art. IX.-1:201 (3) (b) (i) DCFR.

812 Art. IX.-1:201 (3) (c) (ii) DCFR.

813 Art. IX.- 4:102 (1) DCFR; Study Group on a European Civil Code and Research Group on EC Private Law (Acquis Group), *Principles, definitions and model rules of European private law – Draft common frame of reference (DCFR)*, (Munich: Sellier European Law Publishers, 2009), 5401–5402.

814 Art. IX.-3:107 (2)-(3) DCFR.

815 Study Group on a European Civil Code and Research Group on EC Private Law (Acquis Group), *Principles, definitions and model rules of European private law – Draft common frame of reference (DCFR)*, (Munich: Sellier European Law Publishers, 2009), 5404–5405.

816 Study Group on a European Civil Code and Research Group on EC Private Law (Acquis Group), *Principles, definitions and model rules of European private law – Draft common frame of reference (DCFR)*, (Munich: Sellier European Law Publishers, 2009), 5397.

817 See *supra* no. 4.

by Sweden and Article 9 UCC, interested member states could look to these jurisdictions for information on how to delineate acquisition security rights from the other security rights in movable goods. For example, in the United States acquisition financiers are given the advice to transfer the credit directly to the manufacturer or supplier of the acquired good.[818] That way there can be no debate concerning the use of the credit and the status of the acquisition financier.

ii. Retention of ownership devices

168. *Definition of retention of ownership devices* – Retention of ownership devices make up the second group of acquisition finance devices.[819] In the DCFR the term retention of ownership is defined as follows:

> (1) *There is a retention of ownership device when ownership is retained by the owner of supplied assets in order to secure a right to performance of an obligation.*[820]

Furthermore, the drafters explicated a few transactions they automatically consider as retention of ownership devices:

> (2) *The term retention of ownership device includes:*
> (a) *retention of ownership by a seller under a contract of sale;*
> (b) *ownership of the supplier under a contract of hire-purchase;*
> (c) *ownership of the leased assets under a contract of leasing, provided that according to the terms of the contract the lessee at the expiration of the lease period has an option to acquire ownership of, or a right to continue to use, the leased asset without payment or for merely nominal payment (financial leasing); and*
> (d) *ownership of the supplier under a contract of consignment with the intention or the effect of fulfilling a security purpose.*[821]

In the context of the DCFR, I will continue with the term retention of ownership device. Following the DCFR, this term includes traditional retention of title clauses in sale agreements, but also retention of title in hire-purchase, lease agreements with a nominal purchase option and consignment agreements with the intention of securing credit.

---

818 See *supra* no. 48.

819 Art. IX-1:201 (3) (a) DCFR; A. VENEZIANO, 'Security rights in movables in the DCFR: general presentation' in V. SAGAERT, M. E. STORME and E. TERRYN (eds.), *The Draft Common Frame of Reference: national and comparative perspectives*, (Antwerp: Intersentia, 2012), (305) 311.

820 Art. IX. – 1:103, (1) DCFR.

821 Art. IX.-1:103, (2) DCFR.

169. *Justifications for the separate category of retention of ownership devices* – The importance of retention of ownership devices in the DCFR immediately becomes clear in the separate provision that is dedicated to its definition and scope.[822] As mentioned, the drafters of the DCFR did not think it was opportune to abandon the concept of securing supply-side credit on the basis of retaining title and recharacterizing them to acquisition security rights. The main argument for the continued recognition of retention of ownership devices is that owners can generally count on a stronger protection during bankruptcy and execution proceedings brought by other creditors.[823] However, the actual stronger protection of creditors who have retained ownership during bankruptcy and enforcement proceedings in various member states is debatable.[824] For example in Belgium the retention of title-creditor can revendicate the encumbered asset during bankruptcy proceedings but only within a certain timeframe[825] and with return of the already received payments.[826]

Furthermore, the drafters argue that the recharacterization of retention of ownership devices in an acquisition security right would not guarantee that member states would give this new sub-category of security rights the required advantage of super-priority during bankruptcy and enforcement proceedings. This would diminish the value and potential of acquisition security rights to actually replace retention of ownership devices.[827] Therefore, the drafters opted to maintain the concept of retention of ownership device, which they presume automatically have super-priority and additional protections due to their retained title and thus guarantee advantageous protection for acquisition financing during bankruptcy and enforcement proceedings. However, a counter argument is that the DCFR proposes changes to or prefers certain policies in other areas of secured transactions law without hesitating whether this will be adopted with the necessary changes to insolvency and execution law in the adopting states. For example, the DCFR assigns super-priority status to

---

822 Art. IX.-1:103 DCFR.

823 Study Group on a European Civil Code and Research Group on EC Private Law (Acquis Group), *Principles, definitions and model rules of European private law – Draft common frame of reference (DCFR)*, (Munich: Sellier European Law Publishers, 2009), 5397; A. VENEZIANO, 'The DCFR Book on Secured Transactions: some policy choices made by the Working Group' in S. VAN ERP, A. SALOMONS and B. AKKERMANS (eds.), *The future of European property law*, (Munich: Sellier European Law, 2012), (123) 132; U. DROBNIG, 'Security rights in movables' in A. S. HARTKAMP and others (eds.), *Towards a European Civil Code*, (Alphen on the Rhine: Kluwer Law International, 2011), (1025) 1041.

824 A. VENEZIANO, 'A secured transactions' regime for Europe: treatment of acquisition finance devices and creditor's enforcement rights', (2008) 14 Juridica International, (89) 90.

825 Art. XX.194 Belgian Code of Economic Law.

826 Art. 72 SRA.

827 Study Group on a European Civil Code and Research Group on EC Private Law (Acquis Group), *Principles, definitions and model rules of European private law – Draft common frame of reference (DCFR)*, (Munich: Sellier European Law Publishers, 2009), 5397.

acquisition security rights.[828] Evidently, the super-priority status of acquisition security rights also depends on their recognition in insolvency and execution law. The drafters do not explain why they assume that the assignment of super-priority status for acquisition security rights in insolvency and execution law is possible, but a full acceptance of this new category of security rights combined with the recharacterization of retention of ownership devices would not be. Presumably, there is an assumption that some states will not be willing to adopt the DCFR when it advocates for the recharacterization of retention of ownership devices into a more general category of acquisition finance devices. There are different reasons for this possible resistance against a recharacterization approach: a perceived influence from Article 9 UCC and the United States[829] or a general tendency in civil law jurisdictions (which are the majority of European member states) to keep ownership as the most absolute proprietary right in a special category.[830] Therefore, presumably as a compromise, the drafters kept retention of ownership devices as a separate category and merely recommend to upgrade acquisition security rights to a similar super-priority status. If then member states do not adopt the concept of acquisition security rights with super-priority, then at least these states would likely still have some form of retention of ownership devices that grant additional protection to secured creditors based on the retained title and provide additional protection for acquisition financing.

Finally, the category of retention of ownership devices is also preserved to maintain the legal similarity between retention of ownership devices and finance leasing. The latter construction refers to a three-party transaction in which the lessee instructs a lessor to acquire goods from a supplier or manufacturer. In turn the lessor then leases the acquired goods to the lessee for a regular payment. At the end of the agreement, the lessee in most cases has paid the value of the leased good via the rental payments and will generally be given the option to definitively purchase the leased good for a nominal amount. In this form, finance leasing has a strong similarity with a traditional retention of ownership device in a sale agreement. Therefore, the drafters argue that retention of ownership devices should be maintained as a separate category to preserve the legal similarity and economic correspondence between these two mechanisms.[831] However, this argument also suggests that recharacterizing retention of ownership devices to a form of acquisition security right would disturb the legal similarity between

---

828 Art. IX.-4:102 (1) DCFR.

829 G. MCCORMACK, 'The CFR and credit securities – a suitable case for treatment?' in A. VAQUER (ed.), *European private law beyond the Common Frame of Reference*, (Groningen: Europa Law Publishing, 2008), (99) 106.

830 F. MEZZANOTTE, 'The protection of ownership of goods in the DCFR: an "exclusion strategy" at the core of European property law?', (2013) 4 ERPL, (1009) 1019.

831 Study Group on a European Civil Code and Research Group on EC Private Law (Acquis Group), *Principles, definitions and model rules of European private law – Draft common frame of reference (DCFR)*, (Munich: Sellier European Law Publishers, 2009), 5398.

retention of ownership devices in sale agreements and finance leases. This reasoning is incorrect. If the DCFR would opt for a full unitary approach with recharacterization of all retention of ownership devices to acquisition security rights, the recharacterization would not be limited to retention of ownership devices in sale agreements but to all retention of ownership devices in which this mechanism is used to secure acquisition financing. Consequently, in a recharacterization approach finance leases will also be recharacterized to an acquisition security right. In that scenario, retention of ownership devices in a sale agreement and finance leases would still be legally similar in a way that reflects their economic correspondence. Therefore, this argument as a reason not to recharacterize retention of ownership to acquisition security rights does not hold water. Furthermore, the drafters give no further guidance on the actual problem concerning finance leases and retention ownership devices: how finance leases that are retention of ownership devices should be delineated from operational leases.[832] For example, the drafters give no indication on what should be considered a nominal amount and when this threshold is surpassed. Additionally, the drafters only mention the functional similarity between retention of ownership devices in sale agreements and leasing in three-party finance leases. However, a movable good can also be leased in a two-party transaction and sold at the end of the agreement for a nominal amount. What's more, such two-party lease agreements show an even greater similarity with retention of ownership devices in sale agreements. According to the DCFR, these transactions can fall under the scope of retention of ownership devices[833], but the DCFR does not give further indication as to how these leases have to be distinguished from true operational leases. Nevertheless, this is a more relevant issue than whether the legal similarity between retention of ownership devices in sale agreements and finance leases would be disturbed by the recharacterization of retention of ownership devices to acquisition security rights. Therefore, the argument to keep the category of retention of ownership devices to maintain the legal similarity between retention of ownership in sale agreements and finance leases is not convincing, whereas the more relevant issue of delineating finance leases from true leases is not addressed.

832 In an operational or true lease, the lessor has no intention to transfer ownership of the leased good to the lessee at the end of the lease agreement. See, notes on art. IX.-1:103 DCFR in U. DROBNIG and O. BÖGER, *Proprietary security in movable assets (PEL Prop. Sec.)*, vol. 6, (Principles on European Law, Munich: Sellier Publishers, 2015), 250.

833 Study Group on a European Civil Code and Research Group on EC Private Law (Acquis Group), *Principles, definitions and model rules of European private law – Draft common frame of reference (DCFR)*, (Munich: Sellier European Law Publishers, 2009), 5398.

2.3.2. Creation and third-party effectiveness of retention of ownership devices

A. Creation

170. *Distinction between creation and third-party effectiveness* – A primary innovation of the DCFR is the distinction between creation and third-party effectiveness of security rights and retention of ownership devices.[834] First, the creation makes the retention of ownership device and security right effective between the parties to the agreement.[835] However, the mere creation of a retention of ownership device already has proprietary effects against third parties even though the specific requirements for third-party effectiveness[836] have not been fulfilled. For example, a retention of ownership creditor can claim damages from a third person for damage done to the supplied assets. This right does not depend on the third-party effectiveness of the retention of ownership device.[837]

171. *Requirements for the creation of a retention of ownership device* – According to the DCFR, a retention of ownership device is created when four requirements are met:

(a) *the seller, supplier or lessor is the owner of the supplied asset or acts with authority in relation to this asset;*
(b) *the asset is specified in the contract for proprietary security;*
(c) *the secured right exists*[838]*; and*
(d) *the seller, supplier or lessor retains ownership.*[839]

For the most part the requirements for the creation of a retention of ownership device are self-explanatory and do not require additional steps from the retention of ownership creditor. For example, most transactions with a retention of ownership clause already specify which goods are supplied. Consequently, the retention of ownership creditor does not have to take any additional steps in the

834 W. FABER, 'Proprietary security rights in movables – European developments', (2014) 22 Juridica Int'l., (27) 30.

835 Study Group on a European Civil Code and Research Group on EC Private Law (Acquis Group), *Principles, definitions and model rules of European private law – Draft common frame of reference (DCFR)*, (Munich: Sellier European Law Publishers, 2009), 5410.

836 Chapter 3 of Book IX DCFR.

837 Study Group on a European Civil Code and Research Group on EC Private Law (Acquis Group), *Principles, definitions and model rules of European private law – Draft common frame of reference (DCFR)*, (Munich: Sellier European Law Publishers, 2009), 5411.

838 The existence of the secured right refers to the existence of the performance which secured by the retained ownership, such as the payment of the purchase price (see, Study Group on a European Civil Code and Research Group on EC Private Law (Acquis Group), *Principles, definitions and model rules of European private law – Draft common frame of reference (DCFR)*, (Munich: Sellier European Law Publishers, 2009), 5451).

839 Art. IX. – 2:201 (1) (a)-(d) DCFR.

agreement to create the retention of ownership device, unless ownership is only retained for a few goods. In that case, the specific goods covered by a retention of ownership device have to be specified.[840]

172. *Creation as grounds for differentiation between retention of ownership devices and security rights* – The creation of retention of ownership devices is one of the areas where the rules for retention of ownership devices are different from those for the creation of security rights.[841] According to the drafters, some of the main differences between security rights and retention of ownership devices are due to the difference in the methods of creation.[842] However, this view is contradictive to the functional approach in the DCFR. It is difficult to reconcile the continuation of the special status of retention of ownership devices due to their specific method of creation based on retaining title and govern them following separate rules, while simultaneously pursuing the functional approach which aims to transcend these dogmatic differences between retention of ownership devices and acquisition security rights by focusing on their functional similarities over their dogmatic differences. In other words, by continuing to consider the creation of retention of ownership devices as a reason to separate retention of ownership devices from acquisition security rights, the drafters are falling back on dogmatic differences whereas the point of these functional frameworks is to go beyond those and focus on functional similarity and equivalent legal outcomes.

Fortunately, the difference between retention of ownership devices and acquisition security rights due to their difference in creation must not be overstated. In actuality, retention of ownership devices are for the most part regulated by the same rules as acquisition security rights[843] and only in rare cases will the retained ownership result in different outcomes than those for acquisition security rights, such as during enforcement proceedings.[844]

173. *Creating (acquisition) security rights vs. retention of ownership devices* – The requirements for the creation of an (acquisition) security right are not that different from these for retention of ownership devices:

840 Study Group on a European Civil Code and Research Group on EC Private Law (Acquis Group), *Principles, definitions and model rules of European private law – Draft common frame of reference (DCFR)*, (Munich: Sellier European Law Publishers, 2009), 5451–5452.

841 A. J. VAN DER WEIDE, '(On)zekerheden in het DCFR. Boek IX Proprietary security in movable assets', (2011) NTBR, (53) 56.

842 Study Group on a European Civil Code and Research Group on EC Private Law (Acquis Group), *Principles, definitions and model rules of European private law – Draft common frame of reference (DCFR)*, (Munich: Sellier European Law Publishers, 2009), 5449–5450.

843 Art. IX. – 1:104 DCFR.

844 Study Group on a European Civil Code and Research Group on EC Private Law (Acquis Group), *Principles, definitions and model rules of European private law – Draft common frame of reference (DCFR)*, (Munich: Sellier European Law Publishers, 2009), 5663 *et seq.*

(a) the asset exists;
(b) the asset is transferable;
(c) the secured right exists; and
(d) the additional requirements for the creation of a security right by granting, by retention or on the basis of a right of retention of possession are fulfilled.[845]

For the most part, an (acquisition) security right comes into existence the same way as a retention of ownership device. The DCFR does explicate for (acquisition) security rights that the encumbered good has to be transferable (i.e. ownership can be transferred). This requirement is necessary to make sure that in the case of default and enforcement, ownership to the encumbered good can be transferred to the secured creditor.[846] Evidently this step is not necessary for retention of ownership devices, where ownership automatically resides with the retention of ownership creditor. The provision also refers to the additional requirements for granting or retaining a security right or creating one on the basis of a right of retention of possession. These requirements are specific to the method of vesting the security right, but also do not require very many additional steps from the security right holder. The creation of a right of retention of possession only depends upon the additional requirement of the secured creditor being entitled to the retention of possession of an asset as security.[847] In the case of granting a security right the formal requirements are:

(a) the asset to be encumbered is specified by the parties;
(b) the security provider has the right or authority to grant a security right in the asset;
(c) the secured creditor is entitled as against the security provider to the granting of a security right on the basis of the contract for proprietary security; and
(d) the secured creditor and the security provider agree on the granting of a security right to the secured creditor.[848]

174. *Creation of security right by retention of a security right in the encumbered good* – If the security right is created by retaining a security right, then the parties have to take following requirements into account:

(1) In addition to the requirements under Subsection 1, the creation of a security right in a movable asset by retention requires that:
  (a) the secured creditor is entitled as against the transferee to the retention of a security right by virtue of the contract for proprietary security; and

845 Art. IX. – 2:102 DCFR.
846 Study Group on a European Civil Code and Research Group on EC Private Law (Acquis Group), *Principles, definitions and model rules of European private law – Draft common frame of reference (DCFR)*, (Munich: Sellier European Law Publishers, 2009), 5412.
847 Art. IX. – 2:114 DCFR.
848 Art. IX. – 2:105 DCFR.

(b) *the secured creditor transfers its ownership in the asset to be encumbered by the retained security right to the transferee.*[849]

It is interesting that this form of creating a security right exists. In this scenario, the secured creditor owns the movable good and transfers it to the debtor while at the same time retaining a security right in the movable good. One wonders why the DCFR offers this option, when a very similar, if not easier and more logical, result can be achieved by vesting a retention of ownership device. Especially since the DCFR itself points out that the security holder's rights in this scenario are more limited than those of a retention of ownership creditor.[850] A possible reason for providing this method of creating a security right is to leave the door open for a regime in which ownership can no longer be retained, but sellers and other suppliers can transfer ownership while immediately retaining a(n) (acquisition) security right. In such a regime this method of creation can serve a useful purpose, whereas under the current regime it seems more likely that creditors will opt for a retention of ownership device instead of the more round-about way of vesting a security right via retention.

175. *Conclusion* – There are differences between the methods of creation for retention of ownership devices and security rights, but neither the difference in requirements, nor the actual outcomes of these differences should be overstated. For the most part, the creation for both mechanisms is very similar, is not too burdensome on the parties involved and results in quite similar security mechanisms.

B. Third-party effectiveness

176. *Reasons for obtaining third-party effectiveness* – As mentioned, the DCFR introduces a distinction between the creation and third-party effectiveness of security rights and retention of ownership devices.[851] In the majority of cases, the creation of the security right or acquisition finance devices only has an effect between the parties, but not against other holders of proprietary rights in the encumbered asset[852], an execution creditor[853] or the insolvency administrator of

---

849 Art. IX. – 2:113 DCFR.

850 Study Group on a European Civil Code and Research Group on EC Private Law (Acquis Group), *Principles, definitions and model rules of European private law – Draft common frame of reference (DCFR)*, (Munich: Sellier European Law Publishers, 2009), 5442.

851 Study Group on a European Civil Code and Research Group on EC Private Law (Acquis Group), *Principles, definitions and model rules of European private law – Draft common frame of reference (DCFR)*, (Munich: Sellier European Law Publishers, 2009), 5473.

852 Art. IX.-3:101 (1) (a) DCFR.

853 Art. IX.-3:101 (1) (b) DCFR.

the debtor (i.e. security provider)[854] unless additional third-party effectiveness requirements are fulfilled.[855]

177. *Requirements for third-party effectiveness* – Acquisition finance devices, including retention of ownership devices, are only effective against third parties when registered.[856] This requirement is somewhat surprising for retention of ownership devices, since the registration of retention of ownership is far from generally accepted in the European member states.[857] However, under the DCFR retention of ownership and acquisition security rights are treated equally and since acquisition security rights require registration, possession or control for third-party effectiveness this requirement is expanded to retention of ownership devices.[858] However, for practical reasons the third-party effectiveness requirement for acquisition finance devices is limited to registration, since it is unlikely that a debtor would acquire a new good but leave the secured creditor in possession to meet the third-party effectiveness requirement.

Following this registration requirement, the following minimum information has to be submitted in the security rights registry:

- *(a) it is made in respect of an identified security provider;*
- *(b) it contains a minimum declaration as to the encumbered assets;*
- *(c) it is indicated by one or several references to a list of categories of assets to which category the encumbered assets belong;*
- *(d) the requirements of consent are fulfilled; and*
- *(e) it is accompanied by a declaration of the creditor that the latter assumes liability for damages caused to the security provider or third persons by a wrongful registration.*[859]

Interestingly, the DCFR does not impose an obligation to indicate whether the proprietary interest is a security right or an acquisition financing device. This is surprising given the difference the classification of either a security right or acquisition financing device has on the priority rules and can thus be considered

854 Art. IX.-3:101 (1) (c) DCFR.

855 A. VENEZIANO, 'The DCFR Book on Secured Transactions: some policy choices made by the Working Group' in S. VAN ERP, A. SALOMONS and B. AKKERMANS (eds.), *The future of European property law*, (Munich: Sellier European Law, 2012), (123) 129.

856 Art. IX.3:107 and art. IX.3:303 DCFR.

857 E.-M. KIENINGER, 'Evaluation: a common? Convergences, subsisting differences and possible ways for harmonisation' in E.-M. KIENINGER (ed.), *Security rights in movable property in European private law*, (Cambridge: Cambridge University Press, 2004), 658; U. DROBNIG and O. BÖGER, *Proprietary security in movable assets (PEL Prop. Sec.)*, vol. 6, (Principles on European Law, Munich: Sellier Publishers, 2015), 467–469.

858 Study Group on a European Civil Code and Research Group on EC Private Law (Acquis Group), *Principles, definitions and model rules of European private law – Draft common frame of reference (DCFR)*, (Munich: Sellier European Law Publishers, 2009), 5482 *et seq.*

859 Art. IX. – 3:306 (1) DCFR.

as quite relevant information for third parties making use of the security rights registry. The DCFR does mention that when a retention of ownership device is registered, the entry should be adapted to mention a buyer, hire-purchaser, lessee or consignee instead of security provider.[860] This adaptation will indicate to the third-party transferee that the proprietary interest is a retention of ownership device and could qualify for super-priority status. However, for acquisition security rights no such adaptations have to be made, nor any mention of the fact that the security provider is an acquisition financier and has vested an acquisition security right. As a result, the registry leaves out quite relevant information for third parties interested in the encumbrances that have already been vested on the debtor's assets.

178. *Grace period for registration of acquisition finance devices* – Despite the general rule of registration to obtain third-party effectiveness, acquisition financiers are given a 35 day grace period following the delivery of the good to the debtor. Within those 35 days, the acquisition finance device will be considered effective against third parties regardless of the registration. The choice for 35 days is justified by the general practice to grant debtors about 30 days of delay in payment. For such a common practice the drafters did not think it was necessary to register the device, especially when often the payment is made within 30 days and the acquisition finance device disappears at that time. However, if the acquisition financier wants to be sure of his protection against third parties after 30 days, he can register the acquisition finance device and obtain retroactive third-party effectiveness from the day of creation, including super-priority as opposed to third parties.[861] One wonders if the retroactive effect of the registration within 35 days is actually necessary. Acquisition finance devices have super-priority so will automatically surpass earlier vested claims to the encumbered good. Consequently, making the registration effective from the day of creation is unnecessary and inadvertently creates the impression that these acquisition finance devices are surpassed by security rights and claims that became effective before the creation of the acquisition finance device. Therefore, a better way of phrasing this rule would be to state that registration of an acquisition finance device within 35 days entitles the acquisition financier to super-priority.

---

860 Art. IX. – 1:104, (2) DCFR; Study Group on a European Civil Code and Research Group on EC Private Law (Acquis Group), *Principles, definitions and model rules of European private law – Draft common frame of reference (DCFR)*, (Munich: Sellier European Law Publishers, 2009), 5504–5505.

861 Art. IX.-3:107 (2) DCFR; Study Group on a European Civil Code and Research Group on EC Private Law (Acquis Group), *Principles, definitions and model rules of European private law – Draft common frame of reference (DCFR)*, (Munich: Sellier European Law Publishers, 2009), 5482–5483.

Based on the 35 day grace period, the acquisition financier is able to surpass other secured creditors, execution creditors and even insolvency practitioners that have obtained an effective claim to the good during the grace period. However, especially with regards to the super-priority of the acquisition finance device as opposed to the insolvency administrator, this will require a recognition of the 35 day grace period in insolvency proceedings. As mentioned, the drafters of the DCFR are skeptical whether adopting states will make the necessary changes to their insolvency law to accommodate the specific position granted to acquisition financiers. Consequently, the drafters still recommend that acquisition financiers register their acquisition finance device as quickly as possible to avoid debate concerning their super-prioritized position as opposed to claims that came about during the 35 day grace period.[862] Furthermore, if the acquisition financier registers his acquisition finance device outside of the 35 day grace period, then the acquisition finance device will be effective against third parties but it will not enjoy super-priority. In that case the retention of ownership device has priority based on the day of registration, but no longer has super-priority as opposed to previously registered security rights.[863]

179. *Exemptions to requirements for third-party effectiveness* – Finally, the DCFR also provides an exemption from the registration requirement for acquisition finance devices in goods supplied to consumers. The drafters do not explicate why this exemption is provided. Presumably, the reasoning is similar to the one used in Article 9 UCC: the amount of consumer transactions on credit, the burden registration would place on the registration system and the lower value of consumer goods which make the good less valuable to other creditors and third parties.[864] The drafters do explicitly state that the exemption to register only applies to acquisition finance devices in the directly acquired consumer goods, but does not extend to proceeds and other assets different from the supplied asset.[865] The purpose of the provision is to protect acquisitions by consumers, but not to set up a general privilege for all assets owned by consumers.[866] In other words, the acquisition finance device is not exempted because it was granted to a consumer, but because it was vested in a consumer

862 Study Group on a European Civil Code and Research Group on EC Private Law (Acquis Group), *Principles, definitions and model rules of European private law – Draft common frame of reference (DCFR)*, (Munich: Sellier European Law Publishers, 2009), 5484.

863 IX.-3:107 (3) DCFR; Study Group on a European Civil Code and Research Group on EC Private Law (Acquis Group), *Principles, definitions and model rules of European private law – Draft common frame of reference (DCFR)*, (Munich: Sellier European Law Publishers, 2009), 5484.

864 See *supra* no. 59.

865 IX.-3:107 (4) DCFR.

866 Study Group on a European Civil Code and Research Group on EC Private Law (Acquis Group), *Principles, definitions and model rules of European private law – Draft common frame of reference (DCFR)*, (Munich: Sellier European Law Publishers, 2009), 5484.

good. Consequently, acquisition financing devices in the proceeds of the acquired consumer good or other assets belonging to the consumer have to be registered. This raises two questions. First, it is not clear which other assets could be acquired by a consumer that are not consumer goods that would require a registration to make the acquisition financing device effective against third parties. It is unclear whether there is actually a risk that this privilege of exemption of registration could be expanded to all assets of the consumer as the DCFR suggests. Second, the exemption does not apply to proceeds of the acquired consumer goods. Consequently, the acquisition financier has to register the acquisition financing device in proceeds, if he wants to maintain third-party effectiveness. On the one hand, the fact that acquisition financiers have to register their acquisition financing device into proceeds is a significant disadvantage as opposed to other secured creditors for whom the third-party effectiveness of their security right or acquisition financing device in the proceeds of non-consumer goods is automatically provided.[867] On the other hand, given the typical lower value and higher depreciation of consumer goods, it is unlikely that the acquired consumer goods are sold and, even if they were sold, that the proceeds would amount to much. As a result, the fact that automatic third-party effectiveness does not automatically extend to proceeds of the acquired consumer good will likely not affect the acquisition financier very strongly.

2.3.3. Rights of retention of ownership creditors

180. *Overview* – In the next section I assess the rights of retention of ownership creditors according to the DCFR. More specifically, I focus on the extent to which the integration of retention of ownership devices in Book IX of the DCFR has impacted the retention of title ownership's rights and led to equitable legal outcomes between (acquisition) security rights. The different sections cover the retention of ownership creditor's (a) right to dispose, (b) right to trace, (c) super-priority and (d) enforcement.

A. Right to dispose

181. *Right to dispose following a retention of ownership device* – The DCFR makes it very clear that a retention of ownership creditor remains the full owner of the encumbered good.[868] Consequently, the debtor is not able to transfer

---

867 Art. IX. – 3:101 (2) DCFR; Study Group on a European Civil Code and Research Group on EC Private Law (Acquis Group), *Principles, definitions and model rules of European private law – Draft common frame of reference (DCFR)*, (Munich: Sellier European Law Publishers, 2009), 5459–5460.

868 Study Group on a European Civil Code and Research Group on EC Private Law (Acquis Group), *Principles, definitions and model rules of European private law – Draft common frame of reference (DCFR)*, (Munich: Sellier European Law Publishers, 2009), 5484–5485.

title to the encumbered asset to a third party (*nemo dat quod non habet*).[869] Furthermore, one would assume that this means that the retention of ownership creditor can still dispose of the encumbered good. Given that the right to dispose does not reside with the debtor, the logical assumption is that the right to dispose of the good must be with the creditor who retained ownership.

182. *Allocation of the right to dispose between the retention of ownership creditor and debtor* – On the one hand, the DCFR allows the debtor, who is a manufacturer or trader, to dispose of the encumbered goods, designated for sale and lease and products of industrial material, when this occurs in the ordinary course of business. In that case, the encumbered good goes to the third-party transferee free of any encumbrance.[870] The DCFR explicitly states that this provision also applies to retention of ownership devices.[871] In many European states there was already a trend to allow debtors to dispose of goods encumbered with non-possessory security rights, including for retention of title.[872] The proceeds of these goods are often used to pay off the debts secured by the security rights. Consequently, the secured creditor often benefits from the fact that the debtor is allowed to dispose of the encumbered goods in the ordinary course of business.

On the other hand, general contract law principles will likely prevent the retention of ownership creditor from disposing of the encumbered good a second time. When a retention of ownership device is used, the intention is to retain ownership only until the performance of an agreed upon obligation.[873] Consequently, when the debtor performs his obligation, ownership transfers to him. The debtor's claim to the encumbered asset is even made explicit in the DCFR. In Book VIII DCFR, the debtor's right to acquire ownership upon payment of the outstanding obligation is set out and made effective against third parties.[874] If the retention of ownership creditor would dispose again of the encumbered good, he would be in violation of his obligation to perform his agreement in good faith.[875] Therefore, the retention of ownership creditor cannot simply dispose of the encumbered asset a second time based on the theory that he is still full owner of the encumbered good.

---

869 Study Group on a European Civil Code and Research Group on EC Private Law (Acquis Group), *Principles, definitions and model rules of European private law – Draft common frame of reference (DCFR)*, (Munich: Sellier European Law Publishers, 2009), 5401–5402.

870 Art. IX.-5:204 DCFR.

871 Study Group on a European Civil Code and Research Group on EC Private Law (Acquis Group), *Principles, definitions and model rules of European private law – Draft common frame of reference (DCFR)*, (Munich: Sellier European Law Publishers, 2009), 5582.

872 U. DROBNIG and O. BÖGER, *Proprietary security in movable assets (PEL Prop. Sec.)*, vol. 6, (Principles on European Law, Munich: Sellier Publishers, 2015), 641–642.

873 Art. IX.-1:103 (1) DCFR.

874 Art. VIII.-2:307 DCFR.

875 Art. III.-1:103 DCFR.

183. *The debtor's right to dispose of the encumbered good* – These principles mean that retention of ownership does not automatically place the right to dispose with the retention of ownership creditor. On the contrary, the retention of ownership debtor has a pretty strong position to dispose of the encumbered good. The debtor may dispose of the encumbered good free of its encumbrance when the transfer takes place in the ordinary course of business[876] or the third-party transferee acted in good faith when acquiring the good.[877] The criteria for a good faith acquisition are set out in Book VIII DCFR concerning the acquisition and loss of ownership[878]: (1) the standard requirements for transfer of ownership are fulfilled[879] (with the exception of the authority to dispose of the good)[880], (2) the requirements for delivery are fulfilled[881], (3) the good is acquired for value and (4) the transferee did not know, nor could be reasonably expected to know that the transferor had no right or authority to dispose of the good. The rather strict criteria for a good faith acquisition are the result of compromise.[882] On the one hand, the drafters wanted the option for good faith acquisitions of goods so that good faith market participants are protected when acquiring new goods. On the other hand, the drafters wanted to make sure that only under certain circumstances an unauthorized transfer results in a good faith acquisition and the loss of ownership of the actual owner.[883] This balance explains the limitation to for value transactions and the limited interpretation of good faith. The exemption of gratuitous transactions is justified, since in these transactions the disadvantage of the original owner's potential loss of the good outweighs the transferee's disadvantage of not receiving the good despite his good faith. Furthermore, the drafters opted for a strict interpretation, where even the slightest amount of negligence excludes the transferee from a possible good faith acquisition.[884] Additionally, in Book IX DCFR a transfer of ownership to a third-party transferee cannot be in good faith when this good

---

876 Art. IX.-6:102, (2), (a) DCFR.

877 Art. IX.-6:102 *juncto* VIII.-3:102 DCFR.

878 Art. VIII.-3:101 DCFR.

879 Art. VIII.-2:101 (1) (a)-(b), (1) (d), (2)-(3) DCFR.

880 Art. VIII.-2:101 (c) DCFR.

881 Art. VIII.-2:101 (1) (e) DCFR. See also, L. VAN VLIET, 'Acquisition and loss of ownership of goods – Book VIII of the Draft Common Frame of Reference', (2011) ZEUP., (292) 311.

882 W. FABER, 'Book VIII DCFR on acquisition and loss of ownership of goods' in V. SAGAERT, M. E. STORME and E. TERRYN (eds.), *The Draft Common Frame of Reference: national and comparative perspectives*, (Cambridge: Intersentia, 2012), 337.

883 Study Group on a European Civil Code and Research Group on EC Private Law (Acquis Group), *Principles, definitions and model rules of European private law – Draft common frame of reference (DCFR)*, (Munich: Sellier European Law Publishers, 2009), 4154.

884 Study Group on a European Civil Code and Research Group on EC Private Law (Acquis Group), *Principles, definitions and model rules of European private law – Draft common frame of reference (DCFR)*, (Munich: Sellier European Law Publishers, 2009), 4159; W. FABER, 'Book VIII DCFR on acquisition and loss of ownership of goods' in V. SAGAERT, M. E. STORME and E. TERRYN (eds.), *The Draft Common Frame of Reference: national and comparative perspectives*, (Cambridge: Intersentia, 2012), 337.

was encumbered with a security right or retention of ownership device and the encumbrance is registered in the European Security Right Registry, unless the transfer took place in the ordinary course of business.[885] Given the strict interpretation of good faith acquisitions, the retention of ownership creditor still has some chance of recovering the disposed good from the third-party transferee after an unauthorized sale.

Finally, the retention of ownership creditor can explicate that he does not want the encumbered goods to be disposed of.[886] If the debtor in that case does dispose of the encumbered goods despite the retention of ownership creditor's explicit prohibition, then the debtor will be liable for the damages suffered by the retention of ownership creditor following the unauthorized disposition.[887]

184. *Conclusion* – The functional approach limits the retention of ownership creditor's right to dispose. The choice to equate the treatment of retention of ownership devices and acquisition security rights results in permission for the retention of ownership debtor to dispose of the encumbered good under certain circumstances. Furthermore, general contract law principles prevent the retention of ownership creditor to continue to dispose of the encumbered good even though the retention of ownership creditor is technically the owner of the encumbered good. Therefore, the retention of ownership devices in the hands of the creditor does not provide the creditor with any additional protection in this context, while the functional approach equates retention of ownership creditors with security right-holders when dealing with transactions in the ordinary course of business.

B. Right to trace

185. *Overview* – The DCFR takes a moderate approach to the possible extension of retention of ownership devices to goods beyond the originally encumbered good. In these sections, I discuss the possible tracing of retention of ownership devices into the hands of the third-party transferee (i.) proceeds (ii.) and into attachments or mixed goods (iii.).

---

885 Art. IX.6:102 (2) DCFR. See also, Study Group on a European Civil Code and Research Group on EC Private Law (Acquis Group), *Principles, definitions and model rules of European private law – Draft common frame of reference (DCFR)*, (Munich: Sellier European Law Publishers, 2009), 5602–5603; VAN VLIET, 'Acquisition and loss of ownership of goods – Book VIII of the Draft Common Frame of Reference', (2011) ZEUP., (292) 332.

886 Study Group on a European Civil Code and Research Group on EC Private Law (Acquis Group), *Principles, definitions and model rules of European private law – Draft common frame of reference (DCFR)*, (Munich: Sellier European Law Publishers, 2009), 5582 *et seq.*

887 Art. IX.-5:205 (1) DCFR.

i. Tracing into the hands of a third-party transferee

186. *General rules* – A security right or retention of ownership device[888] is terminated or lost when the secured creditor gave permission for the transfer of the encumbered good[889], the third-party transferee acted in good faith when acquiring the encumbered good or the transfer took place in the ordinary course of business.[890] *A contrario*, in other instances the security right or retention of ownership device follows into the hands of the third-party transferee. Notably, due to the registration requirement for retention of ownership devices, the possibility for the third-party transferee to rely on his good faith has become that much harder. Once the retention of ownership device is registered, the third-party transferee can no longer claim he was acting in good faith when he acquired the encumbered good.[891] However, there is an important exception to this rule. If the transfer takes place in the ordinary course of business, then the transferee can rely on his good faith acquisition even though the retention of ownership device was registered in the security rights registry.[892] Regulating otherwise would create too much of an obstacle for commerce.[893]

ii. Tracing into the proceeds

187. *No general extension into proceeds* – The starting point of the DCFR is that security rights do not extend into the proceeds[894] of the originally encumbered good. The reasoning behind this is that other creditors and third parties should have the chance to encumber these goods with their security rights without immediately being surpassed by the secured creditor with a security interest in the original good.[895] However, the DCFR does provide in an exception to

---

888 Study Group on a European Civil Code and Research Group on EC Private Law (Acquis Group), *Principles, definitions and model rules of European private law – Draft common frame of reference (DCFR)*, (Munich: Sellier European Law Publishers, 2009), 5602.

889 Art. IX. – 6:101, (1), (e) DCFR.

890 Art. IX. – 5: 204 DCFR.

891 Study Group on a European Civil Code and Research Group on EC Private Law (Acquis Group), *Principles, definitions and model rules of European private law – Draft common frame of reference (DCFR)*, (Munich: Sellier European Law Publishers, 2009), 5604.

892 Art. IX. – 6:102, (2) (a) DCFR.

893 Study Group on a European Civil Code and Research Group on EC Private Law (Acquis Group), *Principles, definitions and model rules of European private law – Draft common frame of reference (DCFR)*, (Munich: Sellier European Law Publishers, 2009), 5604.

894 *Proceeds is every value derived from an encumbered asset, such as: (a) value realised by sale or other disposition or by collection; (b) damages or insurance payments in respect of defects, damage or loss; (c) civil and natural fruits, including distributions; and (d) proceeds of proceeds* (art. IX. – 1:201, (11) DCFR).

895 Study Group on a European Civil Code and Research Group on EC Private Law (Acquis Group), *Principles, definitions and model rules of European private law – Draft common frame of reference (DCFR)*, (Munich: Sellier European Law Publishers, 2009), 5458–5459.

this rule for both security rights in movable goods, as retention of ownership devices[896], when:

> (1) *A security right extends to rights to payment due to a defect in, damage to, or loss of the originally encumbered asset, including insurance proceeds.*
> (2) *A possessory security right extends to civil and natural fruits of the originally encumbered assets unless the parties agree otherwise.*
> (3) *Other proceeds of the originally encumbered assets are covered only if the parties so agree.*[897]

188. *Third-party effectiveness of extensions into proceeds* – The tracing into proceeds depends on the type of situation. When the tracing into proceeds is automatic (i.e. in the first two scenarios of the provision), then the security right or retention of ownership device automatically extends to these proceeds and the secured creditors do not have to take additional steps.[898] When the tracing is specifically agreed upon between the parties, then the secured creditor has to take additional steps to ensure that the security right or retention of ownership device into proceeds is correctly made effective against third parties.[899]

iii. Tracing into attached or mixed goods

189. *No automatic extension into attached goods* – The DCFR takes as a starting point that security rights or retention of ownership devices cannot be traced in the event the encumbered good is used for production or combination, unless the parties have contractually agreed to the extension of the secured transaction into processed goods.[900] In the event that the parties have agreed to tracing into the newly combined or produced good, the right that the retention of ownership creditor holds, depends on the rights the debtor has in the encumbered good after the production or combination. This is not regulated in Book IX concerning security rights, but in Book VIII concerning the transfer of ownership.[901] Furthermore, the retention of ownership creditor has to ensure that his claim is

---

896 Study Group on a European Civil Code and Research Group on EC Private Law (Acquis Group), *Principles, definitions and model rules of European private law – Draft common frame of reference (DCFR),* (Munich: Sellier European Law Publishers, 2009), 5459.

897 Art. IX. – 2:306 DCFR.

898 Art. IX. – 3:101 DCFR.

899 Study Group on a European Civil Code and Research Group on EC Private Law (Acquis Group), *Principles, definitions and model rules of European private law – Draft common frame of reference (DCFR),* (Munich: Sellier European Law Publishers, 2009), 5460.

900 Study Group on a European Civil Code and Research Group on EC Private Law (Acquis Group), *Principles, definitions and model rules of European private law – Draft common frame of reference (DCFR),* (Munich: Sellier European Law Publishers, 2009), 5468.

901 Chapter 5 of Book VIII DCFR; Study Group on a European Civil Code and Research Group on EC Private Law (Acquis Group), *Principles, definitions and model rules of European private law – Draft common frame of reference (DCFR),* (Munich: Sellier European Law Publishers, 2009), 5467.

correctly made effective against third parties. If that is the case, the retention of ownership creditor retains his super-priority status in the altered good.[902]

In the event the encumbered good is attached to an immovable good, the security right-holder is given the opportunity to register this interest in the land registry and thereby make it effective against potentially conflicting creditors with a claim in the immovable good.[903] The commentary to this provision does not mention whether this rule is expanded to retention of ownership devices.[904] However, this provision is mentioned in the list of provisions which are also applicable to retention of ownership devices, so presumably this provision can be extended.[905]

190. *Extension into comingled goods* – Here, the DCFR takes the position that retention of ownership devices can be traced into a share of the resulting mass or mixture proportionate to the value of the respective goods at the moment of commingling.[906] The retention of ownership device traces into the comingled good without any additional requirements for third-party effectiveness and the retention of ownership device can maintain his super-priority status.[907]

c. Super-priority

191. *First in time, first in right* – In the DCFR a clear choice is made to resolve conflicts between competing creditors on the basis of priority. The general priority rule states that the first security right to be made effective against third parties, via registration, possession or control, takes priority over a security right that was made effective at a later point.[908] For retention of ownership devices the transition to priority is a change. Generally, retention of ownership devices cannot come into conflict with other creditors because the creditor has retained ownership and the debtor does not have sufficient rights in the encumbered

902 Study Group on a European Civil Code and Research Group on EC Private Law (Acquis Group), *Principles, definitions and model rules of European private law – Draft common frame of reference (DCFR)*, (Munich: Sellier European Law Publishers, 2009), 5469–5470.

903 Art. IX. – 3:105 DCFR.

904 Study Group on a European Civil Code and Research Group on EC Private Law (Acquis Group), *Principles, definitions and model rules of European private law – Draft common frame of reference (DCFR)*, (Munich: Sellier European Law Publishers, 2009), 5481.

905 Art. IX. – 1:104 DCFR.

906 Art. IX. – 2:309, (2) DCFR.

907 Study Group on a European Civil Code and Research Group on EC Private Law (Acquis Group), *Principles, definitions and model rules of European private law – Draft common frame of reference (DCFR)*, (Munich: Sellier European Law Publishers, 2009), 5471.

908 Art. IX.4:101 DCFR. See also, Study Group on a European Civil Code and Research Group on EC Private Law (Acquis Group), *Principles, definitions and model rules of European private law – Draft common frame of reference (DCFR)*, (Munich: Sellier European Law Publishers, 2009), 5547 *et seq.*

goods to grant additional claims in the good.[909] However, with the application of a time-based priority regime retention of ownership creditors can now also come into conflict with competing proprietary claims in the same good and be lower-ranking depending on the timing of the fulfillment the third-party effectiveness requirement.[910] The most common example of this conflict is when a bank or other financier vests a security right in all the debtor's current and future inventory. Under a purely time-based priority system, any new inventory would automatically be encumbered with the previously vested security right of the bank and would take priority in time over a later vested retention of ownership device or acquisition security rights in the newly acquired inventory.

192. *Introduction of super-priority for acquisition finance devices* – Nevertheless the choice for a general time-based priority system, the DCFR wants to maintain a stronger protection for acquisition finance devices. One of the ways in which acquisition financing is given preferential treatment over non-acquisition financing is through super-priority. Super-priority means that the retention of ownership creditor surpasses competing claims even if they have been vested at an earlier time than the retention of ownership device.[911] What is new for retention of ownership devices is that the retention of ownership creditor needs super-priority to surpass earlier security rights in the same movable goods. This is somewhat surprising, since one would assume that the retained ownership would avoid any conflict with other creditors and third parties. However, in the DCFR retention of ownership devices only obtain super-priority when the requirements for third-party effectiveness are fulfilled within 35 days of delivery of the good to the debtor.[912] Consequently, the extra protection for retention of ownership creditors is no longer only based on their retained ownership, but also the fulfillment of certain additional requirements. Evidently, the main advantage of basing the protection of retention of ownership devices on an assigned super-priority over the creditor's retained ownership is that now all acquisition finance devices can be given a strong protection on the same basis. All security mechanisms that secure acquisition financing enjoy super-priority if they meet

---

909 Study Group on a European Civil Code and Research Group on EC Private Law (Acquis Group), *Principles, definitions and model rules of European private law – Draft common frame of reference (DCFR)*, (Munich: Sellier European Law Publishers, 2009), 5556; A. VENEZIANO, 'A secured transactions' regime for Europe: treatment of acquisition finance devices and creditor's enforcement rights', (2008) 14 Juridica International, (89) 92.

910 Study Group on a European Civil Code and Research Group on EC Private Law (Acquis Group), *Principles, definitions and model rules of European private law – Draft common frame of reference (DCFR)*, (Munich: Sellier European Law Publishers, 2009), 5548.

911 Study Group on a European Civil Code and Research Group on EC Private Law (Acquis Group), *Principles, definitions and model rules of European private law – Draft common frame of reference (DCFR)*, (Munich: Sellier European Law Publishers, 2009),5555.

912 Art. IX.4:102 *juncto* IX.-3:107 DCFR.

the underlying requirements.[913] This is a clear application of the functional approach where equivalent legal outcomes are generated for functionally equivalent mechanisms.

193. *Super-priority in altered goods* – The DCFR extends super-priority even when alterations have been made to the original good.[914] For example, the DCFR is very clear that priority of a security right or retention of ownership device continues when the original good becomes an accessory to the movable asset[915] or in the good that results from the production or commingling of the original good.[916] Conversely, for an acquisition finance device this translates to super-priority status in the altered goods.[917] However, for this rule to apply the retention of ownership device has to extend to the accessory or commingled good. The extension does not happen automatically, but has to be agreed upon between the contracting parties.[918] When this is the case, then the retention of ownership device extends to altered goods and its super-priority in the good can be maintained.[919]

However, the DCFR does draw a line at the extension of acquisition finance devices in fruits and proceeds of the originally encumbered good.[920] Generally, super-priority does not continue in the fruits and proceeds of the originally encumbered good.[921] The reasoning is that super-priority for acquisition finance devices is partly justified due to the fact that the new goods would not have been acquired by the debtor if not for the acquisition financier.[922] Super-priority in proceeds, however, cannot be justified via that reasoning. Often additional costs have been made to create the fruits and proceeds of a good. Therefore, the acquisition financier is not necessarily the only one who should be given the specific protection in the proceeds or fruits of the acquired goods.[923]

---

913 A. VENEZIANO, 'A secured transactions' regime for Europe: treatment of acquisition finance devices and creditor's enforcement rights', (2008) 14 Juridica International, (89) 92.

914 Study Group on a European Civil Code and Research Group on EC Private Law (Acquis Group), *Principles, definitions and model rules of European private law – Draft common frame of reference (DCFR)*, (Munich: Sellier European Law Publishers, 2009), 5460.

915 Art. IX.-4:103 (1) (a) DCFR.

916 Art. IX.-4:103 (1) (b) DCFR.

917 L. VAN VLIET, 'Acquisition and loss of ownership of goods – Book VIII of the Draft Common Frame of Reference', (2011) ZEUP., (292) 324.

918 Art. IX.-2:308 DCFR.

919 L. VAN VLIET, 'Acquisition and loss of ownership of goods – Book VIII of the Draft Common Frame of Reference', (2011) ZEUP., (292) 323.

920 Art. IX.-4:105 DCFR.

921 Art. IX.-4:105 (1) DCFR.

922 Study Group on a European Civil Code and Research Group on EC Private Law (Acquis Group), *Principles, definitions and model rules of European private law – Draft common frame of reference (DCFR)*, (Munich: Sellier European Law Publishers, 2009), 5566.

923 Study Group on a European Civil Code and Research Group on EC Private Law (Acquis Group), *Principles, definitions and model rules of European private law – Draft common frame of reference (DCFR)*, (Munich: Sellier European Law Publishers, 2009), 5567.

Nevertheless, the DCFR immediately formulates two exceptions to this rule. First, acquisition finance devices continue to enjoy super-priority in the rights to payments due to defects in, damage to or loss of the assets that were originally encumbered. Here the reasoning goes that the proceeds are replacement for the original good and thus the acquisition financier is entitled to super-priority in this good as he was to super-priority in the original good.[924] Second, super-priority is allowed to continue in the proceeds of the sale of the originally encumbered good. The drafters argue that it would be unfair to have a blanket extension of super-priority for acquisition finance devices in the sale proceeds of the originally acquired good. However, if the parties have agreed to the extension of the acquisition finance device to the proceeds, then the acquisition creditor should be protected by allowing the extension of his super-priority in the sale proceeds of the original good.[925] Given these exceptions, it would seem that in many cases the acquisition financier can in fact extend his acquisition finance device and the associated super-priority to the proceeds of the originally encumbered good.

194. *Conclusion* – Due to the functional approach retention of ownership devices can now come into conflict with other creditors and these conflicts are now decided on the basis of priority and super-priority instead of ownership. Notwithstanding this change, little changes for retention of ownership creditors in a practical sense. Super-priority for retention of ownership devices results in the same outcome as before: retention of ownership devices surpass other secured creditors and are given a stronger protection. A potentially big change for adopting member states is that super-priority in most cases hinges on the fulfillment of third-party effectiveness requirements and thus retention of ownership creditors can no longer assume that they automatically have the strongest claim in a good.

D. Enforcement

195. *The various steps to enforcing retention of ownership devices* – Finally, we take a look at the retention of ownership creditor's right to enforcement. Here, the DCFR is also very clear that retention of ownership devices are treated differently from security rights.[926] Due to the creditor's retained ownership, the

---

924 Study Group on a European Civil Code and Research Group on EC Private Law (Acquis Group), *Principles, definitions and model rules of European private law – Draft common frame of reference (DCFR)*, (Munich: Sellier European Law Publishers, 2009), 5567.

925 Study Group on a European Civil Code and Research Group on EC Private Law (Acquis Group), *Principles, definitions and model rules of European private law – Draft common frame of reference (DCFR)*, (Munich: Sellier European Law Publishers, 2009), 5568.

926 Study Group on a European Civil Code and Research Group on EC Private Law (Acquis Group), *Principles, definitions and model rules of European private law – Draft common frame of reference (DCFR)*, (Munich: Sellier Europen Law Publishers, 2009), 5663 *et seq.*

creditor does not have to obtain ownership of the encumbered good and then sell it. The retention of ownership creditor merely has to obtain possession of the encumbered good.[927] This stands in contrast to (acquisition) security rights where the secured creditor has to obtain ownership to the encumbered good in order to sell or appropriate the encumbered good as payment for the outstanding obligation.[928] The reasoning goes that the enforcement of the security right with respect for the debtor's ownership's rights in the encumbered good will likely be more complicated than simply regaining possession of a good that is still owned by the retention of ownership creditor. However, the rules for regaining possession of the encumbered good are the same as those for (acquisition) security rights. For example, the debtor has to give consent for the retrieval of the encumbered good.[929] In other words, the retention of ownership debtor cannot simply come onto the debtor's premises and regain possession of the encumbered goods.[930] Furthermore, if the debtor refuses to give consent, the retention of ownership creditor also has to go through the courts to obtain possession of the encumbered good. In summary, the process to regain possession is not necessarily much easier for a retention of ownership creditor than it is for a security right-holder.

To re-obtain possession of the encumbered good the retention of ownership creditor has to terminate the underlying transaction which contained the retention of ownership device.[931] Alternatively, the retention of ownership creditor may immobilize and preserve the encumbered asset.[932] This is useful in the event the good is too big or heavy to physically move.[933] Furthermore, the retention of ownership creditor has to return the payments he has already received from the debtor.[934] The reasoning goes that the return of the good will satisfy the retention of ownership creditor and that a return of the good in combination of the already received payments would amount to unjust

927 Study Group on a European Civil Code and Research Group on EC Private Law (Acquis Group), *Principles, definitions and model rules of European private law – Draft common frame of reference (DCFR)*, (Munich: Sellier European Law Publishers, 2009), 5663 *et seq.*

928 Study Group on a European Civil Code and Research Group on EC Private Law (Acquis Group), *Principles, definitions and model rules of European private law – Draft common frame of reference (DCFR)*, (Munich: Sellier Europen Law Publishers, 2009), 5614.

929 Art. IX. – 7:302 *juncto* IX. – 7:201 DCFR; Study Group on a European Civil Code and Research Group on EC Private Law (Acquis Group), *Principles, definitions and model rules of European private law – Draft common frame of reference (DCFR)*, (Munich: Sellier Europen Law Publishers, 2009), 5631–5632.

930 Study Group on a European Civil Code and Research Group on EC Private Law (Acquis Group), *Principles, definitions and model rules of European private law – Draft common frame of reference (DCFR)*, (Munich: Sellier Europen Law Publishers, 2009), 5631.

931 Art. IX. – 7:301 (1) DCFR.

932 Art. IX.-7:202 DCFR.

933 Study Group on a European Civil Code and Research Group on EC Private Law (Acquis Group), *Principles, definitions and model rules of European private law – Draft common frame of reference (DCFR)*, (Munich: Sellier European Law Publishers, 2009), 5633.

934 Art. III.-3:511 (2) and (5) DCFR.

enrichment. However, the retention of ownership creditor will be compensated for the use and diminution of encumbered goods for the duration of the agreement.[935] If the returned good is sold, leased or otherwise disposed of, then the retention of ownership creditor is entitled to any surplus value.[936] This is reasonable, since the termination of the original agreement is already accompanied with the return of any payments the retention of ownership creditor received.[937] Consequently, any value the retention of ownership creditor garners in a next agreement, to which the old debtor is not a party, belongs to the retention of ownership creditor.[938]

196. *Enforcement and the functional approach* – According to the DCFR, the retained ownership in retention of ownership devices means that the enforcement of retention of ownership devices must be governed by different rules. At first glance, this view goes against the functional approach, which aims to transcends differences between secured transactions based on dogmatic differences, such as holding title or a limited proprietary interest in the encumbered good, and wants to create equivalent legal outcomes between all secured transactions that perform the same function. Consequently, the continued recognition of ownership in the hands of the retention of ownership creditor impedes the application of the functional approach and the pursuit of equivalent legal outcomes for acquisition security rights and retention of ownership devices. Fortunately, the comparison between the rules governing the enforcement of retention of ownership devices with those for the enforcement of (acquisition) security rights show that many of the rules for the enforcement of security rights are in fact applicable to retention of ownership devices. For example, retention of ownership creditors also have to respect the rules concerning obtaining possession of the encumbered good and cannot unjustly enrich himself when regaining possession of the encumbered good. Consequently, the rules and outcomes of the enforcement retention of ownership devices and acquisition security rights are in fact similar, even though the drafters claim that differences are maintained due to the retained ownership of retention of ownership devices on the one hand and the limited proprietary interest of acquisition security rights on the other hand. This could be viewed

---

935 Study Group on a European Civil Code and Research Group on EC Private Law (Acquis Group), *Principles, definitions and model rules of European private law – Draft common frame of reference (DCFR)*, (Munich: Sellier European Law Publishers, 2009), 5665.

936 A. VENEZIANO, 'Security rights in movables in the DCFR: general presentation' in V. SAGAERT, M. E. STORME and E. TERRYN (eds.), *The Draft Common Frame of Reference: national and comparative perspectives*, (Antwerp: Intersentia, 2012), (305) 311.

937 *Contra*: A. VENEZIANO, 'Security rights in movables in the DCFR: general presentation' in V. SAGAERT, M. E. STORME and E. TERRYN (eds.), *The Draft Common Frame of Reference: national and comparative perspectives*, (Antwerp: Intersentia, 2012), (305) 312.

938 Study Group on a European Civil Code and Research Group on EC Private Law (Acquis Group), *Principles, definitions and model rules of European private law – Draft common frame of reference (DCFR)*, (Munich: Sellier European Law Publishers, 2009), 5666.

as a form of implied functional approach where without making it explicit, the outcomes between functionally similar secured transactions have been made equal.

2.4. *Conclusions*

197. *Main observations concerning the functional approach in the DCFR* – A main characteristic of the DCFR is that it maintains a separate category of retention of ownership devices.[939] Consequently, the DCFR can be seen as an application of the functional approach without recharacterization, which maintains the original terms of retention of ownership but ensures that equivalent legal outcomes are achieved between functionally equivalent mechanisms.[940]

First, retention of ownership devices are for the most part governed by the same rules as general security rights in movable goods.[941] However, the continuation of the concept of retention of ownership devices does result in the drafters maintaining some specific rules for retention of ownership devices in the context of creation, priority and enforcement.[942] Second, retention of ownership devices are placed in a separate category of acquisition financing devices that all guarantee acquisition financing. In this category the legal outcomes of retention of ownership devices are functionally equated with those of specific acquisition security rights. These devices are also subject to certain specific rules, mainly pertaining to super-priority.[943]

198. *Evaluation of the functional approach in the DCFR* – The DCFR's functional approach tries to reconcile two conflicting movements. On the one hand, the drafters want to create a consolidated security right framework that is based on the functional similarity of the different secured transactions in movable goods. On the other hand, the drafters do not want to bring about too much change by recharacterizing retention of ownership devices to acquisition security rights. Consequently, the drafters made a compromise in which retention of ownership devices are treated for the most part as security rights in general and acquisition security rights in particular, but in certain domains remain outside of the general framework for security rights in movable goods and remain governed by their own rules. The choice for the functional approach without recharacterization in the DCFR seems more justified than the UNCITRAL non-unitary approach, since the DCFR at least maintains some of the specific characteristics and rules for retention of ownership devices,

---

939 See *supra* no. 159.
940 See *supra* no. 4.
941 See *supra* no. 159.
942 See *supra* no. 159.
943 See *supra* no. 191.

thereby justifying their separate category. However, by pursuing this approach the DCFR does end up with the minimal amount of equivalence between retention of ownership devices and (acquisition) security rights. Furthermore, Book IX DCFR is not very consistent, nor coherent with its multiple categories of secured transactions which are sometimes, but not always treated similarly. Given these aspects, one wonders whether the functional approach of the DCFR is worth pursuing. The continuation of the concept of retention of ownership devices and maintaining specific rules for them, often on the basis of not very convincing arguments, within a larger security rights framework makes it quite complex to adopt the DCFR. Adopting states will have to find a balance between integrating their retention of ownership devices in the category of acquisition financing devices, while maintaining the inherent characteristics of retention of ownership devices. This will be a delicate exercise after which not much changes for retention of ownership devices, nor the overall coherence and consistency of the security rights framework necessarily improves. Finally, the continuation of the concept of retention of ownership devices may create the false impression that retention of ownership creditors can rely on a much stronger protection when in reality the difference in treatment between retention of ownership devices and (acquisition) security rights is minimal at best. An example of one state's reaction to this approach is discussed in the Part 3 where the application of the different functional approaches to retention of title, including the DCFR approach, in the Belgian Security Rights Act is discussed.

SECTION 3 – CONCLUSIONS ON THE SELECTED FUNCTIONAL APPROACHES AND THEIR APPLICATION TO RETENTION OF TITLE

199. *Overview* – In this section an answer is formulated to the first sub-research question concerning the examples of the functional approach for the Security Rights Act and the way they apply the functional approach to retention of title. More precisely, overarching clarifications are given and conclusions are drawn on the selected functional approaches and their application to retention of title. The focus is on the general characteristics and operation of the selected functional approaches and not on the specific application of the functional approaches in the selected jurisdiction and international instruments. The latter can be found in the conclusions on the functional approach at the end of the sections concerning that jurisdiction or international instrument.

200. *Functional equivalence between retention of title and PMSIs or acquisition security rights* – A first conclusion is that each of the selected frameworks introduces a sub-category of PMSIs (Article 9 UCC) or acquisition security rights

(UNCITRAL Guide and Model Law and DCFR) which perform the specific function of guaranteeing acquisition credit. Because retention of title also inherently guarantees acquisition credit, *PMSIs and acquisition security rights, and not general security rights in movable goods, are the functional equivalent of retention of title.* Consequently, under the functional approach retention of title is either recharacterized to a PMSI (Article 9 UCC) or acquisition security right (UNCITRAL unitary approach) or the legal outcomes for retention of title are functionally equated with those for acquisition security rights (DCFR and the UNCITRAL non-unitary approach). Since PMSIs and acquisition security rights are a sub-category of the general category of security interests or security rights, PMSIs and acquisition security rights are for the most part subjected to the same rules as general security rights in movable goods concerning creation, third-party effectiveness, tracing and enforcement. However, some specific rules and exceptions are reserved for this sub-category of security rights, such as a super-priority protection and certain exemptions from notification requirements for third-party effectiveness.

The interaction of retention of title with the new category of PMSIs or acquisition security rights depends on the type of functional approach that is pursued. In Article 9 UCC and the UNCITRAL unitary approach, retention of title is recharacterized to a PMSI or acquisition security right, respectively, and both the general and specific rules that apply to PMSIs or acquisition security rights, apply to the recharacterized retention of title. In the frameworks that apply the functional approach without recharacterization (the DCFR and the UNCITRAL non-unitary approach), retention of ownership devices or retention of title and finance leases, respectively, are given equivalent legal outcomes as acquisition security rights. In the DCFR, this takes the form of extending the majority of the rules for (acquisition) security rights to retention of ownership devices, whereas in the UNCITRAL non-unitary approach this means adjusting all the rules for retention of title and finance leasing so that they create equivalent legal outcomes to those for acquisition security rights.

201. From title-based mechanism to security right – Second, in each of the functional approaches there is a trend to move retention of title towards security rights with a limited proprietary interest, as opposed to moving functionally equivalent security rights towards a more title-based approach. Generally, title-based characteristics are removed from retention of title, such as the automatic right to revendicate, or limitations are placed on the retention of title creditor, such as the prohibition of unjust enrichment and (further) limitations on the enforcement proceedings. The reform of retention of title to a security right does not necessarily mean that retention of title creditor is less protected. As we saw in the section on Article 9 UCC, the retention of title creditor was already subject to formalities and limitations in the creation, third-party effectiveness, enforcement of his retention of title prior to Article 9 UCC and the recharacterization to a PMSI does not significantly limit the rights of the former retention of title creditors.[944]

202. *Inclusion of leasing following the functional approach* – Third, each of the approaches *includes certain (finance) lease agreements* in the secured transactions framework due to their functional similarity with retention of title in sale agreements. Generally, the application of the functional approach is limited to lease agreements in which title to the leased good is likely to transfer to the lessee at the end of the lease agreement, either automatically or for the payment of a nominal amount (i.e. leases for security purposes). From the moment of inclusion, these leases for security purposes are seen as a form of acquisition security interest or are at least equated with them and are subjected to the requirements for third-party effectiveness for security rights, which in each of the regimes is registration. This means that from that point on the distinction between a (finance) lease which is functionally similar to a sale with retention of title and an operational lease, where the good will always return to the lessor at the end of the agreement, becomes relevant. The lease for security purposes has to be registered to be effective against third parties, whereas the operational lease does not. Consequently, each of the frameworks has to come up with rules to try to distinguish leases for security purposes from operational leases. Given the subtle differences between leases for security purposes and operational leases, creating such rules is quite difficult and their application, in most cases, still require an *in concreto* assessment of the specific case.

203. *Application of the functional approach does not necessarily equal extensive rules and formalities for retention of title* – The functional approach only aims to create equivalent legal outcomes for functionally equivalent mechanisms. However, these legal outcomes do not have to result necessarily in extra formalities or protections for retention of title and its functional equivalent mechanisms. For example, in the DCFR a choice is made to not automatically extend the protection of security rights into the altered goods, but leave this to the parties to be agreed upon contractually. The idea is that the altered goods should not automatically go to the secured creditor with an interest in the originally encumbered good, but that other creditors should have a chance to potentially stake a claim in the altered goods. Following the functional approach these tracing rules are then extended to acquisition financing devices, including retention of ownership devices. Conversely, Article 9 UCC and UNCITRAL Guide and Model Law each implement extensive tracing rules that apply uniformly to their security interests and PMSIs and security rights and acquisition security rights, respectively. Here the reasoning goes that

944 See *supra* no. 110.

secured creditors with an interest in the originally encumbered good should be maximally protected in the event the encumbered good is altered. Both approaches follow from different policy choices, but in each of the selected functional frameworks the functional approach is correctly applied. Similarly, the application of the functional approach does not have to include the introduction of an extensive notification regime for third-party effectiveness for retention of title. Functional frameworks can also choose to opt for a regime with minimal notification requirements to achieve third-party effectiveness. However, like with tracing, once a policy and rules are decided upon with regards to notification requirements, the functional approach requires that these rules are uniformly applied to functional equivalent mechanisms. In practice, the research has shown that in the selected functional frameworks extensive notification requirement and regimes for third-party effectiveness are introduced for all security interests, PMSIs and (acquisition) security rights and extended to retention of title mechanisms in the frameworks that apply the functional approach without recharacterization. The introduction of these extensive notification regimes stems from a desire to create more transparency and uniformity with regards to third-party effectiveness. The expansion of these rules to retention of title and retention of ownership devices is then the result of the functional approach.

204. *Impact of the type of functional approach on the coherence, consistency and complexity of the security right framework* – Finally, I can draw one important distinction between the different functional approaches: the functional approach with recharacterization (i.e. Article 9 UCC and the UNCITRAL unitary approach) allows for a more *coherent and consistent and less complex* system than the functional approach without recharacterization (i.e. the UNCITRAL non-unitary approach and the DCFR). In the former approach, retention of title mechanisms are recharacterized to a PMSI or acquisition security right, respectively, and subjected to the general rules for security interests/rights and the specific rules for PMSIs and acquisition security rights. This leads to one security right framework with one set of unified rules. In the latter approach, states are able to maintain their retention of title mechanisms, but either have to adjust the rules governing these mechanisms to match the outcomes for security rights in general and acquisition security rights in particular or maintain a separate category for retention of title mechanisms that is for the most part governed by the rules for security rights and acquisition security rights, but maintains some of its own characteristics. This evidently creates a complex regime where retention of title mechanisms straddle two worlds at once and it is difficult for creditors to discern what the specific protection for retention of title actually is. Under the UNCITRAL non-unitary approach, there is actually not a specific protection granted to retention of title, but there are specific protections for acquisition security rights with which retention of title mechanisms are fully equated. In the DCFR, retention of ownership devices have some specific rules and protections separate even from their status as acquisition financing devices, but these are very limited. Evidently, this leads to a very complex and sometimes even illogical system where distinctions between retention of title are maintained simply in name (UNCITRAL) or to such limited effect (DCFR) that one wonders what the added value of these approaches are. The added complexity is all the more ironic, since the functional approach without recharacterization is often presented as a method to ease states into the adoption of the functional approach and consolidated security right frameworks. However, the ease of adoption is likely undermined by the actual complexity of achieving equivalence without recharacterization between functionally equivalent mechanisms and the inconsistent and incoherent framework that is the result of following this approach.

205. *Summary* – The basic tenet of the selected functional approaches is to create equivalent legal outcomes between retention of title and functionally similar secured transactions on a general level and on a specific level with regards to secured transactions that guarantee acquisition credit. Each of the selected approaches succeeds in creating unified rules and equivalent legal outcomes for retention of title and functionally similar mechanisms. However, the choice of one specific functional approach over another can have an effect on the coherence, consistency and complexity of the security right framework. A security right framework in which the functional approach with recharacterization is applied, has a cleaner and more coherent look and operation than the framework in which retention of title is not recharacterized and stands alongside functionally similar security rights and is to a greater or lesser extent equated.

CHAPTER 2
THE NON-FUNCTIONAL APPROACH TO RETENTION OF TITLE: GERMANY

206. *Introduction to the non-functional approach* – To better understand the meaning and role of the functional approach with regards to the integration of retention of title in secured transactions law, I also turn my gaze to a jurisdiction that does not apply the functional approach at all: Germany.[945] In this chapter the place and rights of retention of title in German secured transactions law is discussed in order to provide a point of comparison for the application of the functional approach to retention of title in the Belgian Security Rights Act.

SECTION 1 – BACKGROUND TO *EIGENTUMSVORBEHALT*

207. *The gradual evolution of retention of title in Germany* – From a legislative perspective *Eigentumsvorbehalt* (hereafter also, retention of title) in Germany is nearly untouched. This is first evidenced by the minimal regulation of retention of title in the *Bürgerliches Gesetzbuch* (hereafter, BGB).[946] The absence of an extensive regulatory framework for retention of title can be traced back to the fact that historically German property law only recognized possessory *in rem* security rights, such as the possessory pledge (*Faustpfand*).[947] Consequently, the non-possessory retention of title was considered ineffective against third parties and was therefore not legislatively developed.[948] Furthermore, at the outset most transactions in Germany concerning movable goods were conducted on a cash basis which removed the need for retention of title as a means to guarantee

945 M. BRINKMANN, 'The peculiar approach of German law in the field of secured transactions and why it has worked (so far)' in L. GULLIFER and O. AKSELI (eds.), *Secured transactions law reform*, (Oxford: Hart Publishing, 2016), (339) 340.

946 F. FAUST, '§449 – Eigentumsvorbehalt' in H. G. BAMBERGER and others (eds.), *Bürgerliches Gesetzbuch Kommentar*, (4 edn., München: Beck, 2019), 2908.

947 S. KIM, *Die Entwicklung des Anwartschaftsrechts beim Kauf under Eigentumsvorbehalt*, (Dissertation Rechtswissenschaft, Rheinischen Friedrich-Wilhelms-Universität Bonn, 2017), 29.

948 W. SPONER, *Das Anwartschaftsrecht und seine Pfändung*, (Bielefeld: Verlag Ernst und Werner Gieseking, 1965), 33.

credit.[949] Notwithstanding the lackluster regulatory efforts concerning retention of title, some small traces of retention of title regulation can be found as far back as the 1600s[950] and throughout the different iterations of the BGB.[951]

The market's attitude towards sales on credit and the use of retention of title changed when the economy changed. Especially the industrial revolution and the mass production of goods it inspired, led to a significant increase in sales on credit of movable goods.[952] Because the debtor often did not have sufficient valuable assets to guarantee the outstanding debt through a possessory pledge, retention of title was a more pragmatic tool to guarantee the outstanding purchase price.[953] Furthermore, German creditors and debtors were also faced with the inherent disadvantages of only having a possessory pledge as a means to guarantee credit through movable goods. The possessory nature of the pledge would prevent the debtor from using the collateral in his business and would therefore limit the type and amount of assets the debtor could use as collateral to guarantee credit.[954]

Consequently, the use of retention of title grew in popularity, at which point it also became clear that the limited regulation of retention of title in positive law was insufficient to accommodate an ever growing market of consumers.[955] Therefore, manufacturers and suppliers contractually developed new forms of retention of title, such as retention of title that would vertically extend to the receivables that took the place of the original collateral or to the altered encumbered collateral that had been processed by the retention of title debtor.[956]

949 W. SPONER, *Das Anwartschaftsrecht und seine Pfändung*, (Bielefeld: Verlag Ernst und Werner Gieseking, 1965), 32; S. KIM, *Die Entwicklung des Anwartschaftsrechts beim Kauf under Eigentumsvorbehalt*, (Dissertation Rechtswissenschaft, Rheinischen Friedrich-Wilhelms-Universität Bonn 2017), 29.

950 W. SPONER, *Das Anwartschaftsrecht und seine Pfändung*, (Bielefeld: Verlag Ernst und Werner Gieseking, 1965), 33.

951 E. SANDMANN, *Zur Geschichte des Eigentumsvorbehaltes in Deutschland*, (München: Dissertationsdruck Schön, 1972), 110 *et seq.*

952 S. KIM, *Die Entwicklung des Anwartschaftsrechts beim Kauf under Eigentumsvorbehalt*, (Dissertation Rechtswissenschaft, Rheinischen Friedrich-Wilhelms-Universität Bonn 2017), 38.

953 E. SANDMANN, *Zur Geschichte des Eigentumsvorbehaltes in Deutschland*, (München: Dissertationsdruck Schön, 1972), 94–95; S. KIM, *Die Entwicklung des Anwartschaftsrechts beim Kauf under Eigentumsvorbehalt*, (Dissertation Rechtswissenschaft, Rheinischen Friedrich-Wilhelms-Universität Bonn 2017), 39.

954 R. SERICK, *Eigentumsvorbehalt und Sicherungsübertragung*, (Heidelberg: Verlag Recht und Wirtschaft, 1993), 27 – 28; H. H. NÖLL, D. WIEGAND and W. WIEGAND, *J. Von Staudingers Kommentar zum Bürgerlichen Gesetzbuch mit Einführungsgesetz und Nebengesetz*, (C. HERRESTHAL (ed.), Berlin: Sellier, 2018), 3 – 4.

955 S. KIM, *Die Entwicklung des Anwartschaftsrechts beim Kauf under Eigentumsvorbehalt*, (Dissertation Rechtswissenschaft, Rheinischen Friedrich-Wilhelms-Universität Bonn 2017), 89–90.

956 S. KIM, *Die Entwicklung des Anwartschaftsrechts beim Kauf under Eigentumsvorbehalt*, (Dissertation Rechtswissenschaft, Rheinischen Friedrich-Wilhelms-Universität Bonn 2017), 89. For more on the extended forms of retention of title, see *infra* no. 212.

Both the legislator and the BGH turned a blind eye to the use of title as a means to guarantee credit.[957] As a result, title-based mechanisms, such as retention of title and transfer of title (i.e. *Sicherungsübereignung*) became more prominent methods to guarantee credit.[958]

208. *Limited reforms for retention of title* – The second feature that shows the untouched nature of retention of title in German law is the lack of reform with regards to its existing contractual *in rem* security rights in movable goods or *Mobiliarsicherheiten*: the possessory pledge, transfer of title (*Sicherungsübereignung*), assignment of receivables (*Sicherungsabtretung*) and retention of title (*Eigentumsvorbehalt*).[959] *Mobiliarsicherheiten* are transactions in which the creditor obtains or retains a proprietary interest in a movable good to guarantee an outstanding obligation.[960] As mentioned previously, over time it became accepted that title could be used to guarantee an outstanding obligation. Although scholars included retention and transfers of title in the category of *Mobiliarsicherheiten*, these creditors were still considered full owners of the good to which they obtained or retained title.[961] Unlike the previously discussed jurisdictions and instruments, Germany has not enacted any comprehensive reform of its *Mobiliarsicherheiten*. On the contrary, retention of title in Germany has only been modestly amended or reinterpreted in two instances. First, there was the introduction of the European Directive on combating late payment in commercial transactions.[962] This directive includes some minimal provisions concerning retention of title[963], which meant that the German provisions concerning retention of title have to be interpreted in accordance with this European directive.[964] Second, retention of title has been amended in 2001 when it was included in the reformed *Schuldrecht*.[965] In the reformed *Schuldrecht* some aspects regarding the revendication of the encumbered collateral were addressed[966] and the extension of retention of title to cover not only debts

957 H. F. GAUL, 'Lex commissoria und Sicherungsübereignung: – Zugleich ein Beitrag zum sogenannten Innenverhältnis bei der Sicherungsübereignung', (1968) 4 AcP, (351) 357–361.

958 J. RAKOB, 'Germany' in H. C. SIGMAN and E.-M. KIENINGER (eds.), *Cross-border security over tangibles*, (Berlin: Sellier, 2007), (63) 64–65.

959 C. HERRESTHAL, 'Das Recht der Kreditsicherung' in D. KAISER and M. STOFFELS (eds.), *J. von Staudingers Eckpfeiler des Zivilrechts*, (Berlin: Sellier, 2018), par. 14.

960 C. HERRESTHAL, 'Das Recht der Kreditsicherung' in D. KAISER and M. STOFFELS (eds.), *J. von Staudingers Eckpfeiler des Zivilrechts*, (Berlin: Sellier, 2018), par. 14.

961 W. WIEGAND, "Anhang zu §929–931 BGB" in W. WIEGAND (ed.) *J. von Staudingers Kommentar zum Bürgerlichen Gesetzbuch mit Einführungsgesetz und Nebengesetzen*, (Berlin: Sellier, 2017), par. 6.

962 Directive 2011/7/EU of the European Parliament and of the Council of 16 February 2011 on combating late payment in commercial transactions (recast), 48 *Pb.L.*, 48.

963 Art. 9 Directive 2011/7/EU of the European Parliament and of the Council of 16 February 2011 on combating late payment in commercial transactions (recast), 48 *Pb.L.*

964 B. GSELL, 'Der EU-Richtlinienentwurf zur Bekämpfung von Zahlungsverzug im Handelsverkehr', (1998) 37–38 ZIP, (1569) 1577.

965 Gesetz von 26 November 2001 zur Modernisierung des Schuldrechts, (2001) 61 BGBI I, 3138.

966 §449, sec. 2 BGB.

between the retention of title creditor and debtor, but also debts between companies associated with the retention of title creditor and the retention of title debtor (i.e. *Konzernvorbehalt*) were limited.[967] However, this limited reform of retention of title in 2001 was by no means what was initially envisioned by legal scholars and the legislator.[968] The absence of reform is not from a lack of trying. As in other jurisdictions, many authors made suggestions for comprehensive reforms.[969] Central to these reform proposals was the creation of an overarching regime in which the different *Mobiliarsicherheiten* would be reformed into a more unified concept. For LEHMANN and DROBNIG this unified concept was a general non-possessory pledge[970], for WIEACKER it was the expansion of the mortgage principle to movable goods.[971] However, industry practitioners were not convinced of the necessity of such reforms and feared that these would result in the loss of some of the privileges they had gained over the years.[972] Specifically, retention of title creditors had managed to obtain very favorable positions, such as the extension of retention of title to other debts than the outstanding purchase price (i.e. *erweiterte Eigentumsvorbehalt*) which they feared to lose in an extensive reform effort.[973] Despite DROBNIG's initiative to invigorate the debate[974], the system of *in rem* security rights in movable goods in Germany remains largely unreformed.[975]

---

967 §449, sec. 3 BGB. See also, R. M. BECKMANN and others, *J. Von Staudingers Kommentar zum Bürgerlichen Geseztbuch mit Einführungsgesetz und Nebengesetzen*, (M. MARTINEK (ed.), 2 edn., Berlin: Sellier, 2004), 427.

968 M. HABERSACK and J. SCHÜRNBRAND, 'Der Eigentumsvorbehalt nach der Schuldrechtsreform', [2002] JuS, (833) 834.

969 H. LEHMANN, *Reform der Kreditsicherung an Fahrnis und Forderungen* (Stuttgart: W. Rohlhammer Verlag, 1937), 32–38; W. FLUME, 'Der verlängerte und erweiterte Eigentumsvorbehalt', (1950) 22 NJW, (841) 843; W. ASCHER, 'Aufgaben des Gesetzgebers bei einer Neuordnung des Sicherungsgeschäfte des gewerblichen Kreditverkehrs', (1955) 8 DRiZ, (177) 178–179; H. WESTERMANN, 'Gesetzliche Regelung der Sicherungsübereignung und des Eigentumsvorbehalt?' in Verhandlungen des Einundvierzigsten deutschen Juristentags, (Tübingen: J. C. B. Mohr, 1955), 3; U. DROBNIG, *Emphelen sich gesetzlichen Maßnahmen zur Reform der Mobiliarsicherheiten?*, (München: C. H. Beck, 1976), 95; R.REICH, 'Reform der Kreditsicherung', (1976) 15–16 JZ, (463) 464–465.

970 H. LEHMANN, *Reform der Kreditsicherung an Fahrnis und Forderungen* (Stuttgart: W. Rohlhammer Verlag, 1937), 32–38; U. DROBNIG, *Emphelen sich gesetzlichen Maßnahmen zur Reform der Mobiliarsicherheiten?*, (München: C. H. Beck, 1976), 95.

971 F. WIEACKER 'Der Eigentumsvorbehalt als dingliche Vorzugshaftung', (1938) 5 ZAdR, (590) 592.

972 S. KIM, *Die Entwicklung des Anwartschaftsrechts beim Kauf under Eigentumsvorbehalt*, (Dissertation Rechtswissenschaft, Rheinischen Friedrich-Wilhelms-Universität Bonn 2017), 99–101.

973 S. KIM, *Die Entwicklung des Anwartschaftsrechts beim Kauf under Eigentumsvorbehalt*, (Dissertation Rechtswissenschaft, Rheinischen Friedrich-Wilhelms-Universität Bonn 2017), 99.

974 U. DROBNIG, *Emphelen sich gesetzlichen Maßnahmen zur Reform der Mobiliarsicherheiten?*, (München: C. H. Beck, 1976), 95.

975 H. LAMBSDORFF, *Handbuch des Eigentumsvorbehalts im deutschen und ausländischen Recht*, (Frankfurt am Main: Athenäum, 1974), 3; M. BRINKMANN, 'The peculiar approach of German law in the field of secured transactions and why it has worked (so far)' in L.

209. *Conclusion* – From this short overview of retention of title and *in rem* security rights in general, I can deduce that retention of title in Germany remains a contractual construction that has been further fine-tuned in case law. Furthermore, retention of title has not been subjected to any comprehensive reform efforts at which point equivalent legal outcomes between functionally similar secured transactions in movable goods were actively pursued (even though there was noticeable enthusiasm among some German scholars to create such a regime). Given this minimal regulation and lack of reform, the German retention of title provides a good counter-example to compare and contrast the role and meaning of the functional approach as method to integrate retention of title.

SECTION 2 – RETENTION OF TITLE TODAY

210. *Overview* – Two forms of retention of title can be discerned in German law: (1) the *einfaches* or simple retention of title and (2) the *erweiterter/verlängerte* or extended retention of title. Both forms of retention of title are briefly discussed before addressing the associated formalities and the rights of retention of title creditors.

1. SIMPLE RETENTION OF TITLE

211. *Retention of title without any frills* – The simple retention of title or *einfaches Eigentumsvorbehalt* is the retention of title as described in §449 BGB:

> *If the seller of a movable thing has retained title until payment of the purchase price, then in case of doubt it is to be assumed that ownership is transferred subject to the condition precedent that the purchase price is paid in full (retention of title).*[976]

This is retention of title in its purest form. The creditor sells the good, but retains title to the sold good on the condition of full payment of the purchase price. Because the retention of title creditor retains title, he is considered full owner of the encumbered good. Consequently, the retention of title creditor's interest must be distinguished from other *Mobiliarsicherheiten*, such as the possessory

---

GULLIFER and O. AKSELI (eds.), *Secured transactions law reform*, (Oxford: Hart Publishing, 2016), (339) 339.

976 Translation by the Bundesministerium der Justiz und für Verbraucherschutz, online: https://www.gesetze-im-internet.de/englisch_bgb/englisch_bgb.html#p1614 (last checked on January 9th, 2022). The official German version is as follows: *Hat sich der Verkäufer einer beweglichen Sache das Eigentum bis zur Zahlung des Kaufpreises vorbehalten, so ist im Zweifel anzunehmen, dass das Eigentum unter der aufschiebenden Bedingung vollständiger Zahlung des Kaufpreises übertragen wird (Eigentumsvorbehalt).*

pledge or *Faustpfand*, which grants the creditor an *in rem* security right in the encumbered good.[977]

Once the purchase price is paid (i.e. the condition precedent on the transfer of ownership is fulfilled), ownership automatically transfers to the debtor.[978] In this form, retention of title is viewed as a simple and reciprocal form of credit security.[979] Furthermore, this form of retention of title is considered simple, because it does not include clauses in which the protection of the retained title is extended to other collateral or other claims. These more exotic forms of retention of title are discussed in the next sections.

2. CONTRACTUALLY EXTENDED RETENTION OF TITLE

212. *Retention of title with all the trimmings* – Despite the lack of formal legislative reform, the popularity of retention of title among suppliers and manufacturers[980] spurred the contractual development of this security mechanism. More specifically, creditors created ways to contractually extend their protection even if the originally encumbered collateral is no longer present or the originally guaranteed claim is already paid.[981] Two categories of extended retention of title can be discerned: *verlängerte Eigentumsvorbehalt* (2.1.) and *erweiterte*[982] *Eigentumsvorbehalt* (2.2.).

---

977 W. WIEGAND, "Anhang zu §929–931 BGB" in W. WIEGAND (ed.) *J. von Staudingers Kommentar zum Bürgerlichen Gesetzbuch mit Einführungsgesetz und Nebengesetzen*, (Berlin: Sellier, 2017), par. 6–7.

978 H. P. Westermann, *BGB-Sachenrecht*, (Heidelberg: C. F. Müller, 2012), 74.

979 R. M. BECKMANN and others, *J. Von Staudingers Kommentar zum Bürgerlichen Geseztbuch mit Einführungsgesetz und Nebengesetzen*, (M. MARTINEK (ed.), 2 edn., Berlin: Sellier, 2004), 425.

980 H. LAMBSDORFF, *Handbuch des Eigentumsvorbehalts im deutschen und ausländischen Recht*, (Frankfurt am Main: Athenäum, 1974), 9; U. DROBNIG, *Emphelen sich gesetzlichen Maßnahmen zur Reform der Mobiliarsicherheiten?*, (München: C. H. Beck, 1976), 21; H. WEBER, "Reform der Mobiliarsicherheiten", (1976) NJW, (1601) 1605; S. LEIBLE and O. SOSNITZA, 'Grundfälle zum Recht des Eigentumsvorbehalts', (2001) 6 JuS, (244) 244; R. M. BECKMANN and others, *J. Von Staudingers Kommentar zum Bürgerlichen Geseztbuch mit Einführungsgesetz und Nebengesetzen*, (M. MARTINEK (ed.), 2 edn., Berlin: Sellier, 2004), 427; S. LORENZ, 'Grundwissen – Zivilrecht: der Eigentumsvorbehalt', [2011] JuS, (199) 199; S. KIM, *Die Entwicklung des Anwartschaftsrechts beim Kauf under Eigentumsvorbehalt*, (Dissertation Rechtswissenschaft, Rheinischen Friedrich-Wilhelms-Universität Bonn 2017), 14 and 56.

981 H. P. WESTERMANN, *BGB-Sachenrecht*, (Heidelberg: C. F. Müller, 2012), 73; R. M. BECKMANN and others, *J. Von Staudingers Kommentar zum Bürgerlichen Geseztbuch mit Einführungsgesetz und Nebengesetzen*, (M. MARTINEK (ed.), 2 edn., Berlin: Sellier, 2004), 456.

982 Unlike what is sometimes suggested, *erweiterte* retention of title is a specific form of extended retention of title and is not a general term to refer to all forms of extended retention of title. See also, W. FLUME, 'Der verlängerte und erweiterte Eigentumsvorbehalt', (1950) 22 NJW, (841) 841.

2.1. *Verlängerte Eigentumsvorbehalt*

213. *Vertical extension to retention of title* – The *verlängerte Eigentumsvorbehalt* is German law's answer to the use, processing or disposition of the underlying collateral by the debtor. As in other jurisdictions, retention of title implies that the debtor obtains the physical possession of the encumbered collateral. To avoid that retention of title creditors lose their protection due to changes made to the underlying collateral, they will add contractual clauses to the simple retention of title form to ensure their ongoing protection in the altered collateral.

The most common clauses to extend the creditor's protection to new goods are the *Vorausabtretungsklauseln* and the *Verarbeitungsklauseln*. The former clause ensures that the retention of title creditor's right remains protected when the original collateral is sold and replaced by claims on a third-party transferee. The latter clause protects the creditor in the event of alterations made to the originally encumbered good, such as processing or mixing. The extent to which these clauses are upheld and actually protect retention of title creditors has been further fine-tuned in case law.[983]

2.2. *Erweiterte Eigentumsvorbehalt*

214. *Horizontal extension to retention of title* – An additional protection retention of title creditors have created for themselves is the extension of retention of title to other claims between him and the retention of title debtor. The benefit of this is evident, in one contractual clause the retention of title creditor retains his protection as owner not only for the outstanding purchase price, but also for other debts the debtor may owe him. This form of retention of title extension is also referred to as the *Kontokorrentvorbehalt*.[984]

Furthermore, retention of title creditors have also attempted to extend their protection to debts between the retention of title debtor and affiliates of the retention of title creditor (i.e. *Konzernvorbehalt*). The idea here is to bind the debtor and maintain the encumbrance on the sold collateral until all debts between the debtor and the retention of title creditor and all of the associates of the retention of title creditor have been paid. The permissibility of such an extension of retention of title is discussed in more detail when looking into the specific rights of retention of title creditors.[985]

---

983 See *infra* no. 234.

984 M. JUNKER, R. M. BECKMANN and H. RÜSSMANN in M. HERBERGER *et al.* (eds.), *Juris Praxiskommentar BGB*, (9 edn., Berlin: Sellier, 2020), no. 66 (online: https://www.juris.de/r3/document).

985 See *infra* no. 226.

SECTION 3 – SCOPE OF §449 BGB

215. *Overview* – Given the limited regulation concerning retention of title, the scope of retention of title is uncertain. In this section I briefly discuss (1.) the transactions that are covered by §449 BGB, (2.) the type of goods to which title can be retained and (3.) the claims that can be guaranteed by retention of title.

1. TRANSACTIONS TO WHICH §449 BGB APPLIES

216. *Finance vs. operation leasing* – From the language in §449 BGB it is clear that this provision applies to retention of title in sales on credit.[986] The provision does not mention whether the rules concerning retention of title apply to finance leases as well. The BGB does not indicate whether the term retention of title also includes (finance) leasing. In Germany, lease agreements can also be divided in finance and operational leasing. In operational lease agreements the lessor leases a good for a limited amount of time and there is always the intention of both parties for the good to return to the lessor at the end of the lease agreement. The operational lease shows a striking similarity with rental agreements and is therefore governed by the provisions concerning rent and not the provision concerning retention of title.[987] Since operational leases do not have any connection to sale or even *in rem* security rights, operational leases fall outside the scope of this research.

A finance lease is usually a three-party transaction in which the lessee gives instructions to the lessor to purchase a certain good from a manufacturer or supplier. The lessor then leases or rents the good to the lessee for a certain amount of time. During this time the lessee makes regular payments to the lessor. At the end of the leasing agreement the lessee usually has the option to purchase the leased good. In the event the debtor defaults, the retained title in the hands of the lessor gives the lessor a strong protection and allows him to recover the collateral if necessary.[988]

---

986 R. M. BECKMANN and others, *J. Von Staudingers Kommentar zum Bürgerlichen Geseztbuch mit Einführungsgesetz und Nebengesetzen*, (M. MARTINEK (ed.), 2 edn., Berlin: Sellier, 2004), 428.

987 W. FLUME, 'Das Rechtsverhältnis des Leasing in zivilrechtlicher und steuerrechtlicher Sicht', (1972) 1 – 4 DB, (1) 2; M. STOFFELS, 'Leasing' in *J. von Staudingers Kommentar zum Bürgerlichen Gesetzbuch mit Einführungsgesetz und Nebengesetzen*, (Berlin: Sellier, 2018), 20; M. MARTINEK, *Moderne Vertragstypen*, (München: C. H. Beck Verlag, 1991), 67; C. T. EBENROTH, 'Der Finanzierungs-Leasing-Vertrag als Rechtsgeschäft zwischen Miete und Kauf', (1978) 9 JuS, (588) 590.

988 W. FLUME, 'Das Rechtsverhältnis des Leasing in zivilrechtlicher und steuerrechtlicher Sicht', (1972) 1 – 4 DB, (1) 1; M. STOFFELS, 'Leasing' in *J. von Staudingers Kommentar zum Bürgerlichen Gesetzbuch mit Einführungsgesetz und Nebengesetzen*, (Berlin: Sellier, 2018), 19.

217. *Finance leasing as retention of title* – The application of the retention of title provision in the BGB[989] to finance lease agreements is less straight forward. Both the judiciary and doctrine are aware of the differences between finance leasing and operational leasing[990], but they do not see eye to eye with regards to the law that should govern finance lease agreements. Among scholars no formal consensus has been reached on the classification of finance lease agreements and its applicable law. The majority opinion considers finance leases as a type of rental agreement. In this school of thought there only remains some debate on whether finance leases are either a pure[991] or a special type of rental agreement.[992] Only a minority, considers the idea that finance leases show such a similarity with sales on credit with retention of title, that finance leases should be governed by the provisions governing sale (§433 *et seq.* BGB) and even more specifically §449 BGB.[993]

For the moment, the BGH sides with the majority opinion. Since 1975, the BGH considers finance lease agreements as a type of rental agreements[994], a decision that has been upheld as recently as 2013.[995] Consequently, rent law[996] is to be applied to financial leasing and not the provisions concerning sale and retention of title.

218. *Conclusion* – Given the judiciary classification of both finance and operational leasing as a form of rent and not retention of title, leasing cannot be viewed as a form of retention of title in Germany and falls outside of the scope of the term retention of title.

2. GOODS TO WHICH TITLE CAN BE RETAINED IN ACCORDANCE WITH §449 BGB

219. *Goods to which title can be retained* – §449 BGB only refers to the retention of title of movable goods. However, no further direction is provided

---

989 §449 BGB.

990 BGH 11 March 1998, no. VIII ZR 205/97, (1998) 22 NJW, (1637) 1639; M. STOFFELS, 'Leasing' in *J. von Staudingers Kommentar zum Bürgerlichen Gesetzbuch mit Einführungsgesetz und Nebengesetzen*, (Berlin: Sellier, 2018), 19.

991 W. FLUME, 'Das Rechtsverhältnis des Leasing in zivilrechtlicher und steuerrechtlicher Sicht', (1972) 1 – 4 DB, (1) 3 – 4; J. SONNENBERGER, 'Rechtsfragen beim Leasing beweglicher Sachen', (1983) 40 NJW, (2217) 2218–2219; F. WESTPHALEN, 'AGB-Recht im Jahr 2007', (2008) 31 NJW, (2234) 2240.

992 D. REINICKE and K. TIEDTKE, 'Finanzierungsleasing und Sachmängelhaftung', (1982) 19 BB, (1142) 1146.

993 C. T. EBENROTH, 'Der Finanzierungs-Leasing-Vertrag als Rechtsgeschäft zwischen Miete und Kauf', (1978) 9 JuS, (588) 593.

994 BGH 8 October 1975, no. VIII ZR 81/74, (1977) NJW, (195) 196; BGH 29 October 2008, no. VIII ZR 258/07, (2009) MMR, (101) 103.

995 BGH 13 November 2013, no. VIII ZR 257/12, (2014) NJW, 1583.

996 §535 *et seq.* BGB.

with regards to which movable goods exactly title can be retained. Consequently, both jurisprudence and case law have stepped in to fill this vacuum.

According to the jurisprudence in this matter, the movable goods mentioned in §449 BGB include tangible, intangible and accessory goods (*Zubehör*).[997] Accessory goods are movable goods which serve the purpose of the main good without having lost their specificity.[998] Examples of accessory goods are the motor or wheels of a car. Both goods are movable and serve the purpose of the main good, the car, but they have not lost their specificity as movable goods. Consequently, a seller of either the wheels or motor can retain title to these goods and he does not lose his protection due to the fact that these goods are placed in or on the car.[999] Relatedly, §449 BGB also applies to the fruits or gains of a movable good. This follows from the general principle that the gains of a good share the same fate as the good from which the gains came. Therefore, if the main good is encumbered with a retention of title, the same applies to the gains of this good.[1000]

Next, there are also a few paradoxical goods to which §449 BGB applies. For example, title can be retained to consumable goods (*verbrauchbaren Sachen*), but the retained title is lost when the goods are actually used.[1001] Consequently, retaining title to consumable goods is rather inefficient, since retention of title is lost at the moment of the inevitable consumption of the goods.[1002] Furthermore, retention of title to consumable fruits of the originally encumbered collateral is lost when the goods are consumed.[1003] However, if the consumable goods are disposed to a third party, the retention of title creditor can extend his protection to the claim on the third-party transferee that takes the place of the original

997 R. M. BECKMANN and others, *J. Von Staudingers Kommentar zum Bürgerlichen Geseztbuch mit Einführungsgesetz und Nebengesetzen*, (M. MARTINEK (ed.), 2 edn., Berlin: Sellier, 2004), 428; K. VIEWEG and A. WERNER, *Sachenrecht*, (7 edn., München: Verlag Franz Vahlen, 2015), 348.

998 §97 BGB; X. STIEPER, "§97 BGB – Zubehör" in *J. Von Staudingers Kommentar zum Bürgerlichen Geseztbuch mit Einführungsgesetz und Nebengesetzen*, (S. HERRLER (ed.), Berlin: Sellier, 2017), par. 2 (online: https://www.juris.de/r3/document).

999 R. M. BECKMANN and others, *J. Von Staudingers Kommentar zum Bürgerlichen Geseztbuch mit Einführungsgesetz und Nebengesetzen*, (M. MARTINEK (ed.), 2 edn., Berlin: Sellier, 2004), 428.

1000 H. LAMBSDORFF, *Handbuch des Eigentumsvorbehalts im deutschen und ausländischen Recht*, (Frankfurt am Main: Athenäum, 1974), 39 – 40; R. M. BECKMANN and others, *J. Von Staudinger Kommentar zum Bürgerlichen Geseztbuch mit einführungsgesetz und Nebengesetzen*, (M. MARTINEK (ed.), 2 edn., Berlin: Sellier, 2004), 428.

1001 H. LAMBSDORFF, *Handbuch des Eigentumsvorbehalts im deutschen und ausländischen Recht*, (Frankfurt am Main: Athenäum, 1974), 38.

1002 H. LAMBSDORFF, *Handbuch des Eigentumsvorbehalts im deutschen und ausländischen Recht*, (Frankfurt am Main: Athenäum, 1974), 38.

1003 R. M. BECKMANN and others, *J. Von Staudingers Kommentar zum Bürgerlichen Geseztbuch mit Einführungsgesetz und Nebengesetzen*, (M. MARTINEK (ed.), 2 edn., Berlin: Sellier, 2004), 428.

collateral.[1004] For this extension to apply a *verlängerte Eigentumsvorbehalt* has to be contractually agreed upon between the retention of title creditor and debtor.[1005] Another somewhat paradoxical good to which title can be retained are goods that cannot be seized through enforcement proceedings (*unpfändbare Sachen*).[1006] A debtor can use the protection of §811 ZPO to prevent the retention of title creditor from enforcing upon the encumbered goods, even if the goods technically do not belong to the debtor yet.[1007] However, if the retention of title creditor bases his claim on the "*Herausgabeanspruch*" or claim for recovery or revindication, then the retention of title debtor cannot rely on §811, sec. 1 ZPO to prevent enforcement.[1008] This exception explains why retention of title creditors still sell unenforceable goods with retention of title.

Finally, title cannot be retained to a business and its assets as a whole (*Rechtsgesamtheit*) or to a stock of movable goods (*Sachgesamtheit*).[1009] Retaining title to such collections of goods would go against the specificity principle that governs retention of title.[1010] However, as a compromise when title to such a collection of goods is retained, the retention of title clause is considered effective with regards to each of the individual goods within the collection.[1011]

3. *ERWEITERTE EIGENTUMSVORBEHALT*: THE EXTENSION OF RETENTION OF TITLE TO OTHER DEBTS

220. *Contractual horizontal extension of retention of title and its limitations* – Retention of title creditors not only try to extend their retention of

1004 R. M. BECKMANN and others, *J. Von Staudingers Kommentar zum Bürgerlichen Gesetzbuch mit Einführungsgesetz und Nebengesetzen*, (M. MARTINEK (ed.), 2 edn., Berlin: Sellier, 2004), 429.

1005 See *supra* no. 233.

1006 §811 ZPO; H. LAMBSDORFF, *Handbuch des Eigentumsvorbehalts im deutschen und ausländischen Recht*, (Frankfurt am Main: Athenäum, 1974), 40–41; R. M. BECKMANN and others, *J. Von Staudinger Kommentar zum Bürgerlichen Gesetzbuch mit einführungsgesetz und Nebengesetzen*, (M. MARTINEK (ed.), 2 edn., Berlin: Sellier, 2004), 429.

1007 H. LAMBSDORFF, *Handbuch des Eigentumsvorbehalts im deutschen und ausländischen Recht*, (Frankfurt am Main: Athenäum, 1974), 216.

1008 H. LAMBSDORFF, *Handbuch des Eigentumsvorbehalts im deutschen und ausländischen Recht*, (Frankfurt am Main: Athenäum, 1974), 217; R. M. BECKMANN and others, *J. Von Staudinger Kommentar zum Bürgerlichen Gesetzbuch mit einführungsgesetz und Nebengesetzen*, (M. MARTINEK (ed.), 2 edn., Berlin: Sellier, 2004), 452.

1009 H. LAMBSDORFF, *Handbuch des Eigentumsvorbehalts im deutschen und ausländischen Recht*, (Frankfurt am Main: Athenäum, 1974), 40.

1010 R. M. BECKMANN and others, *J. Von Staudinger Kommentar zum Bürgerlichen Gesetzbuch mit einführungsgesetz und Nebengesetzen*, (M. MARTINEK (ed.), 2 edn., Berlin: Sellier, 2004), 429.

1011 H. LAMBSDORFF, *Handbuch des Eigentumsvorbehalts im deutschen und ausländischen Recht*, (Frankfurt am Main: Athenäum, 1974), 40;

title protection vertically, but also horizontally through the *erweiterte Eigentumsvorbehalt*. Typically, this horizontal extension takes the form of a *Kontokorrentvorbehalt* which means that the creditor is allowed to retain title to the originally encumbered good until all the debts between the retention of title creditor and debtor are paid, even though the original claim for the purchase price of the good has been paid off.[1012] The extension of retention of title to other claims than the purchase price has been generally accepted by the BGH.[1013]

However, the extension of retention of title to other claims is not allowed when this is not limited by a release clause (*Freigabeklausel*) that protects the debtor against over-security.[1014] The argument goes that the retention of title creditor cannot hold on to the title to the encumbered good, after payment of the purchase price and its costs, to guarantee a much a smaller debt between the retention of title creditor and debtor. This would unfairly limit the debtor's freedom with regards to the encumbered collateral and would go against the good faith with which the retention of title creditor has to act.[1015] Consequently, any *Kontokorrentvorbehalt* must contain a release clause to avoid the over-security in the hands of the retention of title creditor. The inclusion of a release clause does not necessarily mean that the conditions for over-security and release will be easily fulfilled. According to standing case law of the BGH, the retention of title creditor can retain title to the encumbered collateral for the purchase price and all other claims that can arise from the initial sale agreement.[1016] Consequently, if the retention of title creditor can show that it is likely that more claims will come out of the original sale agreement, such as claims for repair or maintenance, then the retained title will not be considered as over-security and the retained title will not have to be released.[1017]

1012 H. LAMBSDORFF, *Handbuch des Eigentumsvorbehalts im deutschen und ausländischen Recht*, (Frankfurt am Main: Athenäum, 1974), 113; R.REICH, 'Reform der Kreditsicherung', (1976) 15–16 JZ, (463) 466; U. DROBNIG, *Emphelen sich gesetzlichen Maßnahmen zur Reform der Mobiliarsicherheiten?*, (München: C. H. Beck, 1976), 32 and 48; K. TIEDTKE, *Der erweiterte Eigentumsvorbehalt*, (München: Verlag C. H. Beck, 2000), (829) 829; M. HABERSACK and J. SCHÜRNBRAND, 'Der Eigentumsvorbehalt nach der Schuldrechtsreform', [2002] JuS, (833) 837; P. BÜLOW, *Recht der Kreditsicherheiten*, (Heidelberg: C. F. Müller Verlag, 2009), 489; F. FAUST, '§449 – Eigentumsvorbehalt' in H. G. BAMBERGER and others (eds.), *Bürgerliches Gesetzbuch Kommentar*, (4 edn., München: Beck, 2019), 2916.

1013 BGH (1964) NJW 1788; BGH 10 February 1971, (1971) JZ 506; BGH 20 March 1985, no. VIII ZR 342/83, (1985) 31 NJW, 1836; BGH 4 March 1991, no. II ZR 36/90, (1991) 36 NJW, 2285; BGH 9 February 1994, VIII ZR 176/92, (1994) 17 NJW, 1154.

1014 BGH 2 December 1992, no. VIII ZR 241/91, (1993) 8 NJW, (533); BGH 9 February 1994, VIII ZR 176/92, (1994) 17 NJW, (1154) 1155.

1015 BGH 23 November 1977, no. VIII ZR 7/76, (1977) 13 NJW, (632) 632–633.

1016 BGH 14 February 1968, no. VIII ZR 220/65, (1968) 19 NJW, (885) 885; BGH 23 November 1977, no. VIII ZR 7/76, (1977) 13 NJW, (632) 632–633.

1017 P. BÜLOW, *Recht der Kreditsicherheiten*, (6 edn., Heidelberg: C. F. Müller Verlag, 2009), 496.

221. *Horizontal extension of retention of title to the companies associated with the retention of title creditor and debtor* – The other way retention of title creditors try to extend their protection is by retaining title not only until all claims between the retention of title creditor and debtor are paid, but also all the claims between the debtor and all the companies associated with the retention of title creditor. This is also referred to as a *Konzernvorbehalt*.[1018] This practice has been cut short by the legislator in §449, sec. 3 BGB. In this provision it is explicitly prohibited for retention of title creditors to retain title for their claims and the claims of their associated companies. The reasoning behinds this prohibition is that such an extension of the retention of title mechanism would limit the debtor's freedom with regards to this asset too much, since it would basically transfer ownership of the asset for an unspecified time to the retention of title creditor.[1019]

The BGB does not mention the permissibility of the *Konzernvorbehalt* from the perspective of the debtor. In other words, the retention of title until all the debts of the debtor and those of the companies associated with the debtor are paid, seems possible.

SECTION 4 – CREATION AND THIRD-PARTY EFFECTIVENESS OF RETENTION OF TITLE

222. *The bifurcated approach to the creation of retention of title clauses in German civil law* – The BGB does not provide any rules or formalities for the creation or third-party effectiveness of retention of title clauses. Consequently, parties have to rely on general contract law and case law.

The traditional method to retain title is by adding the clause to the underlying sale agreement.[1020] Theoretically, for retention of title to have its full contractual and proprietary effect, it should be created in both the obligation component (i.e. *Verpflichtungsgeschäft* or *schuldrechtlichen Ebene*) and proprietary component

1018 G. KUHN, 'Der Eigentumsvorbehalt im Konkurs', (1972) 8 WM, (206) 209; U. DROBNIG, *Emphelen sich gesetzlichen Maßnahmen zur Reform der Mobiliarsicherheiten?*, (München: C. H. Beck, 1976), 50; M. HABERSACK and J. SCHÜRNBRAND, 'Der Eigentumsvorbehalt nach der Schuldrechtsreform', [2002] JuS, (833) 837; R. M. BECKMANN and others, *J. Von Staudinger Kommentar zum Bürgerlichen Geseztbuch mit einführungsgesetz und Nebengesetzen*, (M. MARTINEK (ed.), 2 edn., Berlin: Sellier, 2004), 467; K. VIEWEG and A. WERNER, *Sachenrecht*, (7 edn., München: Verlag Franz Vahlen, 2015), 363.

1019 G. KUHN, 'Der Eigentumsvorbehalt im Konkurs', (1972) 8 WM, (206) 210; M. HABERSACK and J. SCHÜRNBRAND, 'Der Eigentumsvorbehalt nach der Schuldrechtsreform', [2002] JuS, (833) 838; S. LEIBLE and O. SOSNITZA, 'Grundfälle zum Recht des Eigentumsvorbehalts', (2001) 6 JuS, (244) 558.

1020 S. LEIBLE and O. SOSNITZA, 'Grundfälle zum Recht des Eigentumsvorbehalts', (2001) 6 JuS, (244) 246; R. M. BECKMANN and others, *J. Von Staudingers Kommentar zum Bürgerlichen Geseztbuch mit Einführungsgesetz und Nebengesetzen*, (M. MARTINEK (ed.), 2 edn., Berlin: Sellier, 2004), 428.

(i.e. *Verfügungsgeschäft* or *dinglichen Ebene*) of the sale agreement.[1021] The separation of a sale agreement into its proprietary component, which includes the actual transfer of ownership (i.e. *Übereignung*), and its obligation component is a typical German phenomenon (*Trennungsprinzip*).[1022]

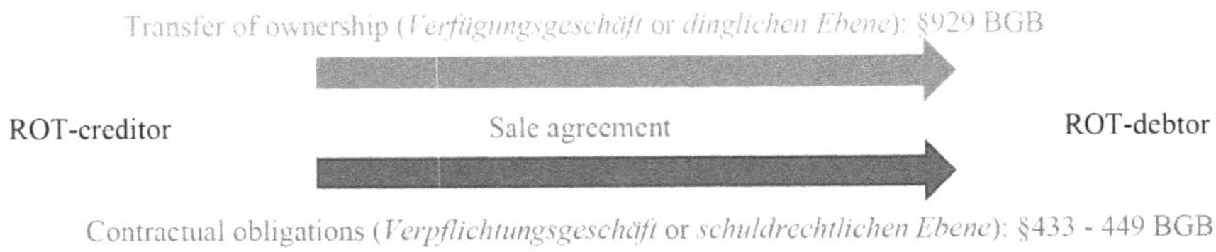

To avoid that the *Trennungsprinzip* obligates sellers to retain title twice (i.e. with regards to the contractual obligations and with regards to the proprietary transfer of the collateral), §449 BGB is so interpreted that the inclusion of the retention of title in the sale agreement is presumed to apply to both the proprietary component and obligation component of a sale agreement.[1023] Beyond the inclusion of retention of title in the sale agreement no further formalities are required.[1024] Furthermore, it is generally accepted that sellers can retain title in their general terms and conditions.[1025] However, in the event the debtor is a consumer stricter rules apply to guarantee that debtors are properly informed about the retention of title clause.[1026]

223. *Implicit retention of title* – Given the flexibility with which retention of title can be created, the question rises whether retention of title can be presumed whenever a good is delivered to a debtor before the purchase price is paid.

1021 K. VIEWEG and A. WERNER, *Sachenrecht*, (7 edn., München: Verlag Franz Vahlen, 2015), 348.

1022 R. SERICK, *Eigentumsvorbehalt und Sicherungsübertragung*, (Heidelberg: Verlag Recht und Wirtschaft, 1993), 58; S. HABERMEIER, 'Das Trennungsdenken- Ein Beitrag zur europäischen Privatrechtstheorie', (1995) 3 AcP, (283) 283; B. AKKERMANS, 'The Role of the (D)CFR in the Making of European Property Law' in V. SAGAERT, E. TERRYN and M.E. STORME (eds.), *The Draft Common Frame of Reference (DCFR): A National and Comparative Perspective*, (Antwerp: Intersentia, 2011), 2.

1023 K. VIEWEG and A. WERNER, *Sachenrecht*, (7 edn., München: Verlag Franz Vahlen, 2015), 348.

1024 U. DROBNIG, *Emphelen sich gesetzlichen Maßnahmen zur Reform der Mobiliarsicherheiten?*, (München: C. H. Beck, 1976), 67; S. LEIBLE and O. SOSNITZA, 'Grundfälle zum Recht des Eigentumsvorbehalts', (2001) 6 JuS, (244) 246.

1025 S. LEIBLE and O. SOSNITZA, 'Grundfälle zum Recht des Eigentumsvorbehalts', (2001) 6 JuS, (244) 246; H. P. Westermann, *BGB-Sachenrecht*, (Heidelberg: C. F. Müller, 2012), 75; K. VIEWEG and A. WERNER, *Sachenrecht*, (7 edn., München: Verlag Franz Vahlen, 2015), 348; F. FAUST, '§449 – Eigentumsvorbehalt' in H. G. BAMBERGER and others (eds.), *Bürgerliches Gesetzbuch Kommentar*, (4 edn., München: Beck, 2019), 2911.

1026 §305, sec. 2 BGB; R. M. BECKMANN and others, *J. Von Staudinger Kommentar zum Bürgerlichen Geseztbuch mit einführungsgesetz und Nebengesetzen*, (M. MARTINEK (ed.), 2 edn., Berlin: Sellier, 2004), 430.

Some authors are of the opinion that this should be possible and should even be considered as the common sense interpretation of a sale agreement in which the debtor obtains possession of a good prior to having paid the full price.[1027] Others suggest that retention of title is only implied and effective against the debtor when there are objectively verifiable indications that the parties agree to sell the good with retention of title[1028] or the retention of title is a common practice in the industry in which the transaction takes place.[1029] Given the questionable status of implied retention of title clauses, retention of title creditors are encouraged to explicitly retain their title in the sale agreement prior to the delivery of the goods to the debtor.[1030]

224. *Retroactive retention of title* – Interestingly, once the sale agreement has been performed and the goods are delivered, an option still exists to vest a retroactive retention of title.[1031] Understandably retaining title in this situation is difficult and even paradoxical; it is hard to retain title to a good when the title is no longer yours to retain. According to case law, the only way for the seller to retroactively retain title is by returning ownership to the original seller and then agree to a conditional transfer of ownership to the buyer.[1032] This approach is very straightforward, but also cumbersome. Parties have to go back on their initial agreement and repeat the transfer with the condition attached. The majority of scholars does not agree with the judiciary approach of passing ownership back and forth between the seller and the buyer, but suggests to simply return ownership without the *Anwartschaftsrecht*[1033] to the seller.[1034] In this approach it takes only one step to switch the original seller and buyer to the position of retention of title creditor and debtor and thus retain title to the underlying good. Finally, a minority opinion simply reclassifies a retroactive retention of title as a transfer of title.[1035] Problematic with such a

---

1027 H. P. WESTERMANN, 'Vereinbarung des Eigentumsvorbehalts, insbesondere durch AGB' in SCHUBERT C (ed.), *Münchener Kommentar zum Bürgerlichen Gesetzbuch*, (8 edn., München: C. H. Beck Verlag, 2018), rn. 15; F. FAUST, '§449 – Eigentumsvorbehalt' in H. G. BAMBERGER and others (eds.), *Bürgerliches Gesetzbuch Kommentar*, (4 edn., München: Beck, 2019), 2911.

1028 K. VIEWEG and A. WERNER, *Sachenrecht*, (7 edn., München: Verlag Franz Vahlen, 2015), 349.

1029 BGH 22 September 2003, II ZR 172/01 (OLG Brandenburg), (2004) NJW-RR, (555) 555.

1030 R. M. BECKMANN and others, *J. Von Staudinger Kommentar zum Bürgerlichen Gesetzbuch mit einführungsgesetz und Nebengesetzen*, (M. MARTINEK (ed.), 2 edn., Berlin: Sellier, 2004), 433.

1031 K. VIEWEG and A. WERNER, *Sachenrecht*, (7 edn., München: Verlag Franz Vahlen, 2015), 349.

1032 BGH 2 October 1952, no. IV ZR 2/52, (1953) 6 NJW, (217) 218.

1033 The *Anwartschaftsrecht* is a specific German concept which refers to the debtor's prospective ownership right in the encumbered collateral. See, *infra* no. 226.

1034 L. RAISER, "Zu BGH 2 Ocotber 1952, no. IV ZR 2/52", (1953) NJW, (217) 217; K. VIEWEG and A. WERNER, *Sachenrecht*, (7 edn., München: Verlag Franz Vahlen, 2015), 349.

1035 H. LAMBSDORFF, *Handbuch des Eigentumsvorbehalts im deutschen und ausländischen Recht*, (Frankfurt am Main: Athenäum, 1974), 34.

recharacterization is that this agreement would lack the parties' intention to create a transfer of title and the necessary specificity.[1036] In a transfer of title agreement the encumbered collateral must be described very precisely.[1037] This specificity may be lacking in an sale agreement in which the parties merely refer to the delivered goods and which is then turned in a transfer of title agreement. Given that the latter two options have not been backed up by case law, I must assume that for the moment it is only possible to retroactively retain title in two steps: 1) by returning ownership to the seller and 2) then transferring it to the debtor on the condition of payment of the purchase price.

225. *Absence of requirements for third-party effectiveness* – Besides the creation of the retention of title clause in the sale agreement, no further formalities are required to retain title in an effective manner. In other words, retention of title clauses do not have to be made public in any way. The idea of creating a non-possessory *in rem* security right with notification requirements has been tossed around[1038], but as of yet has not moved forward. One of the reasons notification requirements, such as the registration in an *in rem* security right registry, are not unanimously viewed as a positive development is that it is considered unnecessary. It is argued that in practice most creditors assume that valuable goods in the debtor's possession are bought under retention of title and are already encumbered.[1039] LAMBSDORFF even goes as far as to say that if you buy or encumber goods in hands of your debtor and you assume that these goods have not yet been encumbered, you deserve not to be protected against other earlier claimants.[1040]

SECTION 5 – RIGHTS OF RETENTION OF TITLE CREDITORS

226. This section will focus on (1.) the right to dispose of the collateral, (2.) the right to trace the collateral, (3.) priority and (4.) the right to revendicate the collateral.

1036 H. LAMBSDORFF, *Handbuch des Eigentumsvorbehalts im deutschen und ausländischen Recht*, (Frankfurt am Main: Athenäum, 1974), 35.

1037 BGH 10 October 1956, no. IV ZR 71/56, (1956) 51–52 NJW, 1918; H. LAMBSDORFF, *Handbuch des Eigentumsvorbehalts im deutschen und ausländischen Recht*, (Frankfurt am Main: Athenäum, 1974), 35.

1038 U. DROBNIG, *Emphelen sich gesetzlichen Maßnahmen zur Reform der Mobiliarsicherheiten?*, (München: C. H. Beck, 1976), 57–58; E.-M. KIENINGER, 'Die Zukunft des deutschen und europäischen Mobiliarkreditsicherungsrechts', (2008) 208 AcP, (182) 210 *et seq.*

1039 H. LEHMANN, *Reform der Kreditsicherung an Fahrnis und Forderungen* (Stuttgart: W. Rohlhammer Verlag, 1937), 7; U. DROBNIG, *Emphelen sich gesetzlichen Maßnahmen zur Reform der Mobiliarsicherheiten?*, (München: C. H. Beck, 1976), 59.

1040 H. LAMBSDORFF, *Handbuch des Eigentumsvorbehalts im deutschen und ausländischen Recht*, (Frankfurt am Main: Athenäum, 1974), 6.

227. *Introduction of the Anwartschaftsrecht* - More than in other jurisdictions, the analysis of the rights of retention of title creditors in German civil law inevitably includes some reference to the rights and position of the retention of title debtor.[1041] This is due to the existence of a specific and legally acknowledged claim the retention of title debtor already has to the encumbered good: the *Anwartschaftsrecht*.[1042] This right is German law's answer to the specific position in which the retention of title debtor finds himself: not quite, but soon to be owner.[1043] The *Anwartschaftsrecht* has not been recognized in codified law.[1044] However, the existence and effects of the *Anwartschaftsrecht* have been generally accepted and deliberated in case law and scholarly works.[1045] The recognition of the *Anwartschaftsrecht* of the retention of title debtor in case law has strengthened the debtor's position with regards to the encumbered good. Furthermore, it has shaped and to some extent limited the retention of title creditor's rights with regards to the encumbered collateral and should therefore be taken into account when assessing his rights.

1. RIGHT TO DISPOSE

228. *Case law limitations on the right to dispose* - The retention of title creditor's right to dispose is rooted in his retained ownership to the encumbered good. Because the retention of title creditor is still owner of the good, he is technically still allowed to dispose of the asset.[1046] However, once the purchase price is paid,

---

[1041] FAUST even goes as far to say that with regards to retention of title, the rights of retention of title-creditor is irrelevant and that one should merely focus on the rights of the retention of title-debtor (F. FAUST, "§449 BGB" in H. G. BAMBERGER, H. ROTH, W. HAU and R. POSECK (eds.), *Bürgerliches Gesetzbuch Kommentar*, (München: Beck, 2019), (2909) 2010).

[1042] *Anwartschaftrecht* is also described as the *Vorstufe zum Eigentum*. Roughly translated it can be referred to as the debtor's prospective ownership right.

[1043] See, BGH 21 September 1959, no. III ZR 103/58, (1960) 1-2 NJW, (34); H. LAMBSDORFF, *Handbuch des Eigentumsvorbehalts im deutschen und ausländischen Recht*, (Frankfurt am Main: Athenäum, 1974), 48; K. MÜLLER and U. P. GRUBER, *Sachenrecht*, (München: Verlag Franz Vahlen, 2016), 309; S. KIM, *Die Entwicklung des Anwartschaftsrechts beim Kauf under Eigentumsvorbehalt*, (Dissertation Rechtswissenschaft, Rheinischen Friedrich-Wilhelms-Universität Bonn 2017), 20 *et seq.*

[1044] S. KIM, *Die Entwicklung des Anwartschaftsrechts beim Kauf under Eigentumsvorbehalt*, (Dissertation Rechtswissenschaft, Rheinischen Friedrich-Wilhelms-Universität Bonn 2017), 22–23.

[1045] For a detailed overview of the scholarly articles and case law concerning the *Anwartschaftsrecht* following the sale with retention of title, see S. KIM, *Die Entwicklung des Anwartschaftsrechts beim Kauf under Eigentumsvorbehalt*, (Dissertation Rechtswissenschaft, Rheinischen Friedrich-Wilhelms-Universität Bonn 2017), 106 *et seq.*

[1046] S. LORENZ, 'Grundwissen – Zivilrecht: der Eigentumsvorbehalt', [2011] JuS, (199) 201; R. M. BECKMANN and others, *J. Von Staudingers Kommentar zum Bürgerlichen Gesetzbuch mit Einführungsgesetz und Nebengesetzen*, (M. MARTINEK (ed.), 2 edn., Berlin: Sellier, 2004), 446; K. VIEWEG and A. WERNER, *Sachenrecht*, (7 edn., München: Verlag Franz Vahlen, 2015), 369.

ownership automatically transfers to the debtor and any transfers the retention of title creditor made after the retention of title sale become ineffective.[1047] Furthermore, the BGH has stated that the retention of title creditor has an obligation to refrain from any behavior that would prevent the transfer of ownership to the debtor.[1048] Consequently, the retention of title creditor's theoretical right to dispose is offset by his contractual obligation[1049] to make sure that the transfer of ownership to the retention of title debtor can take place.

229. *Good faith acquisition and the right to dispose* – Nevertheless, a transfer in good faith to a third party could still jeopardize the debtor's claim to the good. Normally, the third-party transfer is made ineffective by payment of the last installment on the purchase price by the debtor.[1050] However, a third party could be protected against the debtor's claim, if the third party's acquisition complies with the good-faith acquisition rules of §932–936 BGB.[1051] This situation can be avoided through the application of §936, sec. 3 BGB. This provision protects the claim or the *Anwartschaftsrecht* of a possessor over that of a non-possessory good faith transferee. Since in most cases the debtor in a sale with retention of title is in possession of the good, his claim will be stronger than this of a third-party transferee acting good faith. Furthermore, once the debtor makes the final payment for the encumbered collateral, his *Anwartschaftsrecht* transitions into full ownership and further outranks the third party's claim to the collateral.[1052]

2. RIGHT TO TRACE

230. *Overview* – The right to trace refers to the retention of title creditor's right to follow the encumbered good or its replacement goods as it is being processed, mixed, incorporated or disposed of. In this section a distinction is made between (2.1.) tracing without a contractual clause and (2.2.). tracing with a contractual clause.

1047 §161, sec. 1 BGB.

1048 BGH 24 May 1954, no. IV ZR 184/53 (Nürnberg), 1954 NJW, (1325) 1326. See also, A. BLOMEYER, 'Die Rechtsstellung des Vorbehaltskäufers', (1963) 162 AcP, (193) 194–195; S. LORENZ, 'Grundwissen – Zivilrecht: der Eigentumsvorbehalt', [2011] JuS, (199) 200; K. MÜLLER and U. P. GRUBER, *Sachenrecht*, (München: Verlag Franz Vahlen, 2016), 309.

1049 Consequently, LAMBSDORFF does not list retention of title-creditor's the right to dispose, but the retention of title-creditor's obligation to make sure that nothing prevents the transfer of ownership to the retention of title-debtor. See, H. LAMBSDORFF, *Handbuch des Eigentumsvorbehalts im deutschen und ausländischen Recht*, (Frankfurt am Main: Athenäum, 1974), 54.

1050 §161, sec. 1 BGB.

1051 §161, sec. 3 BGB; W. WIEGAND, "§936 BGB" in W. WIEGAND (ed.), *J. von Staudingers Kommentar zum Bürgerlichen Gesetzbuch mit Einführungsgesetz und Nebengesetzen*, (Berlin: Sellier, 2017), 490.

1052 W. WIEGAND, 'Der gutgläubige Erwerb beweglicher Sachen nach §932 ff BGB', (1974) 4 JuS, (201) 211.

2.1. *Tracing without contractual protection*

231. *Tracing into accessions and mixed goods according to general contract law principles* – Tracing without a contractual clause means that the retention of title's extension into the processed, mixed, incorporated or replacement goods is governed by the applicable property law rules.

The impact of attaching or mixing the encumbered collateral with other movable goods are governed in different provisions[1053], but by the same principles. If the encumbered collateral is attached or mixed with another movable good and becomes an essential part of the latter good, then both owners will become co-owners of the assembled or mixed collateral.[1054] A good becomes an essential part of another good when it can no longer be separated from the new good without harming the other components or when separating the two parts would change the essence of the part to which it has been attached or with which it has been mixed.[1055] Furthermore, if a principal good (*Hauptsache*) can be determined[1056], then the owner of the principal good will become the owner of all the goods that have become an essential part of the main good.[1057] If the encumbered collateral has become an essential part of the main good, this would result in the loss of the retained title.

The situation is slightly different, if the encumbered collateral is attached to an immovable good. In the event the encumbered collateral becomes an essential part of an immovable good, the owner of the immovable good will become the owner of the encumbered collateral.[1058] Essential components of immovable goods are buildings, but also goods that are installed in buildings, such as kitchen appliances and bathroom fixtures.[1059]

Finally, when the encumbered collateral is raw material, it can be altered by converting it during a manufacturing process into another good.[1060] In that scenario, the manufacturer becomes the owner of the encumbered raw materials, unless the value of the raw materials is higher than the newly created good.[1061]

1053 §947–948 BGB.

1054 §947–948 BGB.

1055 §93 BGB. See also, BGH 8 October 1955, no. IV ZR 116/55, (1955) NJW, (1793) 1793–1794; BGH 27 June 1973, no. VIII ZR 201/72, (1973) NJW, (1454) 1455; W. WIEGAND, ‹Akzessorietät und Spezialität Zum Verhältnis zwischen Forderung und Sicherungsgegenstand› in *Probleme der Kreditsicherung*, (Bern: Verlag Stämpfli & Cie Ag, 1982), 41.

1056 The determination of what is the main good depends on the customs in that business sector, see BGH 3 March 1956, no. IV ZR 334/55, (1956) 21 NJW, (788) 789.

1057 §947, sec. 2 BGB; F. FAUST, '§449 – Eigentumsvorbehalt' in H. G. BAMBERGER and others (eds.), *Bürgerliches Gesetzbuch Kommentar*, (4 edn., München: Beck, 2019), 2914.

1058 §946 BGB.

1059 §94 BGB; S. LEIBLE and O. SOSNITZA, 'Grundfälle zum Recht des Eigentumsvorbehalts', (2001) 6 JuS, (244) 245; R. M. BECKMANN and others, *J. Von Staudinger Kommentar zum Bürgerlichen Gesetzbuch mit einführungsgesetz und Nebengesetzen*, (M. MARTINEK (ed.), 2 edn., Berlin: Sellier, 2004), 438.

1060 §950 BGB.

1061 BGH 12 January 1972, no. VIII ZR 147/70, (1972) BeckRS, 31126533. See also, S. LEIBLE and O. SOSNITZA, 'Grundfälle zum Recht des Eigentumsvorbehalts', (2001) 6 JuS, (244) 455.

232. *Tracing into the hands of a third-party transferee* – Theoretically, the retention of title creditor should be unaffected by the debtor's disposal of the encumbered collateral. The retention of title creditor is still owner, so the debtor does not have the required authority to transfer the encumbered collateral to a third party. Consequently, the retention of title creditor should have the right to trace the encumbered collateral into the hands of the third-party transferee and to revendicate the encumbered good.[1062] However, there are exceptions to this rule. First, if the retention of title creditor gives his permission to the debtor to dispose of the collateral, the retention of title creditor obviously loses his retained title when the encumbered collateral is sold to a third party.[1063] Furthermore, the permission for the debtor to dispose of the encumbered collateral is even presumed to be given when the debtor is a retailer and when the transfer takes place in the ordinary course of business.[1064] In those cases the debtor is either explicitly or implicitly allowed to transfer the encumbered collateral and the third-party transferee is considered to have acted in good faith.[1065] Conversely, if the debtor transfers the collateral outside the ordinary course of business, the transfer is not authorized and the retention of title creditor cannot claim to have received the collateral in good faith.[1066]

Second, an unauthorized transfer can still result in loss of the retained title if the third-party transferee acted in good faith.[1067] To determine whether the third-party transferee acted in good faith the circumstances of the transfer have to be taken into consideration, such as the customary practices within that industry.[1068] Additionally, an investigatory burden (*Nachforschungspflicht*) is placed on the third-party transferee.[1069] Retention of title has become so ubiquitous in German trade practices that it is very difficult for a third-party transferee to claim that he was unaware of the existence of the retention of title clause.[1070] Consequently, the third-party transferee is expected to conduct a

---

1062 §985 BGB; U. HUBER, 'Gefahren des vertraglichen Abtretungsverbots für den Schuldner der abgetretenen Forderung', (1968) 41 NJW, (1905) 1907.

1063 §185 BGB; R. M. BECKMANN and others, *J. Von Staudinger Kommentar zum Bürgerlichen Gesetzbuch mit einführungsgesetz und Nebengesetzen*, (M. MARTINEK (ed.), 2 edn., Berlin: Sellier, 2004), 87.

1064 §366 Handelsgesetzbuch (HGB); U. HUBER, 'Gefahren des vertraglichen Abtretungsverbots für den Schuldner der abgetretenen Forderung', (1968) 41 NJW, (1905) 1907.

1065 H. LAMBSDORFF, *Handbuch des Eigentumsvorbehalts im deutschen und ausländischen Recht*, (Frankfurt am Main: Athenäum, 1974), 87.

1066 BGH 5 November 1969, no. VIII 247/67, (1970) 3 MDR, (227) 227.

1067 D. REINICKE and K. TIEDTKE, *Kaufrecht*, (München: Carl Heymans Verlag, 2009), 492.

1068 T. WEYER, 'Schutz des Eigentumsvorbehalts und gutgläubiger Erwerb an beweglichen Sachen', (1966) 21 NJW, (959) 959; H. LAMBSDORFF, *Handbuch des Eigentumsvorbehalts im deutschen und ausländischen Recht*, (Frankfurt am Main: Athenäum, 1974), 88.

1069 R. M. BECKMANN and others, *J. Von Staudinger Kommentar zum Bürgerlichen Gesetzbuch mit einführungsgesetz und Nebengesetzen*, (M. MARTINEK (ed.), 2 edn., Berlin: Sellier, 2004), 437.

1070 T. WEYER, 'Schutz des Eigentumsvorbehalts und gutgläubiger Erwerb an beweglichen Sachen', (1966) 21 NJW, (959) 959.; H. LAMBSDORFF, *Handbuch des Eigentumsvorbehalts im deutschen und ausländischen Recht*, (Frankfurt am Main: Athenäum, 1974), 88;

thorough investigation into the existence of a potential retention of title clause. If the third-party transferee fails to comply with this requirement, he will be considered negligent[1071] and a good faith acquisition of the encumbered collateral is ruled out. Furthermore, if the retention of title debtor is considered to have acted in bad faith, he is liable for damages.[1072] Moreover, the retention of title creditor could launch a claim for unjust enrichment against the debtor.[1073] In summary, the obligation for the third-party transferee to thoroughly investigate the potential existence of a retention of title clause offers the retention of title creditor some protection against loss of his retained title due to an unauthorized sale.

2.2. *Tracing with contractual protection*

233. *Overview* – In this section, I look into contractual clauses which explicitly extend the protection of the retention of title creditor after the encumbered collateral has been altered or disposed of. These clauses were developed in industries where alterations to or resale of the encumbered good were necessary and the retention of title creditor did not want to leave his protection to chance.[1074]

2.2.1. *Verarbeitungsklauseln*

234. *The contractual extension of retention of title in manufactured goods* – The *Verarbeitungsklausel* aims to contractually avoid the loss of the retained title that follows the manufacturing of the encumbered collateral into a new good.[1075] In other words, it aims to avoid the application of §950 BGB that assigns ownership to the manufacturer of a good, unless the value of the raw materials is higher than the newly assembled good. There is an ongoing debate whether the application of §950 BGB can be contractually suspended.[1076]

235. *The minority opinion on extending retention of title in manufactured goods* – On the one hand, there are some scholars of the opinion that the application

---

1071 BGH 11 May 1953, no. IV ZR 170/52 1953 NJW, 1139.

1072 §989–990 BGB; R. M. BECKMANN and others, *J. Von Staudinger Kommentar zum Bürgerlichen Geseztbuch mit einführungsgesetz und Nebengesetzen*, (M. MARTINEK (ed.), 2 edn., Berlin: Sellier, 2004), 437.

1073 §816 BGB; H. LAMBSDORFF, *Handbuch des Eigentumsvorbehalts im deutschen und ausländischen Recht*, (Frankfurt am Main: Athenäum, 1974), 63.

1074 H. P. WESTERMANN, *BGB-Sachenrecht*, (Heidelberg: C. F. Müller, 2012), 73; R. M. BECKMANN and others, *J. Von Staudingers Kommentar zum Bürgerlichen Geseztbuch mit Einführungsgesetz und Nebengesetzen*, (M. MARTINEK (ed.), 2 edn., Berlin: Sellier, 2004), 456.

1075 §950 BGB.

1076 R. M. BECKMANN and others, *J. Von Staudinger Kommentar zum Bürgerlichen Geseztbuch mit einführungsgesetz und Nebengesetzen*, (M. MARTINEK (ed.), 2 edn., Berlin: Sellier, 2004), 464.

of §950 BGB can be contractually suspended by the parties.[1077] According to these scholars, §950 BGB should only be invoked when there is an active dispute between the supplier of the raw materials and the manufacturer. However, if the parties have come to an agreement about this conflict, §950 BGB should not be imposed.[1078]

On the other hand, WESTERMANN maintains the view that parties cannot contractually override §950 BGB.[1079] The only way for the retention of title creditor to extend his protection into the newly manufactured goods is by vesting a transfer of title (*Sicherungsübereignung*) of the newly manufactured goods. This reasoning stems from the idea that through the manufacturing process the manufacturer (in this case the debtor) inevitably will become the owner of the new goods. However, parties can agree that ownership to these future goods is immediately transferred to the former supplier in order to guarantee his outstanding claim. Furthermore, the contractual clause that extends the retention of title creditor's claim to the newly manufactured goods (*Verarbeitungsklausel*) can even be recharacterized in a transfer of title clause.[1080] Nevertheless, a recharacterization to transfer of title is not necessarily a full-proof solution. Additional problems can arise, such as the fact that the manufacturer did not intend to vest a transfer of ownership which would lead to the ineffectiveness of the transfer of title clause.[1081]

236. *The majority opinion to the vertical extension of retention of title in manufactured goods* – The majority of scholars and the BGH hold a more nuanced view of the contractual extension of retention of title to newly manufactured goods. The majority finds that parties cannot contractually exclude the application of §950 BGB.[1082] However, some scholars are of the opinion that parties can agree on who should be considered the manufacturer in accordance with §950 BGB.[1083] According to the BGH the manufacturer

---

1077 S. LEIBLE and O. SOSNITZA, 'Grundfälle zum Recht des Eigentumsvorbehalts', (2001) 6 JuS, (244) 455; R. M. BECKMANN and others, *J. Von Staudinger Kommentar zum Bürgerlichen Gesetzbuch mit einführungsgesetz und Nebengesetzen*, (M. MARTINEK (ed.), 2 edn., Berlin: Sellier, 2004), 464.

1078 W. FLUME, 'Der verlängerte und erweiterte Eigentumsvorbehalt', (1950) 22 NJW, (841) 843–844; S. LEIBLE and O. SOSNITZA, 'Grundfälle zum Recht des Eigentumsvorbehalts', (2001) 6 JuS, (244) 455; J. F. BAUR and R. STÜRNER, *Sachenrecht*, (München: C. H. Beck Verlag, 2009), 700–701.

1079 H. P. WESTERMANN, K.-H. GURSKY and D. EICKMANN, *Sachenrecht*, (Heidelberg: C. F. Müller, 2011), 485–486.

1080 H. P. WESTERMANN, K.-H. GURSKY and D. EICKMANN, *Sachenrecht*, (Heidelberg: C. F. Müller, 2011), 486.

1081 W. WIEGAND, '§950 BGB' in W. WIEGAND (ed.), *J. von Staudingers Kommentar zum Bürgerlichen Gesetzbuch mit Einführungsgesetz und Nebengesetzen*, (Berlin: Sellier, 2016), 549.

1082 BGH 15 June 1989, no. IX ZR 167/88, (1989) 50 NJW, (3213) 3213; R. SERICK, 'Kollisionsfälle im Bereiche der Verarbeitungsklauseln', (1975) 9 BB, (381) 382.

1083 R. MÖHRING, 'Konkurrenz von Verarbeitungsklauseln', (1960) 16 NJW, (697) 698; J. RAKOB, 'Germany' in H. C. SIGMAN and E.-M. KIENINGER (eds.), *Cross-border security*

does not have to be the one who actually assembles the good, but can, following industry practices, also be the one who is in charge of the manufacturing process. Consequently, in some cases the supplier of the raw materials can validly be assigned as the manufacturer.[1084] This view was further elaborated in 1956 when the BGH decided that the crucial factor in determining the manufacturer is the opinion of an objective third party, who is familiar with the industry. Therefore, if raw materials are delivered under retention of title and it is agreed between parties that the manufacturing will take place in name of the supplier, generally the suppliers will be considered the manufacturer in accordance with §950 BGB as determined by an objective third party.[1085] Consequently, in most cases the supplier or retention of title creditor will be able to successfully assign himself as manufacturer and maintain his retained title despite the changes made to the encumbered collateral.

This approach has been further specified in doctrine. According to WIEGAND, the extension of retained title to newly manufactured goods is more than the resolution of a conflict between the manufacturer and the supplier. It also concerns other creditors who, through the extension of retention of title, are not able to enforce upon the newly manufactured goods.[1086] Normally when the manufacturer becomes the owner of newly manufactured goods, his other creditors can use these new goods to secure or enforce their claim. However, if the retention of title creditor can maintain his claim on the newly created goods, the other creditors will see their stake in the debtor's estate diminish.[1087] Consequently, the question of whether the retention of title creditor should be allowed to extend his claim in newly manufactured goods should be decided by weighing the interests of the retention of title creditor with those of the other creditors.[1088] Following this reasoning, an extension of the retention of title creditor's protection in the newly manufactured goods to the detriment of the debtor's other creditors is only justified when the manufacturer/supplier takes on significant risk in this transaction. Significant risk in this context refers to an actual risk in the production and/or distribution process.[1089] The added risk for

over tangibles, (Berlin: Sellier, 2007), (63) 67; F. FAUST, '§449 – Eigentumsvorbehalt' in H. G. BAMBERGER and others (eds.), *Bürgerliches Gesetzbuch Kommentar*, (4 edn., München: Beck, 2019), 2915.

1084 BGH 28 June 1954, no. IV ZR 40/54, (1954) BeckRS, 30398959.

1085 BGH 3 March 1956, no. IV ZR 334/55, (1956) 21 NJW, (788) 789.

1086 W. WIEGAND, '§950 BGB' in W. WIEGAND (ed.), *J. von Staudingers Kommentar zum Bürgerlichen Gesetzbuch mit Einführungsgesetz und Nebengesetzen*, (Berlin: Sellier, 2016), 544.

1087 W. WIEGAND, '§950 BGB' in W. WIEGAND (ed.), *J. von Staudingers Kommentar zum Bürgerlichen Gesetzbuch mit Einführungsgesetz und Nebengesetzen*, (Berlin: Sellier, 2016), 546.

1088 W. WIEGAND, '§950 BGB' in W. WIEGAND (ed.), *J. von Staudingers Kommentar zum Bürgerlichen Gesetzbuch mit Einführungsgesetz und Nebengesetzen*, (Berlin: Sellier, 2016), 545.

1089 W. WIEGAND, '§950 BGB' in W. WIEGAND (ed.), *J. von Staudingers Kommentar zum Bürgerlichen Gesetzbuch mit Einführungsgesetz und Nebengesetzen*, (Berlin: Sellier, 2016), 547.

the retention of title creditor would justify his protection over this of the other creditors. However, this approach would also make it more difficult for retention of title creditors to actually extend their claim to the manufactured goods. As of yet, this view has not been adopted by the courts, so there is no precedent as of yet that retention of title creditors have to meet this requirement.

237. *Conclusion* – According to the BGH the contractual extension of retention of title of a supplier in the manufactured goods is not possible *an sich*, but a contractual qualification as manufacturer in accordance with §950 BGB is possible. However, the doctrinal debate in this matter continues, leaving room for further developments in the recognition of the contractual extension of retention of title in manufactured goods.

2.2.2. *Vorausabtretungsklauseln*

238. *Contractual assignment of proceeds of the collateral* – The *Vorausabtretungsklausel* contractually authorizes the retention of title debtor to dispose of the encumbered collateral and simultaneously transfers the claim on the third-party transferee to the retention of title creditor.[1090]

Example

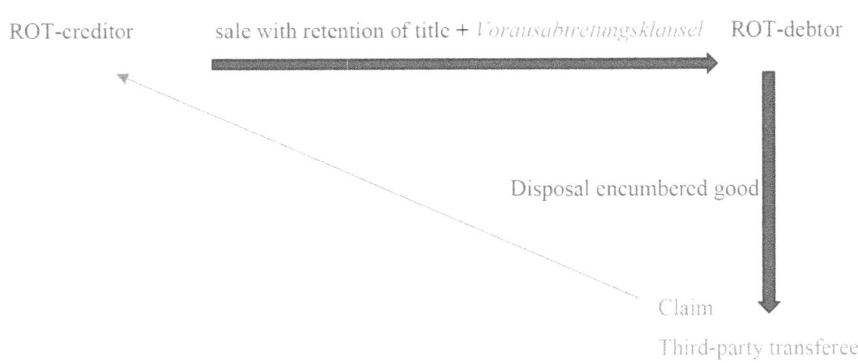

239. *Assignment of future claims to the retention of title creditor* – One of the big issues with this type of contractual extension of the retention of title protection is whether future claims (*künftige Forderungen*) can be assigned. Assets need to be sufficiently defined in order to be assigned.[1091] This can be

[1090] R. M. BECKMANN and others, *J. Von Staudinger Kommentar zum Bürgerlichen Gesetzbuch mit einführungsgesetz und Nebengesetzen*, (M. MARTINEK (ed.), 2 edn., Berlin: Sellier, 2004), 456; F. FAUST, '§449 – Eigentumsvorbehalt' in H. G. BAMBERGER and others (eds.), *Bürgerliches Gesetzbuch Kommentar*, (4 edn., München: Beck, 2019), 2914.

[1091] BGH 25 October 1952, no. I ZR 48/52, (1953) 1 NJW, (21) 21; R. M. BECKMANN and others, *J. Von Staudinger Kommentar zum Bürgerlichen Gesetzbuch mit einführungsgesetz und*

problematic in the case of an assignment clause in a sale with retention of title, because the claim between the debtor and the third-party transferee has not yet come into existence at the moment the assignment clause is agreed upon.[1092] For a long time there was uncertainty among the lower courts concerning the interpretation of the definitive nature of future claims.[1093] The BGH resolved this issue by deciding that a claim is sufficiently defined when at the moment that the claim comes into existence the *Vorausabtretungsklausel* makes it possible to define the claim and its scope *in concreto*.[1094] For example, a claim is sufficiently defined when the assignment refers to the claim on the third-party transferee and is limited to the value of the originally encumbered collateral.[1095] Given the standing case law from the BGH, the validity of *Vorausabtretungsklausln* and their application to future claims is generally accepted. The majority of scholars agrees with the BGH's interpretation of how future claims should be defined.[1096] A minority adheres to a more rigid interpretation and argues that in order for the *Vorausabtretungsklausel* to be valid the claim that is assigned, has to exist the moment the assignment clause is agreed upon.[1097] This would make the use of such assignment clauses very limited, since it is the future claims on third-party transferees that the retention of title creditor would like to have assigned to him.

240. *Requirements for the assignment of claims to the retention of title creditor* - Once the claim on the third-party transferee is assigned to the retention of title creditor, this transaction is treated as a normal assignment of claim clause.[1098]

Nebengesetzen, (M. MARTINEK (ed.), 2 edn., Berlin: Sellier, 2004), 457; F. EICHEL, *Künftige Forderungen*, (Tübingen: Mohr Siebeck, 2014), 373–374.

1092 W. FLUME, 'Der verlängerte und erweiterte Eigentumsvorbehalt', (1950) 22 NJW, (841) 845; H. LAMBSDORFF, *Handbuch des Eigentumsvorbehalts im deutschen und ausländischen Recht*, (Frankfurt am Main: Athenäum, 1974), 142.

1093 For an overview of the older case law, see H. LAMBSDORFF, *Handbuch des Eigentumsvorbehalts im deutschen und ausländischen Recht*, (Frankfurt am Main: Athenäum, 1974), 145–147.

1094 BGH 25 October 1952, no. I ZR 48/52, (1953) 1 NJW, (21) 22; BGH 16 December 1957, no. VII ZR 49/57, (186) 189; BGH 30 April 1959, no. VII ZR 19/58, (1959) 35 NJW, (1533) 1534–1535; BGH 30 June 1959, no. VIII ZR 11/59, (1959) 35 NJW, (1539) 1539; BGH 9 June 1960, no. VII ZR 229/58, (1960) 38 NJW, (1715) 1716. See also, F. EICHEL, *Künftige Forderungen*, (Tübingen: Mohr Siebeck, 2014), 374.

1095 BGH 23 October 1963, no. VIII ZR 150/62, (1964) 4 NJW, (149) 149–150.

1096 W. FLUME, 'Der verlängerte und erweiterte Eigentumsvorbehalt', (1950) 22 NJW, (841) 845; E. LOPAU, 'Die Höchstrichterliche Rechtsprechung zur Forderungsvorausabtretung bei verlängerte Eigentumsvorbehalt', (1973) 31 DB, (1537) 1537; H. LAMBSDORFF, *Handbuch des Eigentumsvorbehalts im deutschen und ausländischen Recht*, (Frankfurt am Main: Athenäum, 1974), 142.

1097 O. FISCHER, 'Der verlängerte Eigentumsvorbehalt in der Krise', (1959) 9 NJW, (366) 367; K. BETTE, 'Der verlängerte Eigentumsvorbehalt in der Praxis', (1973) 16 ZfGK, (793) 794; P. SCHWERDTNER, 'Globalzession und verlängerte Eigentumsvorbehalt', (1974) 40 NJW, (1785) 1788–1789.

1098 §398 BGB; J. BUSCHE, '§398 BGB' in M. LÖWISCH (ed.), *J. von Staudingers Kommentar zum Bürgerlichen Gesetzbuch mit Einführungsgesetz und Nebengesetzen*, (Berlin: Sellier, 2017), 150.

Unlike other civil law jurisdictions, the effectiveness of an assignment clause in the BGB does not depend on the notification of the third-party transferee of the assignment of the claim to the retention of title creditor.[1099] However, practically it will be worthwhile to notify the third-party transferee of the assignment, because until the transferee is notified, the third-party transferee can pay the retention of title debtor in good faith and be freed of his obligation as opposed to the retention of title creditor to whom his claim was assigned.[1100]

Furthermore, if the claim is paid to the debtor, in cash or through a bank transfer, the retention of title creditor will not have a claim to these proceeds.[1101] This is due to the specificity principle. In order for the retention of title creditor to have a proprietary claim to the money or bank transfer that takes the original collateral's place, it needs to be specific or individualized. Once the money is paid to the retention of title debtor, it can no longer be individualized and therefore the debtor becomes the owner of these amounts. However, the retention of title creditor maintains his original claim to the debtor for the originally sold collateral and could even acquire a claim for damages suffered by the retention of title creditor through this third-party transferee.[1102] Unfortunately, without the originally encumbered collateral or the assigned claim the retention of title creditor is an unsecured creditor and only has general enforcement options (i.e. seizure) at his disposal to enforce his claim.

241. *Conflict retention of title creditor with Vorausabtretungsklausel and creditor with a claim to all the debtor's accounts receivable* – Once the extension of retention of title in the claim to the third-party transferee is accepted, the retention of title creditor can come into conflict with the creditor to whom all the debtor's accounts receivable have been assigned (i.e. *Globalzession*). If this conflict were resolved on the basis of the first in time rule, then the creditor to whom all the debtor's present and future accounts receivable have been assigned, would take priority since this agreement generally predates a sale on credit with retention of title and a *Vorausabtretungsklausel.*[1103] To address the nearly automatic priority of the creditor with a *Globalzession,* the BGH intervened. More specifically, the Court reasoned that in most agreements with

1099 J. BUSCHE, '§398 BGB' in M. LÖWISCH (ed.), *J. von Staudingers Kommentar zum Bürgerlichen Gesetzbuch mit Einführungsgesetz und Nebengesetzen*, (Berlin: Sellier, 2017), 153–154.

1100 §407 BGB.

1101 K. VIEWEG and A. WERNER, *Sachenrecht*, (7 edn., München: Verlag Franz Vahlen, 2015), 354.

1102 K. VIEWEG and A. WERNER, *Sachenrecht*, (7 edn., München: Verlag Franz Vahlen, 2015), 354.

1103 BGH 30 April 1959, no. VII ZR 19/58, BGHZ 30, (149) 149; S. LEIBLE and M. F. MÜLLER, §449 BGB – Eigentumsvorbehalt" in M. JUNKER, R. M. BECKMANN and H. RÜßMANN (eds.) *Juris Praxiskommentar BGB – Band 2 Schuldrecht*, (Saarbrücken: Juris, 2020), online: https://www.juris.de/r3/document, par. 56.

a *Globalzession* the debtor is not allowed to assign his accounts receivable a second time to another creditor. However, most suppliers and manufacturers are not willing to sell on credit unless a *Vorausabtretungsklausel* is included in the agreement. This contradiction would lead either to the debtor being unable to buy goods on credit, or in a position where he has to violate his agreement with the creditor with a *Globalzession*. Therefore, the BGH considers an agreement for *Globalzession* in which the debtor is prohibited from buying on credit with a retention of title and *Vorausabtretungsklausel* to go against public policy and thus void.[1104] Given the potential impact of this case law on the *Globalzession* practice, the BGH has further developed its views. Under more recent case law, *Globalzession* of all the debtor's present and future claims does not go against public policy when this does not unreasonably limit the debtor's contractual freedom and there is no threat to the economic interests of future retention of title creditors of the debtor. For example, there is not threat when the agreement with *Globalzession* gives priority to the assignment of the debtor's accounts receivable to retention of title creditors.[1105]

242. *Conclusion* – The retention of title creditor can contractually extend his retention of title by assigning the future claims on third-party transferees to him. However, the retention of title creditor has to remain vigilant that the third-party transferee is notified of the assignment and pays the retention of title creditor and not the retention of title debtor. Consequently, the assignment clause of future claims on the third-party transferees provides some extra protection, but cannot be considered a full-proof protection measure for the retention of title creditor.

3. PRIORITY

243. *Types of conflicts and their outcomes for retention of title creditors in general* – Conflicts between creditors and/or third parties can arise in three scenarios: 1) between two or more creditors that have security rights in the same good, 2) between a secured creditor and a third party with a claim to the encumbered good and 3) between the secured party and another creditor during enforcement proceedings or insolvency proceedings. Notably, the BGB does not provide specific rules that address priority conflicts for retention of title creditors. Consequently, the potential conflicts between retention of title

1104 BGH 28 November 1968, no. VII ZR 157/66, (1969) NJW, 415, par. 20 *et seq.*

1105 BGH 9 November 1978, no. VII ZR 54/77, (1979) NJW, (365) 365; BGH 8 October 1986, no. VIII ZR 342/85, (1987) NJW, 487. See also, S. LEIBLE and M. F. MÜLLER, §449 BGB – Eigentumsvorbehalt" in M. JUNKER, R. M. BECKMANN and H. RÜßMANN (eds.) *Juris Praxiskommentar BGB – Band 2 Schuldrecht*, (Saarbrücken: Juris, 2020), online: https://www.juris.de/r3/document, par. 56.

creditors and other creditors/third parties are resolved via the general provisions in the BGB and on the basis of case law.

244. *Competing secured creditors* – The first potential conflict turns out to be not much of a conflict for the retention of title creditor. Because the retention of title creditor retains title to the encumbered good, the debtor does not have sufficient rights in the encumbered good to vest a more junior security right in the encumbered good.[1106] As a result, it is impossible for a conflicting claim to arise in the encumbered good and the retention of title creditor will always have the highest ranking claim in the encumbered good.[1107] However, the debtor can vest security rights in his *Anwartschaftsrecht*.[1108] The *Anwartschaftsrecht* is the debtor's contingent ownership of the encumbered good which automatically transforms into ownership when he pays the outstanding purchase price.[1109] This prospective ownership right of the good is already worth something and can be transferred or encumbered by the debtor.[1110] However, the transfer or encumbrance of the *Anwartschaftsrecht* does not entail any risk for the retention of title creditor. If the debtor defaults on his obligations, then the retention of title creditor can withdraw from the sale agreement and recover the encumbered good. This ends the retention of title debtor's *Anwartschaftsrecht* and makes the security rights vested in the *Anwartschaftsrecht* without object.[1111] Consequently, the retention of title creditor is not negatively affected by other secured creditors or third parties with an interest in the retention of title debtor's *Anwartschaftsrecht* in the good sold under retention of title.

[1106] M. BRINKMANN, 'The peculiar approach of German law in the field of secured transactions and why it has worked (so far)' in L. GULLIFER and O. AKSELI (eds.), *Secured transactions law reform*, (Oxford: Hart Publishing, 2016), 346.

[1107] J. RAKOB, 'Germany' in H. C. SIGMAN and E.-M. KIENINGER (eds.), *Cross-border security over tangibles*, (Berlin: Sellier, 2007), (63) 70; E.-M. KIENINGER, 'Die Zukunft des deutschen und europäischen Mobiliarkreditsicherungsrechts', (2008) 208 AcP, (182) 215–216.

[1108] M. BRINKMANN, 'The peculiar approach of German law in the field of secured transactions and why it has worked (so far)' in L. GULLIFER and O. AKSELI (eds.), *Secured transactions law reform*, (Oxford: Hart Publishing, 2016), 346; S. LEIBLE and M. F. MÜLLER, §449 BGB – Eigentumsvorbehalt" in M. JUNKER, R. M. BECKMANN and H. RÜßMANN (eds.) *Juris Praxiskommentar BGB – Band 2 Schuldrecht*, (Saarbrücken: Juris, 2020), online: https://www.juris.de/r3/document, par. 23.

[1109] M. BRINKMANN, 'The peculiar approach of German law in the field of secured transactions and why it has worked (so far)' in L. GULLIFER and O. AKSELI (eds.), *Secured transactions law reform*, (Oxford: Hart Publishing, 2016), 346; S. LEIBLE and M. F. MÜLLER, §449 BGB – Eigentumsvorbehalt" in M. JUNKER, R. M. BECKMANN and H. RÜßMANN (eds.) *Juris Praxiskommentar BGB – Band 2 Schuldrecht*, (Saarbrücken: Juris, 2020), online: https://www.juris.de/r3/document, par. 21.

[1110] BGH 10 April 1961, no. VIII ZR 68/60, 35 BGHZ, 85.

[1111] S. LEIBLE and M. F. MÜLLER, §449 BGB – Eigentumsvorbehalt" in M. JUNKER, R. M. BECKMANN and H. RÜßMANN (eds.) *Juris Praxiskommentar BGB – Band 2 Schuldrecht*, (Saarbrücken: Juris, 2020), online: https://www.juris.de/r3/document, par. 30.

245. *Retention of title creditor vs. third-party transferee* – The second conflict can arise when the debtor sells the encumbered good without permission to a third party. This conflict is resolved via the rules concerning good faith acquisitions.[1112] Only when the third-party transferee was unaware of the retention of title, does he acquire the encumbered good in good faith and free from retention of title.[1113] To determine the third-party transferee's knowledge following elements are taken into account: the value of the acquired good, customary nature of retention of title in the industry or knowledge of the seller's weak financial circumstances or commercially dubious behavior.[1114] In other words, in this scenario the resolution of the conflict between the retention of title creditor and the good faith third-party transferee depends on the specific circumstances of the case. Furthermore, the ubiquitous nature of retention of title in many industries means that it is quite difficult for third-party transferees to claim that they were unaware of the retention of title clause. As mentioned, a *Nachforschungspflicht* is placed upon the third-party transferee which obligates him to investigate whether the transferor was allowed to transfer the good to him.[1115] In other words, in the context of retention of title it is very difficult for a third-party transferee to rely on his good faith acquisition.

246. *Retention of title creditor vs. judgement creditor* – Finally, the retention of title creditor can also come into conflict with another creditor, who is enforcing his claim on the debtor's assets including the good encumbered with a retention of title. In this scenario, the retention of title creditor can either initiate proceedings against the enforcement of the encumbered good[1116] or be entitled to preferential satisfaction out of the proceeds following the enforcement.[1117] The majority in scholars and practitioners are of the opinion that the retention of title creditor can start proceedings to halt the enforcement of the encumbered good.[1118] The latter option is considered less convincing, since it

---

1112 §932 *et seq.* BGB; E.-M. KIENINGER, 'Die Zukunft des deutschen und europäischen Mobiliarkreditsicherungsrechts', (2008) 208 AcP, (182) 216. See also, *supra* no. 229.

1113 J. RAKOB, 'Germany' in H. C. SIGMAN and E.-M. KIENINGER (eds.), *Cross-border security over tangibles*, (Berlin: Sellier, 2007), (63) 73; E.-M. KIENINGER, 'Die Zukunft des deutschen und europäischen Mobiliarkreditsicherungsrechts', (2008) 208 AcP, (182) 217; R. M. BECKMANN, "§932 – Gutgläubiger Erwerb von Nichtberechtigten" in M. M. MARITNEK (ed.) *Juris Praxiskommentar – BGB*, (Saarbrücken: Juris, 2020), online: https://www.juris.de/r3/document, par. 10.

1114 E.-M. KIENINGER, 'Die Zukunft des deutschen und europäischen Mobiliarkredit-sicherungsrechts', (2008) 208 AcP, (182) 217.

1115 See *supra* no. 229.

1116 §771 ZPO.

1117 §805 ZPO.

1118 §771 Zivilprozessordnung (hereafter also, ZPO); BGH 1 July 1970, no. VIII ZR 24/69, (1970) 39 NJW, (1733) 1735; S. LEIBLE and M. F. MÜLLER, §449 BGB – Eigentumsvorbehalt" in M. JUNKER, R. M. BECKMANN and H. RÜßMANN (eds.) *Juris Praxiskommentar BGB – Band 2 Schuldrecht*, (Saarbrücken: Juris, 2020), online: https://www.juris.de/r3/document, par.

allows the enforcement of a third party's property and exposes the retention of title creditor to the risks of a public auction in the enforcement process.[1119] However, an important caveat to retention of title creditor's right to halt the enforcement proceedings is that the retention of title creditor has to be aware of the enforcement proceedings. Since the German approach does not prescribe registration, one wonders how a retention of title creditor can be notified of the enforcement proceedings. The lack of publicity of the enforcement proceedings seriously impedes the retention of title creditor's right to halt competing enforcement proceedings on the encumbered good.

4. RIGHT TO REVENDICATE

247. *Right to revendicate and the revocation of the sale agreement* – The retention of title creditor has a right to revendicate the encumbered collateral, but this has been made conditional upon the retention of title creditor revoking the sale agreement.[1120] The obligation to revoke the sale agreement is made explicit in §449 BGB. Before the reform in 2002, the debtor's default was considered a ground for revoking the sale agreement and thus allowed the retention of title creditor to revendicate the collateral from the moment the retention of title debtor defaulted on an installment of the purchase price.[1121]

248. *Revindication and the Trennungsprinzip* – Prior to §449 BGB, the BGH already limited the retention of title creditor's revendication right based on the *Trennungsprinzip.*[1122] In a sale with retention of title there are two components: the proprietary component (*dinglichen Ebene*) and the contractual component (*schuldrechtlichen Ebene*). The proprietary component is the part of the agreement that governs the property right, in this case the transfer of ownership. The retention of title clause, which places a condition on the transfer of ownership, is added to the proprietary component of the sale agreement.[1123] Because the

---

34; S. LEIBLE and O. SOSNITZA, 'Grundfälle zum Recht des Eigentumsvorbehalts', (2001) 6 JuS, (244) 345.

1119 S. LEIBLE and M. F. MÜLLER, §449 BGB – Eigentumsvorbehalt" in M. JUNKER, R. M. BECKMANN and H. RÜßMANN (eds.) *Juris Praxiskommentar BGB – Band 2 Schuldrecht*, (Saarbrücken: Juris, 2020), online: https://www.juris.de/r3/document, par. 34.

1120 H. P. Westermann, *BGB-Sachenrecht*, (Heidelberg: C. F. Müller, 2012), 74; S. LORENZ, 'Grundwissen – Zivilrecht: der Eigentumsvorbehalt', [2011] JuS, (199) 201; F. FAUST, '§449 – Eigentumsvorbehalt' in H. G. BAMBERGER and others (eds.), *Bürgerliches Gesetzbuch Kommentar*, (4 edn., München: Beck, 2019), 2913.

1121 §455 former BGB: *[…] daß der Verkäufer zum Rücktritt von dem Vertrag berechtigt ist, wenn der Käufer mit der Zahlung in Verzug kommt.* See also, P. BUCK, 'Kaufrecht' in *Das Schuldrecht 2002*, (Stuttgart: München, 2002), 180.

1122 BGH 1 July 1970, no. VIII ZR 24/69, (1970) 39 NJW, (1733) 1733.

1123 R. SERICK, *Eigentumsvorbehalt und Sicherungsübertragung*, (Heidelberg: Verlag Recht und Wirtschaft, 1993), 62; K. MÜLLER and U. P. GRUBER, *Sachenrecht*, (München: Verlag Franz Vahlen, 2016), 308.

retention of title clause is part of the *dinglichen Ebene*, ownership remains with the retention of title creditor and the retention of title debtor obtains an *Anwartschaftsrecht*, which protects the retention of title debtor from revendication of the collateral.[1124] The *schuldrechtlichen Ebene* governs the sale agreement itself and governs, among other things, the price and delivery of the good to the retention of title debtor. Furthermore, the *schuldrechtlichen Ebene* also gives the retention of title debtor a right to possession of the collateral.[1125] In the event, the retention of title debtor defaults on the purchase price for the encumbered collateral, the retention of title creditor can enforce the retention of title clause which results in the loss of the retention of title debtor's *Anwartschaftsrecht*. The loss of *Anwartschaftsrecht* in turn results in the loss of this specific protection against revendication. However, the enforcement of the retention of title clause only affects the proprietary component of the sale agreement (*dinglichen Ebene*) and not the contractual part (*schuldrechtlichen Ebene*). Based on the contractual component the retention of title debtor is still entitled to possession of the collateral and protected against revendication.[1126] The retention of title creditor can only revoke this right of possession by revoking the entire sale agreement. This revocation has to be in accordance with the provisions on revoking agreements, such as granting the retention of title debtor a last warning and extension before revoking the agreement.[1127] Only then is the retention of title debtor's right to possession following the sale agreement no longer protected and is the retention of title creditor able to revendicate the collateral.

The above reasoning of the BGH was the inspiration for the new rule in §449 BGB. Since 2002 the provision explicitly states that the retention of title creditor cannot revendicate without revoking the sale agreement.[1128] The fact that the retention of title debtor's default is no longer a ground for the retention of title creditor to revoke the agreement means that the retention of title creditor has to abide by the general rules for contract revocation in the BGB.[1129] The application of revocation rules mainly results in the retention of title creditor having to grant a final extension to the retention of title debtor to allow him to perform his side of the agreement.[1130] However, there are exceptions to this rule, such as

1124 §986, sec. 1 BGB; P. BÜLOW, 'Die isolierte Ausübung des Eigentumvorbehalts nach §449 BGB', (2002) 40 NJW, (2090) 2090.

1125 §868 BGB.

1126 §868 *juncto* §986 BGB; H. LAMBSDORFF, *Handbuch des Eigentumsvorbehalts im deutschen und ausländischen Recht*, (Frankfurt am Main: Athenäum, 1974), 42; P. BÜLOW, 'Die isolierte Ausübung des Eigentumvorbehalts nach §449 BGB', (2002) 40 NJW, (2090) 2091.

1127 BGH 1 July 1970, no. VIII ZR 24/69, (1970) 39 NJW, (1733) 1735.

1128 §449, sec. 2 BGB; K. VIEWEG and A. WERNER, *Sachenrecht*, (7 edn., München: Verlag Franz Vahlen, 2015), 378.

1129 §323 *et seq.* BGB. See also, G. SCHULZE and F. KIENLE, 'Der Kauf unter Eigentumsvorbehalt – eine Kehrtwende des Gesetzgebers?', (2002) 39 NJW, (2842) 2843; P. BÜLOW, 'Die isolierte Ausübung des Eigentumvorbehalts nach §449 BGB', (2002) 40 NJW, (2090) 2090.

1130 323 BGB. See also, M. HABERSACK and J. SCHÜRNBRAND, 'Der Eigentumsvorbehalt nach der Schuldrechtsreform', [2002] JuS, (833) 834.

the deliberate and definitive refusal of the retention of title debtor to perform his side of the agreement.[1131] In that case, the retention of title creditor does not have to grant a final extension before proceeding with revocation. Another exception is §323, sec. 3, 3) BGB which dispenses with the extension for the retention of title debtor, if specific circumstances exist that, after considering the interests of both parties, justify the immediate revocation from the agreement. Under §455 BGB the security aspect (*Sicherungsinteresse*) of retention of title was considered a specific circumstance which allowed the immediate revocation from the sale agreement.[1132] More specifically it was argued that the additional extension for the retention of title debtor would interfere with the execution of the retention of title clause and its underlying collateral. This interpretation is no longer accepted under §449 BGB, but the retention of title creditor's interest in the execution of the collateral can be taken into account to determine and potentially shorten the extension that should be granted to the retention of title debtor.[1133] Finally, parties can also agree that revocation is automatically possible when the retention of title debtor defaults, but for this to apply they have to explicitly agree to this.[1134] In other words, the immediate revocation in the event of default cannot be simply included in the retention of title creditor's general terms and conditions.[1135]

249. *Revindication and return of received payments* – Because the retention of title creditor formally has to revoke the sale agreement in order to revendicate the collateral, the retention of title debtor is entitled to the return of the payments he has already made during the sale agreement.[1136] This return of payments to the retention of title debtor is not rooted in the principle of unjust enrichment, but stems from the contractual relation between the two parties.[1137] More specifically, revoking a reciprocal agreement, such as a sale agreement, means that both parties have to give back what they have received during this agreement.[1138] For a sale agreement with retention of title this means a return

---

1131 §323, sec. 3, 1) BGB.

1132 R. M. BECKMANN and others, *J. Von Staudinger Kommentar zum Bürgerlichen Geseztbuch mit einführungsgesetz und Nebengesetzen*, (M. MARTINEK (ed.), 2 edn., Berlin: Sellier, 2004), 441.

1133 G. SCHULZE and F. KIENLE, 'Der Kauf unter Eigentumsvorbehalt – eine Kehrtwende des Gesetzgebers? ', (2002) 39 NJW, (2842) 2843.

1134 M. HABERSACK and J. SCHÜRNBRAND, 'Der Eigentumsvorbehalt nach der Schuldrechtsreform', [2002] JuS, (833) 834; P. BUCK, 'Kaufrecht' in *Das Schuldrecht 2002*, (Stuttgart: München, 2002), 180.

1135 M. HABERSACK and J. SCHÜRNBRAND, 'Der Eigentumsvorbehalt nach der Schuldrechtsreform', [2002] JuS, (833) 834–835.

1136 H. LAMBSDORFF, *Handbuch des Eigentumsvorbehalts im deutschen und ausländischen Recht*, (Frankfurt am Main: Athenäum, 1974), 44; S. LEIBLE and O. SOSNITZA, 'Grundfälle zum Recht des Eigentumsvorbehalts', (2001) 6 JuS, (244) 245.

1137 §346 BGB.

1138 J. HAGER, '§346' in B. DAUNER-LIEB (ed.), *Nomos Kommentar – BGB Schuldrecht*, (Baden-Baden: Nomos, 2016), 1356.

of the sold collateral to the retention of title creditor and a return of the received payments to the retention of title debtor.

The fact that the revocation implies a return of the received payments to the retention of title debtor means that the retention of title debtor can use this right to repayment to block the revendication by the retention of title creditor. As with the original sale agreement, the duties after revocation have to be performed in a reciprocal manner.[1139] Consequently, if the retention of title creditor refuses to give back the received payments, the retention of title debtor could in return rightfully refuse to give back the encumbered collateral.[1140] However, the retention of title creditor does have some options to override the retention of title debtor's right to refuse revendication without repayment. For example, the retention of title debtor is not able to block the revendication with his claim for repayment if only very few payments have been made to the retention of title creditor and the payments amount to much less than the value of the encumbered collateral. Furthermore, since this idea of returning the received purchase price is rooted in contract law, the parties can also contractually change the reciprocity after revocation. So can the sale agreement include a clause which obligates the retention of title creditor to repayment only after he has revendicated the encumbered collateral. Moreover, the parties can even agree to waive the retention of title debtor's rights to refuse revendication of the collateral until payment of the received payments. Finally, parties can even agree that in the event of default the received payments count towards the damages the retention of title creditor endured. However, retention of title creditors should be cautious since these types of clauses are in danger of being considered to be in bad faith and against public policy, especially when the received payments are much higher than the damages suffered by the creditor.[1141]

SECTION 6 – RETENTION OF TITLE DURING CORPORATE BANKRUPTCY

250. *Overview* – In this section we move on to the protection, or lack thereof, of retention of title during corporate bankruptcy proceedings. As with the other jurisdiction, I start by giving a brief overview of (1.) the main principles of corporate bankruptcy proceedings in Germany. After this (2.) the treatment of retention of title and the rights of retention of title creditors will be set out.

1139 §348 BGB.

1140 H. LAMBSDORFF, *Handbuch des Eigentumsvorbehalts im deutschen und ausländischen Recht*, (Frankfurt am Main: Athenäum, 1974), 40.

1141 H. LAMBSDORFF, *Handbuch des Eigentumsvorbehalts im deutschen und ausländischen Recht*, (Frankfurt am Main: Athenäum, 1974), 45.

1. CORPORATE BANKRUPTCY IN GERMANY

251. *Brief historic background and introduction to German bankruptcy law* – The German corporate bankruptcy procedure was significantly reformed after the reunification of East and West Germany in 1989. More specifically the *Konkursordnung* of the West and the *Gesamtvollstreckungsverordnung* of the East were replaced by the *Insolvenzordnung*. An important change is that the *Insolvenzordnung* provides one procedure that aims at giving creditors the best possible satisfaction through either a liquidation or reorganization of the debtor's estate.[1142] Before, debtors had to decide at the beginning which type of proceeding they wanted: liquidation or reorganization.[1143] Now the choice is made after the bankruptcy proceeding has been opened. Interestingly, the choice between reorganization or liquidation of the bankruptcy estate is made by the creditors and not the debtor.[1144]

Once the petition for a bankruptcy proceeding is filed, a trustee in bankruptcy (*Insolvenzverwalter*) is appointed.[1145] The first phase of the bankruptcy proceeding consists of an assessment on whether the bankruptcy estate has enough funds to cover the costs of the bankruptcy proceeding.[1146] Once this has been established the bankruptcy proceeding is formally opened. The bankruptcy estate consists of all present property of the debtor, wherever located, and all goods acquired by the debtor during the procedure[1147] The trustee in bankruptcy must take possession and make an inventory of all the goods in the debtor's possession, including these that may belong to a third party.[1148] Following the opening of corporate bankruptcy proceedings, a stay of proceedings takes effect thereby halting any enforcement of claims on the debtor's estate.[1149] This stay applies to most creditors[1150], including secured creditors.

1142 C. G. PAULUS, 'The new German insolvency code', (1998) 99 Tex. Int'l. L. J., (141) 143.

1143 C. G. PAULUS, 'The new German insolvency code', (1998) 99 Tex. Int'l. L. J., (141) 143.

1144 C. G. PAULUS, 'The new German insolvency code', (1998) 99 Tex. Int'l. L. J., (141) 143.

1145 §56 (1) InsO; C. G. PAULUS, 'The new German insolvency code', (1998) 99 Tex. Int›l. L. J., (141) 146; D. SCHULZ, B. ULRICH and H. LESSING, *Handbuch Insolvenzrecht*, (4 edn., München: Hauffe Gruppe, 2012), 140.

1146 D. SCHULZ, B. ULRICH and H. LESSING, *Handbuch Insolvenzrecht*, (4 edn., München: Hauffe Gruppe, 2012), 76.

1147 §35 InsO; C. G. PAULUS, 'The new German insolvency code', (1998) 99 Tex. Int›l. L. J., (141) 147; D. SCHULZ, B. ULRICH and H. LESSING, *Handbuch Insolvenzrecht*, (4 edn., München: Hauffe Gruppe, 2012), 178.

1148 BGH 14 December 2000, no. IX ZR 105/ 00, (2001) NJW, (1496) 1497; S. MITLEHNER, *Mobiliarsicherheiten im Insolvenzverfahren*, (2 edn., Köln: RWS Verlag, 2009), 43.

1149 §165–173 InsO; C. G. PAULUS, 'The new German insolvency code', (1998) 99 Tex. Int'l. L. J., (141) 147;

1150 An example of creditors who are exempt from the stay of proceedings are the creditors who can set-off their claim (§94 InsO).

2. RIGHTS OF RETENTION OF TITLE CREDITORS DURING CORPORATE BANKRUPTCY PROCEEDINGS

252. *Overview* – Since retention of title implies that the title of the encumbered good remains with the retention of title creditor, the treatment of retention of title is assessed in both (2.1.) the bankruptcy of the retention of title debtor, as (2.2.) the bankruptcy of the retention of title creditor.

2.1. Bankruptcy of the retention of title debtor

253. *Different stages of the bankruptcy proceeding* – In the event the retention of title debtor goes bankrupt, the impact of the bankruptcy proceeding depends on the phase of the bankruptcy proceeding: the first phase between the request for a bankruptcy proceeding and opening or the second phase once the proceedings have been opened. In the first phase, the trustee in bankruptcy can petition the court to forbid or suspend any enforcement proceedings on the debtor's estate.[1151] Consequently, as long as the trustee bankruptcy has not requested such limitations on the enforcement proceedings, the retention of title creditor can enforce his claim against the debtor.[1152]

254. *Classification of retention of title creditor during corporate bankruptcy proceedings* – Once the bankruptcy proceedings are opened, the retention of title creditor is considered as the full owner of the encumbered good.[1153] The retention of title creditor's status as full owner of the encumbered good is relevant during corporate bankruptcy proceedings due to the position assigned to owners in bankruptcy proceedings. German bankruptcy law makes a distinction between claims that give rise to an *Aussonderungsrecht* or an *Absonderungsrecht*. A claim that gives rise to an *Aussonderungsrecht* (i.e. ownership, some forms of possession[1154] or assignment of receivables) ensures that a good is considered outside of the bankruptcy estate[1155] and forces the trustee in bankruptcy to hand over the good encumbered with the *Aussonderungsrecht*.[1156] Conversely, a claim guaranteed by an *Absonderungsrecht* (i.e. a pledge or transfer of title) only

---

1151 §21 InsO; D. SCHULZ, B. ULRICH and H. LESSING, *Handbuch Insolvenzrecht*, (4 edn., München: Hauffe Gruppe, 2012), 84–85.

1152 §21 InsO; S. MITLEHNER, *Mobiliarsicherheiten im Insolvenzverfahren*, (2 edn., Köln: RWS Verlag, 2009), 34; D. SCHULZ, B. ULRICH and H. LESSING, *Handbuch Insolvenzrecht*, (4 edn., München: Hauffe Gruppe, 2012), 96.

1153 J. RAKOB, 'Germany' in H. C. SIGMAN and E.-M. KIENINGER (eds.), *Cross-border security over tangibles*, (Berlin: Sellier, 2007), (63) 80–81.

1154 §861–862 BGB.

1155 D. SCHULZ, B. ULRICH and H. LESSING, *Handbuch Insolvenzrecht*, (4 edn., München: Hauffe Gruppe, 2012), 174.

1156 D. SCHULZ, B. ULRICH and H. LESSING, *Handbuch Insolvenzrecht*, (4 edn., München: Hauffe Gruppe, 2012), 23.

entitles the holder to satisfy his claim with priority from the proceeds of that particularly encumbered good.[1157]

255. *Treatment of retention of title creditor during corporate bankruptcy* – However, a stay of proceedings is also put in place.[1158] As a result, the retention of title creditor is not able to simply enforce his claim and recover his property. Furthermore, the retention of title creditor has to file his claim and prove his standing.[1159] Interestingly, the provision governing the declaration of claims does not mention claims that are secured by an *Aussonderungsrecht,* but only those with an *Absonderungsrecht* (e.g. claims secured by a pledge or transfer of title).[1160] Nevertheless, the explanatory memorandum to the *Insolvenzordnung*[1161] clearly lists retention of title as a type of secured transaction of which the trustee in bankruptcy should be informed as quickly as possible, since these guarantees are not always clear from the debtor's administration.[1162]

If the retention of title is accepted, the trustee in bankruptcy has the choice between performing or not performing his obligation in the sale agreement.[1163] Until the trustee in bankruptcy makes a decision, the retention of title creditor cannot enforce his claim.[1164] During this time the retention of title creditor is entitled to a right of separation (*Aussonderungssrecht*) that keeps the encumbered good separate from the other goods in the debtor's estate.[1165] If the trustee in bankruptcy choses to perform the sale agreement, the trustee has to make the outstanding payments to the retention of title creditor. If the trustee chooses not to perform, then the retention of title creditor can recover the encumbered good.[1166] In that case the retention of title creditor has to return the payments he already received.[1167] The retention of title creditor is also allowed to recover the

1157 D. SCHULZ, B. ULRICH and H. LESSING, *Handbuch Insolvenzrecht,* (4 edn., München: Hauffe Gruppe, 2012), 22–23.

1158 D. SCHULZ, B. ULRICH and H. LESSING, *Handbuch Insolvenzrecht,* (4 edn., München: Hauffe Gruppe, 2012), 136.

1159 §28, sec. 2 InsO; S. MITLEHNER, *Mobiliarsicherheiten im Insolvenzverfahren,* (2 edn., Köln: RWS Verlag, 2009), 43.

1160 §28, sec. 2 BGB.

1161 Entwurf einer Insolvenzordnung, *BT-Drucks* 12/2443, 119.

1162 S. MITLEHNER, *Mobiliarsicherheiten im Insolvenzverfahren,* (2 edn., Köln: RWS Verlag, 2009), 43.

1163 §107 (2) InsO; J. RAKOB, ‹Germany› in H. C. SIGMAN and E.-M. KIENINGER (eds.), *Cross-border security over tangibles,* (Berlin: Sellier, 2007), (63) 80.

1164 §103 InsO; D. SCHULZ, B. ULRICH and H. LESSING, *Handbuch Insolvenzrecht,* (4 edn., München: Hauffe Gruppe, 2012), 84.

1165 S. MITLEHNER, *Mobiliarsicherheiten im Insolvenzverfahren,* (2 edn., Köln: RWS Verlag, 2009), 41; D. SCHULZ, B. ULRICH and H. LESSING, *Handbuch Insolvenzrecht,* (4 edn., München: Hauffe Gruppe, 2012), 174.

1166 §985 BGB; W. MAROTZKE, ‹Der Eigentumsvorbehalt im neuen Insolvenzrecht', (1995) 17 JZ, (803) 811; D. SCHULZ, B. ULRICH and H. LESSING, *Handbuch Insolvenzrecht,* (4 edn., München: Hauffe Gruppe, 2012), 174.

1167 S. MITLEHNER, *Mobiliarsicherheiten im Insolvenzverfahren,* (2 edn., Köln: RWS Verlag, 2009), 57.

encumbered good, when the retention of title creditor already rescinded the sale agreement prior to the opening of the bankruptcy proceedings. In that case, the rescission of the transaction and the recovery had already been established prior to the bankruptcy procedure and its consequences cannot be reversed.[1168]

256. *Leasing during corporate bankruptcy in Germany* – Interestingly, the provision concerning the treatment of retention of title during bankruptcy proceedings is also considered applicable to lease agreements in which a purchase option is included.[1169] In a lease agreement with purchase option, title to the encumbered good remains with the lessor while possession has transferred to the lessee. The lessee makes regular payments to the lessor for the use of the leased good and has the option to purchase the leased good at the end of the lease agreement. According to certain scholars, the similar structure of a lease agreement with purchase option and a sale with retention of title means that the same bankruptcy provisions should apply.[1170] This is an instance in which German law does allow for an analogous application of retention of title provisions to lease agreements.[1171]

2.2. Bankruptcy of the retention of title creditor

257. *Retention of title and the retention of title creditor's bankruptcy* – Given the fact that title to the encumbered good still resides with the retention of title creditor, the impact of the retention of title creditor's bankruptcy is also taken into account. Once the petition for bankruptcy proceedings has been filed, the trustee in bankruptcy can refuse to deliver the encumbered good to the debtor unless the retention of title debtor already made payments. In that case, the delivery of the encumbered goods has to be performed.[1172]

258. *Impact of the retention of title creditor's bankruptcy on the retention of title* – Once the bankruptcy proceedings are officially opened, the retention of title debtor of the bankrupt retention of title creditor can demand the performance of the sale agreement with retention of title.[1173] As a result, the trustee in bankruptcy cannot simply refuse delivery of the encumbered good or recover

1168 §47 InsO; S. MITLEHNER, *Mobiliarsicherheiten im Insolvenzverfahren*, (2 edn., Köln: RWS Verlag, 2009), 51.

1169 W. MAROTZKE, 'Der Eigentumsvorbehalt im neuen Insolvenzrecht', (1995) 17 JZ, (803) 814; S. MITLEHNER, *Mobiliarsicherheiten im Insolvenzverfahren*, (2 edn., Köln: RWS Verlag, 2009), 61.

1170 BGH 28 November 1994, no. VIII ZR 315/93, (1995) NJW, 519; BGH, 14 December 1989, no. IX ZR 283/88, (1990) NJW, (1113), 1115; S. MITLEHNER, *Mobiliarsicherheiten im Insolvenzverfahren*, (2 edn., Köln: RWS Verlag, 2009), 61.

1171 W. MAROTZKE, 'Der Eigentumsvorbehalt im neuen Insolvenzrecht', (1995) 17 JZ, (803) 814.

1172 S. MITLEHNER, *Mobiliarsicherheiten im Insolvenzverfahren*, (2 edn., Köln: RWS Verlag, 2009), 34.

1173 §107 (1) InsO.

the encumbered good. This option is explicitly given to the debtor to protect his *Anwartschaftsrecht* in the encumbered good[1174] and was a reaction against standing case law of the BGH in which the protection of the retention of title debtor on the basis of his *Anwartschaftsrecht* was denied.[1175] This protection puts the retention of title debtor in a strong position. Moreover, this protection was also extended to lessees in lease agreements with purchase options. Given the functional similarities between a sale agreement with retention of title and a lease agreement with retention of title, the lessee in a lease agreement with retention of title should enjoy the same protection as a debtor in a sale agreement when either the retention of title creditor or lessor, respectively, goes bankrupt.[1176]

However, the protection of the retention of title debtor during the retention of title creditor's bankruptcy only goes so far. First, the *Insolvenzordnung* allows the retention of title debtor to demand performance of the agreement, but only with regards to the transfer of ownership. If other obligations are still outstanding with regards to this agreement, they are not protected under this provision of the *Insolvenzordnung*.[1177] Second, if the retention of title debtor does not perform his obligations in the sale agreement, then the retention of title creditor cannot be made to perform his obligation. In other words, if the retention of title debtor is not making payments, then he cannot demand performance of the obligation from the trustee in bankruptcy. In that case, the trustee in bankruptcy can recover the encumbered good, if it was already delivered to the retention of title debtor.[1178]

SECTION 7 – CONCLUSION ON THE PLACE OF RETENTION OF TITLE IN GERMAN LAW AND THE RIGHTS OF RETENTION OF TITLE CREDITORS

259. *Introduction* – The analysis of retention of title in Germany is aimed at providing a counter example to the previously discussed functional approach as method to regulate retention of title and an interesting point of comparison for

1174 W. MAROTZKE, 'Der Eigentumsvorbehalt im neuen Insolvenzrecht', (1995) 17 JZ, (803) 806; S. MITLEHNER, *Mobiliarsicherheiten im Insolvenzverfahren*, (2 edn., Köln: RWS Verlag, 2009), 39; S. KIM, *Die Entwicklung des Anwartschaftsrechts beim Kauf under Eigentumsvorbehalt*, (Dissertation Rechtswissenschaft, Rheinischen Friedrich-Wilhelms-Universität Bonn 2017), 119, fn. 731.

1175 BGH 9 July 1986, no. VIII ZR 232/85, (1987) JZ, (355) 358.

1176 W. MAROTZKE, 'Der Eigentumsvorbehalt im neuen Insolvenzrecht', (1995) 17 JZ, (803) 807; S. MITLEHNER, *Mobiliarsicherheiten im Insolvenzverfahren*, (2 edn., Köln: RWS Verlag, 2009), 61.

1177 S. MITLEHNER, *Mobiliarsicherheiten im Insolvenzverfahren*, (2 edn., Köln: RWS Verlag, 2009), 39.

1178 S. MITLEHNER, *Mobiliarsicherheiten im Insolvenzverfahren*, (2 edn., Köln: RWS Verlag, 2009), 39.

retention of title and the rights of retention of title creditors across the selected jurisdictions and international instruments. Where the functional approach aims to bring different secured transactions in movable goods together, the non-functional approach in Germany continues strict separations between its different secured transactions in movable goods, including retention of title. Consequently, the German non-functional approach provides a good example of a different approach to retention of title and allows a critical evaluation of the functional approach in the following chapters and what this means for the treatment of retention of title and the rights of retention of title creditors.

260. *Untouched nature of retention of title* – From the analysis of the retention of title and the rights of retention of title creditors in the BGB and bankruptcy law different conclusions can be drawn. First, retention of title remains legislatively untouched. For example, the scope of retention of title remains limited to sale agreements and the German legislator has debated, but never implemented, a unified system of security rights in movable goods in which retention of title is included. However, contractual extensions of retention of title, both vertically and horizontally, have been recognized by the highest courts, thereby extending its general protection.

261. *Title-based protection of retention of title* – Second, the protection of retention of title creditors remains title-based. For example, conflicts between the retention of title creditor and other creditors secured with a potential claim in the encumbered good are considered impossible, since the retention of title debtor does not have sufficient rights in the encumbered good to grant additional claims. Furthermore, during bankruptcy proceedings the retention of title creditor is considered full owner of the encumbered good and granted an *Aussonderungsrecht*. As a result, the encumbered good is considered to fall outside of the bankruptcy estate and the trustee in bankruptcy can be forced to return the good to the retention of title creditor.

However, over time the retention of title debtor has also etched out some protections despite the retention of title creditor's ownership of the encumbered good. For example, the retention of title creditor is theoretically allowed to dispose of the encumbered good a second time due to his retained title, but according to case law from the BGH the retention of title creditor is not allowed to do anything that would prevent the transfer of ownership to the retention of title debtor. Furthermore, the retention of title creditor can revindicate the encumbered good in the event of the retention of title debtor's default, but he has to follow the formalities of rescinding the sale agreement, such as giving the retention of title debtor one more extension, and has to return the payments he already received. Finally, in the event the retention of title creditor goes bankrupt, the encumbered good does not simply revert to the creditor's estate.

The retention of title debtor may demand performance of the sale agreement as long as the retention of title debtor also continues to perform his side of the obligation. This protection of the retention of title debtor during the retention of title creditor's bankruptcy is based on the retention of title debtor's *Anwartschaftsrecht*: a prospective right to ownership that deserves protection. Therefore, the retention of title creditor's retained title does not prevent the retention of title debtor from demanding the transfer of ownership in exchange for the correct performance of the sale agreement.

262. *Summary* – The acceptance of and focus on title-based security mechanisms results in a secured transactions law determined by title instead of limited security rights in movable goods. For example, title in the hands of the retention of title creditor is determinative for the resolution of conflicts with the retention of title debtor and other claimants. Nevertheless, some inroads have been made that limit the protection of the retention of title creditor and further the protection of the retention of title debtor. However, these protections are mainly based on the recognition and protection of the retention of title debtor's budding ownership right in the encumbered good and not on a move from title-based to security right protection for the retention of title debtor (as is the case in the jurisdiction and international instrument with the functional approach). Furthermore, the BGB adheres to a minimalistic legislative approach to the regulation of retention of title, meaning that the courts regularly have to intervene to settle particular protections (e.g. *Anwartschaftsrecht* for retention of title debtors or contractual vertical expansion of retention of title for retention of title creditors) associated with retention of title. Finally, the focus on title-based security mechanisms in German secured transactions law and the very limited use of non-title-based security mechanisms in practice means that there is no tension between the use of title and other security mechanisms that do not rely on title to guarantee credit. This lack of tension between retention of title and other non-title-based security mechanisms explains the lack of incentive in Germany to create a non-title-based and consolidated secured transactions framework, like in Article 9 UCC, the UNCITRAL Guide and Model Law and DCFR.

PART 3

ANALYSIS AND COMPARISON OF RETENTION OF TITLE IN THE BELGIAN SECURITY RIGHTS ACT (2013)

263. *Introduction* – This part provides an answer to the second and third research question of this dissertation. More precisely, retention of title in the Security Rights Act is *analyzed* and the potential impact of the functional approach on retention of title and the rights of retention of title creditors is assessed. Furthermore, the Belgian retention of title is *compared* with retention of title or their functional equivalents (i.e. PMSIs and acquisition security rights) under the functional approaches in the *United States, UNCITRAL Guide and Model Law* and *DCFR* and *contrasted* with the retention of title under the non-functional approach in *Germany*. Based on this comparison conclusions are drawn on the treatment of retention of title in unified security right regimes and *recommendations* are formulated concerning the direction the Belgian legislator could take with regards to the regulation of retention of title.

The section starts with some background to the Security Rights Act (ch. 1) followed by the analysis of retention of title and the application of the functional approach in the Security Rights Act (ch. 2).

CHAPTER 1

BACKGROUND TO THE SECURITY RIGHTS ACT

264. *Overview* – In this chapter the reasons for the reform are set out (section 1), as well as the aspirations and design of the Security Rights Act (section 2).

SECTION 1 – REASONS FOR REFORM

265. *Myriad of reasons to reform secured transactions in movable goods in Belgium* – As the name suggests, the Security Rights Act not only aims to reform retention of title, but also the other existing security rights in movable goods in Belgium. The reform effort was a reaction to the problematic regulation of security rights, and mainly the deplorable state of the pledge regime, prior to the Security Rights Act.[1179] In the explanatory memorandum to the Security Rights Act, the legislator gives the different reasons for the creation of this new framework, such as the abundance of legislative liens, the archaic regulation of security rights in movable goods, use of title to guarantee credit, the enforcement of security rights and the hostile attitude in Belgium against the security trust.[1180] For this dissertation, the archaic and mainly possessory regime for security rights in movable goods (1.) and the limited recognition and enforcement of retention of title (2.) are the most relevant reasons and discussed in more detail.

1179 I. MOREAU-MARGRÈVE, 'Évolution du droit et de la pratique en matière de sûretés' in Les créanciers et le droit de la faillite, (Brussels: Bruylant, 1982),(77) 97–100; A. BRUYNEEL, 'L'évolution du droit des sûretés' in A. BRUYNEEL and A.-M. STRANART (eds.), Les sûretés, (Paris: Feduci, 1984), (5) 18–23; F. GÉORGES, 'La réforme des sûretés mobilières', (2013) 3 Rev. Dr. ULg., (319) 321; M. GRÉGOIRE, 'La modification du code civil en ce qui concerne les sûretés réelles mobilières' in F. GÉORGES (ed.), Insolvabilité et garanties, (Brussels: Larcier, 2014), (10) 10; M. GRÉGOIRE, 'The law of 11 July 2013 amending the Belgian civil code with respect to security interest in movable assets, and repealing various provisions in this area' in B. FOËX (ed.), The draft UNCITRAL model law on secured transactions – why and how?, (Genève: Schulthess, 2016), (171) 172.

1180 Explanatory memorandum for the law to amend the Civil Code concerning *in rem* security rights in movables and abrogation of various dispositions, *Parl. St.* Kamer 2012–13, no. 2463/001, 7–9 (hereafter, explanatory memorandum Security Rights Act, no. 2463/001.

1. ARCHAIC AND POSSESSORY PLEDGE SYSTEM

266. *A panoply of pledges* – Before the Security Rights Act, the secured transactions regime consisted of a variety of different pledges: the pledge on movable goods in the Civil Code[1181], the pledge on movable goods in the Commercial Code[1182], the pledge on business assets[1183], the warrant or warehouse receipt[1184] and the pledge on financial instruments.[1185] This disparity in secured transactions regulation was cause for confusion and burdensome for both creditors and debtors.[1186] For each pledge or pledge-like mechanism different provisions and laws had to be consulted and different formalities fulfilled. Consequently, a case was made for a more streamlined, understandable, predictable and stable secured transactions regime.[1187]

267. *A general aversion towards secured transactions in movable goods with dispossession* – Despite the existence of a few types of non-possessory pledges[1188], dispossession was still the main method to make a pledge in movable, tangible goods effective against third parties. This obviously limited the available collateral. A debtor would only be able to part with a very limited number of assets, which in turn reduced the debtor's options to obtain credit.[1189] In turn, this method of third-party effectiveness was economically inefficient. The debtor had to transfer possession of collateral to the creditor although the asset could probably be put to better use within the debtor's company.[1190] Consequently, the idea of a general non-possessory pledge was put forward that could be used for a larger group of assets without impeding the debtor's use of the collateral.[1191]

1181 Art. 2071 – 2084 CC.

1182 Art. 1–11 Pledge in the Commercial Code.

1183 Business asset Pledge Act 1919.

1184 Warehouse Receipt Act 1862.

1185 Article 7–11 Financial Collateral Act 2004 (Wet van 15 december 2004 betreffende financiële zekerheden en houdende diverse fiscale bepalingen inzake zakelijke-zekerheidsovereenkomsten en leningen met betrekking tot financiële instrumenten, *Belgian State Gazette* 1 February 2005, 2.961).

1186 E. DIRIX, 'Zekerheidsrechten op zoek naar nieuwe wegen' in J. CATTARUZA, W. KUPERS and I. PEETERS (eds.), *Liber Amicorum Achilles Cuypers*, (Brussels: Larcier, 2009), (1) 3; E. DIRIX, 'The new Belgian act on security interests in movable property', (2014) 23 Int Insolv Rev, (171) 172.

1187 M. GREGOIRE, "Les sûretés réelles" in C. BRUYNEEL, J.-P.BUYLE and M. DELIERNEUX (eds.), *Liber Amicorum André Bruyneel – Synthèse de droit bancaire et financier*, (Brussels: Bruylant 2008), (343) 370.

1188 The pledge on business assets and warrant or warehouse receipt.

1189 E. DIRIX, 'Zekerheidsrechten op zoek naar nieuwe wegen' in J. CATTARUZA, W. KUPERS and I. PEETERS (eds.), *Liber Amicorum Achilles Cuypers*, (Gent: Larcier, 2009), (1) 3.

1190 J. BAECK, 'Achtergrond en krachtlijnen van de hervorming' in J. BAECK and M. KRUITHOF (eds.), *Het nieuwe zekerheidsrecht*, (Antwerpen: Intersentia, 2014), (1) 2.

1191 E. DIRIX,'Zekerheidsrechten op zoek naar nieuwe wegen' in J. CATTARUZA, W. KUPERS and I. PEETERS (eds.), *Liber Amicorum Achilles Cuypers*, (Gent: Larcier, 2009) (1) 3–4; J. CATTARUZZA, 'Les grands axes de la réforme des sûretés mobilières', (2013) 4 Dr Banc Fin, (183) 184.

2. LIMITED RECOGNITION AND ENFORCEMENT OF RETENTION OF TITLE

268. *A brief overview of the ups and downs of the judicial and legislative recognition of retention of title* – Initially, there was a hostile attitude towards retention of title in sale agreements in Belgium. Particularly, the third-party effectiveness of retention of title in sale agreements was strongly contested because of its lack of publicity.[1192] Up until 1997, retention of title was merely a contractual clause in sales agreements without any codified rules governing its creation or operation.[1193] This legislative vacuum was problematic, especially when the retention of title creditor wanted to enforce his retention of title clause against third parties. In this context, the Supreme Court decided in 1933 that retention of title was valid *inter partes*, but could not be enforced against third parties.[1194] Consequently, retention of title was not considered effective against third parties during collective insolvency proceedings.[1195] The Court's reasoning in this decision was twofold. First, the Court considered the ostensible ownership problems retention of title posed.[1196] Retention of title

1192 A. DE WILDE, 'Het probleem der tegenstelbaarheid van de afbetalingskoop, aangegaan onder een beding van eigendomsvoorbehoud, ten aanzien van derden; mede in het licht van de wet van 9 juli 1957', (1957–58) RW, (489) 492.

1193 L. SIMONT, 'Essai de classification des sûretés – issues de la pratique et problèmes juridiques qu'elles posent' in A. BRUYNEEL and A. M. STRANART (eds.), *Les sûretés: sûretés traditionnelles, réelles et personnelles, en droit français et en droit belge, sûretés issues de la pratique, droit international privé: colloque de Bruxelles des 20 et 21 octobre 1983*, (Paris: Feduci, 1984), (277) 281–283; I. MOREAU-MARGREVE, 'Faut-il réviser les dispositions du code civil en matière de sûretés et dans l'affirmative, quelles seraient les grandes orientations d'une révision?' in J. ERAUW, B. BOUCKAERT, H. BOCKEN, H. GAUS, M. E. STORME (eds.), *Liber memorialis François Laurent 1810 – 1887*, (Brussels: E. Story – Scientia, 1989), (581) 597–598; E. DIRIX and R. DE CORTE, 'Zekerheidsrechten' in *Beginselen van Belgisch privaatrecht*, (5th edn., Mechelen: Wolters Kluwer, 2006), 409–410; R. DEKKERS, N. CARETTE, G. BAETEMAN, A.-L. VERBEKE and K. VANHOVE, *Handboek brugerlijk recht III*, (Antwerp: Intersentia, 2007), 459.

1194 Cass. 9 February 1933, Pas. 1933, I, 103.

1195 M. WAELBROECK, *Le transfert de la propriété dans la vente d'objets mobiliers corporels en droit comparé*, (Brussels: Bruylant, 1961), 123; F. 'T KINT and P. COPPENS, 'La clause résolutoire et la clause de réserve de propriété dans le contrat de vente', (1979) RRD, (887) 894–895; A. DE CALUWE, 'Verkopen en betaald geraken', (1983) TPR, (243) 256; E. DIRIX, 'Functionele analyse van zekerheidsrechten' in W. PINTENS and others (eds.), *Vigilantibus ius scriptum: feestbundel voor Hugo Vandenberghe*, (Brugge: Die Keure, 2007), (119) 119; I. DURANT, 'Le droit de rétention et la réserve de propriété, deux sûretés réelles mobilières à part entière' in F. GEORGES (ed.), *Insolvabilité et garanties*, (Brussels: Larcier, 2014), (34) 66.

1196 N. CARETTE and J. VAN DE VOORDE, 'Is het bezit als publiciteitsmiddel in verval?' in A. D. BOECK, V. SAGAERT and R. V. RANSBEECK (eds.), *Publiciteit in het zakenrecht*, (Brugge: Die Keure, 2015), (53) 130–131; M. GREGOIRE, 'Questions liées à l'invocation d'une clause de réserve de propriété' in *Mélanges offerts à Pierre Van Ommeslaghe*, (Brussel: Bruylant, 2000), 472; V. SAGAERT, 'Het eigendomsvoorbehoud als volwaardig zekerheidsinstrument' in *Insolventierecht – XXXI Postuniversitaire Cyclus Willy Delva 2004–05*, (Mechelen: Kluwer, 2006), (191) 191; F. 'T KINT and W. DERIJCKE, 'Dessaisissement et situations des creanciers en cas de faillite', *Le nouveau droit du concordat judiciaire et de la faillite: les lois des 17 juillet*

did not require any third-party effectiveness measures, such as registration or dispossession, that would allow third parties to take notice of the retained title.[1197] Other creditors and insolvency practitioners, such as the bankruptcy receiver, had no way of knowing that the encumbered goods still belonged to the retention of title creditor. Consequently, third parties could not be expected to take into account that ownership did not reside with the debtor. Second, the Court was of the opinion that the unpaid vendor's position was legally protected through the unpaid vendor's lien.[1198] Therefore, any contractual alterations to the unpaid vendor's protection through retention of title was considered in violation of public order and not effective against third parties.[1199] This decision of the Supreme Court was confirmed in 1946[1200] and 1994.[1201] The only way the retention of title creditor could enforce his retained title was by notifying the debtor before *concursus* occurred that the retention of title clause would be enforced and the encumbered good revendicated.[1202]

Given the problems relating to retention of title in sale agreements, the legislator took action to create a minimal legal framework.[1203] This translated into

et 8 août 1997, (Brussels: Bruylant, 1997), 204; J. MEERTS, 'Het eigendomsvoorbehoud' in H. BRAECKMANS and others (eds.), *Faillissement & Reorganisatie*, (Mechelen: Kluwer, loosel.) 9–10; A. CUYPERS and P. FRANCOIS, 'Art. 20, 5° Hyp.W' in E. DIRIX, P. FRANCOIS and M. TISON (eds.), *Voorrechten en hypotheken – Artikelsgewijze commentaar met overzicht van rechtspraak en rechtsleer*, (Mechelen: Kluwer, loosel.), 11; E. DIRIX, 'Nieuwe overeenkomsten tot zekerheid', (1988) 2 TPR, (323) 337.

1197 The legislator did not consider retention of title agreements as *in rem* security rights. Therefore, the lack of any notification measures for third-party effectiveness was justified due to the *erga omnes* effectiveness of the ownership in the retention of title-creditor's hands. See V. SAGAERT, *Zakelijke subrogatie*, (Antwerp: Intersentia, 2003), 147.

1198 The unpaid vendor's lien is legally recognized in article 20, °5 of the Mortgage Act (Hypotheekwet van 16 December 1851, *Belgian State Gazette* 22 December 1851, 3.555).

1199 F. 'T KINT and W. DERIJCKE, 'Dessaisissement et situations des creanciers en cas de faillite', *Le nouveau droit du concordat judiciaire et de la faillite: les lois des 17 juillet et 8 août 1997*, (Brussels: Bruylant, 1997), 204; F. 'T KINT, *Sûretés et principes généraux du droit de poursuite des créanciers*, (Brussels: Larcier, 2004), 253; H. VANDENBERGHE, 'Eigendomsvoorbehoud bij leasing', (1980–81) RW, (2761) 2763; A. CUYPERS and P. FRANCOIS, 'Art. 20, 5° Hyp.W' in E. DIRIX, P. FRANCOIS and M. TISON (eds.), *Voorrechten en hypotheken – Artikelsgewijze commentaar met overzicht van rechtspraak en rechtsleer*, (Mechelen: Kluwer, loosel.), 11; P. CALLENS, 'De bescherming van de verkoper van roerende goederen door het eigendomsvoorbehoud – een rechtsvergelijkend overzicht', (1979–80) 16 Jura Falconis, (99) 102; R. DE HEMPTINNE and A. RUYFFELAERE, 'Naar de tegenstelbaarheid van de clausule van eigendomsvoorbehoud' in *Jurist in bedrijf*, (Brussels: Bruylant, 1989), 135.

1200 Cass. 23 May 1946, (1946) Arr. Cass., (195) 198.

1201 Cass. 22 September 1994, (1995) JLMB, 124.

1202 Antwerp 1 March 1988, (1988–89) RW, (575) 576; Kh.Namen 24 November 1994, (1995) TBH, 625 (626); Kh.Kortrijk 11 September 1995, (1996) TBH, (462); E. DIRIX, 'Eigendomsvoorbehoud en samenloop', (1994–95) 37 RW, (1264) 1266; E. DIRIX, 'Art. 101 Faillissementswet' in E. DIRIX, P. FRANCOIS and M. TISON (eds.), *Voorrechten en hypotheken – Artikelsgewijze commentaar met overzicht van rechtspraak en rechtsleer*, (Mechelen: Kluwer, 2011), 11–12.

1203 N. VAN CROMBRUGGHE, 'Belgium' in I. DAVIES (ed.), *Retention of title clauses in sale of goods contracts in Europe*, (Sydney: Ashgate, 1999), (7) 10.

the creation of article 101 of the former Bankruptcy Act. Front and central in this provision was the third-party effectiveness of retention of title in sale agreements and its enforcement via revendication during bankruptcy proceedings. However, given the fact that the provision was included in the Bankruptcy Act, the effectiveness of retention of title outside of corporate bankruptcy proceedings was debated. This debate was resolved by the Supreme Court in 2010 when it decided that retention of title clauses in sale agreements would not be effective against third parties outside of bankruptcy proceedings.[1204] In this case the debtor bought a car on credit and the seller retained title to the car until the purchase price was paid. Thereafter, the debtor became insolvent and initiated non-corporate insolvency proceedings.[1205] At this point the seller reclaimed his car based on his retention of title agreement. However, the Supreme Court refused to allow the revendication, since the recognition and enforcement of retention of title agreement was only legally regulated for corporate bankruptcy proceedings and not for non-corporate insolvency proceedings. Therefore, the Court decided that in the event of a non-corporate insolvency proceeding retention of title agreements remained ineffective against third parties. The seller could only rely on protection based on the unpaid vendor's lien.[1206] This case was met with fervent criticism and disbelief.[1207] Not only did this ruling limit the use of retention of title agreements to one collective insolvency proceeding, it also reinforced Belgian's position as one of the few remaining jurisdictions in Europe where retention of title was not generally recognized.[1208] Moreover, limiting the recognition of retention of title in sale agreements to just corporate bankruptcy proceedings made the distinction between retention of title in sale agreements and finance leasing relevant again. Finance leasing was generally considered effective against third parties. Furthermore, the general acceptance of the third-party effectiveness of finance leasing ensured that during other forms of *concursus*, such as non-corporate insolvency proceedings, the financial lessor

1204 Cass. 7 May 2010, (2010) Arr. Cass., 1334.

1205 Non-corporate insolvency proceedings are regulated in art. 1675/1 *et seq.* of the Code for Civil Procedure.

1206 The unpaid vendor's lien is legally recognized in article 20, °5 Hypotheekwet 16 December 1851, *Belgian State Gazette* 22 December 1851, 3.555 (hereafter, Mortgage Act 1851).

1207 M. E. STORME, 'Eigendomsvoorbehoud en samenloop buiten faillissement: Hof van Cassatie lijdt aan fantoompijn', (2011–12) 5 RW (254) 254; R. FRANSIS, 'Tegenwerpelijkheid van het eigendomsvoorbehoud bij samenloop: de wetgever is opnieuw (dringend) aan zet', (2011) 225 NJW (503) 503; E. DIRIX, 'Art. 101 Faillissementswet' in E. DIRIX, P. FRANCOIS and M. TISON (eds.), *Voorrechten en hypotheken – Artikelsgewijze commentaar met overzicht van rechtspraak en rechtsleer*, (Mechelen: Kluwer, 2011), 17–18; A.-S. GIGOT, 'L'opposabilité de la clause de réserve de propriété en cas de procédures collectives d'insolvabilité', (2011) 6 TBH (511) 511.

1208 E. DIRIX, 'Eigendomsvoorbehoud' (1997–98) 15 RW (481) 481; M. GREGOIRE, *Publicité foncière, sûretés réelles et privilèges*, (Brussels: Bruylant, 2006), 673; E. DIRIX and M. E. STORME, 'Eigendomsvoorbehoud in het ontwerp van faillissementswet: hopeloos onsamenhangend', (1995–96) 41 RW, (1421) 1421; P. VAN OMMESLAGHE, "Les sûretés nouvelles issues de la pratique – Développements récentes, in *Le droit des sûretés*, (Brussels: Du jeune barreau Bruxelles, 1992), (377) 382.

was protected.[1209] As a result, even after the former Bankruptcy Act finance lessors were better protected than sellers with a retention of title. However, the situation did change when the lessor wanted to enforce his finance lease during corporate bankruptcy proceedings after the lessee had lifted the purchase option, but had not yet paid the residual value. In that case, the finance lessor was considered a seller on credit with a retention of title. Consequently, the limited interpretation of article 101, section 2 of the former Bankruptcy Act would also apply to them and would result in the finance lease only being effective during corporate bankruptcy and no other collective insolvency proceedings.[1210]

Nevertheless, the Court stood firm on its decision concerning the effectiveness of retention of title outside of corporate bankruptcy proceedings and maintained that only legislative intervention could expand the protection of retention of title agreements from bankruptcy to all collective insolvency proceedings.

269. *The unchanging nature of the goods encumbered with retention of title* – A second issue with retention of title prior to the Security Rights Act was the *in natura* requirement for the encumbered goods.[1211] One of the benefits of retaining title instead of vesting a pledge, was that the debtor could remain in possession of the collateral and use it in his business. Generally, non-possessory secured transactions are considered economically more efficient because they allow the debtor to make use of his valuable assets which in turn is likely to result in faster repayment of the outstanding debt. However, the requirement that assets remained largely unaltered in the debtor's estate under the Bankruptcy Act, put retention of title at risk and placed a burden on the retention of title creditor to make sure that encumbered good remained *in natura* in the debtor's estate. Although courts intervened to lessen some of the effects of the *in natura* requirement[1212], the fact that alterations to the encumbered good posed a risk to the retention of title undermined its usefulness and made it less attractive as a mechanism to guarantee credit.

1209 J. BEKAERT 'Insolventierechtelijke aspecten van leasing en tegenwerpelijkheid van leasing' in P. BESELAERE, O. LENAERTS, B. TILLEMAN, A. VERBEKE (eds.), *Handboek leasing*, (Brugge: Die Keure, 2007), (591) 594.

1210 J. BEKAERT 'Insolventierechtelijke aspecten van leasing en tegenwerpelijkheid van leasing' in P. BESELAERE, O. LENAERTS, B. TILLEMAN, A. VERBEKE (eds.), *Handboek leasing*, (Brugge: Die Keure, 2007), (591) 595.

1211 Art. 101, sec. 2 Bankruptcy Act 1997: *Daarenboven moeten die goederen zich in natura bij de schuldenaar bevinden. Ze mogen derhalve niet onroerend door incorporatie zijn geworden, noch vermengd zijn met een ander roerend goed.* Translation: *Furthermore, the goods have to remain in natura in the hands of the debtor. Consequently, they cannot become attached via incorporation, nor mixed with another movable good.*

1212 For an overview of the relevant case law see, V. SAGAERT, 'Het 'in natura'-vereiste bij eigendomsvoorbehoud: de gevolgen van de bewerking, vermenging en wederverkoop', (2003) 9 TBH, (773) 781; V. SAGAERT and R. JANSEN, 'Overzicht van rechtspraak – eigendom tot zekerheid', (2012) 3 TPR, (1362) 1368–1369.

SECTION 2 – ASPIRATIONS VS. DESIGN OF THE SECURITY RIGHTS ACT

270. *A call to action for the reform of security rights in movable goods* – Given the problems that had risen after decades of neglecting the efficient regulation of contractual security rights in movable goods, the legislator took action in 2010 and assembled a group of experts to redraft and modernize the contractual security rights in movable goods (i.e. the pledge, retention of title, transfer of title and the right to retention of possession).[1213] In the explanatory memorandum the legislator listed the following underlying objectives of the Security Rights Act[1214]:

- to create effective, flexible and predictable security rights;
- to create a fair balance between the debtor and creditor who agree to a security right;
- to introduce the functional approach[1215];
- to unify security right provisions and laws in the Civil Code;
- to contribute to the harmonization of *in rem* security rights in Europe.

From this list it is clear that the legislator was ambitious in its intended reform. In the experts' ideal version of the Security Rights Act one general (with both possessory and non-possessory third-party effectiveness)[1216] pledge regime would be created, the formerly lesser regulated secured transactions (retention of title, right of retention of possession and transfer of title) would be fully recognized as security rights and the abundance of legislative liens would be reduced.[1217]

271. *Meeting the aspirations for pledges in movable goods* – With regards to the pledge, the legislator comes through on some of his promises. In the Security Rights Act, the pledge is a limited proprietary interest granted by the debtor[1218]

1213 For a detailed overview of the different stages of the legislative process of the Security Rights Act see, F. GÉORGES, 'La réforme des sûretés mobilières', (2013) 3 Rev. Dr. ULg., (319) 321–330.

1214 Explanatory memorandum Security Rights Act, no. 2463/001, 7–9.

1215 The functional approach refers to the theory of treating secured transactions that perform the same function similarly. The application of the functional approach in secured transactions law hails from the United States where the functional approach was used to comprehensively unify their different secured transactions mechanisms (see *supra* no. 35).

1216 W. DERIJCKE, 'La réforme des sûretés réelles mobilières', (2013) 8 TBH, (691) 697; T. DONNEZ and D. GRUYAERT, 'Het nieuwe registerpand in de praktijk: voorwerp, vestiging en uitwerking nader bekeken', (2018) 43 RW, (1683) 1683.

1217 Explanatory memorandum Security Rights Act, no. 2463/001, 12–17.

1218 Third parties can also allow a pledge on one or more of their assets (art. 5 SRA), but this specific form of pledge is outside the scope of this dissertation.

in one or more of his present or future, tangible or intangible, movable assets[1219] to secure a current or future claim.[1220] Since the enactment of the Security Rights Act the pledge in all movable goods can be vested without the creditor having to take possession of the encumbered good.[1221] Consequently, in this regard the Belgian legislator delivered on creating a uniform pledge regime in tangible, movable goods that made much of the former separate pledge regime obsolete.

272. *Failure to deliver on some of the promises concerning the newly reformed secured transactions regime* – First, the legislator does not follow through on the integration effort between the different types of pledge. For example, the pledge on accounts receivable remains governed by its own set of rules.[1222] The most significant distinction between the general pledge regime and the pledge on accounts receivable is that the creation and third-party effectiveness of the pledge on an account receivable is achieved simultaneously, namely when the pledge agreement between the parties is reached.[1223] In other words, for the pledge on accounts receivable no further measures, such as registration or dispossession, need to be taken to make the pledge effective against third parties.[1224] Another example of the existing fragmentation among pledges in the Security Rights Act is the separate regime for security rights in financial collateral. The Financial Collateral Act[1225] includes different rules for the pledge, transfer of title and repo's[1226] in financial instruments. These distinct rules stem from the European directive on financial collateral arrangements[1227] that dictates how security rights in financial instruments should be governed. The European oversight concerning security rights in financial instruments complicates the integration of this separate regime in the Security Rights Act. Therefore, instead of attempting to unify these two regimes, the legislator opted to maintain a clear distinction between security rights in financial collateral and all other movable goods.[1228] These distinctions between different types of

---

1219 Art. 7–8 SRA.

1220 Art. 10 SRA.

1221 Art. 15 SRA.

1222 Art. 60 *et seq.* Security Rights Act (hereafter SRA).

1223 Art. 60 SRA.

1224 F. GÉORGES, 'La réforme des sûretés mobilières', (2013) 3 Rev. Dr. ULg., (319) 354; M. GRÉGOIRE, 'La modification du code civil en ce qui concerne les sûretés réelles mobilières' in F. GÉORGES (ed.), *Insolvabilité et garanties*, (Brussels: Larcier, 2014), (10) 17 *et seq.*; T. DONNEZ and D. GRUYAERT, 'Het nieuwe registerpand in de praktijk: voorwerp, vestiging en uitwerking nader bekeken', (2018) 43 RW, (1683) 1693–1694.

1225 Financial Collateral Act 2004.

1226 A repo is a type of secured transaction in which title to the financial collateral is transferred to guarantee outstanding credit, but the transaction includes the option of the debtor to repurchase the underlying collateral.

1227 Directive 2002/47/EC of the European Parliament and of the Council of 6 June 2002 on financial collateral arrangements, 27 June 2002 *Pb.L.* 168, 43 (hereafter, European Financial Collateral Directive).

1228 Art. 7 of the Financial Collateral Act.

pledges depending on the type of movable good is reminiscent of the disparate regime prior to the Security Rights Act.

Second, the Security Rights Act reduced some, but not all, of the deemed unnecessary legislative liens. Initially, the legislator intended to repeal eleven legislative liens that were considered redundant.[1229] However, in the end the reduction of legislative liens was limited to a few archaic liens[1230], such as the lien for the seeds and costs of harvest[1231] and the innkeeper's lien.[1232] Otherwise, the system of abundant legislative liens in movable goods remains more or less unaltered.[1233]

SECTION 3 – THE FUNCTIONAL APPROACH IN THE SECURITY RIGHTS ACT

273. *Limited application of the functional approach in the Security Rights Act* – Although the functional approach is presented as one of the fundamental cornerstones of the Security Rights Act[1234], the drafters did not elaborate on how the functional approach is actually pursued. In the explanatory memorandum they state that the functional approach in the Security Rights Act means

> *[...] a rational and integrated approach in which similar security mechanisms should have the same legal outcomes despite their conceptual differences.*[1235]

For the pledge, the application of the functional approach takes the form of recharacterizing all the different types of pledges that existed prior to the Security Rights Act[1236] to a general pledge and treating the right of retention of possession[1237] and the transfer of title for security purposes[1238] as a pledge in movable goods. With regards to retention of title, the functional approach is mentioned two more times in the explanatory memorandum. First, the

1229 Explanatory memorandum Security Rights Act, no. 2463/001, 88.

1230 E. DIRIX, 'De nieuwe Pandwet: doelstellingen en uitgangspunten' in M. E. STORME (ed.), *Roerende zekerheden na de Pandwet*, (Antwerpen: Intersentia, 2017), (1) 21–22.

1231 Art. 20, 2° Mortgage Act.

1232 Art. 20, 6° Mortgage Act.

1233 J. CATTARUZZA, 'Les grands axes de la réforme des sûretés mobilières', (2013) 4 Dr Banc Fin, (183) 184; E. DIRIX, 'The new Belgian act on security interests in movable property', (2014) 23 Int Insolv Rev, (171) 180.

1234 Explanatory memorandum Security Rights Act, no. 2463/001, 10.

1235 Explanatory memorandum Security Rights Act, no. 2463/001, 10. Original text: *[...]een rationele en geïntegreerde aanpak bedoeld waarbij gelijkaardige zekerheidsfiguren ongeacht hun conceptuele verschillen dezelfde juridische uitwerking moeten krijgen.*

1236 See *supra* no. 273 and the explanatory memorandum Security Rights Act, no. 2463/001, 15–16.

1237 Art. 73 *et seq.* SRA.

1238 Art. 62 SRA.

classification of retention of title as a full-fledged security right in movable goods is attributed to the functional approach.[1239] Second, the extension of the rules concerning the tracing of the non-possessory pledge into processed, mixed and incorporated goods and proceeds to retention of title[1240] is also credited to the application of the functional approach.[1241]

274. *Comparison of functional approaches across jurisdictions and international instruments* – At first glance, the application of the functional approach to retention of title in the Security Rights Act is quite limited as opposed to the functional approaches in the selected jurisdiction and international instruments. As mentioned, in *Article 9 UCC* and the *UNCITRAL unitary approach* all secured transactions in movable goods that guarantee the purchase price of an asset or credit that enabled the debtor to acquire the encumbered good (i.e. acquisition credit) are recharacterized to a PMSI[1242] or acquisition security right.[1243] Given that retention of title by definition guarantees acquisition credit, this mechanism is automatically recharacterized to a PMSI or acquisition security right and treated by its uniform rules. In the *DCFR*[1244] and under the *UNCITRAL non-unitary approach*, retention of title may not be recharacterized to an acquisition security right, but both instruments go out of their way to explicate that retention of title or retention of ownership devices, respectively, are treated as general security rights and acquisition security rights when specific rules apply to this sub-category of security rights.[1245]

Most striking in the comparison between the Security Rights Act and the other functional approaches is that the Security Rights Act does not provide in a sub-category of PMSIs or acquisition security rights with which retention of title is specifically equated. Consequently, the only immediate functional equivalent of retention of title is the pledge, which in a broad sense performs the same function as retention of title (i.e. guarantee credit by obtaining or retaining a proprietary interest in a movable good) and for which some general rules and legal outcomes can be unified. However, retention of title remains a mechanism that specifically guarantees acquisition credit and, in that sense, a full equation with the pledge is not desirable. How this specific functional approach and treatment of retention of title works out in the Security Rights Act is discussed in the following chapter.

1239 Explanatory memorandum Security Rights Act, no. 2463/001, 30. See also, *infra* no. 277 *et seq*.

1240 Art. 69 SRA.

1241 Explanatory memorandum Security Rights Act, no. 2463/001, 70. See also, *infra* no. 332 *et seq*.

1242 See *supra* no. 46.

1243 See *supra* no. 123.

1244 See *supra* no. 157.

1245 See *supra* no. 125.

CHAPTER 2

RETENTION OF TITLE IN THE SECURITY RIGHTS ACT

275. *Methodological approach* – In this chapter retention of title in the Security Rights Act is analyzed and compared on an internal and external level. On an internal level, the application of the functional approach to retention of title is examined by looking at the extent to which equivalent legal outcomes for retention of title and functionally equivalent mechanisms are achieved. Furthermore, the impact of the functional approach is assessed by comparing retention of title pre- and post-functional approach. On an external level, the functional approach as method for integration of retention of title in security right frameworks is evaluated by comparing and contrasting retention of title in the Security Rights Act to retention of title or their functional equivalents in the other selected jurisdictions and international instruments.

276. *Overview* – The analysis is divided in the classification of retention of title in the Security Rights Act (section 1), the scope of the Security Rights Act (section 2), creation and third-party effectiveness (section 3), rights of retention of title creditors (section 4) and retention of title in corporate bankruptcy proceedings (section 5).

SECTION 1 – CLASSIFICATION OF RETENTION OF TITLE AS A SECURITY RIGHT IN MOVABLE GOODS

277. *Comparison of the classification of retention of title* – Following the functional approach, the Security Rights Act classifies retention of title as a type of security right in movable goods, together with the pledge, the right of retention of possession and the transfer of title for security purposes.[1246] Consequently, the approach in the Security Rights Act can be characterized as type of functional approach without recharacterization, such as in the *UNCITRAL Guide* and *DCFR*, which also maintain retention of title[1247] and

---

1246 E. DIRIX, 'The new Belgian act on security interests in movable property', (2014) 23 Int Insolv Rev, (171) 178.

1247 See *supra* no. 125.

retention of ownership devices[1248], respectively, alongside the security rights in movable goods. However, the Security Rights Act differs from the *DCFR* and the *UNCITRAL Guide*, in that both instruments combine the continuation of the term retention of title or retention of ownership device with clear guidelines (the *UNCITRAL Guide*), or provisions (*DCFR*) on how retention of title and retention of ownership devices should be treated as acquisition security rights. In other words, these instruments attempt to make the treatment of retention of title and retention of ownership devices in the context of secured transactions law clear, despite the lack of an explicit recharacterization of these mechanisms as security rights in movable goods. Conversely, retention of title in the Security Rights Act is only classified as a security right in movable goods without any further indication of what this implies for the concept of retention of title or the rights of retention of title creditors.

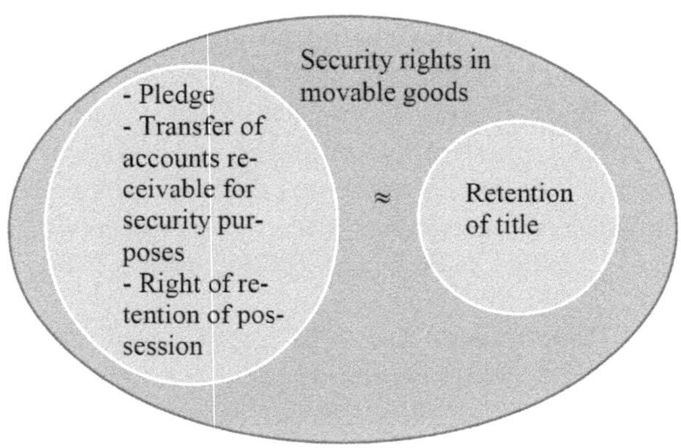

Evidently, the Belgian approach differs from the approach taken in *Article 9 UCC* and *the UNCITRAL unitary approach*. These frameworks do no bother with continuing the term retention of title, but opt for an outright recharacterization of retention of title to PMSIs[1249] and acquisition security rights[1250], respectively.

278. *Impact of the classification of retention of title as security right in movable goods* – The explicit classification of retention of title as a security right in movable goods is a departure from the situation pre-Security Rights Act. In the former Bankruptcy Act of 1997, retention of title was minimally regulated, mainly considered a contract law mechanism and only informally part of secured transactions law in doctrine.[1251] Prior to the Security Rights Act, the

1248 See *supra* no. 168.
1249 See *supra* no. 46.
1250 See *supra* no. 123.
1251 E. DIRIX and R. DE CORTE, 'Zekerheidsrechten' in *Beginselen van Belgisch privaatrecht*, (5th edn., Mechelen: Wolters Kluwer, 2006), 3.

classification of retention of title more resembled the approach now still found in *Germany*, where retention of title is informally listed as a *Mobiliarsicherheit* in doctrine but within the BGB retention of title remains regulated in a singular provision as part of the chapter on Sale and Trade of the BGB.[1252] Now retention of title in the Security Rights Act is explicitly included in the category of security rights in movable goods. Nevertheless, some authors remain skeptical and even refuse to accept the classification of retention of title as a security right and its submission to the typical characteristics of security rights.

1. DOCTRINAL VIEWS ON THE CLASSIFICATION OF RETENTION OF TITLE

279. *Overview* – The acceptance of retention of title as a security right is considered the majority opinion (1.1.). However, a minority of scholars maintains the view that the classification of retention of title as a security right is still debated (1.2.).

1.1. Majority opinion

280. *Outright acceptance of retention of title as security right in movable goods* – The majority of Belgian authors accepts the classification of retention of title as a security right following the legislator's explicit inclusion of retention of title in the category of security rights in movable goods.[1253] The inclusion of retention of title in the category of security rights in movable goods for these scholars also implies that retention of title is determined by the same characteristics as other security rights: the specificity principle, the *numerus clausus* principle, first-in-time principle, subrogation principle, prohibition on unjust enrichment, ex-post judicial control of enforcement and notification principle.[1254]

1252 See *supra* no. 211.

1253 W. DERIJCKE, 'La réforme des sûretés réelles mobilières', (2013) 8 TBH, (691) 719; F. GÉORGES, 'La réforme des sûretés mobilières', (2013) 3 Rev. Dr. ULg., (319) 357; E. DIRIX, 'De nieuwe Pandwet: doelstellingen en uitgangspunten' in M. E. STORME (ed.), *Roerende zekerheden na de Pandwet*, (Antwerpen: Intersentia, 2017), (1) 6; V. NICAISE, 'Rappels des principes, mise en contexte et modifications diverses apportées par la loi du 25 décembre 2016' in I. DURANT (ed.), *Les sûretées mobilières*, (Liège: Anthemis, 2017), (10) 17 and 80; I. DURANT, 'Le droit de rétention et la réserve de propriété, deux sûretés réelles mobilières à part entière' in F. GEORGES (ed.), *Insolvabilité et garanties*, (Brussels: Larcier, 2014), (34) 73; A. APERS and D. GRUYAERT, 'Eigendomsvoorbehoud en onroerende incorporatie volgens de nieuwe pandwet: welk nieuws onder de zon?', (2015) 1 TPR, (83) 87–88; J. CAEYMAEX and T. CAVENAILE, *Manuel des sûretés mobilières*, (3 edn., Brussels: Larcier, 2019), 514.

1254 E. DIRIX and R. DE CORTE, 'Zekerheidsrechten' in *Beginselen van Belgisch privaatrecht*, (5th edn., Mechelen: Wolters Kluwer, 2006), 4–5.

281. *Hints of recharacterization: retention of title as type of non-possessory pledge* – STORME lists specific characteristics of retention of title that are similar to those that can be found in the pledge to not only classify retention of title as a security right, but also consider the right of the retention of title creditor not as title, but as a type of non-possessory pledge.[1255] For example, STORME mentions the fact that retention of title depends for its existence on and is limited for its enforcement to the outstanding debt.[1256] Under the Security Rights Act, retention of title also transfers along with the underlying claim, if it is transferred to a third party.[1257] This connection between retention of title and its underlying claim illustrates the accessory nature of retention of title to the outstanding debt. The accessory nature supports retention of title's classification as a security right, since the accessory nature is seen as a typical characteristic of security rights.[1258]

Furthermore, STORME points out that during corporate bankruptcy proceedings retention of title entitles the creditor more to the value of the encumbered good than the good itself.[1259] This is relevant in the classification debate, because it is often purported that security rights merely entitle the creditor to the value of the collateral, whereas title-based security mechanisms entitle creditors to the encumbered movable good.[1260] However, if the bankruptcy receiver has the ability to block the retention of title creditor's right to revendicate[1261], this would mean that during bankruptcy the retention of title creditor would also be entitled merely to the value of the good and not the good itself.

Finally, in the event the retention of title creditor goes bankrupt, it is generally accepted that the retention of title debtor is unaffected by this and is allowed to continue payments on the collateral.[1262] In other words, the encumbered collateral does not fall into the retention of title creditor's bankruptcy estate. This suggests that the retention of title debtor already has some proprietary interest in the encumbered good that protects him against the bankruptcy of his creditor,

1255 M. E. STORME, *Zekerheden en insolventierecht*, (Ghent, Mariakerke: 2018–19), 411–412.

1256 See *infra* section 4.1. on the right to revendicate.

1257 Art. 23 *juncto* 70 SRA.

1258 I. MOREAU-MARGREVE, 'Evolution du droit et de la pratique en matière de sûretés', *Les créanciers et le droit de la faillite: séminaire organisé à Liège les 17 et 18 novembre 1982*, (Brussels: Bruylant, 1983), (77) 84; M. GREGOIRE, *Publicité foncière, sûretés réelles et privilèges*, (Brussels: Bruylant, 2006), 427; E. DIRIX, 'Nieuwe overeenkomsten tot zekerheid', (1988) 2 TPR, (323) 325.

1259 M. E. STORME, *Zekerheden en insolventierecht*, (Ghent, Mariakerke: 2018–19), 412.

1260 R. JANSEN, 'Eigendomsvoorbehoud' in J. BAECK and M. KRUITHOF (eds.), *Het nieuwe zekerheidsrecht*, (Antwerpen: Intersentia, 2014), (139) 143. See also *infra* no. 370.

1261 Art. XX.201 WER.

1262 This protection of retention of title-debtors has been explicitly recognized in article 10 (2) of the of the former Council Regulation (EC) No 1346/2000 of 29 May 2000 on insolvency proceedings, *Pb. L.*, 160, 1. Recast in article 10, sec. 2 of the European Regulation (EU) 2015/848 of the European Parliament and of the Council of 20 May 2015 on insolvency proceedings (recast), *Pb.L.* 5 June 2015, afl. 141, 19 (hereafter, Insolvency Regulation 2015).

akin to the *Anwartschaftsrecht* of the retention of title debtor in *Germany*.[1263] Based on these characteristics, retention of title is a security right according to STORME and can even be equated with the non-possessory pledge.[1264]

1.2. Minority opinion

282. *Introduction to the minority opinion* – A minority remains skeptical of retention of title's classification as a security right.[1265] Within this minority view two schools of thought can be discerned: 1) retention of title is not a security right and 2) retention of title is not a non-possessory pledge and therefore not a security right.

283. *Retention of title as full ownership* – The first point of view suggests that retention of title does not fall in the category of security rights, because it should be considered as full ownership in the hands of the retention of title creditor. The reasoning goes that retention of title does not merely give you the right to be paid with priority in the event of *concursus* as a security right, but instead retains full ownership in the hands of the creditor.[1266] Consequently, the creditor's retained title allows him to enforce his claim differently than security right creditors, i.e. through revendication, and therefore excludes him from a classification as a security right.[1267]

284. *No non-possessory pledge, no security right* – The second school of thought takes as a starting point that retention of title cannot be equated with the non-possessory pledge and therefore cannot be a security right. Following the distinctions between retention of title and the pledge, it is considered that retention of title is too different from traditional security rights to be classified as one. The leading proponents of this view are SAGAERT, DEL CORAL[1268] and JANSEN.[1269] Interestingly enough these authors use many of the arguments

---

1263 See *supra* no. 257.

1264 M. E. STORME, *Zekerheden en insolventierecht*, (Ghent, Mariakerke: 2018–19), 412.

1265 J. BAECK, 'Achtergrond en krachtlijnen van de hervorming' in J. BAECK and M. KRUITHOF (eds.), *Het nieuwe zekerheidsrecht*, (Antwerpen: Intersentia, 2014), (1) 11; R. JANSEN, 'Eigendomsvoorbehoud' in J. BAECK and M. KRUITHOF (eds.), *Het nieuwe zekerheidsrecht*, (Antwerpen: Intersentia, 2014), (139), 143–144;_V. SAGAERT and J. DEL CORRAL, "Eigendomsvoorbehoud" in *Algemene praktische rechtsverzameling*, (Mechelen: Kluwer, 2015), 8.

1266 J. BAECK, 'Achtergrond en krachtlijnen van de hervorming' in J. BAECK and M. KRUITHOF (eds.), *Het nieuwe zekerheidsrecht*, (Antwerpen: Intersentia, 2014), (1) 11.

1267 Whether the right to revendicate in the of the retention of title-creditor actually distinguishes retention of title from *in rem* security rights will discussed in more detail below (section 3.2.2. right to revendicate).

1268 V. SAGAERT and J. DEL CORRAL, "Eigendomsvoorbehoud" in *Algemene praktische rechtsverzameling*, (Mechelen: Kluwer, 2015), 8.

1269 R. JANSEN, 'Eigendomsvoorbehoud' in J. BAECK and M. KRUITHOF (eds.), *Het nieuwe zekerheidsrecht*, (Antwerpen: Intersentia, 2014), (139), 143–144.

used by STORME in support of retention of title as a security right. However, from the minority point of view these characteristics are now seen as evidence of the incompatibility between retention of title and security rights.

285. *The intrinsic vs. accessory nature of retention of title to the outstanding obligation* – For example, both SAGAERT and JANSEN acknowledge that there is a strong connection between retention of title and the underlying claim. However, for them this does not suggest the accessory nature of retention of title, but rather indicates the intrinsic nature of retention of title to the transaction which performance it guarantees.[1270] For example, a retention of title in a sale agreement only guarantees the outstanding purchase price of the sale agreement and the costs and interests that follow directly from this agreement. As a result, retention of title can only guarantee that specific claim and not any future or other claims unrelated to the agreement in which the retention of title clause was initially included.[1271] Furthermore, retention of title cannot be "vested" for any claim between a creditor and a debtor, but will be retained for the original acquisition credit granted by the retention of title creditor. Because of the intrinsic and not accessory nature of retention of title, the minority opinion concludes that retention of title cannot be considered a pledge that can be vested for any debt between the secured creditor and debtor, and therefore not a security right. However, the strong connection between retention of title and the guaranteed purchase price and its relation to the classification retention of title needs to be further refined. It is true that the nature of retention of title means that title is mainly retained for acquisition credit (i.e. the purchase price and its directly associated costs)[1272] and is usually included in a sale, (finance) lease or functionally similar agreement. However, in *Article 9 UCC*, the *UNCITRAL Guide and Model Law* and *DCFR*, PMSIs and acquisition security rights are considered a specific class of security rights that is only assigned to security interests or rights that guarantee acquisition credit.[1273] In other words, these mechanisms can also not be vested for any and all claims between a creditor and a debtor and only in certain transactions. However, the limitation of the PMSI or acquisition security right status to security right that guarantee certain

---

1270 J. DEL CORRAL, *De leveringsplicht bij de overdracht van roerende lichamelijke goederen*, (Antwerpen: Intersentia, 2013), 159; V. SAGAERT, 'Het eigendomsvoorbehoud (en retentierecht) onder de Pandwet' in M. E. STORME (ed.), *Roerende zekerheden na de Pandwet*, (Antwerpen: Intersentia, 2017), (29) 36; R. JANSEN, 'Eigendomsvoorbehoud' in J. BAECK and M. KRUITHOF (eds.), *Het nieuwe zekerheidsrecht*, (Antwerpen: Intersentia, 2014), (139), 143–144.

1271 Later we will see that in certain mixed transactions the guaranteed debt can be extended to other services outside the purchase price, but they still directly relate to the underlying transaction. Under no circumstance can a retention of title be used to guarantee other debts that have nothing to do with the transaction in which the retention of title clause was originally included. See *infra* no. 295 *et seq*.

1272 See *infra* no. 295.

1273 See for Article 9 UCC, *supra* no. 46, the UNCITRAL Guide and Model Law, *supra* no. 123 and 125 and the DCFR, *supra* no. 167.

debt does not exclude them from the larger category of security rights. It simply places them in a sub-category of security rights which are given certain special protections, such as super-priority. Furthermore, in *Germany*, the contractual, horizontal extension of retention of title to other debts between the retention of title creditor and debtor is allowed (*erweiterte Eigentumsvorbehalt*). Notably, this extensive horizontal extension does not change the retention of title in a type of security right. The German legislator did intervene in the horizontal extension of retention of title when the protection of retention of title is extended to all debts between the retention of title creditor, its associated companies and the retention of title debtor (*Konzernvorbehalt*).[1274] Interestingly, this was not because retention of title thereby converted to a pledge, but because this would in effect turn the retention of title in a transfer of title of the encumbered good for an unspecified amount of time to which the debtor had not agreed.

In summary, the limitation of retention of title in the Security Rights Act to certain claims between the retention of title creditor and debtor due to the nature of the agreement is not a feature that necessarily distinguishes retention of title from *all* security rights, but simply distinguishes retention of title from the security rights that are not vested for acquisition credit.

286. *The right to revendicate and the classification of retention of title* – Additionally, the minority opinion does not agree that the bankruptcy receiver's right to halt the retention of title creditor's revendication by continuing payment on the outstanding debt is a sign that retention of title should be classified as a security right.[1275] On the contrary, the fact that the retention of title creditor has as main method of enforcement the right to revendicate, is for them sufficient to exclude retention of title from the category of security rights. The fact that the pledge-holders also have the option to enforce through appropriation of the collateral does not change these scholars' opinion.[1276] SAGAERT and DEL CORRAL argue that with regards to the pledge this is not the main method of enforcement but the exception to the general enforcement proceedings through forced sale of the good.[1277]

287. *The method of creation as a distinguishing feature* – As the name suggests, retention of title is created by the creditor retaining title to collateral in order to guarantee a claim.[1278] Conversely, a security right in a movable good implies the

---

1274 See *supra* no. 214.

1275 R. JANSEN, 'Eigendomsvoorbehoud' in J. BAECK and M. KRUITHOF (eds.), *Het nieuwe zekerheidsrecht*, (Antwerpen: Intersentia, 2014), (139) 143.

1276 Art. 53 SRA.

1277 V. SAGAERT and J. DEL CORRAL, 'Eigendomsvoorbehoud' in *Algemene Praktische Rechtsverzameling*, (Mechelen: Wolters Kluwer, 2015), 10.

1278 V. SAGAERT and J. DEL CORRAL, 'Eigendomsvoorbehoud' in *Algemene Praktische Rechtsverzameling*, (Mechelen: Wolters Kluwer, 2015), 8–9.

debtor granting a proprietary interest in one or more of his movable assets.[1279] Again the main example here is the pledge: a security right that is granted to the creditor by the debtor in an asset that the debtor or a third party owns.[1280] According to SAGAERT and DEL CORRAL this difference in creation sets retention of title on a different path from the pledge, making it impossible to classify retention of title as a security right.[1281] This reasoning is also applied in the *DCFR,* in which the drafters argue that the different method of creation for retention of ownership devices is one of the main reasons to maintain the distinction between retention of ownership devices and (acquisition) security rights.[1282]

288. *Summary* – Surprisingly, the minority view now seems to be echoed in Book 3 of the new Belgian Civil Code which does not list retention of title as one of the legally determined security rights in movable goods.[1283] However, this goes against the Security Rights Act that is still in effect and the explicit classification of retention of title as a security right in movable goods. Hence, it is advisable that the legislator takes a clear stance in this debate by further clarifying the classification of retention of title and potentially recharacterizing retention of title in the upcoming book 9 of the Civil Code.

2. CONCLUSION

289. *Issues concerning the Belgian application of the functional approach without recharacterization* – The application of the functional approach without recharacterization leaves room for debate on how retention of title should be treated. The continuation of the term retention of title in the Security Rights Act means that all the existing baggage and presumptions concerning the (non-)classification of retention of title as a security right are brought to the Security Rights Act. The reasoning goes that since the name remains the same, the existing theories regarding retention of title can still be applied. These preconceived notions are then used to cast retention of title again in its old terms and distinguish it not only from the other security rights, but from the concept of security right itself. As a result, the inclusion of retention of title in the category of security rights did not result in an increase of clarity and

1279 E. DIRIX and R. DE CORTE, 'Zekerheidsrechten' in *Beginselen van Belgisch privaatrecht*, (5th edn., Mechelen: Wolters Kluwer, 2006), 234.

1280 H. DE PAGE and R. DEKKERS, 'Les biens – les sûretés' in *Traité élémentaire de droit civil Belge*, vol. VI, (Brussels: Bruylant, 1962), 995.

1281 V. SAGAERT and J. DEL CORRAL, "Eigendomsvoorbehoud" in *Algemene praktische rechtsverzameling*, (Mechelen: Kluwer, 2015), 16.

1282 See *supra* no. 172.

1283 Expected art. 3.3 Belgian Civil Code.

coherence with respect of the classification of retention of title, as the legislator intended, but instead continued the contrasting interpretations concerning the classification of retention of title.

The ongoing debate regarding the classification of retention of title is not without consequences. The minority opinion maintains that retention of title is not a security right, but is more akin to full ownership in the hands of the retention of title creditor. However, given the specific protections already given to the retention of title debtor and the limitations placed on the retention of title creditor, it is difficult to accept that retention of title results in traditional full ownership for the retention of title creditor. Consequently, by maintaining that retention of title is not a security right, retention of title falls again in a dogmatic grey area. This situation generates more confusion and case law in which parties try to obtain the classification that bests suit their needs.

290. *Inherent flaw of the functional approach without recharacterization* – The application of the functional approach without recharacterization to retention of title inherently means that the term retention of title continues to be used, while simultaneously equivalent legal outcomes for retention of title and its functional equivalent mechanisms (i.e. acquisition security rights) are pursued. As a result, the term retention of title in a framework with the functional approach without recharacterization continues to cause confusion, since the retention of title creditor is treated less like a full owner and more like the holder of an acquisition security right. This issue can only be avoided by either fully embracing the functional approach with recharacterization or returning to a non-functional system in which the term retention of title truly refers to a title-based security mechanism that is separate from the security rights with a limited proprietary interest in movable goods.

291. *Recharacterization as solution to the classification issues* – Evidently, this debate concerning the classification of retention of title is avoided in *Article 9 UCC* and the *UNCITRAL unitary approach*, where an explicit choice is made to recharacterize retention of title to a PMSI or acquisition security right. In these frameworks, the classification of former retention of title is clear and leaves no room for debate.

Following this approach, in the upcoming Book 9 of the Civil Code retention of title could be recharacterized to an acquisition security right with the following definition:

> *An acquisition security right is every proprietary interest that the creditor retains or obtains in a movable good, which is being acquired by the debtor, to guarantee credit granted by the creditor to the debtor for the acquisition of the movable good.*

In that case the minority opinion can still make the argument that they would have prefered an alignment of retention of title with ownership instead of a recharacterization as an acquisition security right, but they would not be able to undermine the legislator's intention as is the case now.

Similarly, the recharacterization of retention of title can be used as an opportunity to recharacterize the pledge to a more general security right in movable goods. This would align with the approaches in the other frameworks with the functional approach with recharacterization, in which old terminology, such as the pledge, right of retention of title of possession and transfer of title, are abandoned and replaced by an overarching concept of security right in movable goods. The broad definition of this security right would not only encompass the current security rights in movable goods in the Security Rights Act, but could also include some of the legislative liens in the Mortgage Act, such as the lien of the unpaid landlord[1284], the lien for costs made for the preservation of a movable good[1285], and the lien of the carrier.[1286] However, the inclusion of these liens under the definition of security rights would mean that the legislator is open to move towards a system where these preferences are contractually agreed upon instead of being granted automatically by law.

Furthermore, the introduction of a general term of security rights would not only better align with the actual title of the Security Rights Act, but would also make it easier to introduce uniform rules for *all* security rights in movable goods and allow some specific rules for acquisition security rights. Following this approach, a suitable definition for the general category security right in a movable good would be

> *Security rights are all proprietary interests in movable goods that guarantee payment or performance of an obligation between the security right holder and debtor.*

292. *Arguments in favor of the functional approach with recharacterization in the classification debate* – First, this approach would make it easier to include finance leasing in the scope of retention of title.[1287] Second, it would place acquisition credit that is provided by a financier on the same footing as acquisition credit provided by a seller or supplier. Third, this classification would make it clear that retention of title should be treated as other security rights, such as the non-possessory pledge, while leaving room for special treatment specifically for acquisition financing, such as super-priority. Finally, the explicit recharacterization makes it very clear to creditors what they can expect when vesting such an interest. Presumably, such changes were politically too far reaching, leaving us with a retention of title that is stuck between its old and

1284 Art. 20, 1° Mortgage Act.
1285 Art. 20, 4° Mortgage Act.
1286 Art. 20, 7° Mortgage Act.
1287 See *infra* no. 299 *et seq.*

new regime. However, the upcoming Book 9 on secured transactions in the new Civil Code offers a new opportunity to get it right and to clearly classify and characterize retention of title from a functional perspective.

293. *Return to an explicit non-functional classification of retention of title* – Finally, the drafters could return to the system that existed prior to the introduction of the Security Rights Act and still exists in *Germany*: retention of title as an informal part of the security rights in movable goods, but with a clear separation between retention of title and the other security rights and adherence to the title-based nature of retention of title. This approach ensures that parties can rely on the fact that the term retention of title means what it suggests: the creditor has retained title to the encumbered good and is protected as an owner. However, the recognition of the use of title as a form of security can increase tension with the other security rights and secured creditors that cannot make use of title to guarantee credit and cannot enjoy the privileges associated with retaining title. This is less of a problem in *Germany* that has more of a history of title-based security mechanisms and no significant pledge or other security right-based framework. However, in Belgium, the return to an explicit classification of retention of title as title-based mechanism separate from the other security rights could increase the tension between title- and non-title-based creditors and disrupt the coherence of the secured transactions law.

SECTION 2 – SCOPE OF THE SECURITY RIGHTS ACT

294. *Retention of title in more than simple sale transactions?* – The idea to apply retention of title provisions to other transactions, such as mixed transactions and finance leasing is not new, nor uncontested. The following sections describe and compare whether and to what extent the functional approach in the Security Rights Act changes the scope of retention of title and what this means for retention of title creditors. More specifically, I examine the inclusion of mixed transactions (1.) and finance leasing (2.) in the Security Rights Act.

1. INCLUSION OF MIXED TRANSACTIONS – HORIZONTAL EXTENSION OF RETENTION OF TITLE

295. *Irrelevance of the type of transaction in which title is retained* – The Security Rights Act explicitly acknowledges the retention of title creditor's right to revendicate regardless of the transaction in which the retention of title clause

is included.[1288] This is a change from the situation prior to the Security Rights Act, where retention of title outside of pure sale agreements was not accepted.[1289]

In the Security Rights Act, the legislator was intent on making sure that a retention of title clause would not be rejected purely because of the type of agreement in which it was included.[1290] This interpretation aligns with the French Supreme Court case that inspired the legislator's choice to expand the scope of article 69 SRA.[1291] This view is echoed by most authors that agree that the retention of title and the right to revendicate should not be rejected because title was retained in something other than a pure sale agreement.[1292]

296. *Mixed transactions and the horizontal extension of retention of title* – The extension of retention of title to other agreements than sales brought the debate concerning the horizontal extension of retention of title again to the forefront. With the explicit recognition of retention of title in agreements that include sale, but also installation or maintenance of the encumbered good, it seems possible for retention of title to guarantee other claims, such as the cost of installation or maintenance.[1293] This view is confirmed in doctrine which argues that title can be retained for the purchase price and the costs directly associated with the sale, such as packaging costs, delivery costs, taxes and interests.[1294] However most

1288 Art. 69, sec. 3 SRA.

1289 Ghent 10 November 2003, *TBH* 2004, 405. The doctrinal opinions on this issue varied. *Pro:* E. DIRIX, 'Zekerheden, eigendomsvoorbehoud en rangregeling' in H. BRAECKMANS, H. COUSY, E. DIRIX, B. TILLEMAN and M. VANMEENEN (eds.), *Curatoren en vereffenaars: actuele ontwikkelingen*, (Antwerp: Intersentia, 2006), (519) 583; E. DIRIX, 'Art. 101 Faillissementswet' in E. DIRIX, P. FRANCOIS and M. TISON (eds.), *Voorrechten en hypotheken – Artikelsgewijze commentaar met overzicht van rechtspraak en rechtsleer*, (Mechelen: Kluwer, 2011), 7. See also, Fr. Cass. 29 May 2001, (2001) R.T.D. Civ., 930. *Contra*: V. SAGAERT, 'Het eigendomsvoorbehoud als volwaardig zekerheidsinstrument' in *Insolventierecht – XXXI Postuniversitaire Cyclus Willy Delva 2004–05*, (Mechelen: Kluwer, 2006), (191) 193.

1290 Wetsontwerp van 4 december 2012 tot wijziging van het Burgerlijk Wetboek wat de zakelijke zekerheden op roerende goederen betreft en tot opheffing van diverse bepalingen ter zake – amendement, *Parl. St.* Kamer 2012–13, no. 2463/003, 5–6; Wetsontwerp tot wijziging van het Burgerlijk Wetboek wat de zakelijke zekerheden op roerende goederen betreft en tot opheffing van diverse bepalingen ter zake, *Parl.St.* Kamer 2012–2013, no. 2463/005, 31–32.

1291 Fr. Cass. 29 May 2001, (2001) R. T. D. Civ., 930.

1292 R. JANSEN, 'Eigendomsvoorbehoud' in J. BAECK and M. KRUITHOF (eds.), *Het nieuwe zekerheidsrecht*, (Antwerpen: Intersentia, 2014), (139) 147; V. SAGAERT, 'Het eigendomsvoorbehoud (en retentierecht) onder de Pandwet' in M. E. STORME (ed.), *Roerende zekerheden na de Pandwet*, (Antwerpen: Intersentia, 2017), (29) 37; I. DURANT, 'Le droit de rétention et la réserve de propriété, deux sûretés réelles mobilières à part entière' in F. GEORGES (ed.), *Insolvabilité et garanties*, (Brussels: Larcier, 2014), (34) 75; A. APERS and D. GRUYAERT, 'Eigendomsvoorbehoud en onroerende incorporatie volgens de nieuwe pandwet: welk nieuws onder de zon?', (2015) 1 TPR, (83) 93.

1293 D. GRUYAERT, 'Het kredieteigendomsvoorbehoud', 4 (2016) TPR, (1205) 1214.

1294 V. SAGAERT and J. DEL CORRAL, "Eigendomsvoorbehoud" in *Algemene praktische rechtsverzameling*, (Mechelen: Kluwer, 2015), 67; D. GRUYAERT, 'Het kredieteigendomsvoorbehoud', 4 (2016) TPR, (1205) 1214.

authors also agree that retention of title cannot be used to guarantee continuing costs between the retention of title creditor and debtor, such as service or maintenance costs.[1295]

Additionally, the classification of retention of title as a security right in movable goods via the functional approach creates the impression that like the other security rights in movable goods, such as the pledge[1296], retention of title can be vested for all types of debts and not only the purchase price. Nevertheless, the consensus seems to be that retention of title cannot be used to guarantee all existing claims between the retention of title creditor and debtor[1297] (i.e. an all-debts clause)[1298], since this would amount to the illicit creation of a transfer of title agreement. However, retention of title for the purchase price and the installation cost of equipment would likely not be opposed, since this could be considered as a cost directly associated with the sale of the good similar to the delivery cost. Furthermore, retaining title for the installation cost is unlikely to result in a situation where the debtor has already paid off the good, but title remains indefinitely in the hands of the creditor due to ongoing costs between them.

297. *Limitation of retention of title to the purchase price and the functional approach* – At first glance, one could presume that the limitation on the horizontal extension of retention of title is not in line with the functional approach. Pledges can be vested for any and all debts between a creditor and debtor and given the application of the functional approach in the Security Rights Act, one would assume that this should also be possible for retention of title. However, the application of the functional approach to retention of title does not necessarily mean that retention of title can be vested for or extended to any and all claims between a creditor and his debtor, like the pledge. The other selected frameworks that apply the functional approach to retention of title do not state that PMSIs (*Article 9 UCC*)[1299], acquisition security rights, retention of title, finance leases (*the UNCITRAL Guide and Model Law*)[1300] or acquisition financing devices (*DCFR*)[1301] can be vested for any claim between the creditor and debtor. On the contrary, the term PMSI, acquisition security

1295 V. SAGAERT and J. DEL CORRAL, "Eigendomsvoorbehoud" in *Algemene praktische rechtsverzameling*, (Mechelen: Kluwer, 2015), 67.

1296 The pledge can be vested for all sorts of debts as long as there is a maximum amount and the debt is sufficiently determined (art. 10 SRA). See, V. SAGAERT, 'Het eigendomsvoorbehoud (en retentierecht) onder de Pandwet' in M. E. STORME (ed.), *Roerende zekerheden na de Pandwet*, (Antwerpen: Intersentia, 2017), (29) 38.

1297 D. GRUYAERT, 'Het kredieteigendomsvoorbehoud', 4 (2016) TPR, (1205) 1210.

1298 The term all-debts-clause comes from the United Kingdom, where this has been more generally accepted, see *Armour / Thyssen Edelstahlwerke AG* (1991) 2 AC (339) 347.

1299 See *supra* no. 48.

1300 See *supra* no. 123.

1301 See *supra* no. 167.

right or acquisition financing device is limited to secured transactions that guarantee acquisition credit, such as the purchase price of a movable good (i.e. retention of title, finance leases) or specific credit for the acquisition of that good (i.e. PMSIs and acquisition security rights). Moreover, for debts beyond the immediate acquisition credit, such as installation or service costs, it is unclear whether the secured creditor would be allowed to rely on his status as PMSI, acquisition creditor or acquisition financing device. Only *Article 9 UCC* offers some case law and doctrine with an interpretation on what should be considered a purchase money obligation. Mainly this refers to case law where the courts had to determine whether the provided credit was actually used to acquire the encumbered good.[1302] The *UNCITRAL Guide, Model Law* and *DCFR* only mention that acquisition security rights or acquisition financing devices, respectively, guarantee the outstanding purchase price or credit that made the acquisition possible. They do not mention whether the position of acquisition creditor can be extended to other debts between the debtor and acquisition creditor, even those directly associated with the acquisition of the good. What's more, the limitation of PMSIs, acquisition security rights and acquisition financing devices to the outstanding purchase price or credit that directly allowed the acquisition of the encumbered good is actually a consequence of the functional approach. The characterization of a security mechanism as PMSI, acquisition security right or acquisition financing is linked to the acquisition credit this mechanism guarantees and the function it performs. Therefore, allowing acquisition creditors to horizontally extend their position as acquisition creditor to other debts that have nothing to do with the acquisition of the encumbered good would undermine the functional basis upon which this status is assigned.

To further prove the disconnect between horizontal extension and the functional approach, in *Germany* the case law takes the most lenient approach to horizontally extending retention of title to other debts. The BGH sees no issue with the contractual horizontal extension of retention of title for all debts that exist between the retention of title creditor and debtor (*Kontokorrentvorbehalt*).[1303] However, the BGH does draw the line at retaining title for all debts between the retention of title debtor, his retention of title creditor and all the associated companies (*Konzernvorbehalt*).[1304] Not because transfer of title mechanisms are not allowed, but mainly because parties should explicitly agree to such a transaction. As a result, the jurisdiction that does not apply the functional approach to retention of title allows for the most flexibility with regards to the horizontal extension of retention of title.

[1302] See *supra* no. 49.
[1303] See *supra* no. 221.
[1304] See *supra* no. 221.

298. *Conclusion* – In the Security Rights Act retention of title is effective regardless of the type of agreement in which it is included, but can still only be vested for the purchase price of the encumbered good and some of the directly associated costs. The limitation of retention of title to the acquisition credit and potentially the directly associated costs can be seen as a result of the functional approach in order to keep the term retention of title, PMSI, acquisition security right, finance lease or acquisition financing device and its specific protection limited to transactions that guarantee acquisition credit. Therefore, the fact that retention of title in the Security Rights Act can only guarantee acquisition credit (i.e. the purchase price) and not all debts between the retention of title creditor and debtor, like the pledge, does not mean that the functional approach is incorrectly applied.

2. INCLUSION OF FINANCE LEASING

299. *Definition of finance leasing* – Finance leasing is a three party transaction in which the lessee gives instructions to the lessor to purchase a certain good from a manufacturer or supplier. The lessor then leases or rents the good to the lessee for a certain amount of time. During this time the lessee makes regular payments to the lessor. At the end of the leasing agreement the lessee usually has the option to purchase the leased good.[1305] At the moment, finance leasing is only codified in the Royal Decree regarding finance lease corporations of 1967.[1306] This statute lists some characteristics of finance leasing that are used to determine companies that engage in finance leasing. However, this list of characteristics cannot be considered as a legal definition of finance leasing, nor does it classify finance leasing as a specific transaction within the Civil Code.[1307] This lack of legislative guidance has led to ongoing debates among scholars as to how finance lease agreements should be formally classified. Most authors agree

1305 F. 'T KINT, *Sûretés et principes généraux du droit de poursuite des créanciers*, (Brussels: Larcier, 2004), 256; K. VANHOVE, 'Leasing: een complexe bijzondere overeenkomst' in P. BESELAERE and others (eds.), *Handboek leasing*, (Brugge: Die Keure, 2007), (43) 46–47; B. KOHL, 'Le leasing financier en Belgique', (2011) 16 Unif L Rev, (45) 49.

1306 KB 10 november 1967 tot regeling van het juridisch statuut der ondernemingen gespecialiseerd in financieringshuur, *BS* 14 november 1967, 11741.

1307 I. VEROUGSTRAETE, 'Privaatrechtelijke aspecten van finance leasing in België', (1973) 10 TPR, (741) 746–747; L. DE KEYSER, 'Roerende leasing en eigendomsrevindicatie' [1983] TPR, (443) 445 and 554; J. H. HERBOTS, 'Réflexions à propos de la nature du leasing, avant-contrat innomé, typique et fiduciaire (note under Cass. 17 june 1993)', (1996) RCJB, (234) 237; K. TROCH, E. WYMEERSCH and M. DAMBRE, 'Overzicht van rechtspraak – Krediet ', (1999) 4 TPR, (1789) 1815; K. VANHOVE, 'Leasing: een complexe bijzondere overeenkomst' in P. BESELAERE and others (eds.), *Handboek leasing*, (Brugge: Die Keure, 2007), (43) 44–45; F. BRUYNS, *Le location – financement ou leasing mobilier – quarante ans de jurisprudence*, (Brussels: Larcier, 2008), 8; B. KOHL, 'Le leasing financier en Belgique', (2011) 16 Unif L Rev, (45) 56.

that finance leasing cannot be equated with a sale on credit with retention of title, since the debtor does not automatically become owner when he pays the last instalment.[1308] However, there is no consensus on whether finance leases should be classified as a type of rental[1309] or a *sui generis* agreement.[1310] The Supreme Court ruled on this issue in 1993[1311], but the interpretations of this decision vary. Some scholars see the decision as a confirmation that finance leasing should be brought under the scope of rental agreements[1312], whereas others see in the Court's reasoning a confirmation of the *sui generis* nature of finance leasing.[1313] Nevertheless, the debate concerning the classification of the finance lease agreement, the security function of finance leasing is not contested.[1314]

1308 P. DEHAN and L. VINCENT, 'La nature du contrat de "leasing"', [1967] RCJB, (231) 241; I. VEROUGSTRAETE, 'Privaatrechtelijke aspecten van finance leasing in België', (1973) 10 TPR, (741) 748–749; Y. MERCHIERS, 'Enkele nieuwe handelsovereenkomsten', (1979) TPR, (721) 728; H. VANDENBERGHE, 'Eigendomsvoorbehoud bij leasing', (1980–81) 44 RW, (2761) 2766; J. H. HERBOTS, 'Réflexions à propos de la nature du leasing, avant-contrat innomé, typique et fiduciaire (note under Cass. 17 june 1993)', (1996) RCJB, (234) 242; K. VANHOVE, 'Leasing: een complexe bijzondere overeenkomst' in P. BESELAERE and others (eds.), *Handboek leasing*, (Brugge: Die Keure, 2007), (43) 58–59.

1309 I. VEROUGSTRAETE, 'Privaatrechtelijke aspecten van finance leasing in België', (1973) 10 TPR, (741) 746; K. TROCH, E. WYMEERSCH and M. DAMBRE, 'Overzicht van rechtspraak – Krediet ', (1999) 4 TPR, (1789) 1817–1818; H. LIBERT and J. BEKAERT, 'Leasing van roerende goederen' in E. DIRIX and A. VAN OEVELEN (eds.), *Bijzondere overeenkomsten Artikelsgewijze commentaar met overzicht van rechtspraak en rechtsleer*, (Mechelen: Kluwer, loosel.), 7.

1310 P. DEHAN and L. VINCENT, 'La nature du contrat de "leasing"', [1967] RCJB, (231) 243; L. DE KEYSER, 'Onbenoemde overeenkomsten en roerende leasing' in H. HERBOTS (ed.), *Bijzondere overeenkomsten*, (Antwerp: Kluwer, 1980), (439) 454–455; A. DE CALUWE and G. BOGAERT, 'Eigendomsrecht bij leasing', (1981–82) 32 RW, (2129) 2130; L. DE KEYSER, 'Roerende leasing en eigendomsrevindicatie' [1983] TPR, (443) 448; M. VAN WUYTSWINKEL, 'Le leasing mobilier: contrat complexe ou autonome', (1992) Rev. Rég. Dr., (199), 201–202; L. VAN DEN HOLE, 'De roerende leasing – de positie van de lessor bij faillissement', (1996) 40 DAOR, (25) 39–40; F. BRUYNS, 'Chronique de jurisprudence – La location-financement ou leasing mobilier (1999–2003)', (2004) JT, (605) 606; F. BRUYNS, *Le location – financement ou leasing mobilier – quarante ans de jurisprudence*, (Brussels: Larcier, 2008), 35; K. VANHOVE, 'Leasing: een complexe bijzondere overeenkomst' in P. BESELAERE and others (eds.), *Handboek leasing*, (Brugge: Die Keure, 2007), (43) 48–49; B. KOHL, 'Le leasing financier en Belgique', (2011) 16 Unif L Rev, (45) 58; F. BRUYNS and S. CLAEYS, 'Het eigendomsrecht van de leasinggever', (2016) 3 DAOR, (6) 14. For more on *sui generis* agreements in general, see L. DE KEYSER, 'Onbenoemde overeenkomsten en roerende leasing' in H. HERBOTS (ed.), *Bijzondere overeenkomsten*, (Antwerp: Kluwer, 1980), (439) 439–445.

1311 Cass. 17 juni 1993, no. 9405, (1993) Arr. Cass., 601.

1312 M. E. STORME, 'De wijde mantel van de huurovereenkomst biedt ook plaats aan zuivere financieringshuur zonder vrijwaring door de lessor (note under Cass. 17 june 1993)', (1993) R. Cass, (179) 179.

1313 J. H. HERBOTS, 'Réflexions à propos de la nature du leasing, avant-contrat innomé, typique et fiduciaire (note under Cass. 17 june 1993)', (1996) RCJB, (234) 244 *et seq.*

1314 H. VANDENBERGHE, 'Eigendomsvoorbehoud bij leasing', (1980–81) RW, (2761) 2766; L. DE KEYSER, 'Roerende leasing en eigendomsrevindicatie' [1983] TPR, (443) 445; L. DE KEYSER, 'Eigendomsrecht en nieuwe contractvormen: leasing, factoring en franchising', (1983–84) 47 RW, (2407) 2411; L. SIMONT, 'Essai de classification des sûretés

The lessor has financed the acquisition of the movable good and to guarantee this investment the lessor retains title to this good for the duration of the lease agreement. Furthermore, the lessor has no real interest in the goods and usually has no intention in maintaining ownership at the end of the lease agreement.[1315] In the event that the lessee does not lift the purchase option at the end of the lease agreement for the residual price, the lessor would most likely unload the goods as quickly as possible to another potential buyer.[1316] Consequently, the lessor does not retain title because he wants to remain owner of the good, but merely retains title to protect himself in the event the debtor defaults.

300. *Finance leasing prior to the Security Rights Act* – Before the Security Rights Act, only finance leasing was considered effective prior to and during *all* collective insolvency proceedings.[1317] The automatic third-party effectiveness of finance leasing was partly due to the economic importance of the leasing industry.[1318] Denying lessors the ability to rely on their retained ownership of the

– issues de la pratique et problèmes juridiques qu'elles posent' in A. BRUYNEEL and A. M. STRANART (eds.), *Les sûretés: sûretés traditionnelles, réelles et personnelles, en droit français et en droit belge, sûretés issues de la pratique, droit international privé: colloque de Bruxelles des 20 et 21 octobre 1983*, (Paris: Feduci, 1984), (277) 285; H. BRAECKMANS, 'Bankrekeningen, betaal- en kredietverrichtingen', in *Beginselen van Belgisch Privaatrecht*, XIII, Deel 1, Ondernemingsrecht, Vol. B, Brussel, Story-Scientia, 1989, (545) 634; M. VAN WUYTSWINKEL, 'Le leasing mobilier: contrat complexe ou autonome', (1992) Rev. Rég. Dr., (199), 202; J. H. HERBOTS, 'Réflexions à propos de la nature du leasing, avant-contrat innomé, typique et fiduciaire (note under Cass. 17 june 1993)', (1996) RCJB, (234) 256–257; A. VAN OEVELEN, 'De zekerheidsfunctie van het eigendomsrecht bij leasing', *Eigendom/ Propriété*, (Brugge: Die Keure,1996), 21; L. VAN DEN HOLE, 'De roerende leasing – de positie van de lessor bij faillissement', (1996) 40 DAOR, (25) 51; E. DIRIX and R. DE CORTE, 'Zekerheidsrechten', in *Beginselen van Belgisch privaatrecht*, (Mechelen: Kluwer, 2006), 430; D. GRUYAERT, *Exclusiviteit van het eigendomsrecht*, (Antwerp: Intersentia, 2016), 534 and 540; S. BAEYENS, 'De zekerheidsfunctie van het eigendomsrecht van de leasinggever als grondslag voor het verrijkingsverbod bij leasing (note under Cass. 19 december 2019)', (2020) 2 RW, (56) 59.

1315 L. DE KEYSER, 'Eigendomsrecht en nieuwe contractvormen: leasing, factoring en franchising', (1983–84) 47 RW (2407) 2411; E. DIRIX and R. DE CORTE, 'Zekerheidsrechten' in *Beginselen van Belgisch privaatrecht*, (5th edn., Mechelen: Wolters Kluwer, 2006), 430; D. GRUYAERT, *Exclusiviteit van het eigendomsrecht*, (Antwerp: Intersentia, 2016), 541.

1316 F. 'T KINT, *Sûretés et principes généraux du droit de poursuite des créanciers*, (Brussels: Larcier, 2004), 257; E. DIRIX, 'Functionele analyse van zekerheidsrechten' in W. PINTENS and others (eds.), *Vigilantibus ius scriptum: feestbundel voor Hugo Vandenberghe*, (Brugge: Die Keure, 2007), (119) 120; D. GRUYAERT, *Exclusiviteit van het eigendomsrecht*, (Antwerp: Intersentia, 2016), 541.

1317 Cass. 17 June 1993, (1994–95) RW, (1435) 1435; J. H. HERBOTS, 'Réflexions à propos de la nature du leasing, avant-contrat innomé, typique et fiduciaire (note under Cass. 17 june 1993)', (1996) RCJB, (234) 241–243; E. DIRIX, 'Nieuwe overeenkomsten tot zekerheid', (1988) 2 TPR, (323) 340; K. VANHOVE, 'Leasing: een complexe bijzondere overeenkomst' in P. BESELAERE OL, B. TILLEMAN and A. VERBEKE (eds.), *Handboek leasing*, (Brugge: Die Keure, 2007) (41) 46; E. DIRIX, 'Het lot van de realisatiewaarde bij beëindiging van de leasingovereenkomst', (1999–2000) 63 RW, (368) 368; F. BRUYNS and S. CLAEYS, 'Het eigendomsrecht van de leasinggever', (2016) 3 DAOR, (6) 13.

1318 H. VANDENBERGHE, 'Eigendomsvoorbehoud bij leasing', (1980–81) RW, (2761) 2763.

leased goods would jeopardize a thriving part of the economy.[1319] Furthermore, third parties were expected to know that in a finance lease title is retained to guarantee an outstanding claim, because of the inherent nature of the retention of title to finance leasing.[1320] Finance leasing implies that the lessor retains title in order to guarantee his investment so third parties cannot claim to be unaware of this. Finally, it was purported that finance leases serve other purposes than guaranteeing claims, such as insolvency protection and debt collection.[1321] Therefore, it was not merely another type of security right outside the *numerus clausus* principle[1322], but an effective financial transaction that, among other things, guaranteed the outstanding claim through retaining title.[1323] Based on these arguments the third-party effectiveness of retention of title in finance lease agreements during collective insolvency proceedings was accepted despite the fact that finance lease agreements were also not made public in any way.[1324]

301. *Absence of finance leasing in the Security Rights Act* – The drafters seem to consider retention of title mostly as a mechanism for sale agreements, even though the security function of finance leasing and its inherent retention of title to guarantee acquisition credit has been generally acknowledged.[1325] Nevertheless, the different provisions repeatedly refer to the *seller*, the goods *sold* under retention of title, the *purchase* price and the *buyer*.[1326] Only in doctrine do we find reference to the functional approach to make the case that financial leasing is a form of retention of title and falls within the scope of the Security

1319 L. DE KEYSER, 'Roerende leasing en eigendomsrevindicatie' [1983] TPR, (443) 455.

1320 E. DIRIX, 'Nieuwe overeenkomsten tot zekerheid', (1988) 2 TPR, (323) 341.

1321 A. VERBEKE, 'Eigendomsoverdracht tot zekerheid – een genuanceerd beeld' in J. HERBOTS and D. PHILIPPE (eds.), *De trust en de fiduciaire overeenkomst*, (Brussels: Bruylant,1997), (327) 332–333.

1322 This principle prevents parties from contractually creating more security rights than are provided for in the law. For more specifically on the *numerus clausus*-principle, see B. AKKERMANS, *The principles of numerus clausus in European property law*, (Antwerp: Intersentia, 2008), 6–7.

1323 F. BRUYNS and S. CLAEYS, 'Het eigendomsrecht van de leasinggever', (2016) 3 DAOR, (6) 12.

1324 A ministerial decree obligated lessors to identify their leased goods with a tag (art. 2, d ministerieel besluit van 23 februari 1968 tot bepaling van de voorwaarden tot erkenning van de ondernemingen gespecialiseerd in financieringshuur, en waarvan het juridisch statuut door het koninklijk besluit nr. 55 van 10 november 1967 geregeld wordt, *BS* 6 maart 1968, 2212). However, the absence of these tags would not result in the ineffectiveness of the lease agreement with retention of title, but in the loss of the lessor's accreditation to operate as a leasing corporation (Cass. 27 November 1981, (1981–82) RW, (2142) 2151). This decree was later replaced by a new ministerial decree. In the later version there is no mention of placing tags on the leased goods as a requirement to maintain your accreditation as leasing corporation. See also, E. DIRIX and R. DE CORTE, 'Zekerheidsrechten' in *Beginselen van Belgisch privaatrecht*, (5th edn., Mechelen: Wolters Kluwer, 2006), 432; E. DIRIX, 'Nieuwe overeenkomsten tot zekerheid', (1988) 2 TPR, (323) 340.

1325 Cass. 8 november 2002, Arr. Cass. 2002, 2440; Gent 9 January 2006, (2006–07) 33 RW, (1366) 1367; Cass. 19 december 2019, no. C.19.0167.N, (2020–21) 2 RW, 56.

1326 See articles 69–72 Security Rights Act.

Rights Act. For example, DIRIX urges courts to give a functional interpretation to retention of title in the Security Rights Act and include finance leasing within its scope.[1327] Furthermore, the recognition of retention of title regardless of the type of agreement in which it is included could suggest that retention of title in (finance) lease agreements are valid and recognized.[1328]

The choice to only implicitly include finance leasing in the scope of the Security Rights Act is strange. Since the enactment of the Security Rights Act there no longer is a reason from a secured transactions law and insolvency law perspective to distinguish financial leasing from the term retention of title. In the Security Rights Act, retention of title in sale agreements are explicitly made effective against third parties and the integration of retention of title in the former Civil Code ensures its third-party effectiveness in all insolvency proceedings.[1329] In addition, case law already limited the enforcement of leasing via the principle of unjust enrichment and both retention of title and leasing are excluded from notification requirements for their third-party effectiveness[1330], so the inclusion of finance leasing in the Security Rights Act would not result in new limitations on lessors. Moreover, if leasing would also be governed by the Security Rights Act, finance lessors would enjoy the same protection against the negative effects of incorporation as sellers with a retention of title.[1331] Therefore, financial lessors would not be disadvantaged and could potentially even benefit from inclusion in the Security Rights Act.

302. *Debate concerning the inclusion of finance leasing in the scope of the Security Rights Act* – Not everyone agrees with the inclusion of leases in the Security Rights Act as a security right in movable goods. According to BRUYNS and CLAEYS, leasing does not provide the lessor with a security right, since this would go against the *numerus clausus* principle.[1332] Since leasing is not recognized by law as a security or other property right, it cannot be given the same protection as recognized security rights in movable goods, such as the pledge or retention of title in sale agreements.[1333] Consequently, the retained title

1327 E. DIRIX, 'De nieuwe Pandwet: doelstellingen en uitgangspunten' in M. E. STORME (ed.), *Roerende zekerheden na de Pandwet*, (Antwerpen: Intersentia, 2017), (1) 16.

1328 See *supra* no. 295.

1329 R. JANSEN, 'Eigendomsvoorbehoud' in J. BAECK and M. KRUITHOF (eds.), *Het nieuwe zekerheidsrecht*, (Antwerpen: Intersentia, 2014), (139) 147; V. SAGAERT, 'Het eigendomsvoorbehoud (en retentierecht) onder de Pandwet' in M. E. STORME (ed.), *Roerende zekerheden na de Pandwet*, (Antwerpen: Intersentia, 2017), (29) 35; I. DURANT, 'Le droit de rétention et la réserve de propriété, deux sûretés réelles mobilières à part entière' in F. GEORGES (ed.), *Insolvabilité et garanties*, (Brussels: Larcier,2014), (34) 82.

1330 See *infra* no. 360 *et seq.*

1331 See, *infra* no. 340.

1332 F. BRUYNS and S. CLAEYS, 'Het eigendomsrecht van de leasinggever', (2016) 3 DAOR, (6) 10–12.

1333 F. BRUYNS and S. CLAEYS, 'Het eigendomsrecht van de leasinggever', (2016) 3 DAOR, (6) 10–12.

via leasing should be considered as traditional full ownership in the hands of the lessor, much like a landlord's or renter's full ownership[1334] and not ownership for the purposes of guaranteeing a claim. By making this distinction, the title in the lessor's hands is still effective against third parties during collective insolvency proceedings without violating the *numerus clausus* principle and is not submitted to the principles that govern security rights. This interpretation is similar to the approach in *Germany*, where leasing is also still considered a form of rent and not a security right or retention of title.[1335]

303. *Solutions to the leasing issue in the Security Rights Act* – The uncertainty concerning the inclusion of finance leasing in the scope of the Security Rights Act could have been avoided, if the legislator more explicitly included leasing in the security right framework. For example, the legislator could have also mentioned some forms of leasing as a type of retention of title in the Security Rights Act based on their functional similarity with retention of title. This would have effectively forestalled the *numerus clausus* argument against the recognition of leasing as a security right. Once leasing is recognized by secured transactions law, it is added to the limited number of security rights and can be classified and enforced as a security right in movable goods. Furthermore, it would fit neatly with the functional approach of the Security Rights Act which aims to create equivalent legal outcomes for functionally similar mechanisms. Given the functional similarity between retention of title in sale agreements and finance leases for security purposes, the inclusion of finance leasing in the Security Rights Act would fit naturally with this approach.

This is the approach taken in *Article 9 UCC*[1336], *the UNCITRAL Guide and Model Law*[1337] and *DCFR*.[1338] Each of these frameworks explicitly include some form of leasing in the scope of their regime. However, the inclusion of finance leasing in the scope of the Security Rights Act would entail more than simply bringing finance leasing under the term retention of title. In the other functional frameworks, the inclusion of leasing is limited to lease agreements that perform the same function as retention of title in sale agreements. This means that leases for security purposes have to be distinguished from non-security leases. These distinctions are not always easy, as exemplified by *Article 9 UCC* where numerous provisions are dedicated to trying to delineate the very subtle distinction between true or operational leases and leases for security purposes.[1339] However,

1334 See also A. DE CALUWE and G. BOGAERT who emphasize that the lessor remains full owner of the leased good and does not actually retain title like a seller with a retention of title in a sale on credit, A. DE CALUWE and G. BOGAERT, 'Eigendomsrecht bij leasing', (1981–82) 32 RW, (2129) 2129.

1335 See *supra* no. 216.

1336 See *supra* no. 50 *et seq.*

1337 See *supra* no. 124–125.

1338 See *supra* no. 163 *et seq.*

1339 See *supra* no. 52 *et seq.*

in these frameworks the distinction between leases for security purposes and non-security leases is more relevant, since the recharacterization of a lease to a security interests or right in *Article 9 UCC*[1340], the *UNCITRAL Guide and Model Law*[1341] or *DCFR*[1342] in most cases comes with a notification requirement for third-party effectiveness. Consequently, lessors are likely to try to come up with more elaborate schemes to avoid a classification as a security interest to avoid the notification requirement. This is less of an issue in the Security Rights Act, since here the drafters opted to not subject retention of title to a registration requirement. Moreover, under the Security Rights Act the lessor may actually benefit from a classification as retention of title, since it will give him extensive tracing rights in the hands of the debtor or even third-party transferee.[1343]

Alternatively, the Belgian legislator could have opted to recharacterize retention of title as an acquisition security right[1344], that guarantees the outstanding claim for the acquisition of the encumbered good between the creditor and debtor. This would take retention of title as a security mechanism out of a specific sale context and make it clear that any agreement in which a proprietary interest is obtained or retained to guarantee acquisition credit would be considered an acquisition security right and would be governed by the rules and principles governing security rights. On the one hand, this approach is preferable since it casts a wide net and would include all transactions that fit this description. On the other hand, a more generic description could again set off debates among scholars and practitioners whether leasing really fits this description, especially since it is still contested how finance leasing should be formally classified as a transaction. "Anti-inclusion scholars" could focus on the rental or *sui generis* characteristics of leasing to make a claim that the retention of title is not the essential component of finance leasing and could therefore still be excluded from a more general definition of retention of title.

304. *Conclusion and recommendation concerning finance leasing* – The treatment or classification of finance leasing has not explicitly altered following the enactment of the Security Rights Act. The lack of explicit inclusion of finance leasing in the scope of the Security Rights Act runs counter to the application of the functional approach. Belgian case law and doctrine have long acknowledged that certain leases serve a security purpose and are functionally similar to sale agreements with retention of title. Consequently, the Security Rights Act, with its explicit reference to the functional approach as cornerstone, offered the perfect opportunity to explicitly include finance leasing in the Security Rights Act. Nevertheless, the inclusion of leasing in the scope of the Security Rights

1340 See *supra* no. 58.
1341 See *supra* no. 131.
1342 See *supra* no. 176.
1343 See *infra* no. 309.
1344 See *supra* no. 291.

Act is only implicit at best and non-existent at worst, like in *Germany*. For the upcoming Book 9 of the Civil Code on secured transactions a more explicit inclusion of leasing for security purposes is called for. This can be either achieved by explicitly listing leases for security purposes as a type of retention of title, as in the *DCFR* or the *UNCITRAL non-unitary approach*, or by implementing a broadly defined acquisition security right, as in *Article 9 UCC* or the *UNCITRAL unitary approach*, that would also encompass leases for security purposes.

SECTION 3 – CREATION AND THIRD-PARTY EFFECTIVENESS OF RETENTION OF TITLE

305. *No reform concerning the creation and third-party effectiveness of retention of title* – In the Security Rights Act, the rules concerning creation and third-party effectiveness are not unified or extended from the pledge to retention of title or vice versa. Instead, the legislator opted to partially[1345] transplant the provision governing retention of title from the former Bankruptcy Act to the Security Rights Act.

In the following sections, I compare and evaluate the Belgian legislator's choice to maintain minimalistic rules for the creation and third-party effectiveness of retention of title (1.) and the role of registration with respect of the third-party effectiveness of retention of title both in Belgium, the selected jurisdictions and the international instruments (2.).

1. MINIMAL FORMALITIES FOR CREATION AND THIRD-PARTY EFFECTIVENESS OF RETENTION OF TITLE

1.1. Creation

306. *Creation of retention of title before and after the Security Rights Act* – The provision concerning the creation of retention of title in the Security Rights Act[1346] is identical to the provision regarding the creation of retention of title in the former Bankruptcy Act[1347]: the retention of title clause merely has to be added in writing to the agreement prior to delivery of the encumbered good

1345 The part of the provision concerning the creation of retention of title was moved to the Security Rights Act, whereas the part of the provision concerning the enforcement of retention of title during bankruptcy proceedings was moved to the Code on Economic Law (hereafter, CEL).

1346 Art. 69, par. 1 SRA.

1347 Art. 101, par. 2 former Bankruptcy Act.

to be created.[1348] Furthermore, the drafters of the Security Rights Act opted to maintain separate rules for the creation of retention of title and the pledge. The pledge can be created consensually between the two parties[1349], but for evidentiary purposes the encumbered goods, the guaranteed obligations and the maximum amount for which the obligations are guaranteed have to be explicitly mentioned in the pledge agreement.[1350]

The lack of requirements for the creation of retention of title can be explained by the intrinsic nature of the retention of title clause to its underlying agreement. Under the Security Rights Act, retention of title remains closely linked to the transaction which performance it guarantees.[1351] For example, retention of title in a sale agreement can only guarantee the outstanding purchase price (and the costs directly associated with the sale)[1352] and can only encumber the sold collateral. Given that retention of title can only guarantee the performance of this transaction, the sale contract itself already contains all the information regarding the encumbered good (i.e. the sold goods) and the outstanding claim (i.e. the purchase price and its associated costs). Furthermore, since retention of title cannot be extended to guarantee additional claims there is no need to include a maximum amount for which the retained title can be enforced. Conversely, a pledge can be vested for any and all debts between a creditor and debtor. Therefore, the pledge agreement needs to explicate which obligations it guarantees, to what maximum amount and which goods of the debtor's it encumbers.

307. *Comparison of the rules concerning creation* – The creation of retention of title in the Security Rights Act is very similar to the creation of retention of title in *Germany* and retention of ownership devices in the *DCFR* in that they also do not require specific requirements beyond explicitly retaining title in the sale agreement[1353] and a description of the retained asset in the *DCFR*.[1354]

Conversely, *Article 9 UCC* and the *UNCITRAL Guide and Model Law* list explicit information that has to be included in the security right agreement for it be valid between parties. This information is the same for general security interests and PMSIs in *Article 9 UCC*[1355] and security rights and acquisition security rights under the *UNCITRAL unitary approach*.[1356] Since PMSIs

---

1348 Art. 69, par. 1 SRA. The type of document in which the retention of title clause can be included is given a wide interpretation, see explanatory memorandum Belgian Security Rights Act, no. 2463/001, 70.

1349 Art. 2 SRA.

1350 Art. 4 SRA.

1351 V. SAGAERT and J. DEL CORRAL, "Eigendomsvoorbehoud" in *Algemene praktische rechtsverzameling*, (Mechelen: Kluwer, 2015), 67.

1352 See *supra* no. 296–297.

1353 See *supra* no. 223.

1354 See *supra* no. 170.

1355 See *supra* no. 56–57.

1356 See *supra* no. 129.

and acquisition security rights are also security interests and security rights, respectively, it makes sense to have one set of rules for their creation and the formalities required in the (purchase money) security interests or (acquisition) security right agreement. In *Article 9 UCC*, these formalities are quite minimal and only require the description of the encumbered good and a signature from both the creditor and the debtor.[1357] In the *UNCITRAL Guide and Model Law*, the formalities are somewhat more elaborate and include, the identification of the secured creditor and debtor, a description of the secured obligation, description of the encumbered assets and an indication of the maximum amount for which the (acquisition) security is vested.[1358]

Finally, under the *UNCITRAL non-unitary approach*, the rules concerning creation of retention of title and finance leasing have to be so adjusted to match the rules concerning the creation of acquisition security rights.[1359] In practice, it could be that in retention of title or finance lease agreements many of the necessary elements for the creation of an acquisition security rights are already present, so that the rules for creation for these transactions under the *UNCITRAL's non-unitary approach* do not have to be significantly adjusted to achieve equivalent legal outcomes with the rules for creation of acquisition security rights.

308. *Conclusion* – The rules for creating a retention of title have not changed following the integration of retention of title in the Security Rights Act, nor have the rules concerning creation been equated with those for the creation of the pledge. On the one hand, the continuation of the minimal rules for the creation of retention of title makes sense, because in the Security Rights Act retention of title is not recharacterized to an acquisition security right. Consequently, there is not a move towards one set of rules for the creation of (acquisition) security rights with one set of general formalities for the (acquisition) security right agreement. Furthermore, one could argue that retention of title and the pledge in the Security Rights Act do not perform exactly the same function, because retention of title specifically guarantees acquisition credit and the pledge can guarantee any and all debts between a creditor and debtor. Therefore, the application of the functional approach in the Security Rights Act does not necessarily mean that the playing field between retention of title and the pledge must be leveled via the implementation of rules that generate equivalent legal outcomes concerning the creation of retention of title and the pledge. On the other hand, both mechanisms are now classified as security rights in movable goods and in a broad sense they do perform the same function in that they both guarantee credit by obtaining a proprietary interest in a movable good.

1357 See *supra* no. 57.
1358 See *supra* no. 129.
1359 See *supra* no. 130.

The functional similarity in this broad sense could justify the implementation of similar rules for the creation of the pledge and retention of title in order to ensure equivalent legal outcomes between these mechanisms. Moreover, one set of rules for the creation of retention of title and the pledge would certainly simplify the Security Rights Act and would give creditors and debtors one point of reference for the creation of a security right in movable goods. In that case, the introduction of a general category of security rights and acquisition security rights, combined with a recharacterization of retention of title to an acquisition security right, would result in the most coherent and clear approach, since there would only be one set of rules for the creation of all (acquisition) security rights as is the case in *Article 9 UCC* and the *UNCITRAL unitary approach*. This approach is worth considering by the Belgian legislator, when they are drafting the new Book 9 of the Civil Code concerning security rights in movable goods.

1.2. Third-party effectiveness

309. *Absence of notification requirement for third-party effectiveness of retention of title* – The Security Rights Act does not include a uniform regime of notification requirements to achieve third-party effectiveness for all security rights in movable goods. Instead, retention of title is automatically effective against third parties upon its creation in writing.[1360]

310. *Different notification requirements for retention of title and the pledge and the functional approach* – Like with the rules for creation, the difference in notification requirements for retention of title and the pledge in the Security Rights Act does not run counter to the functional approach. The functional approach aims to create equivalent legal outcomes for functionally similar mechanisms. In *Article 9 UCC*[1361], the *UNICTRAL Guide and Model Law*[1362] and the *DCFR*[1363] a choice is made to subject PMSIs or acquisition security rights in movable goods to an extensive notification regime through either registration or dispossession. Following the functional approach, retention of title is then either recharacterized to these mechanisms and subjected to these rules (i.e. *Article 9 UCC* and *UNCITRAL unitary approach*) or the rules for retention of title are so adjusted to match the notification requirements for acquisition security rights (i.e. *DCFR* and *UNCITRAL non-unitary approach*). However, in the Security Rights Act retention of title and the pledge do not specifically perform the same function, since retention of title only guarantees acquisition credit, whereas the pledge can be used to guarantee both acquisition and general

1360 Art. 69 SRA.
1361 See *supra* no. 56.
1362 See *supra* no. 129.
1363 See *supra* no. 173.

credit. Therefore, retention of title and the pledge can be treated differently in the Security Rights Act and still be considered in accordance with the functional approach. Nevertheless, there are advantages connected to the implementation of notification requirements regardless of the functional approach technically allowing a difference in notification requirements for retention of title and the non-possessory pledge.

311. *Arguments in favor of notification requirements for retention of title* – First, the possession of a movable good encumbered with retention of title in the hands of the retention of title debtor has the potential of creating the impression that the retention of title debtor is the owner of the encumbered good and erroneous assessments of the debtor's estate and its encumbrances by third parties (i.e. ostensible ownership issues).[1364] The implementation of notification requirements for retention of title can address the ostensible ownership problems that often plague retention of title mechanisms, as it has in *Article 9 UCC*[1365] and attempts to do via the *UNCITRAL Guide and Model Law*[1366] and the *DCFR*.[1367]

Second, according to Belgian doctrine the notification of third parties of security rights is an essential characteristic of security rights in movable goods.[1368] Consequently, the explicit classification of retention of title as a security right in movable goods provides the perfect opportunity, and one could argue obligation, to implement a notification requirement for retention of title. In the Security Rights Act, notification of third parties of the pledge in tangible goods is achieved via dispossession of the encumbered good[1369] or registration of the security right.[1370] These rules can easily be extended to retention of title. This would not only address the ostensible ownership issues addressed above, but would also create a more coherent and logical notification system for all security rights in movable goods. Furthermore, the implementation of a notification requirement for retention of title does not mean that no exemptions are possible. Like in *Article 9 UCC*[1371], the *UNCITRAL Guide and Model Law*[1372] and the *DCFR*[1373], the Security Rights Act or the new Book 9 of the Civil Code could provide in exemptions to the notification requirements for certain security

1364 E. M. KIENINGER, 'Evaluation: a Common? Convergences, Subsisting Differences and Possible Ways for Harmonisation' in E.-M. KIENINGER (ed.), *Security Rights in Movable Property in European Private Law* (Cambridge: Cambridge University Press, 2004) 652–653.
1365 See *supra* no. 58.
1366 See *supra* no. 131.
1367 See *supra* no. 176.
1368 E. DIRIX and R. DE CORTE, 'Zekerheidsrechten' in *Beginselen van Belgisch privaatrecht*, (5th edn., Mechelen: Wolters Kluwer, 2006), 4.
1369 Art. 39 SRA.
1370 Art. 15 SRA.
1371 See *supra* no. 59.
1372 See *supra* no. 133.
1373 See *supra* no. 179.

rights, certain movable goods or debtors, as is the case for PMSIs and acquisition security rights in consumer goods, respectively. However, a general and more unified notification regime for all security interests in movable goods would be beneficial to the overall coherence, predictability and consistency of the Security Rights Act or in the new Book 9 of the Civil Code.

Finally, the Belgian legislator has already started the process of implementing a general notification regime for retention of title by introducing in 2016[1374] the optional registration of retention of title in the National Pledge Registry[1375] to make retention of title clause public towards third parties.[1376] The legislator acknowledges the possibility of introducing a general and mandatory regime of notification requirements for all security rights in movable goods in the explanatory memorandum to the law that made registration of retention of title in the National Pledge Registry possible. The drafters mention that the option to register retention of title and the possibility for third parties to consult this information[1377] could potentially ease the transition towards a system in which retention of title clauses are also subjected to a compulsory registration requirement for third-party effectiveness.[1378] In other word, the Belgian legislator also sees the value and possibility to introduce a general notification regime for all security rights in movable goods, including retention of title.

312. *Arguments against notification requirements for retention of title* – Despite these arguments in favor, the Belgian legislator still opted against notification requirements for retention of title in the Security Rights Act. There are several reasons for this decision. First, none of Belgium's neighboring countries demand notification requirements to make retention of title effective against third parties. Consequently, if Belgium were to implement notification requirements, such as a registration, it would be singled out and potentially become less attractive for doing business.[1379]

Second, some authors question the ostensible ownership argument in the context of retention of title. These authors are of the opinion that in the current credit economy acquisitions on credit with retention of title are more the rule than the exception and third parties cannot convincingly claim that they did not know or suspect that goods in the debtor's possession do not belong

---

1374 Wetsontwerp houdende de wijziging van verscheidene bepalingen betreffende de zakelijke zekerheden op roerende goederen, *Parl. St.* Kamer 2016–17, no. 2138/001, 10 (Explanatory memorandum regarding amendments to the Security Rights Act, no. 2138/001).

1375 Art. 29, §2 and 30, §2 SRA.

1376 J. CAEYMAEX and T. CAVENAILE, *Manuel des sûretés mobilières*, (3 edn., Brussels: Larcier, 2019), 515.

1377 Art. 31, §2 SRA.

1378 Explanatory memorandum regarding amendments to the Security Rights Act, no. 2138/001, 10.

1379 Explanatory memorandum Security Rights Act, no. 2463/001, 18.

to him.[1380] This reasoning is also used in *Germany* to defend their complete absence of notification requirements for retention of title.[1381] However, saying it is one thing and seeing it in practice is quite another. Even though third parties should be skeptical towards the goods in the debtor's possession, it goes without saying that omitting all notification requirements for retention of title leaves the door open for ostensible ownership issues. Especially, if some security rights are made public through notifications and others are not, this can create confusion on how the goods in debtor's possession should be assessed. This is a problem that does not exists in *Germany*, since there all title-based mechanisms are effective against third parties without notification requirements and the possessory pledge is barely used in practice. Therefore, in *Germany* there is much more of a tradition to assume that the goods in the debtor's possession are already encumbered despite the lack of notification requirements, whereas in Belgium there is a tradition to connect a possible encumbrance of a movable good with a notification requirement, such as the registration requirement for the non-possessory pledge, which stands in contrast with the lack of notification requirements for retention of title.

Finally, some authors are of the opinion that the lack of notification requirements is less important in the case of retention of title. This interpretation follows from the fact that retention of title generally only applies to credit granted by a supplier, seller or manufacturer. Therefore, it should be relatively easy for third parties to verify which debts are owed to these creditors and whether these are guaranteed by a retention of title.[1382] However, this argument seems mostly theoretical, since it is unlikely that third parties will have access to the books of the debtor which allows them to easily verify which claims are guaranteed by a retention of title and which movable goods are encumbered by the retention of title.[1383]

1380 R. DE HEMPTINNE and A. RUYFFELAERE, 'Naar de tegenstelbaarheid van de clausule van eigendomsvoorbehoud' in *Jurist in bedrijf*, (Brussels: Bruylant, 1989), (131) 134–137; G. VERSCHELDEN, "Eigendomsvoorbehoud tussen partijen en tegenover derden", (1998–99) AJT, (821); 834; F. 'T KINT and W. DERIJCKE, 'Dessaisissement et situations des creanciers en cas de faillite', *Le nouveau droit du concordat judiciaire et de la faillite: les lois des 17 juillet et 8 août 1997*, (Brussels: Bruylant, 1997), 200; M. E. STORME, 'Overdracht van roerende goederen, vestiging van pandrecht eigendomsvoorbehoud: een poging tot systematisatie', *Het zakenrecht: absoluut niet een rustig bezit*, (Antwerpen: Kluwer, 1992), (405) 489; J. CAEYMAEX, 'Réflexions sur la réserve de propriété (note under Cass. 22 September 1994)', (1995) JLMB, (126) 128; F. 'T KINT, *Sûretés et principes généraux du droit de poursuite des créanciers*, (Brussels: Larcier, 2004), 242.

1381 See *supra* no. 225.

1382 M.E. STORME, "Paritas creditorum, voorrang en roerende zekerheden", TPR 2006, (939) 978; V. SAGAERT and J. DEL CORRAL, "Eigendomsvoorbehoud" in *Algemene praktische rechtsverzameling*, (Mechelen: Kluwer, 2015), 12; A. APERS and D. GRUYAERT, 'Eigendomsvoorbehoud en onroerende incorporatie volgens de nieuwe pandwet: welk nieuws onder de zon?', (2015) 1 TPR, (83) 90; D. GRUYAERT, *Exclusiviteit van het eigendomsrecht*, (Antwerp: Intersentia, 2016), 500.

1383 I. VAN DE PLAS and M. VANMEENEN, "Third-Party Effectiveness of Retention of Title Agreements: Maintaining the Balance between Creditor-Owners and other Creditors in

313. *Conclusion* – The functional approach in the Security Rights Act does not mean that retention of title automatically has to be subjected to an extensive notification regime for third-party effectiveness as is implemented for the pledge. However, there are definite advantages connected to the implementation of a robust notification regime, most importantly an increase in transparency and the creation of a coherent and unified notification regime for all security rights in movable goods. Furthermore, the introduction of a National Pledge Registry and the optional registration of retention of title therein suggests that the Belgian law is already looking to align itself more with the current trend towards general notification requirements for security rights in movable goods, that we see in *Article 9 UCC*, the *UNCITRAL Guide and Model Law* and *DCFR*, than the system with complete lack of notification requirements that we see in *Germany*. The introduction of a mandatory notification requirement for retention of title would fit with the trajectory of the Belgian law towards more and not less notification requirements for security rights in movable goods.

SECTION 4 – RIGHTS OF THE RETENTION OF TITLE CREDITOR

314. *Overview* – In this section I focus on the specific rights of retention of title creditors within the Security Rights Act, whether any changes to or unification of these rights can be traced back to the application of the functional approach and how these rights compare to the rights of retention of title creditors across the selected jurisdictions and international instruments. More specifically, I discuss the retention of title creditor's right to dispose (1.), the right to trace into altered collateral (2.), the right to super-priority (3.) and the right to revendicate (4.).

1. THE RIGHT TO DISPOSE OF THE ENCUMBERED GOOD

315. *The retention of title creditor's right to dispose prior to and after the Security Rights Act* – Traditionally, the retention of title creditor is considered full owner of the collateral which suggests that he has the right to dispose of the encumbered good a second time. However, property and contract law principles prevented the retention of title creditor from disposing of the encumbered good a second time.[1384] In the Security Rights Act, the drafters do not address the

Bankruptcy Proceedings" in J. GANT (ed.), *Athens INSOL Europe Conference Proceedings Booklet*, (Nothingham: INSOL EUROPE, 2019), (55) 70.

1384 Cass. 10 July 1890, (1890) Pas., I, (259) 260; M. WAELBROECK, *Le transfert de la propriété dans la vente d'objets mobiliers corporels en droit comparé*, (Brussels: Bruylant, 1961), 27; R. JANSEN, *Beschikkingsonbevoegdheid*, (Antwerp: Intersentia, 2009), 445–446;

retention of title creditor's right to dispose. Furthermore, the Security Rights Act does not recharacterize retention of title to an acquisition security right, for which it is clear that ownership resides with the debtor and the creditor has a limited proprietary interest in the encumbered good that does not include the right to dispose. Nevertheless, the same contract and property law principles still apply to the retention of title creditor and limit his theoretical right to dispose of the encumbered good a second time. Therefore, both prior to the and under the Security Rights Act, the retention of title creditor is limited in disposing of the encumbered good a second time.[1385]

316. *The retention of title creditor's right to dispose in comparison* – A similar limitation on the retention of title creditor's right to dispose can also be found in *Germany* and the *DCFR*. In these frameworks, the retention of title or retention of ownership creditor, respectively, is still considered to hold title to the encumbered good but general contract law principles prohibit him from disposing of the encumbered good a second time.[1386] Moreover, in *Germany* the retention of title debtor's claim to the encumbered good is even protected by the debtor's *Anwartschaftsrecht*[1387], a non-codified prospective ownership right that has been recognized by the German BGH.

Alternatively, *Article 9 UCC*[1388] and *the UNCITRAL unitary approach*[1389] recharacterize retention of title to a PMSI or acquisition security right, respectively. As a result, the former retention of title mechanism changes into a construction in which the PMSI debtor is the owner and the creditor only holds a PMSI or acquisition security right, respectively, and no longer title to the encumbered good. This change automatically means that the former retention of title creditor no longer has sufficient rights to the collateral to dispose of it a second time. As a result, these approaches leave much less room for debate concerning the PMSI holder's right to dispose. Furthermore, these approaches are less misleading than the approach in the Security Rights Act, *Germany* and the *DCFR* where the the term retention of title still suggests that the retention of title creditor has the right to dispose of the encumbered good a second time, while general contract law principles implicitly prohibit the retention of title creditor from disposing of the encumbered good a second time.

As a compromise between these two approaches, the *UNCITRAL non-unitary approach* also limits the retention of title creditor's right to potentially dispose a second time of the encumbered good but on the basis of an active reversal of the default rules concerning ownership, such as the right to dispose of the good from

---

1385 M. E. STORME, *Zekerheden en insolventierecht*, (Ghent: 2018–19), 413.
1386 See *infra* no. 182 and 228 *et seq.*
1387 See *infra* no. 227 *et seq.*
1388 See *supra* no. 46.
1389 See *supra* no. 123.

the retention of title creditor to the retention of title debtor.[1390] In other words, this approach combines the continuation of the terms retention of title and finance leasing with an active adjustment of the default assumptions concerning ownership rights to limit the retention of title creditor right to dispose instead of relying on more general contract and property law principles. However, the *UNCITRAL Guide* introduces a category of acquisition security rights, for which it is clear that the security right holder cannot dispose of the encumbered good a second time. Following the functional approach without recharacterization in the *UNCITRAL Guide*, functional equivalent outcomes are then pursued for retention of title, finance leasing and acquisition security rights, resulting in a limitation of the retention of title creditor's or financial lessor's right to dispose. Nevertheless, the continued use of the term retention of title still perpetuates the impression that the retention of title creditor or financial lessor can dispose of the good a second time, even though the default rights concerning ownership have been actively reversed to the retention of title debtor. Therefore, this approach also offers an unclear and misleading approach to the retention of title creditor's right to dispose.

317. *Conclusion* – Under the Security Rights Act the retention of title creditor continues to be unable to effectively dispose of the collateral a second time after having already sold it under retention of title. This limitation is not due to the application of the functional approach with or without recharacterization, but stems from general contract law principles that already applied to retention of title prior to the enactment of the Security Rights Act.

Given that both the pledge holder and retention of title creditor cannot dispose of the encumbered good a second time, despite the retention of title creditor's retained title, one wonders why the Belgian legislator did not push the application of the functional approach further and went for a clear approach where all holders of a security right in movable goods cannot dispose of the encumbered good or the retention of title creditor is explicitly prohibited from disposing of the encumbered good after it has already been sold with retention of title. This approach would certainly improve the clarity of the Security Rights Act for retention of title creditors, debtors and third parties, since it would implement a clear rule and remove all doubt on whether the retention of title creditor can or cannot dispose a second time of the encumbered good.

However, even a uniform rule for all security rights in movable goods regarding the right to dispose or an explicit adjustment for the rules for retention of title with respect of the right to dispose, would not dispel the impression that the term retention of title invokes: the retention of title creditor holds title to the encumbered good and can therefore still dispose of the encumbered good. Such engrained assumptions about the term retention of title and the rights

1390 See *supra* no. 136.

of retention of title creditors are a recurring issue of the functional approach without recharacterization (*DCFR* and the *UNCITRAL non-unitary approach*). This issue can only be addressed by applying the functional approach with recharacterization in which retention of title is recharacterized to a PMIS (*Article 9 UCC*) or acquisition security right (*the UNCITRAL unitary approach*). In these frameworks, there is no debate that the PMSI or acquisition security right holder does not have sufficient rights to the encumbered good to dispose of it.

The existing limitation on the retention of title creditor's right to dispose and the issues associated with maintaining the term retention of title and the right of dispose are further arguments in favor of the implementation of a functional approach with recharacterization in the new Book 9 of the Civil Code. The recharacterization of the retention of title to an acquisition security right would confirm the existing limitations on the pledge holder's and retention of title creditor's right and remove any debate concerning the assumed right of the retention of title creditor to dispose of the encumbered good. Furthermore, this approach would explicate the doctrinal view that retention of title is in fact reduced to a pledge, or security right, in the encumbered good.[1391] Following this interpretation, recharacterizing retention of title to an acquisition security right seems the next logical step in the integration of retention of title.

2. RIGHT TO TRACE INTO ALTERED GOODS

318. *Retention of title and the in natura requirement* – Prior to the Security Rights Act, the continuation of retention of title after alterations to the encumbered goods was not guaranteed due to the *in natura* requirement for the encumbered good in the hands of the retention of title debtor.[1392] This was a hindrance for both the retention of title creditor and debtor. On the one hand, the creditor had to be vigilant to make sure that the encumbered collateral was not altered to such an extent that his protection would be lost. On the other hand, the debtor was limited in his use of the collateral by the creditor who wants to guarantee the protection of his retained title.

319. *Tracing of retention of title under the Security Rights Act* – With the creation of a non-possessory pledge, the issue of protection after alteration of the encumbered good also presents itself for pledge holders. Now the pledgee can be left in possession of the collateral and can make use of the encumbered collateral.[1393] Consequently, the legislator decided to address this issue by

---

1391 M. E. STORME, *Zekerheden en insolventierecht*, (Ghent, Mariakerke, 2018–19), 411–412.

1392 Art. 101 former Bankruptcy Act.

1393 J. BAECK 'Achtergrond en krachtlijnen van de hervorming' in J. BAECK and M. KRUITHOF (eds.), *Het nieuwe zekerheidsrecht*, (Antwerpen: Intersentia, 2014), (1) 13; I. DURANT, 'Le droit de rétention et la réserve de propriété, deux sûretés réelles mobilières à part entière' in F.

significantly expanding the protection of pledge holders after alterations are made to the original collateral.[1394] Following the functional approach, the drafters of the Security Rights Act then extended these protections to retention of title.[1395]

2.1. *Tracing after disposition*

320. *Overview* – The right to trace after disposition means that the retention of title debtor sold or otherwise transferred the encumbered collateral to a third party and received something in return for this good. In the following section, I examine the tracing of retention of title in the hands of the third-party transferee (2.1.1.), followed by the right to trace into the proceeds (2.1.2.).

2.1.1. Tracing into the hands of the third-party transferee

321. *Retention of title and the transfer of the encumbered good before and after the Security Rights Act* – At first glance, the transfer of the encumbered good by the retention of title debtor seems contradictory to the retention of title to the encumbered good. The right to dispose is traditionally viewed as a quintessential ownership right[1396] that resides exclusively with the owner of the good.[1397] Therefore, it was originally understood that the retention of title debtor did not have sufficient rights in the encumbered good to dispose of it free of the encumbrance[1398] and that the retention of title creditor could trace

GEORGES (ed.), *Insolvabilité et garanties*, (Brussels: Larcier,2014), (34) 76; E. HELLEBUYCK, 'Commentaar bij artikel 70 Pandwet' in E. DIRIX and A. VAN OEVELEN (eds.), *Bijzondere overeenkomsten Artikelsgewijze commentaar met overzicht van rechtspraak en rechtsleer*, (Mechelen: Wolters Kluwer, 2019), 2.

1394 Art. 9 and 18–20 SRA.

1395 Art. 70–71 SRA.

1396 Many authors agree that *abusus* is one of the main ownership rights: B. AKKERMANS and W. SWADLING, 'Types of property rights – immovables and movables (goods)' in S. VAN ERP and B. AKKERMANS (eds.), *Cases, materials and text on nationale, supranational and international property law*, (Oxford: Hart Publishing, 2012), (211) 214; J. HANSENNE, 'Les biens: précis' in *Collection scientifique de la Faculté de droit de l'Université de Liège*, vol. I, (Liège: Université de Liège. Faculté de droit, 1996), 581; H. DE PAGE, 'Les biens' in *Traité élémentaire de droit civil Belge*, vol. V (Brussels: Bruylant, 1962), 580; A. KLUYSKENS, 'Zakenrecht' in *Beginselen van burgerlijk recht*, vol. V, (Antwerp: Standaard boekhandel, 1953), 90; W. DELVA, *Overzicht van het Belgisch burgerlijk recht en burgerlijk procesrecht*, (Gent: E. Story – Scientia, 1982), 107–108.

1397 A. KLUYSKENS, 'Zakenrecht' in *Beginselen van burgerlijk recht*, vol. V, (Antwerp: Standaard Boekhandel, 1953), 90–91; H. DE PAGE, 'Les biens' in *Traité élémentaire de droit civil Belge*, vol. V (Brussels: Bruylant, 1962), 786; R. DEKKERS, *Hanboek burgerlijk recht*, (Antwerp: Intersentia, 2005), 60; R. JANSEN, *Beschikkingsonbevoegdheid*, (Antwerpen: Intersentia, 2009), 48.

1398 A. KLUYSKENS, 'Zakenrecht' in *Beginselen van burgerlijk recht*, vol. V, (Antwerp: Standaard Boekhandel, 1953), 90–91; H. DE PAGE, 'Les biens' in *Traité élémentaire de droit civil Belge*, vol. V (Brussels: Bruylant, 1962), 786; R. DEKKERS, *Hanboek burgerlijk recht*, (Antwerp:

the encumbered good in the hands of the third-party transferee. However, over time some exceptions to these principles were allowed.[1399] As a result, retention of title generally followed the encumbered good into the hands of a third-party transferee, unless (1) the goods were transferred with permission of the creditor, (2) the goods were transferred in the ordinary course of business or (3) the third-party transferee acquired the encumbered goods in good faith. In other words, prior to the Security Rights Act, the retention of title creditor was already limited in his ability to rely on his retained title to trace the encumbered good into the hands of a third-party transferee.

The Security Rights Act does not mention the retention of title creditor's right to trace into the hands of the third-party transferee. Given the lack of legislative intervention, the assumption is that the retention of title creditor's right to trace into the hands of the third-party transferee remains governed by the default doctrinal principles concerning tracing.[1400] The lack of explicit rules also means that practitioners and retention of title creditors have to deduce from case law and doctrine to what extent they are protected in the event the encumbered good is transferred to a third party. An important caveat to these tracing rules is when the encumbered goods are sold as part of an enforcement proceeding initiated by an unsecured creditor. In that case, the third-party transferee, who purchases the encumbered good as part of the enforcement proceeding, and thus outside the ordinary course of business, does not have to worry about the potentially retained title and will always obtain the good free of the encumbrance. Furthermore, the bailiff in charge with the enforcement proceeding sale can assume that all the goods in the debtor's possession belong to the debtor and does not have to take into account retention of title, unless the retention of title creditor comes forward.[1401]

322. *The non-possessory pledge and the right to trace into the hands of the third-party transferee* – The right to trace the non-possessory pledge into the hands of the third-party transferee has been made explicit in the Security Rights Act.

> *The pledge will follow the encumbered good in the hands of a third-party transferee and the third-party transferee will be considered the new pledgor. The first section will not apply*

Intersentia, 2005), 60; R. JANSEN, *Beschikkingsonbevoegdheid*, (Antwerpen: Intersentia, 2009), 48.

1399 M. GRÉGOIRE, "Questions liées à l'invocation d'une clause de réserve de propriété" in *Mélanges offerts à Pierre Van Ommeslaghe*, Brussel, Bruylant, 2000, 488;; M. VANDENPLAS, 'De rechtspositie van de verkoper van een onder een beding van van eigendomsvoorbehoud verkocht roerend goed tegenover opvolgende kopers', (2012) TBH, (859) 862.

1400 V. SAGAERT, 'Goederenrecht' in *Beginselen van Belgisch privaatrecht*, vol. V, (Mechelen: Kluwer, 2014), 34–38.

1401 J. LAENENS, D. SCHEERS, P. THIRIAR, S. RUTTEN and B. VANLERBERGHE, *Handboek gerechtelijk recht*, (Antwerp: Intersentia, 2020), 915.

if the pledgor in accordance with article 21 was authorized to dispose of the encumbered goods, or
if the pledgor agreed with the transfer, or
if the third-party transferee is protected by article 3.28 CC.[1402]

The legislator's choice to make the right to trace into the hands of the third-party transferee explicit for the non-possessory pledge and not for retention of title is likely due to the fact that up until the Security Rights Act the pledgor was generally not in possession of the encumbered collateral and could therefore not dispose of the goods.[1403] With the introduction of a non-possessory pledge in the Security Rights Act, the pledgor could potentially dispose of the encumbered good and the consequences of transfers to a third party had to be made clear.[1404] Conversely, in the domain of retention of title the protection of the retention of title creditor and third-party transferee had already been developed in case law and doctrine.[1405] Presumably, the legislator did not think it necessary to explicate these principles for retention of title.

323. *The right to trace into the hands of the third-party transferee in comparison* – In each of the selected jurisdictions and international instruments retention of title or its recharacterized version can be traced into the hands of a third-party transferee unless the encumbered good was sold with permission, in the ordinary course of business or the third party acquired the encumbered good in good faith. What varies amongst the selected jurisdictions and international instruments is the way these rules are established for (former) retention of title creditors.

In *Germany*, the limitations on the retention of title creditor's right to trace into the hands of the third-party transferee have also only been established in case law and doctrine.[1406] The *German* principles concerning tracing of a retention of title into the hands of third-party transferees are similar to those in Belgium.[1407]

Conversely, in the frameworks that apply the functional approach a more explicit effort is made to establish the rules for retention of title creditors to trace into the hands of the third-party transferee. In *Article 9 UCC* or under the *UNCITRAL unitary approach*, retention of title is recharacterized to a PMSI or acquisition security right, respectively, and there is simply one rule regarding

1402 Art. 24 SRA.
1403 Prior to the Security Rights Act the main method to effectively pledge movable goods was to transfer possession to the pledge-holder. See, *supra* no. 267.
1404 J. BAECK, 'Commentaar bij art. 24–25 Pandwet' in E. DIRIX, P. FRANCOIS and M. TISON (eds.), *Voorrechten en hypotheken Artikelsgewijze commentaar met overzicht van rechtspraak en rechtsleer*, (Mechelen: Kluwer, 2015) 44.
1405 See *supra* no. 321.
1406 See *supra* no. 232.
1407 See *supra* no. 321.

tracing of security interests and security rights, including PMSIs and acquisition security rights, into the hands of third-party transferees.[1408]

Alternatively, in the *DCFR* the rules for tracing security rights, including acquisition security rights, into the hands of third-party transferees are explicitly extended to retention of ownership devices[1409], while under the *UNCITRAL non-unitary approach* the rules concerning tracing of retention of title and finance leasing into the hands of a third-party transferee are so adjusted to have the same outcomes as those for acquisition security rights.[1410] As mentioned, a significant difference between the *UNCITRAL Guide* and *DCFR* and the Security Rights Act is that the former group has a sub-category of acquisition security rights, which are functionally equivalent to retention of ownership devices (*DCFR*) or retention of title and finance leases (*the UNCITRAL non-unitary approach*) and for which equivalent legal outcomes have to be established. This explains why these instruments actively take steps to ensure that retention of ownership devices or retention of title and finance leases are treated like acquisition security rights. By contrast, in the Security Rights Act, the non-possessory pledge and retention of title do not perform exactly the same function so their legal outcomes do not have to be equivalent to be in accordance with the functional approach. Furthermore, in the Security Rights Act this sub-category of acquisition security right does not yet exist with which the legal outcomes of retention of title should be equated. However, were the Belgian legislator to introduce an acquisition security right, the explicit creation of equivalent legal outcomes between retention of title and this acquisition security mechanism would not require many additional steps, since the rules concerning tracing into the hands of third-party transferees are already the same for retention of title and the non-possessory pledge and would likely extend to the acquisition security right.

324. *Tracing into the hands of a third-party transferee and registration in the National Pledge Registry* – Nevertheless, the application of either the functional approach with or without recharacterization to retention of title would require the Belgian legislator to address the exception to article 3.28 Civil Code that now exists in the Security Rights Act for a professional third-party transferee of a good registered with a non-possessory pledge. Article 25 of the Security Rights Act states that

> *The registration in the pledge registry excludes third-party transferees, who acted in the course of their business or trade, from the application of article 3.28 of the Civil Code.*

[1408] See *supra* no. 67 and 139.
[1409] See *supra* no. 186.
[1410] See *supra* no. 139.

This provision implements an obligation for professional third-party transferees to check the registry to make sure that the good that is being transferred to them is not encumbered with a non-possessory pledge. The idea is that checking the registry is too cumbersome for consumers, but can be expected of professional third-party transferees.[1411] In other words, professional third-party transferees cannot rely on the adage "*possession vaut titre*" of Article 3.28 of the Civil Code[1412], but will have to verify in the National Pledge Registry whether the good is encumbered with a pledge or not. Interestingly, the Belgian approach goes against the approaches in *Article 9 UCC, the UNCITRAL Guide and Model Law,* and the *DCFR*, which prescribe that a third-party transferee cannot act in good faith when the PMSI, acquisition security right or retention of ownership device, respectively, is registered *unless* when the transfer took place in the ordinary course of business.[1413] This to avoid that transferees would have to constantly check whether a good is free of encumbrances or not, when the transaction clearly takes place in the ordinary course of business. Therefore, it is interesting that Belgium goes in the other direction and prescribes that all professional transferees cannot rely on the presumption of ownership in the hands of the debtor regardless of whether the transfer took place in the ordinary course of business.

If retention of title were to be recharacterized to an acquisition security right, it would automatically be covered by the rules concerning the general security right. If the Belgian legislator were to introduce an acquisition security right and expand the current rules for tracing for the non-possessory pledge to retention of title, this would have to include an expansion of this exception concerning professional third-party transferees to goods encumbered with a retention of title. In any event, if the Belgian legislator were to entertain the idea of making changes, they could also contemplate to lessen the obligation for the professional third-party transferee, by including that in the event of a transfer in the ordinary course of business the professional third-party transferee can rely on art. 3.28 of the Civil Code and does not have to check the National Pledge Registry, as is the case in *Article 9 UCC*, the *UNCITRAL Guide and Model Law* and the *DCFR*. However, the expansion of the rules concerning tracing into the hands of third-party transferees for acquisition security rights to retention of title would also imply the implementation of a general registration requirement for retention of title. Otherwise, the registry would not be an accurate source of information for professional third-party transferees of goods encumbered with a retention of

1411 J. BAECK, 'Commentaar bij art. 24–25 Pandwet' in E. DIRIX, P. FRANCOIS and M. TISON (eds.), *Voorrechten en hypotheken Artikelsgewijze commentaar met overzicht van rechtspraak en rechtsleer*, (Mechelen: Kluwer, 2015), 46.

1412 J. BAECK, 'Commentaar bij art. 24–25 Pandwet' in E. DIRIX, P. FRANCOIS and M. TISON (eds.), *Voorrechten en hypotheken Artikelsgewijze commentaar met overzicht van rechtspraak en rechtsleer*, (Mechelen: Kluwer, 2015), 45.

1413 See *supra* no. 67, 139 and 186.

title. The implementation of a registration requirement would mean a major shift in the regulation of retention of title.[1414] However, the introduction of unified notification requirements for acquisition security rights and retention of title would further the application of the functional approach and would contribute to the coherence, clarity and transparency of the security rights framework.[1415]

325. *Conclusion* – The retention of title creditor's protection after a transfer of the encumbered good to a third-party transferee is equivalent to the protection of a pledge holder. Interestingly, the limitations on the protection of retention of title following a transfer to a third party have not changed following the integration of retention of title in the Security Rights Act, nor are they very different from the protection offered to retention of title creditors in *Germany*. This leads to the conclusion that without the application of the functional approach, there is already a tendency to limit the protection of retention of title creditors in the event the encumbered good is transferred to the third party.

However, the Security Rights Act or the future Book 9 of the Civil Code would likely be better served by having explicit rules for the tracing of retention of title in the hands of third-party transferees, as is the case in the other frameworks that apply the functional approach. This way retention of title creditors and third parties do not have to deduce what their rights are following a transfer to a third party and the functional equivalence between retention of title and a potential acquisition security right would be more clearly established.

2.1.2. Tracing into proceeds

326. *Tracing into proceeds before and after the Security Rights Act* – In the Security Rights Act, the right for the retention of title creditor to trace in the proceeds and the gains of the collateral is uniformly regulated for the non-possessory pledge and retention of title.[1416] This provision is a confirmation of existing case law in which the right to trace retention of title in the proceeds had already been recognized.[1417] Consequently, the protection of retention of title creditors with regards to tracing into proceeds has not changed following the integration of retention of title in the Security Rights Act, but is now generally acknowledged. Furthermore, in the Security Rights Act the extension of the rules concerning tracing of the non-possessory pledge into proceeds to retention of title is explained as a result of the functional approach.[1418] However, given the difference in the specific function between retention of title and the non-possessory pledge, the functional approach does not require the creation of one

1414 See *supra* no. 309.
1415 See *supra* no. 311.
1416 Art. 70 *juncto* 9 SRA.
1417 Brussels 19 November 2002, (2003) 9 TBH, (771) 773.
1418 Explanatory memorandum Security Rights Act, no. 2463/001, 31.

legal outcome for retention of title and the pledge in the Security Rights Act. Nevertheless, the existence of one clear rule concerning tracing of retention of title and the pledge in proceeds certainly increases the clarity and coherence of the Security Rights Act.

327. *Tracing into proceeds in comparison* – The generalization of tracing into proceeds for all security rights in movable goods is a feature that we also encounter in *Article 9 UCC* and the *UNCITRAL Guide* and *Model Law*.[1419] Interestingly, the *DCFR* takes an entirely different stance and does not automatically extend security rights, including retention of ownership devices, into proceeds unless in very specific circumstances or contractually agreed upon. The reasoning in the *DCFR* is that proceeds should be left to other creditors and should not be automatically encumbered by security right holders and retention of ownership creditors.[1420] The contractual option to extend security rights and retention of ownership devices to proceeds in the *DCFR* aligns with the *German* approach which also only allows extension of retention of title into the claims on third-party transferees (*Vorausabtretungsklausel*) when contractually agreed upon.[1421]

328. *Tracing into proceeds and the specificity principle* – Unfortunately, the legal recognition of tracing retention of title into proceeds in the Security Rights Act has not definitively resolved all issues following the transfer of the encumbered collateral.[1422] Although the right to trace into proceeds is now generally recognized for retention of title, it is unclear to what extent the specificity principle still applies. The application of the specificity principle would mean that the retention of title creditor or pledge holder can only successfully trace his secured claim in the proceeds of the encumbered good, if the proceeds remain identifiable in the debtor's estate and a causal link remains intact between the originally encumbered good and the substitute good.[1423] Comparatively, *Article 9 UCC*[1424] and the *UNCITRAL Guide and Model Law*[1425] apply the specificity principle and only allow the extension of PMSIs or acquisition security rights, retention of title or finance leases, respectively, when the proceeds are still identifiably in the debtor's estate. The identification of the proceeds often becomes relevant in the scenario where the debtor deposits the

---

1419 See *supra* no. 69 and 140.

1420 See *supra* no. 187.

1421 See *supra* no. 238.

1422 I. VAN DE PLAS, 'Mis/gebruik in de Pandwet' in A. VAN DE VIJVER (ed.), *Misbruik binnen de onderneming*, (Antwerpen, Intersentia, 2018), (165) 182 *et seq.*

1423 V. SAGAERT, 'Het eigendomsvoorbehoud (en retentierecht) onder de Pandwet' in M. E. STORME (ed.), *Roerende zekerheden na de Pandwet*, (Antwerpen: Intersentia, 2017), (29) 40.

1424 See *supra* no. 70.

1425 See *supra* no. 140.

proceeds of the transfer of the encumbered collateral in a bank account that already contains money belonging to the debtor. In that case, the proceeds will likely become mixed with the money belonging to the debtor which raises concerns on whether the retention of title creditor can sufficiently identify the money as belonging to him. In *Article 9 UCC*, this issue is explicitly addressed via specific tracing rules, such as the lowest intermediate balance rule, that allow the secured creditor to identify his proceeds in such comingled goods.[1426]

329. *Specificity principle and tracing into a bank account in Belgium* – Prior to the Security Rights Act, there would have been no doubt that once the money has been deposited into a bank account, the deposited money can no longer be identified and thus the retained title or pledge would be lost.[1427] Since the enactment of the Security Rights Act, the loss of retention of title or pledge after the money has been deposited into a bank account is no longer so clear-cut. The Security Rights Act provides an expansive protection for the secured creditor in the event his collateral is mixed with either goods belonging to the debtor or goods belonging to third parties.[1428] Basically, the mixing of the encumbered fungible goods with other similar fungible goods does not affect the pledge or retention of title.[1429] One could wonder whether this expansive protection of the pledge and retention of title in the event of mixing could be combined with the tracing of the pledge and retention of title into proceeds. When the secured creditor's right continues into the proceeds (i.e. a fungible good) and is then mixed with other money in the debtor's bank account, the creditor could invoke his protection against mixing. This would mean that the secured creditor could revendicate the same amount in the debtor's possession without having to show that this money is his. In the event the secured creditor would come into conflict with other creditors with claims in the proceeds, the revendication would have to take place in proportion to their rights. Evidently, this interpretation would significantly increase the secured creditor's protection in the event of the transfer of the collateral. Alternatively, the drafters of the Security Rights Act could have taken a page from *Article 9 UCC* and introduced explicit rules that allow secured creditors to trace their proceeds in bank accounts, such as the lowest intermediate balance rule.[1430]

SAGAERT and DEL CORRAL have a narrower interpretation of the protection of retention of title and the pledge into proceeds. They acknowledge that following the Security Rights Act retention of title and the pledge continue into proceeds and mixed goods. However, the strong protection against mixing

---

[1426] See *supra* no. 70.

[1427] Cass. 9 May 1947, (1947) Arr. Cass., (148) 150; V. SAGAERT, *Zakelijke Subrogatie*, (Antwerp: Intersentia, 2003) 380–382.

[1428] See *infra* no. 336.

[1429] Art. 70 *juncto* art. 20 SRA.

[1430] See *supra* no. 70.

only applies to the original moveable good to which title was retained or in which a pledge was vested.[1431] Once the encumbered good has transferred into proceeds, the secured creditor cannot simply invoke his protection against mixing, but he will have to trace his goods in the debtor's estate. Tracing means providing evidence that the replacement good or substitute represents the value of the original moveable good.[1432] The tracing of collateral into bank accounts can become complicated when numerous transactions have taken place in this bank account. In that case, it will be difficult, if not near impossible, for the retention of title creditor to trace the original amount throughout the different transactions and it will become more likely that retention of title is lost.[1433]

Nevertheless, one wonders why the rules concerning mixing would not apply to the proceeds of the original encumbered collateral. In the provision concerning mixing, the Security Rights Act only mentions that the mixing of fungible goods encumbered with a pledge or a retention of title does not affect the pledge or retention of title. It does not limit this application to the original encumbered good. Therefore, it could also apply to the goods that takes its place and through the provision on tracing into proceeds become encumbered with a pledge or retention of title. I concede that this would give a very broad protection to the retention of title creditor and pledge holder. However, a far-reaching protection of retention of title and the pledge following alterations of the collateral is what the legislator envisioned.[1434] Conversely, excluding the proceeds from the protection against mixing would significantly limit the protection of tracing into the proceeds. Once the debtor deposits the proceeds in his bank account, it would be nearly impossible to trace the original proceeds into the debtor's account and throughout multiple transactions in the account. This is also what the legislator wanted to avoid with the protection against mixing. When an original, fungible good, such as grain, is mixed with other fungible goods in the debtor's possession, the retention of title creditor does not have to proof that his specific grain is still in the debtor's possession and has not been processed into breads or even sold and has been turned in the proceeds. The presumption is that the grain in the debtor's possession belongs to the retention of title creditor and can be revendicated. It is unclear why the same rule should not apply when the original collateral has turned into money and has been mixed with other money in the debtor's account.

1431 V. SAGAERT and J. DEL CORRAL, 'Eigendomsvoorbehoud' in *Algemene Praktische Rechtsverzameling*, (Mechelen: Wolters Kluwer, 2015), 131.

1432 V. SAGAERT and J. DEL CORRAL, 'Eigendomsvoorbehoud' in *Algemene Praktische Rechtsverzameling*, (Mechelen: Wolters Kluwer, 2015), 130.

1433 V. SAGAERT and J. DEL CORRAL, 'Eigendomsvoorbehoud' in *Algemene Praktische Rechtsverzameling*, (Mechelen: Wolters Kluwer, 2015), 131.

1434 Explanatory memorandum Security Rights Act, no. 2463/001, 31.

330. *Tracing into proceeds and the authorization of the transfer under the Security Rights Act* – Second, there remains some debate whether the retention of title creditor is able to trace into the proceeds when the transfer of the collateral took place in the ordinary course of business or with the creditor's permission. The majority is of the opinion that the retention of title creditor can always trace into the proceeds, regardless of the authority with which the transfer took place.[1435] Only JANSEN seems doubtful on whether the retention of title creditor has a right to trace when the transfer was authorized. He remains of the opinion that tracing into proceeds is a compensatory measure for wrongful behavior that cannot be automatically extended to all transfers.[1436] SAGAERT refutes this reasoning by pointing out that the provision concerning tracing into proceeds does not make a distinction between transfers with and transfers without authority. Furthermore, SAGAERT refers to other instances where the legislator has allowed tracing into proceeds even though the sale took place with permission of the creditor or within the normal course of business. This is for example the case in article XX.196 of the Code of Economic Law which deals with the goods held in bailment or consignment by the bankrupt. Here the law stipulates that the goods given in consignment or bailment can be revendicated from the bankruptcy estate, if they are present *in natura*. Furthermore, the consignor can even revendicate the price of the goods after they've been sold.[1437] The fact that the owner can revendicate the price of the goods, even though they were sold with permission, can be seen as a sign that tracing into proceeds does not hinge on the authority with which the goods were sold. Nevertheless, the Security Rights Act does not take a stance on this issue, so the protection of retention of title creditor could potentially be called into question here.

331. *Conclusion* – At first glance, the Security Rights Act opted for a broad protection of security rights in movable goods when it comes to tracing into proceeds. The Act implements a blanket extension of the protection to the proceeds of the encumbered good for all security rights in movable goods. In this sense, the Security Rights Act distinguishes itself from *Germany* and the *DCFR*, which leaves it mainly to the secured creditor and debtor to contractually agree upon an extension to the proceeds of the encumbered good. Furthermore, the Security Rights Act even seems to go further than *Article 9 UCC* and the

---

1435 I. DURANT, 'Le droit de rétention et la réserve de propriété, deux sûretés réelles mobilières à part entière' in F. GEORGES (ed.), *Insolvabilité et garanties*, (Brussels: Larcier, 2014), (34) 76–77; V. SAGAERT, 'Het eigendomsvoorbehoud (en retentierecht) onder de Pandwet' in M. E. STORME (ed.), *Roerende zekerheden na de Pandwet*, (Antwerpen: Intersentia, 2017), (29) 41.

1436 R. JANSEN, *Beschikkingsonbevoegdheid*, (Antwerp: Intersentia, 2009), 844–846; R. JANSEN, 'Eigendomsvoorbehoud' in J. BAECK and M. KRUITHOF (eds.), *Het nieuwe zekerheidsrecht*, (Antwerpen: Intersentia, 2014), (139), 153–154.

1437 Art. XX.196, sec. 2 CEL.

UNCITRAL Guide and Model Law in its protection of security rights in proceeds by not explicitly limiting this to the identifiable proceeds. However, doctrinally the unlimited extension of security rights in movable goods in the proceeds is questioned, even though this interpretation runs counter to the extensive protection the Security Rights Act hopes to offer to secured creditors. To address this issue a further clarification of the term proceeds in the Security Rights Act and potentially some additionally guidelines to help tracing into proceeds would further improve the clarity and coherence of the Security Rights Act in this regard.

2.2. *Tracing into altered goods*

332. *Overview* – In the Security Rights Act, the rules concerning tracing into altered goods are explicitly expanded from the non-possessory pledge to retention of title following the functional approach.[1438] This is a significant departure from the regime prior to the Security Rights Act, which adhered to the *in natura* requirement for goods sold under retention of title and thus resulted in a loss of retention of title after most alterations of the encumbered good.[1439] In the following sections I examine the right to trace into processed goods (2.2.1.), mixed goods (2.2.2.) and incorporated goods (2.2.3.).

2.2.1. Tracing into processed goods

333. *Before and after the Security Rights Act* – As with proceeds, the Security Rights Act provides one provision that allows tracing of the non-possessory pledge and retention of title in a processed good.[1440] Prior to the Security Rights Act, the encumbered good had to remain *in natura* in the debtor's hands[1441] and the processing of the encumbered good would in most cases lead to a loss of the retained title.[1442] Evidently, the drafters of the Security Rights Act opted for an increase in the protection of the retention of title creditor.

1438 Art. 70 and 71 SRA. See also, explanatory memorandum Security Rights Act, no. 2463/001, 70.

1439 Art. 101 of the former Bankruptcy Act.

1440 Art. 18 and 70 SRA.

1441 Art. 101 former Bankruptcy Act of 1997.

1442 However, extensive case las was developed to determine when a good was so altered it could no longer be identified. See For an overview of the relevant case law in this regard see, G. VAN HAEGENBORGH, 'Het behoud van voorrechten op samengestelde of bewerkte zaken (note under Cass. 16 december 1994)' (1994–95) 40 RW, (1366) 1367; M. GRÉGOIRE, 'Questions liées à l'invocation d'une clause de réserve de propriété' in *Mélanges offerts à Pierre Van Ommeslaghe* (Brussel: Bruylant, 2000), (465) 478–479; V. SAGAERT, 'Het 'in natura'-vereiste bij eigendomsvoorbehoud: de gevolgen van de bewerking, vermenging en wederverkoop', (2003) 9 TBH, (773) 774–775.

334. *Processing of the encumbered good with or without the authorization of the secured creditor* – The assumption is that the debtor is authorized to manufacture new goods out of the encumbered good and other goods belonging to the debtor.[1443] If the processing is authorized, the retained title or the obtained pledge automatically traces into the newly manufactured good unless the parties agreed otherwise. If the processing of the collateral is unauthorized, then the allocation of title or continuation of the pledge and retention of title in the processed goods is governed by traditional property law principles. More specifically, the Security Rights Act refers for this scenario to articles 3.11 *juncto* 3.56 of the Civil Code.[1444] These provisions contain the traditional property law principles which allocate title to the party who added the most value to the newly manufactured good.[1445] Usually this will be the party who provided the materials (i.e. the retention of title creditor)[1446], but title can also be allocated to the retention of title debtor when the value of the debtor's labor outweighs the value of the materials.[1447]

If the manufacturing process combines the encumbered good with goods belonging to a third party, the authorization to process the encumbered good is not relevant. In this scenario, retention of title and the pledge extend when the encumbered good is considered the main component of the newly manufactured good[1448] or when the encumbered good represents the greatest value in the new good.[1449] Furthermore, this rule is not necessary when the encumbered good can be removed from the newly manufactured good without damage. In that case, the secured creditor can simply revendicate his removable asset.[1450]

The secured creditor, who loses his pledge or retention of title due to the fact that his asset is manufactured into a new good, has a claim on the other party for unjust enrichment.[1451] This claim is limited to the smallest of two amounts: the surplus value the encumbered good gave to the newly manufactured good or the purchase price of the asset.[1452]

1443 Art. 18, sec. 1 SRA.

1444 Art. 18, sec. 2 SRA.

1445 A. L. VERBEKE, V. SAGAERT and B. TILLEMAN, "Wettelijke wijzen van eigendomsverkrijging" in B. TILLEMAN and A. L. VERBEKE (eds.), *Vermogensrecht in kort bestek*, (Brussel: Intersentia, 2020), (226) 241.

1446 Art. 3.56 CC.

1447 Art. 3.57, sec. 1 CC.

1448 Art. 18, sec. 3 SRA *juncto* art. 3.57, sec. 1 CC.

1449 Art. 18, sec. 3 SRA.

1450 V. SAGAERT and J. DEL CORRAL, "Eigendomsvoorbehoud" in *Algemene praktische rechtsverzameling*, (Mechelen: Kluwer, 2015), 143.

1451 Art. 18, sec. 3 SRA. See also, V. SAGAERT and J. DEL CORRAL, "Eigendomsvoorbehoud" in *Algemene praktische rechtsverzameling*, (Mechelen: Kluwer, 2015), 144.

1452 I. CLAEYS and L. VAN VALCKENBORGH, 'Ongerechtvaardigde verrijking ', (2017) 4 TPR, (1455) 1456.

335. *The right to trace into processed goods in comparison* – The Security Rights Act aligns with *Article 9 UCC* and *the UNCITRAL Guide* and *Model Law* which also uniformly extends their PMSIs, acquisition security rights, retention of title and finance leases, respectively, to processed goods.[1453] The *DCFR* opts again for the contrary approach and takes as a default rule that retention of title and security rights in movable goods do not automatically extend to the processed goods unless contractually agreed.[1454] Interestingly, in *Germany* retention of title creditors enjoy a somewhat similar protection as retention of title creditors in the Security Rights Act in that processing the encumbered good does not automatically result in a loss of the retained title. The retention of title also continues when the encumbered good is attached to another movable good (i.e. *Zubehör*).[1455] Furthermore, a contractual extension of retention of title to the processed good (*Verarbeitungsklausel*) has been accepted by the BGH.[1456]

2.2.2. Tracing into mixed goods

336. *Uniform and extensive protection of security rights in mixed goods* – As with processing, the legislator opted to significantly extend the secured creditor's protection in the event the encumbered collateral is mixed with other goods by stating that the mixing of the encumbered collateral does not affect the non-possessory pledge[1457] and by extension retention of title.[1458] In the event that there are multiple secured creditors, they can enforce their rights on the mixed goods in proportion to their respective rights.[1459] This was a significant departure from the previous protection of retention of title which was based on the *in natura* principle and basically led to the loss of the retention of title once the good could no longer be identified in the debtor's hands.[1460]

337. *Doctrinal debate concerning tracing into mixed goods* – Most authors accept this new provision at face value meaning that despite the mixing of the encumbered goods, the retention of title is unaffected and the retention of title creditor can revendicate his goods either fully or in proportion to these rights.[1461]

1453 See *supra* no. 71 and 142.
1454 See *supra* no. 189.
1455 See *supra* no. 219.
1456 See *supra* no. 234.
1457 Art. 20 SRA.
1458 Art. 70 *juncto* art.20 SRA.
1459 Art. 70 *juncto* art.20 SRA.
1460 Art. 101 former Bankruptcy Act of 1997.
1461 R. JANSEN, 'Eigendomsvoorbehoud' in J. BAECK and M. KRUITHOF (eds.), *Het nieuwe zekerheidsrecht*, (Antwerp: Intersentia, 2014), (139), 156–158; I. DURANT, 'Le droit de rétention et la réserve de propriété, deux sûretés réelles mobilières à part entière' in F. GEORGES (ed.), *Insolvabilité et garanties*, (Brussels: Larcier,2014), (34) 79; J. CAEYMAEX and T. CAVENAILE, *Manuel des sûretés mobilières*, (3 edn., Brussels: Larcier, 2019), 514.

This view takes a broad interpretation in which this rule should be considered as a substantial rule that *de facto* eliminates the specificity principle[1462] in the event of mixing. Following this interpretation, the creditor no longer has to trace his collateral in the debtor's estate, but it is sufficient that the goods were once transferred from the creditor to the debtor and can now be found in his possession.

Only SAGAERT and DEL CORRAL raise the possibility of a different interpretation.[1463] The alternative interpretation stems from a debate in France, where a similar rule for the revendication of mixed goods by retention of title creditors exists.[1464] In France, certain authors and courts restrictively interpret this provision by claiming that it only establishes a presumption in favor of the retention of title creditor. According to this interpretation, this provision only suggests that there is a link between the goods in the debtor's possession and the goods the creditor is revendicating. If the debtor or a third party can refute this presumption, then the retention of title creditor would lose his claim to these goods.[1465] However, this interpretation has not been confirmed by the French Supreme Court, that sided with the broader interpretation of the rule concerning tracing into mixed goods.[1466]

Given that the latter interpretation represents a minority opinion in both Belgium and France and was overturned in the latter jurisdiction, it stands to reason that the majority opinion also prevails in Belgium in the application of this provision.

338. *Mixing with goods belonging to the debtor vs. mixing of goods belonging to third parties* – In the event the retention of title creditor's goods are mixed with those belonging to the debtor, the retention of title creditor is allowed to revendicate the amount of goods he is owed without having to show that these are his unpaid goods.[1467]

In the event different suppliers delivered the same fungible goods under retention of title to the debtor, these goods are likely to get mixed. In this case, the different creditors can enforce their claims in proportion to their respective rights.[1468] The limitation of the creditor's claim in proportion to his respective

1462 The specificity principle is considered a general characteristic of property rights, see S. VAN ERP, 'General issues: setting the scene' in S. VAN ERP and B. AKKERMANS (eds.), *Cases, materials and text on national, supranational and international property law*, (Oxford: Hart Publishing, 2012), 52.

1463 V. SAGAERT and J. DEL CORRAL, "Eigendomsvoorbehoud" in *Algemene praktische rechtsverzameling*, (Mechelen: Kluwer, 2015), 114–115.

1464 L.624-16 (Fr.) Code de Commerce.

1465 Paris 12 May 2000, (2000) Dalloz, Act. Jur., 329.

1466 Supreme Court Fr. 5 March 2002, (2002) D., jur. 197.

1467 Art. 20, sec. 1 SRA; V. SAGAERT and J. DEL CORRAL, "Eigendomsvoorbehoud" in *Algemene praktische rechtsverzameling*, (Mechelen: Kluwer, 2015), 116–117.

1468 Art. 20, sec. 2 SRA.

rights is only relevant in the event that there are not sufficient goods in the debtor's estate to satisfy the different claims.

339. *Tracing into mixed goods in comparison* – The general protection of security rights in movable goods in the event the encumbered goods are mixed for all creditors in the Security Rights Act aligns with *Article 9 UCC*[1469] and *the UNCITRAL Guide* and *Model Law*.[1470] Furthermore, the protection in the Security Rights Act is not that different from *German* civil law in that the mixing of the encumbered goods does not automatically result in a loss of the retention of title, but in this jurisdiction depends on the application of general property law principles instead of an automatic extension.[1471] Finally, the *DCFR* again goes in a different direction by not automatically extending their security rights and retention of ownership devices to mixed goods.[1472]

2.2.3. Tracing into incorporated goods

340. *Tracing into incorporated goods prior to and after the Security Rights Act* – Finally, the Security Rights Act also eliminates the formerly negative effect of incorporation to an immovable good on retention of title. Prior to the Security Rights Act, the *in natura* requirement meant that retention of title was lost the moment the good was incorporated in an immovable good.[1473] Once the encumbered collateral was considered incorporated[1474], property law concerning incorporation kicked in and assigned ownership to the owner of the immovable good[1475], unless the encumbered good could be recovered without damaging the immovable good.[1476] In that case, the retention of title creditor could still revendicate the incorporated, encumbered good. If the retention of title creditor lost his protections due to incorporation, the retention of title creditor was entitled to compensation for the value of the collateral he had lost. However, the retention of title creditor's claim would no longer be guaranteed by retention of

1469 See *supra* no. 71.
1470 See *supra* no. 142.
1471 See *supra* no. 231.
1472 See *supra* no. 190.
1473 Art. 554 former Civil Code. See also, V. SAGAERT, 'Het 'in natura'-vereiste bij eigendomsvoorbehoud: de gevolgen van de bewerking, vermenging en wederverkoop', (2003) 9 TBH, (773) 776.
1474 The encumbered collateral was considered incorporated when the encumbered collateral was permanently attached to the immovable good (Cass. 15 September 1988, (1988–89) Arr. Cass., (60) 62).
1475 Art. 554 CC.
1476 Supreme Court Fr. 22 March 1994, (1994) D., I. R. 88; See also, V. SAGAERT, 'Het 'in natura'-vereiste bij eigendomsvoorbehoud: de gevolgen van de bewerking, vermenging en wederverkoop', (2003) 9 TBH, (773) 776.

title.[1477] Now, title is retained to the incorporated collateral, if the retention of title creditor registers his retention of title in the National Pledge Registry.[1478]

341. *Tracing after incorporation of the encumbered good in comparison* – The Security Rights Act aligns again with *Article 9 UCC*[1479] and the *UNICTRAL Guide* and *Model Law*[1480] in that they each allow the extension into incorporated goods. However, in these frameworks the continuation and more importantly the priority as opposed to third parties, including creditors with a security interest in the immovable good, requires the registration of the retention of title, PMSI or acquisition security right, respectively in the land registry in which encumbrances to the immovable good are recorded.[1481] The *DCFR* again offers a contrary approach by only allowing the contractual extension of security rights, and by extension retention of ownership devices, into incorporated goods.[1482] Finally, *Germany* adheres to a more traditional approach and does not allow the extension of retention of title into incorporated goods.[1483]

342. *Tracing into incorporated goods and registration* – Under the Security Rights Act the incorporation of the encumbered collateral does not affect retention of title, if the retention of title clause is registered in the National Pledge Registry.[1484] Evidently, this protection against incorporation requires access to the National Pledge Registry and instructions on how the retention of title clause should be recorded. These provisions were lacking in the original version of the Security Rights Act, but in 2016[1485] additional provisions were introduced that allowed the retention of title creditor to register his retention of title clause and explicated which information the retention of title creditor should enter in the National Pledge Registry.[1486]

The registration requirement to protect retention of title against incorporation follows from the application of the functional approach.[1487] Interestingly, the mechanism with which retention of title is functional equated,

---

1477 V. SAGAERT, 'Het 'in natura'-vereiste bij eigendomsvoorbehoud: de gevolgen van de bewerking, vermenging en wederverkoop', (2003) 9 TBH, (773) 776.

1478 Art. 70 *juncto* 19 SRA.

1479 See *supra* no. 74.

1480 See *supra* no. 142.

1481 See *supra* no. 76 and 142.

1482 See *supra* no. 189.

1483 See *supra* no. 231.

1484 Art. 71 SRA.

1485 Wetsontwerp houdende de wijziging van verscheidene bepalingen betreffende de zakelijke zekerheden op roerende goederen, *Parl. St.* Kamer 2016–17, no. 2138/001, 10 (Explanatory memorandum regarding amendments to the Security Rights Act, no. 2138/001).

1486 Art. 11 wet van 25 december 2016 houdende de wijziging van verscheidene bepalingen betreffende de zakelijke zekerheden op roerende goederen, *BS* 30 december 2016, 91.950. See also art. 30, §2 SRA.

1487 Explanatory memorandum Security Rights Act, no. 2463/001, 16.

is not the non-possessory pledge but the unpaid vendor's lien.[1488] This legislative lien can be maintained in the event of incorporation, if the lien applied to machinery, appliances, tools or other business assets of the debtor.[1489] Initially, to enjoy this protection the unpaid seller had to submit his invoice at the clerk's office of the competent court within 15 days of the delivery of the unpaid goods to the debtor.[1490] To ensure a equivalent legal outcome for the unpaid vendor's lien and retention of title, the drafters of the Security Rights Act also implemented a registration requirement for the continuation of retention of title in the incorporated good.[1491] However, the obligation to submit the invoice for the unpaid goods within 15 days of the delivery of the goods was removed in 2013 in an effort to reduce administrative burdens for the courts.[1492] Consequently, the registration requirement to maintain retention of title in incorporated goods in the Security Rights Act now actually creates dissimilarity between retention of title and the unpaid vendor's lien instead of equivalent legal outcomes. A possible solution to this dissimilarity between two functional equivalent mechanisms would be to remove the unpaid vendor's lien, making retention of title the main and only protection for unpaid vendors. Admittedly, such pursuance of the functional approach will likely be met with resistance from manufacturers and suppliers, because the unpaid vendor's lien is automatic whereas retention of title has to be created by the seller and registered for protection against incorporation. However, this approach does align with the original vision of the drafters of the Security Rights Act, who wanted to significantly reduce the number of legislative liens in movable goods and would better align with the functional approach envisioned in the Security Rights Act.[1493]

Notably, the registration requirement for the continuation of retention of title in incorporated goods does create equivalent legal outcomes between the non-possessory pledge and retention of title. However, it has been established that these two mechanisms do not actually perform exactly the same function and that the functional approach does not require equivalent legal outcomes for retention of title and the pledge.[1494] However, creating a uniform regime for the third-party effectiveness of retention of title in incorporated goods for retention of title and the non-possessory pledge does increase the coherence and clarity of the Security Rights Act. Furthermore, the registration requirement for the

1488 Art. 20, °5 Mortgage Act.

1489 Art. 20, °5, sec. 3 Mortgage Act.

1490 Former art. 20, °5, sec. 4 Mortgage Act. See also, A. CUYPERS and P. FRANCOIS, 'Art. 20, 5° Hyp.W' in E. DIRIX, P. FRANCOIS and M. TISON (eds.), *Voorrechten en hypotheken – Artikelsgewijze commentaar met overzicht van rechtspraak en rechtsleer*, (Mechelen: Kluwer, loosel.), 42.

1491 Explanatory memorandum Security Rights Act, no. 2463/001, 71.

1492 Art. 45 of wet van 14 januari 2013 houdende diverse bepalingen inzake werklastvermindering binnen justitie, *BS* 1 March 2013, 12945.

1493 See *supra* no. 272.

1494 See *supra* no. 274.

tracing of retention of title and the non-possessory pledge in incorporated goods means that there is one point of reference for the determination of the priority conflict with a potential mortgage holder in the immovable good. Now that incorporation does not lead to loss of retention of title or a security right, the secured creditor's claim can come into conflict with the creditor to whom the debtor has mortgaged the immovable good in which the encumbered movable good is incorporated.[1495] By connecting the protection against incorporation to a registration requirement, the mortgage holder can take notice of the retention of title encumbrance and its super-priority status in the incorporated collateral.[1496] A similar approach is followed in *Article 9 UCC*, the *UNCITRAL Guide* and *Model Law* and *DCFR*, where the secured creditor has to make a filing in the registry where the mortgage in the real property is filed, to avoid a conflict with the mortgage holder in the immovable good.[1497]

2.3. Conclusions

343. *Increased protection for retention of title under the expanded tracing rules* – A first conclusion concerning tracing is that the protection of retention of title in altered goods improved as opposed to its protection under the former Bankruptcy Act. Retention of title creditors went from losing their protection once the encumbered good had undergone any alterations, to being protected in most cases when the good has been altered.

344. *Uniform rules for tracing and the functional approach in the Security Rights Act* – In the explanatory memorandum to the Security Rights Act, the drafters give the functional approach as reason for the expansion of the tracing rules from the pledge to retention of title. However, the functional approach does not necessarily require uniform rules for retention of title and the non-possessory pledge. As mentioned, these two mechanisms do not perform exactly the same function, so it could be justified that they do not have the exact same legal outcomes. In that sense, the Security Rights Act differs from the other frameworks that apply the functional approach (i.e. *Article 9 UCC*, the *UNCITRAL Guide and Model Law* and the *DCFR*). In these instruments, retention of title is either recharacterized to a PMSI or acquisition security right which automatically results in one set of rules concerning tracing for

---

[1495] I. DURANT, 'Le droit de rétention et la réserve de propriété, deux sûretés réelles mobilières à part entière' in F. GEORGES (ed.), *Insolvabilité et garanties*, (Brussels: Larcier, 2014), (34) 79–80; A. APERS and D. GRUYAERT, 'Eigendomsvoorbehoud en onroerende incorporatie volgens de nieuwe pandwet: welk nieuws onder de zon?', (2015) 1 TPR, (83) 101. See also, *infra* no. 353.

[1496] V. SAGAERT and J. DEL CORRAL, "Eigendomsvoorbehoud" in *Algemene praktische rechtsverzameling*, (Mechelen: Kluwer, 2015), 146.

[1497] See for more detail *infra* no. 353.

these mechanisms, or retention of ownership devices or retention of title and finance leases functionally equate to acquisition security rights. In the case of the latter approach, the application of the functional approach and the actual functional similarity between retention of ownership devices or retention of title and finance leases on the one hand, and acquisition security rights on the other, results in an expansion of the rules concerning tracing of acquisition security rights to retention of ownership devices or an adjustment of the rules concerning tracing of retention of title and finance leasing to achieve the same legal outcome as the rules for tracing of acquisition security rights. Since retention of title is not recharacterized to an acquisition security right and this concept is not introduced in the Security Rights Act, the rules concerning tracing for the non-possessory pledge and retention of title do not necessarily have to be equated.

However, the implementation of one set of explicit rules for the tracing of all security rights in movable goods undeniably creates a more clear and coherent system. Furthermore, the explicit regulation of the tracing of retention of title in the altered goods for all security rights in movable goods is preferable to the approach in *Germany*. Here the tracing of retention of title in the encumbered goods after alterations is not regulated. Consequently, retention of title creditors and the courts have to come up with quite elaborate alternatives and reasonings to allow the vertical extension of retention of title for retention of title creditors without it encroaching too much on the rights of the retention of title debtor and third parties.

3. SUPER-PRIORITY

345. *Overview* – In the Security Rights Act retention of title creditors' claims are given super-priority status. In this section I delve into the connection between super-priority and the functional approach (3.1.), the specific application of super-priority to retention of title in the Security Rights Act (3.2.) and the extent to which retention of title maintains its super-priority status after alterations to the encumbered good (3.3.).

3.1. Super-priority and the functional approach

346. *Policy behind the assignment of super-priority to all secured transactions that guarantee acquisition financing* – The assignment of super-priority to PMSIs, acquisition security rights and acquisition financing devices is a recurring theme in the selected jurisdiction and international instruments that apply the functional approach. The idea is that *all* secured transactions that guarantee acquisition credit should be given additional protection and should be allowed to surpass more senior security rights in the same goods.[1498] The assignment of super-priority to security rights that guarantee acquisition credit is a policy choice, often to stimulate the distribution of certain credit or to break up certain credit monopolies. In non-functional frameworks, the additional protection of acquisition credit is often based on title and thus reserved for retention of title creditors, who inherently provide acquisition credit due to the nature of the underlying agreement (i.e. a sale agreement or lease), and whose retained title protects them from any conflict with other secured creditors or third parties. This is for example the case in *Germany*[1499] and was the case in Belgium prior to the Security Rights Act.[1500]

In the selected jurisdiction and international instruments with functional approach, this policy is achieved in one of two ways. First, in *Article 9 UCC* and the *UNCITRAL unitary approach* all secured transactions in movable goods that guarantee acquisition credit are recharacterized to a PMSI or acquisition security right, respectively, and given super-priority status.[1501] Second, under the *UNCITRAL non-unitary approach* and the *DCFR*, a sub-category of security rights is created that guarantee acquisition credit (i.e. acquisition security rights) and they are given super-priority status to create a level playing field with retention of title and finance leases in the *UNCITRAL Guide* and retention of ownership devices in the *DCFR*.[1502] In instruments that apply the functional approach without recharacterization, the reasoning remains that retention of title mechanisms in sale and lease agreements can rely on their retained title to ensure that they do not come into conflict with other creditors and thus do not require the explicit assignment of super-priority to provide additional protection for their guarantee of acquisition credit.

3.2. Super-priority for retention of title in the Security Rights Act

347. *Contradiction between retaining title and assigning super-priority* – Given what we now know about the assignment of super-priority in the context of the functional approach, the assignment of super-priority in the Security Rights Act is rather peculiar. In the Security Rights Act, retention of title is granted super-priority status, together with the right of retention of possession of a good for costs made for the preservation of that good[1503], the unpaid vendor's lien and the unpaid sub-contractor's lien.[1504] The explanatory memorandum to the Act only mentions that super-priority status is granted to retention of title, because

[1498] See *supra* no. 81, 144 and 192.
[1499] See *supra* no. 244.
[1500] Art. 101 former Bankruptcy Act.
[1501] See *supra* no. 81 and 144.
[1502] See *supra* no. 144 and 192.
[1503] The super-priority status for the right of retention of possession is limited to the situation in which the retentor is has a claim for the maintenance of the underlying collateral.
[1504] Art. 58 SRA.

without super-priority the seller would be unlikely to grant credit.[1505] From a dogmatic perspective this is a strange explanation, since the retained title in the creditor's hands should normally prevent the retention of title creditor from coming into conflict with other creditors and allow him to avoid any conflict with other creditors. This is the result of the *nemo dat* principle: the debtor cannot grant more rights than he has.[1506] Consequently, it would be impossible to have conflicting claims in goods encumbered with retention of title[1507] and unnecessary to have super-priority status to resolve conflicts.[1508] This is still the case in *Germany*, where as a default retention of title cannot come into conflict with other security rights, since the debtor does not have sufficient interest in the good to vest additional security rights.[1509] Consequently, the BGB does not have any provisions concerning super-priority for retention of title, since the retention of title creditor is presumed to never come into conflict with other creditors.

Alternatively, SAGAERT, STORME and JANSEN see the super-priority status for retention of title as the result of the way retention of title is created. More specifically, retention of title is retained by the creditor, whereas the pledge is granted by the debtor. Consequently, retention of title takes place before the good is transferred to the debtor and the goods transfer to the retention of title debtor with the retention of title clause already attached. Therefore, the retention of title debtor and his creditors always have to take into account the fact that the good is already encumbered with retention of title and retention of title always outranks any other security rights the debtor may vest in the collateral.[1510] In other words, retention of title creditors have an inherent seniority over other security right holders. However, based on this explanation there is again no need for a super-priority rule. Retention of title creditors do not actually surpass other secured creditors in time, but are always protected against earlier claims

1505 Explanatory memorandum Security Rights Act, no. 2463/001, 28.

1506 *Nemo dat quod non habet*: you cannot give what you do not have. The buyer does not have (sufficient) rights in the collateral and can therefore not grant any additional rights or secured transactions in the collateral. See also R Jansen, *Beschikkingsonbevoegdheid* (Antwerp Intersentia 2008) 52–55.

1507 G. SCHRANS, 'Het beding van eigendomsvoorbehoud en zijn externe werking tegenover de schuldeisers van de koper van een zaak', (1982) TPR, (145) 146. The only exception to this rule was the landlord's legislative lien on the furniture. However, this conflict does not stem from the retention of title-debtor being able to grant additional *in rem* security rights in goods encumbered with a retention of title, but stems from the landlord's protection under article 2279 CC. The reasoning goes that the landlord in good faith can presume that all the goods in the tenant's possession belong to the tenant and make up the collateral for the landlord's legislative lien (Cass. 22 September 1938, (1938) Pas. I., 290).

1508 This is the opinion in France where it is considered contradictory to consider the creditor owner and also give him super-priority in a conflict with competing claims. See P. Crocq, *Propriété et garantie* (Paris: LGDJ, 1995) 253 - 254.

1509 See *supra* no. 244.

1510 R. JANSEN, 'Eigendomsvoorbehoud' in J. BAECK and M. KRUITHOF (eds.), *Het nieuwe zekerheidsrecht*, (Antwerpen: Intersentia, 2014), (139), 165; V. SAGAERT, 'Het eigendomsvoorbehoud (en retentierecht) onder de Pandwet' in M. E. STORME (ed.), *Roerende zekerheden na de Pandwet*, (Antwerpen: Intersentia, 2017), (29) 56; M. E. STORME, *Zekerheden en insolventierecht*, (Ghent, Mariakerke, 2018–19), 431.

due to his inherent seniority. The retention of title debtor receives the goods with title already retained and both he and his other creditors have to take this into account regardless of the moment at which other security rights were vested or made effective against third parties. Therefore, the retention of title creditor always has priority and does not need to be explicitly assigned super-priority in a provision to surpass other creditors.

348. *Awkward application of the functional approach regarding the super-priority of retention of title in the Security Rights Act* – From a functional perspective, the assignment of super-priority to retention of title also seems illogical. As mentioned, under the functional approach the assignment of super-priority is mainly a method to create a preferential position for acquisition creditors over general creditors and to create a level playing field between acquisition security rights and retention of title mechanisms. However, in the Security Rights Act, the concept of retention of title is maintained, thereby automatically providing the retention of title creditor with sufficient protection to avoid any conflict with other creditors. Furthermore, the Security Rights Act does not create a separate category of acquisition security rights which perform the same function as retention of title, but on a non-title basis, and would thus require super-priority protection to ensure a level playing field with retention of title. Moreover, the introduction of a new category of acquisition security rights would not entail the assignment of super-priority to retention of title, but to the newly created category of acquisition security rights.

349. *Alternative interpretation of the assignment of super-priority to retention of title* – The assignment of super-priority to retention of title can be interpreted as proof of the implied recharacterization of retention of title to a type of non-possessory acquisition security right. Generally, super-priority is only assigned to security rights because they can come into conflict with other secured creditors and can be overtaken by more senior secured creditors.[1511] Consequently, the assignment of super-priority to retention of title could suggest that the retention of title creditor only has a non-possessory acquisition security right in the encumbered collateral and the retention of title debtor has the option and authority to grant additional security rights in these assets. Without super-priority, the retention of title creditor would then be at risk to be overtaken by other more senior secured creditors. This interpretation aligns with the view expressed by STORME that the retention of title creditor no longer retains full title to the encumbered good, but a type of non-possessory pledge and would allow the retention of title debtor to vest additional security rights in the collateral.[1512] Consequently, competing claims are possible in a good encumbered with retention of title and a priority rule is necessary to resolve

[1511] V. SAGAERT, 'Het goederenrecht als open systeem van verbintenissen? Poging tot een nieuwe kwalificatie van de vermogensrechten', (2005) 3 TPR, (983) 993.

[1512] M. E. STORME, *Zekerheden en insolventierecht*, (Ghent, Mariakerke, 2018–19), 412.

such conflicts. Moreover, it would be possible that more senior, all-encompassing security rights attach to the new goods that come into the debtor's estate under retention of title and could outrank the retention of title based on seniority.

Example

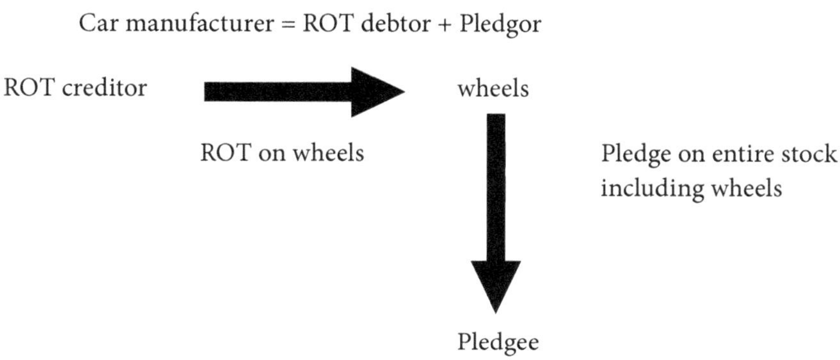

In this example, the pledgee vested and registered his non-possessory pledge in the debtor's present and future stock at time X and the retention of title creditor sold the wheels with retention of title to the same debtor at X+1. In the interpretation that the retention of title creditor only has a pledge, the retention of title creditor could come into conflict with the pledgee. If the conflict is then resolved based on the first in time rule[1513], as is generally the case among security interests in movable goods, including pledges[1514], then the pledgee, who registered at time X, would outrank the retention of title creditor whose retention of title would only become effective the moment the clause was agreed upon in writing at X+1. Given that the legislator aims to prefer creditors who have provided acquisition credit over general creditors, the recharacterized retention of title creditor is given super-priority.

350. *Conclusion* – The assignment of super-priority to retention of title in the Security Rights Act is difficult to explain. First, the application of the functional approach in the Security Rights Act cannot be used as an explanation for the assignment of super-priority to retention of title. Although there is a clear link between assigning super-priority to PMSIs and acquisition security rights and the functional approach in order to create a level playing field, the adoption of the functional approach does not mean that automatically super-priority must be assigned to retention of title. What's more, in the selected frameworks that apply the functional approach without recharacterization, super-priority is usually

---

1513 E. DIRIX, 'The new Belgian act on security interests in movable property', (2014) 23 Int. Insolv. Rev., (171) 178.

1514 E. DIRIX and R. DE CORTE, 'Zekerheidsrechten' in *Beginselen van Belgisch privaatrecht*, (5th edn., Mechelen: Wolters Kluwer, 2006), 4.

assigned to the functional equivalent acquisition security rights to ensure that they enjoy the same protection as retention of title. In other words, the super-priority would not be assigned to retention of title. However, the choice of the legislator to introduce the term super-priority could suggest that they are leaving room for the creation of a sub-category of acquisition security rights that could also be assigned super-priority and would thus obtain the same protection and functionally equivalent outcome as retention of title mechanisms. This would also mean that the retention of title creditor would not lose any protection in conflicts with other creditors following the recharacterization to an acquisition security right. Unfortunately, for now the assignment of super-priority to retention of title in the Security Rights Act seems more like a copy-paste of a term commonly found in frameworks that apply the functional approach, without thoroughly thinking through the implications of this term. In the upcoming Book 9 of the Civil Code, the legislator should bear the issues and inconsistencies concerning super-priority in mind and either leave retention of title out of the group of super-prioritized secured transactions, since they do not need super-priority status, or create a sub-category of acquisition security rights to which super-priority status can be assigned correctly.

3.3. (Super-)priority in altered collateral

351. *Conflicts between the retention of title creditors and competing claimants in the processed or mixed, encumbered goods* – As mentioned, the Security Rights Act vertically extends the retention of title creditor's and pledgor's claim to the mixed or processed goods.[1515] This also means that the retention of title creditor can now come into conflict with other creditors or third parties, who may also have a claim to the processed or mixed goods.

Example

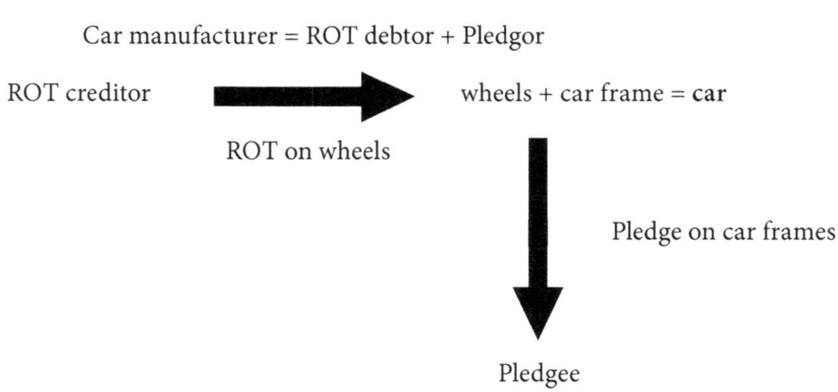

[1515] See *supra* no. 334–335.

For this situation the Security Rights Act provides a solution by granting the retention of title creditor super-priority.[1516] Consequently, in the event the processed or mixed goods are sold off via enforcement proceedings, the retention of title creditor is paid first followed by the pledgees. This approach is similar to the approach in *Germany*, where the retention of title creditor can contractually maintain his protection in altered goods, mainly processed goods (*Verarbeitungsklausel*). Contrary to the approach in Belgium, the German retention of title creditor maintains his superiority over other creditors based on his retained title and not a legislatively assigned status of super-priority. However, the lack of codification of the tracing of retention of title in processed or mixed goods in the BGB also means that due to general property law principles, the retention of title creditor can also lose his extended protection.[1517] In *Article 9 UCC*[1518] and the *UNCITRAL Guide and Model Law*[1519] the extension of super-priority to processed and mixed goods for PMSIs and acquisition security rights, retention of title and finance leases, respectively, is explicitly codified. The *DCFR* also allows the extension of acquisition security rights and retention of ownership, including their super-priority status, in the processed or mixed goods, but only if the parties have contractually agreed to extend their acquisition financing device to the processed or mixed goods.[1520]

352. *Conflict between the retention of title creditor and the mortgage holder* – Following incorporation, the retention of title creditor can come into conflict with the creditor with a mortgage in the immovable good in which the movable and encumbered collateral is incorporated. For this conflict the Security Rights Act has not provided a clear solution. SAGAERT and DEL CORAL see two possible outcomes for this conflict. Either the conflict is resolved based on the first in time rule which would make the solution similar to the solution for the pledge, but would deprive retention of title creditors in this situation from their super-priority.[1521] Or, the super-priority rule is extended to the conflict between retention of title creditors and mortgage holders.[1522] Support for the latter interpretation can be found in the explanatory memorandum to the Security Rights Act, which explicitly gives the retention of title creditor priority over the mortgage holder. However, this interpretation was never translated into an

1516 Art. 58 SRA.
1517 See *supra* no. 234.
1518 See *supra* no. 89–90.
1519 See *supra* no. 146.
1520 See *supra* no. 193.
1521 V. SAGAERT and J. DEL CORRAL, "Eigendomsvoorbehoud" in *Algemene praktische rechtsverzameling*, (Mechelen: Kluwer, 2015), 146–147.
1522 V. SAGAERT and J. DEL CORRAL, "Eigendomsvoorbehoud" in *Algemene praktische rechtsverzameling*, (Mechelen: Kluwer, 2015), 146–147; A. APERS and D. GRUYAERT, 'Eigendomsvoorbehoud en onroerende incorporatie volgens de nieuwe pandwet: welk nieuws onder de zon?', (2015) 1 TPR, (83) 101–102.

explicit provision in the Security Rights Act or Mortgage Act thereby leaving room for interpretation.[1523] The idea to grant the retention of title creditor super-priority over the creditor with a security interest in the immovable good to which the encumbered is attached, can also be found in *Article 9 UCC*[1524], the *UNCITRAL Guide and Model Law*[1525] and *DCFR*.[1526] However, these frameworks all insist on an additional registration of the PMSI, acquisition security right or acquisition financing device, respectively, in the land registry which contains the security rights in the immovable good. This to notify secured creditors with a security right in the immovable good of the conflict with the encumbered attached good. Conversely, the Security Rights Act only requires a registration in the National Pledge Registry to maintain the third-party effectiveness of retention of title against third parties following incorporation without an additional registration in the mortgage registry.[1527]

353. *Conflicts between retention of title creditors and other secured creditors in proceeds* – Finally, the extension of retention of title into the proceeds can also create conflicts with other secured creditors to whom the claims of the debtor on third parties (i.e. accounts receivables) have been pledged or transferred. A possible solution would be to default to the super-priority rule of the Security Rights Act on the basis of which retention of title takes priority over creditor with a pledge in the accounts receivable or to whom they have been assigned. Under the assumption that the extension of retention of title into proceeds means that the retention of title creditor maintains full title to the proceeds, his super-priority in the proceeds as opposed to third parties could be easily established.[1528] However, this solution would require the super-priority provision to be implicitly expanded to conflicts with third-party transferees of the account receivable. Alternatively, according to STORME the retention of title creditor's super-priority as opposed to both the pledgee and assignee is based on the inherent seniority of the retention of title, thereby alleviating the need for a broader provision.[1529] However, STORME points out that the pledgee and assignee are protected against the retention of title creditor's super-priority via the good faith protections for third parties. First, the pledge holder can

---

1523 Explanatory memorandum Security Rights Act, no. 2463/001, 71.

1524 See *supra* no. 75.

1525 See *supra* no. 142.

1526 See *supra* no. 189.

1527 See *supra* no. 342.

1528 Art. 58 SRA. See also, M. E. STORME, 'Zekerheidsrechten op schuldvorderingen op naam' in M. E. STORME (ed.), Roerende zekerheden na de Pandwet, (Antwerpen: Intersentia, 2017), (223) 287.

1529 As mentioned, the implementation of a super-priority rule suggests that the retention of title-creditor no longer has inherent seniority over older *in rem* security rights in the same collateral, but requires an explicit assignment of super-priority to surpass older *in rem* security rights in the same good. See *supra* no. 346.

surpass the retention of title creditor, if the pledge holder in good faith notified the underlying debtor of the pledge. Second, the third-party transferee can still surpass the retention of title creditor's super-priority in the substitute claim, if the transferor was authorized to transfer the claim to a third party and the third-party transferee received the good in good faith.[1530]

Not everyone agrees with this analysis. SAGAERT and DEL CORAL are of the opinion that in a conflict between the retention of title creditor and a pledgee or assignee of an account receivable, priority should always be determined via the first in time rule and not the super-priority rule.[1531] This would mean that the conflict would be resolved based on what happened first: the creation of the retention of title clause for retention of title or the notification of the underlying debtor for the pledge or assignment. It is not further explained why this conflict should be resolved via the first in time rule. SAGAERT's and DEL CORRAL's preference for the first in time rule is especially confusing, since they are both of the opinion that the retention of title creditor should always be given priority, because he has a closer connection to the receivable to which his retention of title has extended than the pledgee or assignee, who often has a right in this asset as a result of broad pledge or assignment agreement in which all the debtor's receivables have been pledged or assigned to him.[1532] By determining this conflict based on the super-priority rule, retention of title would always outrank the pledgee or transferee instead of it being dependent on the moment of notification to the pledged debtor.

354. *Conflicts in proceeds in comparison* – The myriad of approaches to the extension of super-priority into proceeds can also be seen in the selected jurisdictions and international instruments. Similar to the Security Rights Act, the *German* BGB does not offer an explicit solution to any conflicts between the retention of title creditor with a *Vorausabtretungsklausel* and the creditors with a conflicting claim in the same accounts receivable. Therefore, the BGH intervened to avoid that the first in time principle would in most cases give priority to the assignee of the accounts receivable. More precisely, the Court reasoned that the blanket assignment of accounts receivable and the enforcement of non-assignment clauses for future creditors, such as the retention of title creditor, would be in bad faith and go against public policy.[1533]

Conversely, in the other selected frameworks a more explicit approach is chosen to resolve the conflict between retention of title and other creditors

---

1530 M. E. STORME, 'Zekerheidsrechten op schuldvorderingen op naam' in M. E. STORME (ed.), Roerende zekerheden na de Pandwet, (Antwerpen: Intersentia, 2017), (223) 287.

1531 V. SAGAERT and J. DEL CORRAL, "Eigendomsvoorbehoud" in *Algemene praktische rechtsverzameling*, (Mechelen: Kluwer, 2015), 132.

1532 V. SAGAERT and J. DEL CORRAL, "Eigendomsvoorbehoud" in *Algemene praktische rechtsverzameling*, (Mechelen: Kluwer, 2015), 134.

1533 See *supra* no. 241.

in the proceeds. In *Article 9 UCC*, PMSIs are extended into proceeds, but limited to cash proceeds. In other words, extending super-priority to accounts receivables is not possible in order to allow other creditors to vest a competing security interest in these goods.[1534] In the *UNCITRAL Guide and Model Law*, super-priority can be extended to proceeds but only when a distinction is made between proceeds of inventory and equipment. For the proceeds of inventory, the extension of super-priority is limited to cash proceeds. If the distinction between proceeds of inventory and equipment is not made, then the acquisition security rights are extended to the proceeds, but they only enjoy priority and not super-priority status. This rule also applies under the *UNCITRAL non-unitary approach* and thus to retention of title and finance leases. In other words, in that scenario the retention of title creditor or financial lessor is not able to rely on his retained title to surpass more senior creditors, but is recharacterized to a general security right the priority of which is based on time. This approach under the *UNCITRAL non-unitary approach* again confirms that the assignment of super-priority is a policy choice and can vary from transaction to transaction and from good to good. Similarly, retention of title and finance leases under the *UNCITRAL non-unitary approach* are able to trace their claim to the proceeds, but their claim is limited to a security right instead of ownership.[1535] Finally, the *DCFR* simply does not allow the extension of super-priority into proceeds, unless in very specific circumstances.[1536]

355. *Conclusion* – In the Security Rights Act, and most of the other selected frameworks, a choice is made to let retention of title creditors or their functional equivalents (i.e. PMSIs and acquisition security rights) maintain their super-priority status in the altered goods. However, the situation is less clear with regards to extending the super-priority of retention of title to proceeds. The Security Rights Act does not offer clear guidance within doctrine. Different views conflict with each other, making it difficult for the involved creditors to determine what their position will be. Preferably, the Belgian legislator would have made a clearer decision in favor of a specific priority ranking, as in *Article 9 UCC*, the *UNCITRAL Guide and Model Law* and *DCFR*, to bring clarity to this matter and avoid any discussion among the different creditors.

4. ENFORCEMENT

356. *Overview* – In this section I assess the retention of title creditor's right to revendicate as main method of enforcement (4.1.) and the explicit limitation of the right to revendicate through the principle of unjust enrichment (4.2.).

1534 See *supra* no. 87.
1535 See *supra* no. 146.
1536 See *supra* no. 193.

4.1. *The right to revendicate*

357. *Enforcement before and after the Security Rights Act* – The main method of enforcement for the retention of title creditor both in the former Bankruptcy Act and the Security Rights Act has been the right to revendicate.[1537] The right to revendicate is typically associated with the concept of ownership.[1538] The idea is that the owner of a good, including the retention of title creditor, can simply revendicate his property in the event of default by the retention of title debtor. Unlike the tracing rules, the drafters of the Security Rights Act opted against a uniform set of rules for the enforcement of all security rights in movable goods. The pledge is governed by a very specific set of rules that regulate the notification of the pledgor[1539], the sale or appropriation of the encumbered good[1540], judicial oversight of the enforcement proceedings[1541] and the division of the proceeds of the enforcement proceeding.[1542] Conversely, the rules concerning the enforcement of retention of title remain limited to an assignment of the right to revendicate to the retention of title creditor.

358. *The different steps of enforcing retention of title in comparison* – The continuation of the title-based approach to enforcement in the Security Rights Act aligns with the approach in *Germany*[1543] and the *DCFR*.[1544] These frameworks also base the enforcement of retention of title on the ownership to the encumbered good and thus the right to revendicate. Conversely, in *Article 9 UCC*[1545] and the *UNCITRAL Guide and Model Law*[1546], the enforcement of PMSIs or acquisition security rights, retention of title or finance leases, respectively, follows much more strict rules based on the enforcement of security rights for which the debtor is considered owner of the encumbered good and not the creditor.

Under Belgian law, the first step in the revindication process is to notify the debtor of his default and urge him to perform his obligations (*ingebrekestelling*). This step needs to take place before the right to revendicate can be enforced.[1547]

1537 Art. 101 former Bankruptcy Act; Art. 69 SRA.

1538 E. DIRIX, 'Functionele analyse van zekerheidsrechten' in W. PINTENS and others (eds.), *Vigilantibus ius scriptum: feestbundel voor Hugo Vandenberghe*, (Brugge: Die Keure, 2007), (119) 123; R. JANSEN, 'Eigendomsvoorbehoud' in J. BAECK and M. KRUITHOF (eds.), *Het nieuwe zekerheidsrecht*, (Antwerpen: Intersentia, 2014), (139) 163.

1539 Art. 48 SRA.

1540 Art. 51–53 SRA.

1541 Art. 54 and 56 SRA.

1542 Art. 55 SRA.

1543 See *supra* no. 248.

1544 See *supra* no. 195.

1545 See *supra* no. 96 *et seq.*

1546 See *supra* no. 148–149.

1547 Cass. 9 April 1976, (1976) Arr. Cass., (921) 923. See also, V. VERLAECKT, 'Artikel 69 – 72' in D. BLOMMAERT and others (eds.), *Wet en duiding – Economisch recht*, (Brussels: Larcier,

Creditors can contract out of this obligation to notify the debtor of his default[1548], but this does not exempt them from the general obligation to enforce their claims prudently and carefully.[1549] This notification does not have to comply with specific formalities, but at a minimum has to contain the necessary information to allow the identification of the encumbered collateral.[1550] The notification of the intent to revendicate cannot be contractually excluded.[1551] A similar obligation to notify the debtor of the impending enforcement proceedings can be found in the *UNCITRAL Guide and Model Law*[1552] and *Germany*.[1553] Interestingly, *Article 9 UCC*[1554] and the *DCFR*[1555] both do not implement a notification requirement for the enforcement of their PMSI or retention of ownership device, respectively.

Second, the retention of title creditor has to obtain possession of the encumbered good in order to dispose of the good or appropriate it in satisfaction of his outstanding claim. The Security Rights Act does not mention how the retention of title creditor can regain possession of the encumbered good. However, in doctrine it has been clearly established that the retention of title creditor cannot simply go onto the debtor's property and recover what is his. Such forceful revendication of the encumbered collateral could constitute as trespass and potentially abuse of law.[1556] In the event the retention of title debtor refuses to relinquish the encumbered collateral, the retention of title creditor has to turn to the courts and get the necessary approval to forcefully remove the collateral.[1557] Consequently, the retention of title creditor has to

2014), (622) 625; T. VANSWEEVELT and B. WEYTS, 'Nakoming van verbintenissen of betaling ' in T. VANSWEEVELT and B. WEYTS (eds.), *Handboek verbintenissenrecht*, (Antwerp: Intersentia, 2019), (791) 835.

1548 L. DE MEYERE en M. VISSER `Ingebrekestellingsclausules" in *Gemeenrechtelijke clausules*, II in *Contractuele clausules*, (Antwerp: Intersentia, 2013) 1009–1010; V. VERLAECKT, 'Artikel 69 - 72' in D. BLOMMAERT and others (eds.), *Wet en duiding - Economisch recht*, (Brussels: Larcier, 2014), (622) 625.

1549 R. STEENOT, 'De verplichting tot ingebrekestelling (note under Vred. Arendonk 29 September 2009)', (2012) 5 T. Vred., (274) 275.

1550 Ghent 22 October 2007, (2008) TGR-TWVR, (361) 361–362. See also, E. DIRIX, 'Eigendomsvoorbehoud en samenloop', (1994–95) 37 RW, (1264) 1266; G. VERSCHELDEN, 'Eigendomsvoorbehoud tussen partijen en tegenover derden', (1998–99) AJT, (821) 832; V. SAGAERT and J. DEL CORRAL, "Eigendomsvoorbehoud" in *Algemene praktische rechtsverzameling*, (Mechelen: Kluwer, 2015), 79.

1551 V. SAGAERT and J. DEL CORRAL, "Eigendomsvoorbehoud" in *Algemene praktische rechtsverzameling*, (Mechelen: Kluwer, 2015), 79.

1552 See *supra* no. 148.

1553 See *supra* no. 248.

1554 See *supra* no. 95.

1555 See *supra* no. 195.

1556 E. DIRIX, De hervorming van de roerende zakelijke zekerheden, (Mechelen: Kluwer, 2013), 44–45; I. VAN DE PLAS, 'Mis/gebruik in de Pandwet' in A. VAN DE VIJVER (ed.), *Misbruik binnen de onderneming*, (Antwerpen, Intersentia, 2018), (165) 188.

1557 Art. 1462 Civil Procedure Code (CCC). See also, F. 'T KINT, *Sûretés et principes généraux du droit de poursuite des créanciers*, (Brussels: Larcier, 2004), 247; E. DIRIX and R. DE CORTE, 'Zekerheidsrechten' in *Beginselen van Belgisch privaatrecht*, (5th edn., Mechelen:

ask the debtor or the courts for permission to revendicate the collateral. Such limitations on the right to obtain possession of the encumbered good can also be found in the selected jurisdictions and international instruments. Once the retention of title creditor is in possession again of the encumbered good he can choose to dispose of the good or to appropriate it in order to satisfy his outstanding claim. Regardless of whether a retention of title remains a retention of title (*Germany*)[1558], is recharacherized to a PMSI (*Article 9 UCC*)[1559] or acquisition security right (*UNCITRAL unitary approach*)[1560] or equated with an acquisition security right (*UNCITRAL non-unitary approach*[1561] and *DCFR*[1562]), the retention of title creditor is prevented from forcefully entering the debtor's premises and simply retaking the encumbered good as part of the enforcement proceedings.

359. *Conclusion* – The enforcement of retention of title remains based on the right to revendicate both prior to and after the enactment of the Security Rights Act. However, the right to revendicate no longer means that the retention of title creditor can simply take back his property. The retention of title creditor has to respect certain limitations on his right to revendicate, such as notifying the retention of title debtor of the impending enforcement or respecting the retention of title debtor's property when repossessing the encumbered good. As a result, the right to revendicate does not differ so much from the enforcement proceedings of PMSIs and acquisition security rights, which are governed by much more elaborate enforcement rules. Nevertheless, the drafters opted against creating a uniform enforcement regime for all security rights in movable goods, as is the case in *Article 9 UCC* and under the *UNCITRAL unitary approach*. From a coherence and legal certainty perspective the explicit and clear rules concerning the enforcement of PMSIs and acquisition security rights are easier to follow and make it more clear for retention of title creditors what their rights are and how they can be enforced. Therefore, the implementation of one set of rules for the enforcement of all security rights of movable goods in the new Book 9 of the Civil Code would be preferable to the mere assignment of the right to revendicate to retention of title that we have now in the Security Rights Act. Once one set of rules for the enforcement of all security rights in movable goods are recommended, the next logical step would be to simply recharacterize retention of title to an acquisition security right so it can be easily and logically integrated into a general framework for security rights in movable goods.

Wolters Kluwer, 2006), 415; V. SAGAERT and J. DEL CORRAL, "Eigendomsvoorbehoud" in *Algemene praktische rechtsverzameling*, (Mechelen: Kluwer, 2015), 80.

1558 See *supra* no. 248.

1559 See *supra* no. 95.

1560 See *supra* no. 148.

1561 See *supra* no. 148.

1562 See *supra* no. 195.

4.2. *Explicit provision on unjust enrichment*

360. *Unjust enrichment prior to and after the Security Rights Act* – The Security Rights Act comes with an explicit provision on unjust enrichment for retention of title.[1563] The ban on unjust enrichment can be seen as an explication of one of the basic features of security rights in movable goods: that the secured creditor cannot unjustly enrich himself following the enforcement of the encumbered good.[1564] The codification of the ban on unjust enrichment has not changed the protection of retention of title during enforcement proceedings. Prior to the Security Rights Act it was already generally accepted in case law and doctrine that the retention of title creditor could not unjustly enrich himself.[1565] Nevertheless, the explicit provision concerning unjust enrichment for retention of title improves the clarity and legal certainty of the Security Rights Act. Furthermore, it removes any perception that retention of title on the basis of ownership would be entitled to more than the outstanding claim.

361. *Reasoning behind the prohibition on unjust enrichment for retention of title* – The idea that retention of title requires an explicit provision to prevent unjust enrichment can be traced back to the perception that retention of title is more collateral-based and therefore requires an explicit ban on unjust enrichment.[1566] Theoretically, the right to revendicate is aimed at getting the collateral back regardless of the extent to which the value of the collateral succeeds at satisfying the outstanding claim. Consequently, it could be argued that a retention of title creditor does not have to account for any surplus when using the right to revendicate, since this action does not actually relate to the outstanding claim but is simply the recovery of his property. Based on this reasoning it becomes clear why the legislator deemed it necessary to explicitly ban unjust enrichment when retention of title creditors revendicate their collateral, while this is not

1563 Art. 72 SRA.

1564 E. DIRIX and R. DE CORTE, 'Zekerheidsrechten' in *Beginselen van Belgisch privaatrecht*, (5th edn., Mechelen: Wolters Kluwer, 2006), 4.

1565 For the specific application of this principle to retention of title authors turned to a ruling by the French Supreme Court, see Supreme Court 5 March 1996, IV (1996) Bull., 59.Furthermore, the principle was generally accepted as a corrective measure to prevent that one estate would enrich itself without cause to the detriment of another estate. See, H. DE PAGE, 'Les obligations' in *Traité élémentaire de droit civil belge*, III, (Brussel: Bruylant, 1967), 32 *et seq.*; Cass. 19 January 2009, no. C.07.0575.N, concl. MORTIER, (2009) 1 Arr. Cass., (1) 177; E. DIRIX and R. DE CORTE, 'Zekerheidsrechten' in *Beginselen van Belgisch privaatrecht*, (5th edn., Mechelen: Wolters Kluwer, 2006), 27–28 and 414; E. DIRIX, 'Art. 101 Faillissementswet' in E. DIRIX, P. FRANCOIS and M. TISON (eds.), *Voorrechten en hypotheken – Artikelsgewijze commentaar met overzicht van rechtspraak en rechtsleer*, (Mechelen: Kluwer, 2011), 13).

1566 V. SAGAERT, *Zakelijke subrogatie*, (Antwerp: Intersentia, 2003), 131; R. JANSEN, 'Eigendomsvoorbehoud' in J. BAECK and M. KRUITHOF (eds.), *Het nieuwe zekerheidsrecht*, (Antwerpen: Intersentia, 2014), (139) 143.

codified for the enforcement of the other security rights in movable goods. A counterargument for the explicit provision concerning unjust enrichment is that the retention of title can just as easily be explained from a value-based perspective. Like other security rights in movable goods, retention of title is vested to guarantee an outstanding claim. Furthermore, retention of title can only be enforced when the debtor defaults. Therefore, the revendication that follows this default can just as easily be viewed as a means to obtain payment for the outstanding claim and not merely as a tool to recover property. When retention of title is assessed from this perspective, it becomes less clear why the enforcement of a retention of title should be considered different from that of a pledge and unjust enrichment needs to be explicitly prohibited for retention of title and not for the pledge.

362. *Prohibition on unjust enrichment in comparison* – The ban on unjust enrichment for retention of title seems generally accepted across the selected frameworks. In the *DCFR*[1567] and *Germany*[1568], where the term retention of title is maintained, the prohibition is based on general contract law principles that prevent the retention of title creditors from unjustly enriching themselves. Similarly, under the *UNCITRAL non-unitary approach* the rules concerning retention of title and finance leasing are so adjusted to ensure that surplus value returns to the retention of title debtor.[1569] Finally, in the frameworks that apply the functional approach with recharacterization, the prohibition on unjust enrichment for all security rights and security interests, including PMSIs and acquisition security rights, is referred to as the return of any surplus value to the debtor after the distribution of proceeds in the enforcement proceedings.[1570]

363. *Conclusion* – The explicit application of unjust enrichment to retention of title does not actively change the retention of title creditor's position. Furthermore, across the selected jurisdictions and international instruments, retention of title creditors are prohibited from unjustly enriching themselves regardless of whether they have formally retained title or are recharacterized to a PMSI or acquisition security right. However, the explicit nature of the provision on unjust enrichment does remove any misconception that may exist concerning the retention of title creditor recovering the encumbered good and not having to return any of the surplus value.

1567 See *supra* no. 195.
1568 See *supra* no. 249.
1569 See *supra* no. 148.
1570 See Article 9, *supra* no. 96, the UNCITRAL Guide and Model Law, *supra* no. 148.

SECTION 5 – RETENTION OF TITLE DURING CORPORATE BANKRUPTCY PROCEEDINGS

364. *Limitation of the scope to corporate bankruptcy proceedings* – In this section, corporate bankruptcy refers to the liquidation proceeding (i.e. *faillissement/faillite*) as it is set out in Book XX of the Code on Economic Law.[1571] In Belgium, corporate bankruptcy only has the goal to liquidate the company and distribute the proceeds among the different creditors. For the possibility to restructure a company in financial difficulty, Belgian entrepreneurs can rely on a specific corporate restructuring proceeding (i.e. *gerechtelijke reorganisatie/eorganization judiciaire*).[1572]

A choice is made to limit the analysis to retention of title and the rights of retention of title creditors during corporate bankruptcy proceedings, because during this procedure in Belgian law the enforcement and protection of retention of title is most visible. Consequently, in this setting the potential impact of the functional approach on retention of title and the rights of retention of title creditors can be the most clearly ascertained.

365. *Scope of the comparison* – The comparison in this section is limited to *Article 9 UCC* and *Germany*. The reason for this is that the selected international instruments are not linked to a jurisdiction in which retention of title or its (recharacterized) functional equivalents can be assessed during a corporate bankruptcy proceeding.

1. CORPORATE BANKRUPTCY OF THE RETENTION OF TITLE DEBTOR

366. *General recognition of retention of title in collective insolvency proceedings* – One of the biggest developments following the integration of retention of title in the Security Rights Act is that now retention of title is recognized in all collective insolvency proceedings that can befall the retention of title debtor.[1573]

1571 Wet van 11 augustus 2017 houdende invoeging van het Boek XX "Insolventie van ondernemingen", in het Wetboek van economisch recht, en houdende invoeging van de definities eigen aan Boek XX en van de rechtshandhavingsbepalingen eigen aan Boek XX in het Boek I van het Wetboek van economisch recht, *BS* 11 september 2017, 83100 (hereafter, Book XX LEC).

1572 Art. XX.39–97 CEL.

1573 J. CATTARUZZA, 'Les grands axes de la réforme des sûretés mobilières', (2013) 4 Dr. Banc. Fin., (183) 193; W. DERIJCKE, 'La réforme des sûretés réelles mobilières', (2013) 8 TBH, (691) 718; E. DIRIX, 'The new Belgian act on security interests in movable property', (2014) 23 Int. Insolv. Rev., (171) 178; R. HOUBEN and M. VAN DE LOOVERBOSCH, 'Belgium: security interests – moveable assets', (2017) 28 International Company and Commercial Law Review, (67) 69; V. SAGAERT, 'Enkele pijlers van de nieuwe pandwet', *CBR Jaarboek 2013-2014*,

This was in direct response to a 2010 Supreme Court case in which the Court ruled that there was not a general principle that retention of title is effective against third parties during all forms of *concursus*.[1574] Following this reasoning, the court maintained that retention of title could only be enforced during corporate bankruptcy proceedings for which the enforcement of retention of title was regulated.[1575]

With the integration of retention of title in the Security Rights Act and the inclusion of the Security Rights Act in the Belgian Civil Code, the third-party effectiveness of retention of title against third parties both prior to and during all types of *concursus* is confirmed.

367. *Treatment of retention of title during corporate bankruptcy proceedings* – The retention of title creditor's right to revendicate during corporate bankruptcy proceedings can now be found in book twenty of the Code on Economic Law (hereafter, CEL) concerning corporate insolvencies.[1576] As in the former Bankruptcy Act, the CEL upholds the owner's right to revendicate his property out of the bankruptcy estate[1577] and that the right to revendicate has to be enforced prior to the bankruptcy receiver's report on claim verification.[1578] The bankruptcy receiver can only refuse the revendication of the encumbered good in the event that the bankruptcy estate inferred costs from the restitution or detention of the encumbered good and the retention of title creditor refuses to reimburse these costs. In that case, the bankruptcy receiver can invoke his right of retention of possession.[1579] If the encumbered good cannot be revendicated due to, for example, a transfer of the encumbered good to a third party, then the retention of title creditor, who notified the trustee in bankruptcy in a timely manner of his claim and retention of title, is given a preferential claim in the proceeds of this transfer.[1580] In other words, in the context of corporate bankruptcy the retention of title creditor is still viewed as an owner and thus treated separately from the secured creditors with a pledge. However, the

(Antwerp: Intersentia, 2014), (10) 16–17; I. DURANT, 'Le droit de rétention et la réserve de propriété, deux sûretés réelles mobilières à part entière' in F. GEORGES (ed.), *Insolvabilité et garanties*, (Brussels: Larcier,2014), (34) 82; J. CAEYMAEX and T. CAVENAILE, *Manuel des sûretés mobilières*, (3 edn., Brussels: Larcier, 2019), 514.

1574 Cass. 7 May 2010, (2010) Arr. Cass. 2010, 1334.

1575 Art. 101 former Bankruptcy Act.

1576 Wet van 11 augustus 2017 houdende invoeging van het Boek XX "Insolventie van ondernemingen", in het Wetboek van economisch recht, en houdende invoeging van de definities eigen aan Boek XX en van de rechtshandhavingsbepalingen eigen aan Boek XX in het Boek I van het Wetboek van economisch recht, *BS* 11 september 2017, 83100 (hereafter, Book XX LEC).

1577 Art. XX.194, sec. 1 Book XX LEC.

1578 Art. XX.194, sec. 2 Book XX LEC.

1579 Art. XX.194, sec. 3 Book XX LEC.

1580 V. SAGAERT and J. DEL CORRAL, 'Eigendomsvoorbehoud' in *Algemene Praktische Rechtsverzameling*, (Mechelen: Wolters Kluwer, 2015), 96.

difference with the treatment of the pledge during corporate bankruptcy should also not be overstated. Like the retention of title, the enforcement of the pledge is stayed until the bankruptcy receiver has verified the validity and third-party effectiveness of the pledge.[1581] After verification, the pledge holder can enforce his pledge by following the specific enforcement rules set out in the Security Rights Act.[1582] However, unlike retention of title, the bankruptcy receiver can request the court to further stay the enforcement of the pledge, if it is in the best interest of the bankruptcy estate and if it can be expected that the enforcement of the pledge will not disadvantage the pledge holder.[1583] In that case, the priority ranking of the pledge will remain so the pledge holder can still count on some preferential treatment in the distribution of the proceeds of the liquidation proceeding.

368. *Retention of title in corporate bankruptcy in comparison* – Retention of title in *Germany* and PMSIs in the *United States* are both affected by the stay of proceedings of their respective corporate bankruptcy proceedings. However, *Germany* has a similar approach to the one in Belgium, where the retention of title creditor is still considered full owner of the encumbered good and thus the good is considered to fall outside of the bankruptcy estate (i.e. *Aussonderungsrecht*)[1584] and can be revendicated. For *Article 9 UCC*, the effect of the stay of proceedings on PMSIs makes sense, since the recharacterization of retention of title to a PMSI means that title to the encumbered good has transferred to the debtor and the encumbered good has thus become part of the bankruptcy estate.[1585] However, PMSI holders do not lose all agency the moment the corporate bankruptcy proceeding is initiated, since they can also be excluded from the stay of proceedings via the procedures of relief and abandonment.[1586] Furthermore, the super-priority of PMSIs is recognized in corporate bankruptcy proceedings increasing the PMSI holders chance of payment following the liquidation proceedings.[1587]

369. *Conclusion* – After the enactment of the Security Rights Act, the protection of retention of title in Belgian's corporate bankruptcy proceedings has not changed. Moreover, the treatment of retention of title in Belgian corporate bankruptcy proceedings is very similar to the protection to retention of title in *German* corporate bankruptcy proceedings. However, the difference between the treatment of retention of title in Belgium and PMSIs in the United States

1581 Art. XX.121 Book XX LEC.
1582 Art. 47 *et seq.* SRA.
1583 Art. XX.121, sec. 2 Book XX LEC.
1584 See *supra* no. 254.
1585 See *supra* no. 100.
1586 See *supra* no. 104.
1587 See *supra* no. 104.

during corporate bankruptcy proceedings should not be overstated. PMSIs may be slightly more affected by the stay of proceedings, but they also have avenues open to them to avoid the stay of proceedings. Furthermore, the priority status of PMSIs is recognized during corporate bankruptcy proceedings ensuring the preferential treatment and increasing the likelihood of payment during the liquidation of the bankrupt's estate. In that sense, the treatment of PMSIs is very similar to the treatment of the pledge during Belgian corporate bankruptcy proceedings. Given these similarities, the recharacterization of retention of title to an acquisition security right under Belgian law is unlikely to have a significant impact on the treatment of former retention of title creditors during corporate bankruptcy proceedings. Therefore, the potential negative impact of recharacterization of retention of title to an acquisition security right on the protection of former retention of title creditors during corporate bankruptcy proceedings cannot be used as an argument against recharacterizing retention of title.

2. CORPORATE BANKRUPTCY OF THE RETENTION OF TITLE CREDITOR

370. *The concept of retention of title and the retention of title debtor's bankruptcy* – Because retention of title under the Security Rights Act still refers to the ownership in the hands of the retention of title creditor, the bankruptcy of the retention of title creditor can cast doubt on the protection of the retention of title debtor. In the Code on Economic Law the legislator does not take a clear position on whether the corporate bankruptcy of the retention of title creditor has an impact on the rights of the retention of title debtor. Furthermore, the legislator has not provided a provision in which a choice is made for either the protection of the retention of title debtor or the right of the bankruptcy receiver to reclaim the encumbered good following the bankruptcy of the retention of title creditor.

Given this uncertainty in Belgium, there is a possibility that bankruptcy receivers for the retention of title creditor will argue that the encumbered good can be revendicated from the retention of title debtor's hands and can be liquidated as part of the retention of title creditor's bankruptcy proceedings. In that case, it can be presumed that the retention of title debtor will rely on the existing majority opinion in Belgian doctrine that protects the retention of title debtor's nascent ownership in the encumbered good as long as he continues to make payments on the good.[1588] This view is confirmed in the Insolvency Regulation which states that the retention of title debtor is unaffected by the retention of title creditor's corporate bankruptcy proceeding and is allowed to

1588 V. SAGAERT and J. DEL CORRAL, 'Eigendomsvoorbehoud' in *Algemene Praktische Rechts-verzameling*, (Mechelen: Wolters Kluwer, 2015), 70–73.

continue payments on the collateral.[1589] The protection of the retention of title debtor's right in the encumbered good during the retention of title creditor's bankruptcy is also considered as an indication that the retention of title creditor no longer holds absolute title to the encumbered good but merely a security right.[1590]

In *Germany* a slightly different and more convoluted strategy is taken. The BGH intervened to protect the retention of title debtor's *Anwartschaftsrecht* in the encumbered good in order to protect him from the recovery of the encumbered following the retention of title creditor's bankruptcy. However, this protection is revoked in the event the retention of title debtor does not perform his end of the agreement.[1591] In other words, the retention of title creditor technically still holds title to the encumbered good, but the retention of title debtor's budding ownership in the encumbered good (i.e. *Anwartschaftsrecht*) is also protected. Evidently, this problem does not arise in the *United States*, where the recharacterization of retention of title to a PMSI results in a transfer of title to the debtor and there is no debate whether the PMSI debtor can be affected by the PMSI creditor's bankruptcy proceedings.

371. *Conclusion* – The integration of retention of title in the Security Rights Act has not made the position of the retention of title debtor in the event of the retention of title creditor's bankruptcy any clearer. Furthermore, Belgian case law has not yet emerged in which a clear position is taken on the position of the retention of title debtor during the retention of title creditor's corporate bankruptcy proceeding, as was the case in *Germany*. This leaves the position of the retention of title debtor open to interpretation, which is not desirable.

A first step to address this situation, would be to provide a provision clearly stating the retention of title debtor's protection in the event of the retention of title creditor's bankruptcy. However, this would basically entail the introduction of an *Anwartschaftsrecht* into the Belgian legal system, together with all the legal ambiguity the *Anwartschaftsrecht* entails. Alternatively, the recharacterization of retention of title to an acquisition security right, such as in *Article 9 UCC* or the *UNCITRAL Guide and Model Law*, would provide the greatest clarity on this issue and would remove for once and for all the uncertainty following the bankruptcy of the retention of title creditor.

1589 Art. 10 (2) Insolvency Regulation 2015.

1590 M. E. STORME, *Zekerheden en insolventierecht*, (Ghent, Mariakerke: 2018–19), 412.

1591 See *supra* no. 258.

CHAPTER 3
CONCLUSIONS

372. The conclusions to this section are structured in accordance with the second and third sub-research questions of this dissertation.[1592] First, I summarize how the functional approach is applied to retention of title in the Security Rights Act (section 1). This is followed by a summary of the comparison of retention of title across the selected jurisdictions and international instruments (section 2). Finally, I formulate recommendations for the Belgian legislation concerning retention of title following the comparison with the different approaches to retention of title across the selected frameworks (section 3).

SECTION 1 – THE FUNCTIONAL APPROACH OF RETENTION OF TITLE IN THE SECURITY RIGHTS ACT IN BELGIUM

373. *The functional approach and the basic division of security rights in movable goods in the Security Rights Act* – The goal of the functional approach is to achieve equivalent legal outcomes for functionally similar mechanisms. Following this reasoning, the Security Rights Act explicitly classifies the pledge, transfer of title for security purposes of accounts receivable, retention of title and the right of retention of possession as *security rights in movable goods*. Furthermore, the different types of pledges that existed prior to the Security Rights Act are recharacterized to a general pledge. Finally, the transfer of title to accounts receivable for security purposes and the right of retention of possession are treated as a pledge. However, the functional approach in the Security Rights Act does not go so far that all mechanisms that operate like security rights in movable goods are included into the scope of the Security Rights Act. For example, some of the legislative liens in movable goods in the Mortgage Act that perform the same function as a pledge (such as the lien of the unpaid landlord, the lien for costs made for the preservation of a movable good, and the lien of the carrier) are not impacted by the Security Rights Act. Moreover, the unpaid vendor's lien remains untouched by the introduction of the Security Rights Act

[1592] See *supra* no. 8.

and continues as an alternative alongside retention of title. Furthermore, the security rights in financial collateral are not governed by the Security Rights Act, but remain governed by the Financial Collateral Act.

The general classification as a security right in movable goods is a starting point, but needs further refinement. In the Security Rights Act two subgroups can be discerned 1) pledges and security rights that are equated with pledges, and 2) retention of title. It should be noted that the Belgian legislator did not introduce a general subcategory of acquisition security rights that includes retention of title, but holds on to retention of title as a separate subgroup.

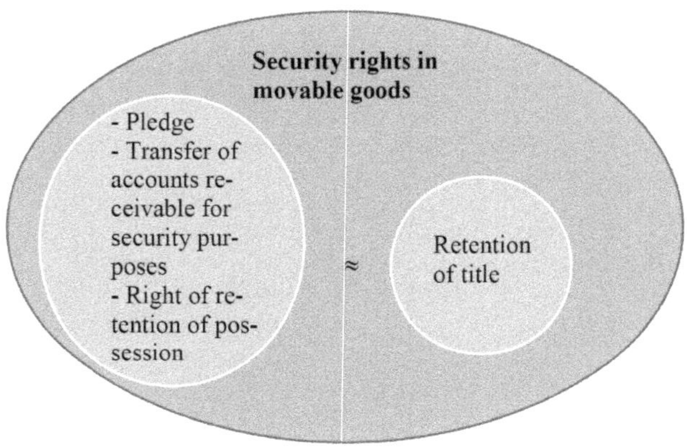

374. *Application of the functional approach to retention of title and the pledge* – In the Security Rights Act, *some equivalent legal outcomes are explicitly pursued* for retention of title and the pledge following the functional approach. For example, the Security Rights Act explicitly creates equivalent legal outcomes with regards to the tracing of retention of title and the pledge in altered goods. Both mechanisms now enjoy protection in the event the originally encumbered good is altered. Similarly, the prohibition of unjust enrichment is now explicitly extended to retention of title to ensure that retention of title creditors cannot retain any surplus value after enforcing their retention of title.

Furthermore, there are also cases where *equivalent legal outcomes for retention of title and the pledge are implicit.* For example, with regards to the right to dispose I established through analysis of case law and doctrine that the retention of title creditor does not have the right to dispose a second time of the encumbered good even though the retention of title creditor supposedly still holds title to the encumbered good. This outcome is equivalent to the pledge holder's inability to dispose of the encumbered good, but is not made explicit. In other words, the legal outcomes are equivalent for retention of title and the pledge in this regard, but this has to be deduced from the case law and doctrine concerning retention of title. A similar situation exists with regards to the rules concerning tracing of the pledge in the hands of a third-party transferee, which are not extended to retention of title. However, again in the case law and doctrine for retention of title, which date back to before the Security Rights Act, it was understood that a retention of title creditor could trace in the hands of the third-party transferee under the same circumstances as the pledge. In other words, only the analysis of case law and doctrine regarding the tracing of retention of title shows that an equivalent legal outcome is achieved with the pledge.

375. *Unequivalent outcomes between retention of title and the pledge* – Beyond the abovementioned examples, the Security Rights Act does not actively pursue equivalent legal outcomes for retention of title and the pledge or any of the other security rights in movable goods. In some cases, the lack of equivalent legal outcomes is due to the continued ownership nature of retention of title in contrast to the limited proprietary interest that follows the creation of pledge in movable goods. For example, the Security Rights Act does not extend the enforcement rules for the pledge to retention of title, but maintains the retention of title creditor's right to revendicate. This choice is informed by the fact that retention of title is title-based and thus authorizes retention of title creditors, in theory, to simply take back their property instead of having to follow specific enforcement rules.

In other instances, the absence of equivalent legal outcomes between retention of title and the pledge is justified by certain policy choices. For example, the Belgian legislator chose to omit retention of title from the notification requirements for third-party effectiveness to avoid being the only jurisdiction with a registration requirement for retention of title in Europe and the reasoning that ostensible ownership problems are not as much of an issue with respect to retention of title as it is with other security rights in movable goods.

Finally, in some cases a difference between the legal outcomes of retention of title and the pledge is maintained due to the difference in credit they guarantee and thus the difference in function they perform. The goal of the Security Rights Act is not to remove all differences between retention of title and the pledge or to turn retention of title into a pledge. The Belgian legislator is aware that retention of title performs a specific function of guaranteeing acquisition credit and because of that should be entitled to specific protection. Therefore, the drafters decided to assign super-priority status to retention of title instead of general priority based on the first in time principle, to ensure that sellers and suppliers will continue the distribution of acquisition credit. However, I have established that the assignment of super-priority to retention of title in the Security Rights Act is difficult to explain. The retained title already guarantees that the retention of title creditor cannot come into conflict with other creditors. Consequently, the assignment of super-priority to retention of title is technically unnecessary, but it does highlight the Belgian legislator's desire to maintain some distinction between retention of title and the pledge due to the different type of credit they guarantee.

376. *Impact of the functional approach on retention of title and the rights of retention of title creditors* – In the few instances where the functional approach is applied, the functional approach does not significantly affect the rights of retention of title creditors. Contrary to what one may expect, subjecting retention of title to some of the rules for the pledge following the functional approach does not result in less protection for the retention of title creditor. For example, the extension of the tracing rules for the pledge to retention of title increases the protection of retention of title creditors in the event the encumbered good is altered. Similarly, in the case of unjust enrichment, retention of title was already subjected to this limitation prior to the Security Rights Act based on case law and doctrine and thus the explicit prohibition of unjust enrichment for retention of title does not significantly change the retention of title creditor's protection. Moreover, in areas where the drafters did not apply the functional approach, such as in the domain of enforcement, the application would not have caused much impact either, since the retention of title creditor's right to revendicate has already been quite limited in case law and doctrine. Furthermore, the lack of a separate category of acquisition security rights, with which retention of title can be fully functionally equated and the continued functional difference between retention of title and the pledge and the security rights that are equated with pledges meant that there was little incentive for the drafters to further unify rules for retention of title and the other security rights in the Security Rights Act. Since retention of title, the pledge and the security rights that are equated with pledges in the Security Rights Act do not perform exactly the same function and are dogmatically different (i.e. retention of title remains title-based and the other security rights are not), a continuation of different rules for retention of title and the pledge and the security rights that are equated with pledges can be justified and explain the very limited impact of the functional approach on the rules and rights of retention of title creditors. What's more, I can conclude that in fact the functional approach is simply very minimally applied and therefore logically does not have a big impact on the rights of retention of title creditors.

377. *Functional approach without recharacterization and its inherent issues* – The Security Rights Act is an example of the functional approach without recharacterization: the original terms of security rights in movable goods are maintained (i.e. pledge, transfer of title for security purposes, retention of title, right of retention of possession) and some equivalent legal outcomes between functional similar mechanisms are pursued. Seeing the application of the functional approach without recharacterization in action in the Security Rights Act confirms the previously made observation that the functional approach without recharacterization results in an *inherently confusing, uncertain and potentially misleading system*. Integral to the functional approach without recharacterization is the continuation of the old term for retention of title, while simultaneously pursuing equivalent legal outcomes for functionally equivalent mechanisms. As mentioned, the pursuit of equivalent legal outcomes should be done explicitly as to remove any doubt concerning the rights of retention of title creditors following the application of the functional approach without recharacterization. Nevertheless, the adherence to the term retention of *title* means that a lot of the baggage and associations with title are brought into the Security Rights Act. This is for example the case with the classification of retention of title as a security right. The explicit inclusion of retention of title in the class of security rights in movable goods should have removed any doubt that retention of title is now a security right and shares the core characteristics with other security rights in movable goods, such as the specificity principle, the *numerus clausus* principle, first in time principle, subrogation principle, prohibition on unjust enrichment, ex-post judicial control of enforcement and notification principle. However, in doctrine we still see debates cropping up concerning the classification of retention of title and to what extent the characteristics of security rights in movable goods can actually be extended to retention of title. Similar issues come up with regards to the right to dispose, trace into the hands of a third-party transferee and enforcement, where the term retention of title creates the impression that the retention of title creditor has absolute authority to do as he pleases with the encumbered good, whereas the case law and doctrine shows that in fact the rights of retention of title creditors are also limited with regards to the encumbered good and in fact are not very different from rights of creditors with a limited proprietary interests, such as an acquisition security right or PMSI, in the encumbered good.[1593]

One could counter the misleading and confusing nature of the functional approach without recharacterization by explicitly listing in the future Book 9 of the Civil Code which principles govern all security rights in movable goods, including retention of title. However, this would still not remove the automatic connotations creditors and other third parties have with the term retention of *title*. No matter how explicit the law, the word title will always bring up certain assumptions and create the impression that the retention of title creditor is entitled to more protection than mere security rights in movable goods.

378. *Summary* – The functional approach is minimally applied in the Security Rights Act in that some equivalent legal outcomes are explicitly established between retention of title and the pledge. However, without the introduction of an acquisition security right, the creation of equivalent legal outcomes between retention of title and acquisition security rights (its true functional equivalent) is not further pursued. Furthermore, the Security Rights Act continues to adhere to the dogmatic difference between retention of title and the pledge, being that one is title-based and the other is not, in both terminology and rules. As a result, the application of the functional approach in the Security Rights Act only amounts to a minimally consolidated and at times even incoherent framework

---

1593 See *infra* no. 379.

with little to no uniform rules, which only minimally improves the operation of the security rights system and the treatment of retention of title creditors.

SECTION 2 – COMPARISON OF THE TREATMENT OF RETENTION OF TITLE ACROSS THE SELECTED JURISDICTIONS AND INTERNATIONAL INSTRUMENTS

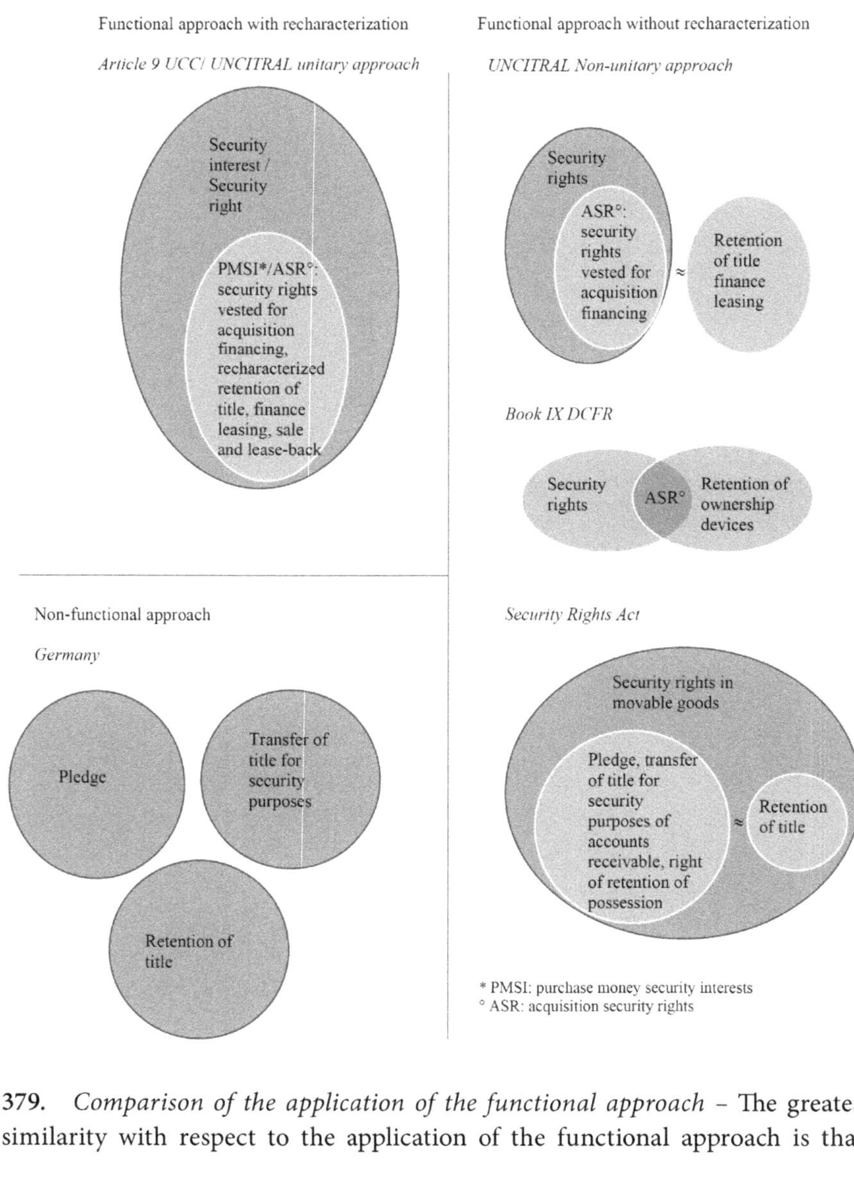

379. *Comparison of the application of the functional approach* – The greatest similarity with respect to the application of the functional approach is that, like in the Security Rights Act, the selected functional frameworks (*Article 9 UCC*, the *UNCITRAL* and *DCFR*) also maintain a distinction between general security rights in movable goods (i.e. security rights and security interests) and security rights that guarantee acquisition credit (i.e. retention of title, finance leasing, retention of ownership, acquisition security rights and PMSIs). These two categories of secured transactions often share some features and rules concerning creation, third-party effectiveness, tracing and enforcement. However, some differences in treatment are maintained for retention of title and acquisition security rights or PMSIs, such as super-priority and exemptions from notification requirements. Unlike the Security Rights Act, the selected functional frameworks either introduce a separate category of acquisition security rights with which the legal outcomes of retention of title are equated (*DCFR* and *the UNCITRAL non-unitary approach*), or recharacterizes retention of title to an acquisition security right or PMSI (*the UNCITRAL unitary approach* and *Article 9 UCC*). The treatment of retention of title like acquisition security rights or their recharacterization to acquisition security rights or PMSIs in these frameworks results in more uniform rules for all secured transactions in movable goods. For example, in each of the selected functional frameworks there are uniform rules for creation, third-party effectiveness, tracing and enforcement of *all* security rights in movable goods, including the sub-categories of retention of title, acquisition security rights and PMSIs.

The notable exception to this approach is the *DCFR*, where equivalent legal outcomes between retention of ownership devices and acquisition security rights are only partially pursued and the dogmatic difference between retention of ownership devices and acquisition security rights is more explicitly maintained, for example in the domains of creation and enforcement. The analysis of retention of ownership devices in the *DCFR* showed that the adherence to such dogmatic differences between retention of ownership devices and (acquisition) security rights is not always based on sound reasoning and often results in incoherent and illogical outcomes for the overall security rights framework. A similar result can be found in the Security Rights Act. The adherence to the term and concept of retention of title in the Security Rights Act also leads to incoherent and misleading outcomes and an unnecessary separation of rules concerning creation, third-party effectiveness and enforcement of retention of title and the other security rights in movable goods.

380. *Comparison of retention of title* – An important result from the analysis and comparison of retention of title across the selected jurisdictions and international instruments is that the rights of retention of title creditors vary very little.[1594] In some cases this is more surprising than others. For example, when comparing PMSIs and acquisition security rights in *Article 9 UCC*

1594 See *infra* Appendix A.

and *the UNCITRAL unitary approach*, one rightfully expects that similarly recharacterized retention of title mechanisms result in security rights that are similarly treated and bestow similar rights on their holders. What is more surprising, is that PMSIs and acquisition security rights show a significant similarity with retention of title under *the UNCITRAL non-unitary approach*, retention of ownership devices in the *DCFR*, retention of title in the Security Rights Act and even retention of title in *Germany*. Especially in the domains where one would expect the retained title to make a difference, for example in the context of enforcement or conflicts with other creditors and third parties, the analysis and comparison of the different iterations of retention of title mechanisms showed that the retained title in the hands of the retention of title creditor does not provide the retention of title creditor with a significant advantage as opposed to the holder of a PMSI or acquisition security right holder. This raises the question, what the added value is of maintaining the term and concept of retention of title if in fact it acts and performs very similarly to acquisition security rights or PMSIs.

SECTION 3 – RECOMMENDATIONS FOR RETENTION OF TITLE IN THE SECURITY RIGHTS ACT

381. *Recommendations based on the functional comparison of retention of title across the selected jurisdictions and international instruments* – The analysis of retention of title and the application of the functional approach in the Security Rights Act showed that the functional approach is only minimally applied to retention of title and not always logically or even correctly. This leads to the question whether the treatment of retention of title should be more modeled after the other approaches to retention of title in the selected jurisdictions and frameworks.[1595]

More specifically, the comparison of retention of title and its functional equivalent mechanisms across the selected frameworks allows for the evaluation of these different approaches to retention of title and the formulation of recommendations on whether the treatment and regulation of retention of title in the Security Rights Act or the future Book 9 of the new Civil Code should

- return to the non-functional approach (*Germany*);
- maintain the dogmatic difference between retention of title, the pledge and the security rights that are equated with pledges based on its title-based nature but with the introduction of an acquisition security right (*DCFR*);

[1595] See overview of different approaches to retention of title in Section 2 – Comparison of the treatment of retention of title across the selected jurisdictions and international instruments.

- introduce a separate category of acquisition security rights and more explicitly and actively pursue their functional equivalence (*the UNCITRAL non-unitary approach*); or
- recharacterize retention of title to an acquisition security right (*Article 9 UCC* and *the UNCITRAL unitary approach*).

1. RETURN TO THE NON-FUNCTIONAL APPROACH

382. *Recap of the non-functional approach* – The non-functional approach refers to a system in which functional equivalence between functionally similar mechanisms is not actively pursued. On the contrary, under the non-functional approach retention of title maintains its specific title-based characteristics that distinguishes it from security rights, even though they may perform the same function. An example of the non-functional approach can be found in *Germany*. There, the few codified secured transactions in movable goods, pledge with dispossession and retention of title, are regulated entirely separate from each other in different parts of the BGB. Furthermore, no additional attempts are made to implement unified rules for the situations in which retention of title and functionally similar security rights perform the same function. On the contrary, retention of title remains a fully title-based mechanism governed by its own specific rules, principles and case law.

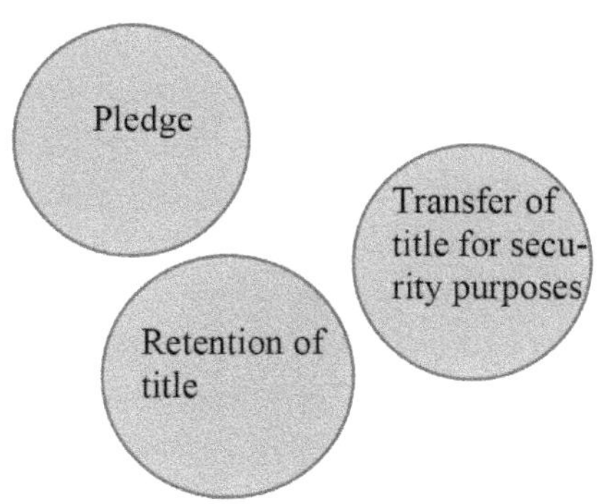

383. *Grounds for the non-functional approach in the Belgian legislation* – The analysis of retention of title in the Security Rights Act showed that the equivalent legal outcomes for retention of title, the pledge and the security rights that are equated with pledges are only minimally pursued. On the one hand, this is due to the fact that retention of title, the pledge and the security rights that are equated with pledges do not fully perform the same function. Furthermore, the Security Rights Act does not introduce a separate category of acquisition security rights with which more equivalent legal outcomes can be pursued. On the other hand, the Security Rights Act adheres to the dogmatic difference between retention of title and other security rights in movable goods, in that retention of title is title-based and the other security rights are not. Additionally, the legislator did not seem intent on pursuing a thorough application of the functional approach to retention of title with or without recharacterization in which retention of title is recharacterized or equated with an acquisition security right. Given this anemic effort to introduce the functional approach in the Security Rights Act, one can wonder whether the Belgian legislation should revert back to the non-functional approach to retention of title.

384. *Application of the non-functional approach to retention of title in Belgian legislation* – First, under the non-functional approach retention of title is maintained as the only mechanism that guarantees acquisition credit. Furthermore, the non-functional approach continues the title-based differences that still exist between retention of title and the other security rights in movable goods. For example, the return to the non-functional approach would mean that the retention of title creditor's right to revendicate in the event of the debtor's default would be justified, since the retention of title creditor would be considered full owner.

Furthermore, a return to the non-functional approach does not mean that there cannot be any similarities between retention of title and other security rights in movable goods. For example, the Belgian legislator could opt to maintain the extended tracing rules into the altered, encumbered goods for retention of title under the non-functional approach even though they are similar to the rules for the non-possessory pledge. As mentioned, in the current Security Rights Act the extension of the rules concerning tracing from the pledge to retention of title are seen as an application of the functional approach. The non-possessory pledge is given extra protection in the event the encumbered goods are altered and to achieve equivalent legal outcomes these rules are extended to retention of title. However, the rules concerning extensive tracing are not unique to security rights and cannot only be extended to retention of title when applying the functional approach. The choice to allow extensive tracing into altered goods is a policy choice to increase creditor protection and to stimulate creditors to distribute credit. Consequently, the choice to allow extensive tracing into altered goods can also be applied to retention of title under the non-functional approach, not from a desire to create equivalent legal outcomes with the pledge or other functionally equivalent security rights in movable goods, but to offer further protections to retention of title creditors in order to stimulate their type of acquisition credit. We saw a similar outcome in *Germany*, where the non-functional approach to retention of title has not stopped the contractual extension of retention of title in processed goods and accounts receivable and the recognition of these extension clauses in case law.

Similarly, the ban on unjust enrichment in the Security Rights Act could be maintained even though one would assume that the retention of title creditor's retained ownership would entitle him to both revendicate the encumbered good and keep any surplus value under the non-functional approach. However, even under the non-functional approach, the retention of title creditor's potential title-based privileges with regards to the surplus value have to be weighed against the general principle against unjust enrichment recognized in Belgian case law and doctrine. Based on this principle, no estate may unjustly enrich themselves at the expense of another without cause. Consequently, even under a non-functional approach in which the title-based nature of retention of title is respected, the unjust enrichment following revindication of the encumbered good can be halted. A similar approach is again found in *Germany*, where the retention of title creditor is also contractually obligated to return any received payments as part of the revindication process even though the retention of title creditor is considered full owner of the good.

However, a logical and coherent application of the non-functional approach in Book 9 of the new Civil Code would require a removal of the retention of title creditor's super-priority status and a return to the resolution of conflicts between retention of title creditors and other creditors and third parties on the basis of the retention of title creditor's retained title. As mentioned, the assignment of super-priority to retention of title only makes sense in the functional approach with recharacterization in which retention of title is recharacterized to a type of acquisition security right and given super-priority to strengthen the protection of security rights for acquisition credit. Conversely, in a system without the functional approach there is no logical reason to assign super-priority to retention of title.

385. *Counterargument to the application of the non-functional approach in Belgian Law* – Belgium, unlike *Germany*, has a strongly developed and widely used security rights, mainly pledge, system that exists alongside retention of title. Consequently, Belgium has a mixed system of secured transactions in movable goods based on title, limited proprietary interests in movable goods (i.e. the pledge and security rights that are equated with the pledge) and the legislative lien for the unpaid vendor. This mixed regime can lead to tension when retention of title creditors, security right holders and lien holders are treated differently even though they are performing the same function. For example, a pledge vested for acquisition credit does not automatically have the same protection as a retention of title vested or legislative lien assigned for the same type of credit.

Conversely, in *Germany* the main secured transactions in movable, tangible goods are title-based: retention of title and the transfer of title for security purposes. Theoretically, secured creditors can make use of the pledge with dispossession, but due to its impractical nature it is hardly ever used. Consequently, in *Germany* all types of credit can be guaranteed by title-based mechanisms and the title-based protection, mainly its strong position in conflicts with other creditors and third parties and during corporate bankruptcy, is not reserved for creditors who provided credit in a sale or lease with retention of title, but can also be granted to financiers who specifically provided credit to acquire a certain good. Therefore, in *Germany* the non-functional approach can continue to apply to retention of title without it causing any meaningful tension with other security rights in movable goods that perform the same function. As a result, there is less tension between these mechanisms than is the case in Belgium where acquisition credit can be guaranteed by the pledge, retention of title and the unpaid vendor's lien, thereby creating tension when there is a difference in treatment. Therefore, the security rights situation in Belgium and *Germany* may not be sufficiently comparable to recommend a *German* non-functional approach for the Belgian security rights framework.

2. RECOMMENDATIONS FOR THE APPLICATION OF THE FUNCTIONAL APPROACH IN THE BELGIAN LEGISLATION

386. *Overview* – The recommendations concerning the application of the functional approach are further divided in recommendations based on the application of the functional approach without recharacterization, like in the *DCFR* and *the UNCITRAL non-unitary approach* (2.1.), and the application of the functional approach with recharacterization, like in *Article 9 UCC* and *the UNCITRAL unitary approach* (2.2.).

2.1. *Recommendations concerning the application of the functional approach without recharacterization*

Book IX DCFR

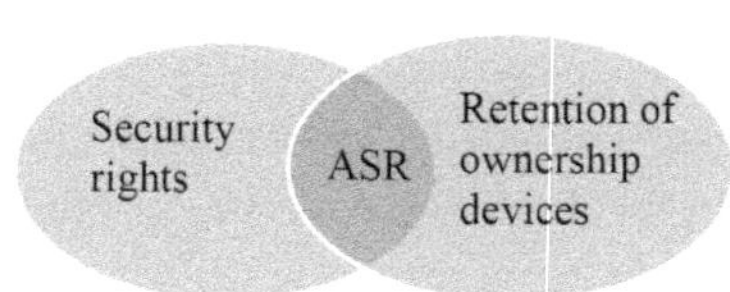

UNCITRAL non-unitary approach

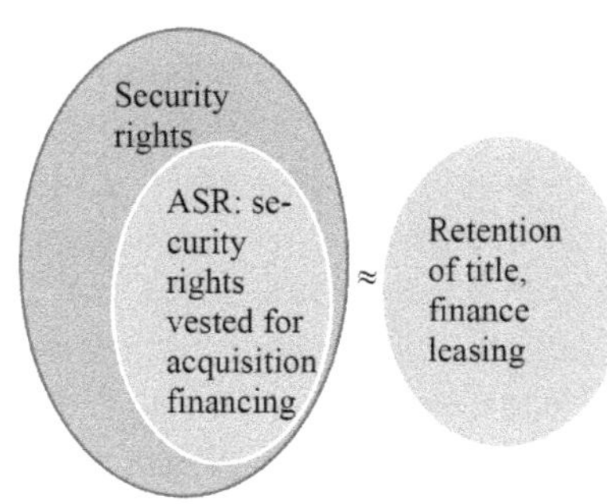

387. *Application of the functional approach without recharacterization in the Security Rights Act* – The application of the functional approach without recharacterization goes further than simply adding retention of title to a larger security rights framework and unifying some rules for functionally equivalent mechanisms. It requires a thorough analysis of retention of title and its functionally equivalent mechanisms, followed by a consistent and explicit adjustment of the rules concerning retention of title. The research showed that simply adding retention of title to the category of security rights in movable goods in the Security Rights Act was not enough to result in a thorough application of the functional approach without recharacterization, nor to create a coherent and logical security rights framework.

388. *Learning from the application of the functional approach without recharacterization in the DCFR and UNCITRAL Guide* – Following the two examples of the functional approach without recharacterization, legislators have the choice between a very exhaustive adjustment of the rules concerning retention of title to create equivalent legal outcomes between retention of title and acquisition security rights (*the UNCITRAL non-unitary approach*), or a partial extension of the rules concerning (acquisition) security rights to retention of ownership devices while maintaining some of the dogmatic differences between retention of ownership devices and acquisition security rights based on the retention of ownership creditor's retained title (*DCFR*). As mentioned, the approach in the Security Rights Act already partially aligns with the approach in the *DCFR* in that it continues the different treatment between retention of title and the other security rights in movable goods, based on the title-based nature of the retention of title. Given this similarity, it would seem sensible to pursue this approach in the new Book 9 of the Civil Code and introduce an acquisition security right with which the rules and rights of retention of title can be equated, while maintaining some of the differences between retention of title and acquisition security right due to the title-based nature of retention of title. However, the analysis of the *DCFR* has shown that the adherence to the dogmatic difference between retention of title and acquisition security rights does not always give the most logical and coherent results and sometimes actively undermines the functional equivalence between retention of ownership devices and acquisition security rights. Therefore, adopting a functional approach without recharacterization like in the *DCFR* is not the most beneficial approach moving forward.

Alternatively, *the UNCITRAL non-unitary approach* offers a much more extensive application of the functional approach without recharacterization by adjusting the rules for retention of title and finance leasing at every stage to result in equivalent legal outcomes for acquisition security rights, retention of title and finance leasing. However, making such extensive changes to retention of title and finance leasing to match the outcomes of acquisition security rights, raises the question whether it would not be easier to recharacterize retention of title to acquisition security rights in order to have one, uniform set of rules for this mechanism instead of painstakingly adjusting the rules for retention of title to macth those for acquisition security rights or copying the rules for acquisition security rights to retention of title. Especially since the continuation of the terms retention of title would still result in the perpetuation of preconceived notions concerning the rights of retention of title creditors and potentially misleading situations in which the term retention of title no longer aligns with the actual rights for retention of title creditors.

2.2. *Recommendations concerning the application of the functional approach with recharacterization*

Article 9 UCC/UNCITRAL unitary approach

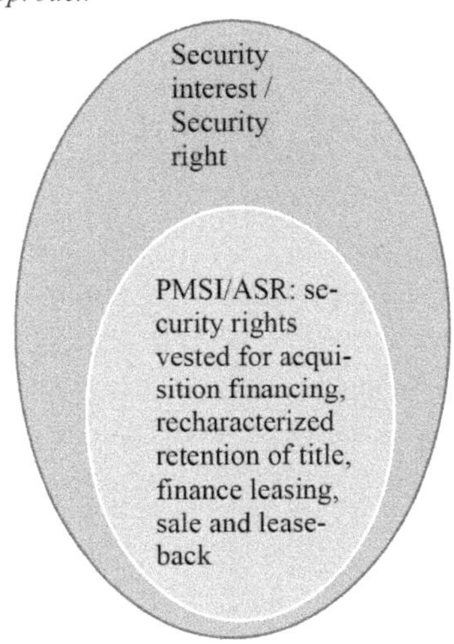

389. *Recap of the functional approach with recharacterization in the selected jurisdiction and international instruments* – Evidently, the functional approach with recharacterization, creates large overarching categories of security rights in movable goods to which secured transactions that meet the definitions of these categories are recharacterized. In *Article 9 UCC* and *the UNCITRAL unitary approach*, every transaction that guarantees payment or performance of an obligation by obtaining a proprietary interest in a movable good is recharacterized to a security interest or security right, respectively. Furthermore, these frameworks have separate categories of PMSIs or acquisition security rights to which retention of title mechanisms are then specifically recharacterized.

390. *Advantages to the adoption of the functional approach with recharacterization* – Given the inherent issues with the application of the functional approach without recharacterization, the logical alternative within the functional realm is to look to the functional approach with recharacterization. The analysis of the frameworks with the functional approach (i.e. *Article 9*

UCC and the *UNCITRAL unitary approach*) showed that there are definitive advantages to the adoption of the functional approach with recharacterization and thus a full recharacterization of retention of title to an acquisition security right.

First, the recharacterization of retention of title to an acquisition security right would finally put the classification debate to rest. No longer could scholars claim that retention of title is dogmatically different from other security rights in movable goods, since it would explicitly be recharacterized to an acquisition security right thereby removing all doubt over its classification and associated rights. It would also address the preconceived notions that retention of title creditors, due to their retained *title*, can count on a stronger protection prior to and during corporate bankruptcy proceedings. Furthermore, it simplifies the inclusion of leasing for security purposes as an acquisition security right, since each lease agreement that would meet the definition of PMSI or acquisition security right is recharacterized as such. However, this simplified inclusion of leasing following the functional approach with recharacterization does not resolve the issue of distinguishing between leases for security purposes and purely operational leases. For this issue the legislator still has to decide whether they regulate this distinction to the best of their abilities, as in *Article 9 UCC*, or leave it up to the courts to deal with the finer points of this distinction, as seems to be suggested in more minimal regulation concerning leasing for security purposes in the *DCFR* and *UNCITRAL Guide and Model Law*. Finally, the recharacterization to an acquisition security right also makes more sense in an international context. Internationally, the term retention of title can create the false impression that creditors retain full title to the encumbered good combined with the absolute rights of an owner, when in actuality the functional approach aims to make their retained right equivalent to acquisition security rights.

Second, the functional approach with recharacterization allows for a more coherent and unified security rights framework. In *Article 9 UCC* and the *UNCITRAL unitary approach*, the recharacterization of retention of title to a PMSI or acquisition security right, respectively, makes it much easier to create a majority of unified rules for all security interests in movable goods and some specific rules for PMSIs and acquisition security rights. More specifically, uniform rules are generally introduced for the creation, third-party effectiveness and enforcement of all (PM)SIs and (acquisition) security rights. This approach would be preferable to the amalgam of rules for retention of title, the pledge and the security rights that are equated with pledges that exist now in the Security Rights Act. What's more, the functional approach with recharacterization aligns with the application of the functional approach with recharacterization that already applies to transfer of title for security purposes to accounts receivable in the Security Rights Act. If the legislator does not see harm in limiting the transfer of title for security purposes in its effect to a pledge, there is no good reason why the legislator should hesitate in recharacterizing retention of title as a super-prioritized acquisition security right. Finally, an explicit choice for two main categories of security rights in movable goods can be a new catalyst for the removal of redundant legislative liens in movable goods in the Mortgage Act that perform the same functions as the security rights in movable goods in the Security Rights Act. The drafters of the Security Rights Act already had the ambition to use the implementation of the Security Rights Act to remove the legislative liens that perform the same function as the pledge and to go to one system for security rights in movable goods. Unfortunately, the drafters only managed to remove a few obscure legislative liens in movable goods, such as the lien for the seeds and costs of harvest and the innkeeper's lien, while many of the other legislative liens in movable goods, such as the lien of the unpaid landlord, the lien for costs made for the preservation of a movable good, the carrier's lien and the unpaid vendor's lien, are maintained. The introduction of two overarching categories of security rights and acquisition security rights with very broad definitions is the perfect opportunity to remove these legislative liens and make a definitive choice for consensual security rights in movable goods as the main method to secure credit. This would not only create a more clear and coherent approach to securing credit, but would also simplify the distribution of proceeds during corporate bankruptcy proceedings, since bankruptcy trustees would not have to take into account various claims to movable goods but could simply look to the Security Rights Act to determine the valid claims to certain movable goods and the order in which payment of their liquidation should be made.

Third, recharacterizing retention of title to an acquisition security right leads to a more logical inclusion of retention of title in the consolidated security right framework. An example is the assignment of super-priority to retention of title in the Security Rights Act. In *Article 9 UCC* and under the *UNCITRAL unitary approach* the assignment of super-priority to PMSIs or acquisition security rights makes perfect sense. Following the recharacterization of retention of title to a PMSI or acquisition security right, respectively, PMSI or acquisition security creditors can no longer rely on their retained title to avoid conflicts with other claimants. Since the drafters wanted to give a special protection to all acquisition creditors, super-priority was created and assigned to them. As mentioned, in the Security Rights Act the assignment of super-priority to retention of title creditors cannot be squared with the functional approach. Even if the drafters wanted to grant special protection to acquisition creditors, the retention of title creditor would not need super-priority since his retained title would make sure that any conflict could be avoided. However, in a system in which all secured creditors that guarantee acquisition credit are recharacterized to an acquisition security right, the assignment of super-priority makes sense to ensure their enhanced protection in conflicts with other creditors.

Fourth, the recharacterization of retention of title to an acquisition security right would also make the expansion of its applicable rules to other functionally similar security rights possible. In *Article 9 UCC* and *the UNCITRAL unitary approach*, the term PMSI or acquisition security right, respectively, covers all security interests that guarantee acquisition credit by obtaining or retaining a proprietary interest in the acquired good. Consequently, this term is not limited to former retention of title creditors or lessors, but applies to all financiers that have provided credit that allowed the debtor to acquire new goods. In the Security Rights Act, the term retention of title only applies to retention of title creditors in sale agreements and potentially to finance lease agreements. As mentioned, the correct and consistent application of the functional approach without recharacterization would require the introduction of a separate category of acquisition security rights, which also enjoy super-priority to ensure equivalent legal outcomes with retention of title. It would be more efficient to simply recharacterize retention of title to an acquisition security right and let this term also cover other security rights that guarantee acquisition credit.

Finally, the application of the functional approach with recharacterization would allow for the introduction of uniform rules for the treatment of (acquisition) security rights during corporate bankruptcy proceedings. Now, under Book XX of the Code of Economic Law (CEL), retention of title creditors are initially stayed by the bankruptcy proceedings, but are allowed to revendicate the encumbered good once their claim has been verified. Likewise, the pledge holder is also stayed by the bankruptcy proceedings and allowed to proceed with enforcement proceedings once his claim has been verified. However, both mechanisms are still governed by different rules even though their treatment during corporate bankruptcy is not that different. In the event of the application of functional approach with recharacterization, Book XX of the CEL could simply have one regime for the treatment of security rights in movable goods during corporate bankruptcy, but assign super-priority to acquisition security rights to continue the specific protection for security rights that guarantee acquisition credit.

391. *Counterarguments for the application of the functional approach with recharacterization* – First, recharacterizing retention of title to an acquisition security right creates the impression that retention of title creditors will lose protection. Obtaining an acquisition security right in a movable good does not sound as strong as retaining title to a good. However, the research has shown that the rights of retention of title creditors in the Security Rights Act are not significantly different from the rights of PMSI creditors or acquisition security right holders. Unfortunately, by changing the name retention of title to acquisition security interest, creditors may get the impression that their rights will be diminished since they are no longer considered as creditors who have retained title. However, this problem is not resolved by maintaining the old terminology. As my research has shown, retention of title creditors are already subjected to limitations regardless of whether they are referred to as retention of title or acquisition security rights. Consequently, in Belgium the continuation of the term retention of title is more deceiving than changing it to a type of acquisition security interest. The latter term would create the correct impression that these creditors have a strong preferential claim guaranteed by a specific good which is further regulated like other security rights in movable goods. Conversely, the adherence to the term retention of title creates the incorrect impression that these creditors retain an absolute title to the encumbered good and are therefore unlimited in their rights. In other words, the argument against the functional approach with recharacterization in order to protect third parties from change actually does them a disservice, since it maintains a system that is no longer in accordance with reality.

Second, one could raise the argument that the application of the functional approach with recharacterization will automatically result in more formalities for the creation and third-party effectiveness of former retention of title mechanisms. Admittedly, this was the case in the *United States* where the functional approach in *Article 9 UCC* entailed the creation of a general security interest which is governed by very detailed rules for its creation and third-party effectiveness and which rules also apply to PMSIs. The unified framework for third-party effectiveness also includes the rule that the default method for third-party effectiveness of non-possessory security interests is registration. In the *United States* the creation of general filing requirement for PMSIs was not a significant change, since registration of conditional sales had already become common prior to *Article 9 UCC*. However, in other jurisdictions where the practice of registering retention of title has not taken hold, the implementation of such a regime would be more daunting. Furthermore, additional formalities will inevitably result in more costs for secured creditors, since creditors will have to dedicate time and resources to fulfill these formalities. Nevertheless, the possibility of a registration requirement is not a sufficient argument to outright reject the functional approach with recharacterization. The application of the functional approach with recharacterization does not necessarily imply the implementation of a registration requirement for former retention of title creditors. Separate rules can be created for different sub-categories of security rights, as is the case in *Article 9 UCC* and *the UNCITRAL unitary approach* where only PMSIs and acquisition security rights, respectively, are given superpriority and PMSIs in consumer goods are automatically effective against third parties. Consequently, jurisdictions considering the legislative integration of retention of title can chose to recharacterize retention of title to a type of acquisition security right and create unified rules for the creation of all security rights, but maintain the exception that acquisition security rights are automatically effective against third parties and automatically obtain super-priority if they guarantee acquisition credit. However, my research has shown that there are significant advantages to the adoption of a robust and uniform notification regime for obtaining third-party effectiveness for all security rights in movable goods that outweigh the disadvantages. Furthermore, within this system some exceptions to notification of certain acquisition security rights or PMSIs can be allowed, such as for PMSIs and acquisition security rights in consumer goods, to unburden the PMSI and acquisition security right holders.

392. *Adoption of the functional approach with recharacterization in Belgium* – After weighing the advantages and disadvantages of the functional approach with recharacterization and the assessment of the inherent issues of the functional approach without recharacterization, the recommendation is to adopt the functional approach with recharacterization, as in *Article 9 UCC* and *the UNCITRAL unitary approach*, in the new Book 9 of the Civil Code. Following this approach, this new regime would not only recharacterize retention of title and other secured transactions for acquisition credit to acquisition security rights, but would also introduce an overarching category of general security rights.

Schematically the structure of security rights in movable goods in the new Book 9 of the Civil Code would look like this:

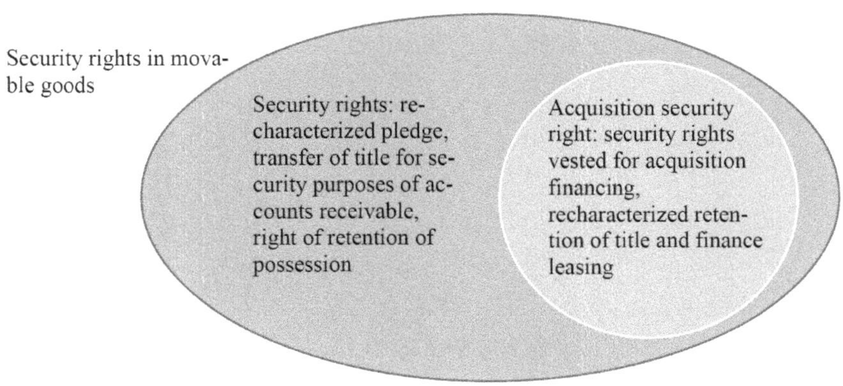

393. *A new security rights system for Book 9 of the Civil Code* – The new categories of secured transactions in movable goods in Book 9 of the new Civil Code would have new, overarching definitions:

> *Security rights are all proprietary interests in movable goods that guarantee payment or performance of an obligation between the security right holder and debtor.*

This category would cover and replace the majority of the current security rights in movable goods in the Security Rights Act, namely the possessory and non-possessory pledge, the right of retention of possession and the transfer of title to accounts receivables.

Furthermore, the main category of security rights would also include a sub-category of acquisition security rights that would have the following definition:

> *An acquisition security right is every proprietary interest that the creditor retains or obtains in a movable good, which is being acquired by the debtor, to guarantee credit granted by the creditor to the debtor for the acquisition of the movable good.*

This category would evidently cover and recharacterize retention of title in sale and finance lease agreements for security purposes to acquisition security rights, but would also cover security rights specifically vested for acquisition credit.

The functional approach with recharacterization would fit with the current title of the Security Rights Act, which places the underlying categories of security rights in movable goods (i.e. pledge, right of retention of possession, transfer of title and retention of title) in the larger category security rights in movable goods. The functional approach with recharacterization would go one step further and actively recharacterize these different secured transactions, and each transaction that meets this definition regardless of its name, to a security right or acquisition security right. Moreover, the choice for overarching categories of consensual (acquisition) security rights could renew the momentum to remove the legislative liens from the Mortgage Act that are functionally equivalent to (acquisition) security rights and make a full commitment to consensual (acquisition) security rights over legislative liens.

PART 4

GENERAL CONCLUSIONS

394. *Overview* – Following the analysis and comparison of the treatment of retention of title across the selected jurisdictions and frameworks, I bring this dissertation to a close with an overview of the main research results. The conclusions are structured following the main and sub-research questions formulated at the beginning of this dissertation.

1. CLARIFICATION OF AND CONCLUSIONS ON THE APPLICATION OF THE SELECTED FUNCTIONAL APPROACHES TO RETENTION OF TITLE

395. *First sub-research question* – The first sub-research question inquired into the functional frameworks that served as inspiration for the Security Rights Act (i.e. *Article 9 UCC, the UNCITRAL Guide and Model Law* and *the DCFR*) in order to better understand and clarify the application of the functional approach to retention of title in Belgium.

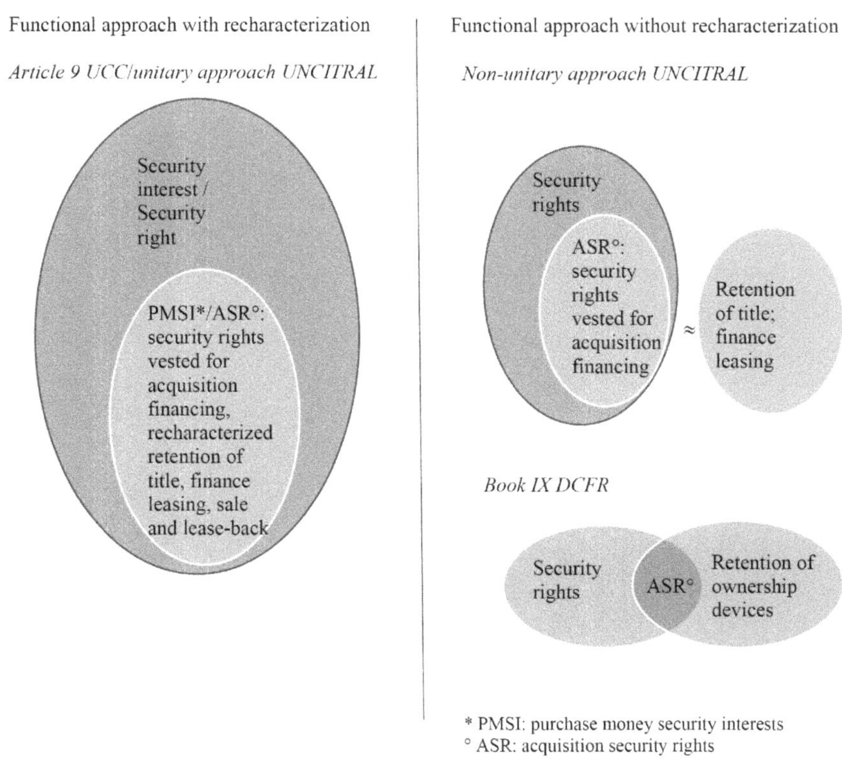

396. *Main distinction between general security rights and security interests versus PMSIs and acquisition security rights* – The research has shown that in each of the selected functional frameworks with and without recharacterization, a distinction is made between general security rights or security interests, that can guarantee any and all debts between a creditor and debtor, and PMSIs and acquisition security rights, that only guarantee credit that was provided to enable the debtor to acquire the encumbered good (i.e. acquisition credit). The PMSIs and acquisition security rights find themselves simultaneously in two categories. On the one hand, PMSIs and acquisition security rights are *security interests* or *security rights*, meaning that they are generally governed by the same rules as security rights or interests with respect to creation, third-party effectiveness, tracing and enforcement. On the other hand, PMSIs and acquisition security rights are a *sub-category of the general security rights or security interests* and perform a specific function of guaranteeing acquisition credit. In each of the selected functional frameworks, the specific function PMSIs and acquisition security rights perform, entitles them to special treatment, such as super-priority in conflicts with other secured creditors and certain exemptions from notification requirements for third-party effectiveness. These special rules for acquisition security rights or PMSIs are generally based on policy choices to favor acquisition credit over general credit and to ensure that acquisition financiers continue to provide this type of credit.[1596]

397. *Retention of title, functionally equivalent mechanisms and the pursuit of equivalent legal outcomes* – The goal of the functional approach in each of the selected frameworks is to create equivalent legal outcomes between functionally equivalent mechanisms. *For retention of title the functionally equivalent mechanism is the PMSI or acquisition security right.* This is the mechanism to which retention of title is recharacterized (i.e. functional approach with recharacterization) or equated with and for which legally equivalent outcomes are pursued (i.e. functional approach without recharacterization). Since PMSIs and acquisition security rights are also security rights or security interests, the treatment of retention of title in these frameworks generally moves from title-based treatment to treatment for security rights with a limited proprietary interest in the encumbered good. However, the research of *Article 9 UCC* has shown that this does not necessarily imply a decrease in protection for retention of title creditors. In most cases the retention of title creditor is already limited in the absolute enforcement of his ownership right in the encumbered good prior to the application of the functional approach and thus the move from title-based to security rights-based protection does not have a significant impact.[1597]

Furthermore, the application of the functional approach does not have to be accompanied with the introduction of extensive formalities or extensive rules for (acquisition) security rights, such as an extensive notification regime for third-party effectiveness, tracing or enforcement rules. The functional

[1596] See *supra* no. 81, 144 and 192.
[1597] See *supra* no. 110.

approach merely aims to create equal legal outcomes for functionally equivalent mechanisms. However, the content of these rules remains the prerogative of the legislator. Once the content of these rules has been decided, be it either extensive rules for third-party effectiveness, tracing or enforcement or not, the functional approach would insist that these rules are uniformly applied to functionally equivalent mechanisms. Therefore, the introduction of notification requirements for third-party effectiveness for (acquisition) security rights in the *UNCITRAL Guide* and *DCFR* in combination with the functional approach meant an extension of these rules to retention of title or retention of ownership devices, respectively. Similarly, the extensive tracing rules for (acquisition) security rights in the *UNCITRAL Guide* are extended to retention of title to guarantee functionally equivalent outcomes between these functionally similar mechanisms, while in the *DCFR* the limitation on automatic tracing in altered goods for (acquisition) security rights are also extended to retention of ownership devices. The last example clearly establishes that the functional approach does not have to be combined with extensive tracing rules for (acquisition) security rights and retention of title mechanisms. Likewise, the functional approach with recharacterization in *Article 9 UCC* and the *UNCITRAL unitary approach* does not have to mean elaborate rules and extensive protections for (PM)SIs and (acquisition) security rights, but in most cases it will. The research shows that most jurisdictions and international organizations use the creation of a consolidated security rights framework based on the functional approach to implement uniform rules for *all* their security rights in movable goods and to increase the protection of secured creditors. Even in Belgium, where the functional approach is so far only minimally applied, the drafters did make a point to create uniform rules with extensive protections for security right holders in the event of alterations to the encumbered good. Furthermore, the drafters introduced an extensive registration regime for the non-possessory pledge, but did not extend this to retention of title. Even though this distinction in third-party effectiveness requirements can be explained by the difference in specific function retention of title and the pledge perform, the research and comparison of retention of title across the selected frameworks has also shown that there is much to be gained from a uniform third-party effectiveness regime, regardless of whether the functional approach requires its implementation.

398. *Functional approach with recharacterization vs. functional approach without recharacterization* – Both the functional approach with and without recharacterization have the same objective: to create equivalent legal outcomes for functionally similar mechanisms. However, the jurisdiction and instruments that apply the functional approach with recharacterization achieve this goal in a more consistent, logical and coherent framework than the instruments that apply the functional approach without recharacterization. As established, the functional approach means that retention of title is either recharacterized to a PMSI or acquisition security right or its legal outcomes are equated with those of a PMSI and acquisition security right. However, in the frameworks that apply the functional approach with recharacterization, *Article 9 UCC* and *the UNCITRAL unitary approach*, retention of title is recharacterized to a PMSI and acquisition security right, respectively, meaning that one set of rules can be created that governs all secured transactions that meet the definition of PMSI or acquisition security right.

Conversely, in frameworks that apply the functional approach without recharacterization, *the DCFR* and *the UNCITRAL non-unitary approach*, the legal outcomes for retention of title are also functionally equated with those for acquisition security rights, but here the rules for acquisition security rights are either expanded to those for retention of title or the rules for retention of title are adjusted in order to achieve the same legal outcome as acquisition security rights and PMSIs. As one can expect, this approach leads to a more convoluted and complex system where retention of title exists alongside the acquisition security rights, but the rules and outcomes for the two mechanisms are made the same. In the *DCFR*, the drafters attempt to justify this approach by adhering very strongly to the title-based nature of their retention of ownership devices and thus maintaining a strong distinction between retention of ownership devices and the acquisition security rights. However, the analysis of the *DCFR* showed that adhering so strongly to the title-based nature of retention of ownership devices only in very few instances leads to significantly different treatment for retention of ownership creditors. Furthermore, continuing this distinction does not add much in the way of protection for retention of ownership creditors, while it does unnecessarily complicate the security rights framework. Interestingly, the *UNCITRAL non-unitary approach* does not even aim to adhere to the title-based nature of retention of title, but simply wants to simplify the introduction of a consolidated security rights framework by allowing adopting states to maintain the terms for retention of title and finance leasing. The preservation of these terms is supposed to ease states into accepting the functional approach as a reform method. However, the continuation of these terms while simultaneously fully adjusting their rules to those for acquisition security rights, means that the term retention of title and finance leasing no longer has any individual meaning or rights associated with it. In other words, the mechanisms only exist in name, but no longer have any specific rights or protections associated to them that separate them from the acquisition security rights. Given the complexity and difficulty of painstakingly adjusting the rules for retention of title and finance leasing to meet the outcomes for acquisition security rights, one can rightfully wonder what the added value is of having a functional approach without recharacterization.

2. APPLICATION OF THE FUNCTIONAL APPROACH IN BELGIUM AND COMPARISON OF RETENTION OF TITLE ACROSS THE SELECTED JURISDICTIONS AND INTERNATIONAL INSTRUMENTS

399. *Second sub-research question* – The second sub-research question examined how the functional approach is applied to retention of title in the Security Rights Act and how this compares to the selected functional and non-functional approaches to retention of title in the selected jurisdictions and international instruments.

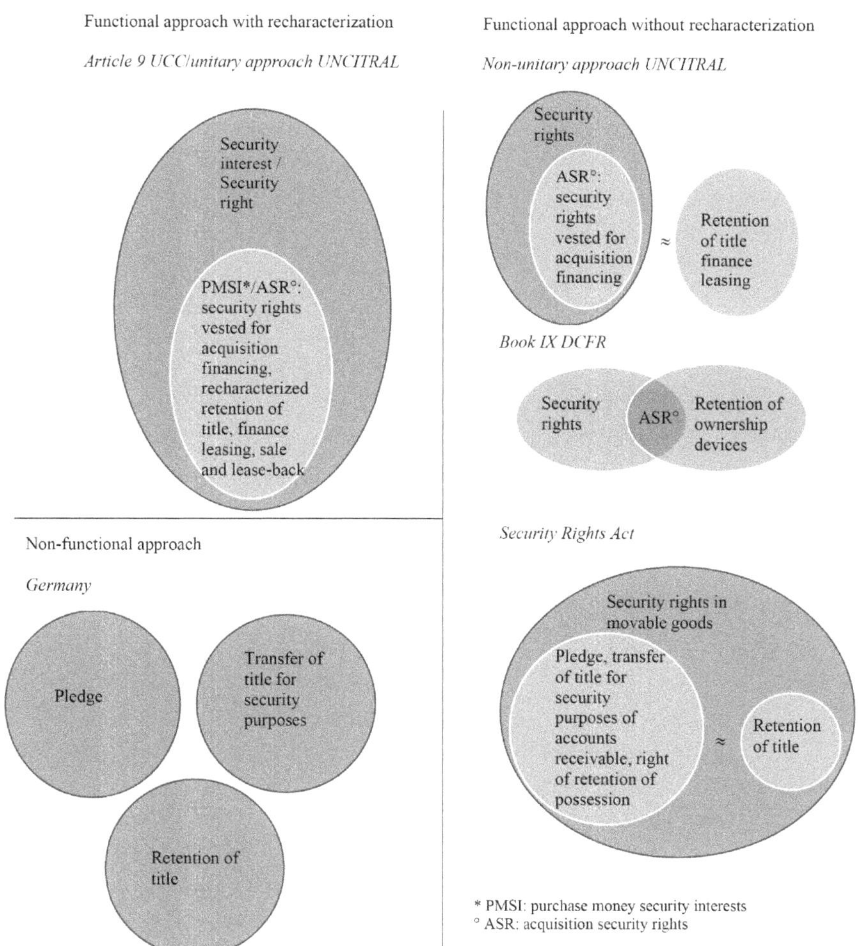

400. *Minimal application with minimal impact of the functional approach to retention of title in the Belgian Security Rights Act* – In the Security Rights Act the functional approach is generally used to (1) classify all the secured transactions listed in the Security Rights Act as security rights in movable goods, (2) to bring together the former amalgam of different pledges in civil and commercial law to one form of possessory or non-possessory pledge and (3) to treat the transfer of title for security purposes of accounts receivable and the right of retention of possession as a pledge. With regards to retention of title specifically, the application of the functional approach to retention of title is limited to the classification of retention of title as a security right and the expansion of the tracing rules for the pledge to retention of title. Given the minimal application of the functional approach, the Security Rights Act distinguishes itself from the other functional approaches where, as mentioned, a separate category of PMSIs or acquisition security rights is introduced to which retention of title is either fully recharacterized or with which each of the rules of retention of title are equated to achieve equivalent legal outcomes.

As can be expected, the minimal application of the functional approach results in a minimal impact for retention of title creditors. Retention of title creditors in Belgium see their rights virtually unchanged compared to prior to the Security Rights Act. Furthermore, in the instances where changes are made following the functional approach, such as the expanded tracing rules the protection of retention of title creditors, the protection for retention of title creditors increases as opposed to the situation prior to the Security Rights Act. In that sense, the Security Rights Act differs from *Article 9 UCC*, which does explicitly recharacterizes retention of title to a PMSI and thus changes the basic structure of the former retention of title mechanism. However, the comparison between retention of title in the Security Rights Act and the PMSI in *Article 9 UCC* and acquisition security right in *UNCITRAL Guide and Model Law* showed that the rights of retention of title creditors in Belgium and PMSI and acquisition holders are very similar to each other. Consequently, one can argue that the recharacterization of retention of title to an acquisition security right in the Belgian legislation would likely not have a significant impact on the rights of retention of title creditors.

401. *The Security Rights Act as an example of the inherent issues of the functional approach without recharacterization* – As established in the previous section, the application of the functional approach without recharacterization comes with some inherent issues, which are on display in the Security Rights Act. For example, the classification of retention of title as a security right in movable goods has not stilled the debate concerning its classification. Despite the explicit classification of retention of title as a security right, some authors continue to distinguish retention of title from the other security rights due to the title-based nature of retention of title. This ongoing debate in the Belgian Security Rights Act concerning the classification of retention of title is a good example of the general issue of *the UNCITRAL non-unitary approach*, where a continuation of the term retention of title is combined with a full adjustment of the rules for retention of title to equate the outcomes of acquisition security rights and thus the term retention of title mechanisms will no longer represent the associations creditors and third parties have with this mechanism.

Similarly, the continuation of the term retention of *title* creates the impression that the retention of title creditor has absolute rights with regards to the encumbered good and, for example, has the option to dispose a second time of the encumbered good, simply revendicate the encumbered good from a third-party transferee or from the retention of title debtor in the event of default. This while the research has shown that the retention of title creditor is also limited in his enforcement and is in actuality treated quite similarly to PMSI or acquisition security right holders. Given these issues, the Security Rights Act exemplifies the problems with the functional approach without recharacterization I observed in the *DCFR*. In this instrument the retention of ownership device is also explicitly maintained in combination with an adherence to its title-based nature. As in the Security Rights Act, this leads to illogical and incoherent outcomes which are exactly what the functional approach aims to improve.

402. *Similarity of retention of title in all its iterations across the selected jurisdictions and international instruments* – When comparing retention of title with its functional equivalent mechanisms across jurisdictions and frameworks, one would expect that the retention of title in the framework with the non-functional approach (*Germany*) would distinguish itself from retention of title or its recharacterized versions, PMSIs and acquisition security rights in the functional frameworks. The former would be a title-based mechanism for which the absolute ownership of the retention of title creditor is recognized, whereas the latter have lost some of the original protections of retention of title since they are now recharacterized to or equated with PMSIs and acquisition security rights which only have a limited proprietary interest in the encumbered good. Nevertheless, the analysis and comparison of these mechanisms shows that the distinctions between retention of title across the selected frameworks are minimal and mainly with regards to the creation and third-party effectiveness of retention of title. Moreover, the rights of retention of title creditors, such as the right to dispose, to trace, the right to preferential treatment in conflict with other creditors or third parties (i.e. priority) and enforcement, are very similar across the selected jurisdictions regardless of whether retention of title continues under its term or is recharacterized to or equated with a PMSI or acquisition security right.[1598]

This result leads to the general conclusion that once title is retained to guarantee credit, retention of title creditors can no longer rely on their retained title as absolute owners but can only use their retained title within the context

1598 See *infra* Appendix A – Table of comparison of retention of title across the selected jurisdictions and international instruments.

of secured transactions law and will have to respect certain limitations on their claim, such as a limitation to dispose of the encumbered good again or the limitation of unjust enrichment following enforcement. This is a strong argument in favor of adopting the functional approach with recharacterization in which retention of title is explicitly recharacterized to an acquisition security right and thus the name better aligns with the actual rights of (former) retention of title creditors.

3. RECOMMENDATIONS FOR THE LEGISLATION OF RETENTION OF TITLE IN THE BELGIAN SECURITY RIGHTS ACT

403. *Third sub-research question* – The final sub-research question aimed to learn from the other approaches to the treatment of retention of title in the selected frameworks and formulate recommendations for the Belgian legislation concerning security rights in movable goods in general and concerning retention of title in particular in the upcoming Book 9 of the Civil Code. The recommendations were based depending on the different approaches to retention of title in the selected jurisdictions and international instruments and the direction the legislator may want to take with the legislation of retention of title: the non-functional approach[1599], the functional approach with recharacterization[1600] and the functional approach without recharacterization.[1601] However, of all the different approaches, the research demonstrated that the functional approach with recharacterization showed the most promise as a method to logically and coherently regulate retention of title in a consolidated security rights framework.[1602] The main advantages of the functional approach with recharacterization are:

(1) removes any doubt concerning the classification of retention of title, since it would be explicitly recharacterized to an acquisition security right;
(2) allows for a broad definition of acquisition security right which can encompass not only retention of title in sale agreements, but also security rights vested for financing granted specifically to acquire a new good and finance leasing;
(3) allows for a more unified system where (acquisition) security rights can for the most part be governed by the same rules both in secured transactions law and corporate bankruptcy proceedings, with a few specific rules for acquisition security rights concerning for example super-priority.

1599 See *supra* no. 382 *et seq.*
1600 See *supra* no. 387 *et seq.*
1601 See *supra* no. 389 *et seq.*
1602 See *supra* no. 390.

Following this approach, I recommend that the security rights in movable goods in the Security Rights Act are structured as follows

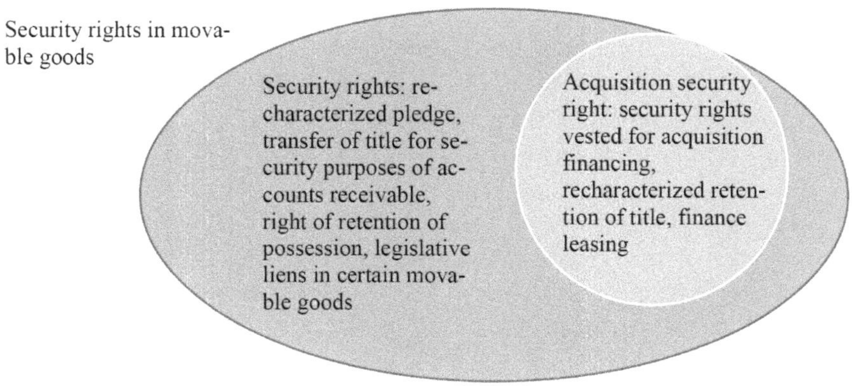

4. THE MEANING, ROLE AND IMPACT OF THE (BELGIAN) FUNCTIONAL APPROACH

404. *Main research question* – Based on the results of research and the conclusions above, I can formulate an answer to the main research question: *What is the meaning and role of the (Belgian) functional approach with regards to retention of title and what is its impact on retention of title creditors?*

With regards to the "Belgian" functional approach, I can conclude that the functional approach was only minimally applied with respect to retention of title in the Security Rights Act. In that sense, *the "Belgian" functional approach is of little meaning, does not play a significant role with regards to retention of title and is of little impact to retention of title creditors.* However, this was more due to the minimal and sometimes incorrect application of the functional approach by the Belgian legislator than the functional approach itself.

The more elaborate functional approaches in the selected jurisdiction and frameworks allow states to go to the *functional core of their secured transactions law regime and re-imagine their secured transactions in movable goods accordingly.* As established in the selected functional frameworks, this leads to a clear-cut division between secured transactions that guarantee general credit (i.e. security rights) and secured transactions that guarantee acquisition credit (i.e. acquisition security rights). As a next step, the functional approach is then used to either recharacterize retention of title to an acquisition security right or equate its legal outcomes with those for acquisition security rights. For a consistent security rights framework this will require a clear set of rules that covers all (acquisition) security rights or a thorough analysis of all the rules and legal outcomes for retention of title and explicitly matching these to the rules for acquisition security rights. Nevertheless, it remains up to the legislators to decide the extent to which they use this opportunity to implement a lot of rules and formalities for their (acquisition) security rights. They can opt for very extensive and more formalistic security rights framework, such as is exemplified in *Article 9 UCC*, the *UNCITRAL Guide and Model Law* and *DCFR*, but they do not have to. Application of the functional approach does not necessarily mean the implementation of extensive rules and formalities. The only requirement from a functional perspective is that the rules and legal outcomes for functional equivalent mechanisms are the same. Consequently, *the role of the functional approach should not be overstated in that it does not automatically result in an extensive and highly formalistic security rights framework.*

Finally, the comparative analysis showed that there is *very little difference between the different forms of retention of title across the selected jurisdictions and international instruments*. This brings me to the conclusion that even in non-functional regimes, such as *Germany*, or minimally functional regimes, such as Belgium, retention of title mechanisms are *de facto* similar to PMSIs and acquisition security rights. Consequently, the adoption of the functional approach with or without recharacterization is *unlikely to have a large impact on retention of title and the rights of retention of title creditors in these jurisdictions*, since they are already quite similar with PMSIs and acquisition security rights. Furthermore, *the functional approach with recharacterization has shown to have significant advantages* over the functional approach without recharacterization and the non-functional approach. Therefore, the application of the functional approach with recharacterization to retention of title should not be viewed as an invasive and necessarily overwhelming reform method with negative effects for retention of title creditors. On the contrary, the application of the functional approach with recharacterization should be viewed as an invitation to reconsider the structure of security rights framework from a functional perspective, which depending on the already existing similarity between retention of title and acquisition security rights, should not have a significant negative impact on the rights of retention of title creditors but will likely have a notable positive impact on the structure, coherence and logic of the security rights framework. I hope that this research will have helped enlarge the insight and understanding into the functional approach and will allow states and legislators contemplating the adoption of a functional approach in their security rights frameworks to make a more informed decision concerning the implementation of the functional approach.

APPENDIX

TABLE OF COMPARISON OF RETENTION OF TITLE ACROSS THE SELECTED JURISDICTIONS AND INTERNATIONAL INSTRUMENTS

	United States	UNCITRAL	DCFR	Germany	Belgium
Classification	Purchase Money Security Right (PMSI)	Unitary: acquisition security right (ASR) Non-unitary: retention of title (RoT)/finance lease (FL)	Retention of ownership device (RoO)	Retention of title	Retention of title
Scope	– conditional sales; – leases for security purposes; – security rights vested for acquisition credit	– Unitary: retention of title finance leases – Non-unitary: retention of title; finance leases; security rights vested for acquisition credit	– Retention of title in sale agreements; – hire-purchase contracts; – leases for security purposes; – consignment contracts	– Retention of title in sale agreements	– Retention of title in sale agreements; (- retention of title in finance leases (debated))
Creation	1) value has been given; 2) the debtor has rights in the collateral or the power to transfer rights in the collateral to a secured party; and 3) the debtor has authenticated a security agreement that provides a description of the collateral and, if the security interest covers timber to be cut, a description of the land concerned	(a) reflect the intent of the parties to create a security right; (b) identify the secured creditor and the grantor; (c) describe the secured obligation; (d) describe the encumbered assets in a manner that reasonably allows their identification; and (e) indicate the maximum monetary amount for which the security right may be	(a) the seller, supplier or lessor is the owner of the supplied asset or acts with authority in relation to this asset; (b) the asset is specified in the contract for proprietary security; (c) the secured right exists; and (d) the seller, supplier or lessor retains ownership	In sale agreement, no specific formalities	In sale agreement, in writing, before delivery of the good to the debtor

	United States	UNCITRAL	DCFR	Germany	Belgium
		enforced, if the State determines that such an indication would be helpful to facilitate subordinate lending			
Third-party effectiveness	Registration or possession, unless PMSI in consumer goods	Registration or possession, unless ASR, RoT or FL in consumer goods	Registration	No notification requirements	No notification requirements
Right to dispose	No right to dispose	No right to dispose	No right to dispose	No right to dispose	No right to dispose
Tracing into hands 3d party transferee	Tracing possible, unless: – permission creditor; – ordinary course of business; – good faith acquisition	Tracing possible, unless: – permission creditor; – ordinary course of business; – good faith acquisition	Tracing possible, unless: – permission creditor; – ordinary course of business; – good faith acquisition	Tracing possible unless good faith acquisition	Tracing possible unless: – permission creditor; – ordinary course of business; – good faith acquisition
Tracing into proceeds	Automatic	Automatic for money, receivables, negotiable instruments and rights to payment of funds credited to a bank account, otherwise additional formalities required	Only contractual extension	Only contractual extension	Automatic extension
Tracing into processed/ mixed goods	Automatic extension	Automatic extension	Contractual extension only	Contractual extension only for processed goods	Automatic extension
Tracing into incorporated goods	Extension after registration in land registry	Extension after registration in land registry	Only contractual extension + registration in land registry	No extension	Extension after registry in Security Rights Registry

	United States	UNCITRAL	DCFR	Germany	Belgium
Super-priority	Yes, only when fulfilment notification requirements (extra notification for inventory)	Yes, only when fulfilment notification requirements (potentially extra notification for inventory)	Yes, only when fulfilment notification requirements	Not applicable due to supremacy of retained title as opposed to third parties	Automatic
Enforcement	Governed by rules enforcement security rights	Unitary: governed by rules enforcement security rights Non-unitary: adjustment RoT and FL to equate outcomes enforcement (A)SR	Mainly governed by rules enforcement security rights, some separate rules for enforcement RoW,	Enforcement based on retained title and sales law	Right to revendicate (in effect very similar to enforcement proceedings pledge)
Bankruptcy	– encumbered good = part bankruptcy estate – application stay of proceedings – bankruptcy PMSI creditor has no impact	NA	NA	– Encumbered good ≠ bankruptcy estate – application stay of proceedings – trustee in bankruptcy decides outcome for retention of title agreement – bankruptcy retention of title creditor impacts retention of title agreement	– Encumbered good ≠ bankruptcy estate – application stay of proceedings – right to revendicate after verification – unclear whether bankruptcy retention of title creditor impacts retention of title agreement

BIBLIOGRAPHY

RELEVANT SOURCES PART 1 – GENERAL INTRODUCTION

AFFAKI, G., 'Increasing access to credit through reforming secured transactions laws' in B. FOËX (ed.), *The draft UNCITRAL model law on secured transactions – why and how?*, (Genève: Schulthess, 2016), (157) p. 203;

ANCEL, J., *Utilité et méthodes du droit comparé*, (Neuchatel: Ides et Calandes, 1971), p. 138;

ARMOUR, J., 'The law and economics debate about secured lending: lessons for European lawmaking', (2008) 5 ECFR, 3;

BELL, J., 'Legal research and the distinctiveness of comparative law' in M. VAN HOECKE (ed.), *Methodologies of legal research*, (Oxford: Hart Publishing, 2011), p. 294;

BRIDGE, M. G. and others, 'Formalism, functionalism, and understanding the law of secured transactions', (1999) 44 McGill L.J., 567;

CARLSON, D. G., 'On the efficiency of secured lending', (1994) 80 Va. L. Rev., 2179

CUMING, R., The internationalization of secured financing law: the spreading influence of the concepts of UCC, Article 9 and its progeny' in R. CRANSTON (ed.), *Making commercial law: essays in honour of Roy Goode*, 499;

DAHAN, F., 'The power of secured transactions law and the challenge of its reform' in O. N. AKSELI (ed.), *Availability of credit and secured transactions in a time of crisis*, (Cambridge: Cambridge University Press, 2013), (101), p. 293;

DANNEMAN, G., 'Comparative law: study of similarities or differences?' in R. REIMANN and R. ZIMMERMANN (eds.), *The Oxford handbook of comparative law*, (Oxford: University Press, 2019), p. 1403;

DAVIES, I., 'Retention of title clauses and non-possessory security interests: a secured credit regime within the European Union?' in I. DAVIES (ed.), *Security interests in mobile equipment*, (Dartmouth: Ashgate, 2002), 335;

DIRIX, E., 'De rol van de rechtsvergelijking in de rechtspraak van het Hof van Cassatie [in de periode 2002–2017]', (2019) 8 TPR, 21;

DROBNIG, U., 'Secured credit in international insolvency proceedings', (1998) 33 Tex. Int'l. L. J., 53;

GRAY, J., 'Commentary on the availability of credit' in N. O. AKSELI (ed.), *Availibility of credit and secured transactions in a time of crisis*, 'Cambridge: Cambridge University Press, 2013), 61;

HIRSCHL, R. 'The question of case selection in comparative constitutional law ', (2005) 53 Am. J. Comp. L., 126;

KESTEMONT, L., *Handbook on legal methodology*, (Antwerp: Intersentia, 2018), p. 97;

KIENINGER, E.-M., 'Introduction: security rights in movable property within the common market and the approach of the study' in E.-M. KIENINGER (ed.), *Security rights in movable property in European private law*, (Cambridge: Cambridge University Press, 2004), 6, p. 777;
KIENINGER, E. M., 'Evaluation: a common? Convergences, subsisting differences and possible ways for harmonisation' in E.-M. KIENINGER (ed.), *Security rights in movable property in European private law*, (Cambridge: Cambridge University Press, 2004), 647, p. 777;
LAWSON, F. H., 'The field of comparative law ', (1949) 61 Jur. Rev. 16;
MCCORMACK, G., 'Secured transactions law reform: UNCITRAL and the export of foreign legal models' in N. O. AKSELI (ed.), *Availability of credit and secured transactions in a time of crisis*, (Cambridge: Cambridge University Press, 2013), 33, p. 293;
MILO, M., 'Retention of title in European business transactions', (2003) 43 Washburn L. J., 121;
MONTI, G., NEJMAN, G. and REUTER, W. J., 'The future of reservation of title clauses in the european community', (1997) 46 ICLQ, 866;
RANK, W., 'Harmonisation of national security rights' in U. DROBNIG, H. J. SNIJDERS and E. J. ZIPPRO (eds.), *Divergences of property law, an obstacle to the internal market?*, (München: Sellier, 2006), 201, p. 240;
REITZ, J. C., 'How to do comparative law?' 46 Am. J. Comp. L., 617;
SAUNDERS, A. and others. 'The economic implications of international secured transactions law reform: a case study', (1999) 20 U. Pa. J. Int'l. Econ. L., 309;
SCHMITTHOFF, M., 'The science of comparative law ', (1939–41) 7 Camb. L. J., 94;
STONE, F. F., 'End to be served by comparative law', (1950–51) 25 Tul. L. Rev., 325;
VENEZIANO, A., 'Security rights in movables in the DCFR: general presentation' in V. SAGAERT, M. E. STORME and E. TERRYN (eds.), *The Draft Common Frame of Reference: national and comparative perspectives*, (Antwerp: Intersentia, 2012), 305, p. 506;
WHITE, J., 'Efficiency justifications for personal property security', (1984) Vand. L. Rev., 473;
ZWEIGERT, K. and KÖTZ, H., *Introduction to comparative law*, (Oxford: Clarendon Press, 1998), p. 714.

RELEVANT SOURCES PART 2 – DIFFERENT APPROACHES TO RETENTION OF TITLE

SECTION 1 – UNITED STATES

1. *Statutes*

1.1. Federal law

Act of 4 April 1800 to establish an uniform system of bankruptcy throughout the United States, 2 Stat. 19;
An act of 19 December 1803 to repeal an act intitled "An act to establish an uniform system of bankruptcy throughout the United States" 2 Stat. 248;

An act of 19 August 1841 to establish a uniform system of bankruptcy throughout the United States, 5 Stat. 440;
An Act of March 3 1843 to repeal the bankrupt act, 5 Stat. 614;
An act of 2 March 1867 to establish a uniform system of bankruptcy throughout the United States, 14 Stat. 517;
An act of 1 July 1898 to establish a uniform system of bankruptcy throughout the United States, 30 Stat. 544;
An act of 25 June 1910 to amend an act entitled An act to establish a uniform system of bankruptcy throughout the United States," approved July-first, eighteen hundred and ninety-eight, as amended by an act approved February fifth, nineteen hundred and three, and as further amended by an act approved June fifteenth, nineteen hundred and six, (1910) 36 Stat., 838;
An act to amend an Act entitled "An Act to establish a uniform system of bankruptcy throughout the United States", approved July 1, 1898, and Acts amendatory thereof and supplementary thereto; and to repeal section 76 thereof and all Acts and parts of Acts inconsistent therewith, (1938) 52 Stat., 840;
An act of 6 November 1978 to establish a uniform law on the subject of bankruptcies, 92 Stat. 2549.

1.2. New York Law

Uniform Conditional Sales Law, Laws of New York (1922), 1766.

2. Doctrine

ACKERMAN, H., 'The Conditional Sales Act', (1915) 10 Bench & B., 356;
ADKINS, L. D. and BARDOS, T. B., 'The leasing transaction', (1962) U. Ill. L. F., 16;
ALBERGOTTI, R. D., *Understanding bankruptcy in the US*, (London: Blackwell, 1992), p. 258;
ANDERSON, T. M., CULHANDE, M. B. and WILSON, C. L., 'Attachment and perfection of security interests under revised Article 9: a nuts and bolts primer', (2001) 9 Am. Bankr. L. Rev., 179;
ARNOLD, C. A., 'The reconstitution of property: property as a web of interests', (2002) 26 Harv. Envtl. L. Rev. 281;
AYER, J. D., 'On the vacuity of the sale/lease distinction', (1983) 68 Iowa L. Rev. 667;
AYER, J. D., 'Further thoughts on lease and sale', (1983) Ariz. St. L. J., 341;
BAILEY, H. J. and HAGEDORN, R. B., *Secured transactions in a nutshell*, (4 edn., St. Paul: West Group, 2000), p. 524;
BAIRD, D. G. and JACKSON, T. H., 'Possession and ownership: an examination of the scope of article 9', (1983) 35 Stan. L. Rev., 175;
BLACK, H. C., 'Corporations under the bankruptcy act of 1898', (1898) 8 Yale L J. 105;
BLUM, B. A., *Bankruptcy and debtor/creditor*, (New York: Aspen publisher, 2006), p. 598;
BOGERT, G. G., 'Proposed uniform conditional sales act', (1917) 3 Cornell L. Rev., 1;
BOGGERT, G. G., 'The evolution of conditional sales law in New York', (1923) 8 Cornell L. Q., 303;
BOWERS, J. W., 'Groping and coping in the shadow of Murphy's law: bankruptcy theory and the elementary economics of failure', (1989–90) 88 Mich L Rev, 2097;

BROOK, J., *Secured transactions*, (5 edn., New York City: Aspen Publisher, 2011), p. 468;
BROWN, R. A., *Law of personal property*, (Chicago: Callahan & Co., 1955), p. 854;
BROWN, J. S., 'Notes – Leases: Security Interests: Uniform Commercial Code', (1963–64) 49 Cornell L. Q., 672;
BULLOCK, W. E. 'Assignments for the benefit of creditors' in D. S. GARLAND DS and L. P. MCGEHEE (eds.), *The American and English encyclopaedia of law*, vol. 3, (2 edn., Northport: Edward Thompson 1897), p. 1196;
BUMP, O., *Fraudulent conveyances – a treatise upon conveyances made by debtors to defraud creditors*, (2 edn., New York: Bakes, Voorhis & Co. Publishers 1876), p. 784;
BURDICK, F. M., 'Codifying the law of conditional sales', (1918) 18 Colum. L. Rev., 103;
CAVENDER, P., 'Notes and comments', (1930) 5 Wash. L. Rev., 65;
CHANDLER, W., 'The revised Bankruptcy Act of 1938', (1938) 24 A. B. A. J., 880;
CHERNUCHIN, C. J., 'Security interests in proceeds of collateral', (2012) 1 Bus. L. Today, 1;
CLARK, B., *The law of secured transactions under the Uniform Commercial Code*, vol. 1, (3 edn., New York City: LexisNexis, 2015), loosel.;
COOGAN, P. F., 'Article 9 of the Uniform Commercial Code: priorities among secured creditors and the floating lien', (1959) 72 Harv. L. Rev., 42;
COOGAN, P. F., 'Security interests in fixtures under the Uniform Commercial Code', (1962) 75 Harv. L. Rev., 1319;
COOGAN, P. F. and GORDON, N. L., 'The effect of the uniform commercial code upon receivables financing – some answers and some unresolved problems', (1963) 76 Harv. L. Rev., 41;
COOGAN, P. F., 'Leases of equipment and some other unconventional security devices: an analysis of UCC section 1-201(37) and Article 9', (1973) Duke L. J., 909;
COOGAN, P. F. 'Leasing and the Uniform Commercial Code' in B. E. FRITCH and A. F. REISMAN (eds.), *Equipment leasing – leveraged leasing*, (2 edn., New York City: Practising Law Institute, 1980), p. 1235;
COOGAN, P. F., 'Is there a difference between a long-term lease and an installment sale of personal property', (1981) 56 N. Y. U. L. Rev., 1036;
COOPER, C., 'Identifying a personal property lease under the UCC', (1988–89) 49 Ohio St. L. J., 195;
COLES, W. D.. 'Bankruptcy legislation in the United States', (St. Louis Law Society, 1898), 1
DALZELL, W. C., 'Lease-contracts as a means of conveying title to chattels', (1921) 1 Ore. L. Rev., 9;
DUKIMINIER, J., KRIER, J. E., ALEXANDER, G. S., SCHILL, M. H. and STRAHILEVITZ, L. J. *Property*, (New York: Wolters Kluwer, 2018), p. 1197;
EPSTEIN, R. A., 'Property and necessity', (1990) 2 Harv. L. J. & Pub. Pol'y., 2;
FENN, A. H., 'Conditional sales', (1890) 24 Am. L. Rev., 64;
FLINT, G. L. Jr., 'Secured transactions history: protecting Holmes' notes through the conditional sales acts', (2013) 44 STM L. J., 317;
FREYERMUTH, R. W., 'Rethinking proceeds: the history of misrepresentation and revision of UCC section 9-306', (1994–95) 69 Tul. L. Rev., 645;
GABRIEL, H. D., *The ABC's of the UCC – Article 2 sales*, (3 edn., Chicago: American Bar Association, 2013), p. 157;

GIBSON, W. E., *A comprehensive overview of revised article 9*, (Durham: Carolina Academic Press, 2007), p. 183;
GILMORE, G. 'The secured transactions article of the Commercial Code', (1951) 16 Law & Contemp. Probs., 27;
GILMORE, G., 'The purchase money priority', (1963) 57 Harv. L. Rev., 1333;
GILMORE, G., *Security interests in personal property*, vol. 1, (Boston: Little Brown and Co., 1965), p. 651
GILMORE, G., *Security interests in personal property*, vol. 2, (Boston: Little Brown and Co., 1965), p. 1508;
GILMORE, G., 'Article 9: what it does for the past', (1965–1965) 26 La. L. Rev. 285;
GILMORE, G., 'Security law, formalism and Article 9', (1968) 47 Neb. L. Rev., 659;
GILMORE, G. and AXELROD, A. 'Chattel security: I', (1947–48) 57 Yale L. J., 517;
GLENN, G., 'The conditional sale at common law and as a statutory security', (1938–39) 25 Va. L. Rev. 559;
GLENN, G., 'The chattel mortgage as a statutory security', (1938–39) 25 Va. L. Rev., 316;
GRIFFIN, A. B. and CURTIS, A. F., *The law of chattel mortgages and conditional sales under the Uniform Conditional Sales Act, adapted to New York State*, (4 edn., Albany: Bender, 1925), p. 304;
GOULD, J. M., *Kent on contracts*, (Boston: Little Brown, 1896), p. 1061;
HALE, W. G., 'The Uniform Conditional Sales Act', (1922–1923) 2 Or. L. Rev., 1;
HALL, H. L., 'Article 2 – from status to contract', (1952) Wis. L. Rev., 209;
HANNA, J., 'The secured creditor in bankruptcy', (1960) 14 Rutgers L. Rev., 471;
HARING, F. B., *The law of conditional sales*, (New York: The Ronald Press, 1907), p. 407;
HAWKLAND, W. D., 'Consignment selling under the Uniform Commercial Code', (1962) 67 Com. L. J., 146;
HAWKLAND, W. D., 'The impact of the Uniform Commercial Code on equipment leasing', (1972) U. Ill. L. F., 446;
HILLER, R. L., 'Security Aspects of Chattel Leases in Bankruptcy', (1965–66) 34 Fordham L. Rev., 439;
HOGAN, W. E., 'The marriage of sales to chattel security in the Uniform Commercial Code: Massachusetts Variety', (1958) 38 B. U. L. Rev., 571;
HOGAN, W. E., 'Financing the acquisition of new goods under the Uniform Commercial Code', (1962) 3 B. C. Indus. & Com. L. Rev., 115;
HUDDLESON, E. E., 'Old wine in new bottles: UCC articles 2A – leases', (1987–88) 39 Ala. L. Rev., 615;
ISAACS, N., 'The economic advantages and disadvantages of the various methods of selling goods on credit', (1923) 8 Cornell L. Q., 199;
ISAAC, M., 'Conditional sale contracts in bankruptcy proceedings', (1902) 10 Am. Law., 535;
ISAAC, M., *Conditional sales in bankruptcy proceedings*, (Atlanta: Foote & Davies, 1905), p. 108;
KENT, J., *Commentaries on American Law*, (4 edn., New York: E. B. Clayton, 1840), p. 828;
KLEPS, R. N., 'Uniformity versus uniform legislation conditional sale of fixture', (1939) 24 Cornell L. Rev., 394;

KRIPKE, H., 'Fixtures under the Uniform Commercial Code', (1964) 64 Colum. L. Rev., 44;
KRIPKE, H., 'Some dissonant notes about articles 2A', (1987–1988) 39 Ala. L. Rev., 791;
LATTY, E. R., 'Sales and title and the proposed code', (1951) 16 Law & Contemp Probs. 3;
LAKIN, L. and BERGER, H. J., 'The secured party: enforcement of his security interest under Article 9 after the debtor's default', (1970) 8 Am. Bus. Law. J., 1;
LAWRENCE, W. H., HENNING, W. H. and FREYERMUTH, R. W., *Understanding secured transactions*, (2 edn., New York City: Matthew Bender, 1999), p. 520;
LEARY, F. J., 'Leasing and other techniques of financing equipment under the U.C.C.', (1968–1969) 42 Temple L. Q., 217;
LEVIN, A. J., 'Intention fallacy in the construction of title retaining contracts', (1925) 24 Mich. L. Rev. 130;
LONG, R. J., 'Conditional sale' in D. S. GARLAND and L. P. MCGEHEE (eds.), *The American and English encyclopaedia of law*, vol. 6, (New York: Edward Thompson Co., 1898), 2;
MAGILL, R. F., 'Legal advantages and disadvantages of the various methods of selling goods on credit', (1923) 8 Cornell L. Q., 210;
MENTSCHIKOFF, S., 'Reflections of a drafter', (1982) 43 Ohio St. L. Rev., 537;
MERRILL, T.W. and SMITH, H. E., *Property – principles and policies*, (3 edn., St. Paul: Foundation Press, 2017), p. 1360;
MEYER, K., 'A primer on purchase money security interests under revised Article 9 of the Uniform Commercial Code', (2001–02) 50 U. Kan. L. Rev., 143;
MILLER, C. R., *A treatise on the law of conditional sales of personal property*, (Cincinnati: R. Clarke, 1888), p. 231;
MOONEY, C. W. Jr., 'The mystery and myth of ostensible ownership and Article 9 filing: a critique of proposals to extend filing requirements to leases', (1987–1988) 39 Ala. L. Rev., 683;
MORRIL, W. W., *Conditional sales and bailments: with forms*, (Albany: Bender, 1901),p. 138;
MOSSOFF, A., 'What is property? Putting the pieces back together' (2003) 45 Ar. L. Rev. 371;
NEWMARK, N., 'Conversion by purchase', (1881) 15 Am. L. Rev. 363;
NOYES GREENE, H., 'Uniform Conditional Sales Act and commentary' in H. NOYES GREEN (ed.), *Uniform laws, annotated*, vol. 2, (Northport: Edward Thompson Co., 1922), p. 376;
PARSONS, T., *Law of contracts*, (Boston: Little Brown, 1864), p. 609;
PEARSON, A. B. and BOYD, H. F., *Benjamin's treatise on the law of sale of personal property*, (Boston: Charles Edson & Co. Publishers, 1888), p. 1330;
PEDEN, J. R., 'The treatment of equipment leases as security agreements under the Uniform Commercial Code', (1971) 13 Wm. & Mary L. Rev., 110;
PENNER, J. E., *The idea of property in law*, (Oxford: Clarendon Press, 1997), p. 240;
PLUMB, W. T., 'The new Uniform Conditional Sales Law', (1922) 27 Com. L. League Bull., 571;
POLLOCK, F., 'What is a thing?', (1894) 10 L. Q. Rev., 318;
POTHIER, M., *A treatise on the law of obligations, or contracts*, vol. 1, (Philadelphia: Robert H. Small, 1839), p. 448;
REISS, W. R., 'Security aspects of equipment leasing', (1962) U. Ill. L. F., 77;

SCHOULER, J., *Treatise on the law of personal property*, (Albany: M. Bender & Co., 1918), p. 886;

SCHROTH, P. W., 'Financial leasing of equipment in the law of the United States', (2010) 16 Unif. L. Rev., 437;

SCHWARTZ, A. 'Security interests and bankruptcy priorities: a review of current theories', (1981) 10 J. Legal Stud., 1;

SHAPIRO, S. L., 'The ABC's of leasing', (1972) U. Ill. L. F., 433;

SPINK, P. M. and ONG, C. A., 'Substance versus form: Anglo-Australian perspectives on title financing transactions', (2004) 63 Cambridge L. J., 199;

STROH, J. H., 'Peripheral security interests – the expanded net of Article 9', (1967) 22 U. Miami L. Rev., 67;

THOMPSON, A. B., 'The bankruptcy act in operation', (1900) 6 W. Res. L. J., 157;

TRAVALIO, G. M., NORDSTROM, R. J. and CLOVIS, A. L., *Nordstrom on sales and leases of goods*, (2nd edn., New York: Aspen law and business, 2000), p. 1128;

VOLD, L., 'Divided property interests in conditional sales', (1929–30) 78 Univ. Penn. L. Rev., 713;

WANGERIN, P., 'Floating liens, proceeds, and PMSIs: perfection and priority in three closely connected cases', (2017) 47 UCC L. J., 287;

WARNER, G. R., 'The anti-bankruptcy act: revised Article 9 and bankruptcy', (2001) 9 Am. Bankr. L. Rev., 3;

WARNER, G. R., 'Article 9's bankruptcy proceeds rule: amending bankruptcy code section 552 through the UCC proceeds definition', (2010) 46 Gonz. L. Rev., 521;

WEINTRAUB, B. and RESNICK, A., "Puncturing the equity cushion – Adequate protection for secured creditors in reorganization cases" 14 UCC L. J., 284;

WELSH, H. M., 'Judicial interpretations of the filing requirements under Article 9 of the Code', (1970) 37 Tenn. L. Rev., 273;

WHITE, R. S., 'Right, duties and remedies of the parties to a sale of personal property which is to be delivered and paid for in instalments', (1897) 7 Yale L. J., 117;

WHITE, J. J. and ISRAEL, D., 'Preference conundrums', (1993) 98 Com. L. J., 1;

WHITE, J. J. and BRUNSTADT, G. E. J., Secured transactions teaching materials, (4 edn, St. Paul: West Publishing, 2013), p. 705;

WHITE, J. J., SUMMERS, R. S. and HILMAN, R. A., *Uniform Commercial Code*, vol. 4, (6th edn., Eagan: Thomson Reuters, 2015), p. 672;

WHITE, J. J. and others, *Principles of secured transactions*, (St. Paul: West Academic Publishing, 2018), p. 291;

WIGMORE, J. H., 'Pledge-idea a study in comparative legal ideas', (1896–97) 10 Harv. L. Rev., 321;

WILCOX, H. S., 'The new amendments to the national Bankruptcy Act', (1910) 9 Okla. L. J., 85;

WILDE, C., 'The Chandler Act', (1938) 14 Ind. L. J., 93;

WILFORD, J., DAVISSON, E. and CHARLES, N., *Lease as a financing and selling device*, (An Arbor: School of Business and Administration, 1951), p. 108;

WINSHIP, P., 'An historical overview of UCC article 9' in L. GULLIFER and O. AKSELI (eds.), *Secured transactions law reform: principles, policies and practice*, (Oxford: Hart Publisher, 2016), 21;
X., 'Conditional sales' (1882) 9 Pac. Coast L. J., 545;
X., *Principles of the law of conditional sales and chattel mortgages: a monograph*, (St. Paul: West Publishing, 1899), p. 28;
X., 'The Uniform Conditional Sales Act', (1922) 22 Colum. L. Rev., (584);
X., 'Defeating the priority of an after-acquired property clause ', (1935) 48 Harv. L. Rev., 474;
X., 'Comments', (1936) 36 Col. L. Rev., (1362);
X., 'The effect of prepayment upon the buyer's right to the goods', (1937) 37 Colum. L. Rev., 630;
X., 'Acquisition of industrial and commercial equipment through leasing arrangements', (1957) 66 Yale L. J., 751;

SECTION 2 – UNCITRAL

1. *UNCITRAL Texts*

UNITED NATIONS COMISSION ON INTERNATIONAL TRADE LAW (UNCITRAL), UNCITRAL Legislative Guide on Secured Transactions, (New York, 2010);
Working Group VI (Security Interests), Draft legislative guide on secured transactions – background remarks, UNCITRAL, (New York, 2007).

2. *Doctrine*

AKSELI, O., *International secured transactions law – Facilitation of credit and international conventions and instruments*, (London: Routledge, 2001), p. 344;
AKSELI O, 'Financial inclusion, access to credit, and sustainable finance: what role for the UNCITRAL Model Law on Secured Transactions?', (2021) 84 Law & Contemp. Probs. 181;
BAZINAS, S., 'Key objectives and fundamental principles of the UNCITRAL legislative guide on secured transactions', (2008) 2 Insolvency & Restructuring Int'l., 42;
BAZINAS, S., 'The work of UNCITRAL on security interest: an overview', (2010) 15 Unif. L. Rev., 315;
BAZINAS, S., 'Acquisition financing under the UNCITRAL legislative guide on secured transactions', (2011) 16 Unif. L. Rev., 483;
BAZINAS, S., 'The utility and efficacy of the UNCITRAL legislative guide on secured transactions' in O. AKSELI (ed.), *Availibility of credit in a time of crisis*, (Cambridge: Cambridge University Press, 2013), 133;
BAZINAS, S., 'The UNCITRAL legislative guide on secured transactions and draft UNCITRAL model law on secured transactions compared' in L. GULLIFER and O. AKSELI (eds.), *Secured transactions law reform*, (Oxford: Hart Publishing, 2016), 481;

BAZINAS, S., 'The draft UNCITRAL model law on secured transactions' in B. FOËX (ed.), *The draft UNCITRAL model law on secured transactions – Why and how?*, (Genève: Schulthess, 2016), 19;

BAZINAS, S., 'The influence of the UNCITRAL Legislative Guide on secured transactions' in F. DAHAN (ed.), *Research handbook on secured financing in commercial transactions*, (Cheltenham: Edward Elgar, 2016), 26;

BEALE, H. 'The UNCITRAL Legislative Guide on Secured Transactions as a model for law reform: some conclusions' in O. AKSELI (ed.), *Availibility of credit and secured transactions in a time of crisis*, (Cambridge: Cambridge University Press, 2013), 275;

CASTELLANO, G. G., 'Reforming non-possessory secured transactions law: a new strategy?', (2015) 78 MLR, 611;

CASTELLANO, G. G., and TOSATO, A., 'Personal property security law: international ambitions and local realities' in L. GHIA (ed.), *International business law*, (Wolters Kluwer, 2019), 283;

COHEN, N., 'Should UNCITRAL prepare a model law on secured transactions', (2010) 15 Unif. L. Rev., 325;

COHEN, N., Harmonizing the law governing secured credit: the next frontier', (1998) 33 Tex. Int'l. L. J. 173;

DROBNIG, U., 'Report of the Secretary-General: study on security interests (A/CN.9/131)', (1977) 8 UNCITRAL Yearbook, 171;

DUNN, J. D., 'UNCITRAL Adopts Legislative Guide on Secured Transactions', (2008) 2 Insolv. & Restruct. Int'l., 40;

GARRO, A. M., 'The creation of a security right and its extension to acquisition financing devices', (2010) 15 Unif. L. Rev., 375;

KLEIN, J., 'UNCITRAL Legislative Guide on Secured Transactions: an introduction and overview', (2009) Am. Bankr. Inst. L. J., 28;

MACDONDALD, R., 'A model law on secured transactions. A representation of structure? An object of idealized imitation? A type, template or design?', (2010) 15 Unif. L. Rev., 419;

MCORMACK, G., 'The CFR and credit securities – a suitable case for treatment?' in A. VAQUER (ed.), *European private law beyond the Common Frame of Reference*, (Groningen: Europa Law Publishing, 2008), 99;

MCCORMACK, G. 'American private law writ large? The UNCITRAL secured transactions guide', (2011) 60 Int'l. & Comp. L. Q., 597;

MCCORMACK, G., 'Secured transactions law reform: UNCITRAL and the export of foreign legal models' in O. AKSELI (ed.), *Availibility of credit and secured transactions in a time of crisis*, (Cambridge: Cambridge University Press, 2013), 33;

MITSDÖRFFER, S., *Sicherungsrechte an Schutzrechten – Ein Vergleich zwischen dem deutschen Recht and dem UNCITRAL Legislative Guide on Secured Transactions*, (Karlsruhe: Mohr Siebeck, 2013), p. 298;

ROVER, J.-H., 'The EBRD's Model Law on Secured Transactions and its implications for an UNCITRAL Model Law on Secured Transactions', (2010) 15 Unif. L. Rev., 479;

SECTION 3 – DCFR

1. DCFR Texts

Study Group on a European Civil Code and Research Group on EC Private Law (Acquis Group), *Principles, definitions and model rules of European private law – Draft common frame of reference (DCFR)*, (Munich: Sellier European Law Publishers, 2009),

2. EU Communications on the DCFR

European Commission, Communication from the Commission to the European Parliament and the Council – A more coherent European Contract Law – An action plan (2003), COM (2003) final, OJ C-63;

Commission of the European Communities, Communication from the Commission to the European Parliament and the Council – European contract law and the revision of the acquis: the way forward (2004);

European Commission, Green Paper from the Commission on policy options for progress towards a European Contract Law for consumers and businesses – Com(2010) 348 final (Brussels, 2010), online: https://eur-lex.europa.eu/legal-content/EN/TXT/?uri=celex%3A52010DC0348;

3. Doctrine

AKKERMANS, B., 'The European Union Development of European property law' in C. GODT (ed.), *Hanse Law School in Perspective – Legal Teaching and Cross Border Research after Lisbon*, (The Hague: Kluwer, 2011), p. 657;

AKKERMANS, B. 'The Role of the (D)CFR in the Making of European Property Law' in V. SAGAERT, E. TERRYN and M.E. STORME (eds.), *The Draft Common Frame of Reference (DCFR): A National and Comparative Perspective*, (Antwerp: Intersentia, 2011), 1;

BEALE, H., 'The European Commission's Common Frame of Reference project: a progress report', (2006) 2 ECLR, 303;

BEALE, H., 'The future of secured credit in Europe: concluding remarks', (2008) 5 ECFR, 375;

BEALE, H., 'The future of the Common Frame of Reference', (2007) 3 ERCL, 257;

BEALE, H., 'The nature and purposes of the Common Frame of Reference', (2008) 14 Juridica International, 10;

BEALE, H., 'Secured transactions', (2008) 14 Juridica International, 96;

BRIDGE, M., 'The scope and limits of security interests', (2008) 5 ECFR, 180;

CASHIN RITAINE, E., 'Common Frame of Reference and property law: a general introduction' in S. VAN ERP, A. SALOMONS and B. AKKERMANS (eds.), *The future of European property law*, (Munich: Sellier European Law, 2012), 1;

COLLINS, H., 'Review – Principles, Definitions and Model Rules of European Private Law: Draft Common Frame of Reference (DCFR)', (2008) 71 Mod. L. Rev., 840;

DROBNIG, U., 'Choosing the right approach for European law making: commentary', (2008) 5 ECFR, 102;
DROBNIG, U. and BÖGER, O. *Proprietary security in movable assets (PEL Prop. Sec.)*, vol. 6, (Principles on European Law, Munich: Sellier Publishers, 2015), p. 990;
DROBNIG, U. 'Security rights in movables' in A. S. HARTKAMP and others (eds.), *Towards a European Civil Code*, (Alphen on the Rhine: Kluwer Law International, 2011), 1025;
EIDENMULLER, H., FAUST, F., GRIGOLEIT, H. C., JANSEN, N., WAGNER, G., ZIMMERMANN, R., 'The common frame of reference for European private law -- policy choices and codification problems', (2008) 28 Oxford J. L. Studies, 659;
ERNST, W., 'Der 'Common Frame of Reference' aus juristischer Sicht', (2008) 208 AcP, 249;
FABER, W. 'Book VIII DCFR on acquisition and loss of ownership of goods' in V. SAGAERT, M. E. STORME and E. TERRYN (eds.), *The Draft Common Frame of Reference: national and comparative perspectives*, (Cambridge: Intersentia, 2012), 323;
FABER, W., 'Proprietary security rights in movables – European developments', (2014) 22 Juridica Int'l., 27;
FLUME, W., 'Das Rechtsverhältnis des Leasing in zivilrechtlicher und steuerrechtlicher Sicht', (1972) 1 – 4 DB, 1;
HAENTJENS, M., 'DCFR en goederenrecht in de praktijk over zekerheid en rafelranden', (2011) NTBR, 54;
HESSELINK, M. W., 'The politics of a European civil code', (2004) 10 ELJ, 675;
HESSELINK, M. W., 'The Common Frame of Reference as a source of European private law', (2009) 83 Tul. L. Rev., 919;
HODGES, C., 'Current discussions on consumer redress: collective redress and ADR', (2012) 13 ERA Forum, 11;
JANSEN, N., 'The authority of an academic 'Draft Common Frame of Reference'' in H. W. MICKLITZ and F. CAFAGGI (eds.), *European private law after the Common Frame of Reference*, (Cheltenham: Elgar, 2010), 147;
KIENINGER, E.-M., 'Introduction: security rights in movable property within the common market and the approach of the study' in E.-M. KIENINGER (ed.), *Security rights in movable property in European private law*, (Cambridge: Cambridge University Press, 2004), 1;
KIENINGER, E.-M., 'Evaluation: a common? Convergences, subsisting differences and possible ways for harmonisation' in E.-M. KIENINGER (ed.), *Security rights in movable property in European private law*, (Cambridge: Cambridge University Press, 2004), 647;
KIENINGER, E.-M., 'The scope and limits of security interests: commentary', (2008) 5 ECFR, (215)
KUNEVA, M., 'Introduction', (2007) 3 ERCL, 239;
LANDO, O. and BEALE, H., *Principles of European Contract Law, Parts I and II*, (The Hague: Kluwer, 2000), p. 561;
LANDO, O. and BEALE, H., *Principles of European Contract Law, Part III*, (The Hague: Kluwer, 2000), p. 291;
LANDO, O., 'The structure and the legal values of the Common Frame of Reference (CFR)', (2007) 3 ECLR, 245;

LETOWSKA, E. and WIEWIOROWSKA-DOMAGALSKA, A., 'The Common Frame of Reference – The perspective of a new member state', (2007) 3 ERCL, 277;

LILLEHOLT, K., 'A European law of lease?' in A. VANQUER (ed.), *European private law beyond the Common Frame of Reference*, (Groningen: Europe Law Publishing, 2008), 57;

MAX PLANCK INSTITUTE FOR COMPARATIVE AND INTERNATIONAL PRIVATE LAW, 'Policy options for progress towards a European contract law – Comments on the issues raised in the Green Paper from the Commission of 1 July 2010, COM(2010) 348 final', (2011) 75 RabelsZ., 371;

MCCORMACK, G., 'The CFR and credit securities – a suitable case for treatment?' in A. VAQUER (ed.), *European private law beyond the Common Frame of Reference*, (Groningen: Europa Law Publishing, 2008), 99;

MEZZANOTTE, F., 'The protection of ownership of goods in the DCFR: an "exclusion strategy" at the core of European property law?', (2013) 4 ERPL, 1009;

ODERKERK, M., 'The CFR and the method(s) of comparative legal research', (2007) 3 ERCL, (315)

RANK, W., 'Harmonisation of national security rights' in U. DROBNIG, H. J. SNIJDERS and E. J. ZIPPRO (eds.), *Divergences of property law, an obstacle to the internal market?*, (München: Sellier, 2006), p. 240;

SEFTON-GREEN, R., 'The DCFR: a technical or political toolbox?' in A. SOMMA (ed.), *The politics of the Draft Common Frame of Reference*, vol. 16, (Alphen on the Rhine: Kluwer Law International, 2009), 39;

SMITS, J. M., 'The Draft Common Frame of Reference for a European private law: fit for purpose?', (2008) 15 Maastricht J. Eur. & Comp. L., 145;

SMITS, J. M., 'The Draft Common Frame of Reference: how to improve it?' in H. W. MICKLITZ and F. CAFAGGI (eds.), *European private law after the common frame of reference*, (Cheltenham: Elgar, 2010), 90;

STADLER, A., 'Die Vorschläge des Gemeinsamen Referensrahmens für ein europäisches Sachenrecht – Grundprinzipien und Eigentumserwerb', (2010) 8 JZ, 380;

STORME, M. E., 'Une question de principe(s)? Réponse à quelques critiques à l'égard du projet provisoire de "Cadre commun de référence"', (2008) 9 ERA Forum, (65)

VAN ERP, S., *European and National Property Law: Osmosis or Growing Antagonism?*, (Leuven: European Law Publishing, 2007), 1;

VAN DER WEIDE, A. J., '(On)zekerheden in het DCFR. Boek IX Proprietary security in movable assets', (2011) NTBR, 53;

VAN VLIET, L., 'Acquisition and loss of ownership of goods – Book VIII of the Draft Common Frame of Reference', (2011) ZEUP., 292;

VENEZIANO, A., 'A secured transactions' regime for Europe: treatment of acquisition finance devices and creditor's enforcement rights', (2008) 14 Juridica International, 89;

VENEZIANO, A., 'Security rights in movables in the DCFR: general presentation' in V. SAGAERT, M. E. STORME and E. TERRYN (eds.), *The Draft Common Frame of Reference: national and comparative perspectives*, (Antwerp: Intersentia, 2012), 305;

VENEZIANO, A., 'The DCFR Book on Secured Transactions: some policy choices made by the Working Group' in S. VAN ERP, A. SALOMONS and B. AKKERMANS (eds.), *The future of European property law*, (Munich: Sellier European Law, 2012), 123;

VON BAR, C., 'Coverage and structure of the academic common frame of reference', (2007) 3 ERCL, 350;
WHITTAKER, S., The 'Draft Common Frame of Reference' - An assessment, (United Kingdom: Ministry of Justice, 2008);

SECTION 4 - GERMANY

ASCHER, W., 'Aufgaben des Gesetzgebers bei einer Neuordnung des Sicherungsgeschäfte des gewerblichen Kreditverkehrs', (1955) 8 DRiZ, 177;
BAUKNECHT, X., "Eigentumsvorbehalt und Anwartschaftsrecht", (1955) 34–35 NJW, 1251;
BAUR, J. F. and STÜRNER, R., *Sachenrecht*, (München: C. H. Beck Verlag, 2009), p. 1086;
BECKMANN, R. M. and others, *J. Von Staudinger Kommentar zum Bürgerlichen Geseztbuch mit einführungsgesetz und Nebengesetzen*, (M. MARTINEK (ed.), 2 edn., Berlin: Sellier, 2004), p. 1135;
BECKMANN, R. M., "§932 - Gutgläubiger Erwerb von Nichtberechtigten" in M. M. MARITNEK (ed.) *Juris Praxiskommentar - BGB*, (Saarbrücken: Juris, 2020), online: https://www.juris.de/r3/document;
BETTE, K.. 'Der verlängerte Eigentumsvorbehalt in der Praxis', (1973) 16 ZfGK, 793;
BLOMEYER, A., 'Die Rechtsstellung des Vorbehaltskäufers', (1963) 162 AcP, 193;
BRINKMANN, M., 'The peculiar approach of German law in the field of secured transactions and why it has worked (so far)' in L. GULLIFER and O. AKSELI (eds.), *Secured transactions law reform*, (Oxford: Hart Publishing, 2016), 339;
BUCK, P., 'Kaufrecht' in *Das Schuldrecht 2002*, (Stuttgart: München, 2002), p. 336;
BÜLOW, P., 'Die isolierte Ausübung des Eigentumvorbehalts nach §449 BGB', (2002) 40 NJW, 2090;
BÜLOW, P., *Recht der Kreditsicherheiten*, (6 edn., Heidelberg: C. F. Müller Verlag, 2009), p. 603;
BUSCHE, J., '§398 BGB' in M. LÖWISCH (ed.), *J. von Staudingers Kommentar zum Bürgerlichen Gesetzbuch mit Einführungsgesetz und Nebengesetzen*, (Berlin: Sellier, 2017), p. 903;
DROBNIG, U., *Emphelen sich gesetzlichen Maßnahmen zur Reform der Mobiliarsicherheiten?*, (München: C. H. Beck, 1976), p. 99;
EBENROTH, C. T., 'Der Finanzierungs-Leasing-Vertrag als Rechtsgeschäft zwischen Miete und Kauf', (1978) 9 JuS, 588;
EICHEL, F., *Künftige Forderungen*, (Tübingen: Mohr Siebeck, 2014), p. 573;
FAUST, F., '§449 - Eigentumsvorbehalt' in H. G. BAMBERGER and others (eds.), *Bürgerliches Gesetzbuch Kommentar*, (4 edn., München: Beck, 2019), p. 3122;
FIKENTISCHER, W. and HEINEMANN, A., *Schuldrecht - Allgemeiner und Besonderer Teil*, (11 edn, Berlin: De Gruyter, 2017), p. 1064;
FISCHER, O., 'Der verlängerte Eigentumsvorbehalt in der Krise', (1959) 9 NJW, 366;
FLUME, W., 'Der verlängerte und erweiterte Eigentumsvorbehalt', (1950) 22 NJW, 841;
GAUL, H. F., 'Lex commissoria und Sicherungsübereignung: - Zugleich ein Beitrag zum sogenannten Innenverhältnis bei der Sicherungsübereignung', (1968) 4 AcP, 351;

GRAVENHORST, W., 'Eigentumsvorbehalt gleich Sicherüngsübereignung?', (1971) 15–16 JZ, 494;

GSELL, B., 'Der EU-Richtlinienentwurf zur Bekämpfung von Zahlungsverzug im Handelsverkehr', (1998) 37–38 ZIP, 1569;

HABERMEIER, S., 'Das Trennungsdenken- Ein Beitrag zur europäischen Privatrechtstheorie', (1995) 3 AcP, 283;

HABERSACK, M. and SCHÜRNBRAND, J. 'Der Eigentumsvorbehalt nach der Schuldrechtsreform', [2002] JuS, 833;

HAGER, J., '§346' in B. DAUNER-LIEB (ed.), *Nomos Kommentar – BGB Schuldrecht*, (Baden-Baden: Nomos, 2016), online;

HEIDLAND, H. 'Verlängerter und erweiterer Eigentumsvorbehalt im Insolvenzverfahren', (1960) 21 KTS, 17;

HERRESTHAL, C. 'Das Recht der Kreditsicherung' in D. KAISER and M. STOFFELS (eds.), *J. von Staudingers Eckpfeiler des Zivilrechts*, (Berlin: Sellier, 2018), online;

HUBER, U., 'Gefahren des vertraglichen Abtretungsverbots für den Schuldner der abgetretenen Forderung', (1968) 41 NJW, 1905;

KUHN, G., 'Der Eigentumsvorbehalt im Konkurs', (1972) 8 WM, 206;

KIM, S., *Die Entwicklung des Anwartschaftsrechts beim Kauf under Eigentumsvorbehalt*, (Dissertation Rechtswissenschaft, Rheinischen Friedrich-Wilhelms-Universität Bonn 2017), p. 161;

KIENINGER, E.-M., 'Nationale, europäische und weltweite Reformen des Mobiliarsicherungsrechts', (2005) 49 WM, 2305;

KIENINGER, E.-M., 'Die Zukunft des deutschen und europäischen Mobiliarkreditsicherungsrechts', (2008) 208 AcP, 182;

LAMBSDORFF, H., *Handbuch des Eigentumsvorbehalts im deutschen und ausländischen Recht*, (Frankfurt am Main: Athenäum, 1974), p. 457;

LEHMANN, H., *Reform der Kreditsicherung an Fahrnis und Forderungen* (Stuttgart: W. Rohlhammer Verlag, 1937), p. 84;

LEIBLE, S. and SOSNITZA, O., 'Grundfälle zum Recht des Eigentumsvorbehalts', (2001) 6 JuS, (244)

S. LEIBLE and M. F. MÜLLER, §449 BGB – Eigentumsvorbehalt" in M. JUNKER, R. M. BECKMANN and H. RÜßMANN (eds.) *Juris Praxiskommentar BGB – Band 2 Schuldrecht*, (Saarbrücken: Juris, 2020), online: https://www.juris.de/r3/document;

LOPAU, E., 'Die Höchstrichterliche Rechtsprechung zur Forderungsvorausabtretung bei verlängerte Eigentumsvorbehalt', (1973) 31 DB, 1537;

LORENZ, S., 'Grundwissen – Zivilrecht: der Eigentumsvorbehalt', [2011] JuS, 199;

MAROTZKE, W., 'Der Eigentumsvorbehalt im neuen Insolvenzrecht', (1995) 17 JZ, 803;

MARTINEK, M., *Moderne Vertragstypen*, (München: C. H. Beck Verlag, 1991), p. 327;

MITLEHNER, S., *Mobiliarsicherheiten im Insolvenzverfahren*, (2 edn., Köln: RWS Verlag, 2009), p. 354;

MÖHRING, R., 'Konkurrenz von Verarbeitungsklauseln', (1960) 16 NJW, 697;

MÜLLER, K. and GRUBER, U. P., *Sachenrecht*, (München: Verlag Franz Vahlen, 2016), p. 850;

NÖLL, H. H., WIEGAND, D. and WIEGAND, W., *J. Von Staudingers Kommentar zum Bürgerlichen Gesetzbuch mit Einführungsgesetz und Nebengesetz*, (C. HERRESTHAL (ed.), Berlin: Sellier, 2018), p. 515;

PAULUS, C. G., 'The new German insolvency code', (1998) 99 Tex. Int'l. L. J., 141;

RAKOB, J., 'Germany' in H. C. SIGMAN and E.-M. KIENINGER (eds.), *Cross-border security over tangibles*, (Berlin: Sellier, 2007), 63;

RAISER, L., 'Zu BGH 2 October 2010, nr. IV ZR 2/52', (1953) 6 NJW, 217;

REICH, R., 'Reform der Kreditsicherung', (1976) 15-16 JZ, 463;

REINICKE, D. and TIEDTKE, K., 'Finanzierungsleasing und Sachmängelhaftung', (1982) 19 BB, 1142;

REINICKE, D. and TIEDTKE, K., *Kaufrecht*, (München: Carl Heymans Verlag, 2009), p. 763;

SANNWALD, R., *Der Finanzierungsleasingvertrag über bewegliche Sachen mit Nichtkaufleuten*, (Berlin: Duncker & Humblot, 1982), 73;

SCHULZ, D., ULRICH, B. and LESSING, H., *Handbuch Insolvenzrecht*, (4 edn., München: Hauffe Gruppe, 2012), p. 343;

SCHULZE, G. and KIENLE, F., 'Der Kauf unter Eigentumsvorbehalt - eine Kehrtwende des Gesetzgebers? ', (2002) 39 NJW, 2842;

SCHWERDTNER, P., 'Globalzession und verlängerte Eigentumsvorbehalt', (1974) 40 NJW, 1785;

SERICK, R., *Eigentumsvorbehalt und Sicherungsübertragung*, vol. I, (Heidelberg: Recht und Wirtschaft, 1963), p. 543;

SERICK, R., 'Kollisionsfälle im Bereiche der Verarbeitungsklauseln', (1975) 9 BB, 381;

SERICK, R., *Eigentumsvorbehalt und Sicherungsübertragung*, (Heidelberg: Verlag Recht und Wirtschaft, 1993), p. 341;

SONNENBERGER, J., 'Rechtsfragen beim Leasing beweglicher Sachen', (1983) 40 NJW, 2217;

STOFFELS, M., 'Leasing' in *J. von Staudingers Kommentar zum Bürgerlichen Gesetzbuch mit Einführungsgesetz und Nebengesetzen*, (Berlin: Sellier, 2018), p. 228;

TIEDTKE, K., *Der erweiterte Eigentumsvorbehalt*, (München: Verlag C. H. Beck, 2000), (829) p. 1075;

VIEWEG, K. and WERNER, A., *Sachenrecht*, (7 edn., München: Verlag Franz Vahlen, 2015), p. 671;

WEBER, H., 'Reform der Mobiliarsicherheiten', (1976) 36 NJW, 1601;

WESTERMANN, H. P., 'Gesetzliche Regelung der Sicherungsübereignung und des Eigentumsvorbehalt?' in Verhandlungen des Einundvierzigsten deutschen Juristentags, (Tübingen: J. C. B. Mohr, 1955), p. 80;

WESTERMANN, H. P., *BGB-Sachenrecht*, (Heidelberg: C. F. Müller, 2012), p. 281;

WESTERMANN, H. P., 'Vereinbarung des Eigentumsvorbehalts, insbesondere durch AGB' in C. SCHUBERT (ed.), *Münchener Kommentar zum Bürgerlichen Gesetzbuch*, (8 edn., München: C. H. Beck Verlag, 2018), online source: https://beck-online.beck.de/?vpath=bibdata%2Fkomm%2FMuekoBGB_8_Band4%2FBGB%2Fcont%2FMuekoBGB%2EBGB%2Ep449%2Ehtm, rn;

WESTPHALEN, F., 'AGB-Recht im Jahr 2007', (2008) 31 NJW, 2234;

WEYER, T., 'Schutz des Eigentumsvorbehalts und gutgläubiger Erwerb an beweglichen Sachen', (1966) 21 NJW, 959;

WIEGAND, W., 'Der gutgläubige Erwerb beweglicher Sachen nach §932 ff BGB', (1974) 4 JuS, 201;

WIEGAND, W., 'Akzessorietät und Spezialität Zum Verhältnis zwischen Forderung und Sicherungsgegenstand' in *Probleme der Kreditsicherung*, (Bern: Verlag Stämpfli & Cie Ag, 1982), p. 198;

WIEGAND, W., '§950 BGB' in W. WIEGAND (ed.), J. von Staudingers Kommentar zum Bürgerlichen Gesetzbuch mit Einführungsgesetz und Nebengesetzen, (Berlin: Sellier, 2016), p. 835;

WIEGAND, W., "Anhang zu §929–931 BGB" in W. WIEGAND (ed.) J. von Staudingers Kommentar zum Bürgerlichen Gesetzbuch mit Einführungsgesetz und Nebengesetzen, (Berlin: Sellier, 2017), online;

WESTERMANN, H. P., GURSKY, K.-H. and EICKMANN, D., Sachenrecht, (Heidelberg: C. F. Müller, 2011), p. 1079.

RELEVANT SOURCES PART 3 – BELGIUM

AKKERMANS, B., *The principles of numerus clausus in European property law*, (Antwerp: Intersentia, 2008), p. 657;

APERS, A. and GRUYAERT, D., 'Eigendomsvoorbehoud en onroerende incorporatie volgens de nieuwe pandwet: welk nieuws onder de zon?', (2015) 1 TPR, 83;

BAECK, J., 'Achtergrond en krachtlijnen van de hervorming' in J. BAECK and M. KRUITHOF (eds.), *Het nieuwe zekerheidsrecht*, (Antwerpen: Intersentia, 2014), 1;

BAECK, J., 'Commentaar bij art. 24–25 Pandwet' in E. DIRIX, P. FRANCOIS and M. TISON (eds.), *Voorrechten en hypotheken Artikelsgewijze commentaar met overzicht van rechtspraak en rechtsleer*, (Mechelen: Kluwer, 2015), loosel.

BAECK, J., 'Het nieuwe pandrecht', (2016) 31 RW, 1209;

BAEYENS, S., 'De zekerheidsfunctie van het eigendomsrecht van de leasinggever als grondslag voor het verrijkingsverbod bij leasing (note under Cass. 19 december 2019)', (2020) 2 RW, 56;

BECUE, P., "De wet van 11 juli 2013 met betrekking tot de hervorming van zakelijke zekerheden op roerende goederen (nieuwe pandwet). Principes en impact op de verzekeringssector. Het eigendomsvoorbehoud in Belgie komt tot volledige maturiteit", (2014) T. Verz., 352;

BEKAERT, J., 'Insolventierechtelijke aspecten van leasing en tegenwerpelijkheid van leasing' in P. BESELAERE, O. LENAERTS, B. TILLEMAN, A. VERBEKE (eds.), *Handboek leasing*, (Brugge: Die Keure, 2007), 591;

BOGAERT, G., 'Beëindiging van de leasingovereenkomst' in P. BESELAERE and others (eds.), *Handboek leasing*, (Brugge: Die Keure, 2007), p. 697;

BONTINCK, L., 'Het pandregister' in M. E. STORME (ed.), *Roerende zekerheden na de Pandwet*, (Antwerpen: Intersentia, 2017), 203;

BOONEN, H., 'De rechtsschijn', (1950–51) 8 RW, 289;

BOUCKAERT, F., 'Note under Cass. 7 mei 2010', (1995) 12 T. Not., 576;

BRAECKMANS, H., 'Bankrekeningen, betaal- en kredietverrichtingen', in *Beginselen van Belgisch Privaatrecht*, XIII, Deel 1, *Ondernemingsrecht*, Vol. B, Brussel, Story-Scientia, 1989, 545;

BRUYNS, F., 'Chronique de jurisprudence – la location-financement ou leasing mobilier (1993–1998)', (1999) 118 JT, 201;

BRUYNS, F., 'Chronique de jurisprudence – La location-financement ou leasing mobilier (1999–2003)', (2004) JT, 605;

BRUYNS, F., *Le location – financement ou leasing mobilier – quarante ans de jurisprudence*, (Brussels: Larcier, 2008), p. 63;

BRUYNS, F. and CLAEYS, S., 'Het eigendomsrecht van de leasinggever', (2016) 3 DAOR, 6;

CAEYMAEX, J., 'Réflexions sur la réserve de propriété', (1995) JLMB, 126;

CAEYMAEX, J. and CAVENAILE, T., *Manuel des sûretés mobilières*, (3 edn., Brussels: Larcier, 2019), p. 915;

CALLENS, P., 'De bescherming van de verkoper van roerende goederen door het eigendomsvoorbehoud – een rechtsvergelijkend overzicht', (1979–80) 16 Jura Falconis, 99;

CARETTE N. and VAN DE VOORDE, J., 'Is het bezit als publiciteitsmiddel in verval?' in A. D. BOECK, V. SAGAERT and R. V. RANSBEECK (eds.), *Publiciteit in het zakenrecht*, (Brugge: Die Keure, 2015), 53;

CATTARUZZA, J., 'Les grands axes de la réforme des sûretés mobilières', (2013) 4 Dr. Banc. Fin., 183;

CLAEYS, I. and VAN VALCKENBORGH, L., 'Ongerechtvaardigde verrijking ', (2017) 4 TPR, 1455;

COLLE, P. and VAN DEN BRANDE, B., 'Het eigendomsvoorbehoud verbintenisrechtelijk bekeken en tegenwerpelijkheid van het beding in de verschillende samenloopsituaties' in B. Tilleman and P. A. Foriers (eds.), *De Koop/La Vente* (Brugge: Die Keure, 2002), (163) p. 305;

CUYPERS, A. and FRANCOIS, P. 'Art. 20, 5° Hyp.W' in E. DIRIX, P. FRANCOIS and M. TISON (eds.), *Voorrechten en hypotheken – Artikelsgewijze commentaar met overzicht van rechtspraak en rechtsleer*, (Mechelen: Kluwer,), loosel.;

DAVREUX, F., 'Dévelopments récents à propos de la clause de réserve de propriété, utilité du privilège du vendeur et position du founisseur et du prestataire de services' in C. BIQUET-MATHIEU (ed.), *Le point sur le droit des sûretés*, (Liège: Formation permanente CUP, 2000), 277;

DE CALUWE, A. and BOGAERT, G., 'Eigendomsrecht bij leasing', (1981–82) 32 RW, 2129;

DE CALUWE, A., 'Verkopen en betaald geraken', (1983) TPR, 243;

DE CONINCK, B. 'La clause de réserve de propriété et son opposabilité en cas de concours' (2005) 5 TBBR, 241;

DEHAN, P. and VINCENT, L., 'La nature du contrat de "leasing"', [1967] RCJB, 231;

DE HEMPTINNE, R. and RUYFFELAERE, A.. 'Naar de tegenstelbaarheid van de clausule van eigendomsvoorbehoud' in *Jurist in bedrijf*, (Brussels: Bruylant, 1989), (131) p. 518;

DE KEYSER, L., 'Onbenoemde overeenkomsten en roerende leasing' in H. HERBOTS (ed.), *Bijzondere overeenkomsten*, (Antwerp: Kluwer, 1980), 439;

DE KEYSER, L., 'Roerende leasing en eigendomsrevindicatie' [1983] TPR, 443;

DE KEYSER, L., 'Eigendomsrecht en nieuwe contractvormen: leasing, factoring en franchising', (1983–84) 47 RW, 2407;

DEKKERS, R., CARETTE, N., BAETEMAN, G., VERBEKE, A.-L. and VANHOVE, K., *Handboek brugerlijk recht III*, (Antwerp: Intersentia, 2007), p. 820;

DEL CORRAL, J., *De leveringsplicht bij de overdracht van roerende lichamelijke goederen*, (Antwerpen: Intersentia, 2013), p. 629;

DEL CORRAL, J., 'Eigendom tot zekerheid' in H. BRAECKMANS and others (eds.), *Faillissement & gerechtelijk akkoord*, (Mechelen: Kluwer), loosel.;

DE PAGE, H. and DEKKERS, R., 'Les bien – les sûretés' in *Traité élémentaire de droit civil Belge*, (Brussels: Bruylant, 1962), p. 1048;

DE PAGE, H. and DEKKERS, R., 'Les principaux contrats usuels', *Traité élémentaire de droit civil Belge*, vol. V, (Brussels: Bruylant, 1975), p. 1167;

DERIJCKE, W., 'La réforme des sûretés réelles mobilières', (2013) 8 TBH, 691;

DE WILDE, A., 'Het probleem der tegenstelbaarheid van de afbetalingskoop, aangegaan onder een beding van eigendomsvoorbehoud, ten aanzien van derden; mede in het licht van de wet van 9 juli 1957', (1957–58) RW, 489;

DIRIX, E., 'Nieuwe overeenkomsten tot zekerheid', (1988) 2 TPR, 323;

DIRIX, E., 'Eigendomsvoorbehoud en samenloop', (1994–95) 37 RW, 1264;

DIRIX, E. and STORME, M. E., 'Eigendomsvoorbehoud in het ontwerp van faillissementswet: hopeloos onsamenhangend', (1995–96) 41 RW, 1421;

DIRIX, E., 'Eigendomsvoorbehoud' (1997–98) 15 RW, 481;

DIRIX, E., 'De uitoefening van het eigendomsvoorbehoud bij faillissement', (1999–2000) 30 RW, 1038;

DIRIX, E., 'Het lot van de realisatiewaarde bij beëindiging van de leasingovereenkomst', (1999–2000) 63 RW, 368;

DIRIX, E., 'De uitoefening van het eigendomsvoorbehoud bij faillissement', (1999–2000) 30 RW, 1038;

DIRIX, E., 'Faillissement en lopende overeenkomsten', (2003) 67 RW, 201;

DIRIX, E. and DE CORTE, R. 'Zekerheidsrechten' in *Beginselen van Belgisch privaatrecht*, (5th edn., Mechelen: Wolters Kluwer, 2006), p. 519;

DIRIX, E., 'Zekerheden, eigendomsvoorbehoud en rangregeling' in H. BRAECKMANS, H. COUSY, E. DIRIX, B. TILLEMAN and M. VANMEENEN (eds.), *Curatoren en vereffenaars: actuele ontwikkelingen*, (Antwerp: Intersentia, 2006), 519;

DIRIX, E., 'Effect of security rights vis-à-vis third persons' in U. DROBNIG, H. J. SNIJDERS and E. J. ZIPPRO (eds.), *Divergences of property law, an obstacle to the internal market?*, (München: Sellier, 2006), 69;

DIRIX, E., 'Functionele analyse van zekerheidsrechten' in W. PINTENS and others (eds.), *Vigilantibus ius scriptum: feestbundel voor Hugo Vandenberghe*, (Brugge: Die Keure, 2007), 119;

DIRIX, E., 'Art. 101 Faillissementswet' in E. DIRIX, P. FRANCOIS and M. TISON (eds.), *Voorrechten en hypotheken – Artikelsgewijze commentaar met overzicht van rechtspraak en rechtsleer*, (Mechelen: Kluwer, 2011), loosel.;

DIRIX, E., De hervorming van de roerende zakelijke zekerheden, (Mechelen: Kluwer, 2013), p. 317;

DIRIX, E., 'The new Belgian act on security interests in movable property', (2014) 23 Int Insolv Rev, 171;

DIRIX, E., 'België kiest voor een centraal pandregister', (2014) 5 Tijdschrift voor Insolventierecht, 6;

DIRIX, E., 'The Belgian reform on security interests in movable property' in L. GULLIFER and O. AKSELI (eds.), *Secured transactions law reform*, (Oxford: Hart Publishing, 2016), 391;

DIRIX, E., 'De nieuwe Pandwet: doelstellingen en uitgangspunten' in M. E. STORME (ed.), *Roerende zekerheden na de Pandwet*, (Antwerpen: Intersentia, 2017), 1;

DIRIX, E., "Beslag" in *Algemene Praktische Rechtsverzamling*, (Mechelen: Kluwer, 2018), p. 615;

DIRIX, E., 'De rol van de rechtsvergelijking in de rechtspraak van het Hof van Cassatie [in de periode 2002-2017]', (2019) 8 TPR, 21;

DIRIX, E., 'Art. 47 - 56 Pandwet' in E. DIRIX, P. FRANCOIS and M. TISON (eds.), *Voorrechten en hypotheken Artikelsgewijze commentaar met overzicht van rechtspraak en rechtsleer*, (Mechelen: Kluwer, loosel.);

DONNEZ, T. and GRUYAERT, D., 'Het nieuwe registerpand in de praktijk: voorwerp, vestiging en uitwerking nader bekeken', (2018) 43 RW, 1683;

DUMON, Y.; 'La Loi d 8 Août 1997 sur les faillites - Loi interprétative du 12 mars 2000 concernant l'article 101, alinéa 3, énonçant les modalités d'exercice du droit de revendication', (2000) 26 JT, 556;

DURANT, I., 'Le droit de rétention et la réserve de propriété, deux sûretés réelles mobilières à part entière' in F. GEORGES (ed.), *Insolvabilité et garanties*, (Brussels: Larcier,2014), 34;

FELTKAMP, R., 'Overdracht tot zekerheid van schuldvorderingen: een bijzonder(e zeker)heid?', (2017) 4 TBBR, 215;

FRANSIS, R., 'Tegenwerpelijkheid van het eigendomsvoorbehoud bij samenloop: de wetgever is opnieuw (dringend) aan zet' (2011) 225 NJW, 503;

GEORGE, F., "L'incidence de la faillite sur la contrat de factoring" (2013) 119 RDC 741;

GÉORGES, F., 'La réforme des sûretés mobilières', (2013) 3 Rev. Dr. ULg., 319;

GÉORGES, F., 'Opposabilité des sûretés réelles mobilières et conflits de rang' in I. DURANT (ed.), *Les sûretés réelles mobilières*, (Liège: Anthemis, 2017), 84;

GIGOT, A.-S., 'L'opposabilité de la clause de réserve de propriété en cas de procédures collectives d'insolvabilité', (2011) 6 TBH, 511;

GRÉGOIRE, M., 'Questions liées à l'invocation d'une clause de réserve de propriété' in *Mélanges offerts à Pierre Van Ommeslaghe* (Brussel: Bruylant, 2000), (465) p. 1092;

GRÉGOIRE, M.,, *Publicité foncière, sûretés réelles et privilèges*, (Brussels: Bruylant, 2006), p. 798;

GRÉGOIRE, M., "Les sûretés réelles" in C. BRUYNEEL, J.-P.BUYLE, M. DELIERNEUX (eds.), *Liber Amicorum André Bruyneel - Synthèse de droit bancaire et financier*, (Brussels: Bruylant 2008), 343;

GRÉGOIRE, M., 'La modification du code civil en ce qui concerne les sûretés réelles mobilières' in F. GÉORGES (ed.), *Insolvabilité et garanties*, (Brussels: Larcier, 2014), 10;

GRÉGOIRE, M., 'The law of 11 July 2013 amending the Belgian civil code with respect to security interest in movable assets, and repealing various provisions in this area' in B. FOËX (ed.), *The draft UNCITRAL model law on secured transactions - why and how?*, (Genève: Schulthess, 2016), 171;

GRUYAERT, D., '[Roerende leasing en faillissement] Het Hof van Cassatie geeft zeer (te?) ruime interpretatie aan de bevoegdheid tot revindicatie', (2013-14) 15 RW, 579;

GRUYAERT, D., 'Het kredieteigendomsvoorbehoud', 4 (2016) TPR, 1205;

GRUYAERT, D., *Exclusiviteit van het eigendomsrecht*, (Antwerp: Intersentia, 2016), p. 890;

HEENEN, J., 'Les garanties du vendeur de meubles et leurs avatars (note under Cass. 18 November 1971)', (1973) RCJB, 9;

HELLEBUYCK, E., 'Commentaar bij artikel 70 Pandwet' in E. DIRIX and A. VAN OEVELEN (eds.), *Bijzondere overeenkomsten Artikelsgewijze commentaar met overzicht van rechtspraak en rechtsleer*, (Mechelen: Wolters Kluwer, 2019), loosel.;

HERBOTS, J., 'Réflexions à propos de la nature du leasing, avant-contrat innomé, typique et fiduciaire (note under Cass. 17 june 1993)', (1996) RCJB, 234;

HERBOTS, J. and others. 'Overzicht van rechtspraak – Bijzondere overeenkomsten – Leasing', (2002) 1 TPR, 897;

HOUBEN, R. and VAN DE LOOVERBOSCH, M., 'Belgium: security interests – moveable assets', (2017) 28 International Company and Commercial Law Review, 67;

JANSEN, R., *Beschikkingsonbevoegdheid*, (Antwerp: Intersentia, 2009), p. 931;

JANSEN, R., 'Eigendomsvoorbehoud' in J. BAECK and M. KRUITHOF (eds.), *Het nieuwe zekerheidsrecht*, (Antwerpen: Intersentia, 2014), (139), p. 177;

KOHL, B., 'Le leasing financier en Belgique', (2011) 16 Unif. L. Rev., 45;

J. LAENENS, D. SCHEERS, P. THIRIAR, S. RUTTEN and B. VANLERBERGHE, *Handboek gerechtelijk recht*, (Antwerp: Intersentia, 2020), p. 969;

LEBON, C., 'Non nudis pactis dominia rerum transferuntur. Kritische bemerkingen omtrent de consensualiteit van de overdracht van eigendom en de vestiging van beperkte zakelijke rechten', (2004) TPR, 409;

LENEP, R. 'De rechtspraak van het Hof van Cassatie en het afbetalingscontract', (1932–33) RW, 440;

LIBERT, H. and BEKAERT, J., 'Leasing van roerende goederen' in E. DIRIX and A. VAN OEVELEN (eds.), *Bijzondere overeenkomsten Artikelsgewijze commentaar met overzicht van rechtspraak en rechtsleer*, (Mechelen: Kluwer), loosel.

MALEKZADEM, J., 'Uitwinning van de pandrechten na de hervorming' in M. E. STORME (ed.), *Roerende zekerheden na de Pandwet*, (Antwerpen: Intersentia, 2017), 157;

MCGUIRE, M.R., *Transfer of title concerning movables*, II, National report: Germany, (Frankfurt am Main: P. Lang, 2006), 78;

MEERTS, J., 'Het eigendomsvoorbehoud' in H. BRAECKMANS and others (eds.), *Faillissement & Reorganisatie*, (Mechelen: Kluwer), loosel.;

MERCHIERS, Y., 'Enkele nieuwe handelsovereenkomsten', (1979) TPR, 721;

MOREAU-MARGREVE, I., 'Evolution du droit et de la pratique en matière de sûretés', *Les créanciers et le droit de la faillite: séminaire organisé à Liège les 17 et 18 novembre 1982*, (Brussels: Bruylant,1983), 77;

NEELS, L., 'Eigendomsvoorbehoud bij leasing', (1980–81) 44 RW, 2075;

NICAISE, V., 'Rappels des principes, mise en contexte et modifications diverses apportees par la loi du 25 décembre 2016' in I. DURANT (ed.), *Les sûretées mobilières*, (Liège: Anthemis, 2017), p. 237;

RONSE, J., 'Het risico bij verkoop op afbetaling met beding van eigendomsvoorbehoud', (1953–54) 41 RW, 1897;

SAGAERT, V., *Zakelijke subrogatie*, (Antwerp: Intersentia, 2003), p. 793;

SAGAERT, V., 'Het 'in natura'-vereiste bij eigendomsvoorbehoud: de gevolgen van de bewerking, vermenging en wederverkoop', (2003) 9 TBH, 773;

SAGAERT, V., 'Het goederenrecht als open systeem van verbintenissen? Poging tot een nieuwe kwalificatie van de vermogensrechten', (2005) 3 TPR, 983;

SAGAERT, V., 'Het eigendomsvoorbehoud als volwaardig zekerheidsinstrument' in *Insolventierecht - XXXI Postuniversitaire Cyclus Willy Delva 2004-05*, (Mechelen: Kluwer, 2006), 191;

SAGAERT, V. and JANSEN, R., 'Overzicht van rechtspraak - eigendom tot zekerheid', (2012) 3 TPR, 1362;

SAGAERT, V., 'Goederenrecht' in *Beginselen van Belgisch privaatrecht*, vol. V, (Mechelen: Kluwer, 2014), p. 785;

SAGAERT, V. and DEL CORRAL, J., 'Eigendomsvoorbehoud' in *Algemene Praktische Rechtsverzameling*, (Mechelen: Wolters Kluwer, 2015), p. 178;

SAGAERT, V., 'Het eigendomsvoorbehoud (en retentierecht) onder de Pandwet' in M. E. STORME (ed.), *Roerende zekerheden na de Pandwet*, (Antwerpen: Intersentia, 2017), 29;

SCHRANS, G., 'Het beding van eigendomsvoorbehoud en zijn externe werking tegenover de schuldeisers van de koper van een zaak', (1982) TPR, 145;

SIMONT, L., 'Essai de classification des sûretés - issues de la pratique et problèmes juridiques qu'elles posent' in A. BRUYNEEL and A. M. STRANART (eds.), *Les sûretés: sûretés traditionnelles, réelles et personnelles, en droit français et en droit belge, sûretés issues de la pratique, droit international privé: colloque de Bruxelles des 20 et 21 octobre 1983*, (Paris: Feduci, 1984), 277;

STEENOT, R., 'De verplichting tot ingebrekestelling (note under Vred. Arendonk 29 September 2009)', (2012) 5 T. Vred., 274;

STEENNOT, R., 'Algemene regeling van het pand' in J. BAECK and M. KRUITHOF (eds.), *Het nieuwe zekerheidsrecht*, (Antwerp: Intersentia, 2014), 27;

STORME, M. E., 'Overdracht van roerende goederen, vestiging van pandrecht eigendomsvoorbehoud: een poging tot systematisatie', *Het zakenrecht: absoluut niet een rustig bezit*, (Antwerpen: Kluwer, 1992), 405;

STORME, M. E., 'De wijde mantel van de huurovereenkomst biedt ook plaats aan zuivere financieringshuur zonder vrijwaring door de lessor (note under Cass. 17 june 1993)', (1993) R. Cass., 179;

STORME, M.E., "Paritas creditorum, voorrang en roerende zekerheden", TPR 2006, 939;

STORME, M.E., 'Eigendomsvoorbehoud en samenloop buiten faillissement: Hof van Cassatie lijdt aan fantoompijn' (2011-12) 5 RW, 254;

STORME, M.E., 'Zekerheidsrechten op schuldvorderingen op naam' in M. E. STORME (ed.), *Roerende zekerheden na de Pandwet*, (Antwerpen: Intersentia, 2017), 223;

STORME, M.E., *Zekerheden en insolventierecht*, (Ghent, Mariakerke, 2018-19), online;

STOUFFLET, J., 'L'usage de la propriété à des fins des garantie' in A. BRUYNEEL and A.-M. STRANART (eds.), *Les sûretés*, (Paris: Feduci, 1984), p. 595;

'T KINT, F. and COPPENS, P., 'La clause résolutoire et la clause de réserve de propriété dans le contrat de vente', (1979) RRD, 887;

'T KINT, F. and DERIJCKE, W., 'Dessaisissement et situations des créanciers en cas de faillite', *Le nouveau droit du concordat judiciaire et de la faillite: les lois des 17 juillet et 8 août 1997*, (Brussels: Bruylant, 1997), 173;

'T KINT, F., *Sûretés et principes généraux du droit de poursuite des créanciers*, (Brussels: Larcier, 2004), p. 467;

’T KINT, F. and DERIJCKE, W., *La faillite*, (Brussels: Larcier, 2006), p. 436;
TROCH, K., WYMEERSCH, E. and DAMBRE, M., ‘Overzicht van rechtspraak – Krediet’, (1999) 4 TPR, 1789;
VANBELLE, J., ‘De revendicatie van onroerende en roerende goederen’, (1994–95) Jura Falconis, 31;
VAN CROMBRUGGHE, N., ‘Belgium’ in I. DAVIES (ed.), *Retention of title clauses in sale of goods contracts in Europe*, (Sydney: Ashgate, 1999), 7;
VANDENBERGHE, H., ‘Eigendomsvoorbehoud bij leasing’, (1980–81) RW, 2761;
VAN DEN HOLE, L., ‘De roerende leasing – de positie van de lessor bij faillissement’, (1996) 40 DAOR, 25;
VAN DE PLAS, I., ‘Mis/gebruik in de Pandwet’ in A. VAN DE VIJVER (ed.), *Misbruik binnen de onderneming*, (Antwerpen, Intersentia, 2018), 165;
VANDENPLAS, M., ‘De rechtspositie van de verkoper van een onder beding van eigendomsvoorbehoud verkocht roerend goed tegenover opvolgende kopers’, (2012) 9 TBH, 859;
VAN DE VOORDE, J., *De verkrijgende verjaring. De nalatenschap van Rome heroverwogen*, (Doctor of Laws, University of Antwerp, 2017), p. 982;
VAN ERP, S., ‘General issues: setting the scene’ in S. VAN ERP and B. AKKERMANS (eds.), *Cases, materials and text on national, supranational and international property law*, (Oxford: Hart Publishing, 2012), 34;
VAN GERVEN, W. and VAN OEVELEN, A., *Verbintenissenrecht*, (Leuven: Acco, 2015), p. 728;
VAN HAEGENBORGH, G., ‘Het behoud van voorrechten op samengestelde of bewerkte zaken (note under Cass. 16 december 1994)’ (1994–95) 40 RW, 1366;
VANHOVE, K., ‘Leasing: een complexe bijzondere overeenkomst’ in P. BESELAERE and others (eds.), *Handboek leasing*, (Brugge: Die Keure, 2007), 43;
VAN OEVELEN, A., ‘De zekerheidsfunctie van het eigendomsrecht bij leasing’, *Eigendom/Propriété*, (Brugge: Die Keure,1996), p. 385;
VAN OEVELEN, A., ‘Schadebedingen in leasingovereenkomsten en de zekerheidsfunctie van het eigendomsrecht van de leasinggever (note under Cass. 8 November 2002)’, (2003–04) 37 RW, 1459;
VAN OMMESLAGHE, P., “Les sûretés nouvelles issues de la pratique – Développements récentes”, in *Le droit des sûretés*, (Brussels: Du jeune barreau Bruxelles, 1992), 377;
VANSWEEVELT, T. and WEYTS, B., ‘Nakoming van verbintenissen of betaling ‘ in T. VANSWEEVELT and B. WEYTS (eds.), *Handboek verbintenissenrecht*, (Antwerp: Intersentia, 2019), 791;
VAN WUYTSWINKEL, M., ‘Le leasing mobilier: contrat complexe ou autonome’, (1992) Rev. Rég. Dr., 199;
VAN WYNSBERGHE, M., ‘Eigendomsvoorbehoud en bewerking of vermenging van de onbetaalde goederen’, (2010–11) 4 Jura Falconis, 29;
VERBEKE, A., ‘Eigendomsoverdracht tot zekerheid – een genuanceerd beeld’ in J. HERBOTS and D. PHILIPPE (eds.), *De trust en de fiduciaire overeenkomst*, (Brussels: Bruylant,1997), 327;
VERBEKE, A. L., SAGAERT, V. and TILLEMAN, B., “Wettelijke wijzen van eigendomsverkrijging” in B. TILLEMAN and A. L. VERBEKE (eds.), *Vermogensrecht in kort bestek*, (Brussel: Intersentia, 2020), 226;

VERLAECKT, V., 'Artikel 69 – 72' in D. BLOMMAERT and others (eds.), *Wet en duiding – Economisch recht*, (Brussels: Larcier, 2014), 622;
VEROUGSTRAETE, I., 'Privaatrechtelijke aspecten van finance leasing in België', (1973) 10 TPR, 741;
VEROUGSTRAETE, I., *Manuel de la continuité des entreprises et de la faillite*, (Waterloo: Kluwer, 2011), p. 1010;
VERSCHELDEN, G., 'Eigendomsvoorbehoud tussen partijen en tegenover derden', (1998–99) AJT, 821;
WAELBROECK, M., *Le transfert de la propriété dans la vente d'objets mobiliers corporels en droit comparé*, (Brussels: Bruylant,1961), p. 246;
ZENNER, A., *Dépistage, faillites & concordats*, (Brussels: Larcier, 1998), p. 1184;
ZENNER, A., 'Faillite et concordats – la réforme de la réforme et sa pratique', *Les dossiers du journal des tribunaux*, (Brussels: Larcier, 2002), p. 492;

INDEX

L

M

N

O

P

R

S

www.ingramcontent.com/pod-product-compliance
Ingram Content Group UK Ltd.
Pitfield, Milton Keynes, MK11 3LW, UK
UKHW061858100926
8556IPUK00009B/921

9 781839 703